Smart City Emergence

Smart City Emergence
Cases From Around the World

Edited by

Leonidas Anthopoulos
Professor, University of Thessaly, Volos, Greece

Elsevier
Radarweg 29, PO Box 211, 1000 AE Amsterdam, Netherlands
The Boulevard, Langford Lane, Kidlington, Oxford OX5 1GB, United Kingdom
50 Hampshire Street, 5th Floor, Cambridge, MA 02139, United States

Copyright © 2019 Elsevier Inc. All rights reserved.

No part of this publication may be reproduced or transmitted in any form or by any means, electronic or mechanical, including photocopying, recording, or any information storage and retrieval system, without permission in writing from the publisher. Details on how to seek permission, further information about the Publisher's permissions policies and our arrangements with organizations such as the Copyright Clearance Center and the Copyright Licensing Agency, can be found at our website: www.elsevier.com/permissions.

This book and the individual contributions contained in it are protected under copyright by the Publisher (other than as may be noted herein).

Notices
Knowledge and best practice in this field are constantly changing. As new research and experience broaden our understanding, changes in research methods, professional practices, or medical treatment may become necessary.

Practitioners and researchers must always rely on their own experience and knowledge in evaluating and using any information, methods, compounds, or experiments described herein. In using such information or methods they should be mindful of their own safety and the safety of others, including parties for whom they have a professional responsibility.

To the fullest extent of the law, neither the Publisher nor the authors, contributors, or editors, assume any liability for any injury and/or damage to persons or property as a matter of products liability, negligence or otherwise, or from any use or operation of any methods, products, instructions, or ideas contained in the material herein.

British Library Cataloguing-in-Publication Data
A catalogue record for this book is available from the British Library

Library of Congress Cataloging-in-Publication Data
A catalog record for this book is available from the Library of Congress

ISBN: 978-0-12-816169-2

For Information on all Elsevier publications
visit our website at https://www.elsevier.com/books-and-journals

Publisher: Joe Hayton
Acquisition Editor: Brian Romer
Editorial Project Manager: Ali Afzal-Khan
Production Project Manager: Kamesh Ramajogi
Cover Designer: Mark Rogers

Typeset by MPS Limited, Chennai, India

Contents

List of contributors		xv
Foreword		xix
Introduction		xxi

1. Project management guidelines/frameworks in the era of agility and complexity — 1
Vyron Damasiotis and Panos Fitsilis
- 1.1 Introduction — 1
- 1.2 Project management standards — 2
  - 1.2.1 International project management association individual competence baseline guide — 2
  - 1.2.2 Project IN controlled environment — 3
  - 1.2.3 The ISO21500:2012 — 5
  - 1.2.4 The project management body of knowledge guide — 6
  - 1.2.5 Project management standards' comparison — 11
- 1.3 Project complexity and project management — 12
  - 1.3.1 Types of complexity — 13
  - 1.3.2 Approaches to complexity — 13
  - 1.3.3 Software project complexity — 15
- 1.4 Conclusion — 16
- About the authors — 17
- References — 17

2. The smart city of Évora — 21
J. Seixas, S.G. Simoes, J.P. Gouveia and L. Dias
- 2.1 Introduction — 21
- 2.2 Background — 23
  - 2.2.1 Évora InovCity — 23
  - 2.2.2 Integrated city planning toward Évora Action Plan for sustainable energy — 25
  - 2.2.3 "Smart cities" memorandum of understanding — 26
- 2.3 Research methodology: case study — 27
  - 2.3.1 Scope — 28
  - 2.3.2 Integration — 29
  - 2.3.3 Organization — 34
  - 2.3.4 Time — 39
  - 2.3.5 Cost — 39

		2.3.6	Risks	43
		2.3.7	Discussion—the fringes	44
	2.4	Conclusions		46
	Acknowledgments			47
	About the authors			47
	References			48
	Further reading			50
3.	**The smart city of Torino**			**51**
	Chiara Delmastro, Rocco De Miglio, Alessandro Chiodi,			
	Maurizio Gargiulo and Paola Pisano			
	3.1	Introduction		51
	3.2	Background		53
	3.3	Research methodology: the case study		53
		3.3.1	Scope	56
		3.3.2	Integration	57
		3.3.3	Organization	59
		3.3.4	Time	60
		3.3.5	Cost	65
		3.3.6	Quality	67
		3.3.7	Risks	70
		3.3.8	Procurement	74
		3.3.9	Discussion—the fringes	75
	3.4	Conclusion		77
	Acknowledgments			77
	About the authors			77
	References			78
	Further reading			81
4.	**The smart city of Leuven**			**83**
	Roel Heijlen and Joep Crompvoets			
	4.1	Introduction		83
		4.1.1	Objective and structure of the chapter	84
	4.2	Background		85
		4.2.1	Context	85
		4.2.2	Focus areas	86
	4.3	Analysis of the case		87
		4.3.1	Scope	89
		4.3.2	Integration and organization	90
		4.3.3	Time	92
		4.3.4	Costs and funding channels	92
		4.3.5	Criteria regarding quality and procurement	94
		4.3.6	Risks and anticipation	94
	4.4	Discussion		99
		4.4.1	Strategy	100

		4.4.2	Multidisciplinarity (and cocreation)	100
		4.4.3	Appropriation	101
		4.4.4	Road map	101
		4.4.5	Technology	101
	4.5	Conclusion		102
	Acknowledgments			102
	About the authors			102
	References			103
5.	**The smart city of Vienna**			**105**
	Vasja Roblek			
	5.1	Introduction		105
	5.2	Background		106
	5.3	Research methodology: case study		118
		5.3.1	Scope	118
		5.3.2	Integration	120
		5.3.3	Organization	123
		5.3.4	Time	123
		5.3.5	Discussion—the fringes	125
	5.4	Conclusions		126
	About the author			126
	References			126
6.	**A smart city needs more than just technology: Amsterdam's Energy Atlas project**			**129**
	Zulfikar Dinar Wahidayat Putra and Wim van der Knaap			
	6.1	Introduction		129
	6.2	Background		130
		6.2.1	Theoretical approach for Amsterdam Smart City	132
		6.2.2	Organization of Amsterdam Smart City	135
	6.3	Research methodology: case study		136
		6.3.1	Scope	136
		6.3.2	Integration	137
		6.3.3	Organization	138
		6.3.4	Timescale	140
		6.3.5	Cost	140
		6.3.6	Quality	141
		6.3.7	Risks	141
		6.3.8	Procurement	142
		6.3.9	Discussion	142
	6.4	Conclusions		144
	6.5	Remarks		145
	About the authors			145
	References			146
	Further reading			147

7.	**The smart city of Trikala**		**149**
	Leonidas Anthopoulos		
	7.1	Introduction	149
	7.2	Background	152
	7.3	Research methodology: case study	158
		7.3.1 Project mission statement	158
		7.3.2 Resource-based motivation	163
		7.3.3 Life-cycle management	164
		7.3.4 Project coalition management	166
		7.3.5 Discussion—the fringes	167
	7.4	Conclusion	169
	Acknowledgments		170
	About the author		170
	References		170
	Further reading		171
8.	**The evolution of smart city policy of Korea**		**173**
	Jae Yong Lee and Ji-in Chang		
	8.1	Introduction	173
	8.2	Background	175
	8.3	Research methodology: a case study	176
		8.3.1 Scope	177
		8.3.2 Integration	179
		8.3.3 Organization	181
		8.3.4 Time	184
		8.3.5 Cost	186
		8.3.6 Quality	187
		8.3.7 Risks	188
		8.3.8 Procurement	188
		8.3.9 Discussion—the fringes	189
	8.4	Conclusion	192
	Acknowledgment		192
	About the authors		192
	References		193
9.	**The smart city of Hangzhou, China: the case of Dream Town Internet village**		**195**
	Iraklis Argyriou		
	9.1	Introduction	195
	9.2	Background	196
		9.2.1 The Dream Town smart project in Hangzhou: a designated space for promoting innovation-based urbanization	196
		9.2.2 Theoretical context and organization schemas	198

	9.3	Research methodology: case study	200
		9.3.1 Scope	201
		9.3.2 Integration	203
		9.3.3 Organization	203
		9.3.4 Time	205
		9.3.5 Cost	208
		9.3.6 Quality	208
		9.3.7 Risks	209
		9.3.8 Procurement	210
		9.3.9 Discussion—the fringes	210
	9.4	Conclusions	214
	Acknowledgments		216
	About the author		216
	References		216
	Appendix A: Actors interviewed for the Dream Town smart city case		218
10.	**The smart city of Changsha, China**		**219**
	Qiaomei Yang		
	10.1	Introduction	219
	10.2	Background	222
		10.2.1 National strategy: informationization development in China and electronic government	222
		10.2.2 The organizational scheme of smart city construction	223
		10.2.3 The outline for construction of new smart city and optimization of public service modes	225
		10.2.4 The impacts of urbanization step onto the era 3.0 and Changsha is practicing to construct smart city	228
		10.2.5 Huawei internet of things (IOT) platform development tendency in the arena of smart city	228
	10.3	Research methodology: case study	229
		10.3.1 Scope	229
		10.3.2 Time series for the diffusion of smart city evolution	231
		10.3.3 Discussion—the fringes	235
	10.4	Conclusions	237
	Acknowledgment		239
	About the author		239
	References		239
	Further reading		240
11.	**Smart city evolution in India: the cases of Dehradun, Nagpur, and Allahabad**		**243**
	Vinay Kandpal		
	11.1	Introduction	243
	11.2	Background	244

	11.3	Research methodology		246
		11.3.1 Dehradun		246
		11.3.2 Nagpur city		249
		11.3.3 Allahabad		252
	11.4	Conclusions		256
	Acknowledgment			257
	About the author			257
	References			257
	Further reading			258
12.	**The smart city of Pune**			**261**
	Zeenat Rehena and Marijn Janssen			
	12.1	Introduction		261
	12.2	Background		263
	12.3	Major challenges		265
	12.4	Smart city of Pune		267
		12.4.1 Scope		269
		12.4.2 Integration		269
		12.4.3 Organization		272
		12.4.4 Cost		273
		12.4.5 Quality		275
		12.4.6 Risks		276
		12.4.7 Procurement		277
		12.4.8 Discussion—the fringes		279
	12.5	Conclusion		280
	About the authors			280
	References			281
	Further reading			282
13.	**The smart city of Nara, Japan**			**283**
	Narutoshi Sakano			
	13.1	Introduction		283
	13.2	Background		285
	13.3	Research methodology: case study		286
		13.3.1 Utilizing renewable energies in the three major projects		286
		13.3.2 Evaluation		287
	13.4	Conclusion		290
	About the author			291
	Reference			293
	Further reading			293
14.	**A smart city case study of Singapore—*Is Singapore truly smart?***			**295**
	Marianna Cavada, Miles R. Tight and Christopher D.F. Rogers			
	14.1	Background		295
	14.2	Singapore's vision—a smart nation		296

14.3	Research methodology: the Smart Model Assessment Resilient Tool		296
	14.3.1	Introduction to assessment of Smart Model Assessment Resilient Tool	296
	14.3.2	Integration	298
	14.3.3	Organization	298
	14.3.4	Timescale	299
	14.3.5	Singapore's smart initiatives	300
	14.3.6	Reach—star ratings of Singapore's initiatives	303
	14.3.7	Risks	304
	14.3.8	Procurement	304
	14.3.9	Benefits of Singapore's initiatives on liveability actions	304
	14.3.10	Direct impact on lenses	306
	14.3.11	Indirect impact on lenses	307
14.4	Conclusions and recommendations		308
Acknowledgments			310
About the authors			310
References			311
Further reading			314

15. The smart city of Newark, NJ: data analytics platform for economic development and policy assessment — 315
Soon Ae Chun, Kevin Lyons and Nabil R. Adam

15.1	Introduction		315
15.2	*Smart city* data analytics platform		317
	15.2.1	Smart city platform architecture	317
15.3	Case studies: analytics for information needs and decision support		318
	15.3.1	Analysis for Newark industrial manufacturing	318
	15.3.2	Anchor institution analysis	319
	15.3.3	Smart city governance analytics	320
	15.3.4	Anchor Institution—Beth-Israel Medical Center	321
	15.3.5	City government—economic impact analysis	321
15.4	Discussions		324
	15.4.1	Scope	324
	15.4.2	Integration	326
	15.4.3	Organization	327
	15.4.4	Time	327
	15.4.5	Cost	328
	15.4.6	Quality	328
	15.4.7	Risks	328
	15.4.8	Procurement	329
15.5	Conclusion		329
Acknowledgments			329
About the authors			330

	References	331
	Further reading	331
16.	**The case of Quayside, Toronto, Canada**	**333**
	Pamela Robinson and Steven Coutts	
	16.1 Introduction	333
	16.2 Background	335
	16.2.1 History	335
	16.2.2 Theoretical context	337
	16.3 Research methodology: case study	338
	16.3.1 Scope	338
	16.3.2 Integration	339
	16.3.3 Organization	340
	16.3.4 Time	341
	16.3.5 Cost	342
	16.3.6 Quality	342
	16.3.7 Risks	342
	16.3.8 Procurement	343
	16.3.9 Discussion—the fringes	344
	16.4 Conclusions	345
	Acknowledgment	346
	About the authors	346
	References	347
17.	**The Brazilian smart cities: a national literature review and cases examples**	**351**
	Luiz Pinheiro Junior	
	17.1 Introduction	351
	17.2 Smart cities—background theoretical	353
	17.3 Research methodology: literature review and cases cited	356
	17.3.1 Brazilian literature and cases about smart cities	356
	17.3.2 Smart cities discussion in the Brazilian context	358
	17.4 Conclusions	360
	Acknowledgments	361
	About the author	361
	References	362
	Further reading	365
18.	**Porto Alegre, Brazil: the smart health case of Gerint**	**367**
	Paulo R. Miranda, Clarice S. Porciuncula and Maria A. Cunha	
	18.1 Introduction	367
	18.2 Background	369
	18.2.1 The Brazilian health service	370
	18.2.2 The regulation of access to health services	371
	18.2.3 Dimensions of the regulation of health services	371

	18.3	Research methodology: case study	372
		18.3.1 Porto Alegre Smart City	372
		18.3.2 Scope	375
		18.3.3 Integration	381
		18.3.4 Organization	382
		18.3.5 Time	383
		18.3.6 Cost	383
		18.3.7 Quality	384
		18.3.8 Risks	384
		18.3.9 Procurement	385
		18.3.10 Discussion—the fringes	385
	18.4	Conclusions	386
	Acknowledgments		387
	About the author		387
	References		388
	Further reading		390

19. Smart city of Algiers: defining its context — 391
Kamila Ghidouche Aït-Yahia, Faouzi Ghidouche and Gilles N'Goala

	19.1	Introduction	391
	19.2	Background	392
		19.2.1 Concept evolution	392
		19.2.2 Definitions and dimensions	393
		19.2.3 Smart city limits	393
	19.3	Project definition methodology	394
		19.3.1 Study area	394
		19.3.2 Integration and organization	395
		19.3.3 Schedule	396
		19.3.4 Funding	396
	19.4	Research methodology: the case of Algiers	397
		19.4.1 Methodological approach	397
		19.4.2 Emerging results and discussion	398
	19.5	Conclusion	403
	About the authors		403
	References		404
	Further reading		405

20. The smart city of Johannesburg, South Africa — 407
Kelvin Joseph Bwalya

	20.1	Introduction	407
	20.2	Background	409
	20.3	Research methodology: case study	411
		20.3.1 Scope and timeline	412
		20.3.2 Integration	413
		20.3.3 Organization	413

		20.3.4	Time	414
		20.3.5	Cost	414
		20.3.6	Discussion—the fringes	415
	Conclusions			416
	Acknowledgments			417
	About the authors			417
	References			418
21.	**The smart city of Tunisia**			**421**
	Aroua Taamallah, Maha Khemaja and Sami Faiz			
	21.1	Introduction		421
	21.2	Background		422
	21.3	Research methodology: case study		423
		21.3.1	Scope	423
		21.3.2	Integration	426
		21.3.3	Organization	428
		21.3.4	Time	429
		21.3.5	Cost	429
		21.3.6	Quality	430
		21.3.7	Risks	430
		21.3.8	Procurement	430
		21.3.9	Discussion	430
	21.4	Conclusions		431
	Acknowledgments			431
	About the authors			432
	References			432

Conclusions: putting "sustainable" in smart cities	**435**
Author index	**439**
Subject index	**447**

List of Contributors

Nabil R. Adam Rutgers University, Newark, NJ, United States

Kamila Ghidouche Aït-Yahia Ecole des Hautes Etudes Commerciales — EHEC, Kolea, Algeria

Leonidas Anthopoulos University of Thessaly, Volos, Greece

Iraklis Argyriou UMR 8504 Geographie-cites, French National Center for Scientific Research (CNRS), Paris, Paris Region, France

Maria Cristina Bueti International Telecommunications Union, Geneva, Switzerland

Kelvin Joseph Bwalya University of Johannesburg, Johannesburg, South Africa

Marianna Cavada University of Birmingham, Birmingham, United Kingdom

Ji-in Chang Graduate School of Smart City Science Management, Hongik University, Sejong City, Korea

Alessandro Chiodi E4SMA, Torino, Italy

Soon Ae Chun City University of New York, New York, NY, United States

Steven Coutts Civic Sandbox: Research and Practice Group, Toronto, ON, Canada

Joep Crompvoets KU Leuven Public Governance Institute, Leuven, Belgium

Maria A. Cunha Getulio Vargas Foundation (FGV), Center for Studies in Public Administration and Government, São Paulo, Brazil

Vyron Damasiotis General Sciences Department, University of Thessaly, Larissa, Greece

Rocco De Miglio E4SMA, Torino, Italy

Chiara Delmastro Department of Energy, Politecnico di Torino, Torino, Italy

L. Dias CENSE—Center for Environmental and Sustainability Research, NOVA School of Science and Technology, NOVA University Lisbon, Campus de Caparica, Caparica, Portugal

Sami Faiz ISAMM, University of Tunisia, Sousse, Tunisia

Panos Fitsilis General Sciences Department, University of Thessaly, Larissa, Greece

Maurizio Gargiulo E4SMA, Torino, Italy

Faouzi Ghidouche Ecole des Hautes Etudes Commerciales — EHEC, Kolea, Algeria

J.P. Gouveia CENSE—Center for Environmental and Sustainability Research, NOVA School of Science and Technology, NOVA University Lisbon, Campus de Caparica, Caparica, Portugal

Roel Heijlen KU Leuven Public Governance Institute, Leuven, Belgium

Chris Ip International Telecommunications Union, Geneva, Switzerland

Marijn Janssen Delft University of Technology, Delft, The Netherlands

Vinay Kandpal University of Petroleum & Energy Studies, Dehradun, India

Maha Khemaja ISSATS, University of Soussa, Sousse, Tunisia

Jae Yong Lee Smart & Green City Research Center, Korea Research Institute for Human Settlements, Sejong City, Korea

Kevin Lyons Rutgers University, Newark, NJ, United States

Paulo R. Miranda Procempa, ICT Services Company of the Municipality of Porto Alegre, Porto Alegre, Brazil

Gilles N'Goala Montpellier Management Institute — MOMA Institute, Montpellier, France

Luiz Pinheiro Junior Positivo University, Curitiba, Brazil; Getulio Vargas Foundation - FGV-EAESP, São Paulo, Brazil

Paola Pisano Municipality of Torino, Torino, Italy

Clarice S. Porciuncula Procempa, Gerint Project, Porto Alegre, Brazil

List of Contributors

Zulfikar Dinar Wahidayat Putra Urban and Regional Planning Study Program, Gadjah Mada University, Yogyakarta, Indonesia

Zeenat Rehena Aliah University, Kolkata, India

Pamela Robinson School of Urban and Regional Planning, Ryerson University, Toronto, ON, Canada

Vasja Roblek Faculty of Organizational Studies, Novo Mesto, Slovenia

Christopher D.F. Rogers University of Birmingham, Birmingham, United Kingdom

Narutoshi Sakano Public Sector Consulting Division, Fujitsu Research Institute (FRI), Tokyo, Japan

J. Seixas CENSE—Center for Environmental and Sustainability Research, NOVA School of Science and Technology, NOVA University Lisbon, Campus de Caparica, Caparica, Portugal

S.G. Simoes CENSE—Center for Environmental and Sustainability Research, NOVA School of Science and Technology, NOVA University Lisbon, Campus de Caparica, Caparica, Portugal

Aroua Taamallah ISITCom, University of Soussa, Sousse, Tunisia

Miles R. Tight University of Birmingham, Birmingham, United Kingdom

Wim van der Knaap Landscape Architecture and Spatial Planning Group, Wageningen University, Wageningen, The Netherlands

Qiaomei Yang Department of Public Administration and Sociology, Erasmus School of Social and Behavioral Sciences, Erasmus University Rotterdam, Rotterdam, The Netherlands

Foreword

Smart city ... what do you recall when you encounter this phrase? What type of city do you imagine? It might be, for example, city where residents live with happiness, city where residents can access to the public transportation wherever/whenever they want, or city where residents can obtain necessary information whenever they wish. The answers toward all these questions might be "YES." These days, there are plenty national/regional/international projects regarding the smart city all over the world. Not a single day has passed without me watching/listening the articles/news about the smart city. Discussions are coming from various sectors, including information and communications technologies, security, safety, environment, etc. The smart city may be the ideal world for all of us to live with the real sustainability.

Standardization can contribute to make cities smarter. There are three biggest internationally recognized standardization bodies in the world: IEC; ISO (International Organization for Standardization); and International Telecommunication Union, Telecommunication Standardization Sector. They are producing some sets of standards within their expertise. I am deeply involved in ISO technical work; ISO has standardization committee whose title is "Sustainable Cities and Communities." You can check what type of standards this committee addressed via ISO website.[1]

Allow me to introduce some projects under ISO. ISO currently focuses on two types of standards regarding smart city, "management system for sustainable city (including some sets of indicators)" and "smart infrastructure as a city service." In addition to these, recently standardization of managing "data" is hot topics to us. City (including infrastructure) has multifarious information, and handling those information is critical issue for us.

Through my long career involving in the international standards development, I have no doubt that standardization provides the daily business scene with effective tools, but on the other hand, to be honest, standardization is just one of the business tools. Standard itself is not law/legislation and should be used as "voluntary" basis in its nature. Due to this inherent nature of standard, people definitely need "motivation" to utilize these standards in their daily business.

This book provides you with several smart city case studies from around the world, which follow alternative approaches and technologies, an event that validates how important the corresponding standards are to the smart city emergence. The investigated cases are presented in a standardized manner in this book, with the use

---

[1] https://www.iso.org/committee/656906.html.

of common project management knowledge areas, which demonstrate the cases from the owner perspective and analyze their scopes, technologies, and methodologies.

I am determined that this book can help the cities that are trying/will try to implement their smart city projects, in terms of learning from alternative experiences and from competitive solutions, while they can look up for standards that can assist them in adopting these solutions. Although the smart city cannot be realized within 1 day, 1 month, or 1 year, I am sure that these smart city projects will bring all of you to a long but fascinating journey, which may bring a bright future to all of us.

Yusuke Chiba
Japanese Standards Association, Tokyo, Japan

Introduction

Smart city (SC) has emerged during the last two decades to a broad scientific domain and a dominant industrial market, which attract an interdisciplinary attention. All the scientific fields—from the information and communications technologies (ICT) to the economics and environmental studies or even the humanities—and all the industries—from the ICT again, to automotive and construction or even health—have joined their forces and provide with innovative products, services, and business models the urban sector.

SC appears to play a significant role for governments too, due to their economic and environmental impact, and modern strategies utilize its potential for dealing with critical challenges, such as local growth, poverty, social coherence, climate change, and resilience. The governments struggle to provide with economic support the SC development at national, supranational, and international levels, while they have employed the standardization bodies to clarify and homogenize the SC context. After all these efforts the SC has become a competitive arena for both the big industrial vendors and the new entrants, but also for cities, which self-claim to be smart or which synthesize coalitions to achieve in several common goals.

In this regard the cities follow several development frameworks or partner with vendors to gain support for their SC development, which appears to have evolved to a local digital transition that affects all the key players and stakeholders. Nevertheless, even today, it is still unclear the scope, the tools, and the models that are being adopted by different cities under their SC mission. This event is normal, since not all the SC solutions are suitable for all the cities, while scale plays a major role for the SC development.

The aim of this book is to collect and present information from several cities around the globe with regard to their SC development. More specifically, it presents how different cities have approached the SC; the vision that they defined for their SC and the problems they wanted to solve with the corresponding smart solutions; the projects that were launched and the timeline for their development; the corresponding budgets and the implementation methodologies, etc. In this regard the purpose of the book is not to compare different SC cases but to collect information whether the cities appear to converge to a common SC purpose or they utilize the SC for different reasons and directions.

In order for this book to achieve in this mission, it has been considered that the SC is owned by the city (municipality, local government, or other owner), and in this regard, the owner perspective to the SC project(s) has been requested by the contributors. Otherwise, due to the different stakeholders' interests to the SC, different types of information would be depicted from different points of view.

Moreover, in order for the collected information to be homogenized, specific kinds of data were requested by the contributors, which match the knowledge areas of the project management body of knowledge. In this regard, information for the 10 knowledge areas (scope, time, cost, risk, stakeholders, etc.) was gathered for each of the presented cases, except if something was missing or unclear. I considered this approach critical, since the SC—even as a portfolio—is a complex project in numerous terms—context, competitive interests, size, duration, uncertainties, innovation, etc.—and from this point of view, a project-based approach can simplify its understanding and can shed light to its particularities, status, and fringes.

The collected material is impressive, since it highlights how different cities approach the SC. Similarities and variances deal not mainly with the geography or the community but particularly with the SC vision and the city mission that affected the SC definition. For instance, several cities prioritized energy efficiency, and corresponding interventions appear in the SC scope; others focused on local growth or social cohesion, and the SC was employed to bring new ideas, investments, or to soften the community's divergencies; finally, others view a leading role in the SC arena and combine smart solutions with the local strengths and the international role that a city plays, etc.

Moreover, this book is valuable since it contains stories both from known (e.g., Amsterdam, Vienna, and Singapore) SC but also, not that famous cases (e.g., Algiers, Torino, and Trikala), which come from both the developed and the developing world. As such, a beautiful "puzzle" with SC pieces of 20 cities from all the continents has been structured with this volume, which is expected to guide the future SC development with the provision of ideas, approaches, problems and solutions, successes and failures, visions and methodologies. It is also of high importance that both small- and large-scale cases are contained, while others are at their beginning (e.g., from Algiers and Tunisia), since it is depicted whether and how the SC projects have been defined and evolved, especially after this quite long SC lifecycle, which started in the early 1990s.

I would like to thank all the contributors for their time and effort they gave and the quality of work that they delivered to this volume. I hope you will find this book useful and important for your study (if you are a researcher or student), your inspiration (if you are a government senior or industry's key player), and your guidance (if you are a manager or developer).

Leonidas Anthopoulos
University of Thessaly, Volos, Greece

Project management guidelines/frameworks in the era of agility and complexity

Vyron Damasiotis and Panos Fitsilis
General Sciences Department, University of Thessaly, Larissa, Greece

Chapter Outline

1.1 Introduction 1
1.2 Project management standards 2
    1.2.1 International project management association individual competence baseline guide 2
    1.2.2 Project in controlled environment 3
    1.2.3 The ISO21500:2012 5
    1.2.4 The project management body of knowledge guide 6
    1.2.5 Project management standards' comparison 11
1.3 Project complexity and project management 12
    1.3.1 Types of complexity 13
    1.3.2 Approaches to complexity 13
    1.3.3 Software project complexity 15
1.4 Conclusion 16
About the authors 17
References 17

1.1 Introduction

A project is a set of activities, tasks, and processes executed together in order to achieve specific project objectives under certain constraints in terms of time, cost, and resources (Kerzner, 2013). For the successful execution of these elements and meeting the project objectives, we need to establish a set of project management (PM) processes. Initially, the term "project management" was introduced at the US aerospace-sector large projects during 1950s and at that time led to the development of two scheduling models: the critical path method and the program evaluation and review technique (Hornstein, 2015). In subsequent years, the need to manage large software projects forced the PM community to develop advanced methodologies and techniques more suitable for large projects. Currently, the application of PM techniques is considered as "sine qua non" in achieving projects goals. The Project Management Institute (PMI), one of the most popular PM professional associations worldwide, defines PM in PM body of knowledge (PMBOK) as the "application of knowledge, skills, tools, and techniques to project activities to meet the project requirements" (PMI, 2017). However, PMBOK is not the only framework focusing on PM. Several PM frameworks have been introduced with the most popular of them being the International Project Management Association (IPMA) Competence Baseline [Individual Competence Baseline (ICB)] (IPMA, 2015), Projects IN a Controlled Environment (PRINCE2) (Axelos, 2017), ISO21500—Guidance on project management (ISO, 2012), etc. In the following sections we will offer a short introduction to each of the aforementioned PM frameworks.

1.2 Project management standards

1.2.1 International project management association individual competence baseline guide

The IPMA issued its first guide in PM named ICB in 1998. IPMA (2015) delivered the fourth version of ICB guide, which reflects latest development in PM. The ICB guide, unlike other PM approaches, is focused on the soft skills required by individuals for effective PM rather than on the hard skills (e.g., methods and techniques). More specifically, ICBv4 guideline describes a comprehensive list of competencies that each individual should have or should develop for a successful management of a project, program, or portfolio. However, ICBv4 does not describe in detail the competencies required for each specific project roles, as it considers that the required competencies for each role may differ according to project type, organization, or industry that undertake the project (Vukomanović, Young, & Huynink, 2016).

ICBv4 identifies 29 competence elements which are divided into three competence areas as follows (IPMA, 2015):

1. *People competencies:* Includes 10 personality/behavioral traits required by PMs needed in the context of a project, program, or portfolio management. Therefore in this category, competences such as communication, leadership activities are included.
2. *Practice competencies:* Includes 14 elements describing the methods, tools, and techniques that should be used in the management of projects, programs, or portfolios to realize their success. A person working in a project needs to master skills such as how to manage the scope and the requirements or how to develop a schedule. These skills are related mainly with technical aspects of the management of a project.
3. *Perspective competencies:* Includes 5 elements describing the methods, tools, and techniques required to support the development of projects, programs, and portfolios, through which individuals interact with the environment. For example, knowing the cultural traits of the project stakeholders is an important asset for the project managers.

In Table 1.1 the elements that are included in each competency area are presented.

It should be made clear that ICBv4 was developed to be the global standard for individual competencies in project, program, and portfolio management, and it can be used supplementary to other popular PM standards. It focuses on the ability of individuals to acknowledge disciplines from the side of the processes, methodology

Table 1.1 Competency elements per competency area.

People competencies	Practice competencies	Perspective competencies
Self-reflection and self-management	Design	Strategy
Personal integrity and reliability	Goals, objectives, and benefits	Governance, structures, and processes
Personal communication	Scope	Compliance, standards, and regulation
Relationships and engagement	Time	Power and interest
Leadership	Organization and information	Culture and values
Teamwork	Quality	
Conflict and crisis	Finance	
Resourcefulness	Resources	
Negotiation	Procurement	
Results orientation	Plan and control	
	Risk and opportunity	
	Stakeholders	
	Change and transformation	
	Select and balance	

tools, and techniques, and to apply them successfully to projects, programs, and portfolio in order to enhance the possibilities for project success (Vukomanović et al., 2016).

1.2.2 Project in controlled environment

PRINCE2 is among the most known and widely used PM methodology around the globe, used by a wide range of people, organizations, and industries in both public and private sectors. Initially PRINCE2 was introduced in 1996 by the Office of Government Commerce in the United Kingdom, as a generic PM method and increasingly became very popular and de facto methodology for PM worldwide. Since 2013, the ownership and the responsibility for the development and promotion of PRINCE2 were transferred to a company named AXELOS Ltd. PRINCE2 was updated in 2017 in order to adopt the latest changes in business practices and to capitalize the feedback received by the PRINCE practitioners. This PRINCE update was aiming to provide trusted guidance and authority to customers and project stakeholders in a dynamic project environment with continuously raised expectations and new emerging technologies (Axelos, 2017). Currently, PRINCE2 can be used as a guide for managing projects regardless of their type or size. It consists of four basic but integrated elements: project environment, principles, themes, and processes. These elements are described and defined in PRINCE2 as follows (Axelos, 2017).

The processes consist of the core of PRINCE2 framework, describing the main steps that should be followed during the project life cycle. Seven process groups have been identified, which are:

1. starting up the project,
2. directing a project,
3. initiating a project,
4. controlling a stage,
5. managing product delivery,
6. managing stage boundaries, and
7. closing a project.

For each one of these processes, checklists with recommended activities, responsibilities, and guidance for tailoring the process to the specific project environment are provided.

One of the main constructs of PRINCE2 is the theme. The themes are the parts of the project which need to be continually tackled throughout the project. They are knowledge areas on a specific PM areas (e.g., the business case, planning, quality). For each theme, PRINCE2 provides the necessary guidance on how to apply them into projects and defines the minimum requirements needed to be fulfilled in each theme. The PRINCE2 themes are the following:

- *Business case:* It refers to the creation and maintenance of appropriate records for the justification of project business case.
- *Organization:* It concerns the definition of the roles and responsibilities of the project team members.
- *Quality:* It defines the specification of the quality requirements, the way quality will be measured, and how these will be applied to the project deliveries.
- *Plans:* It describes the steps needed to be followed to develop the plans and the techniques that should be used during project execution.
- *Risk:* It is concerned with project risk identification.
- *Change:* It defines how a project manager should assess and react on project changes.
- *Progress:* It describes the way the project should be executed, the performance and ongoing viability of project plans.

Further, PRINCE2 defines a set of principles which are considered as the baseline where processes and themes are built on. They are defined as the good practices and guiding requirements that are mandatory to be followed in order to be considered that a project is genuinely being managed by following the PRINCE2 guides. PRINCE2 defines seven such principles, namely:

1. the continued business justification,
2. learn from experience,
3. defined roles and responsibilities,
4. manage by stages,
5. manage by exception,
6. focus on products, and
7. tailor to suit the project environment.

Finally, the project environment is the space in which all the other elements are operating. Further, in an attempt to adapt to emerging agile management trends, a PRINCE2 Agile guide was developed. It combines agile practices and PRINCE2 best practices, providing to the PM practitioners with a detailed guide on how to apply agile methods on PRINCE2. PRINCE2 Agile guide focuses to the following principles (Axelos, 2016):

- Be on time and hit deadlines.
- Protect the level of quality.
- Embrace and adapt to change.
- Keep project teams stable.
- Manage stakeholders' expectation so that they accept that they do not need everything.

In conclusion, PRINCE2 is a process-based, structured PM methodology that can be tailored to any type of project, program, or project portfolio, aiming in providing practitioners with the necessary awareness and guidance to apply methods and techniques that are crucial to successful project completion.

1.2.3 The ISO21500:2012

ISO21500:2012—Guidance on project management is an international standard developed by the International Organization for Standardization (ISO). It is a guidance for PM able to be used by any type of organizations either public or private and for any type of project. The aim of ISO21500 is to provide a guide to both new and experienced project managers on how to apply PM disciplines into a business environment in order to enhance the possibilities for better business results and project success. A fundamental aspect in this effort is the use of the same language and processes by all project stakeholders, which improves communication and cooperation. ISO21500 provides a high-level description of concepts and processes that are considered to form good practices in PM but does not provide detailed guidance on the management of programs and project portfolios (Gasiorowski-Denis, 2012). The structure of ISO21500 is similar to PMBOK guide, but the design of this standard took into consideration the requirement for alignment with the other ISO-related standards such as ISO10006:2003, Quality management systems—Guidelines for quality management in projects; ISO10007:2003, Quality management systems—Guidelines for configuration management; ISO31000:2009, Risk management—Principles and guidelines; and some sector-specific complementary standards for industries such as aerospace and IT (Gasiorowski-Denis, 2012).

Specifically, ISO21500 identifies 5 process groups and 10 management areas called subject groups as presented in Table 1.2.

It has also identified 39 processes divided into the 10 project subject groups. The concepts and their relation that are described and discussed in ISO21500 playing a significant role during project execution are, namely, the project, PM organizational strategy and projects, project environment, project governance, projects and operations, stakeholders and project organization, competencies of project personnel,

Table 1.2 ISO21500 structure.

Process groups	Subject groups
Initiating Planning Implementing Controlling Closing	Integration Scope Resource Time Cost Quality Communication Risk Procurement Stakeholders

project life cycle, project constraints, and relationships between PM concepts and processes.

ISO21500 does not address any guidance for agile PM. Zandhuis and Stellingwerf (2013) criticize that ISO21500 process groups are based on the Deming's circle Plan—Do—Check—Act, in order to support continuous improvement and adaptation to change. However, its processes are considered closer to a cascade way of development, it is a "waterfall" life cycle, than an iterative way and as such is not considered suitable for project-oriented organizations (Rehacek, 2014).

In conclusion, ISO21500:2012 is a PM guide that is trying to incorporate the best practices in PM and present them in a way able to be understood by all project stakeholders. Therefore it is limited to the introduction of the processes, their inputs, and their outputs, and do not describe any specific tools and techniques.

1.2.4 The project management body of knowledge guide

PMBOK has gained global acknowledgment and is the standard PM framework that is used in the United States and many other countries. It is adopted by many international organizations such as ANSI (Holtzman, 1999), IEEE (2011), and ISO (2012). The evolution of PMBOK is characterized by its editions. The first version of PMBOK was published in 1996, and it was based on a white paper issued in 1983 called "Ethics, Standards, and Accreditation Committee Final Report." The second edition was published in 2000, and in 2004 the third edition was published, which was significantly revised from the previous versions. Its fourth edition was published in 2008. In this edition, PMBOK acknowledges five process groups, namely (1) initiating, (2) planning, (3) executing, (4) monitor and controlling, and (5) closing, which are similarly to ISO21500 project groups. Further, it defines nine PM knowledge areas, namely (1) scope PM, (2) integration PM, (3) risk PM, (4) time PM, (5) cost PM, (6) quality PM, (7) communication PM, (8) human resources PM, and (9) procurement PM. In its fifth edition published in 2013, PMBOK acknowledging the significance of project stakeholders in project progress supplements the existing management knowledge areas with another area, the stakeholders' management knowledge area. In September 2017, the sixth edition was issued.

1.2.4.1 Project management body of knowledge areas

The sixth edition of PMBOK is divided in two major parts. The first part is entitled "A guide to the project management body of knowledge," and the second part is entitled "The standard from project management." In the first part the importance of PM and the role of project environment are discussed. In continuation the focus is placed on the role of the project manager and specifically to the skills and competencies project managers should have in order to operate effectively in various organizational environments. Table 1.3 presents the 10 management knowledge areas of PMBOK as defined in its sixth edition.

In PMBOK for each knowledge area, the corresponding processes, activities, tools, and techniques are presented in detail. Specifically, for each knowledge area the following aspects are covered:

- *Key concepts:* Describes the key concepts of PM in the specific area.
- *Trends and emerging practices:* Information regarding what is considered as good practice is briefly presented in this section. This information is significantly revised as most of what was considering as good practices in the previous editions were removed since they were not used in projects.
- *Tailoring considerations:* Because each project is unique, project manager should consider what approaches and processes are postappropriate for the specific project.
- *Consideration for agile/adaptive environments:* Since many projects use agile development methods, this section highlights the approaches need to be followed in order to allow project managers to integrate agile practices into their projects.
- *Process description:* In this section, the processes defined in each knowledge area are presented in detail. Specifically, the inputs, tools and techniques, and outputs that can be used in each process are described. At this point, it should be noted that not all the tools and techniques are mandatory to be used but their usage is depended on the needs of specific project. They should be considered as a guide or pool of best practices.

In the second part of the sixth edition of PMBOK, the PM process groups are presented. It starts with the definition of good practices, the key PM concepts and by presenting the relationships of PM with organizational strategy, portfolio management, project governance, project success and benefits management, project life cycle, project stakeholders, and project manager role. The following sections are organized according to five process groups defined in PMBOK describing the key benefits, inputs, and outputs for each PM process.

1.2.4.2 Project management body of knowledge and agile

The sixth edition of PMBOK gives emphasis to iterative and adaptive development methods in an attempt to be aligned with emerging new practices. In the previous PMBOK versions, agile principles were integrated within all knowledge areas;

Table 1.3 Project management (PM) body of knowledge areas (PMI, 2017).

Knowledge area	Description
Project integration management	Includes the processes and activities to identify, define, combine, unify, and coordinate the various processes and PM activities within the PM process groups. Seven key processes are identified in the project integration management knowledge area, namely (1) to develop the project charter, (2) to develop the PM plan, (3) to direct and to manage the PM plan, (4) to direct and to manage the project work, (5) to manage project knowledge, (6) to monitor and to control the project work, (7) to perform change management, and (8) to close a project or a project phase
Project scope management	Includes the processes required to ensure that the project includes all the work required, and only the work required, to complete the project successfully. Five key processes are identified in the project scope management knowledge area, namely (1) to plan scope management, (2) to collect the requirements, (3) to define project scope, (4) to create the WBS, and (5) to validate project scope and to control project scope
Project schedule management	Includes the processes required to manage the timely completion of the project. Six key processes are identified in the project schedule management knowledge area, namely (1) to plan the project scheduling activities, (2) to define project activities, (3) to sequence the project activities, (4) to estimate project activities duration, (5) to develop the project schedule and to control the schedule
Project cost management	Includes the processes involved in planning, estimating, budgeting, financing, funding, managing, and controlling costs, so that the project can be completed within the approved budget. Four key processes are identified in the project cost management knowledge area, namely (1) to plan cost management, (2) to estimate project costs, (3) to develop the project budget, and (4) to control project costs
Project quality management	Includes the processes for incorporating quality policy of the organization regarding planning, managing, and controlling project and product quality requirements in order to meet stakeholders' objectives. Three key processes are identified in the project quality management knowledge area, namely, (1) to plan project quality, (2) to manage project quality, and (3) to control project quality
Project resource management	Includes the processes to identify, acquire, and manage the resources needed for the successful completion of the project. Six key processes are identified in the project resource management knowledge area, namely (1) to plan project resource management, (2) to estimate project resources, (3) to acquire the needed resources, (4) to develop the project team, (5) to manage project team, and (6) to control project resources

(*Continued*)

Table 1.3 (Continued)

Knowledge area	Description
Project communications management	Includes the processes that are necessary to ensure that the information needs of the project and its stakeholders are met through development of artifacts and implementation of activities designed to achieve effective information exchange. Three key processes are identified in the project communication management knowledge area, namely (1) to plan project communications, (2) to manage project communications, and (3) to monitor the project communications
Project risk management	Includes the processes of conducting risk management planning, identification, analysis, response planning, response implementation, and monitoring risk on a project. Seven key processes are identified in the project risk management knowledge area, namely (1) to plan risk management, (2) to identify the project risks, (3) to perform qualitative risk analysis, (4) to perform quantitative risk analysis, (5) to plan project risk responses, (6) to implement project risk responses, and (7) to monitor project risks
Project procurement management	Includes the processes necessary to purchase or acquire products, services, or results needed from outside the project team. Three key processes are identified in the project procurement management knowledge area, namely (1) to plan project procurements, (2) to conduct project procurements, and (3) to control project procurements
Project stakeholder management	Includes the processes required to identify the people, groups, or organizations that could affect or be affected by the project, to analyze stakeholder expectations and their impact on the project, and to develop appropriate management strategies for effectively engaging stakeholders in project decisions and execution. Four key processes are identified in the project stakeholder management knowledge area, namely (1) to identify project stakeholders, (2) to plan stakeholder engagement, (3) to manage stakeholder engagement, and (4) to monitor stakeholder engagement

WBS, work breakdown structure.

however, the agile approach was not recognized as a main PM trend. In the sixth edition of PMBOK, PMI recognized the increasing popularity of agile approaches, and in cooperation with the Agile Alliance, issued the "Agile Practice Guide." The guide provides PMs with a better description and explanation of agile concepts, tools, techniques, and approaches for successful adoption of this methodology to management processes.

1.2.4.3 The role of project manager

PMI acknowledges the critical role of project managers, in successful project execution, devotes a full chapter in PMBOK guide sixth edition, for defining the role of project managers. PMBOK defines project manager as "the person assigned by the performing organization to lead the team that is responsible for achieving the project objectives" (PMI, 2017). Its role is clearly visible through the project and is clearly distinguished from the role of other managers, for example, operation manager or functional manager.

The role of project manager can differ between organizations as it is tailored to fit the organization needs. Usually a project manager is involved in a project from its start to its end. However, there are cases that a project manager can be engaged in a project before its start, in initial project activities such as the analysis and the evaluation of project feasibility or in consulting activities with executive and business leaders, in order to define project strategic objectives that will satisfy customer needs of improve organizational performance. Also, in some cases, a project manager can evaluate and analyze the final project outcomes.

The multifaceted role of project managers does not imply that project manager should have the knowledge and skills to perform every activity of the project. Project manager should have the knowledge, the skills, and the experience to perform the management processes and be able to coordinate project team members, to provide leadership and effective planning of the work have to be done. Furthermore, project manager is the person that stands between various project stakeholders, team members, and project sponsor. This role is critical, as it is responsible to draw, share, and give direction to the common vision for project success. Therefore the ability of project manager in behavioral skills such as in communicating, in managing people, in controlling and balancing their conflicts, and in revealing the consensus and common ground among them is crucial for the successful execution of their role. The effective communication of a project manager with the various project team members and stakeholders requires the ability of the project manager to understand the communication needs of various types of stakeholders, to plan and maintain communication plans, to have skills in using various communication forms (e.g., verbal, written), and to communicate in a clear, concise, complete, and easy to understand way. Project managers, within the same organization, negotiate for shared resources, for assigning priorities, for the alignment of the goals of the project with the goals of the organization beyond communication and leadership skills, and need to have knowledge of the project domain. PMI identifies three key skills that a project manager should know as PMI talent triangle.

- *Technical PM skills*, referring to knowledge and behaviors related to specific project domain.
- *Leadership ability*, which refers to knowledge, skills, and behaviors required to guide, motivate, and direct a team toward project and/or organization goals.
- *Strategic and business management* capacity that implies the domain knowledge and expertise required by project managers in order to enhance project/organization performance and business outcomes.

In summary the role of project manager in both a project and an organization is multifaceted and critical to project success and organization improvement. A project manager should have a very good knowledge of the project and business domain in order to lead; should be able to assign roles and responsibilities to project members; and should be able to communicate effectively and guide the project to success completion while keeping it aligned with organizational goals.

1.2.5 Project management standards' comparison

In the earlier sections, some of the most globally known and widely used PM frameworks were presented. Most of them are process oriented (PMBOK, ISO21500, PRINCE2), and only one (ICB) is focused on the competencies required by individuals for managing projects. Each of the above frameworks approaches the subject of PM within its own perspectives and focuses on different aspects of management process.

ICBv4 focus on the competencies required by project managers or project stakeholders generally in order to be able to manage or participate in a project successfully. ICBv4 role is considered as supplementary to other word most known PM frameworks (Vukomanović et al., 2016).

ISO21500 is a PM framework providing a high-level description of concepts and processes without provide any detailed guidance on how to perform PM. It has a structure that is very similar to PMBOK, but its aim is to provide a common knowledge and understanding of PM aspects between various project stakeholders, in order to enhance stakeholders' communication and through this project success.

PMBOK is a detailed guide describing methods, processes, and tools that are required for an effective PM. It follows a descriptive approach and identifies a wide list of PM knowledge areas that cover almost all aspects of PM, with a detailed description of processes and tools needed to be followed in every step of PM. However, PMBOK does not describe how to apply the available tools and techniques, leaving that to the judgment of project manager.

PRINCE2 is as well a process-based management framework but follows a prescriptive approach in PM, describing in detail how PM techniques should be structured and implemented. This is done through the definition of the processes, themes, and principles that should be followed during project execution.

We can observe many similarities between PMBOK and PRINCE2 into their processes definitions, project planning methodologies, and project required documentation. However, there are significant differences too, such as that PMBOK planning is focused on processes, while PRINCE2 is focused in dividing project into phases and to the delivery of the final product. Furthermore, PMBOK emphasizes to the role of project manager and considers it as the main authority that has to make the decisions about the project in order to meet project goals, while in PRINCE2 the management authority can be delegated to other senior managers (Matos & Lopes, 2013). PRINCE2 does not cover all aspects of PM as PMBOK does, and it does not define tools and techniques. On the other hand, the PMBOK in some cases can be considered as quite complex and overly detailed in describing some of its elements. According to several project managers' view, PMBOK and PRINCE2 are not mutually exclusive but can be considered supplementary. That is not only because they are filling the gaps of each other in the description of management areas and management team responsibilities, but also to the extent that one is a guide referring to what should be known to manage a project successfully, and the other is a methodology referring to what should be done to managed a project successfully.

1.3 Project complexity and project management

Projects are used by organizations as a means to implement their strategy, to implement changes increasing their competiveness, their presence in the market, to provide new services, and generally to fulfill the expectations of their clients and stakeholders. However, some projects, due to their temporary and unique nature, have a number of characteristics that can endanger their success. A number of studies attempted to define project success and concluded that project success relates mainly on two factors: the accomplishment of a successful project product and the successful execution of a PM process (Baccarini, 1999; Prabhakar, 2008; Sudhakar, 2012). A successful product is one that fulfills all its initially defined requirements, while a successful PM process is the execution of a project within a determined scope, budget, schedule, and quality. Thus the study of project failure sources should enable both factors.

The CHAOS report indicated that among the main factors affecting project result in terms of failure, challenge or success, are factors that are related to PM issues. A careful analysis of software project failure factors, from various researchers such as the Standish Group (1995, 2009, 2015), Molina and Toval (2009), Charette (2005), indicates that among the main factors affecting project failure, challenge or success, are factors which are related to PM issues and that many of these issues arise at the early stages of project design, for example, during the project scope definition and the requirements elicitation stage. This implies that the basis for a successful project is set at the initial steps of project design and goes through successful and efficient PM. Despite the progress of PM practices, a project will still fail, with most of these failures to be attributed to the complexity of projects. The relationship between complexity and PM practice is still blur (Geraldi, Maylor, & Williams, 2011; Kiridena & Sense, 2017).

Very often people have difficulties in distinguishing between the terms complex and complicated, considering them as synonyms (Geraldi et al., 2011). A project, even large in scale, that is self-contained, well-defined, with clear and structured steps to solution, can be complicated but not complex. For example, the wiring of a skyscraper can be complicated but not complex since it follows a clear methodology, specific design, and structured steps during its implementation. On the other hand, the definition of the term complex, in addition, should include interaction between structural and dynamic elements (Whitty & Maylor, 2009). A project, of any size, that is highly dependent on its environment (e.g., political, economic, legal) with stakeholders having conflicting interests or demanding continuous changes in requirements, strategies, and decisions can be considered complex (Chapman, 2016). For example, a project concerning the development of smart cities and their each subcomponent can be a complex project, since it has several parameters that cannot be completely understood and predicted, for example, adoption of the system by the citizens or different requirements of priorities between internal and external project stakeholders.

The distinction between the terms "complex," "complexity," and "complicated" is important to be fully understood in order to move on to the study of project complexity and its sources. In projects the sources of complexity vary and are more than one, including ambiguity in requirements, lack of scope clarity, communication barriers, resulting in different levels and types of complexity for each project (Remington, Zollin, & Turner, 2009). According to the Association for Project Management (https://www.apm.org.uk), the complexity in a project stems from the interactions between organizations forming project organization, the interaction of various units within the same organization, the requirement for coordination between various project elements, and the use of a wide range of PM tools, methods, and techniques (Association for Project Management, 2008).

1.3.1 Types of complexity

There are two major approaches to complexity. The first one is called descriptive complexity and describes complexity as a property of a system. The second approach is called perceived complexity, and it is described as the subjective complexity that someone experiences through the interaction with the system. Hagan, Bower, and Smith (2011) and Baccarini (1996) state that considering complexity as a subjective issue that can change according to the observer implies difficulty in understanding and dealing with a problem or situation, and for that reason, it is not a reliable basis for further research analysis.

On the other hand, a number of researchers argue that the perception of complexity is dependent on the cognitive level (knowledge, experience, background, personality) of the people involved (Fioretti & Visser, 2004; Jakhar & Rajnish, 2014; Remington et al., 2009). According to them it is possible for some people to identify complexity in a system, for some other to identify complexity but have different understanding of it, and for some other to be unaware of its existence. Another characteristic of complexity that should be considered is that the perception of an observer toward complexity can change over time. This change may be due to experience and/or knowledge that is gained over time, making a project that was initially perceived as complex, to look less complex if performed repeatedly or followed by more ambitious projects (Chapman, 2016).

1.3.2 Approaches to complexity

Complexity can exist in both aspects of project success, as was defined earlier. A significant number of studies have been undertaken in recent years in order to understand, define, and determine the concept of project complexity

(Bakhshi, Ireland, & Gorod, 2016; Bosch-Rekveldt et al., 2011; Chapman, 2016; Damasiotis, 2018; Damasiotis & Fitsilis, 2015; Dombkins & Dombkins, 2008; Geraldi & Adlbrecht, 2007; Hass, 2007; Lu et al., 2014; Maylor, Vidgen, & Carver, 2008; Nguyen, Nguyen, Long, & Dang, 2015; Qazi, Quigley, Dickson, & Kirytopoulos, 2016; Vidal & Marle, 2008; Vidal, Marle, & Bocquet, 2011; Williams, 2002). They proposed various approaches in defining project complexity and determining areas that are sources of complexity. Some of these studies are theoretical while others attempt to identify characteristics of complexity that are measurable and in that way to define complexity models that allow the assessment of project complexity in order to increase the chances of project success.

However, despite that a significant number of researchers are studying complexity in projects (Bakhshi et al., 2016), there is still no consensus on defining project complexity, resulting in a variety of approaches and definitions of it (Ireland et al., 2013; Nguyen et al., 2015; Sedaghat-Seresht, Fazli, & Mozaffari, 2012; Standish Group, 2009, 1995; Vidal & Marle, 2008), indicating that even though progress has been done, there is, still, significant work to be done (Oehmen, Thuesen, Ruiz, & Geraldi, 2015).

Although there is no consensus on the definition of complexity, there is consensus on the project aspects that affect complexity. Uncertainty is probably the most common factor which is identified as a main source of complexity, either implicitly or explicitly, in the proposed frameworks. Uncertainty is related to managerial complexity, considering to be the factor that reflects the ambiguity associated with many project aspects such as data, lack of clarity, lack of structure, unpredictable behavior among project stakeholders, uncertainty in goals related to the requirements elicitation, resource limitation, and task complexity (Geraldi et al., 2011; Ward & Chapman, 2003; Williams, 1999). Also the uncertainty stemming from the means used to carry out the project is acknowledged as an important dimension of project complexity (Lu et al., 2014; Xia & Lee, 2005). Williams (1999) states that uncertainty adds to project structural complexity, which relates to project size, variety, and interdependence (Geraldi et al., 2011). Xia and Lee (2005) and Baccarini (1996) identify two dimensions of structural complexity, one related to organizational issues and the other related to the technology being used. Organizational and technological factors are next to uncertainty, the most commonly identified complexity factors among the researchers. The organizational factor is related to project staffing, coordination of stakeholders, contract management project planning and scheduling, organization departments, hierarchy structure, etc., and has received great attention by researchers during the previous years (Baccarini, 1996; Bosch-Rekveldt et al., 2011; Lu et al., 2014; Nguyen et al., 2015; Vidal et al., 2011; Xia & Lee, 2005). Vidal et al. (2011) suggest that organizational complexity is the most significant source of project complexity. The technological factor refers to relationships between technology elements, the variety of technology platforms, technology novelty, newness of project technology, technology changes, and has also attracted attention from other researchers (Baccarini, 1996; Bosch-Rekveldt et al., 2011; Lu et al., 2014; Nguyen et al., 2015; Remington et al., 2009; Vidal et al., 2011; Xia & Lee, 2005). Two aspects of project technology, which are the newness of technology being used in projects and the technology immaturity, are identified by PMI (2013) among the most important factors of the complexity of projects and their management.

1.3.3 Software project complexity

Software complexity relates to both the software product and the software development process (SDP). Several approaches of software complexity have been proposed by researchers according to the domain where they originated from.

Zuse (1990) approached software complexity from a programmer's psychological perspective and defined it as the difficulty to analyze, maintain, test, design, and modify software. Along the same lines, Kushwaha and Misra (2006) defined software complexity as the degree of difficulty to understand and verify a system or a component. Keshavarz, Modiri, and Pedram (2011) stated that although there were different approaches for defining software complexity, most of them comply with Zuse's approach. Ribbers and Schoo (2002), in their research for complex software implementation programs, examined complexity through the prism of implementation complexity and identified three complexity dimensions: variety, variability, and integration. Variety is defined as the different states a system can take. Variability of a system is defined as the dynamics of its elements and the interrelations between them. Finally, integration is referred to as the planned changes during the implementation program including IT systems and business processes.

Considering the best approach to measure software complexity, Ghazarian (2015) states that the existence of more classes, control flows, or modules in a code does not necessarily mean that it is more complex than another one with less of these characteristics, and therefore a more rigorous approach is needed. In addition Khan, Mahmood, Amralla, and Mirza (2016) in their research compared several complexity measurement models based on code characteristics and identified that different models produce different results as they capture different aspects of a software code. Focusing on SDP, Sharma and Kushwaha (2010) and Keshavarz et al. (2011) in their approach on software complexity measurement stated that software complexity measures based on code are not the best approach to assess software complexity if we would like to have a proactive approach in measuring complexity, as the code of the software is produced at the later stages of software development. They proposed a complexity framework based on requirements engineering documents that utilize software aspects such as functional and nonfunctional requirements, technical expertise, design constraints, number of interfaces, number and type of inputs, and outputs and number of users and locations that will be deployed by a software system.

In the same line Damasiotis (2018), Fitsilis and Damasiotis (2015) proposed an innovative approach in measuring software project complexity through the prism of PM by identifying 11 complexity areas with their corresponding complexity metrics, 10 of which are related to management areas of a project as they are defined in PMBOK, and one is related to technical aspects of SDP. Using the specified complexity model, project managers as well as other project stakeholders can assess expected project complexity by assessing 35 complexity metrics using a scale ranging from 0 to 10. The overall complexity is calculated by the sum of products of each metric weight and metric value as assessed by project manager. The complexity level of the overall project is expressed in values between 0 and 10 with higher values indicating higher complexity.

1.4 Conclusion

PM is of considerable and increasing importance in project execution during the last decades. Many studies proposing various PM approaches have been introduced during all these years. They approached PM from different viewpoints and attempted to respond in various management challenges. It is noticeable in the literature that the concept of PM during these years was moved from a rather static and mechanistic approach to more dynamic, adaptive, and holistic approach (Svejvig & Andersen, 2015). Several standards or best practice guides in PM have been introduced with some of them to gain global acknowledgment. Most of them through continuous updates try to catch the latest developments in the field and assist project managers and project stakeholders in their operations in order to overcome the barriers and the obstacles they face toward a successful project completion. Project complexity was identified as one of the main barriers in successful project execution and has attracted the attention of several researchers over the last decade. The multidisciplined and multifaceted notion of project complexity led in several different approaches to it. However, most of them are limited to just conceptual approaches while studies considering the practical assessment and evaluation of project complexity are still limited. Therefore most effort is need in that way as the identification and practical assessment of the expected complexity of a project, in a way that is straightforward, simple, reliable, and compatible with the way projects are executed and managed, are among the challenges of PM for the next years.

To cope better with project globalization and continuously increasing project complexity, project managers should have a set of skills and competencies that require an efficient and effective education and training. The role of education and training is also revealed from the aforementioned PM guides and standards, as they are based on the knowledge, experience skills, and competencies that a project manager should have in order to successfully utilize these standards and apply them to projects. This implies the need for a closer cooperation between industry and academia in order to improve the education and training practices.

The increasing adoption of agile development methods in software projects and the special characteristics that an agile approach has, have led PM organizations, such as PMI, to update their PM guides in order to adapt to agile practices. However, more effort is still needed as agile practices are still not incorporated in PM guides but are mainly provided as supplementary guides.

About the authors

Dr. *Vyron Damasiotis* is a lecturer at University of Thessaly, Greece. He served as a lecturer of Distributed Information Systems at the University of Applied Sciences of Thessaly, School of Business and Economics, Department of Accounting and Finance for 12 years. He also worked as a software developer in various research projects and a part-time lecturer at the University of Applied Sciences of Thessaly. His research interests include software development, project management, computer networks, information systems security, etc.

Prof. Dr. *Panos Fitsilis* is a professor at the University of Thessaly. He also served at the University of Applied Sciences of Thessaly (UAST), School of Business and Economics, Greece, and is a visiting professor at Innopolis University, Kazan, Russian Federation. He has extensive project management experience with the development and deployment of large IT systems and extensive management experience in various senior management positions such as Director of School of Business and Economics at UAST, Vice President of UAST Research Committee, Head of Project Management Department at UAST, Head of Business Unit at Intrasoft International, an international IT company.

References

Association for Project Management. (2008). *APM competence framework*. Bucks, UK: Association for Project Management.

Axelos. *PRINCE2 Agile|PRINCE2|*. (2016). Available from <https://www.axelos.com/best-practice-solutions/prince2/prince2-agile>.

Axelos. *PRINCE2 2017 update*. (2017). Available from <https://www.axelos.com/prince2-2017>.

Baccarini, D. (1996). The concept of project complexity—A review. *International Journal of Project Management, 14*(4), 201–204.

Baccarini, D. (1999). The logical framework method for defining project success. *Project Management Journal, 30*(4), 25–32.

Bakhshi, J., Ireland, V., & Gorod, A. (2016). Clarifying the project complexity construct: Past, present and future. *International Journal of Project Management, 34*(7), 1199–1213.

Bosch-Rekveldt, M., et al. (2011). Grasping project complexity in large engineering projects: The TOE (Technical, Organizational and Environmental) framework. *International Journal of Project Management, 29*(6), 728–739.

Chapman, R. (2016). A framework for examining the dimensions and characteristics of complexity inherent within rail megaprojects. *International Journal of Project Management, 34*(6), 937–956.

Charette, R. N. (2005). Why software fail. *IEEE Spectrum, 42*(9), 42–49.

Damasiotis, V., (2018). Modelling software project management complexity—An assessment model (Ph.D. thesis). Stoke-on-Trent, UK: Staffordshire University.

Damasiotis, V., & Fitsilis, P. (2015). Assessing software project management complexity: PMCAT tool. In K. Elleithy, & T. Sobh (Eds.), *New trends in networking, computing,*

E-learning, systems sciences, and engineering (pp. 235–242). Bridgeport, CT: Springer International Publishing.

Dombkins, D., & Dombkins, P. (2008). *Contracts for complex programs: A renaissance of process.* Charleston, SC: Booksurge Publishing.

Fioretti, G., & Visser, B. (2004). A cognitive interpretation of organizational. *E:CO Special Double Issue*, 6(1–2), 11–23.

Fitsilis, P., & Damasiotis, V. (2015). Software project's complexity measurement: A case study. *Journal of Software Engineering and Applications*, 8, 549–556.

Gasiorowski-Denis, E. *New ISO standard on project management.* (2012). Available from <https://www.iso.org/news/2012/10/Ref1662.html>.

Geraldi, J., & Adlbrecht, G. (2007). On faith, fact, and interaction projects. *Project Management Journal*, 38(1), 32–43.

Geraldi, J., Maylor, H., & Williams, T. (2011). Now, let's make it really complex (complicated): A systematic review of the complexities of projects. *International Journal of Operations & Production Management*, 31(9), 966–990.

Ghazarian, A. (2015). A theory of software complexity. In: *IEEE/ACM fourth SEMAT workshop on a general theory of software engineering* (pp. 29–32).

Hagan, G., Bower, D., & Smith, N. (2011). Managing complex projects in multi-project environments. In C. Egbu, & E. Lou (Eds.), *Proceedings of the 27th annual ARCOM conference* (pp. 787–796). Bristol, UK: Association of Researchers in Construction Management.

Hass, K. (2007). Introducing the project complexity model. A new approach to diagnosing and managing projects. Part 1 of 2. *PM World Today*, 9(7), 1–8.

Holtzman, J. (1999). Getting up to standard. *PM Network*, 12(44–46), 13.

Hornstein, H. (2015). The integration of project management and organizational change management is now a necessity. *International Journal of Project Management*, 33(2), 291–298.

IEEE, 2011. *IEEE guide—Adoption of the Project Management Institute (PMI(R)) standard: A guide to the project management body of knowledge (PMBOK(R) guide)—IEEE Std 1490-2011* (4th ed.). s.l.:s.n.

IPMA. (2015). IPMA competence baseline, Version 4.0. s.l.: PMI Publishing.

Ireland, V., et al. (2013). A contribution to developing a complex project management BOK. *IPMA Project Perspectives*, 35, 15–25.

ISO. *ISO21500:2012: Guidance on project management.* (2012). Available from <http://www.iso.org/iso/catalogue_detail?csnumber = 50003> Accessed 11.03.18.

Jakhar, A. K., & Rajnish, K. (2014). Measuring complexity, development time and understandability of a program: A cognitive approach. *International Journal of Information Technology and Computer Science*, 6(12), 53–60.

Kerzner, H. *Project management: A systems approach to planning, scheduling, and controlling.* (2013). Available from <http://books.google.com/books?hl = en&lr = & id = 4CqvpWwMLVEC&oi = fnd&pg = PR21& dq = PROJECT + MANAGEMENT&ots = LMsOnvwrZs& sig = A5eMH8KDDUN-pEVx8EKNhauXhko> Accessed 09.03.18.

Keshavarz, G., Modiri, N., & Pedram, M. (2011). Metric for early measurement of software complexity. *International Journal on Computer Science and Engineering (IJCSE)*, 3(6), 2482–2490.

Khan, A. A., Mahmood, A., Amralla, S. M., & Mirza, T. H. (2016). Comparison of software complexity metrics. *International Journal of Computing and Network Technology*, 4(1), 19–26.

Kiridena, S., & Sense, A. (2017). Profiling project complexity: Insights from complexity science and project management literature. *Project Management Journal*, *47*(6), 56−74.

Kushwaha, D. S., & Misra, A. K. (2006). A complexity measure based on information contained in software. *Proceedings of the fifth WSEAS International Conference on software engineering, parallel and distributed systems* (pp. 187−195). Madrid, Spain: WSEAS.

Lu, Y., et al. (2014). Measurement model of project complexity for large-scale projects from task and organisation perspective. *International Journal of Project Management*, *33*(3), 610−622.

Matos, S., & Lopes, E. (2013). Prince2 or PMBOK—A question of choice. *Procedia Technology*, *9*, 787−794.

Maylor, H., Vidgen, R., & Carver, S. (2008). Managerial complexity in project based operations: A grounded model and its implications for practice. *Project Management Journal*, *39*(S1), S15−S26.

Molina, F., & Toval, A. (2009). Integrating usability requirements that can be evaluated in design time into model driven. *Advances in Engineering Software*, *40*(12), 1306−1317.

Nguyen, A. T., Nguyen, L. D., Long, L., & Dang, C. N. (2015). Quantifying the complexity of transportation projects using the fuzzy analytic hierarchy process. *International Journal of Project Management*, *33*(6), 1364−1376.

Oehmen, J., Thuesen, C., Ruiz, P., & Geraldi, J. (2015). Complexity management for projects, programmes, and portfolios. An engineering systems perspective. *PMI Global Congress 2015—EMEA*. London, England: Newtown Square, Project Management Institute.

PMI. (2013). *A guide to the project management body of knowledge (PMBOK® guide)* (5th ed.). s.l.: Project Management Institute, Inc.

PMI. (2017). *Project management body of knowledge: A guide to the project management body of knowledge*. Newtown Square, Project Management Institute.

Prabhakar, G. P. (2008). What is project success: A literature review. *International Journal of Business and Management*, *3*(9), 3−10.

Qazi, A., Quigley, J., Dickson, A., & Kirytopoulos, K. (2016). Project complexity and risk management (ProCRiM): Towards modelling project complexity driven paths in construction projects. *International Journal of Project Management*, *34*(7), 1183−1198.

Rehacek, P. (2014). Standards ISO 21500 and PMBoK guide for project management. *International Journal of Engineering Science and Innovative Technology*, *3*(1), 288−295.

Remington, K., Zollin, R., & Turner, R. (2009). *A model of project complexity: Distinguishing dimensions of complexity from severity. The ninth international research network of project management conference (IRNOP-IX)*. Berlin: IRNOP.

Ribbers, M. A., & Schoo, K. C. (2002). Designing complex software implementation programs. In: *Proceedings of the 35th annual Hawaii international conference on system sciences* (pp. 3391−3401).

Sedaghat-Seresht, A., Fazli, S., & Mozaffari, M. M. (2012). Using DEMATEL method to modeling project complexity dimensions. *Journal of Basic and Applied scientific Research*, *2*(11), 11211−11217.

Sharma, A., & Kushwaha, D. (2010). A complexity measure based on requirement engineering document. *Journal of Computer Science and Engineering*, *1*(1), 112−117.

Sudhakar, G. P. (2012). A model of critical success factors for software projects. *Journal of Enterprise Information Management*, *25*(6), 537−558.

Svejvig, P., & Andersen, P. (2015). Rethinking project management: A structured literature review with a critical look at the brave new world. *International Journal of Project Management, 33*(2), 278−290.

The Standish Group. (1995). *Charting of information technology—Chaos*. West Yarmouth, MA: The Stadish Group International.

The Standish Group. *CHAOS summary 2009. The 10 laws of CHAOS*. (2009). Available from <https://www.classes.cs.uchicago.edu/archive/2014/fall/51210-1/required.reading/Standish.Group.Chaos.2009.pdf> Accessed 23.10.16.

The Standish Group. (2015). *CHAOS report*. West Yarmouth, MA: The Standish Group.

Vidal, L., & Marle, F. (2008). Understanding project complexity: implications on project management. *Kybernetes, 37*(8), 1094−1110.

Vidal, L. A., Marle, F., & Bocquet, J. (2011). Using a Delphi process and the analytic hierarchy process (AHP) to evaluate the complexity of projects. *Expert Systems with Applications, 38*(5), 5388−5405.

Vukomanović, M., Young, M., & Huynink, S. (2016). IPMA ICB 4.0—A global standard for project, programme and portfolio management competences. *International Journal of Project Management, 34*(8), 1703−1705.

Ward, S., & Chapman, C. (2003). Transforming project risk management into project uncertainty management. *International Journal of Project Management, 21*(2), 97−105.

Whitty, S. J., & Maylor, H. (2009). And then came complex project management (revised. *International Journal of Project Management, 27*(3), 304−310.

Williams, T. (2002). *Modelling complex projects*. London: John Wiley & Sons.

Williams, T. M. (1999). The need for new paradigms for complex projects. *International Journal of Project Management, 17*(5), 269−273.

Xia, W., & Lee, G. (2005). Complexity of information systems development projects: Conceptualization and measurement development. *Journal of Management Information Systems, 22*(1), 45−83.

Zandhuis, A., & Stellingwerf, R. (2013). *ISO21500 guidance on project management—A pocket guide (1st ed.)*. Zaltbommel: Van Haren Publishing.

Zuse, H. (1990). *Software complexity measures and models*. New York: de Gruyter and Co.

The smart city of Évora

J. Seixas, S.G. Simoes, J.P. Gouveia and L. Dias
CENSE—Center for Environmental and Sustainability Research, NOVA School of Science and Technology, NOVA University Lisbon, Campus de Caparica, Caparica, Portugal

Chapter Outline

2.1 Introduction 21
2.2 Background 23
    2.2.1 Évora InovCity 23
    2.2.2 Integrated city planning toward Évora Action Plan for sustainable energy 25
    2.2.3 "Smart cities" memorandum of understanding 26
2.3 Research methodology: case study 27
    2.3.1 Scope 28
    2.3.2 Integration 29
    2.3.3 Organization 34
    2.3.4 Time 39
    2.3.5 Cost 39
    2.3.6 Risks 43
    2.3.7 Discussion—the fringes 44
2.4 Conclusions 46
Acknowledgments 47
About the authors 47
References 48
Further reading 50

2.1 Introduction

Europe is a highly urbanized continent where over 73% of the population to live in cities, two-thirds of which live in urban settlements of less than 500,000 people (United Nations, 2014). The UN also estimates that urban areas account for 60%–80% of global energy consumption and around the same share of CO_2 emissions. In order to achieve the goal of the 2015 UN Paris Agreement on Climate Change to limit average global temperature rise to well under 2°C, concerted action will therefore be needed in cities to manage energy consumption and reduce greenhouse gas (GHG) emissions.

As more people move to cities, energy demand is expected to grow accordingly, along with demand for transport, so the scale of the challenge is increasing over time, while the need to substantially reduce energy and emissions grows ever more

Smart City Emergence. DOI: https://doi.org/10.1016/B978-0-12-816169-2.00002-X
© 2019 Elsevier Inc. All rights reserved.

apparent. At the same time, many urban areas are already experiencing some of the impacts of climate change with more frequent and intense heat waves and floods, where the most socially vulnerable are particularly at risk.

Cities are increasingly aiming to become sustainable and smart, to reduce energy consumption and related costs, and to contribute to mitigate climate change by reducing or avoiding GHG emissions. Innovation in energy is supported in many cities and across different economic sectors in response to a range of drivers. Mostly, energy-related smart solutions contribute to increase the sustainability of the city, in environment, economic, and social aspects. Municipalities, local stakeholders, and citizens are increasingly aware of their role in helping to meet the demand for energy in a more efficient and sustainable manner that reduces their impact on the climate. Therefore cities should act in planning their future development by considering common challenges on energy and climate: they must become "smart" and sustainable and provide secure, affordable, and eco-friendly energy solutions.

We argue that energy smart solutions should be identified through an integrated approach, considering the different types of energy consumers, as well as the existing and the potential energy producers. Only taking the city energy system as a whole, it is possible to identify the cost-effective and socially accepted measures.

This chapter presents the case of Évora, in Portugal, equipped with more than 34,000 smart meters that provide a high volume of electricity consumption data. We'll show that this information will gain new insights from a door-to-door survey, to identify consumers' clusters. A 3-year project was conducted through a close collaboration between a technical and scientific team and the technicians from the city governance bodies, to leverage the way that smart energy measures are identified, ranked, and selected as the most prominent to implement.

Energy consumption data collection and analysis, beyond smart meters, was hard, and in some cases impossible to be performed. Moreover, it was a challenge to define the appropriate methods to analyze data with different time resolution and provide useful knowledge. Energy consumption changes dynamically during a day, a week, and a year due to a wide range of reasons that range from climate to economic and cultural. In this regard, high-resolution data collection and analysis are necessary in order for the motivations behind consumers' profiles and patterns to be discovered at households, transportation, services, or utilities (e.g., water and wastewater treatment plants).

This case shows the benefits to approach the energy smart potential through an integrated framework to address the efficiency of energy flows across various city sectors with regard to economic, environmental, and social criteria, in order to identify the optimum mix of short-, medium-, and long-term measures for a sustainable energy future.

The remainder of this chapter is organized as follows: the following Section 2.2 contains the background information of the examined case and the particular environment that affects it. Then, Section 2.3 analyzes the case study in terms of the project management body of knowledge and excludes useful outcomes that address city's smart energy system. Finally, Section 2.4 contains some conclusions.

2.2 Background

Évora is a middle-sized city, with circa 53,000 inhabitants, located in the southern inner mainland. Due to its well-preserved old town center, still partially enclosed by medieval walls, and a large number of monuments dating from various historical periods, including a Roman temple, Évora is a UNESCO World Heritage Site, and a member of the Most Ancient European Towns Network. These characteristics present peculiar conditions for the integration of renewables and energy efficiency solutions in the buildings, while cultural distinctive features condition the expectation of its inhabitants regarding living conditions and mobility in the inner center of the city. There are cities in southern Europe with similar characteristics as Évora, and thus the outcomes of this chapter may be of direct interest for them, both for technicians and policy bodies.

During the last decade, several initiatives have been developed over the city of Évora, transforming it gradually into a smart city with positive impacts on the local quality of life, economic development, and environmental sustainability. This section presents three selected milestones that have paved the way toward Évora smart city, focusing on its smart energy systems. We use the concept of smart energy systems, by taking an integrated holistic focus on the inclusion of several energy demand and supply sectors (electricity, heating, cooling, industry, buildings, and transportation), allowing for the identification of more achievable and affordable solutions to the transformation into future renewable and sustainable energy solutions. Where smart grids focus primarily on the electricity sector, the smart energy system concept represents a scientific shift in paradigms away from single-sector thinking to a coherent energy systems understanding on how to benefit from the integration of all sectors and infrastructures (Lund, Østergaard, Connolly, & Mathiesen, 2017).

2.2.1 Évora InovCity

Évora was the first Iberian smart city to test a new way of conceiving the distribution and production of electricity, through the Inovgrid project—Évora InovCity. The project provided smart meters to the electricity consumers in Évora Municipality (not only the city), free of charge. These smart meters collect data about individual consumption profiles and collective grid demands. After a few years of data collection the project enables and optimizes the smooth integration of decentralized energy production and electric vehicles (EVs) (charging infrastructure) into the grid. The project also promotes automated grid management, the improvement of the quality of energy services, the reduction of grid operating costs, and the promotion of energy efficiency and sustainability while simultaneously reducing national energy dependence (Carvalho, 2011). Évora InovCity comprises several features, such as smart metering, public lighting, charging infrastructure for EVs, energy efficiency, and client interaction interfaces.

One can underline that Évora InovCity was the first project to initiate the transformative process of the city toward a smart city. The project was implemented in

2010 by the distribution system operator (DSO) (EDP Distribuição S.A.) and included the installation of 35,000 energy boxes (smart meters), corresponding to 54,000 consumers, plus 340 distribution transformer controllers, and the respective integration with the company's systems. Simultaneously, new public lighting was installed in Évora city, including light-emitting diodes (LEDs) and light regulators along with remote management systems. Traditional lights were replaced by LEDs in some central places paying special attention to the numerous historical locations (world heritage). Light regulators, movement sensors, and more flexible public light controls operated by the customer (municipality) via web portal were also introduced within this project.

Regarding demand-side management functionalities, 3550 facilities are fitted with demand response or energy-efficient solutions, comprising different customer profiles, including residential and commercial buildings, and small industries. The project also includes 70 vehicle-to-grid-enabled EV charging points, 250 distributed generation (DG) monitoring and control units, and 2 primary distribution substations. A great number of stakeholders adopted new technologies and services, namely, prosumers (i.e., person who consumes and produces electricity); universities, municipalities, subcontractors, and service providers. In parallel, with the installation of this hardware, the project has proceeded with the definition of working groups dedicated to the analysis and quantification of the potential benefits of the installed technologies.

Évora Municipality was chosen to implement the Inovgrid pilot project by EDP Distribuição S.A., because of its size, the network diversity, and the willingness of the customers to support a thorough evaluation of an innovative pilot smart grids initiative. Sociological studies allowed for the understanding of the client's expectations about the feedback information on energy efficiency and satisfaction with the hardware installation.

Taking the definition of "smart cities" as the use of smart electricity grids, where digital technology solves the problems of traditional grids with several advantages, one may underline the following features achieved with Évora InovCity.

At home, consumers were able to identify when, how, and where energy is used during the day precisely, while they can (1) access their bills based on actual consumption, allowing consumer control via a computer or smartphone; (2) program appliances to operate in the most convenient periods; (3) manage consumption in real time, minimizing costs; (4) take advantage of new services and price plans tailored to each consumer profile; (5) use integrated home automation solutions to interact with domestic consumption devices; (6) remotely activate services, such as electricity tariff and power changes; (7) produce energy at home, for own use or for sale to the network, by installing photovoltaic (PV) solar panels or small wind turbines at home; and (8) manage energy more efficiently by checking online the difference between what it is spent and what it is produced. Moreover, the project allowed a greater grid capacity to integrate renewable energy and EVs (charging stations), and to improve the ability to detect and resolve failures of the electricity distribution network.

At public spaces, Évora InovCity enabled (1) traditional lamps' upgrades to LED technology that resulted to a 40%−50% electricity costs' reduction; (2) lighting adjustment according to natural light conditions (i.e., lights switch on automatically on dusks and gradually light intensity increases and minimizes unnecessary consumption); (3) light intensity decreases between 2:00 a.m. and 5:00 a.m., leaving enough for minimum security purposes; (4) light dimming according to the approach or presence of vehicles or pedestrians, ambient luminosity, and atmospheric conditions. For instance, the remote light switch off in the absence of visitors in museum rooms resulted to an overall energy savings of approximately 12% (EDP, 2017).

2.2.2 Integrated city planning toward Évora Action Plan for sustainable energy

Évora was one of the four European cities' partners of the Integrative Smart City Planning (InSMART) project (http://www.insmartenergy.com/) that was implemented from 2014 to 2017 with a mission to compose sustainable energy action plans (SEAPs) for each city using a comprehensive and integrated approach. A mix of sustainable energy measures to enhance energy efficiency and reduce GHG emissions of each city was introduced, by approaching the whole city energy system through specialized tools and models, and a series of participative workshops with local stakeholders.

In 2012 Évora delivered its Sustainable Action Plan (CME, 2012) to the Covenant of Mayors. According to this plan, CO_2 emissions were estimated to be 4.87 tCO_2/inhabitant, where residential and commercial buildings (35%) were the highest emitters, followed by private and commercial transportation (32%) and waste management processes (31%). Several actions were proposed to reduce 20% of CO_2 emissions in 2020, including information and financial incentives, and urban planning regulation for buildings, technological substitution in public lighting, public transportation and alternative modes and vehicles incentives for mobility sector, and recycling and waste production prevention. The InSMART project was implemented under a close collaboration with the team in charge at Évora Municipality in order to revise and compose the next SEAP version, and with a high-level political support, advanced with regard to the methods to identify, assess, and rank a set of measures toward cost-effective low-carbon options up to 2030.

The InSMART project is explained in the next section and returned the benchmarking of the Évora Municipality for different reasons: (1) it relied on the Évora InovCity project (cf. Section 2.1) data infrastructure; (2) the city energy system included all the energy sectors, from energy producers to all type of energy consumers, organized in a well-structured reference system; (3) more than 30 stakeholders, from public bodies to private companies were engaged and participated in three workshops; (4) a detailed economic analysis of the mid-term measures was undertaken, identifying all relevant investment indicators; and (5) a detailed, realistic, and applicable mid-term implementation plan was developed including the timeline and the monitoring indicators for each city.

InSMART approaches the urban challenges of energy and climate change by considering the city energy system as an integrated network of energy flows

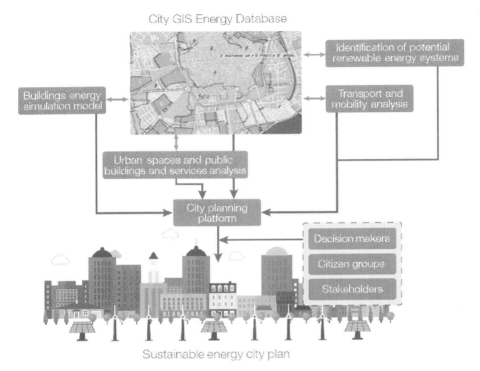

Figure 2.1 Integrated city energy planning framework.
Source: Adapted from Giannakidis, G., Seixas, J., Gouveia, J.P., Simões, S., Dias, L., Robinson, D., et al. (2017). *INSMART – Integrative Smart City Planning. Project book.* Available from: <www.insmartenergy.com> (Giannakidis et al., 2017).

connecting energy providers with buildings, public spaces, transport, and utilities, while taking into account spatial differentiation (Giannakidis et al., 2018; Gouveia, Seixas, & Giannakidis, 2016). The detailed analysis of the local energy system with simulation tools, accompanied by the active participation of decision-makers and stakeholders, reflects the cornerstone of the InSMART Integrated City Energy Planning Framework, as illustrated in Fig. 2.1. We may state that the InSMART project provided the framework, tools, and practice to influence the conceptualization of a smart city for the case of Évora, covering the aspects of intelligent energy, reduction in GHG emissions, and local empowerment and development.

2.2.3 "Smart cities" memorandum of understanding

In 2016 the Municipality of Évora, together with the Central Alentejo Intermunicipal Community (CIMAC), nine municipalities in the Alentejo region, the Alentejo Regional Development Agency and companies, such as CISCO, PT, CEIIA, EDP Distribuição, Decsis, or Phillips, signed the "Smart Cities"

Memorandum of Understanding (MoU). This commitment intended to concern a starting point for the promotion of opportunities in the region and in Évora, with reference to the concept of "Smart & Connected Communities (S + CC)," which defines a community that synergistically integrates intelligent technologies with natural and built environments, including infrastructure, in line with the concept of smart cities (Villa & Mitchell, 2010).

The vision of S + CC changes the way urban areas are planned and managed to achieve economic, social, and environmental sustainability. In this regard, that MoU foresees the promotion of joint activities and explores potential collaborations in the areas of mutual interest in sustainable urbanization, such as the identification of new urban services where new or existing solutions and architectures can be implemented in pilot experiments. These services may include parking, waste, lighting, water, public safety, energy efficiency, and mobilization of citizens, among others, always aiming at improving the living conditions of populations. The innovation of this initiative relies on the commitment of many public entities of the Alentejo region, with governance responsibilities, which makes the implementation of innovative services easier and effective for a wide proportion of the local population.

2.3 Research methodology: case study

The city of Évora has a well-preserved old town center, which is still partially enclosed by medieval walls. A large number of monuments that are dated from various historical periods are located in the city, including a Roman temple, which made Évora a UNESCO World Heritage Site, and a member of the Most Ancient European Towns Network. It is located in the Alentejo region of Portugal covering an area of 1307 km^2, with a population of 57,000 inhabitants (INE, 2011). Around 80% of the inhabitants of the municipality live in the city. The Municipality of Évora is a strong and dynamic regional hub due to its demographic and economic potential and its concentration of industrial and logistic activities. Évora's economy is mainly based on the services sector, including decentralized services of the central government, and recently it has become a major international tourist attraction. Industry includes electronics and electromechanical components and civil construction. The countryside is open wide with extensive cereal fields, pasture, and remarkable forest patches of cork and holm oak, often with cereals and pastures under cover, as well as olive groves, and vineyards, making agriculture an important activity in the municipality.

As stated previously, Évora has been selected as the case study of this chapter because it is a city where several initiatives take place. In this section, we present the approach, tools, and results of the FP7 European-funded project, InSMART—Integrated Smart City Planning project, which involved four European cities: Évora (Portugal), Cesena (Italy), Nottingham (United Kingdom), and Trikala (Greece), with the support of scientific and technical organizations of the same countries. The project run from 2014 to 2017 and contributed to push Évora city planning toward a smart and sustainable city, mostly related with its energy system. Gargiulo et al. (2017) disclose selected results to the four cities.

The project was developed within a close collaboration between Center for Environmental and Sustainability Research (CENSE) at NOVA University of Lisbon and the Municipality of Évora, in particular the presidency body and the departments of local development and energy maintenance. A set of local stakeholders were engaged and participated in the project under a comprehensive framework: 6 stakeholders are regional public authorities, 7 are local authorities, 7 are business and private sectors, and 10 come from the local community, including academia and nongovernmental organizations.

2.3.1 Scope

The Évora case study focuses on energy as the main scope. The deployment of low or neutral carbon technologies for sustainable energy production and use requires the active engagement of local and regional communities. Several programs and plans (e.g., CoM, 2012; IDB, 2011) have involved cities that work toward sustainable development, decarbonization, and quality of life enhancement. Cities' activities affect the environment in both negative and positive ways (Dodman, McGranahan, & Dalal-Clayton, 2013) that lead to the need of cities to address climate change, reduce energy consumption, and increase the use of renewable energy sources through the development of holistic plans that respect environmental, societal, and economic aspects. To allow for city authorities to curb increasing energy demand to dealt with demographic changes and infrastructure maintenance, it is fundamental to make use of the appropriate methods and data analysis throughout the urban development value chain (WEF, 2018).

Although the growing availability of advanced computing and sensing capabilities facilitates the access to big data repositories that contain city information (Sanz et al., 2015), it still requires decision-makers to trust and understand the indicators and tools behind them. In the presented case, we depict the collection of different data sources and its analysis and portray the interoperability of diverse types of data (with different temporal and spatial dimensions), to provide useful and comprehensive information and knowledge to an integrated energy planning tool while considering all city demand sectors and its spatial patterns.

The project InSMART approaches the city energy system as an integrated network of energy flows that connect energy providers with energy consumers (buildings, public spaces, transport, and utilities), while considering spatial differences, being the residential buildings and transport object of a detailed analysis. Fig. 2.2 presents the Municipality of Évora that consists of 21 sectors, with regard to the mobility patterns identified through diary registries survey and road networks.

The InSMART integrative planning approach includes the analysis of energy consumption beyond residential buildings and transport. The following sectors were studied, and the energy consumption profiles were identified: municipal buildings, tertiary buildings, urban spaces, water and sewage systems, and the municipal solid

The smart city of Évora

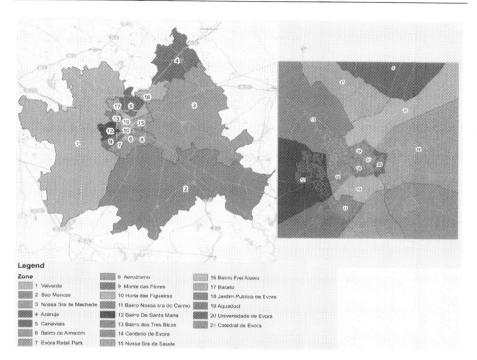

Figure 2.2 Évora city districts regarding the mobility patterns (Dias, Gouveia, Seixas, Bilo et al., 2015).

waste (MSW) collection and process (Dias, Gouveia, Seixas, Bilo, & Valentim, 2015). Future energy-saving potential, both technology based (e.g., improve efficiency of waste water treatment plants) and behavioral (e.g., impact of increasing MSW recycling rates), was assessed.

2.3.2 Integration

A structured analytical framework was developed and implemented to integrate multiple data sources and methods, with different temporal and spatial resolution (e.g., door-to-door surveys, smart meters, stakeholders' engagement, energy statistics), models (on transport and mobility, buildings simulation, energy system optimization), and analysis tools [statistical, common geographic information systems (GIS) platform], which able to support the integrated city energy modeling tool. A comprehensive extensive data capture and modeling processes to integrate all the interactions of energy use and production in the city was essential to deliver future sustainable energy pathways, while considering the participation and validations with the local stakeholders.

Integrated energy planning involves the economic, social, and environmental dimensions of a city and depicts all the energy demand sectors. We argue that a coherent and robust database of city indicators enables city decision-makers to efficiently achieve in their sustainable energy and climate targets. The most definitive aspect in energy planning and effective policy execution is the availability of adequate data, combined with detailed modeling and simulation to improve the knowledge of existing systems, namely, on energy flows among different consumers and city districts and on alternative energy measures (Brandoni & Polonara, 2012).

We make use of the massive electricity smart metering system installed in Évora (EDP Distribuição, 2016), to advance on a high-resolution data-based tool for integrated energy city planning. The Municipality of Évora calculates per capita annual energy consumption to the approximate amount of 48 GJ that can be compared to the average value of 61 GJ of the country of Portugal (DGEG, 2016). Oil products for transportation and agriculture, together with electricity for residential buildings, services, and industry are the major energy sources of the municipality. There is a high potential to decarbonize the energy system, namely, by providing endogenous renewable resources, mostly solar-based solutions. A conservative estimate of technical potential of solar PV at utility scale, taking into account spatial planning regulations, points to more than 2 TW h/year (Lourenço, 2014), corresponding to ninefold the annual electricity consumption of Évora Municipality. Also, for rooftop solar PV, conservative potential estimations point out to around 40 MW (Dias, Gouveia, & Seixas, 2015). Currently, 2.4 MW of utility-scale projects are already installed, and almost 1.2 GW h produced by rooftop decentralized solutions (EDP Distribuição, 2016).

The integrated analytical framework bridges the gap between data requirements and their availability through their collection from the ground up and analysis for all the urban energy sectors (i.e., residential buildings, transport and mobility, and other energy demand sectors and supply side) in selected geographical units of a city (i.e., spatial districts). The framework makes use of multiscale data of diverse types and granularity including (1) 15 minutes' electricity consumption data from smart meters, (2) monthly/annual statistical energy production and consumption values, (3) detailed energy modeling of buildings archetypes, (4) transportation characteristics and mobility flows, and (5) door-to-door surveys. The Integrated City Energy Planning Tool is rooted in technological-economic model (TIMES model) and makes use of all this data to generate representations of the city energy system in a base year and predicting future low-carbon and sustainable pathways by 2030.

The city energy indicators are mapped into a web-based GIS platform allowing geospatial analysis, bringing forward the awareness and participation of different levels of city stakeholders, namely, municipal technicians, planners and decision-makers, utilities, transportation companies, citizen groups, and market associations. The stakeholders' participation along the process, namely, through a multicriteria assessment tool, is an essential of the smart and sustainable city planning, in assembling an acceptable, realistic, and mostly beneficial city action plan. Fig. 2.3 shows the different data and methods that were used to generate future smart and sustainable pathways for Évora energy system.

The smart city of Évora

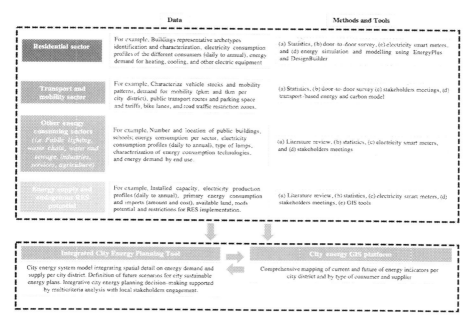

Figure 2.3 Integrated framework of data and methods to generate future smart and sustainable pathways for Évora energy system.

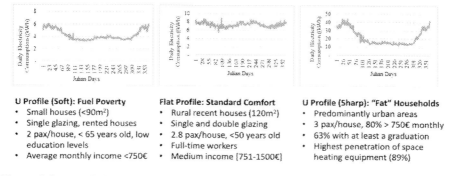

U Profile (Soft): Fuel Poverty
- Small houses (<90m²)
- Single glazing, rented houses
- 2 pax/house, < 65 years old, low education levels
- Average monthly income <750€

Flat Profile: Standard Comfort
- Rural recent houses (120m²)
- Single and double glazing
- 2.8 pax/house, <50 years old
- Full-time workers
- Medium income (751-1500€)

U Profile (Sharp): "Fat" Households
- Predominantly urban areas
- 3 pax/house, 80% > 750€ monthly
- 63% with at least a graduation
- Highest penetration of space heating equipment (89%)

Figure 2.4 Annual electricity consumption profiles for three clusters (2011–14 average). *Source:* Adapted from Gouveia, J.P., & J. Seixas (2016). Unraveling electricity consumption profiles in households through clusters: Combining smart meters and door-to-door surveys. Energy and Buildings 116, 666–676.

Considering the case of smart meter registries available, we were able to link 64% of the collected households' door-to-door surveys (i.e., 389), with the respective smart meters (275), while preserving the confidentiality of the house owners. The combination of these two sources of information allowed the identification of 10 comprehensive and coherent households' clusters (Gouveia & Seixas, 2016), three of which are illustrated in Fig. 2.4. This information coupled with energy simulation of buildings typologies allowed the disclosure of the households potentially under fuel poverty conditions, and those with potential excess consumption where it is essential to develop smart solutions, either policy instruments or energy products (Gouveia, Seixas, & Long, 2018). In addition, the smart metering data were also identified as a valuable tool to assess households' behavior for climatization (both space heating a cooling) (Gouveia, Seixas, & Mestre, 2017). All this research highlighted has significant for roles and activities of DSOs (Nunes, Gouveia, Rodrigues, & Simão, 2017).

Mobility patterns were also assessed via door-to-door surveys and travel diaries, to produce maps of energy consumption with hotspots of mobility demand. Likewise, the energy profiles of public spaces, and of water, wastewater, and waste systems were considered in the integrated energy system model, a technology-based optimization tool (TIMES_Evora) (Simoes, Dias, Gouveia, & Seixas, 2016a), as illustrated in Fig. 2.5.

Future pathways for Évora were generated after envisioning "Smart Évora," with no changes on energy consumption profiles for the each of the consumers' groups (e.g., residential, services, and transport), but with an increase of soft mobility options in selected areas. Moreover, the impact of the construction of the new mall and sports store, and the relocation of the municipality technical services, the

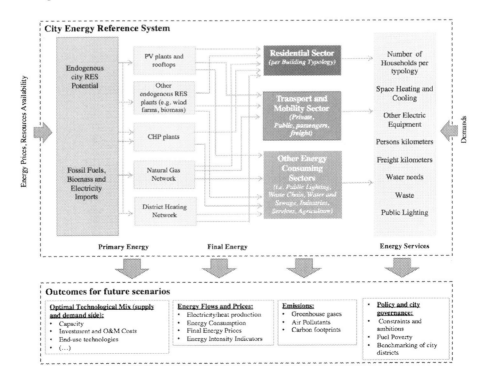

Figure 2.5 Structure of the TIMES_Evora model, including main inputs and outputs, used to generate future smart and sustainable pathways for Évora energy system.

construction of a new district hospital, new roads, and the expansion of the industrial park were considered. The technological options were tested with the integrated modeling tool are listed in Table 2.1.

The impact in terms of energy efficiency, emissions reduction, and costs of investment, and operation and maintenance was assessed through the integrated modeling tool TIMES_Evora considering the whole energy system of the city,

Table 2.1 Technological options tested in TIMES_Evora model for the Smart Évora vision.

Name	Description	Code
Public lighting		
Changing luminaires with more efficient lamps	Change 80% public lighting to LEDs by 2020 Change all public lighting to LEDs by 2030	PL1 PL2
Residential buildings		
Solar thermal	Install solar thermal hot water panels in 10% of dwellings by 2020	RSD1
	Install solar thermal hot water panels in 40% of dwellings in 2030	RSD2
Solar PV	Solar PV installed corresponding to 10% of maximum feasible potential by 2020	RSD3
	Solar PV installed corresponding to 30% of maximum feasible by 2030	RSD4
Insulation windows	Double glazing in 80% of dwellings by 2030	RSD6
Insulation infiltration	Small-scale insulation solutions in 50% of dwellings by 2030	RSD7
Insulation walls and roofs	Wall & Roof insulation combined in 60% of dwellings by 2030	RSD8
Waste, water, and waste water		
Increase recycling	Increase by 35% the share of recycled MSW after 2020	R1
Decrease MSW production	Decrease MSW production per capita in 20% from 2013 values	R2
Energy efficiency in water system	Improve energy efficiency in water treatment plants in 50% by 2030/2009	R3
Energy efficiency in waste water treatment	Improve energy efficiency in waste water treatment plant in 30% by 2030/2009	R4
Transport		
Promotion of cycling	Extension of the existent 7 km cycling lanes combined with making city bikes available from 2020 onward	TRA1

(Continued)

Table 2.1 (Continued)

Name	Description	Code
City centre traffic restrictions	Duplicate parking fees in historic center from 2020 onward	TRA2
	Interdiction for all type of vehicles and concerning all purposes to the Évora Acropolis from 2020 onward	TRA3
Speed reductions	Speed limitation to 30 km/h, for all vehicles in diverse zones from 2020 onward	TRA4
Electric vehicles	5% of passenger cars are electric by 2030	TRAelc
Biofuel buses	All buses use biofuels by 2030	TRAbus
Increase historic center parking—concentrated	Construction of three parking lots with a total of 500 parking spaces for nonresidents in the historic center from 2020 onward	TRA7
Increase historic center parking—disperse	300 new parking spaces for residents in the historic center from 2020 onward	TRA8
Public transportation	Shift of 15% from private cars mobility to public transportation from 2020 onward	TRA9
Systemic		
CO_2 emission cap	Reduction of total CO_2 emissions in 2030 of 30% from 2030 baseline values	CAP

LED, Light-emitting diode; *MSW*, municipal solid waste.

while it respected the existing typologies of buildings, the current spatial mobility patterns, and the profiles of electricity consumption along the year, as well as the endogenous energy resources of the municipality. For illustrative purposes, Fig. 2.6 shows the energy savings (higher limit) and CO_2 emissions (lower limit) in 2030 obtained with each option when compared to the baseline scenario.

2.3.3 Organization

InSMART is based on a participatory design and development approach. All city stakeholders were invited to collaborate and contribute in the consultation process about alternative energy futures: the municipal authorities, commercial and professional associations, private companies, and citizens. Each stakeholder group contributed to the vision for the city's development in the next 15 years, through three sequential workshops: (1) Scenarios definition, (2) Results discussion, and (3) evaluation criteria definition and weighting, then ranking the city's energy measures.

After the identification and analysis of a wide set of multiple options conducting to smart and sustainable pathways for the city, there is the need to identify the optimal sustainable path of city. The energy system is complex and is conditioned by a wide range of actors, with different responsibilities and roles, and therefore, the organization and selection of the smart options must be approached through a

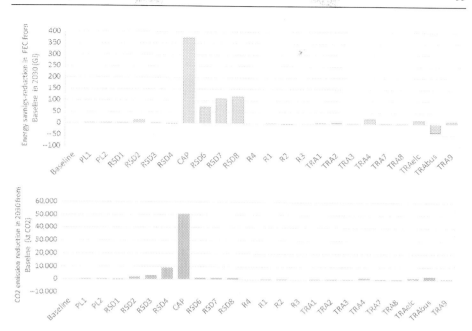

Figure 2.6 Energy savings and CO_2 emissions reduction in 2030 for each modeled option (cf. Table 2.1), when compared to the baseline (Simoes et al., 2016a).

coherent and inclusive method, to ensure the representativeness and effectiveness of the selected smart solutions that will be implemented.

We used a multicriteria decision analysis (MCDA), which is a generic framework, able to use to inform and support complex decision-making situations with multiple and often conflicting objectives "that stakeholders' groups and/or decision-makers value differently" (Saarikoski et al., 2016). Both energy and environmental policies involve large numbers of stakeholders with different views and preferences. Due to the numerous attributes of the policy alternatives that are nonmarket valued, the multiple views of the stakeholders cannot always be determined in advance or with certainty (Greening & Bernow, 2004). The use of MCDA allows a better alternative to cost/benefit or cost-effectiveness-based methods (Greening & Bernow, 2004; Wang, Jing, Zhang, & Zhao, 2009). The PROMETHEE method (Brans, 1984) was applied in energy planning and used the outranking principle to rank the alternatives. It is well adapted to problems where a finite number of alternatives require ranking while it considers several, sometimes, conflicting, criteria (Terrados, Almonacid, & Perez-Higueras, 2009; Wang et al., 2009).

In a typical MCDA process applied to energy planning, it usually includes four main stages (Wang et al., 2009): (1) alternatives' formulation and criteria selection, (2) criteria weighting, (3) evaluation, and (4) final treatment and aggregation. PROMETHEE was applied in the city of Évora and provided a ranking of the alternative options for smart energy planning actions, ranging from the best to the worst (in the context of compromising the mix of evaluation criteria) possible interventions (Simoes, Dias, Gouveia, & Seixas, 2016b). Table 2.2 lists the criteria that were used in our analysis, which characterized each of the options that were modeled, which were the data for criteria A, B, and C being provided by the TIMES_Evora model, and for criteria D and E taken from expert guess of the InSMART Portugal team, based on literature data and bilateral consultation with Évora stakeholders.

Table 2.2 Performance of each criterion (Simoes et al., 2016b).

Criterion	Indicator(s) to assess performance
A. Reduction of energy consumption	PJ of saved final and primary energy
B. Reduction of GHG emission	t CO_2 of avoided emissions
C. Financial effort	€ of total investment cost + € of annual operation and maintenance cost
D. Contribution for local development	*High*—New jobs creation, foreseen involvement of local companies providing services/products in the implementation, and no potential for the creation of new businesses *Medium*—No jobs are created, foreseen involvement of local companies providing services/products in the implementation, and no potential for the creation of new businesses *Low*—No jobs are created, no foreseen involvement of local companies providing services/products in the implementation, and no potential for the creation of new businesses
E. Contribution for improving comfort and quality of life	*High*—Significant improvements in indoor thermal comfort, mobility services (including congestion and parking), and public lighting *Medium*—Moderate improvements in indoor thermal comfort, mobility services (including congestion and parking), and public lighting *Low*—No foreseen improvements in indoor thermal comfort, mobility services (including congestion and parking), and public lighting
F. Feasibility of implementation	*High*—Directly involves less than 100 end targets as implementers, permitting process entails approval of a maximum of two different institutions, estimated implementation time is lower than 1 year, will not create social opposition *Medium*—Directly involves more than 1000 end targets as implementers, permitting process entails approval of a maximum of four different institutions, estimated implementation time is longer than 1 year, most probably will not create social opposition *Low*—Directly involves more than 5000 end targets as implementers, permitting process entails approval of at least four different institutions, estimated implementation time is longer than 2 years, potentially will create social opposition

Table 2.3 Results of the criteria weight allocation made during the stakeholder workshop (Simoes et al, 2016b).

Group	Allocated weight (1−5) to each criterion					
	A.	B.	C.	D.	E.	F.
Average						
Local authorities	5	3	4	4	4	3
Civil society	5	4	3	4	4	3
Public services and regional authorities	5	5	3	5	3	2
Private sector	3	4	4	3	4	3
Consensus						
Local authorities	No consensus was obtained, median was used					
Civil society	No consensus was obtained, median was used					
Public services and regional authorities	5	5	3	5	3	2
Private sector	3	5	4	1	4	2

Each criterion was weighted with 25 stakeholders in a workshop in Évora, with a value that ranged from 1 to 5, where 1 stands for "very low relevance criterion" and 5 for "highly relevant criterion." During the workshop in Évora the stakeholders were organized in four groups: (1) local authorities (e.g., departments of the Municipality of Évora and several civil parishes), (2) civil society representatives (e.g., GARE—Association for the Promotion of a Culture of Road Security, DECO —Portuguese Association for the Defense of the Consumer, Évora University), (3) public services and regional authorities (e.g., ADRAL—Regional Development Agency of Alentejo, GESAMB—Environment and Waste Management, CIMAC— Intermunicipal Community of Central Alentejo), and (4) private sector (e.g., EDP S.A., EDIA S.A., Cycloid) (Simoes et al., 2016b).

The stakeholders initially discussed the criteria in order to achieve a first common basis of understanding on their meaning and then to allocate the weights in an individual basis. This was then followed by another discussion period to try to achieve consensus on the weights, which was only possible for two of the stakeholder groups. The results in the weighing are presented in Table 2.3. In conclusion, Table 2.4 presents the classification of the acceptable (Phi > 0) and the three worst (lowest negative Phi) actions for each stakeholder group together with the ones obtained by the compromise problem.

MCDA analysis provided the following results, reflecting a compromise among all stakeholder groups' preferences:

1. Acceptable measures:
   a. TRAelc—Shift of 15% from private cars mobility to public transportation from 2020 onward;
   b. TRAbus—All buses use biofuels in 2030;
   c. R2—Decrease MSW production per capita in 20% from 2013 values;

Table 2.4 Summary of the alternatives per stakeholder group ranked per Phi value (Simoes et al, 2016a).

#	Local authorities	Regional authorities	Private	Civil society
	\multicolumn{4}{c}{**Best performing solutions**}			
1	[a]Electric cars (TRAelc)	[a]Electric cars (TRAelc)	[a]Electric cars (TRAelc)	[a]Electric cars (TRAelc)
2	[a]Decrease MSW production (R2)	[a]Speed reductions (TRA4)	[a]Biofuel buses (TRAbus)	[a]Speed reductions (TRA4)
3	[a]Speed reductions (TRA4)	[a]Biofuel buses (TRAbus)	[a]Light insulation (RSD7)	[a]Biofuel buses (TRAbus)
4	[a]Light insulation (RSD7)	[a]Decrease MSW production (R2)	[a]Wall & Roof insulation (RSD8)	[a]Decrease MSW production (R2)
5	[a]Wall & Roof insulation (RSD8)	[c]Increase parking fees (TRA2)	[b]Solar PV roof up to 30% potential (RSD4)	[c]Increase parking fees (TRA2)
6	[a]Biofuel buses (TRAbus)	[a]Light insulation (RSD7)	[a]Speed reductions (TRA4)	[a]Light insulation (RSD7)
7	[c]Increase parking fees (TRA2)	[c]City center traffic restrictions (TRA3)	[b]Solar PV up to 10% maximum feasible (RSD2)	[a]Wall & Roof insulation (RSD8)
8	[c]City center traffic restrictions (TRA3)	[a]Wall & Roof insulation (RSD8)	[a]Decrease MSW production (R2)	[c]City center traffic restrictions (TRA3)
9	[a]Increase recycling (R1)	[a]Double glazing windows (RSD6)	[a]Double glazing windows (RSD6)	[a]Increase recycling (R1)
10	[a]Double glazing windows (RSD6)	[a]Solar thermal (RSD2)	[a]Solar thermal (RSD2)	[a]Double glazing windows (RSD6)
11	[a]Solar thermal (RSD2)	[a]Increase recycling (R1)	[a]Increase recycling (R1)	[a]Solar thermal (RSD2)
	\multicolumn{4}{c}{**Three worst solutions**}			
	[d]PL2	[d]TRA7	[d]TRA1	[d]TRA7
	[d]RSD1	[d]TRA8	[d]TRA8	[d]TRA8
	[d]TRA8	[d]RSD1	[d]RSD1	[d]RSD1

MSW, Municipal solid waste.
[a]Solutions acceptable by all stakeholder groups.
[b]Solutions acceptable by at least two stakeholder groups.
[c]Actions reflecting at least two stakeholder groups' preferences.
[d]Actions among the three worst ones for all stakeholder groups.

    d. TRA4—Speed limitation to 30 km/h, for all vehicles in diverse zones from 2020 onward;
    e. RSD7—Small scale insulation solutions in 50% of dwellings by 2030;
    f. RSD8—Wall & Roof insulation combined in 60% of dwellings by 2030;
    g. RSD6—Double glazing in 80% of dwellings by 2030;
    h. RSD2—Install solar thermal hot water panels in 40% of dwellings in 2030;
    i. TRA2—Duplicate parking fees in historic center from 2020 onward;
    j. TRA3—Interdiction for all type of vehicles and concerning all purposes to the Évora Acropolis from 2020 onward.
2. Worst measures:
    a. TRA8—Increase historic center parking disperse with 300 new disperse parking spaces for residents in the historic center from 2020 onward;
    b. RSD1—Install solar thermal hot water panels in 10% of dwellings by 2020;
    c. PL2—Change all public lighting to LEDs by 2030.

We may comment on the apparent nonrational disregard of measure PL2, due to its known cost-effectiveness, by saying that the stakeholders departed from their own perspective that does not include public lightning and assumed the public lighting substitution by LEDs is likely an obvious decision, taking the current state of the art, so it does not require additional effort in terms of decision-making.

2.3.4 Time

The InSMART project required a 10 years' implementation plan, including a timeline, allocation resources, and a monitoring system. Due to the exploratory nature of the selected measures identified within the project (i.e., they have to be detailed and approved by a formal local governance process), the 10-year period was taken in three steps for the implementation: immediate (1–2 year), meaning a high priority for the municipality, intermediate (3–5 years), and further ahead (6–10 years). Table 2.5 illustrates the split of the selected measures into the three periods of the 10-year timeline.

A set of key performance indicators that were used to monitor the plan's implementation is provided in Table 2.6. Data were collected from several municipal services, including the municipal financial and operational departments, on an annual basis.

2.3.5 Cost

The acceptable measures resulting from the integrated TIMES_Evora modeling tool assessment, and from the MCDA decision-making analysis, were further developed to estimate its costs. Some of the success of acceptable measures requires the willingness of the municipal governance bodies to promote them, while others depend mostly on the consumers' decision and, at some extent, the willingness of the national government bodies. Therefore for simplicity we select those requiring actions from local governance bodies to estimate the costs involved. Table 2.7 illustrates the performance and investment costs for the selected measures. We included

Table 2.5 Timing of implementation.

Measures:	TIMING		
	Immediate (1–2 years)	Intermediate (3–5 years)	Further ahead (6–10 years)
R2—Decrease MSW production per capita in 20% from 2013 values	X		
RSD7—Small-scale insulation solutions in 50% of dwellings by 2030	X		
RSD8—Wall & Roof insulation combined in 60% of dwellings by 2030			
RSD6—Double glazing in 80% of dwellings by 2030			
RSD2—Install solar thermal hot water panels in 40% of dwellings in 2030			
TRA1: Extension of the existent 7 km cycling lanes combined with making city bikes available from 2020 onward	X		
TRAelc—Shift of 15% from private cars mobility to public transportation from 2020 onward		X	
TRAbus—All buses use biofuels in 2030		X	
TRA2—Duplicate parking fees in historic center from 2020 onward;			X
TRA3—Interdiction for all type of vehicles and concerning all purposes to the Évora Acropolis from 2020 onward			X
TRA4—Speed limitation to 30 km/h, for all vehicles in diverse zones from 2020 onward			X

the extra measure TRA9 although it was not selected as one of acceptable measures by consensus, but by the local governance bodies. For the case of consumers' decision, costs indicators were estimated for the case of the historic center of the city, which may be taken as an indication of the magnitude of the incentives the local governance bodies may put in place. For these cases the savings reflect a combination of the three measures and were modeled with TIMES-Evora, while the investment costs were estimated via a survey of insulation options available in the Portuguese market and estimating its application considering the building typologies available in the historic center.

Table 2.6 Évora InSMART key performance indicators.

Sectors	Key performance indicators	Unit
Energy		
Transport	Variation of FEC	GJ
	FEC per capita	J/inhab
Residential buildings	Variation of FEC	GJ
	FEC per capita	J/inhab
Public buildings	Variation of FEC	GJ
	Energy intensity	J/public employers
Public lighting	Variation of FEC	GJ
	Share of LED over total lighting	%
Waste services	Variation of FEC in waste systems	GJ
	FEC per capita	J/inhab
Integrated city	Variation of TPEC	GJ
	New PV installed capacity in roof tops	MW
	New utility-scale PV installed capacity	MW
Carbon emissions		
Transport	Variation of GHG emissions in transport	tCO$_2$e
Residential buildings	Variation of GHG emissions in residential buildings	tCO$_2$e
	Average household carbon intensity	kgCO$_2$/household
Public buildings	Variation of GHG emissions in public buildings	tCO$_2$e
	Average buildings carbon intensity	kgCO$_2$/m^2
Public lighting	Average carbon intensity	
Waste services	Variation of GHG emissions in waste systems	tCO2e
	Average carbon intensity	kgCO$_2$/inhab
Integrated city	Variation of GHG emissions	% change from base year
	Emissions per capita	tCO$_2$e/inhab
	Total GHG emissions	tCO$_2$e
Financial		
Transport	Investment in transport measures	M€
Public buildings	Investment in public buildings measures	M€
Public lighting	Investment in public lighting measures	M€
Waste services	Investment in sectoral measures	M€
Other		
Transport	Extension of bike lanes	km
	Public bikes	No
	EV charging points	No
	New parking lots	No

(Continued)

Table 2.6 (Continued)

Sectors	Key performance indicators	Unit
Public buildings	Zero-energy buildings	No
Public lighting	New automated management	No
Waste services	Variation of waste production	t
	Variation of recycling rate	% from base year

EV, Electric vehicle; *FEC*, final energy consumption; *GHG*, greenhouse gas; *LED*, light-emitting diode; *PV*, photovoltaic; *TPEC*, total primary energy consumption.

Table 2.7 Performance of the modeled measures for all zones of Évora considered in InSMART. The energy savings and CO_2 emission reduction values are a relative difference to a baseline case in 2030 where the respective measure is not implemented.

Code	Reduction of energy consumption in 2030 (GJ)	Reduction of CO_2 emission in 2030 (t)	Investment for the whole period of the investment (€ 2015)
R2: Decrease MSW production per capita in 20% from 2013 values[a]	951	89,661	300,000
TRA1: Extension of the existent 7 km cycling lanes combined with making city bikes available from 2020 onward[a]	2959	197,633	1190,000
TRA2: Duplicate parking fees in historic center from 2020 onward[a]	3695	261,207	—
TRA3: Interdiction for all type of vehicles and concerning all purposes to the Évora Acropolis from 2020 onward[a]	1617	109,703	15,000
TRA4: Speed limitation to 30 km/h, for all vehicles in diverse zones from 2020 onward[a]	18,341	1303,333	20,000
TRAbus: All buses use biofuels by 2030[b]	−37,400	2272,948	1802,423
TRA9: Shift of 15% from private cars mobility to public transportation from 2020 onward[a]	9218	657772	10,000

(*Continued*)

Table 2.7 (Continued)

Code	Reduction of energy consumption in 2030 (GJ)	Reduction of CO_2 emission in 2030 (t)	Investment for the whole period of the investment (€ 2015)
Indicators for the historic center of Évora city			
RSD6: Double glazing in 80% of dwellings by 2030[b]	5 918	1 112 240	11 388 164
RSD7: Small-scale insulation solutions in 50% of dwellings by 2030[b]			5 633 622
RSD8: Wall & Roof insulation combined in 60% of dwellings by 2030[b]			355 505

The financial effort was estimated via different approaches as indicated. *MSW*, Municipal solid waste.
[a]Project-based estimates.
[b]TIMES_Évora model estimates.

The measures considered herein contributing to transform Évora city into a more sustainable city setup mostly on clean mobility, and urban planning and retrofitting at the historical center. The reason for this relies on the local government's ambition to revitalize the historical center toward a smart and sustainable one. Having said that, the economic viability of the estimated investments has been approached as a public investment and not as a market-based private investment. Within this context, funding schemes available in Portugal for sustainability, development, and climate mitigation existing may be considered to boost the needed investment, namely, the Portugal 2020, as part of the European Regional Development Funds, the National Energy Efficiency Fund, the European Union LIFE Programme, the JESSICA Holding Fund Portugal, and the ELENA mechanism from the European Investment Bank.

In addition to the investments on sustainable solutions a great effort is calling to add smart solutions through Internet-based technologies boosting innovation in terms of efficient and clean energy consumption.

2.3.6 Risks

The case presented in this chapter refers to the production of a huge amount of information and knowledge on the city energy system, following a comprehensive methodology, instead of a digital technology or feature. The risks identified along the 3-year project mostly referred to data availability and were treated through alternative data gathering, as surveys or interviews. However, the risk we want to stress on this section points to the availability of the information and knowledge acquired to the market or to policy bodies. This information and knowledge is partially included in standard reports and scientific published papers, but most of it is not easily available to the city actors.

Energy indicators, spatially explicit per city sector, are available through a GIS web platform (http://beta.cres.gr/insmart/gis_evora.html). Indicators include for example the energy consumption for building typologies, road network with speed limits, bike lanes, energy consumption for transportation, energy consumption for water, wastewater and waste treatment, solar PV potential, for the base year (2013), as well as energy maps for the measures toward sustainable pathways. The GIS available energy maps have the purpose of visualization of the impact of such measures that mostly benefit the political and social actors.

However, there is the risk that the huge amount of detailed information on energy consumption in a myriad of activities in Évora is not likely available to other actors, although it could support the development of new digital solutions to make the city smarter in terms of energy consumption and production. This risk is a tangible one, and it is not easy to overcome, because of the data property issue, and unavailable data infrastructure. We underline this risk, as a hot issue regarding projects with massive data production pipelines.

2.3.7 Discussion—the fringes

> "Évora is the first city in Portugal to have a massive implementation of smart energy meters with over 35,000 being installed, which opens the possibility of adjusting energy consumption to the real necessities and, fundamentally, to change the standards of energy consumption with a view to greater sustainability and efficiency. This is also accompanied by other municipal projects to adapt to climate change and the development of intelligent solutions, in line with Évora's commitment to the Covenant of Mayors to reduce its GHG emissions by 2020. With InSMART we could deepen this commitment! The project has helped us to better assess options for energy use in a more sustainable way, while improving the well-being of our citizens and the competitiveness of our businesses." By Carlos Pinto de Sá—Mayor of Évora. Fig. 2.7 presents an air view of the city of Évora.

We may underline the lessons learnt and key innovations achieved with InSMART for the city of Évora, which could be expanded to other cities. Regarding the innovation in the city's energy system knowledge, the following aspects were achieved:

1. Improved knowledge on energy consumption, in particular for electricity consumption in the residential sector, supported by an in-depth analysis of smart meter data. As a spin-off to this it was possible to
    a. characterize fuel-poor consumers and
    b. identify complementarities between potential PV-generated electricity and daily consumption profiles of end users in commercial, residential, and industry sectors.
2. Detailed characterization of the residential building stock, through building typologies and in-depth assessment of its energy-saving potential.

Figure 2.7 Air view of the city of Évora.
Source: Évora Municipality.

3. Detailed mapping of solar thermal and solar PV technical potential (first city in Portugal with this information).
4. Mobility analysis, including for major infrastructure planned (the new ring road or shopping malls) and modeling of impact of transport-related measures.

Regarding the innovation in the city's energy system planning, the following points can be listed:

1. The engagement of external stakeholders in the energy planning process of the city, whereas before only municipal staff were doing this task. This clearly promoted synergies, by considering new perspectives on visioning the future of the municipality and increased awareness of energy planning.
2. A prospective thinking about energy consumption in Évora as an "integrated urban energy system" highlighted new priorities instead of those traditionally taken under municipal management, which is a challenge for a new generation of local energy policies.
3. The use of methods, such as MCDA, and engaging different groups of external stakeholders enabled convergence around a set of sustainable energy measures that are both scientifically sound and socially acceptable for the future of the municipality.

The achievements for the city gained by the InSMART project are of high value regarding the knowledge acquired but deserve a better commitment from the political framework that governs the city. Although much of the data and analysis that supported the project was obtained through a very close collaboration with the municipal services, and the measures identified within a participatory process with regional and local authorities, business, and academia, the implementation of such measures are dependent from political decision framework. A huge amount of knowledge on Évora sustainable energy system was produced and is available to the high-level political will and decision. Furthermore, this knowledge is also available for the market to inspire new and useful digital solutions on energy use targeted to the different consumers' clusters. However, it should be underlined that these potential features require further efforts to be real and effective. Therefore we advocate that the data and knowledge produced should be made easily available, more than in the usual standard reports and published papers. Additional insights on integrated modeling for the four cities are extensively discussed in Simoes et al. (2018). It was found that energy modeling at urban level brings with it a new set of challenges since, for a well-known territory, transparency, and effective communication with local decision-makers are even more important than at national or transnational level. Special efforts should be paid to making model results geographically explicit, and urban modeling results should expect scrutiny by local agents. Smart energy systems demand to close the gap between the scope for action of local energy planners, and the most energy intensive urban sectors, which highlighted new priorities instead of those traditionally taken under municipal management.

2.4 Conclusions

Évora was the first Iberian smart city to be included in the Inovgrid project—Évora InovCity, providing the installation of 35,000 energy boxes (smart meters) free of cost, corresponding to 54,000 consumers. This feature allowed to install new abilities, such as smart metering, intelligent public lighting controlling, charging infrastructure for EVs, energy efficiency, and client interaction interfaces. For these reasons, Évora was elected as one of the four European cities, to be the test case of the InSMART project that aimed to push forward innovative and sustainable solutions for the whole energy system.

The InSMART methodology offered the city an integrated and participatory process to explore and examine the energy consumption sectors together with potential local energy generation options and come up with a smart development plan for energy that is supported by all stakeholders. It can be integrated into the process of developing a SEAP or a Sustainable Energy and Climate Action Plan by municipalities participating in the Covenant of Mayors for Climate and Energy and offered the advantage of concrete scientific approaches in local energy planning, contributing to the realization of the EU's energy and climate goals.

InSMART identified the optimum mix of short-, medium-, and long-term measures for a sustainable energy future in Évora, by addressing the efficiency of energy flows across various city sectors with regards to economic, environmental, and social criteria and paving the way toward an actual implementation of priority actions and a more sustainable city planning. The selected measures cover the areas of clean and soft mobility, waste reduction, and energy efficiency solutions in buildings, totaling more than €20 million for the next 10 years, while reducing 6 $MtCO_2$.

The participation of the city's stakeholders proved to be vital both to increase the awareness of the scientific terms on the city's specific challenges to be tackled by the modeling tools and to the acceptance of the final ranking of options for the sustainable energy development of each city.

A considerable amount of new knowledge and information on Évora energy system was produced, some of it at a very detailed temporal resolution, and it is available both to the high-level political will and decision and to the market actors. Therefore there is a high potential both to advance on policies to promote some of the measures, mostly those seen as public investments or with positive impacts in local development, as well as on new digital solutions on energy use targeted to the different consumers' clusters.

Acknowledgments

The work supporting this chapter was partially funded by the EU project InSMART— Integrated Smart City Planning, under grant agreement no. 314164. The authors want to thank the other InSMART project members for their multiple and diverse contributions to the framework presented in this paper. The authors also want to thank the interviewers and citizens that made possible the accomplishment of the surveys and to the city stakeholders for the detailed data collection, in particular Nuno Bilo and António Valentim from Évora Municipality. We would also like to acknowledge the support given to CENSE by the Portuguese Foundation for Science and Technology through the strategic project UID/AMB/04085/2013.

About the authors

Júlia Seixas is a professor at the Faculty of Science and Technology of NOVA University of Lisbon (FCT NOVA), being currently the president of the Department of Environmental Sciences and Engineering. She coordinates the Energy & Climate line, at the CENSE at FCT NOVA, dedicated to the research of carbon neutral energy futures, and its linkages with climate change. She is a member of the scientific committee of the UL−UNL Joint PhD Program on Climate Change and Sustainable Development Policies. She uses to coordinate studies for energy and climate mitigation public policies, as well as for private companies. She has more than 50 publications in international scientific journals and is often invited to speak at conferences on sustainable energy and climate change futures.

Sofia Simões is a senior researcher on energy systems modeling, at the CENSE at FCT NOVA. Her work focuses on low-carbon energy systems, namely, on energy technological transitions, new policy approaches, and on the vulnerability and adaptation of energy systems to climate change, mostly using the ETSAP-TIMES model. She worked as a researcher for the European Commission—Joint Research Centre Institute for Energy and Transport modeling the EU energy system. She has a PhD from Leiden University (NL) and a MSc in Environmental

Management and Policy from Lund University (SE). Her BSc Degree is in environmental engineering from NOVA University. Sofia has 15 peer-reviewed publications in scientific journals and more than 30 publications in peer-reviewed conferences.

João Pedro Gouveia is an integrated member of the CENSE at FCT NOVA. He holds a PhD in Climate Change and Sustainable Development Policies—Sustainable Energy Systems (NOVA University of Lisbon/Lisbon University).

His topics of research are on smart cities, energy transitions, low-carbon energy technologies, and related economic and policy analysis, energy efficiency topics, energy poverty, and thermal comfort mapping, and smart meters data mining. He has 15 indexed publications in Scopus, and he is a coauthor of the New York Times Best Seller book: "DRAWDOWN: The Most Comprehensive Plan Ever Proposed to Reverse Global Warming." He has more than 30 presentations in national and international peer-reviewed conferences.

Luís Dias is currently a PhD student in the PhD program in Global Studies, a joint program between the Faculty of Sciences and Technology and the Faculty of Social Sciences and Humanities, both from NOVA University of Lisbon. At the CENSE at FCT NOVA, dedicated his research career to energy and climate mitigation studies and integrated analysis with air pollutants policies. He has worked for around 10 years in energy—environment modeling at different scales of action, from local to national and European levels. He has four publications in international scientific journals and more than 20 presentations in national and international peer-reviewed conferences.

References

Brandoni, C., & Polonara, F. (2012). The role of municipal energy planning in the regional energy-planning process. *Energy (2012)*, *48*(1), 323–338.

Brans, J. (1984). Operational research '84. In J. P. Brans (Ed.), *Proceedings of the Tenth International Conference on Operational Research/Actes de la Dixième Conférence Internationale de Recherche Opérationelle de l'IFORS, 1984* (pp. XIX, 1100). Amsterdam, New York, Oxford: North-Holland /Elsevier.

Carvalho, J. (2011). Lessons learned in implementing the InovGrid smart city project in Évora. Metering & Smart Energy International. Available from: <www.metering.com/lessons-learned-in-implementing-the-inovgrid-smart-city-project-in-vora/>.

CME (2012). *Plano de Ação para a Energia Sustentável de Évora. Évora Carbono Zero*. Camara Municipal de Évora. Available from: <http://www.cm-evora.pt/pt/site-viver/Habitar/ambiente/PublishingImages/Paginas/Evoracarbonozero/PAES_Evora2012.pdf>.

CoM (2012). *Covenant of Mayors official website*. Available from: <www.eumayors.eu/>.

DGEG. (2016). *Energy statistics*. Directorate for Energy and Geology. Available from: <www.dgeg.pt>.

Dias, L., Gouveia, J. P., & Seixas, J. (2015). Analysis of the cities' energy systems and networks. In *Internal report 5 assessment of RES potential at city level—The case of solar technologies. INSMART Integrative Smart City Planning project (ENER/FP7/314164)*. Available from: <www.insmartenergy.com>.

Dias, L., Gouveia, J. P., Seixas, J., Bilo, N., & Valentim, A. (2015). Analysis of the city energy system—Évora. In *Deliverable 4.1. INSMART Integrative Smart City Planning project (ENER/FP7/314164)*. Available from: <www.insmartenergy.com>.

Dodman, D., McGranahan, G., & Dalal-Clayton, B. (2013). *Integrating the environment in urban planning and management. Key principles and approaches for cities in the 21st century*. United Nations Environment Programme.

EDP (2017). *Évora Inovcity*. Available from: <https://www.edp.com/en/stories/evora-inovcity>.

EDP Distribuição. (2016). *Electricity Registries from Évora's Smart Meters database*. Lisbon, Portugal: InovGrid Évora. EDP Distribuição S.A.

Gargiulo, M., Chiodi, A., De Miglio, R., Simoes, S., Long, G., Pollard, M., . . . Giannakidis, G. (2017). An integrated planning framework for the development of sustainable and resilient cities—The case of the InSMART project. *Procedia Engineering, 198*, 444–453.

Giannakidis, G., Gargiulo, M., De Miglio, R., Chiodi, A., Seixas, J., Simoes, S. G., . . . Gouveia, J. P. (2018). Challenges faced when addressing the role of cities towards a below 2-degree world. In G. Giannakidis, K. Karlsson, M. Labriet, & B. Ó. Gallachóir (Eds.), *Limiting global warming to well below 2°C: Energy system modelling and policy development. Lecture notes in energy 30* (pp. 373–389). Springer International publishing. https://doi.org/10.1007/978-3-319-74424-7_22.

Giannakidis, G., Seixas, J., Gouveia, J. P., Simões, S., Dias, L., Robinson, D., et al. (2017). *INSMART – Integrative Smart City Planning. Project book*. Available from: <www.insmartenergy.com>.

Gouveia, J. P., & Seixas, J. (2016). Unraveling electricity consumption profiles in households through clusters: Combining smart meters and door-to-door surveys. *Energy and Buildings, 116*, 666–676.

Gouveia, J. P., Seixas, J., & Giannakidis, G. (2016). Smart City Energy Planning: Integrating data and tools. In *Proceedings of the 25th International Conference Companion on World Wide Web (WWW '16 Companion). International world wide web conferences steering committee, Republic and Canton of Geneva, Switzerland* (pp. 345–350). doi: https://doi.org/10.1145/2872518.2888617.

Gouveia, J. P., Seixas, J., & Long, G. (2018). Mining households's energy data to disclose fuel poverty: Lessons for southern Europe. *Journal of Cleaner Production., 178*, 534–550.

Gouveia, J. P., Seixas, J., & Mestre, A. (2017). Daily electricity profiles from smart meters - Proxies of active behaviour for space heating and cooling. *Energy, 141*(2017), 108–122.

Greening, L., & Bernow, S. (2004). Design of coordinated energy and environmental policies: Use of multi-criteria decision-making. *Energy Policy, 32*(6), 721–735.

IDB. (2011). *Emerging and sustainable cities initiative*. Inter-American Development Bank. Available from: <www.idb.org>.

INE (2011). *CENSUS 2011*. Lisbon, Portugal: Statistics Portugal. Available from: <www.ine.pt>.

Lourenço P. (2014). *Electricity production from large-scale solar PV and CPV in the rural areas of the municipality of Évora: Available area and technical potential*. Faculdade de Ciências e Tecnologia, Universidade Nova de Lisboa.

Lund, H., Østergaard, P. A., Connolly, D., & Mathiesen, B. V. (2017). Smart energy and smart energy systems. *Energy, 137*, 556–565.

Nunes, V., Gouveia, J. P., Rodrigues, A. M., & Simão, T. (2017). InSMART—Towards the new distribution systems operators potential role in low carbon future and integrated frameworks for smart cities. CIRED, International Conference in Electricity Distribution. *Open Access Proceedings Journal* (1) 2797–2799.

Saarikoski, H., Barton, D. N., Mustajoki, J., Keune. H., Gomez-Baggethun, E., & J. Langemeyer (2016). Multi-criteria decision analysis (MCDA) in ecosystem service valuation. In M. Potschin & K. Jax (Eds.), *OpenNESS ecosystem services reference book. EC FP7 grant agreement no. 308428*. Available from: <www.opennessproject.eu/library/reference-book>.

Sanz, L., Rallo, E., Gasa, S., Lahoz, L., Forcadell, J., Gil, R., ... Isern, A. (2015). *City anatomy indicators*. City Protocol Society.

Simoes, S., Dias, L., Gouveia, J. P., & Seixas, J. (2016a). Report on optimum sustainability pathways – ÉVORA. D-WP 5 – Deliverable D5.3 InSMART Integrative Smart City Planning. In *Coordination and support action (Coordinating action). FP7-ENERGY-SMARTCITIES-2012*. Available from: <http://www.insmartenergy.com/wp-content/uploads/2014/12/D5.3-Optimum-Sustainable-Pathways-Evora.pdf>.

Simoes, S., Dias, L., Gouveia, J. P., & Seixas, J. (2016b). Report on the multicriteria methodology, the process and the results of the decision making – Évora, Portugal. D-WP 5 – Deliverable D5.7. In *INSMART Integrative Smart City Planning. Coordination and support action (Coordinating action). FP7-ENERGY-SMARTCITIES-2012*. Available from: <http://www.insmartenergy.com/wp-content/uploads/2014/12/D5.7-Report-on-the-Multicriteria-methodology-Evora.pdf>.

Simoes, S., Dias, L., Gouveia, J. P., Seixas, J., De Miglio, R., Chiodi, A., ... Giannakidis, G. (2018). INSMART—Insights on modelling EU cities decarbonisation pathways. *Energy Strategy Reviews, 20*, 150−155.

Terrados, J., Almonacid, G., & Perez-Higueras, P. (2009). Proposal for a combined methodology for renewable energy planning. Application to a Spanish region. *Renewable and Sustainable Energy Reviews, 13*, 2022−2030.

United Nations. (2014). *World urbanization prospects: The 2014 revision, highlights (ST/ESA/SER.A/352)*. Department of Economic and Social Affairs, Population Division. Available from: <https://esa.un.org/unpd/wup/publications/files/wup2014-highlights.pdf>.

Villa, N., & Mitchell, S. (2010). *Connecting cities, achieving sustainability through innovation. White paper*. Cisco Internet Business Solutions Group (IBSG).

Wang, J., Jing, Y., Zhang, C., & Zhao, J. (2009). Review on multi-criteria decision analysis aid in sustainable energy decision-making. *Renewable and Sustainable Energy Reviews, 13*, 2263−2278.

World Economic Forum (2018). *Inspiring future cities and urban services shaping the future of urban development and services initiative. REF 250815*. Available from: <http://www3.weforum.org/docs/WEF_Urban-Services.pdf>.

Further reading

InSMART (2017). *Findings and lessons learnt for European cities from the InSMART project: A new methodology for smarter energy planning, tested in four EU cities. InSMART (Integrative Smart City Planning) project book* (36 pp.). Available from: <http://www.insmartenergy.com/wp-content/uploads/2014/11/54263_Insmart-brochure_36pp_FINAL_LR.pdf>.

The smart city of Torino

Chiara Delmastro[1], Rocco De Miglio[2], Alessandro Chiodi[2], Maurizio Gargiulo[2] and Paola Pisano[3]
[1]Department of Energy, Politecnico di Torino, Torino, Italy, [2]E4SMA, Torino, Italy, [3]Municipality of Torino, Torino, Italy

Chapter Outline

3.1 Introduction   51
3.2 Background   53
3.3 Research methodology: the case study   53
    3.3.1 Scope   56
    3.3.2 Integration   57
    3.3.3 Organization   59
    3.3.4 Time   60
    3.3.5 Cost   65
    3.3.6 Quality   67
    3.3.7 Risks   70
    3.3.8 Procurement   74
    3.3.9 Discussion—the fringes   75
3.4 Conclusion   77
Acknowledgments   77
About the authors   77
References   78
Further reading   81

3.1 Introduction

The European Union is showing its strong commitments in smart cities by developing instruments, such as the Horizon 2020, to support its strategy to 2020 in which smart cities cover a key role. In 2011 the situation of smart cities was mapped by the European Union revealing that 240 over the 468 EU-28 cities with population larger than 100,000 habitants can be classified as a smart city, and Italy is among the Countries with a larger number of smart cities[1] (Beretta, Cattolica, & Trieste, 2018). Furthermore, thanks to the Covenant of Mayor Initiative (European Commission); many European municipalities developed their energy plan SEAP (Sustainable Energy Measures Plan). This initiative promotes the vision to 2050 of

---

[1] Although the definitions of "smart city" are many and varied.

Smart City Emergence. DOI: https://doi.org/10.1016/B978-0-12-816169-2.00003-1
© 2019 Elsevier Inc. All rights reserved.

"accelerating the decarbonization of their territories, strengthening their capacity to adapt to unavoidable climate change impact, and allowing their citizens to access secure, sustainable and affordable energy" (European Commission), thus moving toward smarter uses of the energy, which is a widely accepted key indicator of city smartness. The Municipality of Torino joined the Covenant of Mayor Initiative in 2009. In this framework the municipality developed the most recent energy plan "TAPE—Turin Action Plan for Energy" (Città di Torino, 2012) in which it is planned to reduce urban carbon emissions to 40% by 2020 (referring to 1990 emission level). During this activity the energy balance of the city in 1990 and 2005 has been accounted, and the related carbon emissions have been estimated with the goal of identifying actions in the different sectors for reaching the 2020 emission reduction goal.

The Municipality of Torino also joined the European Innovation Partnership "Smart City & Communities" (European Commission, 2011) launched in 2011 by the European Community. In this framework the municipality declared its aim in becoming a smart city by means of novel solutions in the urban space. These solutions should respect the environment, reduce energy consumption in buildings, improve urban mobility conditions and management, and guarantee to its citizens a better quality of life. Some keywords of this activity are, therefore, energy, environment, mobility, accessibility, inclusiveness, and lifestyle. The city also participates at the Smart City National Observatory (Associazione Nazionale Comuni Italiani) created by ANCI (National Association of Italian Municipalities) to share knowledge, best practices, and guidelines among public, research and private institutions related to urban innovation and sustainability. Furthermore, the municipality confirmed its engagement in the smart city concept (in its energy-related area) by joining the energy center initiative (Borchiellini et al., 2017). This initiative aims at strengthening the cooperation among political, scientific, and business actors through the construction of a physical headquarter (Politecnico di Torino, 2017) where they could collaborate on R&D themes related to energy. In particular, one of the main activities of the energy center, in which the municipality confirmed its commitment, is represented by a smart city and smart infrastructure.

The objective of this book chapter is twofold: (1) to provide a pool of evidence of the most relevant actions of the city of Torino in order to be considered smart through literature evidence, exploration of projects and official websites and (2) to collect the performance of the "city smartness" making the use of city-specific indicators in accordance with the methodology provided by the World Council of City Data (WCCD) ISO 37120 [International Organization for Standardization (ISO), 2014]. Starting from the description of background activities in Section 3.2, this chapter will describe the smart city context and the research methodology in Section 3.3. The evaluation of the "city smartness" indicators is performed in Section 3.3.6 while Section 3.4 propose a discussion to identify rooms of improvement. The discussion is supported by the involvement of a municipality official. The final part of the chapter is devoted to the conclusion, highlighting how the city meets its initially grounded objectives and the related learning outcomes to reconceptualize the vision.

3.2 Background

The approach to the "smart city" concept in Torino followed a standard path, the preparation of the SEAP, the participation to the EU initiatives, etc. and quite standard (top-down) approaches (definitions of high-level targets and target-oriented analyses) and priorities (GHG reduction, renewables) on the example of national and supranational entities. It was not driven by specific problems or challenges of the city (from the bottom), at least in the first phase, and recently (from 2013) only a more targeted approach, as well as a more city-specific awareness, is being considered and implemented.

In 2013 the municipality, together with the Torino Smart City Foundation (Torino Smart City Foundation) and Torino Wireless (Fondazione Torino Wireless), developed a smart city master plan "SMILE—Smart Mobility, Inclusion, Life&Health, Energy." The SMILE plan aimed to identify a set of sustainable "actions" (rather than targets) by developing a business model and key performance indicators (KPIs) and to provide the city with a decision support tool to guide the city of Torino in identifying key projects and in supporting the development of a local strategy both in the short and the medium-long term. An overview of some of the main smart "initiatives" undertaken during years and related to the principal pillars of SMILE is presented in the next chapters together with a discussion of main strengths, weaknesses, and possible future developments.

3.3 Research methodology: the case study

Based on literature evidence and exploration of projects and official websites, this chapter describes the main elements of the smart city story of Torino (approach, examples, and key figures), and after all, it attempts to measure the benefits of the undertaken "actions" against the "core" ISO 37120 indicators (used to steer and measure the performance of city service and quality of life).

The city of Torino is the capital of the Piedmont Region, sited in the Northeast part of Italy, in a continental climatic zone (2617 heating degree days at 20°C) occupying an area of roughly 130 km^2. In 1991 the population amounted to 979,839 inhabitants, and it has been reduced (moved to adjacent municipalities) over the following years, accounting for approximately 896,818 inhabitants in 2002 and 899,455 in 2014, slightly increasing the number foreigner citizens. Indeed, in the last decades, the city experienced an economic, cultural, and urban transformation mostly related to the decentralization of automotive production in other areas. This generated the abandonment of some urban areas, in particular to the ones closed to the main railway links. Therefore the city went through a period of urban renewal by reconverting the abandoned areas of workers and urban infrastructures. Hosting the 2006 Winter Olympics was another significant driver of urban renovation through the recovery of historical heritage and the improvement of transport infrastructures that brought Torino to the current condition. Some of the city characteristics (as collected in a report of the Italian National Institute of Statistics), identified as the most relevant indicators to describe the city conditions in Comune di Torino (2015), are listed in Table 3.1. By looking at the indicators of the city against the national (average) values, it is easy to get first general insights on the "good" and "bad" performances, and hints for the future area of "smart" improvement.

Table 3.1 Indicators of the city of Torino.

Indicators	Year	Unit	Torino	Italy
Available income per capita of consumer households	2012	Euro (€)	20,454.8[a]	17,307.2
Employment rate	2013	Per 100 person in an age range of 20–64	65.9[a]	59.8
Specialization in knowledge-intensive productive sectors	2011	Per 100 employees	10.7	4.4
Families with broadband Internet connection	2011	Per 100 households	46.4	44.9
Losses of the pipe network for the distribution of water to the consumers	2012	Percentage of water lost on the volume of water introduced	36.9	37.4
Urban air quality	2013	Number of exceedances of the daily limit value of PM10	126.0	n.a.
Noise pollution	2013	Noise controls with at least one record exceeding the limit for 100,000 inhabitants	4.1	4.4
Urban green space availability	2013	m^2 per inhabitant	24.1	32.2
Total density of green areas (protected natural areas and urban green areas)	2013	Fraction of the municipal surface	19.8	18.2
Urban vegetable gardens	2013	m^2 per 100 inhabitants	220.7	18.4
District heating	2012	m^3 per inhabitant	58.3	10.8
Cars with emission standards lower than the Euro 4 class	2013	Per 1000 inhabitants	393.9	311.8
Urban waste sent to landfill	2013	Percentage of total municipal waste produced	58.5[a]	36.9
Separate collection of urban waste	2013	Percentage of total municipal waste	51.0[a]	42.3

(Continued)

Table 3.1 (Continued)

Indicators	Year	Unit	Torino	Italy
Time dedicated to mobility	2011	Average time—minutes	26.9	23.4
Density of urban networks of local public transport	2012	Seats—km per inhabitant	7144.8	4794.0
Density of cycle paths	2013	Per 100 km^2 of municipal area	137.4	18.9
Availability of pedestrian areas	2012	m^2 per 100 inhabitant	45.8	33.4

[a]Data at Province level.
Source: From Comune di Torino (Servizio Statistica e Toponomastica Città di Torino). (2015). *Rapporto Urbes 2015, Il benessere equo e sostenibile nelle città*.

Table 3.2 2005 Energy consumption and CO$_2$ emissions data for the city of Torino (Città di Torino, 2012).

	Energy consumption (MW h/year)			CO$_2$ emissions	
	Electricity	Fossil fuels	Total	t/year	%
Built environment	2682,364	8463,086	11,145,450	2856,778	56
Municipal buildings	61,491	313,035	374,526	70,034	1
Service buildings	1441,580	1303,084	2744,664	997,163	20
Residential buildings	1092,488	6846,967	7939,455	1744,790	34
Public lighting	86,805	/	86,805	44,791	1
Industry	1631,392	3207,568	4838,960	1508,716	30
Transportation	28,641	287,474	316,115	734,852	14
Total	4342,397	11,958,128	16,300,525	5100,346	

One of the most critical indicators is related to the urban air quality, exceeding the daily limit value of PM10 for 126 days in 2013. This indicator has not improved in the recent years; only reactive measures are taken to cope with the problem (concentrations above thresholds) in the short term, while a clear strategy for the medium term is still lacking.

As for the energy-related area, the most recent energy balance of the city was prepared in 2010 (and refers to 2005 data) accounting a consumption of 16,600 GW h/year with related carbon emissions of 5100 ktCO$_2$/year (Città di Torino, 2012) as shown in Table 3.2. According to the energy balance, 56% of total CO$_2$ emissions were related to the built environment, 30% to industry, and 14% to mobility. The built environment represents a key consumption and CO$_2$ emissions voice taking into account that more than 80% of buildings predate the energy regulation law (around 1980). According to the most recent census data, Torino construction stock is composed by 62,643 occupied buildings (Municipality of Torino), fully characterized with the support of geographic information system (GIS) tools in the works of Fondazione Torino Wireless, Torino Social Innovation, URBACT European Program, and it is constituted by approximately 213 Mm^3 volume of the buildings, of which almost 83% is residential and 17% nonresidential (approximately 7.6 Mm^3 of non-municipal buildings). Furthermore, in this area of Italy, the energy consumption of majority of the buildings is related to thermal needs, accounted for 2015 in the work of Mutani, Delmastro, Gargiulo, and Corgnati (2016), and set as 9.19 TW h of which 62% residential consumption (average space heating consumption of 174 kW h/m^2) and 38% nonresidential.

In 2015 57 Mm^3 of the urban building's volume was supplied by an entirely gas-based district heating system managed and operated by a single company, where there are still possibilities of expanding the network (Delmastro, Martinsson, Dulac, & Corgnati, 2017; Guelpa, Mutani, Todeschi, & Verda, 2017). The heat generation mix is composed of 740 MW of natural gas combined heat and power (CHP), 1000 MW of gas auxiliary boilers, and 12,500 Mm^3 of daily storage delivering about 2000 GW h$_{th}$ together with 950 GW h$_{el}$ (Delmastro et al., 2017). The buildings that are not connected to the district heating network are mostly supplied by natural gas boilers (more than 80%), some fuel oil boilers, ($\sim$11%) and electricity ($\sim$3%). Fig. 3.1 shows some maps relative to the city population and urban building stock distribution.

3.3.1 Scope

"Innovation" in the city arose from the need to cope with economic and social changes. In the last 20 years, following this vocation, the city of Torino, with its strong manufacturing background, was able to reinvent and relaunch itself with a process that has seen the participation of all the stakeholders of the ecosystem and in which the role of the public administration was central. The city in 2016 won the second prize in the "European Capital of Innovation" contest, awarded by the European Commission. This attestation followed a planning phase first, the master plan for Torino Smart City, and second, an operational phase that involved innovation projects developed by the city. The current administration has decided to relaunch the path started to drive Torino in becoming a smart city and a reference point for social innovation. The objectives that Torino pursues as smart city are as follows:

- Give more efficient services to citizens, simplifying and digitizing their access, and promoting new skills and work processes within the administration.
- Promote industrial development and economic growth of the ecosystem, starting from start-ups and small businesses, through which open innovation can collaborate with large companies, and favoring new business models that can facilitate the transition to a circular economy and sustainable development.
- Respond to citizens' requests for transparency and participation by promoting information, dialogue, and bottom-up approach, both online and offline.
- Find innovative solutions that bring a balance between citizens' lifestyle and the impact it has on the environment, defending the health and the quality of life.

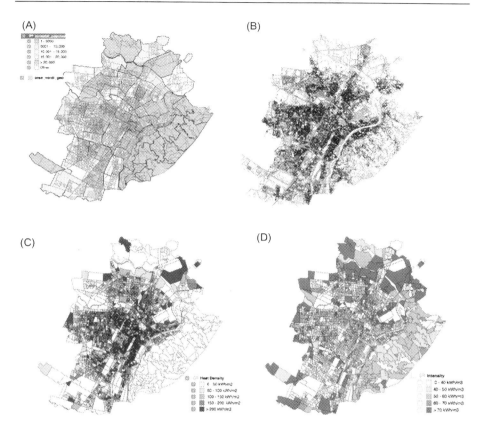

Figure 3.1 Maps of the city of Torino related to (A) population distribution and green areas (Municipality of Torino); (B) buildings and street map (Municipality of Torino); (C) heat density per unit on land use on census section areas (Mutani et al., 2016); and (D) heat density per unit of heated building volume (Mutani et al., 2016).

- Enhance and boost the use of public transport and soft mobility solutions by rethinking them in a more efficient and integrated way as a service.
- Promote projects with a strong social impact to respond to emerging needs in our city and create a more inclusive society.
- Protect common goods and promote their access by taking the full advantage of the potential offered by new technologies.
- Improve the urban environment starting from the suburbs, giving new life to public spaces and areas, promoting safety, and combating degradation.

3.3.2 Integration

In late 2012 the city of Torino and the Torino Smart City Foundation chose a local government-supported agency [Torino Wireless (Fondazione Torino Wireless)] for innovation and information and communications technology (ICTs) as coordinator for a project to develop a "plan for smart city." The project SMILE (Mobility, Inclusion, Life and health, Energy, and Integration) aimed to provide the city with a decision support tool able to guide Torino in identifying key projects and in supporting the development of a strategy both in the short and in the medium-long term according to a model of extended participation and the involvement of institutions, research bodies, and local companies. 66 bodies, among which 28 companies, 5 R&D institutes, 23 public agencies, 10 no profit associations, all enrolled for free, were actively engaged during a period of 150 working days to produce the first clear and shared strategic project developed by an Italian city depicting a pathway toward a more simple, secure, sustainable, and modern city. Such extended engagement allowed to collect a rich set of proposals based on the strategic priorities of the city and on the stakeholders' views. Four strategic areas of development were identified: mobility (intelligent transportation system (ITS), cycling, and freight logistics), social inclusion (digitalization, public housing, employment and social innovation, and social participation), health and well-being (public security, waste management, building management, tourism, lifestyle, and food), energy (building efficiency, smart grid, and public lighting), while at the end of the works, 45 were the proposals contained in the master plan. Some of those ideas have already been implemented or are currently under implementation, others look at the resources of the European Horizon 2020 program. Among the key prioritized actions the following are the most interesting ones covering a wide spectrum of sectors and typologies:

- Participative mobility management (new data acquisition systems, sharing and use of transport-related data).
- Cycling (new bike lanes, info-mobility, and bike sharing).
- Digitalization of the services (digital literacy of population, a digital time-based local exchange trading system, etc.).
- Urban requalification of public spaces and security enhancement through urban regeneration as a measure of social support, and through communication and citizen involvement.
- Reorganization of the catering services in the schools (short food chain: low emissions, local products, etc.).
- The creation of a monitoring system to analyze, benchmark, and visualize key indicators at municipal and submunicipal (district) level.
- Promotion of energy conservation and environmental sustainability for private buildings, through the adoption of technical standards for the definition and verification of energy requalification of buildings.
- Intelligent urban public lighting, using LED lamps, remote controllers, and automatic adjustments of the intensity according to natural lighting.

Some of the proposed actions are common in the SMILE and SEAP/TAPE plans, though the two programs have a different genesis and follow different approaches in terms of timing (short term vs 2020), coverage (many urban-related areas vs energy-related areas only), design (actions designed from the bottom vs targets forced from the top and inherited by the national example), scope (smart city vs low-carbon city), and engagement (more stakeholders-based the first and more technical experts-based the second).

3.3.3 Organization

Once declaring the objective of becoming a smart city in 2011, the Municipality of Torino was already involved in 16 sectoral plans, 25 European projects, 20 national projects, and 24 local projects. As previously explained, in late 2012, the SMILE project was conceptualized by means of the cooperation among the Municipality of Torino, the Torino Smart City Foundation, and Torino Wireless. In this smart city program a strong leadership of the municipality was highlighted: the municipality devoted specific internal expertise and structures to develop and manage the program autonomously; involving the other partners during the operative and executive phases. The Torino Smart City Foundation was created to coordinate and manage the initiatives of Torino Smart City. The goals of the foundation are to promote research activities at the national and international level and to coordinate collaborative projects with the private sector. In particular the Foundation acts to develop information programs to the citizens, and other institutions promote innovation and "smart" events throughout the city and encourage the exchange of good practices among several realities. In February 2013 the activities for concretizing the SMILE strategic plan started. As shown in Fig. 3.2, the activities lasted for 150 working days, and the process involved 350 people divided into 5 technical thematic working tables (Mobility, Inclusion, Life and Health, Energy, and Integration). More than 100 proposals derived from this process among which 45 were selected by the stakeholders to be presented to the municipality that in December 2013 defined the "top" actions to be included in the SMILE master plan. Among the 45 proposed actions, 7 were related to mobility (info-mobility, cycling, and logistics), 9 were related to inclusion (digitalization, social innovation, and participation), 12 were related to life and health (safety, wastes, urban renovation, culture and tourism,

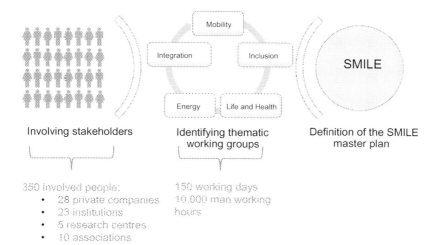

Figure 3.2 Schematic of the pillars of the SMILE strategic program. *SMILE*, Smart Mobility, Inclusion, Life&Health, Energy.

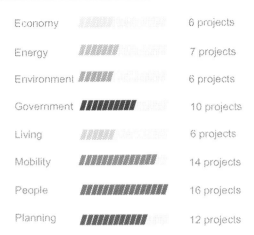

Figure 3.3 Project situation in 2017.
Source: Adapted from Associazione Nazionale Comuni Italiani (ANCI) & Istituto per la Finanza e l'Economia Locale (IFEL). *Piattaforma Agenda Urbana*. <http://osservatoriosmartcity.it> Accessed December 2017.

lifestyle, and alimentation), 10 were related to energy (smart grids, building retrofit, and public lighting), while 7 are transversal (data gathering, KPIs, infrastructures, and communication).

The TAPE actions are instead completely managed by the municipality. To date, many of the proposed actions have been implemented. In 2015 more than 60 projects were ongoing involving 28% life and health, 27% inclusion, 19% energy, 15% mobility, and 10% integration. In 2017 a total of 77 projects [Associazione Nazionale Comuni Italiani (ANCI) & Istituto per la Finanza e l'Economia Locale (IFEL)] are accounted as summarized in Fig. 3.3. The centrality of the citizens is evident, being "people" the voice with a higher number of projects (e.g., Apps for citizens, urban gardens, etc.).

3.3.4 Time

As previously described, the SMILE "master plan" for smart city focused on six main pillars. The whole SMILE process lasted 5 months in 2013 (Fig. 3.4), many projects are continuously implemented, and some have been already concluded, while others are still ongoing with a target year in 2020.

An overview of some of the major activities and projects of both the SMILE and TAPE master plans are summarized in Fig. 3.5 (starting date of the action). Some of the most interesting projects for each pillar of the SMILE master plan, together with the main TAPE actions and objectives, are presented in the following subsections, while all the information related to the 77 ongoing and concluded projects can be found in UIA.

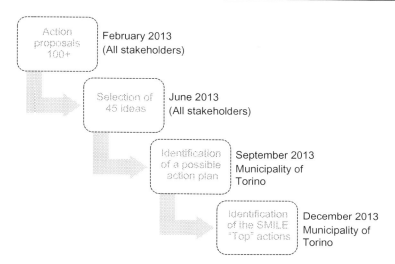

Figure 3.4 Duration and steps of the process for the definition of the SMILE master plan. *SMILE*, Smart Mobility, Inclusion, Life & Health, Energy.

3.3.4.1 Smart mobility

Great attention is devoted to mobility, starting from 2010 many initiatives were undertaken in order to reduce traffic intensity and improve urban logistics. The bike-sharing service (Fig. 3.6B) accounts 116 places (Fig. 3.6A), and it is continuously improving: other private free-floating services are present in the city since 2017 (e.g., GoBike). Attention was also devoted to security and traffic logistics by allowing the citizen to plan their bicycles paths through a website [B.U.N.E.T., Bike's Urban Network in Torino project (5T C di T)] started in 2014. An electric car-sharing service is present since 2013 while in 2015 the ENI company promoted the Enjoy (ENI) car-sharing service (Fig. 3.6C). From 2018 a carpooling service will be activated thanks to the social car project (ANCI & IFEL, 2017). In addition the city of Torino is characterized by a restricted traffic zone (ZTL), an area where cars are controlled with special permits in order to minimize traffic and facilitate pedestrians and cyclists. Furthermore, it may support the monitoring of traffic in the city center to facilitate projects related to new traffic logistic [e.g., PUMAS project—Planning Sustainable Regional/Urban Mobility in the Alpine Space (Città di Torino) that has the goal of redefining the logistics of goods transportation].

3.3.4.2 Smart environment

The municipality pays considerable attention to the urban environment for improving citizens' life quality. From 2011 to 2015 an important activity of urban regeneration has been launched in the suburban neighborhood "Barriera di Milano" (Città di Torino) for triggering the overall (physical-environmental, social-cultural, and economic-employment) improvement of the area. The program fostered interactions

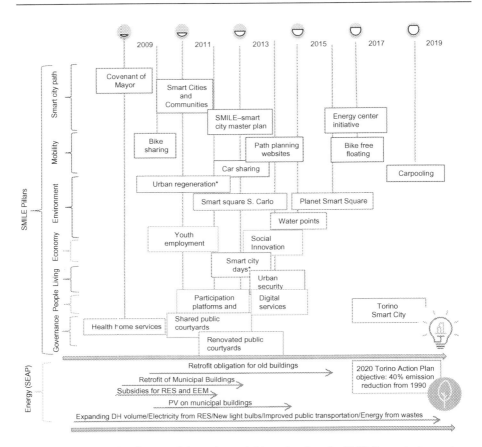

Figure 3.5 Schematic of some of the major activities related to the SMILE smart city master plan and the TAPE. * is related to concluded initiatives: RES, DH, EEM, PV. *RES*, renewable energy sources; *DH*, District heating; *EEM*, energy efficiency measures; *PV*, photovoltaic; *RES*, renewable energy sources; *SMILE*, Smart Mobility, Inclusion, Life & Health, Energy.

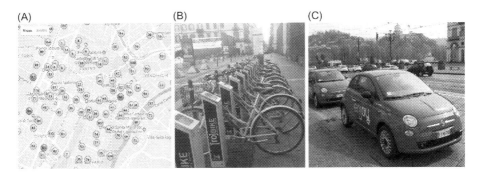

Figure 3.6 Images of the (A) pick up and drop off points distribution of the ToBike service, (B) a [To] Bike pick up/drop off point, and (C) an Enjoy car.

Figure 3.7 Images of the Planet Smart Square: (A) the smart bench and (B) the urban garden. *Source*: From Planet Idea. *Planet Smart Square*. (2016). <https://www.planetsmartcity.com/smartsquare/index.html> Accessed December 2017.

among all urban actors with a total of 34 strategic interventions (e.g., the redefinition of new and existing public spaces, employment reintegration, and collective public art). Furthermore, "water points" were placed in the urban area in 2015 (Società Metropolitana Acque Torino, 2015) for supporting the consumption of tap water for food purposes.

Other important activities are related to "smart squares." In 2013 the first square was related to the Civic Lab Piazza San Carlo in which an innovative lighting system and free Wi-Fi are provided. The second recent initiative, inaugurated in 2016, is represented by the "Planet Smart Square" (Planet Idea, 2016) in which the square space is improved thanks to the actions integrating innovations and people engagement. Some of the interventions involve technology (e.g., emergency pillar to call public intervention/police), architecture [e.g., smart bench to charge the phone, free Wi-Fi (Fig. 3.7A)], environment (e.g., photovoltaic tiles), and social inclusion [e.g., urban garden (Fig. 3.7B), bookcrossing].

3.3.4.3 Smart economy

Activities related to the smart economy are mostly related to social innovation and youth employment. In 2014 the "FaciliTo Giovani e Innovazione Sociale" (Torino Social Innovation) was launched to support the start-ups of entrepreneurial projects related to social needs and proposed by young individuals from 18 to 40. The service offers financial (<80 k€), technical, and informative support (e.g., business models, training) and helps 71 projects (46 financed) over the 255 received.

Another project related to the smart economy is the European project "My Generation@Work" (URBACT European Program) of the URBACT program, started in 2012 and concluded in 2017, that developed the social innovation platform to encourage a collaborative form of dialogue related to public goods and services. The commitment of Torino continues with other two projects: BoostInno (Program UE) and Co-City (UIA) aiming to redesign Torino Social Innovation and to involve citizens to comanage public services, respectively. The local authority has the role of facilitating innovation, and the general idea is to contribute to the creation of new jobs and new enterprises reducing urban poverty (currently 7% of the total population).

3.3.4.4 Smart living

The smart living dimension includes projects related to initiatives for raising citizen awareness, safety, and health-related services.

In 2013 the municipality organized the Smart City Days, showing "smart city" as the best practices in some urban squares in order to raise citizen awareness on smart initiatives: sustainable mobility, scientific research, energy savings, healthy nutrition, and green public areas. Moreover, the municipality has been involved in many projects with the goal of creating innovative safety solution exploiting data received from sensors, workers, or citizens [e.g., Sensing Safety at Work (SEeS@W) (Sensing Safety at Work) and the FIWARE European project (FIWARE, 2014)] Another interesting project is represented by the OPportunites for an active and healthy LONgevity—OPLON project (OPLON, 2014) and focused on the development of monitoring systems to promote "active aging" by allowing fragile elderly to spend as much time as possible in their home rather than in hospitals.

3.3.4.5 Smart people

The "smart people" pillar includes all the actions directly related to citizens' digital services and participation platforms. Some activities allowed sharing georeferenced territorial real-time information, photo, videos (e.g., the "Uptu-It's up to you" platform created in 2012) Furthermore, in 2013 during the Smart City Days, an app (App4Torino) was launched for searching new app ideas from which 20 project ideas have been selected for application in the national Smart City & Communities tender (Ministero dell'Istruzione dell'Università e della R). Other apps have been developed for helping tourists and citizens moving throughout the city. From 2013 to 2015 the "Guardando la Città Metro per Metro" (S[m2]art, 2013) project started with the aim of offering digital services at both citizens and public administrations. The "smart" aspects of the project are due to the architectural integration of urban furnishings and technologies and to the implementation of innovative and existing digital services in the furnishings. The main impacts include improving the well-being of people in urban areas (inclusion, accessibility, and safety) and improving the quality of public administration services.

3.3.4.6 Smart governance

Smart governance is related to the creation of new services and public spaces for citizens. Among the most relevant initiatives the "Radiologia domiciliare—R@dhome" activated in 2008 is highlighted. By means of this initiative, patients have a mobile radiology unit to do exams directly at home and sending them to the X-ray units of hospitals. In 2011 the "GerOs—Networking in Osteoporosi" started. This service provides treatment to those who live in remote areas and suffer from fracture osteoporosis. An IT platform in cloud computing has allowed the creation of a network between the various peripheral specialist structures and the regional reference center for the diagnosis and treatment plan. Other projects related to the opening to the population (as public spaces) the courtyards of the schools owned by the city of Turin. The courtyards of schools have also been the object of another project focused on experimenting new design solutions developed together with users in a unitary design that harmonizes building interventions, furnishings, innovative solutions for gaming and socializing, and green accommodations (Città di Torino, 2013).

3.3.4.7 Torino Energy Action Plan

The TAPE energy plan was developed in 2009 and includes actions lasting from 2009 to 2020. Among the most relevant the proposed actions from 2010 to 2020 include the energy retrofit of municipal buildings (-1.75 ktCO_2/year from 2010 to 2013) and of residential buildings (-103 ktCO_2/year at the regional level from 2010 to 2016), the installation of PV panels on municipal building rooftops (-619 tCO_2/year from 2010 to 2015), energy production from renewable energy sources (-31.7 ktCO_2/year from 2007 to 2020), increasing the district-heated volume of roughly 4 Mm^3 (-4.4 ktCO_2/year from 2009 to 2020), substitution of inefficient individual boilers (-40 ktCO_2/year at the regional level from 2009 to 2020), substitution of inefficient lamp bulbs (-4 ktCO_2/year from 2009 to 2020) and LED usage in traffic lights (-8.6 ktCO_2/year from 2009 to 2020), the retrofit of public transport vehicles (-13.5 ktCO_2/year from 2009 to 2020), increasing the use of bicycles in urban areas (-22 ktCO_2/year from 2009 to 2020), and increasing the electricity production from urban solid waste (-165 ktCO_2/year from 2009 to 2020).

3.3.5 Cost

The 77 projects required a total investment of approximately 211 M€ (ANCI & IFEL, 2017). The SMILE master plan required a total investment of 500 k€ covered

Table 3.3 Summary of the investments (global cost of the project) related to the project involving the Municipality of Torino.

Pillar of the activity	Projects		Total budget (investment)		Average budget/project (M€/project)
	Number	%	M€	%	
Environment	6	7.8	15.6	7.4	2.60
Energy	7	9.1	61.2	79.4	8.74
Economy	6	7.8	7.6	9.9	1.27
People	16	20.8	8.3	10.8	0.52
Living	6	7.8	18.0	23.4	3.00
Mobility	14	18.2	65.2	84.7	4.66
Government	10	13.0	9.619	12.5	0.96
Planning	12	15.6	25.56	33.2	2.13
Total	77		211.1		2.74

by the municipality, while the TAPE energy plan was directly developed by the municipality. As summarized in Table 3.3, considering the number of projects, the energy-related ones are activities requiring higher investments followed by the mobility-related ones. Investments in the energy sector are mostly related to the commitment of the municipality in constructing the new energy center building (19 M€) (Borchiellini et al., 2017), in retrofitting existing schools (15 M€), in monitoring energy consumptions (9 M€), and in retrofitting public lighting system (14 M€). Detailed information about all the projects can be found in ANCI and IFEL (2017).

Tenders from the European Commission and the Italian Government mostly supported the promotion of the smart city objectives. Together with the previously presented projects, some relevant examples and the related funds are described in this paragraph.

The municipality won the European tender Competitive and Innovation Program—Entrepreneurship and Innovation Program (CIP—EIP) with the 2 M€ Pro-LITE project (Procurement of Lighting Innovation and Technology in Europe, 2012—16). During this period the municipality searched for innovative solutions to substitute existing traffic lights with LED lamps. Another funded project (roughly 263 k€) within the CIP—EIP tender was the 2013 Innocat project devoted to the implementation of coordinated eco-innovation contracts in the collective catering sector. In the framework of the CIP—ICT Policy Support Programme the CROSS project aimed to creating a platform and an app for managing monetary and nonmonetary transactions related to the economic sphere of subsidiarity and public services.

In 2012 in the framework of EU-FP7 research program the TRIBUTE project ("Take the energy bill back to the promised building performance," 300 k€) aimed at reducing the gap between measured and attended energy performance of commercial buildings through new predictive algorithms. The 5-year projects involved

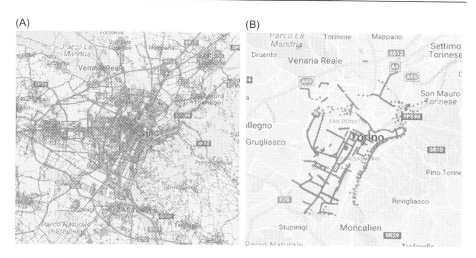

Figure 3.8 Snapshots from the OPTICITIES platform to check: (A) average traffic routes and (B) cycle paths (CSI Piemonte).

16 partners with a total cost of 9.9 M€. A case study building was "smart" monitored and accordingly managed.

Another project related to mobility was OPTICITIES (2013–16, a total budget of 13 M€), it integrates data related to traffic with public transportation, carpooling, and bicycles into an online platform (Fig. 3.8).

The smart city ambition of the city was also supported by funding from the Ministry for Research, University, and Instruction (MIUR) through the Smart City & Communities tender in which a total of 183 M€ was allocated for projects related to safety, smart grids, education, and sustainable architecture. Another tender launched by the MIUR, the "Social Innovation" tender, allocated 7 M€ to territorial projects started from a partnership between young people (below 30 years old) and the municipality. In Table 3.4 information related to the presented projects are summarized.

3.3.6 Quality

Assessing the level of performance in the area of "smart cities" is not trivial. The definition itself of words such as "smart" (according to which criteria?) or "innovation" (on which level of complexity?) is often subjective and approached in different ways by cities and by analysts, thus limiting the possibility to make a direct and consistent comparison or to have clear benchmarks. The international debate focuses on the definition of a smart city for many years (Dall'O, Bruni, Panza, Sarto, & Khayatian, 2017). So far, the city has not developed its own "smartness" evaluation metric yet, but every single project impact is currently "self-evaluated" by qualitative ranking from 1 to 5 against three dimensions of sustainability (ANCI & IFEL, 2017): economic dimension (intended as the ability to generate income and work for the population), social dimension (intended as

Table 3.4 Cost information related to the presented projects.

Project name	Duration	Cost of the project (k€)	Source of funding
Smart mobility			
Bike sharing [TO]Bike	2010—ongoing	3793	Regional, national, municipal, PPP
B.U.N.E.T project	2014 (completed)	26.5	Municipal
Electric car sharing	2013—ongoing	580	National, municipal, PPP
OPTICITIES project	2013—16	13,011	European
Social car	2015—18	5385	European
Smart environment			
Urban regeneration (Barriera di Milano)	2011—15	35,000	Regional, municipal, European
Water point	2015—ongoing	4400	Unclear
Pro-LITE	2012—16	2059	European, Municipal
Smart economy			
FaciliTo	2014—15	2000	Municipal
My Generation@Work	2012—15	701.74	European
Smart living			
SEeS@W	2014—15	1305	Structural
OPLON	2014—16	9000	National
FIWARE	2014	150	European
Smart people			
Uptu-It's up to you	2012	8.49	Municipal
s[m2]art	2013—15	8000	National
TRIBUTE	2013—17	9914	European
Smart governance			
Opening school courtyards	2012	26	Municipal
New design solutions for school courtyards	2013	2440	Municipal
CROSS	2012—16	5472	European

B.U.N.E.T., Bike's Urban Network in Torino; *PPP*, Public—Private Partnership.

the ability of guarantee an equally distribution of well-being by class and gender), and environmental dimension (intended as the ability of maintaining the quality and reproducibility of natural resources). An example of the previously analyzed projects is provided in Fig. 3.9.

The smart city of Torino

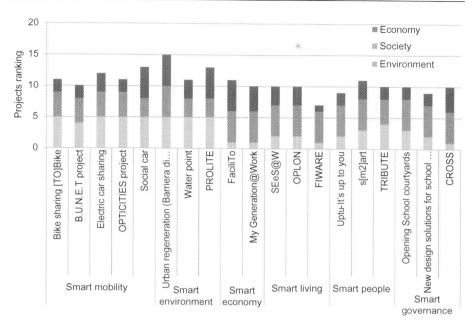

Figure 3.9 The municipal self-evaluation of projects in terms of three dimensions of sustainability: economy, society, and environment (ANCI & IFEL, 2017).

The municipality is now working in the direction of evaluating project results through iterative cycles. These cycles are based on a feedback process that has so far mainly involved the administration itself, which had to absorb its logic, but which will increasingly involve citizens through participation platforms. In addition, indicators (KPIs) will be defined which will measure progress on the different objectives of the city. The quality of the initiatives to make the city "smarter" will be measured by tracking the identified key indicators over the time, by benchmarking the city performance with other reference cities, and by making more information available to the citizens, thus submitting to the judgment of citizens about the actual changes and signs of progress of the city.

Meantime, the smart city activities of the city have been ranked according to two Italian protocols: the ICity rate (Forum Pa srl, 2017) and the smart city index (EasyPark, 2017).

The ICity rate protocol takes into account 15 sustainability dimensions represented by 113 indicators. The city of Torino has been ranked as seventh over 106 Italian cities, accounting 532.9 points. According to the ICity rate report, the criticality points (lower than Italian average) of the city include land use and green areas, tourism, public Wi-Fi, elderly care, local air pollution (PM10 and NO_2), pedestrian areas, electric mobility, and traffic limitation. As major strengths of the city can instead be highlighted: mobility planning, little accidents, wastewater treatments, evictions, early leavers, waste management, open data, innovation, high efficiency of the courts, voluntary homicides, and shared administration.

The smart city index (EasyPark, 2017) analyzed each city according to the following major dimension: transport and mobility, sustainability, governance, innovation economy, digitalization, living standard, and expert perception. According to the smart city index, Torino is in 69th position. In this more international comparison the problems related to the Italian context are being more visible. These critical points can be identified in public transportation, digitalization of the government, digital and business ecosystems. As a result, the estimated living standard average (dependent on the average sum spent, average net salary) is quite low compared to other European cities.

As stated in the introduction, one of the goals of the chapter is to collect the smart city indexes according to a more *international* standard, the WCCD ISO 37120 (ISO, 2014). This standard enables cities to be measured in terms of economic, environmental, and social indicators (46 "core" and 54 "supporting") considering major 17 fields: economy, education, energy, environment, finance, fire and emergency response, governance, health, recreation, safety, shelter, solid waste, telecommunication and innovation, transportation, urban planning, wastewater, water and sanitation, reporting and record maintenance and aim to assist cities in setting targets and monitoring achievements. The ISO certifications rank cities on five levels from "aspirational medal" to "platinum medal," depending on the number and quality of indicators. In Table 3.5 the collected core indicators (only) for the city are presented and are used to measure the performance of Torino against two European cities (Porto and Valencia). Both the cities of Porto and Valencia were selected as the benchmark being highly ranked, located in South European countries, and well-described with numerical details in the Global Cities Registry.

Such comparison reveals a few numbers of important points to be considered, they are as follows:

- For a meaningful international benchmark a more comprehensive set of indicators must be monitored at city level (e.g., education related, ICT and innovation related, transportation related, and economy related);
- For many social and economic indicators the city of Torino performs even better than "gold" and "platinum" ranked cities (e.g., indicators about education);
- Stand-alone energy-related indicators may be misleading and cannot be used to reliably evaluate the city smartness;
- The city of Torino is still far from the best performances with respect to the local pollutants and the (associated) indicator of private vehicles dependency, as well as with respect to the digitalization;
- The relatively low number of (available and trackable) indicators, together with the current low performance on important (core) indicators, would not allow obtaining a high-level certification (gold, platinum) for the city.

3.3.7 Risks

As far as authors are aware, there is no explicit reference to risk management procedures in the two key programs analyzed (neither in the SMILE project nor in the TAPE). In the former the uncertainty and the risk associated with potential

Table 3.5 ISO 37120 core indicators.

Core indicator	Torino Value	Year	Source	Porto certification level: *Gold* (ISO, 2014)	Valencia certification level: *Platinum* (ISO, 2014)
City's unemployment rate	7.20%	2011	ISTAT (n.d.)	17.6% (2011)	21.7% (2015)
Percentage of living population living in poverty	7%	2017	UIA	19.5% (2015)	26.2% (2014)
Percentage of students completing secondary education	Not available	29.2% share of population completing secondary education in 2011 (ISTAT, n.d.)		78.7% (2015)	72.4% (2014)
Primary education students/teacher ratio	8.3	2017[a]	ISTAT (2017)	13.1 (2015)	21.4 (2013)
Total yearly residential electricity use per capita (kWh/capita)	1213.1	2005	Città di Torino (2012)	1852.2 (2015)	1433.1 (2014)
Yearly energy consumption per m³ of public buildings (kWh/m³)	48.86	2017	Comune di Torino	19.5 (2015)	47.4 (2014)
Percentage of total energy derived from renewable sources as a share of city's total energy consumption (%)	Not available			20.8% (2015)	4.7% (2014)
Total yearly electricity use per capita (kWh/capita)	4820.9	2005	Città di Torino (2012)	5549.8 (2015)	3233 (2013)
Fine particulate matter concentration PM 2.5 (μg/m³)	18	2016	ARPA Piemonte (n.d.)	5.1 (2015)	12 (2014)
Particulate matter concentration PM10 (μg/m³)	28	2016	ARPA Piemonte (n.d.)	18 (2015)	23.5 (2014)
GHG emissions (t/capita)	5.7	2005	Città di Torino (2012)	4.84 (2015)	3.55 (2012)
Debt service ratio (debt service expenditure as a percentage of the municipality's own source revenue)	252.20%	2008	Associazione artigiani e piccole imprese Mestre CGIA Mestre	0.8% (2015)	20.78% (2014)
Number of firefighters per 100,000 population	50	2017[a]	Comando Provinciale dei Vigili del Fuoco di Torino	99.8 (2015)	36.2 (2014)

(*Continued*)

Table 3.5 (Continued)

Core indicator	Torino Value	Year	Source	Porto certification level: *Gold* (ISO, 2014)	Valencia certification level: *Platinum* (ISO, 2014)
Number of fire-related deaths per 100,000 population	0.034	2007[b]	D'Addato (2011)	0 (2015)	0.63 (2014)
Number of natural disaster-related deaths per 100,000 population	Not available			0 (2015)	0 (2014)
Voter participation in last municipal elections (as percentage of eligible voters)	54.41%	2016	Comune di Torino	52.6% (2013)	72.2% (2015)
Woman as a percentage of total elected to city level office	44.23%	2017	Comune di Torino	23.1% (2016)	39.4% (2015)
Average life expectancy	85	2017	Costa, Stroscia, Zebgarini, & Demaria (2017)	81 (2012)	82.7 (2012)
Number of inpatient hospital beds per 100,000 population	330	2013[b]	Annuario Statistico del Servizio Sanitario Nazionale (2013)	1640 (2015)	525 (2012)
Number of physicians per 100,000 population	Not available			2094 (2015)	619 (2012)
Underage 5 mortality per 1000 live birth	2.5	2015	Comune di Torino (2015)	9.73 (2015)	3.26 (2013)
Square meters of public indoor recreation space per capita	Not available			6.48 (2015)	1.37 (2014)
Square meters of public outdoor recreation space per capita	Not available			1.77 (2015)	51.2 (2014)
Number of police officers per 100,000 population	118	2011[b]	Fondazione Filippo Caracciolo (2011)	469.5 (2014)	208.25 (2013)
Number of homicides per 100,000 population	1.1	2012	Comune di Torino (2015)	2.31 (2015)	0.51 (2014)

Percentage of city population living in slums (%)	0.28% (associated to nomad communities)	2015	Aragona (2015)	0% (2015)	0% (2014)
Percentage of city population with regular solid waste collection (residential)	100%	2017	Authors' assumption	98% (2016)	100% (2014)
Total collected municipal solid waste per capita (t/capita)	0.404	2017	Amiat—Azienda Multiservizi Igiene Ambientale	0.63 (2016)	0.39 (2013)
Percentage of city solid waste that is recycle	42.70%	2016	Amiat—Azienda Multiservizi Igiene Ambientale	17.7% (2016)	36.5% (2014)
Number of Internet connections per 100,000 population	46,400	2011	Comune di Torino (2015)	49836 (2016)	63000 (2013)
Km of high capacity public transportation system per 100,000 population	1.5 (underground metro system only)	2017	Comune di Torino	18.85 (2015)	14.43 (2014)
Km of light passenger public transportation system per 100,000 population	137.9	2017	CSI Piemonte	289.12 (2015)	58.72 (2014)
Annual number of public transport trips per capita	Not available			636.5 (2015)	158.45 (2014)
Number of personal automobile per capita	0.619	2015	Comuni Italiani	0.33 (2011)	0.59 (2014)
Green area (hectares) per 100,000 population	241	2013	Comune di Torino (2015)	133.2 (2014)	46.9 (2014)
Percentage of city population served by wastewater collection	100%	2011	ISTAT (n.d.)	99.2% (2015)	99.7% (2013)
Percentage of city population with potable water supply service	100%	2011	ISTAT (n.d.)	100% (2015)	100% (2014)
Total domestic water supply per capita (L/day)	189	2011	Società Metropolitana Acque Torino (n.d.)	134 (2015)	101 (2013)

[a]Data at national level.
[b]Data at regional level.

smart city actions were somehow controlled and mitigated by the engagement of a large number of stakeholders through which key actions were identified and selected. In the latter case the target-oriented approach to 2020 only looks at the energy savings, emission reductions, and costs (three main criteria) from a technical perspective without analyzing the corresponding elements of uncertainty and risks. The only action that may be highlighted is the engagement of citizens through surveys related to mobility in order to better shape mobility policies (Comune di Torino).

It is therefore evident that there is still room for making the local planning activity more "robust," taking into explicit consideration other criteria in the evaluation of smart city strategies, for example:

- The potential legal issues. Legal and regulatory concerns relating to the implementation of an action. For example, congestion charging schemes or low-carbon zones may have legal issues related to their implementation. Expansion of the district heating network can be affected by environmental/urban regulations.
- The social acceptability to assess the degree to which a specific initiative will be socially acceptable to citizens. Those with low social acceptability might include ones increasing citizen's economic burden, interruption of transport networks, or the introduction of new regulations relating to citizen's energy behavior. Conversely, subsidies for new energy infrastructure or retrofit schemes might have high social approval.
- The financial issues, meaning the existence of backup solutions, of flexibility in the project design to cope with an unexpected lack of budget, and of accurate procedures against money losses.

3.3.8 Procurement

As reported in Table 3.3, most of the project funding derives from the participation of European, national and regional tenders or have been funded by the municipality itself. Few cases were driven by public–private partnership (PPP) contracts while on the front of the research support for short-term funds, a center of competence on civic crowdfunding will shortly be activated by the municipality for social innovation projects.

During the last years the municipality also gained experience in public procurement. Starting from 2009, networks for fostering good practices exchange related to public procurements were launched. In particular the city became a partner of the SCI-Network project (sustainable construction and innovation network through public procurement), running from 2009 to 2012 with the goal of connecting public authorities to explore European best practices in construction procurement and to share and encourage innovative and sustainable solutions in construction projects. From November 2011 to March 2012 a training program was established by the city on how to foster innovation at each stage of the procurement procedure, with a focus on the construction sector. The city of Torino was considered a relevant case at the European level for a multidisciplinary training course on how to foster innovation in construction procurements; the course involved municipal department heads and other public operators for 28 hours and covered strategy settings, legal and administrative issues, and technological skills.

3.3.9 Discussion—the fringes

From the smart city "narrative," it is evident that the municipality dedicated lots of efforts to rapidly attempt to transform Torino into a smart city. This strong commitment allowed reaching some achievements in terms of citizen services and urban life quality. At the same time, major challenges are still to be faced in order to address the emerged critical points, such as high levels of particulate concentration, low tourism, free Wi-Fi areas, and digitalization. In order to completely build the smart city vision and address the criticalities identified in Section 3.6, it is still necessary to work on some key pillars that the municipality identified as fundamental for the coming years. Supported by the previous analysis and by a direct feedback of the administration, the recognized intervention axes to invest in next years in order to pursue the objectives of the smart city are as follows:

- The valorization of data, their analysis, and their diffusion, in order to evaluate the policies of the city, make services more efficient and support the ecosystem.
- The development of physical infrastructure, both in terms of connectivity and of Internet of Things (IoT), to collect data and create a suitable territory for innovation.
- The digitization of the services offered by the administration to citizens and internal processes within the administration itself, favoring the establishment of civic technologies and solutions that guarantee common goods by design (such as solutions based on block chain).
- The promotion and encouragement of citizen participation by boosting bottom-up decision-making processes and faster feedback cycles compared to public policies.
- The acceleration of new technologies experimentation on the territory, making the city an open-air laboratory that attracts new companies.

Torino keeps working in the transformation toward a smart city. Starting from the list of the recognized intervention axes, the local administration will focus in the coming years on prioritizing the ideas that maximize the benefits for citizens in terms of new services, social impact and attraction of new experiments and the impact on the administration in terms of efficiency, better decision-making, and evaluation of its policies. These actions will see the coordination between the use of the PON (National operative program for Research and Competitiveness) funds, the funds coming from the announcement for the suburbs with AxTO (Città di Torino) and European projects, such as Co-City and ProGiReg. New ideas have been already recently preassessed, and a number of new projects have just been started (in 2017).

Among the recent projects the 2017 "Torino as a Platform" project involves the structuring and development of a city data platform. The importance of data sharing and an approach that sensitizes this direction is one of the foundations on which the Torino Smart City project is based. The data become public and available to all the city's stakeholders, encouraging the emergence of innovative solutions able to respond to the needs of citizens. Furthermore, making data produced by urban and interoperable metabolism allows policies to be evaluated effectively and becomes a crucial support for decision-making. In addition, making available and interoperable the data produced by the urban ecosystem makes it possible to effectively evaluate policies and becomes a fundamental support for decision-making. In addition the decomposition of data silos produced by the administration allows, from an operational point of view, to obtain efficiency, effective evaluation processes, and greater synergies between the sectors of the city. Another ongoing project started in May 2017 is "IoTorino" (Città di Torino) that is linked to networks and sensors. The project starts from school buildings (primary and lower secondary schools) with a restricted pilot involving 14 schools. The feedback gathered in this pilot by an interdepartmental working group constituted by the city have allowed a greater planning structure that will lead, during 2018 and 2019, to a significant extension on to other school buildings with the ambitious goal to reach all the elementary and middle schools in the coming years. The philosophy of the project moves on three different directions: monitor the consumption of the school community in order to activate pedagogical–educational plans aimed at young people, school staff, and more extended to families. These activities both in frontal mode and through recreational activities (gamification) and multimedia will aim to spread behaviors that encourage and spread issues related to sustainability, starting from the students and arriving to the families, starting from schools as a neighborhood technology hub. Starting from the extension of the Wi-Fi network, in the coming years, schools will be at the center of a series of experiments concerning IoT. Another project in 2017 is DecidiTorino (Decidi Torino, 2017). Each area of the administrative activity must be oriented toward a participatory approach This is why the city has adopted an open-source participation platform with the possibility to welcome debates, project proposals from citizens, share the initiatives of the local administration, and structure participatory budget processes. To date the platform has been put online, and the rules will be defined by operating the platform through iterative processes.

With the WeGovNow project [Towards We-Government (Città di Torino)], funded under the Horizon 2020 program with 4195 k€ of which 236 k€ to the city of Torino, a new platform for codesigning public services will be tested. The city internally has adopted collaborative work tools that can facilitate the sharing of knowledge, communication, and agile work. The integration between the sectors of the local administration is a fundamental step for a more efficient administration, and that gives quick and effective answers to the needs of the territory. To further encourage the entry of new knowledge by the administration, two doctoral scholarships have been created on data analysis and on the circular economy. A memorandum of understanding (MOU) has been stipulated through which the 5G of the Telecom Italia, is an Italian telecommunications company (TIM) phone company will be tested. Furthermore, the new platform, Torino Social Impact, was launched as an open community hub. Finally, the administration continues to support initiatives through two technical and financial support measures that have been activated: the 3.3.1.A of the Pon Metro (Agenzia per la coesione territoriale, 2017) and the 3.0.3 of the AxTO Program (Città di Torino, 2017). The activities of the Innovation Center of the City of Turin, Open Incet (Innovation Center Torino), are also entering into the system with the imminent opening of Impact HUB.

3.4 Conclusion

Based on the analysis of the smart city story of Torino, in the previous sections, authors have summarized the relevant findings (current state of the art and next challenges) at the "operational"-like level. As a conclusion, few more strategic-oriented and approach-related considerations are presented with the aim to highlight the further room of improvement for the city of Torino and for its pathway toward a smart development in the next years.

Although the general awareness of the municipality and citizens about the concepts of sustainability, innovation, and participation (pillars of the smart city concept), and about some evident of "smart" changes in the city in the recent years (e.g., bike sharing, and urban regeneration), Torino will need, in the future, a medium-to-long planning platform and vision. Actions are still generally thought, designed, and implemented looking at the short term (e.g., 2020) without a clear and comprehensive objective, which might be improved by structuring current activities into longer term frameworks. Nowadays, there is a very limited talk (and ideas) about the actions and programs to 2030 and beyond, and the transformation of Torino into a smart city is not approached like a continuum of steps (knowing/understanding/planning/designing/acting/monitoring/informing) to iterate, repeat, and improve time by time, but rather like spot initiatives of public/private stakeholders running for short time. Implementing a more structured a systemic long-term planning practice may improve the monitoring mechanisms and the communication channels of the city smartness[2], as well as supporting a more informed decision-making.

Another key drawback of the current approach to city smartness is that actions and initiatives are not designed to tackle city-specific problems but look more like inspired by the examples of other cities and experiences. The attempted international benchmark (making use of the WCCD certification system) has clearly confirmed the need for the city to "act" and improve in specific areas in order to make Torino smarter and closer to the best cities in terms of sustainability, city services, and quality of life.

Acknowledgments

The authors would like to thank Prof. Stefano Paolo Corgnati (DENERG, Politecnico di Torino) for the precious support provided during the drafting of the chapter.

About the authors

Chiara Delmastro holds a PhD in energy engineering from Politecnico di Torino. She is specialized in urban energy planning and energy modeling for the analysis of

---

[2] For the entire time of writing the paper the official communication platform of Torino smart city (the website http://www.torinosmartcity.it/) has been down (for maintenance).

policy-oriented scenarios. She is currently working as a research fellow in Politecnico di Torino with main focus on energy access in developing countries and decarbonization of heat and power sectors.

Rocco De Miglio is an expert in the development and the application of decision support systems in the energy/environmental sector, and in the analysis of all integrated dimensions of the energy governance concept at different scales. With E4SMA he has an extensive experience in modeling and policy analysis projects, and as individual experts in internationally funded technical assistance activities.

Alessandro Chiodi is an energy analyst and modeler. He collaborates from 2010 with E4SMA for activities involving the implementation of decision supporting tools (models) in the energy and environmental space, the development of integrated scenario analysis and technology assessments, and the support and review of policy-making processes at various levels of governance.

Maurizio Gargiulo holds an MSc degree in environmental engineering at the Politecnico di Torino. He has 15 years of experience in energy system modeling and in particular with the TIMES model generator. Since 2002 he has collaborated with national and international institutions on energy system modeling and scenario analysis. Since the beginning of 2010 he is leading E4SMA, as senior energy modeler and analyst. He has been involved in several international activities, collaborating with public and private institutions, on energy model design, implementation, and scenario analysis.

Paola Pisano is the deputy mayor for Innovation, Smart City, Demographic and Statistical Services and Information Systems of the City of Torino. She holds a PhD in business administration, and is a professor of innovation management at the University of Torino, director of IcxT's Smart City laboratory at the University of Turin, representative for the city of Torino in the incubator of the Politecnico di Torino (I3P—5th European incubator), in the Torino Wireless Technological Cluster and in the advisory board of energy center. She has been visiting lecturer at Glasgow Caledonian University London and at the University of Westminster, and she has published more than 70 papers on the subject of innovation and business models.

References

5T C di T. *B.U.N.E.T. project 2014.* <https://www.bunet.torino.it> Accessed December 2017.
Agenzia per la coesione territoriale (2017). *Programma Operativo Nazionale (PON) "Città Metropolitane 2014—2020.*
Amiat—Azienda Multiservizi Igiene Ambientale. *Amiat—Azienda Multiservizi Igiene Ambientale 2016.* <http://www.amiat.it/cms/servizi/16-raccolta-e-smaltimento-rifiuti> Accessed December 2017.
Annuario Statistico del Servizio Sanitario Nazionale. (2013). *Direzione Generale della Digitalizzazione del Sistema Informativo Sanitario e della Statistica Ufficio di Statistica.* Roma: Annuario Statistico del Servizio Sanitario Nazionale.

ARPA Piemonte. *AR per la PA*. (n.d.). Indicatori Online <http://www.arpa.piemonte.gov.it/reporting/indicatori-on_line/componenti-ambientali/aria_particolato-pm2-5-media-annua> Accessed December 2017.

Aragona, E. *La mappa dei rom in Italia. La comunità conta 150/170 mila persone*. Sole 24 Ore 2015.

Associazione artigiani e piccole imprese Mestre (CGIA Mestre). *E' Torino il comune più indebitato d'Italia 2014*. <http://www.cgiamestre.com/2011/01/29/e-torino-il-comune-piu-indebitato-ditalia/> Accessed December 2017.

Associazione Nazionale Comuni Italiani. *Smart City National Observatory*. <http://osservatoriosmartcity.it/cos-e/> Accessed December 2017.

Associazione Nazionale Comuni Italiani (ANCI) & Istituto per la Finanza e l'Economia Locale (IFEL). *Piattaforma Agenda Urbana*. <http://osservatoriosmartcity.it> Accessed December 2017.

Beretta, I., Cattolica, U., & Trieste, V. (2018). The social effects of eco-innovations in Italian smart cities. *Cities*, 72, 115−121. Available from https://doi.org/10.1016/j.cities.2017.07.010.

Borchiellini, R., Corgnati, S. P., Becchio, C., Delmastro, C., Bottero, M. C., Dell'Anna, F., et al. (2017). The energy center initiative at Politecnico di Torino: Practical experiences on energy efficiency measures in the Municipality of Torino. *International Journal of Heat and Technology*, 35. Available from https://doi.org/10.18280/ijht.35Sp0128.

Città di Torino. *PIANO D' AZIONE L' ENERGIA SOSTENIBILE. Turin Action Plan for Energy*. 2012.

Città di Torino. *PUMAS project*. <http://www.comune.torino.it/relint/inglese/progetti/tc0713/pumas.shtml> Accessed December 2017.

Città di Torino. *Urban Barriera Project*. <http://www.comune.torino.it/urbanbarriera/> Accessed December 2017.

Città di Torino. *Progetto Unitario Cortili Scolastici*. 2013. <http://www.comune.torino.it/iter/servizi/laboratorio_citta_sostenibile/progetto_cortili_scolastici.shtml> Accessed December 2017.

Città di Torino. *Azioni per le periferie torinesi—AxTo*. <http://www.axto.it/> Accessed December 2017.

Città di Torino. *Progetto Io Torino 2017*. <http://www.comune.torino.it/cittagora/in-breve/torino-sensorizzata.html> Accessed December 2017.

Città di Torino. *WeGovNow project 2017*. <http://www.comune.torino.it/relint/inglese/progetti/programmi1420/wegovnow.shtml> Accessed December 2017.

Comando Provinciale dei Vigili del Fuoco di Torino. *Comando Provinciale dei Vigili del Fuoco di Torino 2017*. <http://www.vvf.torino.it/organizzazione/organizzazione.html> Accessed December 2017.

Comune di Torino (Servizio Statistica e Toponomastica Città di Torino). (2015). *Rapporto Urbes 2015, Il benessere equo e sostenibile nelle città*.

Comune di Torino. <http://www.comune.torino.it/> Accessed December 2017.

Comune di Torino. *Politecnico di Torino. Indagine sulla mobilità 2017*. <http://www.comune.torino.it/trasporti/archivio-news/venerdi-11-agosto-strada-traforo-del-pino-chiusa-a-5.shtml> Accessed December 2017.

Comuni Italiani. *Parco Veicolare Provincia di Torino 2015*. <http://www.comuni-italiani.it/001/statistiche/veicoli.html> Accessed December 2017.

Costa, G., Stroscia, M., Zebgarini, N., & Demaria, M. (2017). *40 anni di salute a Torino di salute a Torino* (1st ed.). Milano: Inferenze scarl.

CSI Piemonte. *OPTICITIES project*. <http://www.opticities.co> Accessed December 2017.

D'Addato, M. *STUDIO SUGLI INCENDI IN ITALIA DAL 2007 AL 2011*. 2011.
Dall'O, G., Bruni, E., Panza, A., Sarto, L., & Khayatian, F. (2017). Evaluation of cities' smartness by means of indicators for small and medium cities and communities: A methodology for Northern Italy. *Sustainable Cities and Society, 34*, 193−202. Available from https://doi.org/10.1016/j.scs.2017.06.021.
Decidi Torino. (2017). <https://www.deciditorino.it> Accessed December 2017.
Delmastro, C., Martinsson, F., Dulac, J., & Corgnati, S. P. (2017). Sustainable urban heat strategies: Perspectives from integrated district energy choices and energy conservation in buildings. Case studies in Torino and Stockholm. *Energy, 138*, 1209−1220. Available from https://doi.org/10.1016/j.energy.2017.08.019.
EasyPark. *Smart City Index 2017*. (2017). <https://easyparkgroup.com/smart-cities-index/> Accessed December 2017.
ENI. *Enjoy car sharing service*. <https://enjoy.eni.com/it> Accessed December 2017.
European Commission. *Covenant of Mayor Initiative*. <http://www.conventiondesmaires.eu/index_en.html> Accessed December 2017.
European Commission. *Smart City & Communities*. (2011). <http://ec.europa.eu/eip/smartcities/index_en.htm> Accessed December 2017.
FIWARE. *FIWARE project*. (2014). <https://www.fiware.org> Accessed December 2017.
Fondazione Filippo Caracciolo. (2011). *LA POLIZIA LOCALE IN ITALIA Dai grandi ai piccoli Comuni* (pp. 1−24).
Fondazione Torino Wireless. <https://torinowireless.it> Accessed December 2017.
Forum Pa srl. *ICity rate 2017—La classifica delle città intelligenti italiane*. (2017). <http://www.icitylab.it/il-rapporto-icityrate/edizione-2017/> Accessed December 2017.
Guelpa, E., Mutani, G., Todeschi, V., & Verda, V. (2017). A feasibility study on the potential expansion of the district heating network of Turin. *Energy Procedia, 122*, 847−852. Available from https://doi.org/10.1016/j.egypro.2017.07.446.
Innovation Center Torino. <http://openincet.it> Accessed December 2017.
International Organization for Standardization (ISO). (2014). *ISO 37120:2014. Sustainable development of communities—Indicators for city services and quality of life*.
ISTAT. *dati Istat*. (n.d.). <http://dati.istat.it/> Accessed December 2017.
ISTAT. (2017). *Studenti e Scuole dell' Istruzione Primaria e Secondaria in Italia*. Roma: ISTAT. <https://www.istat.it/it/files/2017/04/Studenti-e-scuole.pdf> Accessed December 2017.
Ministero dell'Istruzione dell'Università e della R. *Smart Cities and Communities*. <http://hubmiur.pubblica.istruzione.it/web/ricerca/smart-cities-and-communities-and-social-innovation> Accessed December 2017.
Municipality of Torino. *Geoportale del comune di Torino*. <http://www.comune.torino.it/geoportale/> Accessed December 2017.
Mutani, G., Delmastro, C., Gargiulo, M., & Corgnati, S. P. (2016). Characterization of building thermal energy consumption at the urban scale. *Energy Procedia, 101*, 384−391. Available from https://doi.org/10.1016/j.egypro.2016.11.049.
OPLON. *OPLON project, OPportunites for an active and healthy LONgevity*. (2014). <http://www.oplon.eu/en_US/> Accessed December 2017.
Planet Idea. *Planet Smart Square*. (2016) <https://www.planetsmartcity.com/smartsquare/index.html> Accessed December 2017.
Politecnico di Torino. *Energy Centre*. (2017). <http://www.energycenter.polito.it> Accessed December 2017.
Program UE. *BoostInno project*. <http://urbact.eu/boostinno> Accessed December 2017.

SCI-Network. *SCI-Network project.* <http://www.sci-network.eu/home/> Accessed December 2017.
Sensing Safety at Work. *Smartdatanet.* SEeS@W. <https://www.smartdatanet.it/ecosistema/bando/progetti-bando/sicurezza/sees-w.html> Accessed December 2017.
S[m2]art. *Smart Metro Quadro: guardando la città metro per metro.* (2013). <http://www.smartcityitalia.net/projects/sm2art/> Accessed December 2017.
Società Metropolitana Acque Torino. *S. Punti Acqua SMAT.* (2015). <http://www.smatorino.it/servizi_idrici_integrati_14> Accessed December 2017.
Società Metropolitana Acque Torino. *S. ISTAT rileva un consumo pro capite di 175 litri di acqua al giorno.* (n.d.). <http://www.smatorino.it/notizia_558> Accessed December 2017.
Torino Smart City Foundation. *Torino Smart City Foundation.* <http://www.torinosmartcity.it> Accessed December 2017.
Torino Social Innovation. *FaciliTo and Social Innovation.* <http://www.torinosocialinnovation.it/azioni/facilito-giovani/> Accessed December 2017.
UIA. *Co-City project.* <http://www.uia-initiative.eu/fr/uia-cities/turin> Accessed December 2017.
URBACT European Program. *My Generation @Work.* <http://urbact.eu/my-generation-work> Accessed December 2017.

Further reading

Consorzio per il Sistema Informativo. *CSI Piemonte.* <http://www.csipiemonte.it/web/it/> Accessed December 2017.
Delmastro, C., Mutani, G., & Corgnati, S. P. (2016). A supporting method for selecting cost-optimal energy retrofit policies for residential buildings at the urban scale. *Energy Policy, 99*, 42−56. Available from https://doi.org/10.1016/j.enpol.2016.09.051.
Moovit Insight. (2017). *Informazioni e statistiche sui mezzi pubblici nell'area Torino e Asti. Italia.* <https://moovitapp.com/insights/it/Analisi_Moovit_sull_indice_per_la_mobilità_pubblica_Italia_Torino-222> Accessed December 2017.
Mutani, G., & Vicentini, G. (2015). Buildings' energy consumption, energy savings potential and the availability of renewable energy sources in urban spaces. *Journal of Civil Engineering and Architecture Research, 2*, 1102−1115.

The smart city of Leuven

Roel Heijlen and Joep Crompvoets
KU Leuven Public Governance Institute, Leuven, Belgium

Chapter Outline

4.1 Introduction 83
    4.1.1 Objective and structure of the chapter 84
4.2 Background 85
    4.2.1 Context 85
    4.2.2 Focus areas 86
4.3 Analysis of the case 87
    4.3.1 Scope 89
    4.3.2 Integration and organization 90
    4.3.3 Time 92
    4.3.4 Costs and funding channels 92
    4.3.5 Criteria regarding quality and procurement 94
    4.3.6 Risks and anticipation 94
4.4 Discussion 99
    4.4.1 Strategy 100
    4.4.2 Multidisciplinarity (and cocreation) 100
    4.4.3 Appropriation 101
    4.4.4 Road map 101
    4.4.5 Technology 101
4.5 Conclusion 102
Acknowledgments 102
About the authors 102
References 103

4.1 Introduction

On October 23, 2017 the City Council of Leuven, a Belgian medium-sized city, adopted a statement of intent to transform Leuven into a "futureproofed smart city" (Belga, 2017a). In the months before this symbolic and formal event of adoption took place, the focus areas, goals, and actions of Smart City Leuven were outlined by a steering group and a working group including members of all segments of Leuven's Triple Helix model. By Triple Helix model, we refer to government—university—industry interactions leading to emerging innovation systems (Leydesdorff & Deakin, 2011). The members of the steering group and working group for Smart City Leuven consisted of representatives of the city hall, the city administration, the socioeconomic development organization Leuven MindGate, research institutions (*Imec, KU Leuven, UC Leuven-Limburg*), and the companies Cronos & Commscope.

In the academic literature, there is no consensus about the definition of a smart city (Ben Letaifa, 2015; Meijer & Rodriguez Bolivar, 2016). Broadly stated, it refers to urban innovation that deals with urban challenges by employing modern ICT infrastructure and techniques (e.g., sensors, cameras, data platforms, and big data analytics) and stakeholders participation (Ballon, 2016; China Academy of Information and Communication Technology, 2016; Townsend; 2013). Some cities give their own meaning to the hyped but vague concept (Lee, Hancock, & Hu, 2013). Analyzing its statement of intent and the vision document, Leuven considers cities to become *smart* when smart technology, smart citizens, and smart policy collaborate together. The purpose of this collaboration is the creation of a pleasant environment to live, to learn, to work, and to relax. This ultimate aim for Smart City Leuven is summarized as "a futureproof liveable urban setting for inhabitants and city visitors with specific attention for social inclusion." In this chapter we line up with the meaning of a smart city given by Leuven, but we will also refer to typical definition elements as mentioned above, namely, the tackling of urban challenges, a strong focus on technology and data, the strive for stakeholders participation and additionally economic development.

As there is no "one-size-fits-all" format for smart cities and each city has its own characteristics and issues (China Academy of Information and Communication Technology, 2016; Hollands, 2015; Kitchin, 2015; Meijer & Rodriguez Bolivar, 2016), the outlining of Smart City Leuven integrated on the one hand the cities' unique selling points and on the other hand some specific challenges. The unique selling points comprise Leuven's large student population, the presence of world-renowned research institutions and open innovation pioneers, a compact city center and its central location within Belgium. Specific challenges deal for instance with the pursuit to keep city shopping in Leuven attractive and data integration within the city administration.

Now that the vision for Smart City Leuven has reached ground, next steps will focus on the formalization of the smart city organization, the coordination of smart city initiatives, the implementation and expansion of projects, and the monitoring of the objectives. These steps include various challenges such as

- evolving toward a Quadruple Helix model by involving citizens in the smart city story;
- further reflection on financial stimuli for smart city projects;
- enthusing companies to contribute to making Leuven smarter;
- creating a data governance framework for the city administration;
- engagement, new task allocations, and novel practices inside the city administration; and
- putting social inclusion aspirations into practice.

4.1.1 Objective and structure of the chapter

The aim of this chapter is to present the case of Smart City Leuven and to execute a primarily evaluation of its smart city vision.

In the next sections at first more background information on Smart City Leuven will be provided to gain insight into the context that drove involved parties to create a smart city initiative and the chosen topics the actors of the Triple Helix want to focus on. Second, the results of our case study research on the conceptualization of Smart City Leuven are presented. This presentation includes the analysis of a smart city's key elements, such as scope, integration, organization, time, costs, funding channels, quality criteria, procurement aspects, risks, and anticipation of risks. In the third section, strengths, weaknesses, and outstanding questions of Leuven's smart city vision will be discussed by using elements of the SMART model of Ben Letaifa. Finally, the chapter ends with a conclusion section.

4.2 Background

The idea for Smart City Leuven did not grow out of thin air. Grasping the context of its emergence and the selection of focus areas for smart projects provides a better understanding of the conceptualization of Smart City Leuven. Therefore this section, aimed at the provision of more background information on Smart City Leuven, explores the following questions:

- Which factors led to the idea of transforming Leuven into a smart city?
- Which topics have been selected to converge Leuven's smart city projects?

4.2.1 Context

The main forces behind the choice to develop a smart city vision for Leuven were the lack of coherence in innovative urban projects, the historical existence of a functioning Triple Helix model and ambitions concerning economic growth.

Before its smart city vision the city of Leuven, well aware of the worldwide smart city trend, realized they were already executing or planning projects that could be labeled "smart." Examples are experiments with road pricing (Tibau, 2011) and the city program to become a climate neutral city by 2030, including inter alia projects concerning district heating (Leuven 2030, 2017). However, there was a lack of coherence in these different projects. The city of Leuven wanted to avoid following blindly the trend of smart cities. Therefore they first took time to study and delineate the concept of smart cities in order to design its own coherent vision.

To elaborate this vision, various partners from the city, knowledge institutions, and companies were brought together. The city of Leuven and the University of KU Leuven have already a long tradition of collaboration. Being a smaller city, short lines of communication between the city and Leuven's business circle are present to cooperate on common interests. This resulted for instance in 2016 in the founding of a socioeconomic development organization called Leuven MindGate. Leuven MindGate acts to promote, consolidate, and enforce Leuven as a one of the world's prime regions for health, high tech, and creativity (Leuven MindGate, 2017). The members of this organization comprise all segments of the Leuven's Triple Helix model (government—knowledge institutions—industry). Considering these existing historical and structural partnerships among the city, knowledge institutions and corporations, the ideal ecosystem was available to design and implement a smart city vision for Leuven. Strong leadership inside the segments of the Triple Helix model, convinced about the benefits of working together to address Leuven's urban challenges, facilitates the processes related to futureproof city innovations.

Another driver for jumping on the smart city train was ambitions concerning economic growth. The city department of economics and trade, which is a key actor within the smart city partnership, believes that smart city developments, inter alia through new technologies and novel ideas, will create job opportunities and has potential to strengthen commercial activities in the city. Therefore the smart city vision also contains actions to anticipate on current and future economic needs.

4.2.2 Focus areas

The partners of Smart City Leuven identified five focus domains for smart development. These domains integrate on the one hand existing initiatives. For instance, the priority sectors of the socioeconomic organization Leuven MindGate (namely, health, high tech, and creativity), and their interplay are reflected in the selected topics. Likewise, the program to become a climate neutral city by 2030 shows elements in the focus domains. On the other hand, new subjects are also introduced related for instance to the inclusion of inhabitants with low incomes or low digital literacy. The five focus areas that will frame the smart city initiatives of Leuven behold the following:

1. *Optimization of streams:* Leuven has the ambition to optimize by 2030: (a) mobility streams, such as distribution of goods and human transport, and (b) energy streams regarding warmth, gas, electricity, and water. This requires reliable and proficient information streams.
2. *Smart service delivery:* By using smart processes and IT-capacity, which will enable inter alia city data sharing, the city wants to proactively accommodate to the needs of inhabitants and city visitors with specific attention for social inclusion.
3. *Smart health(care):* Taking the advantage of the presence of high-quality, internationally renowned health(care) actors in Leuven, the city will serve as an ideal platform to test new healthcare technologies.
4. *City experience:* Oriented toward a pleasant urban environment, Leuven will employ measurements and new technologies to increase social cohesion and experiential value for inhabitants and city visitors.
5. *Talent:* Leuven wants to deploy the competences of his inhabitants taking into account each person's talents. This includes on the one hand being an attractive environment for highly skilled people who can be triggered to innovate for urban challenges. On the other hand, lifelong learning activities and technology need to diminish the digital divide between inhabitants in order to avoid a dual economy/society.

4.3 Analysis of the case

Leuven is a medium-sized city in Belgium (Fig. 4.1). Since the beginning of 2017, it has become the 10th Belgian city and the 5th city in Flanders, the northern region of Belgium, which has more than 100,000 inhabitants (Belga, 2017b). The continuing population growth represents a real challenge for Leuven as its surface is limited to 56.63 km^2 (Vlaanderen, 2017). To cope for instance with the increased mobility streams that a growing population entails, the city introduced in 2016 a new traffic circulation plan. This plan included inter alia an extension of the pedestrian zone in Leuven's small, medieval city center (Heijlen & Crompvoets, 2017). Besides its regular inhabitants the city houses approximately 35,000 students who

Figure 4.1 Map of Belgium (Leuven situated by square).
Source: CIA World Fact Book (2018).

Table 4.1 Facts and figures of Belgium, Vlaams-Brabant and the city of Leuven.

Amount of inhabitants Belgium	11,322,088
Average amount of inhabitants per Belgian municipality	19,223
Amount of inhabitants province Vlaams-Brabant	1129,234
Amount of inhabitants Leuven	100,121 regular inhabitants plus approximately 35,000 students
Surface of Belgium	30,528 km^2
Surface of province Vlaams-Brabant	2106 km^2
Surface of Leuven	56.63 km^2
Amount of districts of Leuven	5: Heverlee, Kessel-Lo, Leuven, Wilsele, and Wijgmaal

Source: Statistics Belgium. *Structuur van de bevolking volgens woonplaats: grootste gemeenten*. (2017). <http://statbel.fgov.be/nl/statistieken/cijfers/bevolking/structuur/woonplaats/groot/> Accessed 03.01.18 (in Dutch) (Statistics Belgium, 2017), *Vlaanderen. Gemeenten en provincies. Vlaams-Brabant. Leuven*. (2017). <https://www.vlaanderen.be/nl/gemeenten-en-provincies/provincie-vlaams-brabant/leuven> Accessed 18.12.17 (in Dutch), and Leuven's city administration.

besides its regular inhabitants the city houses approximately 35,000 students who live most parts of an academic year in Leuven but have their domicile somewhere else. This unique rate between inhabitants *(approx. two-thirds of the residents)* and students *(approx. one-third of the residents)* makes of Leuven the biggest student city of Belgium. Table 4.1 provides an overview of demographic and surface information.

Since the University of KU Leuven dates back from the year 1425, the city has a long academic history. The presence of the university and a university hospital stimulates economic growth in the region as they generate numerous spin-offs, of which many operate in the sectors of health and high tech. Another important sector for the economic fabric of Leuven comprises creativity and culture. Therefore the city has recently invested to transform a former run-down area into a neighborhood with affordable space for creative entrepreneurs. Considering that Leuven is also the capital of the province of Vlaams-Brabant, its economic and cultural meaning expands the city borders toward a larger region.

Now that some facts and figures of Leuven have been briefly sketched, we examine the following elements to grasp the conceptualization of Smart City Leuven: scope, integration, organization, time, costs, funding channels, quality criteria, procurement aspects, risks, and anticipation of risks.

The analysis is based upon document analysis and interviews with persons concerned from the city hall, the city departments, and the socioeconomic organization Leuven MindGate. The documents that were analyzed consisted inter alia of the smart city vision document, the statement of intent of Smart City Leuven, communications from the City and Leuven MindGate, articles from newspapers and government webpages containing information on smart city initiatives. The interviews were semistructured discussing themes, such as stakeholders, coordination, challenges, financial aspects, data exchange, technologies, and future steps.

4.3.1 Scope

While discussing the focus areas for Smart City Leuven, the members of the Triple Helix partnership also determined some actions or projects toward smartness. Some of these actions and projects were already planned and have been embedded in the smart city vision. Other actions and projects are completely new. Table 4.2 offers examples of actions and projects that are identified to give content to Smart City Leuven. For each focus area of Smart City Leuven the table provides illustrations of smart city projects that have been chosen to incorporate, to explore, or to prospectively implement in order to execute Leuven's smart city vision. As Smart City Leuven is only in its initial stage, many work still needs to be done. In addition, more actions and projects will grow as new opportunities will be looked for.

Table 4.2 Examples of actions and projects of Smart City Leuven.

Focus area	Examples of actions and projects
Optimization of streams	• Smart and sustainable city logistics: employing small electric vehicles and e-bikes for "last mile" deliveries in the city center in order to diminish freight traffic, noise, and air pollution • Test ground smart street lights: testing of sensors measuring air quality, noise and traffic streams attached to city street lights • Preparing the introduction of a semiautonomous bus shuttle connecting different parts in the city by 2020 • Innovative bike-sharing systems • Applying to become a city test environment for 5 G internet • Enforcing the policy of shop & go parking spaces (maximum 30 min) by using sensors • STORY: a research project on interoperability between energy smart grids • Integrating smart energy applications within the building constructions of a new city block
Smart service delivery	• Employing an integrated, uniform data platform to optimize information processes within the city administration • Creation of an Open Data platform to share data with citizens and entrepreneurs in order to create social and economic value • The Digital Citizen of Leuven: the creation of a digital profile for each citizen to allow for instance the automatic allocation of social benefits • Introducing blockchain pilots • An application to notify defects concerning city playgrounds
Smart health (care)	• InnovAGE: a living lab where companies and organizations can test and improve health(care) innovations • Construction of a new health site in the city center (including i.a. service flats for elderly), which will employ novel health technologies • Leuven Vital City: city support for innovative initiatives that stimulate inhabitants to have an active lifestyle • Testing wearables to improve the health of the city's personnel

(Continued)

Table 4.2 (Continued)

Focus area	Examples of actions and projects
City experience	• Hands-free shopping • Introduction of the internationally renowned city pass app in collaboration with other cities in Flanders
Talent	• PIP: an education format from the University of KU Leuven whereby an interdisciplinary team of students collaborate during a full academic year to deliver a solution for a task given by the project sponsor (i.a. the city administration) • Leuven International House: actions to enhance Leuven's working and living climate for international knowledge workers • Test ground "start-ups in residence" to assist the start-ups scene in Leuven • Supporting initiatives that offer access to technology and help with computer problems for disadvantaged groups

PIP, Product Innovation Project.
Source: Smart City Leuven's vision document, interview data & Leuven's city administration.

Each action or project needs to have a link with the selected focus areas and Leuven's smart city goal to improve the conditions of living, studying, working, and relaxing. However, the projects and actions can vary according to the following:

- *Initiator:* a city department, a research institution, Leuven MindGate, a corporation wanting to test an innovation, a health organization, or other actors (for instance a public bus company)
- *Target group:* inhabitants, students, workers in Leuven, entrepreneurs, city visitors, and tourists
- *Required infrastructure*: For example, electronic vehicles, smart energy equipment (i.a. smart grids), sensors, solid internet connections, apps, data platforms, blockchain technology, futureproof buildings
- *Sponsorship:* public funding, public–private partnerships, private funding, or external subsidies

Overviewing the actions and projects, running or scheduled, a typical mix of smart city elements can be noticed, such as the tackling of urban challenges (i.a. city traffic problems, energy scarcity), the importance of data streams, and being competitive (i.a. attracting international talent and start-ups).

4.3.2 Integration and organization

As already mentioned, Smart City Leuven is conceptualized by a Triple Helix model. The actors involved in the creation of smart city vision included are the representatives of

- the city council: the aldermen responsible for economy, trade, and environment;
- the city administration: inter alia the departments of economy and trade, social affairs, data management, spatial planning, sustainability and mobility;

- knowledge institutions: the University of KU Leuven, the university college UC Leuven-Limburg and Imec *(=a R&D and innovation hub in nanoelectronics and digital technologies);*
- the socioeconomic organization Leuven MindGate; and
- the companies Cronos *(=consultancy regarding innovative entrepreneurship)* and CommScope *(=a network infrastructure provider).*

All actors subscribed the statement of intent, comprising a summary of the smart city vision for Leuven and the following engagement: "The proposers wish to actively connect with the five focus domains for Leuven and all commit themselves to support minimum one of these domains with the required resources subjected to further clarification, arrangements and agreement about the employment of these resources."

To elaborate this statement of intent and the vision of Smart City Leuven, a large steering group with all members of the Triple Helix model and a smaller writing committee were established. Since the vision has been set out, an organization guiding the implementation of Smart City Leuven will be formalized in the next months. To coordinate the various different actions and projects related to the smart city vision, two project coordinators will be hired soon and financed by the city hall. One project coordinator has the task to coordinate the smart city initiatives across the various city departments. He or she shall work within the city hall. The other project coordinator, more focused on the other actors of the Triple Helix model, will work at the socioeconomic organization Leuven MindGate. He or she acquires the responsibility to maintain contacts with companies in the field of high tech, health, and creativity, which can contribute in making Leuven a smarter city. Both coordinators are expected to closely consult each other in order to align. Taking into account the existing structure, the coordination plans, the focus areas, and some specific projects, the future organization might be formed as illustrated in Fig. 4.2.

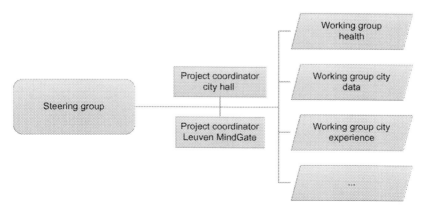

Figure 4.2 Potential future structure of Smart City Leuven.
Source: Interview data & Leuven's city administration.

Figure 4.3 Timeline smart city vision Leuven.
Source: Interview data, Leuven's city administration and Belga (2017a, October 24). Leuven wil uitgroeien tot smart city. *Knack Datanews*, <http://datanews.knack.be/ict/nieuws/leuven-wil-uitgroeien-tot-smart-city/article-normal-916443.html> Accessed 27.10.17 (in Dutch).

As will be discussed later in this chapter, the current actors concerned also intend in the near future to involve citizens in order to evolve toward a Quadruple helix model for Smart City Leuven.

4.3.3 Time

The operation to design, approve, and announce the vision of Smart City Leuven lasted approximately 9 months. Steps included procedures related to debating, writing, voting, and communicating on Leuven's smart city vision as also some linked expenses. The timeline in Fig. 4.3 shows an overview of key events and entities involved.

This timeline focuses only on the settled process regarding the vision of building of Smart City Leuven. Other parts in this chapter have outlined or will discuss the next steps more broadly. These next steps comprise inter alia the formalization of the organizational structure, the hiring of personnel to coordinate smart city initiatives, attracting new fund and participants, and the setup of data governance. Later in the discussion part, we will argue that the development of a road map is desirable to streamline the several identified smart city projects.

4.3.4 Costs and funding channels

The implementation of Smart City Leuven will be accompanied with costs for the city such as

- the recruitment of two project coordinators;
- data infrastructure: inter alia a sensor system for the shop & go parking spaces, an Open Data platform and blockchain technology;
- engagement in collaborative innovative projects: for example, the PIP whereby the city hall sponsors a novel education format of the university;
- the employment of smart energy tools in new building constructions in which the city is involved; and
- potentially extra personnel needs within the city administration (for instance to cope with new challenges on city data management).

Besides public financing, for instance to coordinate the smart city initiative or innovate public service delivery, the city intends to stimulate smart city projects through funds for public—private partnerships. Recently, such a project started whereby a company and the city are testing smart sensors attached on cities' street lights to measure air quality. These public—private partnerships aimed to support innovations require financial contributions by the private partners (e.g., companies). Further reflections about the funds for public—private partnerships are planned within the city. Some projects will however not include any city cofinancing as the city might only be involved by allowing innovations to be real life tested in the public domain of Leuven. Apart from the city and companies, knowledge institutions also have already embedded projects with their own financial support within the smart city initiatives (e.g., The STORY project of the university college UC Leuven-Limburg). As noted in the statement of intent of Smart City Leuven, all proposers engage themselves to contribute with (financial or other) sources to at least one focus area.

In addition, the city of Leuven explores new opportunities regarding

1. external budgets or support for smart city initiatives, awarded by programs from the provinces, the regional Government of Flanders, the European Union, or private initiatives (e.g., financial institutions) and
2. external collaborations with other Belgian cities or international cities.

An example of external support is for instance an initiative from the Flemish provinces to offer cities in Flanders a uniform data platform infrastructure to process and visualize statistics and other city information. The city administration will use this infrastructure allowing the different departments to integrate their data. In addition, the city will apply for subsidies from the Smart Flanders program of the Flemish Government. This program supports Flemish cities to open their data in order to stimulate the creation of smart services and applications through city data reuse. Other supportive actions from the Flemish Government comprise the payments of travel costs of Flemish cities' delegates to attend international expos about smart cities and subsidies for innovative business networks. Leuven MindGate recently participated in a proposal for the Flemish Agency for Innovation and Entrepreneurship for the foundation of an innovative cluster in the field of smart cities, linking the companies in Flanders, which are active in this area.

The city of Leuven is convinced that in the case of certain smart initiatives, a collaboration between cities is strongly desirable. The exploration of such collaborations has been incorporated in the statement of intent of Smart City Leuven. More partnerships, around smart urbanism in order to avoid fragmentation and to create efficiency gains, have also been proclaimed by smart city scholars pointing at the similar challenges cities face (Ballon, 2016; Fraefel, Haller, & Gschwend, 2017). Also, the Smart Flanders program plays on common city needs and the economies of scale by stimulating intercity collaboration.

On a national level, Leuven desires for instance intercity collaboration concerning the introduction of the international city pass app in Flanders and educational activities for city officials regarding big data. It has also recently worked together with the Flemish city of Kortrijk regarding a group purchase that included a sensor system for shop & go parking places. Concerning the international level, the city of Leuven disposes since 2013 of an India House to promote Leuven–Indian partnerships. Regarding the presence of this India House, the city recently identified Indian smart cities to cooperate with. Furthermore, the city has applied for particular Horizon 2020 projects of the European Union, which stimulate collaboration between European cities.

4.3.5 Criteria regarding quality and procurement

As the concept of smart city gained momentum and cities are getting overwhelmed with various project calls and offers from companies concerning smart solutions, the identified focus areas of Smart City Leuven need to serve as a guiding tool for enabling selections. Guidance is necessary as one of the aldermen stated "We do not want gadgets just to have gadgets" referring to the objective that chosen technologies for Smart City Leuven should contribute to the quality of life of people.

Besides the focus domains and the impact on the living environment of citizens and other important quality criteria for future selections of smart city projects might, based on interviews with persons concerned, involve

- the visibility of the project;
- the range;
- committing to or proceeding with existing projects;
- the level of uniqueness or media appeal;
- the futureproof approach;
- the degree of risks; and
- the costs.

Next steps in the implementation will show how such criteria will be formalized in the procedures of the steering committee, working groups, or other organizational bodies responsible to take decisions on project choices and distribution of resources.

Considering future procurements, the sharing of data will become the norm for the city of Leuven. In the plans toward city data integration and an Open Data environment, new contracts with private partners are expected, when relevant, to contain clauses on societal use of data. Contracts concerning the exploitation of public city parking places are a typical example. Data on the occupancy rate of these parking places offer interesting information for the city administration to monitor mobility streams and for app developers to support city visitors finding available parking space. However, in the past such data sharing was not always easy to obtain in Leuven. Clear contractual agreements with private partners must end potential restrictions to data access.

4.3.6 Risks and anticipation

In order to achieve the goals of Leuven's smart city vision, awareness on potential risks and if possible anticipation of these risks requires due consideration. Which are the risks, how does Leuven plan to deal with these risks, and which are the relevant questions for the future? Risks include privacy matters and other data sensitivities, low involvement from stakeholders, exclusion mechanisms, and reluctance to intercity collaboration.

4.3.6.1 Privacy matters and other data sensitivities

The use of ICT is considered to be a key element of smart urbanism. Nevertheless, critical literature on smart cities warns for the so-called dark side of ICT referring for instance to mass surveillance through city cameras and sensors, misuse of personal data, and vulnerabilities concerning hacking (Castelnovo, Misurac, & Savoldelli, 2016; Hollands, 2008; Kitchin, 2014). A recently launched test ground in Leuven on smart street lights with sensors (Belga, 2017a; Mertens, 2017) raises some questions about such concerns.

The sensors attached to the street lights measure in this first phase the quality of air. In addition, in a later phase, other sensors attached to the street lights will measure warmth and movements to monitor for instance mobility streams or the availability of parking spaces. Data from the sensors will be shared through the future Open Data platform of Leuven. However, how do people living close to these street lights feel about the sensors in their neighborhood? Warmth sensors might for instance indirectly provide information on the presence of someone living across a streetlight. Keeping in mind privacy matters, the city will work together with the architecture department of the University of KU Leuven to examine the experience of inhabitants concerning the presence of these sensors (Fig. 4.4).

Other privacy matters are related to the plans of data integration within the city administration. The city department of data management is currently preparing a data governance model. Batini (2010) defines data governance as "the formal orchestration of people, processes, and technology to enable an organization to leverage data as an asset." Privacy is a particular domain of data governance besides domains, such as security, ethics, the data life cycle, data quality, ownership, access rights, and stakeholders (see, for example, Otto, 2011). Reflections and agreements seem necessary regarding the questions such as

1. which data within the city administration can be shared cross-departmental taken into account privacy of citizens (but also other aspects as the relevancy and the reliability of data), and
2. which city data can be shared publicly through the Open Data platform?

Despite the worldwide enthusiasm on open data, it is claimed to be a myth that all data should be made publicly available (Janssen, Charalabidis, & Zuiderwijk, 2012; Walravens, 2012). For instance, some data, which at a first glance may seem innocent and appropriate for sharing, could however by the application of data mining techniques (mis)used to identify individuals or groups (Bannister & Connoly, 2011). As such, caution should be exercised in order to not unintentionally releasing confidential data. Furthermore, opening some particular data sets behold societal risks and political choices. For instance, in comparison with another Flemish city a member of the City Hall of Leuven stated that he does not intend to publicize crime

Figure 4.4 Pictures of Leuven's smart street lights test ground.
Source: Roel Heijlen.

statistics per region as he believes that comparisons by citizens regarding these data may lead to needless public anxiety.

4.3.6.2 Low involvement from stakeholders

Although the approval of the statement of intent to transform Leuven into a "future-proofed Smart City" by the city council received some media attention, at this moment Leuven's smart city vision is not yet widely known among all stakeholders. The vision of Smart City Leuven has been prepared by a small but important circle of believers within the Triple Helix model. However, to become successful the vision requires in the following stages more publicity and adoption by a larger group of stakeholders (citizens, civil servants, and companies). In other words a lack of a broad basis for Smart City Leuven can undermine the achievement of the smart city goals. How to engage more stakeholders?

4.3.6.2.1 Citizens
To avoid a smart city approach, which is too technocratic or too corporate, several researchers dealing with urban innovation call for the inclusion of citizen

participation and point at interesting participatory projects in some existing smart cities (e.g., Baccarne, Mechant, & Schuurman, 2014; Castelnovo et al, 2016; Hollands, 2015).

The city of Leuven has experience with citizen participation regarding programs on climate neutrality and social economy initiatives. However, in the context of Smart City Leuven, the city is still looking how to evolve toward a Quadruple Helix model by involving the citizens. Receiving a lot of offers from consultants and companies presenting themselves as participation experts or providers of must-have participatory tools (e.g., discussion e-platforms for citizens), Leuven faces the challenge of selecting valuable offers and experiments. In addition, as noted by one of the interviewees, participation includes challenges regarding representation. Due consideration to inclusive methods must lower or prevent the risk that participation only favors the most assertive and well-off citizens.

4.3.6.2.2 Civil servants

Although the steering group and the working groups of Smart City Leuven behold different civil servants from various city departments, many civil servants within the city administration are not yet fully familiar with the vision and actions regarding Smart City Leuven. The civil servants who are involved consider the extension of internal support and cultural change within the organization as challenge that needs to be addressed. Related to these items, interviewees referred for instance to issues such as

- the willingness to share data across city departments;
- the establishment of a collective "data hygiene" mind-set referring to the shared responsibility to keep city data qualitative and secure; and
- the conquest of potential fear that new technologies (e.g., blockchain projects) might lead to internal job losses.

Kitchin, Coletta, Evans, Heaphy, and Mac Donncha (2017) already described the problem that smart city ideas and policies run into inertia and resistance by managers and workers from the city administration inter alia fueled by doubts concerning the maturity, the utility, the affordability, and the practicality of technologies.

Considering the involvement of civil servants questions for the near future are as follows:

- Will information sessions and other internal communication activities make large parts of the city personnel enthusiastic for Smart City Leuven?
- Will the future smart city project manager within the city administration be able to guard over sufficient internal support for the smart city vision and actions across the different city departments?
- How to overcome potential barriers to organizational change?

4.3.6.2.3 Companies

At the moment, two companies (namely, Cronos and CommScope) are directly involved with Smart City Leuven being members of the steering and working groups. The ambition is nevertheless to attract the attention of more companies that can contribute in making Leuven smarter regarding the selected focus areas. To fulfill this ambition, different actions are planned, for example,

- information sessions on Smart City Leuven at business associations in Leuven,
- the recruitment of a smart city project manager at the socioeconomic development organization Leuven MindGate to continuously promote Smart City Leuven toward private actors and liaise with potential partners active in the sectors of healthcare, high tech, and creativity, and
- the release of funds for public—private partnerships regarding smart city projects and the provision of the public domain for testing grounds.

Based on the interviews, the impression exists that increased engagement of companies will show less challenges than the engagement of citizens and civil servants. A partial explanation of this observation lays in the ability of the city of Leuven, which is small in surface, to benefit from close connections with Leuven's business circle in order to disseminate information and to find interested parties for projects.

4.3.6.3 Exclusion mechanisms

As smart cities are often driven by new technologies and ideas from high-skilled people, they could lead to social polarization within the city population (Hollands, 2008; Rosati & Conti, 2016). Although Leuven has a large amount of highly educated citizens, parts of the city population with lower education levels or in vulnerable situations should however not be neglected.

One exclusion mechanism involves the lack of knowledge and skills to cope with new technology or the lack of financial resources to buy certain technological infrastructure. Being aware of these risks, the focus area of Leuven's Smart City on talent includes lifelong learning activities and actions to facilitate access to technologies. This means inter alia the support of locations and initiatives offering computer access and help with computer problems for disadvantaged groups. Furthermore, the city aims to employ technology to proactively anticipate on social needs. Kanter and Litow (2009) illustrated how technology in urban settings can provide opportunities from the affluent to the at risk. The city of Leuven is for instance interested in smart solutions to automatically allocate certain social benefits to right holders. Certain social benefits for citizens with a low income, such as free city trash bags or discounts on cultural or sporting activities, are currently underused. Automated allocation has the potential to increase its use by avoiding application processes or problems regarding awareness about these social benefits.

Another exclusion mechanism concerns labor market needs causing possible disparities between high-skilled and low-skilled workers. While some profiles experience a growth in job demands and income, others are confronted with factory closedowns and unemployment (Rosati & Conti, 2016). These differences could threaten social cohesion within smart cities, such as Leuven, which are very attractive for the knowledge industry. Can future projects related to the focus area of city experience, a focus area inter alia intended to strengthen social cohesion, diminish segmentation between population groups differing in skills and income?

Within the objective to become a worldwide prime region for health, high tech, and creativity, and within the context of global competition for talent, the Triple Helix of Smart City Leuven aims to attract knowledge workers to the city. Notwithstanding, this quest for high-skilled workers, Smart City Leuven also comprises actions to enforce job positions for low-skilled workers. As local trade in the city center provides a great amount of jobs to low-skilled workers, the city of Leuven wishes to strengthen its appeal and enhance the comfort of city shoppers in order to keep competing with online shops and exurban shopping malls.

4.3.6.4 Reluctance to intercity collaboration

Each city has its own characteristics and specific needs, but several challenges are similar. As mentioned earlier, the city of Leuven is convinced that intercity collaboration on particular smart projects is desirable. Nevertheless, to accomplish such cooperation, Leuven depends on the willingness of other (national and international) cities. Lack of collaboration risks cause fragmentation, efficiency losses, and a fortified position for consultants and other firms. Considering the current avalanche of offers cities currently receive, strong intercity partnerships might enhance the bargaining power of cities toward suppliers of smart city advice, services, or products. Among some other cooperative activities, Leuven engages in projects of other policy levels that facilitate intercity collaboration. Will ongoing and future initiatives from provincial, Flemish, and European authorities further stimulate intercity collaboration?

4.4 Discussion

Now that the conceptualization of Smart City Leuven has been sketched, this section will reflect on strengths, weaknesses, and outstanding questions of Leuven's smart city vision. We must however keep in mind that Smart City Leuven is still in an early stage. The reflection is founded on the current situation that still needs much implementation work.

In order to structure our reflection, inspiration in smart city literature was sought to decide which elements are relevant to evaluate a smart city vision and approach. Although many studies on smart cities or parts of smart cities (e.g., governance and data aspects) are available, not many encompass practical frameworks regarding smart city vision design. An exception concerns the SMART model of Ben Letaifa showing urban leaders where to start and what steps to follow regarding the design and implementation of strategies for building smart cities.

To evaluate the vision and approach of Smart City Leuven, we will discuss the five strategic steps identified in the SMART model of Ben Letaifa (Ben Letaifa, 2015). These steps include

- strategy: defining a common vision of the city based on knowledge about the community and its needs;
- multidisciplinarity: mobilizing multidisciplinary stakeholders and resources for the smart city cocreation;

- appropriation: gaining social acceptability among stakeholders of the smart city projects;
- road map: an implementation strategy containing details of the activities' workflow; and
- technology: identifying enabling technologies the smart city requires.

4.4.1 Strategy

Specific characteristics and issues of Leuven are embedded in its smart city story. The Steering Group of Smart City Leuven designed a smart city vision that integrated Leuven's unique selling points. In addition, the group listed focus areas to offer guidance for smart city projects. These included some particular needs of Leuven regarding for instance the challenges for local trade, the evolvement toward data integration within the city administration, and aspects regarding social cohesion. The focus domains are rather broad and vague. Within the steering group, there was debate if more delineation of the focus domains was necessary, but eventually the broad descriptions were chosen.

One might criticize these descriptions as being too large to have clear selection criteria to steer the smart city vision. On the other hand a too rigid smart city vision could also inhibit creativity and interesting initiatives. As Townsend (2013) noticed "Smart cities need to be efficient but also preserve opportunities for spontaneity, serendipity, and sociability."

4.4.2 Multidisciplinarity (and cocreation)

Smart City Leuven has the advantage to employ existing partnerships and structures between the city, knowledge institutions and corporations, such as the socioeconomic organization Leuven MindGate. By allying present collaboration structures the stakeholders avoid fragmentation.

The socioeconomic organization Leuven MindGate, covering all representatives of a Triple Helix model, provides an ideal ecosystem to mobilize various disciplines for smart city projects. Leuven MindGate promotes for instance the interplay between the disciplines of high tech, health, and creativity, which are also reflected in the smart city vision. Multidisciplinarity is also present in the variety of city departments (e.g., economy, social affairs, and data management) involved in the Steering Group of Smart City Leuven and the availability of various private or academic experts (e.g., regarding architecture and energy) to develop and implement projects, inter alia within the focus area of optimization of streams.

While the Triple Helix partnership seems solid, an important smart city actor, namely, the citizen, is currently missing. Well aware of the importance of citizen participation the partnership of Smart City Leuven aims to evolve toward a Quadruple Helix model. However, in this stage the partners are still investigating which ways are suited to engage citizens. The near future will show if Smart City Leuven succeeds in building a functioning Quadruple Helix model. As citizens of Leuven were not involved in the design of the smart city vision, question is if the vision requires some adaptation based on citizens input.

Considering other stakeholders, the explicit desire of Smart City Leuven and actions to collaborate with other cities regarding certain smart city projects prove to be promising in the light of economies of scale. Can Leuven and its partner cities grow out to be examples of exemplary intercity collaborations?

4.4.3 Appropriation

Leuven's smart city vision stipulates general warnings concerning the limits and vulnerabilities of technology and the need for privacy protection regulations. At first sight most projects that are currently selected as part of Smart City Leuven appear less controversial. The test ground smart street lights with sensors which potentially could reveal sensitive information is, by contrast, an exception. As mentioned, the architecture department of the University of KU Leuven will examine in collaboration with the city the experiences of inhabitants living nearby these street lights. Will the results of this study influence the city's choice for certain technologies? Although the execution of this study shows that the city is concerned about social acceptance, it is at this moment unknown how it will approach other projects comprehending for instance ethical and privacy issues. Who decides if projects are socially acceptable and how (e.g., through participatory methods)? Will each project be assessed separately or is there a need for a general framework to assess social acceptability? If the amount of projects rises, these questions might become more pressing.

4.4.4 Road map

During the elaboration of the "Smart City Leuven" vision, for each focus domain, various actions and projects were identified. However, at this moment a detailed implementation plan of the numerous identified activities is lacking. The draw up and follow-up of an implementation plan might be the task of the two smart city project coordinators who will be hired in the next months.

Some projects are already running or have just been started, while others still need to be developed. An implementation plan may contribute to preserve a global overview. On the one hand, such a plan can offer a state of affairs of Smart City Leuven and its future developments. On the other hand, it might also facilitate the monitoring and the evaluation of Leuven's smart city objectives. The latter raises another question to address: How will Leuven evaluate its road toward smartness?

4.4.5 Technology

Smart City Leuven has already chosen some technologies to support for instance smart service delivery. The data platform to integrate data within the city administration of Leuven and the future Open Data platform to share data with the public are two examples. However, as studies on electronic government show, success or failure of IT projects within the public sector is often not caused by the provided technology itself but relating to contextual factors (Van Cauter, 2016). Will Leuven learn from the lessons of other cities concerning data integration and open data challenges, such as change averse, new roles and responsibilities, information quality (e.g., Dong, Singh, Attri, & El Saddik, 2017; Janssen et al 2012; Schol & Alawadhi, 2016). The development of a data governance model for the city administration is planned. However, since data governance concerns several domains, the city will have to determine which domains require first priority. Another decision involves the selection of data sets that can be easily publicized on the future Open Data platform. As not all data can be opened immediately and at the same time, it is recommended to set out some quick wins (European Data Portal, 2017).

Regarding technologies, such as sensors, smart energy meters, and wearables, in other focus areas of Smart City Leuven, such as optimization of streams, smart health, and city experience, data governance, will also need to be addressed. Stakeholders responsible for the technology (e.g., companies, health organizations, knowledge institutions, and city departments) may vary per project, and each project comprises own particularities. However, similar data challenges are possible. Can future exchange on data governance policies and practices between the different smart city projects be enriching and can it align certain principles?

4.5 Conclusion

Being a young member of the "smart cities" club and finding itself in the early stage of implementing a smart city vision and identified actions, Leuven has the advantage to learn from the existing experiences of "older" smart cities. Moreover, this position as a newcomer offers the city an opportunity to anticipate some of the concerns *(e.g., undue techno-optimism, technocratic governance, and dual societies)* in critical literature about the smart cities rhetoric. Anticipation of these critics are reflected in Smart City Leuven through the particular attention for social inclusion, investigations regarding future citizen participation, the strong desire for intercity collaboration, and a study concerning technological vulnerabilities. However, the road toward smartness for Leuven still contains many implementation challenges, among them, the creation of broad support within the city administration and the development of effective data governance models.

Acknowledgments

We would like to thank the people from the city hall, the city administration, and Leuven MindGate, who were very helpful to support us in gathering information for this book chapter.

About the authors

Roel Heijlen is researcher at the KU Leuven Institute of Public Governance. His research fields include big data and the government, data governance within the public sector and smart cities. His background is in political science. Before he started as an academic, he worked as a policy adviser on e-health.

Prof. Dr. Ir. Joep Crompvoets holds a chair in "Information Management in the Public Sector" at KU Leuven, Belgium, and is secretary-general of the EuroSDR—an European spatial data research network linking national mapping agencies with research institutes and universities for the purpose of applied research. Joep has been involved in numerous research projects related to the spatial data infrastructures, GIS, public sector innovation, and e-governance. He has written numerous publications about these topics.

References

Baccarne, B., Mechant, P., & Schuurman, D. (2014). Empowered cities? An analysis of the structure and generated value of the Smart City Ghent. In R. P. Dameri, & C. Rosenthal-Sabroux (Eds.), *Smart City*. Switzerland: Springer, Progress in IS.

Ballon, P. (2016). *SmartCities. Hoe technologie onze steden leefbaar houdt en slimmer maakt*. Leuven: LannooCampus, [*in Dutch*].

Bannister, F., & Connolly, R. (2011). The trouble with transparency: A critical review of openness in e-government. *Policy and Internet, 3*(1), Article 8.

Batini, C. (2010). Data governance. In G. Viscusi, C. Batini, & M. Mecella (Eds.), *Information systems for egovernment* (pp. 21–41). Berlin, Heidelberg: Springer.

Belga (2017a, October 24). Leuven wil uitgroeien tot smart city. *Knack Datanews*, <http://datanews.knack.be/ict/nieuws/leuven-wil-uitgroeien-tot-smart-city/article-normal-916443.html> Accessed 27.10.17 (in Dutch).

Belga (2017b, June 13). Leuven doorbreekt kaap van 100.000 inwoners. *Metro*, <https://nl.metrotime.be/2017/06/13/news/leuven-doorbreekt-kaap-van-100-000-inwoners/> Accessed 03.01.18 (in Dutch).

Ben Letaifa, S. (2015). How to strategize smart cities: Revealing the SMART model. *Journal of Business Research, 68*, 1414–1419.

Castelnovo, W., Misurac, G., & Savoldelli, A. (2016). Smart cities governance: The need for a holistic approach to assessing urban participatory policy making. *Social Science Computer Review, 34*(6), 724–739.

China Academy of Information and Communications Technology. (2016). EU-China Policy Dialogues Support Facility II *Comparative study of smart cities in Europe and China 2014*. Berlin, Heidelberg: Springer Current Chinese Economic Report Series.

Dong, H., Singh, G., Attri, A., & El Saddik, A. (2017). Open data-set of seven Canadian cities. *IEEE, 5*, 529–543.

European Data Portal. *How to build an Open Data Strategy*. (2017). <www.europeandataportal.eu/nl/providing-data/goldbook/how-build-open-data-strategy> Accessed 22.12.17.

Fraefel, M., Haller, S., & Gschwend, A. (2017). Big data in the public sector. Linking cities to sensors. In M. Janssen, et al. (Eds.), *Electronic government. EGOV 2017. Lecture notes in computer science* (Vol. 10428). Cham: Springer.

Heijlen, R., & Crompvoets, J. (2017). Clean data for cleaner air? Case study research about data streams concerning low-emission zones and car-free zones. *Zenodo*. Available from https://doi.org/10.5281/zenodo.884076.

Hollands, R. G. (2008). Will the real smart city please stand up? Intelligent, progressive or entrepreneurial? *City, 12*(3), 303–319.

Hollands, R. G. (2015). Critical interventions into the corporate smart city. *Cambridge Journal of Regions, Economy and Society, 8*, 61–77.

Janssen, M., Charalabidis, Y., & Zuiderwijk, A. (2012). Benefits, adoption barriers and myths of open data and open government. *Information Systems Management, 29*, 258–268.

Kanter, M. R., & Litow, S. S. (2009). *Informed and interconnected: A manifesto for smarter cities. Working paper 09-141.* Harvard Business School.

Kitchin, R. (2014). The real-time city? Big data and smart urbanism. *GeoJournal, 79*, 1–14.

Kitchin, R. (2015). Making sense of smart cities: addressing present shortcomings. *Cambridge Journal of Regions, Economy and Society, 8*, 131–136.

Kitchin, R., Coletta, C., Evans, L., Heaphy, L. & Mac Donncha, D. (2017). Smart cities, urban technocrats, epistemic communities and advocacy coalitions. In *The programmable city working paper 26.* <http://progcity.maynoothuniversity.ie/>.

Lee, H. J., Hancock, M. G., & Hu, M. (2013). Towards an effective framework for building smart cities: Lessons from Seoul and San Francisco. *Technical Forecasting and Social Changes, 89*, 80–99.

Leuven 2030. *Onze projecten.* (2017). <https://www.leuven2030.be/onze-projecten> Accessed 20.12.17 (in Dutch).

Leuven MindGate. (2017). <www.leuvenmindgate.be> Accessed 15.11.17.

Leydesdorff, L., & Deakin, M. (2011). The triple-helix model of smart cities: A neo-evolutionary perspective. *Journal of Urban Technology, 18*(2), 53–63.

Meijer, A., & Rodriguez Bolivar, M. P. (2016). Governing the smart city: A review of the literature on smart urban governance. *International Review of Administrative Science, 82*(2), 392–408.

Mertens, B. (2017, November 4). Leuven test slimme lantaarnpalen. *HLN.* <https://www.hln.be/regio/leuven/leuven-test-slimme-lantaarnpalen~ae767246/> Accessed 05.01.18.

Otto, B. (2011). A morphology of the organisation of data governance. In: *ECIS 2011 proceedings. Paper 272.*

Rosati, U., & Conti, S. (2016). What is a smart city project? An urban model or a corporate business plan? *Procedia—Social and Behavioral Sciences, 223*, 968–973.

Scholl, H. J., & Alawadhi, S. (2016). Creating smart governance: The key to radical ICT overhaul at the City of Munich. *Information Polity, 21*, 21–42.

Statistics Belgium. *Structuur van de bevolking volgens woonplaats: grootste gemeenten.* (2017). <http://statbel.fgov.be/nl/statistieken/cijfers/bevolking/structuur/woonplaats/groot/> Accessed 03.01.18 (in Dutch).

Tibau, F. (2011, January 14). Leuvense experiment met rekeningrijden van start in voorjaar. *Knack Datanews.* <http://datanews.knack.be/ict/nieuws/leuvense-experiment-met-rekeningrijden-van-start-in-voorjaar/article-normal-277671.html> Accessed 20.12.17 (in Dutch).

Townsend, A. (2013). *Smart cities: Big data, civic hackers, and the quest for a New Utopia.* New York: W.W. Norton & Company.

Van Cauter, L. (2016). *Government-to-government information system failure in Flanders: An in-depth study* (Doctoral dissertation). Katholieke Universiteit Leuven.

Vlaanderen. *Gemeenten en provincies. Vlaams-Brabant. Leuven.* (2017). <https://www.vlaanderen.be/nl/gemeenten-en-provincies/provincie-vlaams-brabant/leuven> Accessed 18.12.17 (in Dutch).

Walravens, N. (2012). Mobile business and the smart city: Developing a business model framework to include public design parameters for mobile city services. *Journal of Theoretical and Applied Electronic Commerce Research, 7*(3), 121–135.

The smart city of Vienna

Vasja Roblek
Faculty of Organizational Studies, Novo Mesto, Slovenia

Chapter Outline

5.1 Introduction   105
5.2 Background   106
5.3 Research methodology: case study   118
   5.3.1 Scope   118
   5.3.2 Integration   120
   5.3.3 Organization   123
   5.3.4 Time   123
   5.3.5 Discussion—the fringes   125
5.4 Conclusions   126
About the author   126
References   126

5.1 Introduction

In the last few years a discourse about urban development strategies emerged, which includes some innovative solutions of technological companies that have become an important stakeholder in cities' smart urban strategies. Especially IBM, Cisco and Siemens are very important players in cooperation with several municipalities in providing new solutions for smart city initiatives (Niaros, Kostakis, & Drechsler, 2017). In their consulting capacity, they do offer several proposals for creating smart models of urban management to the involved municipalities with the goal to solve the problems of sustainability in urban environments, which are then expected to be resolved in the long run (e.g., the city strategies are preparing until 2050) (Söderström, Paasche, & Klauser, 2014).

In the 21st century we have found different concepts and theories about smart cities (e.g., sustainable cities) in Europe. The smart cities' practice and theory are still in a phase of formation (Angelidou, 2015; McNeill, 2015; Violi, 2014; Yigitcanlar, 2015). The literature is divided into two main categories. We have studies that are focused on the technological side, especially on energy efficiency regarding carbon emission, etc. The second group is dealing with analyzing the importance of the ICT infrastructure, e-government, mobile applications (public transport), e-health, and e-drive mobility. These articles aim at increasing competitiveness, administrative efficiency, and social inclusion (e.g., applications and portals for the senior citizens). The critical review of the literature after 2011 has exposed the phenomenon of smart cities from different viewpoints: socioeconomic, ecologic, political, science and technology studies, governmentally studies, and ideological criticism (Morozov & Bria, 2018).

Based on the municipalities' strategies it can be seen that the infrastructure played a crucial role in enabling urbanization and facilitating growth and development. The smart city concept should be understood as a complex mechanism, where we begin to realize the often unintended interplay of human, environmental, social, and economic factors of a technological and engineering led mechanism (Anthopoulos, 2017). The latest thinking regarding smart urban projects reflects on the comprehension of the smart and sustainable infrastructure as a networking link between places and people in order to create a more sustainable, healthy, and resilient future for these citizens (e.g., project of a Vienna suburbia Aspern). In these urban projects that transfer the smart city idea to a project level global socioeconomic factors, processes of the innovation of new technology, the constant adaptation both in the public and private sectors as well as the diversity of internal and external qualified resources need to be addressed adequately. This particularly refers to the development of the "Internet of Things," "Internet of Services," artificial technologies, blockchain technologies, new sustainable materials, new economic models (sharing economy, cycling economy), smart processes (e-mobility, e-health, e-governance), etc., which lead to continuous development and semantic features of the smart city (Han & Hawken, 2018; Roblek, Erenda, & Meško, 2018; Santonen, Creazzo, Griffon, Bódi, & Aversano, 2017).

It is reasonable to expect that smart urban regions will have more industrial competences in the future, and for their development, universities spin-offs and start-ups might be important by helping to compensate for negative effects of smart technologies (e.g., the reduction of the number of employees). This will be supported by investing in smart technology social innovation projects that will also improve citizens' well-being and the overall development of society.

This chapter is structured as follows: it starts with the theoretical background of the smart urbanization and the concept of the smart city, as is has been given by different authors. In the second section, we define the research problem. The following third section presents the utilized research methodology. Finally, the main research results are presented, discussed, and conclusions, including limitations and directions for future research, are given and recommended.

5.2 Background

The Austrian smart cities technology platform was established in 2011. It was launched with the goal to represent the interests of Austrian industry and stakeholders from the research in the SET Plan Industry Initiative Smart Cities and Communities and in the EIP-SCC, which emerged from it in 2013.

The Austrian Federal Ministry of Transport, Innovation and Technology (BMVIT) initiated together with the Climate and Energy Fund and the Austrian Association of Cities and Towns the Smart Cities and Regions Platform in 2013. Together with stakeholders from research and industry, the platform works out issues of shared interest to the Austrian municipalities in the field of smart cities and developing requirements to apply to the progress of technology (Smart Cities—Intelligent Cities in Europe, 2018).

Vienna's smart city activities are embedded in various transnational and European programs. Vienna cooperates with other European cities and international business and research partners namely with

- the project TRANSFORM (Transformation Agenda for Low Carbon Cities, partially funded within the EU's 7th Framework Program for Research). In this project Vienna was cooperating with the Amsterdam, Copenhagen, Genua, Hamburg, and Lyon. "TRANSFORM plus" pilot projects are implemented in "smart" city districts, and the overall urban strategy is advanced with the support of the Climate and Energy Fund.
- the program CapaCity—the city of Vienna and its organizations are cooperated with the other cities in the Danube region. The city of Vienna is focused on the internationalization of its ideas of the integrated urban development as holistic smart city approach to other cities in the region with aim to generate common project ideas.

It is apparent from the framework strategy development that there were several different stakeholders who were involved in the smart city Wien framework development process. Those different stakeholders comprised members from public (e.g., Office of Mayor, Vienna Business Agency, MA21—municipal department for district planning and land use, MA20—municipal department for energy planning, MA18—municipal department for urban development and planning, MA22—environmental protection, MA53—municipal department for press and information services, Social housing services, Wiener Wohnen, Viena science and technology fund) or public enterprises (e.g., transportation utility Wiener Linien, energy utility Wien Energie, research and innovation department of Vienna utilities, utility for gas, electricity, and thermal grids Wiener Netze), private organizations (e.g., Aspern Smart City Research, Consultants ETA, etc.), semipublic organizations (TINA Vienna Urban Technologies + Strategies), research organizations (Smart City Expert Advisory Board, Technical University Vienna, Vienna University of Economics and Business, and Non-University Research) and of course citizens in order to ensure a bottom-up and user-centered approach.

The Vienna smart city strategy includes the stakeholder's opinion and gives the possibility of their involvement in the projects. In the past years different initiatives were established that formed the R&D project groups. In Table 5.1 the R&D programs are described and presented with the initiatives and R&D groups.

Table 5.1 presents the initial and implemented projects of Vienna that have been funded under the smart cities initiative of the Climate and Energy Fund since the first call in 2010. The project topics include: mobility, communication and information, energy networks, supply and disposal, buildings, the city as a system and green and—free space.

Table 5.1 Initial and implementation projects of Vienna that have been funded under the smart cities initiative of the Climate and Energy Fund since the first call in 2010.

Project name	Consortium	Project description	Date of project	Project value
Biotope City is smart—Coca-Cola Areal in Wien	Universität für Bodenkultur Wien—Institut für Landschaftsplanung (Konsortialführung) BauXund Forschung und Beratung GmbH Stichting Biotope City Rüdiger Lainer + Partner Architekten ZT GmbH Mag. Janos Karasz Dr. Raimund Gutmann	On the former Coca-Cola site right next to the Wienerberg, a new district with around 900 apartments is being built. The planning model was "Biotope City," which includes a wide range of landscaping measures. The "Biotope City is smart" study analyzed the obstacles to the implementation of this model and developed proposals for their structural removal. The study also explored ways to optimize landscaping plans	September 1, 2016—October 31, 2017	€251,322
BuildyourCity2gether Wien Aspern	United Creations (Konsortialführung) Plenum—Gesellschaft für ganzheitlich nachhaltige Entwicklung GmbH Universität für Bodenkultur Wien—Institut für Landschaftsplanung TB Obkircher OG Forschungsinstitut für biologischen Landbau Österreich Institut für partizipative Sozialforschung Gartenpolylog—GärtnerInnen der Welt kooperieren	The objective of "BuildYourCity2gether" is to gather information on a collaborative, self-built, energy-efficient, multistory, low-tech building project. The legal and planning requirements will also be explained. In order to answer practical implementation questions, a one-story prototype will be constructed by laymen supervised by experts. A training program is being implemented, and a crowdfunding program set up for financing. This will be included in an overall implementation concept for a multistory demo project that will be constructed either on the Seestadt Aspern test grounds or at an alternative site	March 6, 2017–March 5, 2018	€156,908
Green future for schools	Technische Universität Wien—Institut für Hochbau und Technologie (Konsortialführung) Universität für Bodenkultur Wien—Institut für Ingenieurbiologie und Landschaftsbau B-NK GmbH	In the "GRÜNEzukunftSCHULEN" (green future schools) demo project, "greening" approaches for schools are being developed and modified on a theoretical basis at three Vienna school locations. At two of these locations (BRG 16 at Schuhmeierplatz in Ottakring and BRG 15, Diefenbach Gymnasium, in Rudolfsheim-Fünfhaus), these ideas are also actually	March 1, 2017–February 29, 2020	€938,540

	Dipl.-Ing. Ralf Dopheide e.U.	being implemented. The focus is on energy and water usage in maintaining green spaces and the effect of these green areas on the building, the indoor climate and the microclimate of the site. In addition to implementing and evaluating green spaces, the result is intended to provide guidelines for green architecture in school construction	May 1, 2011 bis June 30, 2012	€139,242
GUGLE Wien Penzing und Alsergrund	PORR (Wien) Siemens (Wien) Wiener Linien (Wien) Wien Energie Stromnetz (Wien) Wien Energie Gasnetz (Wien) Wien Energie Fernwärme (Wien) Energiecomfort (Wien) iC Consulenten (Wien) TU Wien-EEG (Wien) 4ward Energy (Wien)	The upgrading of urban areas in general and the Viennese districts Penzing and Alsergrund in particular by modernizing existing buildings, integrating renewable energy production, and more sustainable approaches to mobility will contribute in the short term to reducing greenhouse gas emissions in the city districts below the level of 1990, and in the medium term, showcase projects can increase the pace of the desired market expansion based on empirical results. The future scenarios proposed in the GUGLE master plan and measures are not new. The value of this work (the master plan and the publishable final report) consists of the coordination with key stakeholders who are core members of the GUGLE team and in the specification and quantification for implementation on the widest possible scale in both districts		
HEAT_re_USE.vienna Probing for the systematic use of waste heat potentials in Vienna	AIT Austrian Institute of Technology GmbH, Energy Department	The use of waste heat sources is an effective way to increase the energy efficiency of municipal energy systems. The project aims to identify potential operational waste heat sources and to evaluate their usefulness directly in the neighborhood or for district heating systems. Implementation options and developing concepts will be discussed with stakeholders from businesses and potential local clients during workshops in selected test case areas (architects, contractors) and finally, utilization concepts will be developed and evaluated on an economic basis	June 1, 2015–November 30, 2016	€221,322

(Continued)

Table 5.1 (Continued)

Project name	Consortium	Project description	Date of project	Project value
ICT Integration for Buildings and Electrical Grid Wien-Aspern	Siemens Aktiengesellschaft Österreich (Consortial leader) AIT Austrian Institute of Technology GmbH Energiecomfort Energie—und Gebäudemanagement GmbH Wiener Netze GmbH Wien Energie GmbH	The exploration of Aspern examines ways in which to realize the potential to increase energy efficiency by taking an interconnected view of the infrastructure levels of buildings and electrical power networks and to integrate renewable energy sources and storage technologies. The central objective of exploration is the creation of the overall technical concept for a selected test bed in the seaside town of Aspern, which will be implemented subsequently in the lead project. Through definition of applications, the requirements are derived for the technical overall concept, including the basic structure of the ICT architecture (hardware and software) as well as the technical infrastructure (heat pumps, photovoltaic systems, etc.).	January 7, 2013—June 30, 2014	€414,515
Collaborative urban structures and spatial strategies of sharing and exchange—Pocket Mannerhatten	tatwort Nachhaltige Projekte GmbH (Konsortialführung) Technische Universität Wien—Department für Raumplanung Technische Universität Wien—Institut für Energiesysteme und Elektrische Antriebe DDr. Gebhard Klötzl Florian Niedworok	Urban development around the world is faced with the challenge of population growth on the one hand and the associated increasing pressure on space and space (structures) on the other as well as shrinking and restructuring requirements on the other. The increased settlement pressure makes it necessary, especially in densely populated areas, to provide additional public spaces, green and open spaces, footpaths, or cycle paths. These can currently—if at all—be integrated into the existing urban structures only with high costs or through demolitions and thus the loss of uses and areas. Moreover, there is a lack of innovative methods and strategies to solve this challenge	July 1, 2016—June 30, 2017	€272,575
Make your city smart—Wien Aspern	Technische Universität Wien—Continuing Education Center (Konsortialführung) Käferhaus G.m.b.H.	The "Make your city smart" project, located in Vienna Aspern, researched and developed a tool kit for do-it-yourself builders, which is intended to support construction initiatives by lay people, planners, and	March 1, 2016—August 31, 2017	€210,988

	Institut für Höhere Studien (IHS) asbn—Austrian Strawbale Network (Österreichisches Netzwerk für Strohballenbau) RWT plus ZT GmbH	craftsmen and women, and help them to shape their environment together in future, in a way that reflects their own needs. The tool kit includes sketches of possible approaches for do-it-yourself construction, addresses various construction methods and materials, and offers reference examples for do-it-yourself projects. In the near future the tool kit with be available from the ICP (TU Wien) and is to be used as a planning guidance catalogue		€1,544,647
Mischung: Nordbahnhof	Technische Universität Wien—Institut für Architektur und Entwerfen (Konsortialführung) Technische Universität Wien—Department für Raumplanung Studiovlay ZT GmbH Erste gemeinnützige Wohnungsgesellschaft Heimstätte Gesellschaft m.b.H. morgenjungs GmbH Architekturzentrum Wien	The principles of sustainable mixed use for new districts were developed in the "Mischung: Possible!" (Mixing possible!) exploratory study, which focused on three Vienna case studies (Wienerberg City, North Station, and Seestadt Aspern). These are now being further developed and implemented in Vienna's North Station district in the "Mischung: Nordbahnhof" ("North Station mix") demo project. A central starting point is the transformation of an existing warehouse into an urban experimentation area for the new district: Innovative workplaces, cultural events, a coworking space, open workshops, and multifunctional event spaces are intended to attract new creative uses and other "nonresidential uses" to the district on a sustainable basis. The overarching objective is to encourage innovative construction, integrate new stakeholders into development-related management of the area, and enhance ecological sustainability	January 1, 2017–December 31, 2019	
Mischung: Possible!	Technische Universität Wien—Institut für Architektur und Entwerfen (Konsortialführer) Technische Universität Wien—Department für Raumplanung STUDIOVLAY ZT GMBH DI Andrea Mann	The focus is on the socially, economically, and ecologically sustainable interaction of working and living in densely built-up urban neighborhoods by integrating the fields of action of buildings and urban mobility against the background of social and societal change. The aim of the project is to establish the connection between conceptual demands on the variety of uses and the implementation of urban planning as well as everyday world appropriation	October 1, 2015–November 30, 2016	€214,378

(Continued)

Table 5.1 (Continued)

Project name	Consortium	Project description	Date of project	Project value
Pocket Mannerhatten—Implementation of collaborative urban structures and spatial sharing strategies in "Block 61"	tatwort Nachhaltige Projekt GmbH (Konsortialführer) Arch. DI Florian Niedworok Technische Universität Wien—Department für Raumplanung—Fachbereich Soziologie Technische Universität Wien, Institut für Energiesysteme und Elektrische Antriebe (EEG) Rechtsanwalt DDr. Gebhard Klötzl GrünStattGrau Forschungs—und Innovations—GmbH	Mixture: Possible! Therefore it pursues a participative approach and thus facilitates a transfer of knowledge between the actors involved (institutions, planners, property developers, users) and learning processes with the aim of making innovation feasible. As a result, innovation scenarios and three derived and implementable impulse models for new open-access residential areas are worked out A convincing strategy for facing the challenge of population growth on the one hand and shrinking and restructuring requirements on the other hand is the approach of a sensitive renewal and densification of existing neighborhoods. In Vienna the growth quarters (Gründerzeitviertel) are especially recommended for a small-scale adaption of existing uses and infrastructures as well as the integration of multiple expectant social groups and sociocultural contexts in action. However, there is a lack of innovative methods to solve these issues. Pocket Mannerhatten aims to meet this challenge with a socially innovative participatory organized urban development strategy based on the idea that small-scale and adjacent plots are linked with each other regarding several functions and uses (space sharing). In an innovative way such building areas and functions, underground, open and green areas as well as energy and building services systems are linked. The architectural theory of conception of "collaboration options" (Niedworok 2014) in compound with a bonus system serves as basis for the project as well as the result of the interdisciplinary research study Smart Cities Demo	January 1, 2018–December 12, 2020	€1,083,364

		(finished in 2017). The later included an intensive participatory process and the identification of a project site and interested owners for the one-to-one implementation of the concept as pilot project. On the basis of a concrete-built realization, further questions concerning participation and stakeholder processes, construction law, urban planning and architecture solutions, cost and financing issues and the development for an innovative administration process as well as a nonprofit business model for a long-term implementation should be answered. The results of the collaboration of interdisciplinary research with the city of Vienna, and relevant stakeholders should then be merged into a design manual and the long-term implementation in city renewal strategies in Vienna and other cities		
Energy monitoring and intelligent plant control in the Smart AirportCity	Denkstatt GmbH (Konsortialführer) Flughafen Wien AG denkstatt & enertec GmbH msg systems GmbH Technische Universität Wien, Institut für Hochbau und Technologie	At the city/commercial district of Vienna Airport, an integrative approach of energy monitoring and building-wide energy monitoring and proactive, intelligent plant control including user involvement is implemented. This reduces energy consumption, CO_2 emissions and loads on the infrastructure in the overall energy-building-user system	February 1, 2018–January 31, 2020	€779,110
Smart Block Step II Wien	BURTSCHER—DURIG ZT GmbH (Konsortialführung) Österreichische Gesellschaft für Umwelt und Technik komobile W7 GmbH Martin Gruber Zeininger Architekten	Given the current renovation rate of around 1%, the treatment of existing unrenovated housing is a problem for metropolitan areas, since such housing will continue to make up the majority of properties. Vienna's "Smart Block II Energy" exploratory study looks into cross-property processes as a block. In a pilot project on Hernalser Gürtel (major road in Vienna's Hernals district), sustainable solutions were developed in the areas of energy and mobility, and the added value of operations shared between several properties was assessed	April 1, 2016–June 30, 2017	€271,456

(*Continued*)

Table 5.1 (Continued)

Project name	Consortium	Project description	Date of project	Project value
Smart Cities Demo Aspern	Aspern Smart City Research GmbH & Co KG Siemens Aktiengesellschaft Österreich AIT Austrian Institute of Technology GmbH Käferhaus G.m.b.H. WIENER NETZE GmbH WIEN ENERGIE GmbH Magistratsabteilung 18 Stadtentwicklung und Stadtplanung SERA energy & resources e.U. MOOSMOAR Energies OG Magistratsdirektion—Stadtbaudirektion MD-BD—Projektleitung Seestadt Aspern	The flagship project "SC Demo Aspern" intends a large-scale implementation of a system optimizing approach between buildings, power grids, users, and comprehensive ICT solutions. This innovative combination is integrated into test beds in the development area Aspern Vienna's Urban Lakeside consisting of three construction sites (residential building blocks, student's dormitory, kindergarden and school building). Findings from the demonstration are utilized to improve operation and control strategies of buildings and power grids as well as to innovate the interaction with users for optimal usage of energy and CO_2 reductions		€7,917,051
Smart City im Gemeindebau				
Smart City Vienna—Liesing Mitte	Magistrat der Stadt Wien—MA 22 (Wien) Wirtschaftskammer Wien (Wien)	There is a great opportunity in the target region during the period of the SET plan (through 2020) to establish a model city quarter in Liesing Mitte together with leading cities in Europe—Copenhagen, Hamburg, Amsterdam, and Gran Lyon—one of which will be visible in Europe and around the world as a best practice showcase for a "smart" city	April 1, 2011–March 31, 2012	€125,000
Smart City Vienna Laxenburger Straße	ÖBB-Immobilienmanagement Gesellschaft mbH (Consortial leader) Österreichisches Ökologie-Institut Vasko + Partner, Ingenieure, Ziviltechniker für Bauwesen und Verfahrenstechnik Ges.m.b.H.	Smart city X examines the potential for the implementation of a smart city at the urban development area Laxenburger Straße/Landgutgasse, located nearby the new Vienna Central Station. This leads to the integrative concept of a Smart City, which must be done in close collaboration with the necessary authorities, project promoters, and of course potential clients. The experience and results from the project can then be used for the development of demonstration projects	January 6, 2014—May 31, 2015	€208,917

Smart City Wien	Municipal Department 20—Energy Planning, Wiener Stadtwerke Holding AG (Wien) 3420 Aspern Development AG (Wien) Siemens AG Österreich (Wien) Österreichisches Forschungs—und Prüfzentrum Arsenal Ges.m.b.H. (Wien) raum & kommunikation GmbH (Wien) Vienna University of Technology (Wien) Energieinstitut der Wirtschaft GmbH (Wien) Austrian Institute of Technology GmbH (Wien)	The enormous human capital available in Vienna is best leveraged by a comprehensive process of mobilization in business, research, and administration and particularly in the population The experience of the Vienna Smart City project has shown that large industrial and research institutions are also partners in financial respects and intend to assume this role even more in the future. The primary objective here is to develop new solutions and technologies jointly with the city of Vienna and to implement showcase and pilot projects. In 2012 a platform event was initiated to be held at least twice a year for business, administration, and research to optimize networking A particular advantage of the Vienna Smart City project is its emphasis on spatial urban development with the objectives of greater energy efficiency and improved climate protection. Thus the Vienna smart city process, the vision of the future developed from it for energy management and climate protection in Vienna, and the associated test projects stand for the definition of a new, intelligent path of development for Vienna, which is closely connected to the creation of the new urban development plan	April 1, 2011–February 29, 2012	€141,852
Smart life on the water—recovery of the Danube bank Vienna	SB gruppe	The Danube Flats construction project on the site of the former Cineplexx Reichsbrücke in Vienna's 22nd district had the image of an urban oasis as its goal, and the "Smartes Leben am Wasser" ("Smart living on the waterside") exploratory study did the necessary groundwork. The priorities were adding greenery to the high-rise building itself, water management, and innovative and multifunctional design for landscaping and open spaces. The project also explored how the quality of life in and around this high-rise apartment building could be optimized with the help of digital solutions	September 5, 2016–September 4, 2017	€195,063

(Continued)

Table 5.1 (Continued)

Project name	Consortium	Project description	Date of project	Project value
Smart living for generations	Caritas der Erzdiözese Wien—Hilfe in Not (Konsortialführung) Österreichisches Institut für Nachhaltige Entwicklung Österreichische Energieagentur—Austrian Energy Agency Schwarztal Gemeinnützige Wohnungs- & Siedlungsanlagen GmbH Wohnbauvereinigung der Gewerkschaft Öffentlicher Dienst Gemeinnützige Gesellschaft m.b.H	The Vienna exploratory study worked with elderly residents to develop opportunities for active involvement in the modernization of their residential areas. Two housing complexes in the 19th and 22nd districts, originally built in the 1960s and 1970s and housing predominantly older residents, served as a test bed. The study resulted in catalogues of generation-appropriate technological, social, and structural modernization measures and specific action plans for implementation projects in the two housing complexes	July 1, 2016—July 31, 2017	€203,284
TRANSFORM +	ÖIR GmbH (Consortium leader) Magistratsabteilung 18 Stadtentwicklung und Stadtplanung Magistratsabteilung 21 B Stadtteilplanung und Flächennutzung Süd-Nordost (Bezirke 10-13 und 21-23) Magistratsabteilung 21 A Stadtteilplanung und Flächennutzung Innen-West (Bezirke 1-9 und 14-20) Magistratsabteilung 20—Energieplanung Siemens Aktiengesellschaft Österreich AIT Austrian Institute of Technology GmbH ETA Umweltmanagement und Technologiebewertung Gmb ENERGIECOMFORT Energie- und Gebäudemanagement GmbH	The subsequent TRANSFORM + project facilitates and deepens the Austrian research field in the scope of the FP7 project TRANSFORM through a concrete comprehensive smart city development concept, through the content-rich and organizational configuration of the smart city stakeholder processes at the city level, as well as concrete data-analysis and planning projects in two urban sectors, so-called Smart Urban Labs (Liesing and aspern Seestadt). Here, sound decisions for a location-specific optimized smart energy system shall be made and implemented by a medium-term, concrete implementation plan. Two pilot applications, the so-called Smart Citizen Assistant and an "e-delivery" project will be implemented in the two smart urban labs under TRANSFORM. In order to make all of the results from TRANSFORM and TRANS-FORM + widely available and applicable to other Austrian cities, the preparations and communication of these results are included in the scope of the projet.	January 1, 2013—February 29, 2016	€1,900,000

Urban Cool Down—cool places for growing city quarters	Wirtschaftsuniversität Wien—Institut für Transportwirtschaft und Logistik WIENER NETZE GmbH wien 3420 Aspern Development AG Technische Universität Wien—Institut für Verkehrswissenschaften WIENER STADTWERKE Holding AG WIEN ENERGIE GmbH Neue Urbane Mobilität Wien GmbH ARAC GmbH MK Landschaftsarchitektur e.U. (Konsortialführung) B-NK GmbH Research & Data Competence OG MJ Landschaftsplanung e.U. Dipl.-Ing. Ralf Dopheide e.U.	"Urban Cool Down" considered integrative measures for summer cooling in growing urban districts. It investigated the urban climate effects of green spaces, conducting numerous on-site activities. In addition, cooling options were introduced to Vienna districts and subjected to an evaluation process. A roadmap for practical implementation was also prepared. The applications catalog, which can be downloaded at www.urbancooldown.at, lists technically and socially feasible design solutions and strategies for cooling measures, with detailed visualizations	November 1, 2016—October 31, 2017	€271,045

ICP, Institute for Convivial Practices.
Source: The Smart Cities initiative of the Climate and Energy Fund. 2018 available at: http://www.smartcities.at/city-projects/smart-cities-en-us/#projects

5.3 Research methodology: case study

An analysis of the case "smart city Vienna" is undertaken in order to understand this complex concept and to gain an in-depth understanding of its context. At first we present and analyze the city extensively (history, demographics, facts and figures of its economy, etc.) and answer how it is governed and characterizes the stakeholders, etc. The smart city case is being presented in a project management form.

5.3.1 Scope

The city of Vienna is facing challenging times ahead. The population in the federal capital is growing, and in Greater Vienna it will reach the three million mark in the course of the coming 25 years. This development goes hand in hand with a rising demand for energy, a demand for affordable and functional housing, and a need for strong traffic concepts.

According to the Smart City Wien Framework Strategy, the smart city projects are organized under several topics: education, digital, energy, buildings, health, infrastructure, innovation, mobility, social affairs, urban development, and environment. We are presenting the main characteristics of these individual topics and attaching links to individual projects.

5.3.1.1 Education

Vienna wishes to become a top research location in the framework of the smart city strategy. Therefore the emphasis of the municipal education policy bases on preparing research, technology and innovation yields, as well as new smart technical and social solutions. The main purpose is the implementation of these solutions with a goal to provide new employments.

The main educational projects include the following:

- Vienna Research Festival: This enables children and young people to become acquainted with the latest technologies and knowing the research processes.
  Site: https://smartcity.wien.gv.at/site/en/vienna-research-festival/
- Vocational orientation workshop with future: The young scholars between 13 and 14 years old are getting knowledge about the future jobs related to robotics, applications development, and renewable energy solutions. Youngsters are on workshops exchanging their knowledge with people who work in these sectors.
  Site: https://smartcity.wien.gv.at/site/en/future-jobs/
- Digital city. Wien initiative is an independent and not-for-profit initiative of the city and committed ICT companies in Vienna. They prepare various educational programs in the field of ICT.
  Site: https://digitalcity.wien/

5.3.1.2 Digital

The Smart City Wien Framework Strategy is exposing the ICT as a central driver of innovation and strength of Vienna. Both the public and private sectors are including ICT solutions in their business processes. Vienna wishes to become by 2020 the most progressive European city with respect to an open government and to cover all city districts with a comprehensive wireless LAN (WLAN) in future.

Some of the most important ICT solutions, which serve as showcases for the city and its economy are as follows:

- "Sag's Wien" application: This application allows citizens to report their concerns directly to the city administration in 30 seconds. The clear goal is to strengthen the "digital competence" of the public as well as of its citizens, and it represents a part of the Digital Agenda Vienna.
  Site: https://www.wien.gv.at/sagswien/index.html
- Digital Agenda Vienna: The Digital Agenda Vienna initiative is a result of a collective working process. Interested citizens were involved interactively in the development of ideas via an online participation platform. From the Digital Agenda Vienna, there are already numerous implemented projects and applications, such as the official wien.at live app, the initiative DigitalCity.Wien, or a smart infrastructure for everyone (more than 400 wien.at public WLAN hotspots).
  Site: https://smartcity.wien.gv.at/site/en/digital-agenda-vienna/
- e-Government and virtual municipal authority: The city digital service enables citizens' online business registration, dog registration, information about historical certificates of registration. The Viennese accommodation companies are using online service for the legally required notifications for the tourism statistics.
  Citizens can identify themselves with the citizens' card or mobile signature digital identity.
  Sites: https://www.wien.gv.at/amtshelfer/index.html
  https://www.buergerkarte.at/en/index.html
- The wien.at live app: This application includes an offline city map, information about the weather and public transport as well as a refugee relief function.
  Site: https://www.wien.gv.at/live/app/

5.3.1.3 Energy

The most important Vienna strategy goals in the area of energy include increasing the energy efficiency and the decreasing the final energy consumption per capita in Vienna by 40% by 2050 (compared to 2005). At the same time the per capita primary energy input should drop from 3000 to 2000 W. In 2030 over 20%, and in 2050, 50% of Vienna's gross energy consumption will originate from renewable sources.

Projects include the following:

- Wien Energie as a pioneer in the energy industry: They are researching the use of blockchain technology for the decentralized, uncomplicated handling of transactions in the energy industry. They were carried out in 2017 as a pilot project for gas trading. As partners in the project the oil companies BP and Eni, the business consultant Ernst & Young and the blockchain start-up BTL were involved.
  Site: https://www.wienenergie.at/eportal3/
- Clean heat and a stable power grid: The Power-2-Heat plant in Leopoldau converts the excess electricity into heat and thus contributes to energy being used intelligently and more efficiently.
  Site: http://www.wienenergie.at/

- Energy from metro brakes: A pilot system was used to find out how to use the energy generated from metro brakes more efficiently. The energy was using in the metro stations for elevators, lighting, and escalators. The goal is to reduce energy consumption. The tests were successfully completed in January 2018.
   Site: https://www.wienerlinien.at/eportal3/ep/contentView.do?pageTypeId = 66526& channelId = -47186&programId = 74577&contentId = 1800243&contentTypeId = 1001
- Smart traffic lights: Through weather and environmental sensors that are mounting to Viennese traffic lights, a dense grid of measuring stations is formed, which provides valuable data for diverse applications.
   Site: https://www.wien.gv.at/verkehr/ampeln/index.html

5.3.1.4 Health and social affairs

- ICT is utilized in the treatment process and patient management in accordance with the e-health strategy that includes projects such as mHealth (future project), the electronic health record (Elga), telemedicine services, particularly including mobile monitoring equipment (e.g., home monitoring), decision support systems, the tools for the analysis of anonymized data for planning, control, and transparency of the provision of services in the health field as well as for medical−epidemiological research. The goal of the strategy is to decrease patient's time in hospitals and ambulatory setting.
   Site: https://www.wien.gv.at/gesundheit/einrichtungen/planung/ehealth/
- Viennese active and assisted living test region (Waalter): Various integrated technologies with accompanying services are being tested in 83 Viennese households. Among others, tablets and apps are used to enable and facilitate communication and to support the people in planning and realizing social activities in groups or on their own. Moreover, mobile emergency systems, indoor tumble detection sensors, tumble prevention systems, health information, and telemedicine are being tested in order to further drive security and health in the daily routine. The project runs from December 2016 until November 2019.
   Site: https://smartcity.wien.gv.at/site/en/waalter-2/

5.3.2 Integration

Vienna is not only the capital of Austria but also a metropolitan region where the headquarters of the Austrian multiregional companies, universities, and institutes are located. As a result of that, this region is consequently presenting a high level of research and development activities. According to the Austrian Federal Government Strategy for Research, Technology and Innovation, Vienna is being prepared since 2008 to meet this trend, as reflected by the first European Research, Technology and Innovation (RTI) document "Vienna—Thinking the Future" (Wien denkt Zukunft). In 2014 the framework strategy "Smart City Vienna" (smart city Wien) was adopted, and in 2015 the strategy "Innovative Vienna 2020" was put forward. (Innovatives Wien 2020).

The framework strategy of smart city is not just a focus on technological issues but represents one of the main pillars for the concept of smart city Vienna, considering the factors as quality of living, resources, and innovation (Fig. 5.1). For the sustainable development of the smart city Vienna, it is important to establish the

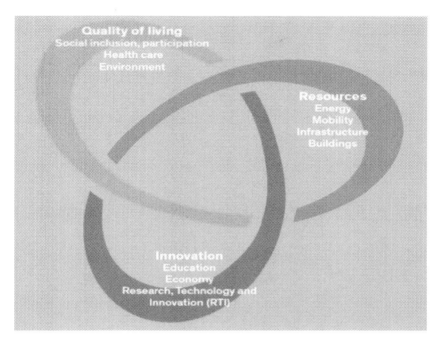

Figure 5.1 The smart city Wien principles.
Source: Smart City Wien Framework Strategy, 2014.

balance between the efficient use of resources, quality of life and innovation. No field can perform in a sustainable, integrated, and thus smart way without respecting the other categories (Smart City Wien Framework Strategy, 2014).

The main triggers of the objective "quality of life" are social inclusion, participation, environment, and health. To ensure the quality of life for citizen's each smart city needs to enable the intelligent usage of resources and energy efficiency regarding mobility, buildings, urban infrastructure (waste, water, and ICT), and the grid. Innovation as the next key topic includes education, economic prosperity, science and technology. They all present the important and vital drivers for the transformation of the Vienna into a smart city. The optimized and reasonable use of resources is defined as objectives that aim to reduce the consumption of energy, increasing e-mobility, etc. (Table 5.2).

Vienna includes two important goals for the development Vienna as a R&D center in the central European region. The first goal is to position Vienna until 2050 as a one of the top five research centers in Europe. The second goal is oriented toward the development of an innovative triangle region Vienna–Brno–Bratislava. The Smart City Vienna Framework Strategy objectives refer primarily to the future, which challenges will strongly affect the city and the region (Table 5.2) according to the smart city Vienna principles are defined their strategy objectives.

Table 5.2 Smart city Vienna strategy objectives.

Smart city Vienna: objectives	
Resources	
• Reduction of CO_2 emissions per capita: till 2030 at least 35% and till 2050 at least 80% • Energy efficiency: reduce energy consumption per capita by 40% in 2050 • 20% gross energy consumption in 2030 from renewable sources and 50% in 2050 • Most innovative city in open government by 2020 • Broad wireless network and 100 new Apps in the next 3 years • 2000 W steady power supply per capita, 1 t CO_2 per capita	• Motorized traffic: 20% share of all trips till 2025 and 15% till 2030 • Motorized traffic: new engine technologies till 2030 (e.g., e-mobility), and no more internal combustion engines till 2050 • City logistic 100% CO_2 free till 2030 • Nearly zero energy standard new buildings 2018/2020 • Building efficiency: refurbishment leads to 1% annual energy reduction in building stock • 10% energy reduction for external commuter traffic till 2030 • Continuation with highest standards of Vienna's infrastructure in future • ICT infrastructure showcases
Quality of life	
• Highest quality of life and highest happiness of all European cities • Keeping today's 50% of the city as green space • Affordable housing and attractive residential environment • Healthy conditions and health competences for all people • Top and efficient health care, in public ownership	• Diversity and social inclusion for all groups and society • Suitable wages for all employees to be able to meet needs of life • Considering gender aspects in all processes of decision, planning, and implementation • Satisfaction with spare time—quantitative and qualitative • 270 saved tonnes of CO_2 in waste systems till 2020
Innovations	
• Between the 5 cities in science and innovations until 2050 • Additional research headquarters till 2030, and magnet for top—science and international students • Twice as much direct investments from and to Vienna	• Innovation region Vienna—Bruno—Bratislava one of the most prospering in Europe by 2030 • One of the top 10 wealthiest cities in Europe in GDP • Vienna strengths for middle and south-east Europe • 80% share of technology on exports by 2050 (from 60% in 2012)

Source: Smart City Wien Framework Strategy, 2014.

5.3.3 Organization

The Vienna smart city approach is divided into two primary levels of implementation. The first level is mainly political and includes the political priorities and defining policies in the light of increasing complexity coupled with tight resources.

The second level is on an operative level where many tasks are being handled with help of the individual organizational units of the city of Vienna, and it is carried out with the cooperation within and outside of the municipal administration. The outside cooperation includes consultation processes with the Federal Provinces of Lower Austria and Burgenland (e.g., regarding mobility, regional development issues).

The constitution of the Vienna smart city initiative is involving municipal and public institutions in a governmental structure. It is also establishing cooperation with private and civil actors in a governance structure for implementation (Fig. 5.2). On the operational level the smart city Wien initiative is managed by a steering group that consists of administrative groups and representatives of public enterprises. The steering group is also involving an external advisory board for consultation. Activities are coordinated by the working group whose members are coming from a project management office at the urban development department. This department is in charge of the strategical preparation for the smart city. The TINA Vienna is steering and supporting this working group. The agency is also closely working together with both internal and external stakeholders of the city who are participating by preparing the realization of smart projects (Vienna Administration, 2016).

5.3.4 Time

The city of Vienna started with the smart city stakeholder process in 2011 beginning with the thematic workshops and interviews with the stakeholders from different municipal departments and various experts in the city. Because of their ideas and proposals, the Smart City Wien Framework Strategy was prepared, which will subsequently come into practice until the year of 2050. It encompasses all areas of the municipal administration, urban policy, guidelines for the development smart city initiatives and projects. The strategy includes three lines: "quality of living," "resources," and "innovation." Each line is structured-specific associated topics and goals (Vienna City Administration, 2016).

In 2011 the smart city TINA Vienna was established, which effectively got a service mandate in 2012 by the city of Vienna as official Smart City Vienna Agency (TINA, 2018). In January 2017 TINA Vienna and Europa forum Wien were merged into a new competence center for future urban issues, which is called Urban Innovation Vienna (formally organized as a public limited company).

In 2013 a memorandum of understanding was signed between Vienna and the Federal Republic of Austria to advance the smart city cause. The objectives lie in initiating projects and to obtain European Union funding (Vienna City Administration, 2016).

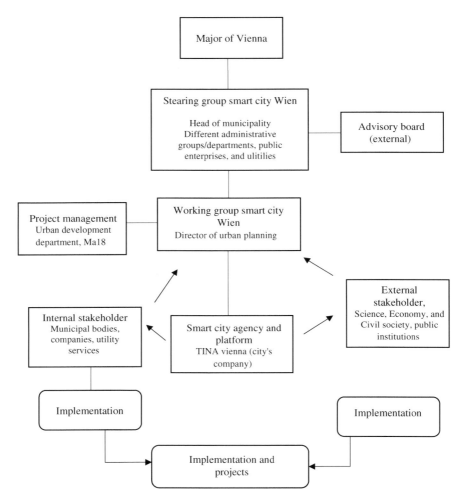

Figure 5.2 Government–governance structure of smart city Wien.
Source: The Organisation of the Vienna City Administration.

The Vienna council adopted the strategy of the Smart City Vienna on June 2014. This strategy presents a legally binding document for the cities' activities. According to this strategy TINA Vienna becomes a Smart City Wien Agency (SCWA). Its main role is to be a link between all relevant initiatives and programs of the city of Vienna in the implementing the Smart City Wien Framework Strategy. Moreover, the SCWA is also active on an international level, where it takes into account the relevant aspects of international and European policy-making (Tinavienna, 2018).

The strategy was created based on the assumptions that its elementary goals are to integrate and cross-link these areas: energy, mobility, urban planning and governance. The essential purpose of connecting these areas was to provide the implementation of ecological and social aspects of urban society and a participatory approach (Step 2025, 2014). The strategy is also based on the context of environmental protection on the EcoBusiness Plan that was launched in 1998 by the Municipal Department for Environmental Protection. The goal of this plan is to support companies in the implementation of environmental measures (The Vienna EcoBusiness Plan, 2018).

According to the fundamental intention the EcoBusiness Plan, the process of connecting all areas is to create a smart city as an environment where stakeholders can develop, produce, and use the "smart" innovations with an important goal to provide the energy efficiency and climate protection. Therefore the strategy for the development of a smart city contains goals that should be reached by 2050, as they wish to reduce its per capita greenhouse gas emissions to 80% of 1990 levels (Vienna City Administration, 2016).

The next step, which is important for the development a Vienna as a smart city, was a preparation of the Vienna digital agenda (2014−15). In the year 2014 the initiative the Digital City Wien had been established. Interested citizens, external experts, representatives from both the private sector and the municipal administration are driving this initiative in close cooperation. The goal of the initiative is the strengthening of Vienna as an ICT hub, to position it strategically, and to promote them regionally and internationally. The involved stakeholders had been preparing projects which topics cover data security, digital competences, and literacy services (education app, elderly people app), services (e.g., e-health, app for public transport, building initiative, women in IT, refugee's initiative, industry and makers, and digital city web platform (Digital City Wien, 2018) from 2014 until the 2017.

The prevalent challenge for the municipal government represents the expected increase of the population in the federal capital and its greater area. It is expected that the population will reach the 3 million people mark in next 25 years. The urbanization is exposing Vienna to the challenge of balancing the rising demand for energy, affordable housing, and public transportation options, while reducing greenhouse gas emissions. This is one of the reasons why it had been decided to begin in 2010 with the preparation of the process and in 2013 with the construction of a new smart city project in the suburb of Aspern. In order to ensure sustainable mobility Aspern is connected to Vienna by a metro system. The project is recognized as a "city within a city" and will eventually house 20,000 inhabitants by 2030, according to the planners. Urbanists wish to use Aspern as case for other new urban projects in the greater area of Vienna. The main purpose of this new smart suburb is that citizens are living in newly built houses that are erected using sustainable principles—using the appropriate materials, local construction, and smart building principles (Buntz, 2016).

5.3.5 Discussion—the fringes

It can be estimated according to a scoping literature and documents review that Vienna is really transforming into a smart city. The municipality is—together with all the involved stakeholders—currently implementing or has even already completed several smart projects. The city is currently collaborating with the stakeholders and project owners, beginning from the preparing of the common strategy to its realization in practice. The main point of the city case is that it is based on the sustainable and environmental adaptations that have also to be sustained in economical results of the projects (e.g., costs saving, value added, return of investment, etc.).

5.4 Conclusions

The smart city Vienna strategy can be divided in two core aspects: the first one includes projects and policies that focus on the technological side, especially on the energy efficiency, carbon emission, etc. The second aspect focuses on analyzing on the importance of the ICT infrastructure, e-government, mobile applications (public transport), e-health, and e-drive mobility.

Most of the technological solutions of Vienna's smart city are not visible to the individual who is walking across the city. The most favored is e-mobility, which, through e-car sharing, is gaining increased popularity across Europe, which can be seen as both locals and tourists use the wien.at live app. Most of the other solutions are embedded in buildings and are therefore invisible. In addition, most of the projects are still in the process of research and testing and are therefore limited to exclusive parts of the city.

Based on the municipality strategy, it can be seen out that the infrastructure played a vital role in enabling urbanization and facilitating growth and development.

About the author

Vasja Roblek is an assistant researcher at Higher Institution Fizioterapevtika. He completed his bachelor's studies in banking, the Faculty of Economics, University of Ljubljana, Slovenia and finished his master of science degree at the Faculty of Management, University of Primorska, Slovenia. He is a professional consultant with extensive experience in strategy and business development. His current research areas are smart city, knowledge management, health management and sustainability. He has published several scientific papers in the international journals and he is a coauthor of the two book chapters (Springer) and book on sustainable development. He is an editorial assistant of the *International Journal of Markets and Business Systems*, published by Inderscience.

References

Angelidou, M. (2015). Smart cities: A conjuncture of four forces. *Cities*, *47*, 95−106.
Anthopoulos, L. (2017). Smart utopia VS smart reality: Learning by experience from 10 smart city cases. *Cities*, *63*, 128−148.

Buntz, B. (2016). *Meet Austria's smart city of the future.* Vienna: Internet of Things Institute. Available at <http://www.ioti.com/smart-cities/meet-austria-s-smart-city-future>.

Digital City Wien. (2018). Available at <https://digitalcity.wien/category/projekte/>.

Han, H., & Hawken, S. (2018). Introduction: Innovation and identity in next generation smart cities. *City, Culture and Society, 12,* 1–4. Available from https://doi.org/10.1016/j.ccs.2017.12.003.

McNeill, D. (2015). Global firms and smart technologies: IBM and the reduction of cities. *Transactions of the institute of British geographers, 40*(4), 562–574.

Morozov, E., & Bria, F. (2018). *Rethinking the smart city.* New York: Rosa Luxemburg Stiftung.

Niaros, V., Kostakis, V., & Drechsler, W. (2017). Making (in) the smart city: The emergence of makerspaces. *Telematics and Informatics, 34*(7), 1143–1152.

Roblek, V., Erenda, I., & Meško, M. (2018). The challenges of sustainable business development in the post-industrial society in the first half of the 21st century. In D. R. Leon (Ed.), *Managerial strategies for business sustainability during turbulent times* (pp. 1–22). Hershey, PA: IGI Global.

Santonen, T., Creazzo, L., Griffon, A., Bódi, Z., & Aversano, P. (2017). *Cities as living labs: Increasing the impact of investment in the circular economy for sustainable cities.* Brussels: European Commission.

Smart Cities—Intelligent Cities in Europe. (2018). Available at <http://www.smartcities.at/home-en-US>.

Smart City Wien Framework Strategy (2014). *Vienna city administration,* Vienna. Available at <https://www.wien.gv.at/stadtentwicklung/studien/pdf/b008384b.pdf>.

Söderström, O., Paasche, T., & Klauser, F. (2014). Smart cities as corporate storytelling. *City, 18*(3), 307–320.

Step 2025. (2014). *Urban development plan Vienna.* Vienna: Vienna City Administration. Available at: https://www.wien.gv.at/stadtentwicklung/studien/pdf/b008379b.pdf.

Tinavienna. (2018). Available at <http://alt.tinavienna.at/en/smartcitywienagency>.

The Vienna EcoBusiness Plan. (2018). Available at <https://www.wien.gv.at/english/environment/protection/eco/>.

Vienna Administration. (2016). Available at <https://www.wien.gv.at/english/administration/organisation/pdf/administration.pdf>.

Vienna City Administration. (2016). *Smart city framework strategy* (2nd ed.). Vienna: Vienna City Administration. Available at <https://smartcity.wien.gv.at/site/en/the-initiative/framework-strategy/>.

Violi, P. (2014). *Smart city between mythology, power control and participation. New semiotics: Between tradition and innovation* (pp. 1125–1131). Sofia: New Bulgarian University, 16–20 September.

Yigitcanlar, T. (2015). Smart cities: An effective urban development and management model? *Australian Planner., 52*(1), 27–34.

A smart city needs more than just technology: Amsterdam's Energy Atlas project

Zulfikar Dinar Wahidayat Putra[1] and Wim van der Knaap[2]
[1]Urban and Regional Planning Study Program, Gadjah Mada University, Yogyakarta, Indonesia, [2]Landscape Architecture and Spatial Planning Group, Wageningen University, Wageningen, The Netherlands

Chapter Outline

6.1 Introduction 129
6.2 Background 130
    6.2.1 Theoretical approach for Amsterdam Smart City 132
    6.2.2 Organization of Amsterdam Smart City 135
6.3 Research methodology: case study 136
    6.3.1 Scope 136
    6.3.2 Integration 137
    6.3.3 Organization 138
    6.3.4 Timescale 140
    6.3.5 Cost 140
    6.3.6 Quality 141
    6.3.7 Risks 141
    6.3.8 Procurement 142
    6.3.9 Discussion 142
6.4 Conclusions 144
6.5 Remarks 145
About the authors 145
References 146
Further reading 147

6.1 Introduction

Many governments are adopting specific technologies to harness the power and influence of Information and Communication Technology to meet complex urban challenges and improve the quality of life of their citizens (Ojo, Dzhusupova, & Curry, 2016). The resulting "smart city" concept has become widespread since the European Union launched the Europe 2020 Strategy in 2010, which stimulated governments to use the smart city concept as a key development pathway (Cocchia, 2014).

Amsterdam was a smart city long before the term was used. In 1611 the establishment of the Hendrick de Keyser Exchange Centre marked Amsterdam as the first smart city in the world since merchants could exchange any information about trade in there (Baron, 2012). In 1994 city's activists built a digital network for citizens to deliver their protests and notions to politicians (Anthopoulos, 2017), further establishing Amsterdam as a smart city. The city tried to formalize its smart city status in 2009 by establishing a partnership organization, Amsterdam Smart City (ASC), which includes businesses, societal research groups ("middle ground" organizations), knowledge institutions, and local government institutions, who collaborate to develop smart city projects [Amsterdam Smart City (ASC), 2011; van Winden, Oskam, van den Buuse, Schrama, & van Dijck, 2016]. ASC was initiated by a knowledge-based economy organization, the Amsterdam Innovation Motor (AIM), together with the electricity company Alliander, the Amsterdam Municipality, and an independent research institute, Nederlandse Organisatie voor Toegepast Natuurwetenschappelijk Onderzoek (TNO) (ASC, 2011), who established the ASC framework based on citizen-oriented strategies (Dameri, 2017). They focused on three main areas, namely, innovative technology, behavioral change, and sustainable economic investment (ASC, 2011). The key idea of this smart city approach is to connect all partners, including citizens, and create a collaborative ecosystem among them to develop and test various small-scale projects in the greater Amsterdam area. The most successful projects could then be scaled up in three ways, namely, via rollout, expansion, or replication (van Winden et al., 2016). Using this approach, ASC expects to contribute to the goals of Amsterdam City and demonstrate successful projects to the rest of the world.

The focus of this chapter is to describe the smart city of Amsterdam, and this study aims to explore the ASC organization by investigating its mission and a specific smart city project developed within it. An elaboration of this topic will give readers more of an insight into the smart city concept and its practice in Amsterdam. For this purpose, we focused on the Energy Atlas project, one of the many projects developed by ASC. It is an open-data map containing the baseline and potential for using renewable energy in the city.

6.2 Background

In 2010 the European Union prepared a strategic policy document that specified an agenda for achieving smart, sustainable, and inclusive growth by 2020 (European Commission, 2010). Targets in line with those goals were formulated, including the aim of coping with climate challenges by reducing CO_2 emissions by 20% compared with 1990, generating 20% of energy using renewable sources, and improving energy efficiency by 20%. In the Netherlands, these targets were adapted as follows (as an agenda toward 2020): 30% reduction in CO_2 emissions compared with 1990, 20% of energy to come from renewable energy sources, and a 2% increase in energy efficiency per year (Šťáhlavský, 2011). Amsterdam signed the "Covenant of

A smart city needs more than just technology: Amsterdam's Energy Atlas project

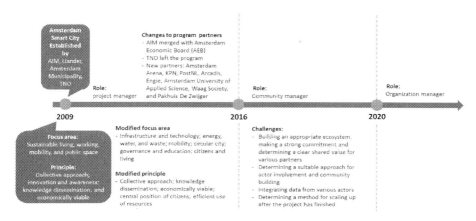

Figure 6.1 ASC timeline. *ASC*, Amsterdam Smart City.

Mayors,"[1] thereby adopting a policy with the following goals (as an agenda toward 2025): a 40% reduction in CO_2 emissions compared with 1990, climate-neutral municipal institutions before 2015, and 20% of energy generated using renewable energy sources (Capra, 2014). Based on these European national and local targets, the ASC was established to contribute to the accelerated achievement of these targets (Capra, 2014). This is one of the reasons why, during its initiation phase, ASC only focused on climate and energy targets.

ASC has grown quickly since it was established in 2009. This is visible in the changes that have been made to its program partners, principles, roles, and focus areas (see Fig. 6.1). Regarding the program partners, the AIM was merged with the Amsterdam Economic Board (AEB), and TNO no longer acts as a program partner; however, other partners have joined. In 2018 ASC comprises 11 program partners divided into four categories, namely, the City of Amsterdam, the private sector, knowledge institutions, and citizen-oriented organizations (ASC, 2017). The City of Amsterdam consists of the Amsterdam Municipality, represented by the Chief Technology Officer (CTO) and the AEB, while the private-sector partners consist of Alliander, Amsterdam Arena, KPN, PostNL, Arcadis, and Engie. Amsterdam University of Applied Science is the knowledge institution, and the citizen-oriented group consists of Waag Society and Pakhuis De Zwijger. The websites of these organizations can be found in Section 6.5 at the end of this paper.

The principles of ASC have also been modified since 2009. Its framework was initially based on four principles; collective approach, innovation and awareness, knowledge dissemination, and being economically viable. Havelaar (2016) stated that there are now five principles within ASC, as "innovation and awareness" has been removed and two new principles, the "central position of citizens" and "efficient use of resources," have emerged. It seems that, going forward, the

---

[1] A communal commitment of the Mayors of many European cities to implement a European strategy on Climate and Energy (https://www.covenantofmayors.eu/).

organization wants to focus more on involving citizens and developing small-scale projects to use resources more efficiently and build more citizen awareness.

Havelaar (2016) explained that there have been three changes to the roles played by ASC. From 2008 to 2016, ASC played the role of a project manager that positioned the city at the front of innovation by focusing on milestones. From 2016 until 2020, ASC has taken the role of a community manager that positions its partners at the front by focusing on making small projects a success. Finally, from 2020, its role will be as an organizational manager that positions the citizens at the front by focusing on the project and its upscaling method.

The focus areas were also improved. At its outset, ASC only focused on four areas: sustainable living, working, mobility, and public spaces. These were based on intelligent grid management principles and were in line with the main interest of one of its initiators, the electricity provider Alliander. Today, the focus areas have expanded to incorporate other themes, such as digital city, energy, mobility, circular city, governance and education, and citizens and living (ASC, 2018). These themes are flexible, and program partners can add or remove a theme based on the market's needs. Developments in these focus areas also transform the goals of the organization, from reducing CO_2 emissions by saving energy to becoming a future-proof and liveable city by addressing local challenges.

Regarding the challenges that should be tackled, van Winden et al. (2016) stated that there are four areas that need to be explored by ASC. First, building an appropriate ecosystem based on strong commitment, while determining a clear shared value for its various partners; second, determining a suitable approach for actor involvement and community building; and third, integrating data from various actors, finally, determining a method of scaling up projects after they finish. The ASC community manager mentions that the organization is still looking for a way to measure the impact of finished projects, which also includes determining the best way to fund projects in the future.

6.2.1 Theoretical approach for Amsterdam Smart City

Our observation of the ASC framework reveals its unique combination of an urban innovation system (public−private−people partnership), a living lab, and a developing business model. In the next subsections, we describe some theoretical aspects of these three elements.

6.2.1.1 Urban innovation system

The innovation process in the ASC organization could well be described as an urban innovation system. According to Markatou and Alexandrou (2015), there is currently no consensus on the definition of an innovation system, which can come under four approaches: national, regional, sectoral, and technological innovation systems.

van Winden, Braun, Otgaar, and Witte (2014) proposed an urban innovation system framework based on the regional innovation system approach. They stated that

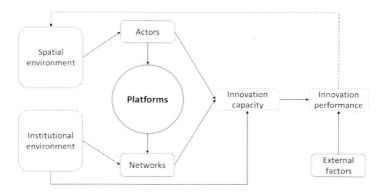

Figure 6.2 The components of an urban innovation system.
Source: Adapted from van Winden, W., Braun, E., Otgaar, A., & Witte, J.-J. (2014). In S. M. Christopherson, M. Feldman, G. Grabher, R. Martin, & M. Perry (Eds.), *Urban innovation systems: What makes them tick?* (1st ed.). New York: Routledge.

there are six components that influence the innovation capacity and performance of such a system, namely, the actors, networks, organizations, spatial environment, institutional environment, and external factors. A wide range of institutions can be considered actors in the ASC, and its existence as a platform suggests that this framework best represents the ASC case (see Fig. 6.2).

Urban innovation systems are run by actors, who can be firms, knowledge institutions, governments, and/or communities. The combination and commitment of different actors are important for building a strong urban innovation system. Networks refer to the interactions among the actors, which can change in different innovation phases, while platforms are intermediary actors that organize the other actors and their networks. These intermediary actors can consist of a building, organization, meeting or exhibition, website, or even venture capital (see also van Winden et al., 2014). The spatial environment of an urban innovation system includes its geographic location, accessibility, amenities, and "brand name" of a city, while the institutional environment refers to the laws, traditions, and cultures of the city. The external factors include market and technology opportunities, market circumstances, and local demand. In this context, ASC can be seen as the platform to connect actors and build networks to increase the innovation capacity and performance in Amsterdam.

6.2.1.2 Urban living lab

The ASC is based on the urban living lab concept, which describes a user-centered open innovation structure that engages users as active contributors to an innovation process (Scholl et al., 2017). According to Steen and van Bueren (2017), an urban living lab has four characteristics. First, the context is related to a real-life use. Second, the participants are users, private and public actors, and knowledge institutions, each of whom has the same decision power in every innovation phase.

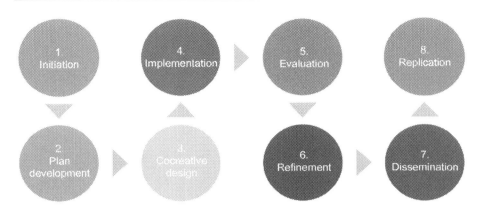

Figure 6.3 Urban living lab process.
Source: Adapted from Steen, K., & van Bueren, E. (2017). *Urban living labs: A living lab way of working* (1st ed.). Amsterdam: AMS Institute.

Third, the activities are related to innovative developments using a cocreation platform. This is an iterative process, meaning that feedback on an innovation result is used to make further improvements, resulting in an improved product, service, application, process, or system (see also Steen and van Bueren, 2017). Finally, its goal is to innovate, to develop knowledge for replication, and to support urban sustainability. Steen and van Bueren (2017) also formulated an eight-step process for using an urban living lab (see Fig. 6.3).

6.2.1.3 Business model

ASC needs a business model to guide its operation. According to Diaz-Diaz, Muñoz, and Pérez-González (2017), the most cited business model definition comes from Osterwalder and Pigneur (2010) who stated that a business model is a tool to describe the rational way by which an organization creates, delivers, and captures value. Business model frameworks have been developed to help organizations explain their business strategy, with the most used framework, also developed by Osterwalder and Pigneur (2010), focusing on nonprofit organization and public administration. This framework consists of nine blocks describing the organization's resources and value proposition, customers, and finances. Osterwalder and Pigneur (2010) also stated that there are five possible patterns of a business model, namely, unbundling, long-tailed, multisided, FREE, and open business models. It seems that ASC mostly uses the FREE and the open business model, which makes at least one customer segment free of charge for all time, with an open business model for the innovation process, which is assembled in a collaborative way between ASC and external organizations to create and deliver a value proposition. Based on our observations, the essential value proposition of ASC itself is to provide a platform where different parties can connect and solve related urban problems. Unfortunately, we could not find any relevant illustrations of the business model currently being used by ASC.

6.2.1.4 Concluding remark on the theories

The elaboration of each of these theories enables their interlinkage in ASC to be identified. The ASC is an ecosystem of actors, networked and organized in an urban innovation system, who use an urban living lab approach to conduct the innovation process. The innovation products are implemented based on a specific business model, which may be either a FREE or open business model.

6.2.2 Organization of Amsterdam Smart City

ASC (2017) stated that its organization is a public–private–people partnership, where all parties are responsible for all activities in the organization. The public and private parties collaborate as program partners and in turn collaborate with people to develop particular projects.

Havelaar (2016) stated that from 2016 to 2020, the role of the organization is more of a community manager, transforming the governance of the organization. There is no recent information available regarding its current organizational structure; therefore we will use the structure as presented by Šťáhlavský (2011) here (see Fig. 6.4).

The 11 program partners show their commitment by forming steering committees, by providing human resources to the project group, and by paying an annual fee to

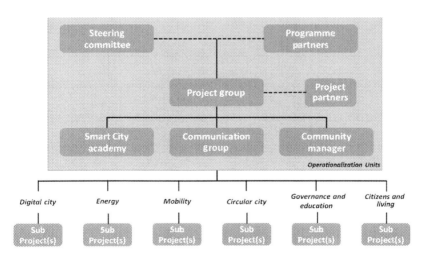

Figure 6.4 Interpretation of the current ASC organizational structure. *ASC*, Amsterdam Smart City.
Source: Based on Amsterdam Smart City (ASC). (2018). *Amsterdam Smart City*. From <amsterdamsmartcity.com>. Retrieved 12.09.17. Šťáhlavský, R. (2011). *Amsterdam Smart City project overview*. Prague: Accenture.

ASC. In the project group, several project partners are involved in the different phases of project development. This group is supported by the Smart City Academy, a communication group, and a community manager. Each project group has its own activities that fall into one of the six themes, with subprojects for different solutions such as Vehicle2Grid and City Data (digital city subproject); City-zen: Virtual Power Plant and Energy Atlas (energy); Together and Foodlogica (mobility); Ecube Labs and Bundles (Circular City); Powow and StartUp in Residence (Governance and Education); and Civocracy and Transformcity (Citizens and Living) (ASC, 2018).

6.3 Research methodology: case study

Historically, Amsterdam was the center of one of the world's largest commercial hubs (Gray, 2008). The city even became a "smart city" in 1611 with the establishment of the Hendrick de Keyser Exchange Centre (Baron, 2012), which enabled traders to exchange trade information and increased the volume of trades that could be conducted. Amsterdam has a long history of innovation, with the municipality even declaring that innovation is the DNA of the city (Amsterdam Municipality, 2016). This claim was supported by the European Commission, which awarded the city the title of the innovation capital city of Europe (I-Capital) in 2016.

At present, Amsterdam's innovative culture is used to tackle the city's challenges and provide solutions for its total population of around 855,000 people (Amsterdam Municipality, 2018). About 68% of these citizens are economically productive (aged between 20 and 64) and influence the economy of the city. Around 25% of all workers in Amsterdam provide professional services (SEO Economisch Onderzoek, 2009).

The government of Amsterdam is based on an open-system governance model, with a focus on innovation and change as well as differentiation and decentralization (see Putra, 2018; Newman, 2001). The city council, the college of Mayors and Alderpersons, and the district committees form the municipality (Amsterdam Municipality, 2018), which focuses on four service clusters, economic, social, community, and administrative, and their respective departments. Smart city–related topics are the responsibility of departments within the economic cluster. The main municipality stakeholders for the smart city are the CTO and the AEB, although other departments can be involved in a smart city project by contacting the CTO or ASC directly (see Fig. 6.5).

To provide a clearer insight into the smart city project and the role of different stakeholders in Amsterdam the management of a smart city project conducted by ASC, the Energy Atlas project, will be explored in the following sections.

6.3.1 Scope

According to van Winden et al. (2016), ASC focuses on three themes during its innovation process; energy, mobility, and the circular economy. Amsterdam is currently

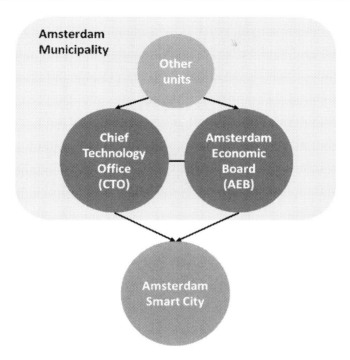

Figure 6.5 The involvement of Amsterdam Municipality departments in ASC. *ASC*, Amsterdam Smart City.

focusing to implement an energy transition to cope with climate-related issues (van Winden et al., 2016); therefore we decided to pick a project from the energy theme to present the innovation scope and project management within ASC. We selected the Energy Atlas project as our case study based on data availability (primary and secondary), the continuity and complexity of the project, and the success story behind it.

Energy Atlas is an interactive open-data map containing the baseline current usage and prospects for renewable energy usage in the city (see Fig. 6.6). This project was begun in 2012 to provide information to all stakeholders in the city under the ASC organization. The Energy Atlas project was led by an officer from the sustainability and planning department of the municipality, who said that the use of this map enables stakeholders to quickly identify their business case for applying renewable energy in a particular area (van Winden et al., 2016). This project also aimed to help the city to accelerate its energy transition to reduce CO_2 emissions. It can be accessed through this link: https://maps.amsterdam.nl/open_geodata/ under the "sustainability" label.

6.3.2 Integration

Amsterdam agreed to a 40% reduction in CO_2 emissions by 2025, which requires an energy transition involving the substantial reduction of nonrenewable energy

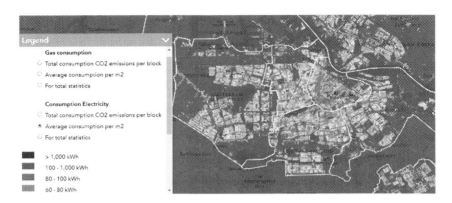

Figure 6.6 Amsterdam Energy Atlas visualization.
Source: From Amsterdam Municipality. (2014). Energy-use of gas and electricity energy. From <https://maps.amsterdam.nl/energie_gaselektra/?LANG = en>. Retrieved 27.05.18 (Amsterdam Municipality, 2014).

usage in the city. The municipality therefore needed a baseline dataset to provide insights into the current energy usage and provide a tool to highlight the potential use of all types of renewable energy in the city. The ultimate goal of this project was to provide an open-data resource for all stakeholders in the city, enabling them to quickly determine which types of renewable energy can be applied in a certain area.

After signing a memorandum of understanding (MoU) between the European cities that joined "TRANSFORM," a carbon reduction program from the European Commission, the Amsterdam Municipality had more power to engage related stakeholders to further develop the Energy Atlas. Initially, the municipality cooperated with Liander, an energy company and a key partner in ASC, to provide the energy data. Under an agreement between the stakeholders the municipality began to collaborate with other public utility providers and housing corporations to obtain energy data without impacting customer privacy. After aligning all data formats and building the system the Energy Atlas was successfully launched and made publicly accessible in 2014.

6.3.3 Organization

The Energy Atlas was organized by the municipality alongside public utility providers and nongovernmental organizations (NGOs), with additional collaboration from private companies and knowledge institutions (see Fig. 6.7) (van Winden et al., 2016).

Each partner in the organization has their own level of influence and interest in the project. A stakeholder analysis can be drawn based on this (see Fig. 6.8).

Most of the stakeholders are key players, yet possess different levels of influence and interest. The most powerful and interested stakeholder is the public

A smart city needs more than just technology: Amsterdam's Energy Atlas project 139

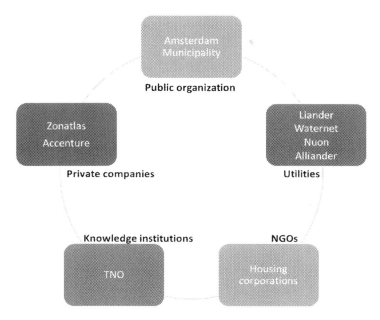

Figure 6.7 Energy Atlas project stakeholders.
Source: Adapted from van Winden, W., Oskam, I., van den Buuse, D., Schrama, W., & van Dijck, E. (2016). *Organising Smart City projects: Lessons from Amsterdam*. Amsterdam.

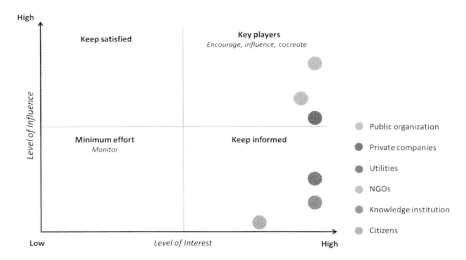

Figure 6.8 Energy Atlas project stakeholder analysis.
Source: Based on van Winden, W., Oskam, I., van den Buuse, D., Schrama, W., & van Dijck, E. (2016). *Organising Smart City projects: Lessons from Amsterdam*. Amsterdam.

organization, the municipality. They can encourage the public utility providers to share their data and cocreate in this project, which also provides these companies with significant levels of influence as the providers of the main resource, the energy database. The public utility providers became more interested in the project when the municipality gave them clear information about the long-term benefits of sharing their data (van Winden et al., 2016), which was also true of the NGOs (housing corporations). Two other stakeholders, the private companies and the knowledge institution, were simply kept informed by the key players, as they had limited power in the implementation of this project. The private company Accenture was hired by the Amsterdam Municipality as a consultant to organize the project management, while Zonatlas helped the key players to identify the potential rooftops suitable for solar panels in Amsterdam. The knowledge institution TNO offered to conduct research on the implementation of the project to support the key players.

6.3.4 Timescale

The Energy Atlas was developed between 2012 and 2014 and was quickly implemented when the municipality joined the EU-funded program "TRANSFORM" (van Winden et al., 2016). During this period the Energy Atlas was developed by encouraging the involvement of key stakeholders (public utility providers and housing corporations), integrating all the gathered data into one database, and analyzing the data for energy simulation. In 2014 the Energy Atlas was published as an online map. The overall timeline of the Energy Atlas development is presented in Fig. 6.9.

6.3.5 Cost

The cost for the Energy Atlas was mostly covered by the European Commission through the "TRANSFORM" program. We could not find the exact budget allocation for the development of the Energy Atlas, but we identified the parties who funded the project (see Table 6.1). The project leader mentioned that most of the cost came from outside of the municipality, meaning the budget use could be tangibly controlled by external parties. The key parties therefore used their

Figure 6.9 Timeline of Energy Atlas project development.
Source: Adapted from van Winden, W., Oskam, I., van den Buuse, D., Schrama, W., & van Dijck, E. (2016). *Organising Smart City projects: Lessons from Amsterdam*. Amsterdam.

Table 6.1 Cost of energy atlas.

No.	Budget	Total (€/month)	Remark
Income			
1	European Commission (TRANSFORM Program)	n/a	*No specific data given*
2	Amsterdam Investment Fund	n/a	*No specific data given*
3	Energy loan	n/a	*No specific data given*
4	Involved organizations	n/a	*No specific data given*
Total			
Outcome			
1	Exploration of project ideas	10,000	*Based on the source*
2	Energy Atlas development • Human resources (majority of cost) • Technology	180,000	*Based on the source*
Total		± 190,000	*Interpreted from the source*

Source: Data from Boogert, G., Mantel, B., Mollay, U., & Schremmer, C. (2015). *TRANSFORM synthesis report: Final version*. Belgium.

budget efficiently, which could be one of the reasons why this project finished on time and with good quality. The long-term economic viability of the project was secured by Energy Fund, an institution that was established in 2015 after the publication of the Energy Atlas (Amsterdam Municipality, 2015).

6.3.6 Quality

Several general standards were used for the Energy Atlas project, including for the data gathering, analysis, and visualization. Data gathering was based on an agreement between the municipality and the public utility providers and housing corporations. The data had to meet specific legal requirements from each party, that is, user data privacy and security, and the location of critical infrastructure. The data analysis had to be in line with the project aims, and the information could therefore only be used for providing the baseline, prospects, and simulation of the energy use of Amsterdam. The data visualization had to be user-friendly. The project leader said that no specific standards had to be taken into account when the stakeholders developed the project, such as contract penalties or warranty periods.

6.3.7 Risks

The project team had to overcome several risks, such as data privacy and security. The municipality decided to only use general energy data, because publishing individual customer data from public utility providers is too sensitive. An agreement was also made for the location of the critical infrastructure, in which they decided to publish only the energy infrastructure without its critical points (van Winden et al., 2016).

6.3.8 Procurement

The Energy Atlas was built using a public−private partnership agreement. The European Commission provided the initial funds for the project through the "TRANSFORM" program, enabling the municipality to work with Liander to create a prototype of the Energy Atlas as a tool to present to other stakeholders. The prototype successfully helped the municipality to encourage other public utility providers and housing corporations to share their data. The published Energy Atlas can now be used to create business plans for small open innovation activities targeting energy use.

6.3.9 Discussion

The overview presented in Fig. 6.10 provides a clearer insight into the development of the Energy Atlas project, one of the smart city projects in ASC. As Boogert, Mantel, Mollay, and Schremmer (2015) outlined, this project provided several key insights into such projects:

1. Stakeholder management was necessary for the implementation of the project. It was necessary for the municipality to encourage the public utility providers and housing corporations to share their energy data by highlighting the benefits to them. In this phase the role of ASC is crucial for connecting all partners and facilitating their roles during the project development.
2. Collaboration between the municipality, industry, and research institutions was fundamental for successful research during the project development. The municipality has to convince the stakeholders to take part and therefore requires scientific research materials that can be presented to the stakeholders.

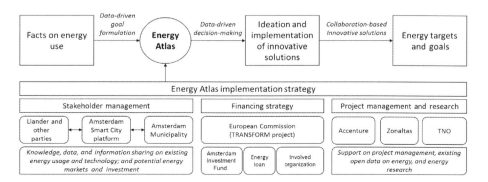

Figure 6.10 Overview of the development of the Energy Atlas project.

3. A prototype of the Energy Atlas was helpful to share the project idea. The prototype became a tool for convincing stakeholders, especially in terms of their decision to make a long-term investment in the project by freely sharing their data.
4. The project is still focused on the energy use, prospects, and networks at a residential/building scale, so innovative solutions may only emerge at that scale.
5. The data in the Energy Atlas are static and require ongoing updating. ASC therefore plays a crucial role in ensuring that the energy data are kept updated by the stakeholders in the future.

Overall, the project met its initial objective of publishing energy data as a tool for users to quickly develop innovative energy solutions. Another achieved objective was to gather energy data from several different providers in the city. This successful cooperation between the municipality and the stakeholders was established with the help of ASC, who makes connections between the actors, and facilitated their collaboration.

As the Energy Atlas is an open-data map, no feedback has currently been recorded from its end users. The project leader clarified that no publication or media outlet has reflected on the use of the Energy Atlas; however, an organization based on a public−private−people partnership between various parties in South-East Amsterdam, ZO Circular, has demonstrated the benefit of the Energy Atlas (Boogert et al., 2015). They used the data and tools from the Energy Atlas to guide interventions regarding heat usage and the implementation of solar projects in their district, which helped them to build a strategic plan for a more sustainable South-East Amsterdam. This reveals that the Energy Atlas has helped its users in decision-making processes and in their development of business strategies based on energy transition.

As the Energy Atlas is the only freely accessible system providing real energy usage data, it may attract the attention of parties all over the world (Boogert et al., 2015). The reliability and usability of its data mean the Energy Atlas could be used to attract investments for energy transitions and define new challenges for innovation by enabling people to make innovative business decisions to cope with energy challenges.

This project is based on the collaboration and a MoU between European cities. Amsterdam can use this coalition to increase the competitiveness of Energy Atlas usage at the regional scale, which is even being scaled up toward the national level (the Netherlands). This project can therefore successfully compete in the international smart city competition, enabling more cities all over the world to learn from Amsterdam.

In an official document containing frequently asked questions, ASC (2017) stated that it is an innovative organization for future-proof city development, which acts by identifying and connecting parties and accelerating breakthrough ideas to address city challenges. They facilitate the innovation process based on the collaboration of a public−private−people partnership, providing an actor network for the stakeholders. The collaborative principle of ASC based on public−private partnerships was implemented well in the development of the Energy Atlas project, as highlighted by the collaboration between the municipality and the private stakeholders who possess the energy data. The public body (the municipality) acted as an initiator and coordinator for the project, helping the private parties (particularly the public utility providers and housing corporations) to realize the benefit of sharing their data and act as providers for the project. ASC fulfilled its claim of being a facilitator for stakeholders to collaborate and develop innovations. They helped the municipality to connect with its key partner, Liander, and enabled them to accelerate the development of the Energy Atlas; however, the citizens of Amsterdam were not represented well during the process. This was accepted because the development of the project did not require any feedback or assistance from individuals. Now that the Energy Atlas has been published, the people of Amsterdam can contribute by providing feedback to the municipality regarding its data and tools. We can therefore conclude that ASC successfully operationalized their working concept.

6.4 Conclusions

ASC reports at least four lessons learnt from the implementation of the Energy Atlas project. (1) A smart city is not only about developing an advanced technological solution but also the empowerment of actors in the city to innovate in response to recent city challenges. (2) Technology is only one tool for tackling city challenges. The Energy Atlas, as an innovative technology, is a medium to enable people to create and adapt business ideas to contribute to tackling energy challenges. (3) To innovate, actors need to collaborate based on an agreement and trust each other. (4) A partnership organization such as ASC is required for a smart city to connect the relevant actors, facilitate cocreation processes, and accelerate innovations.

Summing up the lesson learnt, ASC has taught us that technology is not the end goal of a smart city but only one of the tools needed to achieve the goals. The essential "smart" ideas come from the people in the city, who create innovative solutions to cope with contemporary city challenges and effectively manage them. An innovative solution involves not only technology but also nontechnological advances, such as a new community system or different ways of financing. From ASC, we also learned that a collaborative ecosystem is important for facilitating innovation.

It should be stressed that there is a wide range of projects across the ASC themes, all with different purposes, setups, and impacts. Some of them are already successful, while others are still in the development phase. The Energy Atlas is a very successful example, and its usability and possibilities have begun to be translated to other fields of innovation within ASC. The collaboration within the Energy Atlas project is more between organizations and businesses (public−private) than a partnership with the citizens themselves; however, which would likely not be possible for some of the other smart city projects. In the future, it seems likely that ASC will adjust their role and focus to not only connect partners in a collaborative way but also to build an effective measurement of impact and develop processes for scaling up successfully implemented smart city projects.

The Energy Atlas project almost failed to encourage stakeholders to share their energy data but was able to continue because the "TRANSFORM" program from the European Commission strengthened the position of the Amsterdam Municipality to involve energy stakeholders. This shows that political and financial commitments from higher levels of government will help smart city projects to run well. The EU trigger and institutional backup have been demonstrated to be important aspects in the implementation of smart city projects.

All actors focusing on the smart city concept, such as governments, private organizations, and scholars, need to be aware that a smart city must be driven by people as well as technology in order to cope with contemporary city challenges. Smart cities trigger an innovative and collaborative ecosystem; therefore, future research should focus more on the innovation process and actor engagement in these projects.

6.5 Remarks

Amsterdam Smart City	https://amsterdamsmartcity.com/
Alliander	https://www.alliander.com/
Liander	https://www.liander.nl
Nederlandse Organisatie voor Toegepast Natuurwetenschappelijk Onderzoek	https://www.tno.nl
Amsterdam Economic Board	https://www.amsterdameconomicboard.com
Amsterdam Arena	https://www.johancruijffarena.nl/home-1.htm
KPN	https://www.kpn.com
PostNL	https://www.postnl.nl
Arcadis	https://www.arcadis.com
Engie	https://www.engie.nl
Amsterdam University of Applied Science	http://www.amsterdamuas.com/
Waag Society	https://waag.org
Pakhuis De Zwijger	https://dezwijger.nl

About the authors

Zulfikar Dinar Wahidayat Putra studied Urban Environmental Management with a specialization in Land Use Planning at Wageningen University, the Netherlands. He is an urban planner, specializing in smart city and innovation systems. His thesis concerned the interaction between smart city projects as local initiatives and government environmental policies, with a focus on Amsterdam. He was a Sustainable Development Goals (SDGs) Innovation Officer in the United Nations for Development Program in Indonesia before taking on a new role as a research assistant in the Urban and Regional Planning Study Program at Gadjah Mada University, Indonesia. He also has experience with climate action research, gained by participating in the Venlo Circular Challenge held by Sustainable Motion Netherlands, as well as from a summer school called "Journey" organized by Climate-KIC, European Institute of Innovation and Technology, European Union. He is an experienced urban planner and works on urban and regional planning, mapping, urban design, innovation systems, and SDG projects in consultancy firms and in the United Nations agency in Indonesia. For further correspondence, make contact via zulfikar.dinar@gmail.com.

Wim van der Knaap studied Landscape engineering at Wageningen University, the Netherlands, and is now an assistant professor in the university's Landscape Architecture and Spatial Planning Group, specializing in planning aspects for urban/rural fringe developments, especially in the metropolitan area. He thereby focuses on planning processes around contemporary issues such as the impacts of climate change and water-related topics. His main interests are in the participation processes related to the technological developments and impacts related to these planning processes, and he has participated in several projects across Europe to study rural/urban developments and their accompanying issues. For further correspondence, make contact via Wim.vanderKnaap@wur.nl.

References

Amsterdam Municipality. (2014). *Energy-use of gas and electricity energy*. From <https://maps.amsterdam.nl/energie_gaselektra/?LANG = en> Retrieved 27.05.18.

Amsterdam Municipality. (2015). *Sustainable Amsterdam: Agenda for renewable energy, clear air, a circular economy, and a climate-resilient city*. Amsterdam.

Amsterdam Municipality. (2016). *Amsterdam and Europe: Historical ties*. Amsterdam.

Amsterdam Municipality. *The governing bodies of Amsterdam*. (2018). From <https://www.amsterdam.nl/en/governance-city-hall/governing-bodies/> Retrieved 25.05.18.

Amsterdam Smart City (ASC). (2011). *Smart stories: AmsmarterdamCity*. Amsterdam.

Amsterdam Smart City (ASC). (2017). *Frequently asked questions: AmsmarterdamCity*. Amsterdam.

Amsterdam Smart City (ASC). (2018). *Amsterdam Smart City*. From <amsterdamsmartcity.com> Retrieved 12.09.17.

Anthopoulos, L. G. (2017). In C. G. Reddick (Ed.), *Understanding smart cities: A tool for smart government or an industrial trick?* Cham: Springer International Publishing.

Baron, G. (2012). *Amsterdam Smart City*. Amsterdam: Amsterdam Municipality.

Boogert, G., Mantel, B., Mollay, U., & Schremmer, C. (2015). *TRANSFORM synthesis report: Final version*. Belgium.

Capra, C. F. (2014). *The smart city and its citizens governance and citizen participation in Amsterdam Smart City*. Erasmus University Rotterdam.

Cocchia, A. (2014). Smart and digital city: A systematic literature review. In R. P. Dameri, & C. Rosenthal-Sabroux (Eds.), *Smart city: How to create public and economic value with high technology in urban space* (pp. 13–43). Cham: Springer International Publishing. Available from https://doi.org/10.1007/978-3-319-06160-3.

Dameri, R. P. (2017). *Smart city implementation: Creating economic and public value in innovative urban systems* (1st ed.). Cham: Springer International Publishing. Available from https://doi.org/10.1007/978-3-319-45766-6.

Diaz-Diaz, R., Muñoz, L., & Pérez-González, D. (2017). The business model evaluation tool for smart cities: Application to SmartSantander use cases. *Energies*, *10*, 1−30. Available from https://doi.org/10.3390/en10030262.

European Commission. (2010). *EUROPE 2020: A European strategy for smart, sustainable, and inclusive growth*. Brussels.

Gray, J. (2008). *Amsterdam lonely planet* (1st ed.). Amsterdam: Lonely Planet.

Havelaar, R. (2016). *Best practices and lessons learned from a global village with 8 years' experience in citizen engagement*. Seminar Presentation, Thurgau: Suisse Energie. Retrieved from <http://www.smartcity-suisse.ch/fileadmin/user_upload/SmartCity/de/Dateien/Praesentationen_StGallen_2016/2_Rogier_Havelar_Amsterdam_Smart_City_web.pdf>.

Markatou, M., & Alexandrou, E. (2015). Urban system of innovation: Main agents and main factors of success. *Procedia − Social and Behavioral Sciences*, *195*, 240−250. Available from https://doi.org/10.1016/j.sbspro.2015.06.355.

Newman, J. (2001). *Modernizing governance: New labour policy and society* (1st ed.). London: SAGE Publications Ltd.

Ojo, A., Dzhusupova, Z., & Curry, E. (2016). Exploring the nature of the smart cities research landscape. In J. R. Gil-Garcia, T. A. Pardo, & T. Nam (Eds.), *Smarter as the new urban agenda: A comprehensive view of the 21st century city* (1st ed., pp. 23−47). Cham: Springer International Publishing. Available from https://doi.org/10.1007/978-3-319-17620-8.

Osterwalder, A., & Pigneur, Y. (2010). *Business model generation* (1st ed). New Jersey: Wiley.

Putra, Z. D. W. (2018). *The interaction between non-government-based smart city projects and government-based environmental management: The case of Amsterdam*. Wageningen University. Available from https://doi.org/10.13140/RG.2.2.13651.48161.

Scholl, C., Ablasser, G., Eriksen, M.A., Baerten, N., Blok, J., Clark, E., Friendrich, Z. (2017). In C. Scholl, M. A. Eriksen, N. Baerten, E. Clark, T. Drage, T. Hoeflehner, P. Wlasak (Eds.), *Guidelines for urban labs*. Antwerp: URB@exp.

SEO Economisch Onderzoek. (2009). *Amsterdam, Netherlands: Self-evaluation report*. Amsterdam.

Šťáhlavský, R. (2011). *Amsterdam smart city project overview*. Prague: Accenture.

Steen, K., & van Bueren, E. (2017). *Urban living labs: A living lab way of working* (1st ed.). Amsterdam: AMS Institute.

van Winden, W., Braun, E., Otgaar, A., & Witte, J.-J. (2014). In S. M. Christopherson, M. Feldman, G. Grabher, R. Martin, & M. Perry (Eds.), *Urban innovation systems: What makes them tick?* (1st ed.). New York: Routledge.

van Winden, W., Oskam, I., van den Buuse, D., Schrama, W., & van Dijck, E. (2016). *Organising smart city projects: Lessons from Amsterdam*. Amsterdam.

Further reading

Athey, G., Nathan, M., Webber, C., & Mahroum, S. (2008). Innovation and the city. *Innovation: Management, Policy & Practice*, *10*(2), 156−169.

The smart city of Trikala

Leonidas Anthopoulos
University of Thessaly, Volos, Greece

Chapter Outline

7.1 Introduction   149
7.2 Background   152
7.3 Research methodology: case study   158
   7.3.1 Project mission statement   158
   7.3.2 Resource-based motivation   163
   7.3.3 Life-cycle management   164
   7.3.4 Project coalition management   166
   7.3.5 Discussion—the fringes   167
7.4 Conclusion   169
Acknowledgments   170
About the author   170
References   170
Further reading   171

7.1 Introduction

Smart city (SC) is a radically evolving domain, whose grassroots go back to the early 1990s (Anthopoulos, 2017) and keep on evolving as a multidisciplinary domain with the engagement of almost all the scientific fields and industries. Among the numerous SC definitions, an indicative that combines international standards' ones concerns *the utilization of information and communications technologies (ICT), and innovation by cities (new, existing or districts), as a means to sustain in economic, social and environmental terms and to address several challenges dealing with six (6) dimensions (people, economy, governance, mobility, environment, and living)* (Anthopoulos, 2017).

Today, the SC domain seems to mature with the engagement of international standardization bodies that define SC standards for several purposes: the International Standards Organization (ISO) for instance, introduced among others the ISO37101 series that provides with definitions, indexes, and specifications the SC (ISO, 2016). Moreover, SC can be observed around the world, while almost all cities can claim that they are smart. In this respect numerous city coalitions have been structured, which share a common vision or purpose (Anthopoulos, 2017). For instance, the World Council for City Data[1] aims to certify data quality that is used for city evaluation via specific key performance indicators; Eurocities[2] aims to deal with common challenges that cities in the European Union (EU) share; Open and Agile Smart Cities focus on smart-city data and services; etc. The conceptualization and development of a SC are not an easy process. Instead, several models and architectures can be located. An indicative unified conceptual model (Anthopoulos, Janssen, & Weerakkody, 2016) views several smart service groups that integrate facilities, with ICT and environment, while it recognizes the significant role of governance and management for SC development. On the other hand, an indicative architecture (Fig. 7.1) comes from the International Telecommunication Union (ITU) (Anthopoulos, Gemma, Fathy, & Sang, 2015) and views service flow between several architecture layers, while the British Standards (BSI, 2016) defines the entities between which data flow occurs.

SC emerged dramatically during the last 20 years after the initial appearance in literature. During this evolution, the SC changed its initial purpose and scope and several versions appeared in this timeline (Anthopoulos, 2017). This chapter aims to present the case of Trikala, Greece, which was initially grounded in late 2003 by the Municipality of Trikala. The case envisioned an interconnected city and a local information society, and defined several projects that would be invested in order to establish this mission (Table 7.1). Trikala was officially entitled "the First Greek Digital City" in December 2004 due to its numerous information systems; it evolved to a wireless city in 2005 and then to broadband city in 2007. The overall development and operation was managed by a municipal company (e-Trikala), which was a state-owned enterprise. This evolution is depicted in Fig. 7.2 but a decline occurred right after and until 2014. This failure was expressed in lack of public interest and maintenance difficulties, which were based on the national fiscal crisis that Greece experienced this period.

When the municipal leadership changed in 2014, several efforts were undertaken to recover the intelligent infrastructure and gain back local interest. These efforts resulted to its current form, which has integrated previous infrastructure with a set of brand-new information systems and smart services. Today, Smart Trikala offers numerous smart services, which range from complaints' registration to smart lighting and smart parking. The overall portfolio is being managed by municipal units and some resources from e-Trikala. The purpose of today's Smart Trikala is to *become a modern city that offers useful services to the local community, which enable growth and enhance sustainability, while future generations are being supported to adopt today's and future services.* This is a prestigious case, which corresponds to the description of a SC development in a typical medium-sized city and depicts how it can become successful, even under hard conditions.

The rest of this chapter is organized as follows: Section 7.2 explains the background of the case, while Section 7.3 analyzes Smart Trikala with the use of the

---

[1] http://www.dataforcities.org/.
[2] http://www.eurocities.eu/.

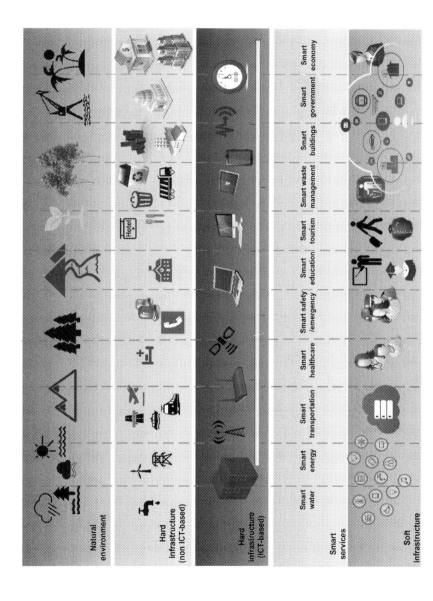

Figure 7.1 SC meta-architecture (Anthopoulos, 2017). SC, Smart city.

Table 7.1 The initial project portfolio of the digital city of Trikala (until 2014).

	Project title	Budget (€)	Start
1	Public Wi-Fi network that interconnects several municipalities	22,375,570	6/11/2008
2	Broadband penetration support in Trikala	7200,000	24/5/2005
3	Metropolitan area fiber-optic network in the city of Trikala	112,000,000	8/3/2007
4	E-government systems	25,100,000	1/3/2006
5	Telecare systems	10,543,400	13/4/2006
6	GIS of Trikala	169,702,81	22/10/2007
7	Web portal for the Commercial Chamber	30,599,600	28/2/2007
8	Digital initiatives organized by the Commercial Chamber	73,308,000	1/8/2012
9	Mobile service provision for tourists (XENAGOS)	55,062,000	23/12/2009
10	Intelligent transportations system	61,996,999	5/6/2006
11	Digital public service provision	28,385,534	3/9/2008
12	Web portal development	32,803,594	10/1/2008
13	Culture content development	8000,000	10/8/2003
14	Public consultations (e-Politis)	18,789,480	27/2/2014

Figure 7.2 The evolution timeline of Smart Trikala.

Project Management Body of Knowledge (PMBOK) (PMI, 2013) knowledge areas. Finally, Section 7.4 contains some conclusions and future thoughts.

7.2 Background

Trikala is a medium-sized city with approximately 80,000 residents, which is located in the region of Thessaly, in Central Greece (Fig. 7.3). Its history goes back to the third millennium BCE, while Trikala is famous for its music and creativity: the city was the birthplace of many famous Greek folk musicians; a museum has been grounded to honor famous musician Vassilis Tsitsanis[3]; a music studio is open

---
[3] http://www.mouseiotsitsani.gr/.

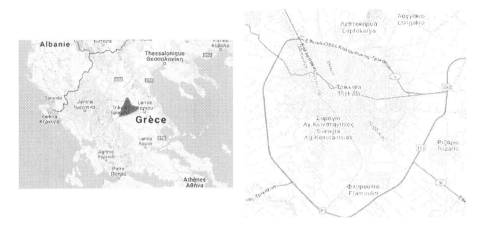

Figure 7.3 A geographic map with the city of Trikala and its downtown.

to young musicians; more than 20 small schools offer music and dance lectures, which occupy more than 200 young entrepreneurs; and more than 600 creative activities take place on an annual basis in Trikala, that attract people from all over Greece.

Creative activities transformed Trikala to an attractive winter touristic destination in 2010, when it started hosting the biggest Greek national Christmas thematic village (the Elves Mill[4]). More than 1 million tourists visit Trikala during Christmas, which supports the local market, experience surrounding sightseeing even at distances of 20 km from the city, and encourage the organization of many parallel events and the local creative industry's growth. Evidence from the municipality and the Regional Bank of Thessaly shows steady GDP during the fiscal crisis and a 6.8% increase of the local GDP, with 1% annually and basically during December (all facts since 2010), which demonstrates the effect of all the above activities on the local economy.

Trikala is a typical Greek city, with narrow streets, traffic congestion, and both old and new buildings, while several parks—and the river of Litheos that crosses the city—leave many open spaces (Fig. 7.4). The city has a dense network of pedestrian areas and cycling lanes; it is supported by the local public transportation system (bus) that mainly connects downtown with surrounded districts and villages, while it has undertaken several initiatives for sustainable mobility (e.g., car parking slots' release for cycling lanes, smart parking system's installation to encourage car avoidance). The city is governed by the Municipality of Trikala, which is supervised by a regional authority (Region of Thessaly) and the national central government. According to the latest legal framework (Kallikratis), the Municipality of Trikala incorporated 37 communities around the city—even 20 km away from the main urban system.

---

[4] http://milosxotikon.gr/.

Figure 7.4 A view of Trikala city and the river of Litheos.

The municipality is responsible to install and maintain all the types of utilities and services in the area {i.e., water and sewage [offered by the municipal company(DEYAT) partner in this proposal], streets, public lighting and traffic lights, public buildings} and authorizes/supervises the remainders (education, health, telecommunications, public transportation, etc.), except from the energy (they are offered by natural gas and electricity providers) and telecommunication services. Nevertheless, the city owns several photovoltaic stations installed in municipal areas and public buildings' roofs, as well as the longest municipal fiber-optic network of 24 km length, which serves the public organizations in the city and a municipal Mesh Wi-Fi network that covers the city. Trikala is connected with all the nearby big cities, regional capitals, and the capital of Greece (Athens) via a network of national roads and the railway network. Public transportation services in the municipal area are offered by a local transportation provider, which collaborate with the city, while another private company offers bus connections with other cities (KTEL).

The city is surrounded by agricultural landscapes that support corresponding economic activities. An amount of approximately 800 small and medium-sized enterprises are located in the city, which mainly deal with commercial and other types of services. Moreover, the holly area of Meteora and other important mountain areas are close to the city (all at a distance of approximately 20 km), which attract a significant and relevant touristic market. All economic activities in the city (including the local ICT industry) are supervised by the local Commercial Chamber and the local Commercial Union (both are partners in this proposal), while all major national banks have branches in the city.

Education services of all levels are offered in the city—ranging from more than 50 primary and high schools to university (Department of Sport Science) and university of applied science (Department of Civil Engineering). Future university planning views three university departments in Trikala, all of which to deal with sports and dietary. These tertiary-education schools collaborate with the municipality in several innovative activities (i.e., sustainable mobility planning in the city), while they are partners in other activities (i.e., smoking prohibition in public spaces, summer schools, and volunteer activities).

Furthermore, a public hospital is located in the city, while the municipality organized and supervises social-care services and the networks of volunteers. These services treated more than 500 poor people from all over the region during the last 5 years, while it welcomed and provided shelter in the city to immigrant waves of more than 500 people—in collaboration with the UN Refugee Agency in July 2017. A telecare center was installed in 2008 in the city, which supported more than 20 people with disabilities distantly. Recently, the local network of volunteers installed 20 defibrillators in the city for heart-attack support. Volunteers adopted a mobile app (named PLISION[5]), which enables instant notification and response against such events. In addition, a court of justice is located in the city, while safety services are offered by police and municipal police, fire brigade station, and a civil service hosted in the Town Hall. The local volunteer network has become eligible to respond to natural disasters and the use of a commercial third-party app (PLISION) has been upgraded accordingly. Finally, the municipality operates the main local cultural and sport facilities [sport centers (5), public libraries (1), galleries (2), and museums (5)].

The local economy is mainly based on agricultural activities and on an increasing creative industry, while local GDP is among the lowest in Greece and in Europe, and the average unemployment rates are approximately equal to the average Greek ones (27% in 2016). The overall city figures are presented in Table 7.2.

In general it has to be underlined that Trikala experienced—like the entire country—an enormous fiscal crisis period since 2008, but with extreme effects after 2015. Nevertheless, the above activities, which were mainly guided by the municipality, strengthened the social coherence, responded effectively to immigrant waves of more than 500 people, engaged the community and the creative industry, and corresponding activities resulted to a steady local GDP during the last 5 years, which is something unique for the Greek conditions.

It was presented before that the city of Trikala has a long "smart" history. The project portfolio (Table 7.1) that was funded by the Greek Information Society Framework program focused on the development of the local information society, and they highly achieved in this mission. This project portfolio was accompanied by the participation of Trikala in numerous consortiums of corresponding European projects, all related to digital development and local ICT transformation. Although the above involvement of Trikala sounds "opportunistic" and "fragmented," it was not, since it had prioritized specific directions, which aligned to national and EU policies such as (1) the development of the local information society; (2) social and

---

[5] https://play.google.com/store/apps/details?id = eu.plision and https://itunes.apple.com/gr/app/plision/id1273877162?mt = 8.

Table 7.2 Figures of the city of Trikala.

Figure	Value
City population	62,154
Metropolitan area population (e.g., an area consisting of a densely populated urban core and its less-populated surrounding territories, sharing industry, infrastructure, and housing)	81,355
Average annual population growth during the last 5 years (since 2013)	+1.12%
Average population's age (years)	43
Aging index	1.41
Male population's proportion	49.3%
Population with higher education diplomas	37.32%
Population that graduated from a university	27.56%
Population with special needs (disabled, homeless, and immigrants)	6.44%
Employment rate (ratio of employed to working-age population from 15 to 64 years)	80.4%
Economically active population's proportion	38.7%
Main economic sectors	*Agriculture activities:* 12.04% of the employed population *Industry (mainly the food sector):* 17.31% of the employed population *Service sector (public sector, education, health, banking, tourism, etc.):* 70.65% of the employed population
Fiber-optic municipal network (km)	24.3
Metro Wi-Fi network city coverage (%)	88.3
Students per STEM kit at public schools	7
Students per PC at public schools	1.5

STEM, Science, technology, engineering, and mathematics; *PC*, personal computer.

business engagement in ICT activities; and (3) municipal efficiency's and effectiveness' enhancement.

After 2014 the municipality realized the importance of digital transformation and aligned its policies to its context, as follows:

1. *Big data and digital platforms:* The city has installed a central city-monitoring platform (Cisco Connected Digital Platform[6,7]), which integrates several cyber-physical systems (sensors and controllers with regard to smart public lighting, mesh Wi-Fi, smart parking,

---

[6] https://www.cisco.com/c/en/us/solutions/industries/smart-connected-communities/kinetic-for-cities.html.
[7] https://www.cisco.com/c/dam/m/ru_ru/training-events/2017/cisco-connect/pdf/Lev_Levin_Cisco_Connected_Digital_Platform.pdf.

and smart environment), while it plans to install and integrate smart-bins and municipal fleet control. All collected big data streams will be offered to the public via the city data portal[8] that is under development with a plan to launch by March 2018. The system analyzes all the collected data and visualizes smart service performance. Moreover, other platforms collect and analyze data via the municipal processes.

2. *Digital skills:* The municipality offers many training ICT programs within its organization, and it has partnered with vocational training schools to support ICT business training. Recently, it has launched *corresponding efforts with public schools with regard to science, technology, engineering, and mathematics (STEM), which enhance youth creative and algorithmic thinking, problem solving, and team working.* A parallel effect of this initiative was that within a 2-month period only; more than 10 local robotics academies were grounded in the city, which validate the potential that lies behind such initiative.

3. *Cities and regions:* The municipality realized its leading role with regard to ICT transformation and defined the following policies: (1) data industry's development: it defined its open data policy, collects data streams, and opens them centrally on its data portal (see footnote 8); (2) partners with stakeholders in terms of calculating performance with the ICT, initiating training programs and undertaking common activities (i.e., Elves Mill and virtual open mall) and space sharing; (3) simplifies government transactions: it defined the city call center, it launched the self-service citizen machine, and measures G2B services' performance. Moreover, the municipality became a fellow city of the EU Digital Cities Challenge[9] and gains coordinated support with regard to the definition of a local Digital Transformation Strategy.

4. *ICT standardization:* The city of Trikala in collaboration with the Greek standardization body tries to standardize the SC ecosystem.[10] The leader of this proposal's project team is the leader of these standardization efforts, and he is the same person who supervises the smart initiatives in Trikala after 2014. In addition, it updated its internal organization with the definition of the SC department, which aims to standardize all the internal processes with the use of ICT, while it aims to standardize processes that involve the other city stakeholders (i.e., construction project development in the city). Standardization will be monitored with the ICT, such as with open project management tools.

The above initiatives have been supported only with municipal funding and in partnership with vendors that want to develop and test their artifacts under real conditions. Moreover, the commercial union collaborated with the municipality and created a virtual open mall that operates over the municipal Wi-Fi. This "virtual" mall disseminates offers to the Wi-Fi users that are being launched by the local retailers and enables the provision of personal marketing campaigns. In addition, the municipal company for water utility service provision developed a smart water system for network monitoring, while it participated in a EU-funded collaboration activity to calculate city's energy efficiency (InSMART[11] FP7 project).

---

[8] http://data.trikalacity.gr.
[9] https://www.digitallytransformyourregion.eu/cities.
[10] http://www.elot.gr/1397_ELL_HTML.aspx.
[11] www.insmartenergy.com.

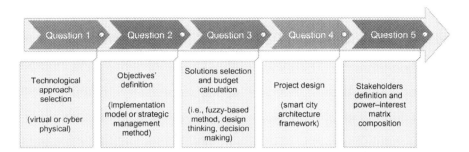

Figure 7.5 Project mission definition (Anthopoulos, 2017).

7.3 Research methodology: case study

This case is analyzed with the use of four project management processes (Winch, 2009), which aggregate the 10 PMBOK knowledge areas as follows:

1. *Project mission statement:* It includes the integration and scope management areas.
2. *Resource-based motivation:* It contains human resource and procurement management areas.
3. *Life-cycle management:* It addresses time, cost, quality, and risk management areas.
4. *Project coalition management:* It explains communications and stakeholders management areas.

7.3.1 Project mission statement

Scope definition is critical where requirements, deliverables, duration, and budget are being specified (Fig. 7.5). This process is analyzed in the following steps: (1) client needs' definition; (2) stakeholders' management. These steps determine project organization and emphasize on information flow. The first question that the client answers deals with the technological approach of the SC (virtual or cyber-physical). Virtual approaches limit the SC scope to software and applications, while the cyber-physical extends it to infrastructure and embedded systems (e.g., networks, IoT). Smart Trikala (Fig. 7.6) adopted the cyber-physical approach with the following systems:

1. A cyber-physical subsystem that offers the following services
   a. Smart lighting (upgrades to LED and motion sensors)
   b. Smart parking with underground sensors that react with parking slots.
   c. Smart environment with sensors that measure temperature, humidity, and emissions.
   d. Enhanced public Wi-Fi with fiber-optic connections with the access points.
   e. Municipal fleet management system (with GSM sensors for vehicle tracking).
   f. Smart waste management system, with smart-bin sensors installed downtown.
   g. Smart water-metering and management system, with the installation of smart-meters downtown. Smart water and smart waste sensors are being connected via a LoRa network.[12]

---

[12] https://lora-alliance.org/.

Figure 7.6 Smart Trikala components.

Figure 7.7 Citizen self-service system with even door-to-door delivery.

    h. Traffic lights' and water pumps' monitoring for malfunction detection and instant response by the municipal services.
    i. Citizen self-service system for certificate public printing, which can be delivered with a door-to-door service (Fig. 7.7).
2. A virtual environment with
    a. An end-to-end city management system that has been developed and deployed by CISCO (Kinetic) and operates as a cloud-based service.
    b. Wi-Fi login system (Purple) developed by SiEBEN, which supports the operation of the open mall (Fig. 7.8), and operates as a cloud-based service too.
    c. Fleet analysis system that depicts vehicles' position and routes, and it is being offered as a service by Vodafone.
    d. Geographical information system (GIS) system with several layers with geospatial information, which is based on ESRI^R ArcGIS^R platform as a cloud-based service too.
    e. Complaints registration system that operates via phone, web, and mobile App (Fig. 7.9), which is the official municipal App entitled Trikala Check App.[13]

---

[13] https://www.trikalacity.gr.

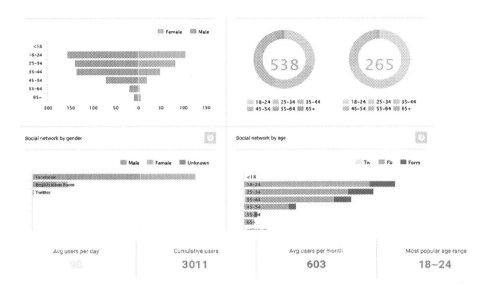

Figure 7.8 A snapshot of the Purple logger's dashboard.

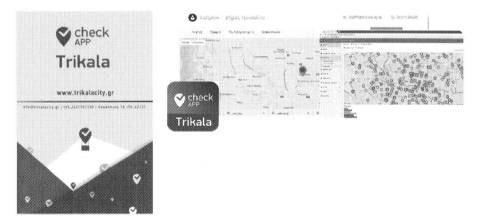

Figure 7.9 The complaints' registration system and the official municipal mobile application.

- **f.** Public consultations and social brain-storming service, which are being offered as a service by Crowdpolicy vendor.
- **g.** Digital payments that are being offered in collaboration with a banking system, while the citizens are being authenticated in association with the national tax system (TAXIS).
- **h.** Parking analytics, which is a dashboard that collects and analyzes data from the parking slots.

All the above services are being monitored and are also being demonstrated in a control room that is located at the town hall (Fig. 7.10). In order for the above systems and services to be available, the following past smart infrastructure that was installed via previous projects (Table 7.1) are being utilized:

1. The metropolitan fiber-optic network, which interconnects the IoT gateway and the Wi-Fi access points.
2. The previous Wi-Fi network.
3. The old GIS data that was registered in 2008.
4. Fiber-optic and Wi-Fi infrastructure that was installed for the purposes of the self-driving bus that was deployed and tested under the EU Project CityMobil2[14] (Fig. 7.8).

Beyond the above systems, Smart Trikala uses data and functionalities from the following information systems:

1. Municipal systems for document and financial management
2. Public consultation and brainstorming system[15]
3. Smart water management system
4. Telecare system for people with special needs

The second question that the client answers has to do with target definition of the project. This query respects the project ecosystem's perspectives (e.g., location, community) Anthopoulos and Tsoukalas (2006) introduced a development framework for a digital city, which recognizes four axes of precedence for local growth (economy, education and training, quality of life, culture and tourism) and five perspectives for project definition (social, technological, informative, ethical, and economical). This development framework aligns to the project integration knowledge area of PMBOK, because it performs a detailed analysis of the local characteristics and makes a gap analysis that the SC can close.

Figure 7.10 The control room for Smart Trikala.

---

[14] https://cordis.europa.eu/result/rcn/191677_en.html.
[15] http://hello.crowdapps.net/open-trikala.

An alternative approach to the above framework can be the strategic management of a SC (Lysons & Farrington, 2006). This approach requires the definition of the entire SC life cycle and more specifically (1) strategic analysis (David, 2011); (2) synthesis [e.g., with Porter's (1996) five forces; the 7p Marketing Mix (Ivy, 2008; Rafiq & Ahmed, 1995); or the strategy map (Kaplan & Norton, 1996)]; (3) strategic implementation; (4) evaluation; and (5) revision. The case of Smart Trikala emphasized on

1. The reduction of energy spending in the city
2. Traffic congestion reduction
3. Air quality improvement
4. Sold waste management
5. Municipal efficiency with regard to responses to the city's requirements

The third question deals with the solutions' selection for the SC. This process is crucial since not all the available SC solutions are appropriate for each city. Smart Trikala selected several types of smart services as they were presented above. The solution selection that could enable them was based on the following criteria:

1. Infrastructure (sensors) with software and application programming interfaces (APIs) that are compatible and able to integrate and exchange data with the city management platform.
2. Equipment that was available in the market to be supplied for the SC project.

The fourth question deals with project planning, which is affected by the architecture framework that is being selected for the SC. The architecture that was selected for Smart Trikala was service oriented architecture (SOA), since each subsystem is independent to the others and can be connected to the city management system.

Another crucial question deals with the viability assessment of the SC project. In this regard the SC project has to meet the expectations of the interested parties. For this reason, a stakeholder's analysis was performed with the use of the power—interest table (Table 7.3). The case of Trikala experienced a failure in terms of social adoption due to the fact that such an analysis was not performed, while a

Table 7.3 Power—interest table for Smart Trikala.

Power to influence	Level of interest	
	Low	High
Low	Local banks, international community, researchers	Political opponents in the council, citizens, enterprises, environmental, schools, local universities, church
High	ICT industry, standardization bodies, European organizations, central government	Municipality, regional government, local chambers, providers, media

communication of the SC targets to the community had not been performed, in combination with the political opposition and the local digital divide. This time, Smart Trikala followed

1. Project communication with the central government (major ministers visited the case and experienced the offered services).
2. Project communication from the usefulness point of view (e.g., solid waste management opportunities were demonstrated during the project initiation, where a corresponding conference took place in Trikala).
3. The engagement of the commercial chamber as a significant project partner.

The above process succeeded during project start, and stakeholders' trust has been gained with regard to the project potential.

7.3.2 Resource-based motivation

This process enables the project owner to choose the procurement system and the payment methods that will be followed during project implementation. Three separate steps are contained in this process: (1) project coalition's composition; (2) coalition's motivation; and (3) supply chain management. In case the SC is a public project, the owner is the local government that follows the public-procurement system. In case the SC is the outcome of a public–private partnership (PPP), the procurement system's selection is based on (1) who funds the SC project; (2) who is the project deliverables' owner; and (3) what is the coalition form and the corresponding procurement legal framework.

The owner of Smart Trikala is the Municipality of Trikala and the project outcome is being developed under partnerships that develop pilot projects. Each pilot is being authorized by the local council and a memorandum of understanding (MoU) is signed by the partners. The following companies synthesized the coalition of Smart Trikala:

1. Space Hellas S.A.: Installed, parameterized, and integrated sensors, gateways, and access points.
2. Cisco International Limited: Supplied the project with sensors, antennas, access points, and the city management system. Moreover, it played the role of the coalitions' project manager.
3. Kafkas S.A.: Supplied the project with the upgraded street lighting system and with LED lights.
4. SiEBEN: Installed the Wi-Fi logger (Purple), performs the data analytics, and supports the local retailers for their marketing campaigns.
5. ParkGuru: Developed the software and app for parking management.
6. Unixfor S.A: Developed the citizen self-service system.
7. Enstruct: Developed the GIS system.
8. Egritos Group S.A.: Integrated the subsystems with the Municipal-information systems.
9. Cicicom S.A.: Installed LoRa and interconnected waste-bin and water-meter sensors with it. Moreover, it performs data analytics with regard to their performance.
10. Gridnet: Performs data analytics with regard to smart-parking behavior.

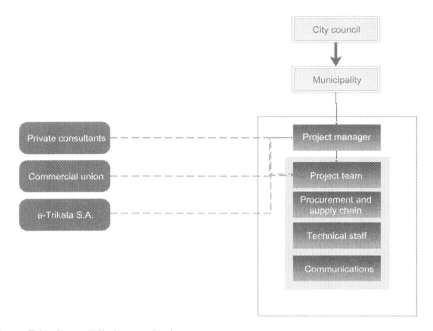

Figure 7.11 Smart Trikala organization.

11. E-Trikala S.A. (municipal company): Installed fiber-optic network that integrated the new access points and gateways with the rest fiber-optic network.

On the other hand, the municipality of Trikala developed the control room and offered its resources for construction activities (e.g., vehicles and human resource), while it operates and maintains the overall system. Moreover, it was the project manager and communications manager of Smart Trikala (Fig. 7.11).

7.3.3 Life-cycle management

This process is being executed by the project manager in an attempt to control the project implementation in terms of budget, time, quality, and risk. The following activities belong to this process: (1) minimize client surprise; (2) problem estimation and solution determination; (3) cost management; (4) time management; (5) quality management; (6) risk management; and (7) communications management. Moreover, project integration and scope management are also involved in this process.

The first question that is asked and has to be answered under this process concerns the definition of project owner, his effectiveness to lead to the project, and his power against the project organization. The municipality of Trikala owns Smart Trikala and was authorized to lead the overall project implementation, as well as to secure the project continuation after its completion. Several contractors had to undertake individual missions that were specified in the MoUs, while only the political opposition in the council was skeptical against the project and performed checking on the municipal authority, but it did not hold enough power to change the SC project.

The second question that has to be asked concerns the project management method that is being followed, in order for the time, scope, risk, quality, and information flow to be secured. Surprises were small during the implementation of Smart Trikala, since the initially grounded objectives were established, with the following exceptions:

1. Smart parking sensors could be installed both sides in the selected zone, since some high-voltage cables were there and affected their measurements.
2. The installation of traffic-congestion cameras was not authorized due to legal conditions.
3. The self-service machine simulated public service execution, since some changes to the legal framework are required to enable their real operation.

Nevertheless, all the above smart services are being offered, while some of them are under testing (self-service machine and smart parking) in order for being optimized and to meet legal framework's requirements. The PMBOK knowledge areas were followed from the project manager and order for the MoU obligations to be respected by all the parties and scope, time, and cost requirements were completely respected. The project timeline was extremely short (Table 7.4) and numerous interdependent project activities were executed (Table 7.5), respectively. The rest of the systems that were planned for the smart-bin and smart-meters, and several analytics were followed; they are still under testing and finalization until the end of 2018, and they are not included in the following tables.

With regard to quality management, only the previously explained (one to three) deliverables did not meet the initially grounded specifications.

The third question that has to be answered under this process is the project operation, maintenance, and continuation. Although the Smart Trikala's lifecycle was short, the project was complex due to the following reasons:

1. Complexity: Several subsystems have to interoperate.
2. Uncertainty: None of the systems had been previously tested in real-city environments.
3. Technological complexity: Different technologies are being followed by different subsystems (e.g., LoRa and Wi-Fi).

Table 7.4 Project timeline and project phases.

	2017			2018		
A: case study analysis						
B: implementation						
C: testing						
D: production						
E: project extension						

Table 7.5 Project activities.

WP/activity	May 2017				June 2017			
	Week 1	Week 2	Week 3	Week 4	Week 1	Week 2	Week 3	Week 4
A: case study analysis								
A.1: on site testing								
A.2: detailed analysis								
B: implementation								
B.1: MoU completion								
B.2: fiber-optic connections								
B.3: network infrastructure								
B.4: parking sensors								
B.5: lighting upgrades								
B.6: environmental sensors								
B.7: purple service launch								
B.8: smart parking app								
B.9: integration with kinetic								
B.10: GIS								
B.11: self-service machine								
B.12: integration with others								
C: pilot								
C.1: applications testing								
C.2: system migration								

MoU, Memorandum of understanding.

4. Legal restrictions: Some of the solutions demand legitimate changes.

The SC operation's and maintenance's planning respected the above complexity sources and gave flexibility for their completion in the requested time frame. For instance, although the parking sensors were installed on time, the corresponding mobile app was launched for testing 4 months later in October 2017, and 6 months later in December 2017, it was under full operation. The citizen self-service machine is still under demo operation.

7.3.4 Project coalition management

This final process deals with the human resource management PMBOK knowledge area and helps the project manager to control human resources via the definition and guidance of the project organization (Anthopoulos, Ipsilantis, & Kazantzi, 2014). Two questions that have to be answered under this process concern the organization schema and the leadership style. The Smart Trikala organization had to do with a PPP agreement, which was signed by more than 10 private companies, the municipal company (e-Trikala), and the Municipality of Trikala. Moreover, the organization involved the local commercial union for the purposes of the open mall. This agreement exceeds the project implementation and includes a significant production period, where the smart services are being offered and evolved.

The organization schema of the project management team was complex, since technical representatives and engineers of all the private partners contributed to the project development, while all of them referred to their employer only and not to the project manager. The project manager simply applied for the project demands to the representatives of the partners, who gave orders to their engaged staff. With regard to the leadership style, the project manager applied a friendly and open style, due to the numerous partners and only during crisis events (deadlines and technical failures) behaved authoritarian.

7.3.5 Discussion—the fringes

Smart Trikala is a representative SC case that was deployed in a typical medium-sized European city that was affected by an extreme fiscal crisis. It shows that a SC can deploy even without extensive funding, but only if it secures a strong political commitment and if it aligns to a clear strategic planning. The case had to utilize the existing ICT facilities and to avoid experiencing similar to the past failures, via meeting the following objectives:

1. *Align with recent ICT policies and deal with recent challenges* (social coherence and climate change)
2. *Support transforming the city to a smart* (in terms of internal operation); *sufficient* (in terms of politics, finance, and food); *resistant* (against political, fiscal, and other types of crisis); *agile* (align to changes easily); and *sustainable* one (in terms of environment, transportation, economy, and planning).

In this regard, the municipality prioritized and met with Smart Trikala the following:

1. Policy making: focus on local needs instead of technology.
2. Citizen first: meet citizen expectations.
3. Usefulness and simplicity: easy to use and solve community's problems.
4. Engagement: design for the people with the people.
5. Secure funding: mainly small projects to be funded by the city; pilot solution testing; and European funding.

Until today, some tangible outcomes of Smart Trikala can be documented:

1. *Stakeholders' engagement:* The municipality collaborates with city's key players (creative activities; open mall; open dialogs and data).
2. *Access to technologies:* Demos such as the self-driving bus (CityMobil2); smart project's deliverables (i.e., the city's monitoring center (control room); the self-service machine for certificate issuing).
3. *Online community:* More than 100 users access the public Wi-Fi on a daily basis, while most local retailers post offers on the virtual open mall.

4. *Creative economy:* More than 200 cultural events and 432 cultural activities take place per annum and more than 20 new-born companies deal with creativity.
5. *ICT professionals:* More than 10 full-time jobs have been created in the municipality for ICT professionals during the last 3 years; more than 10 new robotics academies have installed in the city.
6. *Local business growth:* An amount of 6.3% per annum has been documented, mainly supported by visitors and the touristic activities, which were all strengthened by the local ICT performance.
7. *Municipal debt's decrease:* An amount of €4.2 million per annum has been saved by the municipal spending due to the internal efficiency's upgrade, which was based on the ICT (internal information systems, complaints' registration, and response, etc.)
8. *Energy savings:* The installed LED lights with the accompanied smart controllers that enabled lighting automation have documented over 70% energy savings during their operation (since June 2017); fleet management and GIS have saved over 20% of fuel by the municipal vehicles.
9. *Better digital and cyber-physical infrastructures at city level:* Metro-Wi-Fi has been upgraded and improved its performance; a beacon's network supports visitors' mobility; 48 parking slots are being monitored with sensors and a smart application; more than 50 smart-bins will be installed in the city by early 2018.
10. *Improved municipal services:* Complaints center collects over 50 messages and applications per day, 85% of which concern typical response for street damages, lights' replacement, animal collection, and green issues. The installed center has decreased the municipal response's time from 2 months to up to 7 days. Moreover, the citizens receive instant responses to their claims with regard to the estimated response time, and they can rate the quality of service. The system is being supported by cross-border information systems, which are cloud-based and redundant.
11. *Open data streams:* Today, 38 open data streams have been launched and deliver data to central government's data portal (opendata.gov.gr). The municipality has drafted its open data policy, and the municipal portal will launch by the end of 2017.
12. *Geospatial services:* After more than 10 years of efforts, the city of Trikala has launched its GIS portal and prepares open geospatial information. The system will be fully operational by the end of 2017.
13. *STEM training in schools:* All public schools in the city will be equipped with kits for educational robotics (i.e., Mindstorms, Arduino, and Raspberry). The initiative was launched and supported by the municipality to launch in late 2017 in collaboration with the administrations of education.
14. *Online public consultation:* More than 200 citizens registered their opinions during the first online-deliberation sessions that took place during 2017. This number will be attracted to emerge rapidly with the forthcoming upgraded portal and the participation of the Wi-Fi-based online community, while the updated platform has been launched.
15. *Sustainable mobility:* A network of bicycle lanes of over 6 km has been developed in the city and is going to double its size by 2019. Car avoidance is expected to be encouraged further with the smart parking and smart traffic management services, when drivers will be obliged to pay for parking slots—something that does not happen today.
16. *Environmental monitoring:* A sensor collects and measures several types of emissions in downtown, and corresponding data are stored in the municipal ICT assets.

7.4 Conclusion

The case of Smart Trikala belongs to the "Trikala 2025" strategic planning that envisions a smart, coherent, and resistant city. Its analysis in project management terms returned useful findings from the project-owner perspective. The adopted four processes incorporate all the 10 PMBOK knowledge areas and demonstrated the extensive scope of a representative SC project. Moreover, some remarks deal with the following:

1. This analysis clarifies the project scope and definition. Moreover, details are being provided with regard to the project's schedule, cost, and quality, while information of the ecosystem are collected (stakeholders and their power and organization schema).
2. A SC project is complex in terms of components' plethora, technological demands, and organization. Smart Trikala showed that the service deployment in a typical medium-sized city that addresses four of the SC dimensions, involved more than 10 vendors and technologies that have to be integrated {governance: complaints' registration, citizen self-service machine, and public consultations; economy: open mall; mobility [smart parking and traffic lights monitoring and analytics; and environment (lighting, sensing)]}.
3. A SC project attracts the vendors' interest at multidisciplinary levels. In the case of Smart Trikala, numerous partners collaborated, which mostly belong to the ICT and the construction sectors.
4. A SC project can experience project failures (e.g., in terms of time and quality), regardless the managerial experience of the owner and the engaged developers. Smart Trikala had to launch in an extremely tight 2-month timeline, from highly experienced vendors (e.g., CISCO) in a city with a long "smart" history (Trikala). Nevertheless, innovative technologies that had been not tested before, the particularities of the project site and legal restrictions (e.g., new kinds of parking sensors that were affected by high-voltage waves; citizen self-service machine; congestion management with cameras) affected the on-time completion.

However, Smart Trikala keeps on evolving with numerous components, initiatives, and services. For instance, the 5G pilot that was announced in 2017 is going to launch within 2018; the open data portal has been launched and extends its content; the regional open lab is going to launch and transform to a local innovation hub; while smart cards' use is planned to be encouraged with benefits' allocation to their owners and with accessibility to facilities and services. All this planning goes beyond 2019, while the project aims to attract corresponding investments in an attempt to secure its viability beyond 2025.

One of the most critical parameters to avoid missing the social interest is community's training on ICT skills. In this regard, several campaigns have been launched that concern the following: unemployed free-of-charge training (e.g., TechTalents School), CISCO Academy operation for talents' attraction and staying in Trikala, close collaboration with schools (e.g., STEM support, code competitions hosting), and professional training to commercials, which is planned to be provided by big vendors (e.g., Google and Amazon). It remains to see whether these initiatives will succeed in their mission.

Acknowledgments

Parts of this chapter were included in the proposal that Trikala submitted to the EU Digital Cities Challenge,[16] with which it became a fellow city. Some more evidence were collected under the MSc. Thesis developed by Yannis Koutsikos, under the postgraduate program in project and program management, of the TEI of Thessaly, Greece.

About the author

Dr. Leonidas Anthopoulos is a professor in e-business at the Business School of the University of Thessaly, Greece, and director of the Postgraduate Program in Project and Program Management. Dr. Anthopoulos has extensive research, planning, and management experience with the development and deployment of complex IT projects. Among them, it is worth mentioning the Smart City of Trikala (e-Trikala) and the central web portal for the Hellenic Ministry of Foreign Affairs etc. He is a member of various committees; worth mentioning are the ITU Smart City Focus Group and the United for Smart and Sustainable Cities, associate editor of the IJPADA journal (IGI-GROUP) and editor of book collections. He is the author of numerous articles published in scientific journals, chapter collections, and international conference proceedings. Some of his articles can be found on *ACM Computing Surveys*, *Government Information Quarterly* (Elsevier), *Cities* (Elsevier), *Technological Forecasting and Social Change*, *Information Polity* (IOS Press), *International Journal of Electronic Government Research* (IJEGR), *Transforming Government*, etc. His research interests concern, among others, smart city, e-government, enterprise architecture, strategic management.

References

Anthopoulos, L. (2017). Understanding smart cities—A tool for smart government or an industrial trick? In *Public administration and information technology* (Vol. 22). New York: Springer Science + Business Media. ISBN: 978-3-319-57014-3 (Print) 978-3-319-57015-0 (Online).

---

[16] https://www.digitallytransformyourregion.eu/.

Anthopoulos, L., Gemma, P., Fathy, R. A., & Sang, Z. (2015). *Technical specifications on "Setting the framework for an ICT architecture of a smart sustainable city"*. <https://www.itu.int/en/ITU-T/focusgroups/ssc/Documents/website/web-fg-ssc-0345-r5-ssc_architecture.docx> Retrieved 25.10.18.

Anthopoulos, L., Ipsilantis, P., & Kazantzi, V. (2014). The project management perspective for a digital city. *International Journal of Information Technology Project Management (IJITPM)*, *5*(1), 45−62.

Anthopoulos, L., Janssen, M., & Weerakkody, V. (2016). A unified smart city model (USCM) for smart city conceptualization and benchmarking. *International Journal of E-Government Research (IJEGR)*, *12*(2), 76−92.

Anthopoulos, L., & Tsoukalas, I. A. (2006). The implementation model of a digital city. The case study of the digital city of Trikala, Greece. *Journal of E-Government*, *2*(2), 91−109.

British Standards Institute (BSI). (2016). *Mapping smart city standards: Based on a data flow model*. <https://www.bsigroup.com/LocalFiles/en-GB/smart-cities/resources/BSI-smart-cities-report-Mapping-Smart-City-Standards-UK-EN.pdf> Retrieved 25.10.18.

David, R. F. (2011). *Strategic management (concepts and cases). Global* (13th ed.). Pearson Higher Education.

International Standards Organization (ISO) (2016). Sustainable development in communities. Retrieved from https://www.iso.org/files/live/sites/isoorg/files/archive/pdf/en/iso_37101_sustainable_development_in_communities.pdf.

Ivy, J. (2008). A new higher education marketing mix: The 7Ps for MBA marketing. *International Journal of Educational Management*, *22*(4), 288−299. Available from https://doi.org/10.1108/09513540810875635.

Kaplan, S. R., & Norton, P. D. (1996). *Translating strategy into action. The balanced scorecard* (pp. 8−12). Library of Congress Cataloging-in-Publication Data, 30−32.

Lysons, K., & Farrington, B. (2006). *Purchasing and supply chain management*. Prentice Hall Publishing.

Porter, M. (1996). What is strategy? *Harvard Business Review*. Retrieved from <http://www.ipocongress.ru/download/guide/article/what_is_strategy.pdf>.

Project Management Institute (PMI). (2013). *A guide to the project management body of knowledge*. Atlanta, GA: PMI.

Rafiq, M., & Ahmed, K. P. (1995). Using the 7Ps as a generic marketing mix: An exploratory survey of UK and European marketing academics. *Marketing Intelligence & Planning*, *13*(9), 4−15. Available from https://doi.org/10.1108/02634509510097793.

Winch, G. (2009). *Managing construction projects. An information processing approach*. Oxford, UK: Blackwell Publishing.

Further reading

International Organization for Standardization. (2017). *ISO and smart cities*. <https://www.iso.org/publication/PUB100423.html> Retrieved 25.10.18.

The evolution of smart city policy of Korea

Jae Yong Lee[1] and Ji-in Chang[2]
[1]Smart & Green City Research Center, Korea Research Institute for Human Settlements, Sejong City, Korea, [2]Graduate School of Smart City Science Management, Hongik University, Sejong City, Korea

Chapter Outline

8.1 Introduction   173
8.2 Background   175
8.3 Research methodology: a case study   176
    8.3.1 Scope   177
    8.3.2 Integration   179
    8.3.3 Organization   181
    8.3.4 Time   184
    8.3.5 Cost   186
    8.3.6 Quality   187
    8.3.7 Risks   188
    8.3.8 Procurement   188
    8.3.9 Discussion—the fringes   189
8.4 Conclusion   192
Acknowledgment   192
About the authors   192
References   193

8.1 Introduction

The smart city has become a new megatrend in urban policy worldwide. Since the inauguration of President Moon's government in 2017, smart city has emerged as an important focus of attention in Korea. On January 29, 2018, the Korean government announced its new smart city implementation strategy across all ministries of the government. The decision for this 5-year project was announced by the Presidential Committee on the Fourth Industrial Revolution, composed of 30 members from the private and public sector with the mission of harnessing cutting-edge technology to achieve economic growth. The smart city implementation plan is distinctly different from the smart city implementation strategy pursued since the 2000s in Korea, as it has incorporated important aspects of international smart city discourse since the 2010s. This presents a new opportunity to reinvent the smart city in Korea. For the newly formulated smart city strategy to be successful, it is necessary to review the history of the smart city in Korea and to reevaluate the performance and the limitations so far.

Since the early 2000s, the smart city was regarded as an engine for future growth of Korea. Ambitious plans to make urban management more efficient through the use of information and communication technology (ICT) garnered national and international attention. In 2003, the smart city was conceptualized as a viable commercial venture for the first time when urban service solutions, such as the bus information system, integrated traffic control center, CCTV for crime prevention, were implemented in Hwaseong–Dongtan New Town, located about 30 km to the south of Seoul. However, after the initial aggressive building of infrastructure using cutting-edge technology and the provision of service solutions, there has been hardly any major progress in substance since then in Korea. In contrast, both economically developed and developing countries in the world have adopted the smart city as a new paradigm on which their national agenda is based. In recent years, as the fourth industrial revolution is gaining recognition as a new megatrend, interest in smart cities has increased exponentially.

Even though numerous smart cities are constructed and are being discussed, the concept of the smart city is still subject to numerous interpretations. Scholars and experts on smart cities have not been able to agree on the most basic concepts and constituting elements, even while it continues to evolve rapidly with each day. This failure to come to an agreement at the conceptual level has become an obstacle at the implementation level.

Currently, the smart city concept varies depending on economic conditions and policies adopted by different countries at national, regional, and municipal levels. This is probably because the smart city concept did not originate from one distinct country or one small group of scholars. The smart city was conceptualized and developed from specific needs of different countries and cities. For example, for European countries, the smart city was discussed in terms of sustainable development, and therefore, the smart city concept is defined broadly. In other words, the concept incorporates not only an ICT-based approach but also encompasses the political, economic, social, and cultural aspects of sustainability. In contrast, the smart city in Korea began as a ubiquitous city (hereafter called U-City) which originated from the idea of providing smart solutions based on cutting-edge ICT and, therefore, was defined with some specificity.

It is difficult to argue for or against defining the smart city either broadly or specifically because each definition has advantages and disadvantages. If a broad definition is adopted, the advantage is that the overall characteristics of the city are considered and comprehensive projects become possible. However, the characteristics of smart city become ambiguous, and project implementation can become difficult. If a specific definition is adopted, smart city projects can be implemented relatively easily in short term, but the effect can be limited to specific projects. Smart city values can be difficult to realize in the long term.

For this reason, this chapter looks back on the causes for the creation of the smart city in Korea and the environmental changes in the course of its evolution. In the case of Korea, the central government plays a much greater role than individual local governments or the private sector in the implementation of smart cities. Instead of choosing one particular city, this chapter looks into the overall changes of the Korean government's smart city policy and discusses the accomplishments, limitations, and ways of overcoming the challenges. At the end of the chapter, future directions for the smart city will be discussed.

8.2 Background

The "U-City" was a brand name adopted for the Korean smart city to build the initial infrastructure and to pursue technology-oriented policies. The U-City was a concept based on advanced infrastructure, construction, and technology that gradually expanded to incorporate governance and innovation as well. These changes eventually resulted in the revision of the "U-City Act" in 2018, at which time the term "U-City" was legally abandoned after 17 years since its conception.

Smart cities were implemented in Korea in the early 2000s, even before smart cities became the subject of interest internationally. There were three major changes in Korea's smart city policy since 2003. The first occurred between 2003 and 2013 and can be characterized as "the construction stage," which involved the building of smart city infrastructure and operating smart services. During this period in 2008, "Act on the Construction etc. Of Ubiquitous Cities" (hereafter referred to as U-City Act) was enacted. It focused on ICT applied to new city and town development. The second change, which can be called "the connecting stage," occurred between 2014 and 2016. During this period, the focus was on connecting smart city services and building governance structure. The third and current "enhancement stage" is planned for the period from 2017 to 2020. It focuses on innovating smart city and creating a smart city ecology.

Korea's pursuit of the U-City strategy was based on domestic circumstances at that time and thus is distinguished from the international discourse revolving around global environmental problems and problem seeking. At the beginning of the 2010s, the Korean government was looking for ways to utilize an oversupply of high-speed internet networks crisscrossing the country. The timing coincided with the government's plan to construct numerous new towns in the capital region as well as numerous innovation cities throughout the nation under the banner of balanced economic development. As more than 20 new towns were to be built within a relatively short time throughout Korea, it seemed only logical to incorporate the existing internet networks as an integral part of the new towns in order to achieve more effective urban management. The government instituted policies encouraging new towns to incorporate cutting-edge technology in urban infrastructure, notably in transportation and safety/security sectors. The high-tech infrastructure was financed by profits gained through real estate development in new cities.

From 2014 onward, the Korean government has sought to integrate previously independent operating services and systems, such as public transportation, crime prevention, infrastructure management, into one smart city platform. It has actively encouraged cities throughout the country to establish smart city platforms through financial incentives and technical support. By bringing separately provided services into one integrated system, the possibility of connecting disparate services has opened new horizons. For example, CCTV originally installed solely for traffic management purpose can now be used in multiple ways, such as crime prevention and catching tax evaders by tracking their license plate number.

From 2016 onward, the Korean smart city concept is being reconstructed to actively accommodate relevant perspectives and viewpoints originating from Europe and the United States. In addition to technological aspects, there is a national consensus in Korea that a smart city needs to provide space for innovative job creation as well as provide efficient solutions for urban problems. Strategies to meet these new goals are currently being formulated.

Regarding policy, there was a comprehensive review of legislation concerning Korea's smart city in 2016. The "U-City Act" was revised to the "Smart City Act." The formal name has been changed from "Act on the Construction etc. Of Ubiquitous Cities" to "Smart City Construction and Industrial Vitalization Act." The purpose was to allow a greater number of participants from more diverse fields of specialization to participate in smart city projects. The name and some content of legislation were amended to readjust the focus from smart city construction not only to smart city management/operation but also to the cultivation of new innovative industries. In particular, there have been active attempts to create a smart city that incorporates greater socio-environmental aspects than previously realized in Korea.

Regarding fostering new industries, Sejong City and Busan have been selected as nationally designated urban pilot cities in 2018, making them recipients of concentrated investments in cutting-edge technology and infrastructure. Another benefit is the institution of a "legislative sandbox" in these cities, freeing industries to implement projects from previously restrictive regulations. Institutional support measures, such as special exemption laws for industries, more liberal location requirements, and financial support packages, are being prepared in order to stimulate participation by private companies. Through these measures, Sejong City and Busan have gained the exclusive privilege to implement and test cutting-edge technologies, such as self-driving cars and drones. Compared to other Korean cities, these two cities are now able to build new foundations for future urban technologies.

The implementation of smart city technology in Korea is freed of limitations to newly built cities. Deteriorating older cities and city centers are being transformed into smart environments that enable citizens to participate in finding solutions to urban problems. Compared to earlier practices in Korea, smart city policies are being implemented that reflect local context and characteristics. This two-pronged approach is expected to bring benefits to older cities which were excluded from smart city policies in the past.

8.3 Research methodology: a case study

This section looks at the evolution of U-City to smart city policies of the Korean government and does not focus on one city. As Korea's cities were generally built according to what can be described as "one-model-fits-all" process, most U-Cities share more commonalities than differences. It gives an overview that describes the interrelation and integration of service organization and governance strategy, strategic implementation to set up the smart city ecology.

8.3.1 Scope

The U-City concept did not make a sudden appearance. As Table 8.1 shows, there were numerous ICT projects underway in Korea before the U-City made its first appearance. In fact, the beginnings of the U-City can be traced to the increased use of geographic information. In order to use large amounts of newly created information, the government began to build information systems. As more institutions began to access these systems for management of building facilities, the government implemented "ubiquitous computing," which can be described as an early version of the current internet of things (IoT) network. With this development, the U-City began to be discussed seriously.

The early 2000s was a time in Korea when the Second National High-Speed Communication Network Installation Project was completed, and GIS projects laid the foundation for better management of urban facilities through better access to location-based information. At that time, numerous massive construction projects were starting or were about to start. The Korean government was masterminding the construction of these second-generation new cities, which were mostly

Table 8.1 Smart city policy—related policy before U-City.

	Background	Major characteristics
National GIS established (1995—)	Need for national geographic information highlighted by a succession of underground gas explosions on subway construction site in Seoul (1994) and Daegu (1995)	Focused on the distribution and use of information. Municipalities create their own geographic information databases. Information management system followed by widespread use of GIS in the public sector
	UIS established due to greater use of geographic information	
UIS established (2000—)	Increased demand for location information of underground infrastructures, such as electricity, gas, telecommunication	Detailed and comprehensive GIS developed to locate and manage underground pipes and ducts so as to prevent fire, explosion, gas leakage, etc.
	The beginnings of U-City appear	
IT839 Strategy (2004)	Implementation of ubiquitous city concepts and the increased demand for a strategic approach to U-City	As IT began to be part of everyday life, the government proposes a national future vision where ICT creates added value to society
	Drawing up of U-Korea Master Plan	

GIS, Geographic information system; *UIS*, Urban Information System; *ICT*, information and communication technology.

concentrated in the capital region. Whereas the first-generation new cities in the 1980s were built primarily to provide much-needed housing, potential residents of the second-generation new cities demanded the city to be designed for higher living conditions. In order to provide greater convenience for future residents, innovative urban development methods were required. One of these innovations was the incorporation of ICT in urban planning. At the same time, under the banner of nationwide balanced development, newly built cities, such as innovation cities and Sejong New Administrative City, were planned all over the Korean peninsula. As the construction of high-tech infrastructure was relatively easy to incorporate in new city development, all 56 new cities slated for development were designated as U-Cities.

The early conceptualization of the U-City involved collecting information regarding urban infrastructure and facilities which would eventually evolve into a comprehensive urban management system. In other words, the system would be set up to manage underground infrastructure at the beginning, but its scope would be expanded to include all urban infrastructure in a city. This becomes evident in the legal definition of the U-City. In the definition, urban infrastructure is combined with the ubiquitous technology. This information is managed and utilized using an information platform called an Integrated Operation Control Center (IOCC) (Fig. 8.1).

This concept was much broader than just managing underground infrastructure by grafting ICT on building construction. In order to proceed with urban planning as well as building high-tech facilities and systems, the existing legislative structure with separate laws and regulations for ICT and building construction was difficult to circumnavigate. Red tape encompassing numerous laws concerning disparate fields, such as ICT, real estate, urban planning, and new city development construction, was almost insurmountable in terms of time and substance, if dealt on an

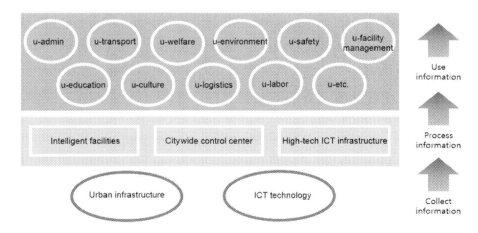

Figure 8.1 Korea's U-City concept.
(Ministry of Land, Transport and Maritime Affairs. (2008). *The first ubiquitous comprehensive plan: 2009–2013*. Seoul, Korea: Ministry of Land, Transport and Maritime Affairs. (In Korean); adapted by Ji-in Chang)

individual basis. Not only were there procedural problems, but there were difficulties incorporating the new concept of U-City and U-City infrastructure within the existing legislative framework. In addition, as U-City construction had already started in 38 areas in Korea, such as Hwaseong−Dongtan, Yongin, Pyeongtaek, Paju, Seongnam, and Suwon, the legal basis for these projects needed to be urgently provided. Considering all these factors, the Korean government judged that it would be more efficient to bring the planning, development, management, and operation of U-Cities under one comprehensive legislation. Thus the U-City Act was enacted in 2008.

In the early implementation stage, the role of the central government was to establish a legal system, to support local government projects, and to provide technology and manpower, while the role of the local government was to build and manage smart cities (Fig. 8.2). Local governments in Korea have been conservative in introducing new technologies due to their concerns about possible budget waste and desire to minimize trial and error. Therefore in this context, Korea's central government adopted the approach where they initiated pilot projects to support local governments in finance, administration, and technology and promoted their success stories after implementation. Currently, many local governments are developing their own ecosystems, because a positive consensus on smart cities has been reached.

8.3.2 Integration

The U-City Act was the first of its kind worldwide. As can be discerned by its official name, the focus was on construction. Its focus was on providing a procedure for the construction of U-Cities. Korea's U-City Act delineates the process and provides a model for financing urban infrastructure needed to create a smart city. In the case of "cities built from scratch," development profit was restituted in order to finance urban infrastructures, such as roads, parks, and other amenities. The U-City Act mandated that U-City urban infrastructure is considered as part of urban infrastructure, thus qualifying it for urban infrastructure financing. According to the U-City Act, U-City infrastructure includes intelligent facilities, ICT infrastructure, and IOCCs among others. The "National Land Planning and Using Act" provided a connecting bridge between the existing urban planning system and the newly created U-City planning system. When looking at the definition of intelligent facility, the "National Land Planning and Using Act" specifies U-City infrastructure to be any public facility of construction and ICT convergence. This includes facilities related to traffic, emergency, health and welfare, environment, logistics, culture, and space among others.

After the U-City Act took effect, U-City districts were typically located at the center of newly built cities. The construction cost for the aforementioned U-City infrastructure, which generally includes intelligent facilities, ICT infrastructure, IOCCs, depends on the size of the district in which they are located, but on average ranged between US$372 million and US$558 million (40 billion won and 60 billion won), which only amount to 1%−3% of the total new city construction cost.

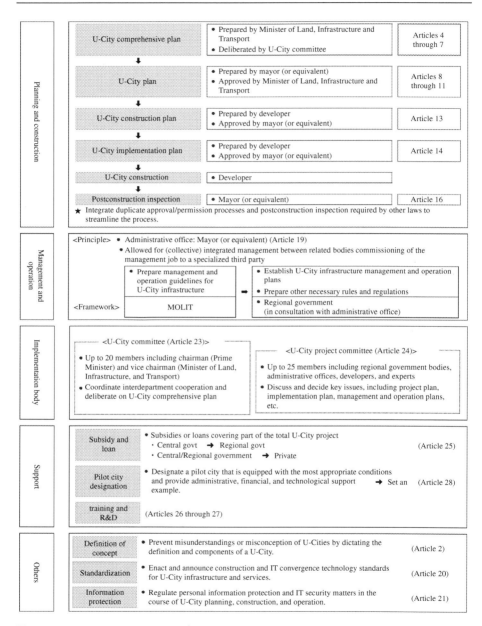

Figure 8.2 The legal framework for U-City construction.
(Shin, D. (2013). *A primer on Korean planning and policy: Smart city. PKPP 2013-11.* Korea Research Institute of Housing Settlements (KRIHS)) (Shin, 2013)

The evolution of smart city policy of Korea   181

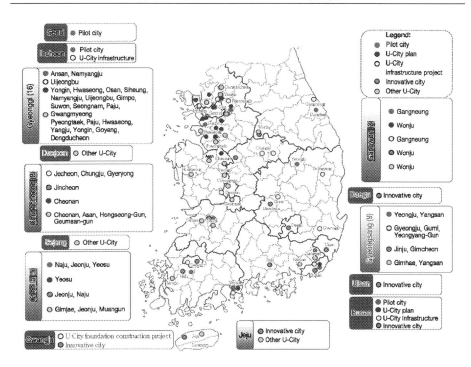

Figure 8.3 U-Cities in 2012.
(Shin, D. (2013). *A primer on Korean planning and policy: Smart city. PKPP 2013-11.*
Korea Research Institute of Housing Settlements (KRIHS)) (Shin, 2013)

As this model of financing, U-City infrastructure allowed construction without additional support from the national or local government, all newly built cities which met required conditions took advantage of the opportunity to become a U-City. In this way, the number of smart cities multiplied at a much faster rate in Korea compared to overseas. From the private developer's point of view, developing a U-City at only 1%–3% greater cost compared to existing practices presented an attractive option. Thus the national government, the local government, and the private sector all came to participate actively in the construction of U-Cities in Korea.

The number of U-Cities in Korea increased more rapidly than anywhere else in the world. In less than 4 years after the enactment of the U-City Act, 50 cities and counties, which is almost one-third of all 163 cities and counties in Korea, had implemented some form of the U-City project by 2012 (see Fig. 8.3).

8.3.3 Organization

According to the initial U-City legal framework, cooperation among various government agencies and departments was assumed. However, there are limitations that needed to be overcome. Providing interconnected services by new combinations of already existing information and systems was a new exciting development in terms of creating a low-cost high-efficiency service solution. However, even though it was a relatively easy concept theoretically and technically, there were several obstacles to overcome to implement it in real life. Ironically, the clearly defined subdivisions and distinct roles of Korea's government organizations and institutions, which had been instrumental in the Korean economy's rapid and productive development since the 1970s, acted as barriers in the age of economic growth through a convergence of diverse functions in the 2000s.

In order for interconnected services to function effectively, collaboration among relevant government departments is essential. For example, the effect of a truly interconnected fire emergency service would compensate by many times the cost of investment incurred. However, institutionally, safety and transportation services are under the jurisdiction of the police department, while facility management and administrative services are provided by local government. In addition, health-care and welfare services are administered by hospitals. Cooperation and collaboration among independent departments are absolutely required for interconnected services to operate effectively, but there are real difficulties with this. Furthermore, in cases of security CCTVs and administrative services, there are legal aspects, such as regulation regarding personal privacy, that need to be resolved. For these reasons, despite discussions of innovative ideas and scenarios which may be highly effective, it would take much time and effort for it to be implemented.

In terms of interconnected services which are beyond the scenario stage, progress has been made concerning the interconnection of information systems and increasing cooperation between relevant departments and institutions. Specifically, regarding fire emergency services, legal and governance problems needed to be resolved for live video of ongoing fires captured by CCTV cameras to be shared with the relevant fire station. First, concerning legal restrictions, as security CCTV is closely associated with individual privacy, it was illegal to share CCTV videos with other institutions. Also, only authorized persons were allowed to monitor CCTVs. Without resolution of these legal barriers, it was impossible to provide interconnected services. Therefore the institutional modifications allowing for "information to be transmitted to relevant organizations in case of emergency" resolved this issue. Only after the National Emergency Management Agency and Ministry of Land, Infrastructure, and Transport (MLIT) had signed an MOU to build collaborative governance between themselves was it possible to share services. Currently, MLIT is working on providing services and supporting local government in building up interconnected services through IOCCs. At the same time, it is working on improving and pursuing MOUs with relevant institutions so that these interconnected services can expand through these platforms.

Due to the barriers described above, urban integrated platforms and interconnected services are currently confined to five major areas where smart city services are provided in support of relevant authorities (Table 8.2). Even though interconnected services provide high efficiency at low cost as they increase in diversity, governance and legislative problems tend to increase with each interconnection. The Korean government is currently working on improving the institutional

Table 8.2 The smart city urban-integrated platform and interconnected services.

Socially disadvantaged	112 emergency videos (fire station)	112 emergency fire dispatch	119 emergency dispatch (rescue center)	Emergency quick reaction force
In case of an emergency involving children and patients with dementia, IOCC, based on in-location information received from telecommunication companies ascertains the exact position through CCTVs and transmits the information to police or fire department	In case of reports of kidnaping, robbery, and assault, IOCC transmits real-time videos to police	In the case of hit-and-run accidents, IOCC provides police with videos at the time of the accident and any information on escape routes taken by suspect's car, etc.	In case of fire, rescue, and first-aid, IOCC provides fire department with real-time video and traffic information crucial to helping within the "golden hour"	In case of major national disaster and catastrophe, IOCC provides videos for rapid assessment and transmission, recovery, relief, etc.

IOCC, Integrated Operation Control Center.

framework, and awareness of the many benefits accruing to collaboration among disparate organizations is increasing. For these reasons, the future outlook for interconnected services seems positive.

8.3.4 Time

Policy changes and implementation from 2008 to 2010 have been described already in the sections above. Policy changes and implementation from 2003 to 2017 are shown in Fig. 8.4.

After 2010, the U-City business model had come under increasingly sharp criticism domestically. Due to Korea's urban policy changes, U-City projects were rapidly declining. It was in contrast to the active discussions on smart cities starting worldwide. With 2013 as the turning point, countries expanded their national funding for building smart cities. In Korea, the smart city was considered as providing a low-cost, high-efficiency alternative to U-Cities, but there were no serious deliberations on large-scale investment.

However, the new government led by President Moon Jae-in included the smart city as part of the national agenda in 2017. Consequently, the scope of smart city policy was greatly expanded. International discussion issues were introduced into Korean discourse and diverse policy tools were considered with renewed interest. Just the year before, in 2016, the fourth industrial revolution had been at the forefront of discussions in Davos Forum, with smart cities regarded as promising engines of economic growth.

As mentioned earlier, the smart city was constructed in the 2000s to make urban management more efficient through the creation of high-tech infrastructure. The

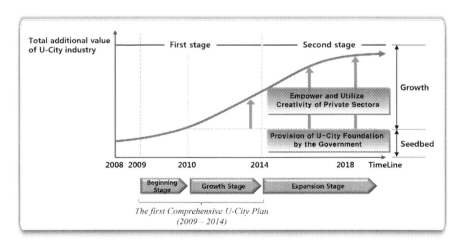

Figure 8.4 Timeline of U-City.
(Lee, J. Y. (2012). Implementation of the smart city in Korea. In *Presentation at National World Habitat Day 2012*) (Lee, 2012)

Smart City Concept in Korea

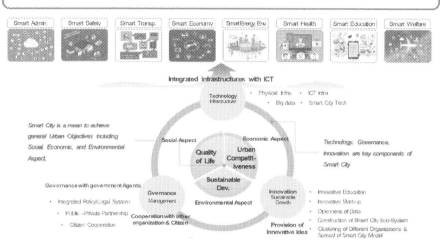

Figure 8.5 The smart city concept.
(Lee, J. Y. (2018). *Catalyzing the evolution of ICT based growth ecosystems in cities.* Korea Research Institute of Housing Settlements (KRIHS)) (Lee, 2018).

important keyword at this time was "construction," and the main goal was to realize convergence between city construction and ICT. At this time, separate institutional and organizational systems were restructured to accept convergence of different technologies and infrastructures. With the international discourse of the fourth industrial revolution, the focus has shifted to innovative job creation. One of the important new objectives of the smart city under Korea's new president has become the creation of space enabling this innovative job creation.

The smart city concept has greatly expanded due to domestic changes and expectations of meeting global standard of the smart city. The legal definition of the U-City, based on combining urban infrastructure with ICT, has been revealed through trial and error to be restrictive in regards to creating a truly successful comprehensive model of the smart city. Only when the convergence of institutions and governance is realized can smart city management and operation function effectively. With the advent of the fourth industrial revolution, innovative job creation has become part of smart city's requirements. Fig. 8.5 shows the expansion of the smart city concept.

The effort to expand the concept of the smart city began with the revision and renaming of the "U-City Act" to "Smart City Act." As the renaming clearly indicates, it is not simply modifying the terminology but redirecting the focus from technology and infrastructure to institutions and governance. In addition, Korea's smart city vision has been narrowed down to efficient urban problem-solving and creation of innovative jobs. This new reformulation of the vision and goals is connected to detailed strategic plans.

8.3.5 Cost

The cost of smart city construction can be divided into categories. Generally, there is the new city development model in which the smart city infrastructure financing is built-in. Another source of financing is to use the national government budget. The construction of a new smart city is mainly financed through funds utilizing the development profit. Depending on the size of the development project, a stable budget of 50 billion won to 60 billion won (about 44.3−53.1 million USD) per project area covers the initial construction cost. In contrast, in the case of urban regeneration projects, the central government secures a welfare budget for new smart infrastructure deemed necessary to solve problems related to cities experiencing urban decline. More specifically, the central government selects five local government projects each year and provides each one with financial support exceeding 3 billion won (about 2.7 million USD). In some cases, private funding in the form of BTL (build−transfer−lease) is implemented.

This section discusses models for funding smart city construction cost from various angles. While the strategy of securing reliable financing based on development profits of new cities has greatly contributed in the building of high-tech infrastructure and increasing the number of U-Cities in Korea, it has also brought with it numerous limitations. The greatest limitation is that new cities were favored above existing cities due to the ease of financing. The limitations are as follows:

First, there was a lack of clear vision and objectives in pursuing the U-City strategy. As described above, the beginning of the U-City can be ascribed to the confluence of two major factors in the early 2000s: the completion of a nationwide high-speed information network construction project and the start of a national construction plan to build new cities. Korea's high competitiveness in construction and information technology contributed to a vague expectation that their convergence would create new industries and lead to higher quality of life for the people by providing solutions to urban problems. After almost 15 years, the general consensus is that the U-City fell short of delivering satisfactory results. Instead of creating new industries, the construction of U-Cities was unable to expand beyond increasing the supply of high-end apartment complexes. While urban problems are concentrated in existing cities, information technology services were concentrated in well planned new cities with relatively few urban problems. Without specific goals based on a vague vision, policies that were implemented proved inadequate to demonstrate substantive results.

Second, there was no financial model for existing cities, where urban problems usually occur, and thus U-City services could not be extended beyond newly built cities to old city centers. There was no differentiated service model which recognized the distinct characteristics of different cities. Also, there was no development of services which allowed the participation of citizens and the private sector to find solutions for urban problems based on diversity of ideas. In fact, in the case of new cities, there was no distinct identity accrued over time and no residents living in them at the time of construction that warranted a distinct participatory model for development. For reasons of cost reduction, a "one-model-fits-all" approach has been adopted that centered on a menu of standardized services, such as transportation and security.

Third, U-City projects were focused on the actors involved in the implementation. In most cases, public corporations were responsible for the construction of U-Cities. For this reason, the private sector was sidelined, which prevented new injection of ideas and procedures into the system. In other words, instead of producing a new ecology which may have evolved into creating a virtuous cycle of service innovations and new industries, U-City construction followed a formula centered on limited solutions. Overall, this prevented the sustained evolution of U-Cities beyond the stage of early implementation.

Fourth, U-City is subject to new city construction. Without the construction of new cities, U-Cities were unable to secure financing. When government policy changed its course to favor urban regeneration over building new cities, U-City projects could no longer be pursued.

After the transformation of the "U-City Act" into "Smart City Act," however, the smart city is being touted again as a low-cost, high-efficiency solution for urban problems. The domestic smart city policy has two clear goals. The low-cost and high-efficiency aspect of urban problem-solving is accomplished by using information communication technology to provide useful information in real time to relevant actors. In this respect, the approach to the problem-solving for smart city can be thought of as diagnosing the exact problem, identifying the most effective solution, deriving objective performance criteria for reviewing effectiveness, and supporting the diffusion of excellent solutions.

8.3.6 Quality

Since 2010, smart city has been attracting domestic and international attention because it was the most efficient model to solve urban problems in the foreseeable future. Most notably, European countries have introduced strategies to solve urban problems, such as increasing citizen participation, introducing living labs, quantifying and accumulating problem-solving achievements, identifying and disseminating successful solutions based on intercity networks, and diversifying financing models that serve as benchmarks for Korea's new approach to smart cities.

First, citizens' participation and living labs are based on the idea that problems of a city are best known by the citizens who live there. Also, the success of a smart city is determined by the level of the citizens. At present, citizen participation is essential for the promotion of smart city, and there is a consensus that the living lab is the most effective model to implement it.

Second, quantification and accumulation of problem-solving achievements were also important factors of the smart city. Because the smart city approach to addressing urban problems has never been possible before, it is difficult to be certain how effective each individual solution will be. Therefore it is imperative to present quantitative results (15% reduction of traffic congestion within 3 years, 10% reduction in energy consumption within 3 years) and monitoring them during the initial project.

Third, the identification and diffusion of successful solutions based on intercity networks are also important for smart cities to solve urban problems. It is impossible to introduce and test all the solutions in one city. Therefore if the solution introduced in each city is integrated and monitored through the intercity network, successful urban solutions can be shared through the intercity network to contribute to overall success.

Fourth, the greatest problem in finding solutions to urban problems in the declining urban areas is the financing scheme. In the case of providing public services in declining cities, profit generation becomes a problem. This is the reason why these services rely on government funding, but there is a limit to government support. Therefore it is necessary to search for new financing methods, such as citizen crowdfunding and make efforts to find efficient solutions against investment cost.

8.3.7 Risks

The smart city is a new model that has only recently been developed. For this reason, the risk is high. In contrast, focusing on risk factors will hinder innovation, and thus mechanisms to overcome these problems need to be discussed. In Korea, the government first tests and verifies new technology before proceeding with widespread implementation. Almost all municipalities in Korea have an integrated operation center. Relatively speaking, the infrastructure of smart cities in Korea is cutting edge. This means that the next concern is to create services for the more efficient use of existing infrastructure. One major problem for Korean cities is that their management and operating expenses are high because the infrastructure is not built gradually but provided at once by the national government.

The validity of the European model in the Korean context needs to be tested. For example, Seoul Hanok Village, a district consisting of traditional Korean style houses, can be called European style in its implementation. The Seoul Metropolitan Government provides telecommunication facilities for the area or short-range wireless network, while the remaining private companies select ideas and participate in the process. It began with smart services for parking lots and garbage cans. This model does not apply in the areas where the existing urban infrastructure upgrade has been done. In new cities, the high-tech infrastructure is there, and it is a matter of connecting different parts together. The smart city needs to be viewed comprehensively; urban solutions should not be limited to one zone. In new cities, new infrastructure can be laid with much less money than in existing cities. The biggest problem in providing smart solutions in old cities concerns land. It is, therefore, important to make policy connections.

8.3.8 Procurement

So far, Korea's smart cities are supported by the national government, at the same time as development, with testbed evaluation of technology that has mainly undergone with some contents concerning cooperation with the private sector. Previously, the U-City Act covered only residential land development projects. An important issue in the U-City Act was the size of land of 1.65 million m^2. Any U-City on a lesser scale than 1.65 million m^2 was ineligible for national government support. The advantage of this financing model was that the cost of constructing U-City could be recovered by selling housing to new residents. After the infrastructure was built, Korea Land & Housing Corporation (LH) handed the smart city over to the local government. The management of the infrastructure became the responsibility of the local government. The private sector became involved after the government laid out the masterplan by providing services. The problem with this model is that without large-scale residential development projects, financing becomes difficult. Also, since the most preferred public services are crime prevention and traffic management, the government provided a set menu of smart city services, leading to cookie-cutter cities throughout Korea.

When applying smart city solutions to existing cities, citizen participation becomes natural because it is necessary to have a dialogue with citizens and gain consensus. Cooperation with private companies becomes necessary. Business is promoted with private corporate money. BTO (build–transfer–operate) and BTL methods are used when it is difficult to raise funds early in a large project. In the case of BTL, it is long-term repayment model. BTL projects are also being carried out in Ansan and Gwangju in Gyeonggi Province. There are many requests for the expansion of crime prevention CCTV. Not only security CCTV equipment but also the underground infrastructure needs to be constructed. The cost amounts to about 110 billion won, which is difficult for the municipality to secure. The municipality can then make plans for a 10- or 30-year repayment model. The BTO method of financing is often used in tunnels. It is a way to cover business expenses while building and operating.

8.3.9 Discussion—the fringes

The reason why the smart city is receiving worldwide attention since 2010 is that it is perceived to present the most effective model to counter urban problems in the future. Internationally, cities are deploying different strategies, such as greater participation of citizens, living labs, monitoring the management of performance using empirical data, finding solutions through cooperation between cities, among others.

Recently, Korea's smart city policy has taken a new direction. The new smart city policy is engaging with urban problems in the existing cities while incorporating policies from abroad. The biggest problem in Korea's past U-City policy has been a record of trial and error, which arose from a mismatch of goals, means, and target locations. Measures to correct this problem require distinguishing between different types of smart cities (Table 8.3). Taking a mid to long-term perspective, the new smart policy strives to create a city that can simultaneously provide solutions to urban problems and create jobs. However, in the early stage of the smart city, identifying and adopting appropriate

Table 8.3 Different types and goals of the smart city.

Type	Goal	Key element	Method	Target area
Problem-solving smart city	Low-cost, high-efficiency solutions for urban problems	Exploring urban problems and solutions based on citizen participation	– Living Lab based on citizen participation – Problem-oriented quantitative performance criteria and measures – Sharing performance through city networks – Individual solutions capable of problem solutions and matching	City centers and declining areas with urban problems
Opportunity-creating smart city	Creation of innovative new industries	Creation of industries based on innovative ideas and data	– Liberalizing regulation, i.e., a legislative sandbox – Creating industries taking into account product value – Creating a global market using a global network – Establishing information communication infrastructures based on an integrated open data platform	New city suited to construct high-tech infrastructure and new spaces

measures is necessary. Also, the tools are also very different depending on the goals that the smart city intends to achieve.

In order to create innovative jobs, it is necessary to understand the characteristics of industries in the fourth industrial revolution. Already, the physical space and virtual space is being connected based on information. In many cases, the newly created jobs will not be totally new but will involve the connecting and converging of existing industries through ICT. These industries will probably be characterized by short life cycles. Instead of expending much time inventing new industries, convergence enables new industries to be created within a short time frame. In terms of variety of new industries created, convergence can be applied to all industries without any perceivable limits. Today's industries can be described as Lego blocks. If existing industries are Lego blocks, the combination of these blocks is unlimited. In other words, sustained creation is possible as long as new ideas exist. Therefore the appearance of new industries is almost unpredictable as new ones are created at lightning speed.

The role of the government in this scenario is to provide an environment in which new industries can be created. The characteristics of convergence will require a very different industrial structure than the existing one which is based on mass production. For this reason, regulations and structural management based on traditional industries need to be reviewed to eliminate barriers and stumbling blocks. In other words, it is important for smart cities to implement programs to liberalize legislation, establish open data policy to increase citizen participation, development of citizen-led models, setting up global networks to facilitate market shares overseas.

Regarding the goal of making a smart city for opportunity creation, the industrial characteristics of the fourth industrial revolution era need to be understood in order to nurture a new industry. The characteristics of the fourth Industrial Revolution era features a linkage of virtual space and physical space, rapidly changing technology, the horizontal integration of individual industries, a start-up based on innovative ideas and data. The fourth Industrial Revolution era will have a structure that cannot be supported by the existing system. However, in terms of linking virtual space and physical space, it is the city where people, data and innovative ideas are concentrated. The problem is that the most regulated space is also the city. Therefore it is impossible to experiment using the city as a target space. A regulatory sandbox in which legislative restrictions are suspended for a certain period is required where new industries can be tested.

A data platform that enables free data sharing and data integration is also an essential part of creating innovative workplace creation because new industries are created based on data and innovative ideas. With open data, horizontal integration between previously separated industries can create new industries. In this process, cooperation among various private sector companies becomes important. In order to secure new markets, linking smart cities are also necessary for the sustainability of the industry.

8.4 Conclusion

Through the early construction of U-City, Korea attracted international attention by challenging the practice of city management based on ICT. However, construction-oriented policies targeting only new cities were promoted, and it became increasingly alienated from the global smart city debate since 2010. However, the smart city in Korea has begun accepting various models which have been discussed abroad, and smart city promotion is getting a new start.

In 2003, Korea pursued a national policy of building ubiquitous cities from scratch or retrofitting existing city infrastructure with high technology. As "a built environment where any citizen can get any services, anywhere and anytime through ICT devices to improve the citizens' quality of life and city competitiveness" (Ministry of Land, Transport and Maritime Affairs, 2008, 3), the U-City incorporated the goals of efficiency and economy through the use of technology. Sejong, the new administrative capital of Korea, and Songdo district in Incheon are well-known U-City cases. Even though the Korean government had a head start with its own brand, "U-City" was regarded as being too focused on technology and the term was abandoned in 2016 in favor of a more universally accepted "smart city." The smart city was thought to incorporate a stronger social dimension as shown in the EU's definition, "a smart city is a city seeking to address public issues via ICT-based solutions on the basis of multistakeholders, municipality-based partnership" (European Parliament, 2014, 9).

Thus in the foreseeable future, smart city policies are expected to focus on solving urban problems that people face in existing cities and on fostering high-tech new industries through regulatory sandbox policies. These are already being implemented in Busan Eco Delta City and Sejong 5-1 District. At the same time, the government is busily laying a solid foundation for the development of new high-tech industries. Programs are being developed through various R&D projects and living labs to tackle social problems and sustainability issues.

Acknowledgment

This research was supported by a grant (18AUDP-B070726-06) from Architecture & Urban Development Research Program funded by Ministry of Land, Infrastructure and Transport of Korean government.

About the authors

Jae Yong Lee is Director of Smart & Green City Research Center of the Korea Research Institute for Human Settlements (KRIHS), Korea. He is also a member of the Presidential Committee on the Fourth Industrial Revolution as well as the National Smart City Committee. He has been in charge of smart city national planning and smart city legal system projects since 2008, receiving numerous awards and honors, including one Commendation by the Minister of Land, Transport and Maritime Affairs in 2012 and one Commendation of the Prime Minister in 2015. He has published extensively in Korea and overseas on Korean smart city policies. Lee received his Ph.D. degree from Ohio State University (Geography), his Master degree from Texas A&M University (Urban Planning) and his Bachelor degree from Korea University (Geographic Education). Topics of particular interest include smart cities, spatial information, open data policy and innovative industry.

Ji-in Chang is Assistant Professor at the Graduate School of Smart City Science Management, Hongik University, where she is teaching courses on smart cities and environmentally friendly housing. Chang holds degrees from Seoul National University (Ph.D. in Urban Planning), Massachusetts Institute of Technology (M. Sc. in Architecture Studies), and University of New South Wales (B.Arch., Honors). Before joining Hongik University, she was a Visiting Research Fellow at the Megacity Research Center of Seoul Institute, a think tank of the Seoul Metropolitan Government. She also worked as a practicing architect. Topics of particular interest include smart cities, sustainable development, transnationalism, and gendered urbanism.

References

European Parliament. (2014). *Mapping smart cities in the EU. Policy department A: Economic and scientific policy study.* http://www.europarl.europa.eu/studies Retrieved 01.10.15.
Lee, J. Y. (2012). Implementation of the smart city in Korea. In *Presentation at National World Habitat Day 2012.*
Lee, J. Y. (2018). *Catalyzing the evolution of ICT based growth ecosystems in cities.* Korea Research Institute of Housing Settlements (KRIHS).
Ministry of Land, Transport and Maritime Affairs. (2008). *The first ubiquitous comprehensive plan: 2009–2013.* Seoul, Korea: (In Korean).
Shin, D. (2013). *A primer on Korean planning and policy: Smart city. PKPP 2013-11.* Korea Research Institute of Housing Settlements (KRIHS).

The smart city of Hangzhou, China: the case of Dream Town Internet village

Iraklis Argyriou
UMR 8504 Geographie-cites, French National Center for Scientific Research (CNRS), Paris, Paris Region, France

Chapter Outline

9.1 Introduction 195
9.2 Background 196
    9.2.1 The Dream Town smart project in Hangzhou: a designated space for promoting innovation-based urbanization 196
    9.2.2 Theoretical context and organization schemas 198
9.3 Research methodology: case study 200
    9.3.1 Scope 201
    9.3.2 Integration 203
    9.3.3 Organization 203
    9.3.4 Time 205
    9.3.5 Cost 208
    9.3.6 Quality 208
    9.3.7 Risks 209
    9.3.8 Procurement 210
    9.3.9 Discussion—the fringes 210
9.4 Conclusions 214
Acknowledgments 216
About the author 216
References 216
Appendix A Actors interviewed for the Dream Town smart city case 218

9.1 Introduction

Chinese cities of various administrative status and geographical locations pursue innovation policies to enact social and economic progress (Fang, Ma, Wang, & Li, 2014). A recent smart project in the Internet area that reflects China's contemporary efforts to promote innovation-driven urbanization is the so-called Dream Town Internet village in the city of Hangzhou, the provincial capital of the Zhejiang Province, located in the southeast part of the country close to the Shanghai metropolis. Aiming at emulating territorialized spaces of high-technology innovation at the international level such as the Silicon Valley in California, the Dream Town incubation space for Internet startups is a key delivery platform of the Zhejiang Hangzhou Future Sci-Tech City (FSTC)—a scientific and technological innovation zone located in the western area of Hangzhou. The Dream Town thus represents a flagship Chinese smart project aiming at promoting economic development and quality of life through Internet-related startup innovation. Both the FSTC and Dream Town were driven by multilevel governmental priorities. Specifically the FSTC was initiated in 2010 by the Chinese Central Organization Department and State-owned Assets Supervision & Administration Commission of the State Council as a key implementation mechanism of China's National Strategy on Talents (Douay & Henriot, 2016). The FSTC comprises three distinct platforms with the goal of promoting innovation as well as serving as a base for talented individuals and young professionals offering to develop their ideas into technological products. One of the platforms is Dream Town. In response to state rationales for innovation policymaking, the Internet village was strongly promoted by the Hangzhou municipal government and the Zhejiang provincial government. The Dream Town site was foreseen by these subnational governments as potentially forming a new motor of the information economy capable of promoting economic growth, innovation abilities, and social progress at the citywide and provincial-wide level. Besides serving as a test-bed site in the Hangzhou territory, Dream Town aims to become a new norm of Internet incubation for smart development throughout China. To date the site's operation has been smooth and progress on programmatic goals has been well on track. At the same time the project has encountered two main challenges: (1) the market promotion of produced innovation; and (2) the integration of economic, social, and environmental considerations, as envisaged in the Dream Town master plan. This chapter proceeds as follows: Section 9.2 sets the broader context for the Dream Town project, and the theoretical context for the empirical analysis. Section 9.3 includes key data for Dream Town, as well as the results of the case study analysis by focusing on the policy and actor organizational frameworks critical for the planning and implementation of the Internet village. Section 9.4 presents the conclusions.

9.2 Background

9.2.1 The Dream Town smart project in Hangzhou: a designated space for promoting innovation-based urbanization

Since the introduction of China's regime restructuring in the late 1970s, the urbanization process has contributed largely to the country's social and economic progress. With the urban population projected to reach over 1 billion by 2030, Chinese cities are expected to play an increasingly important role for China's future prosperity (The World Bank and Development Research Center of the PRC State Council, 2014). This is also evident in national policy documents such as the 13th National Five-Year Plan for Economic and Social Development 2016–20

(Part XIII: New Urbanization) (PRC Central Committee of Communist Party, 2016). At the same time the National Five-Year Plan and supplementary strategic documents emphasize the central role of innovation, including the Internet sector, for the country's growth prospects (PRC State Council, 2016). In fact the emphasis of the Chinese central government on local innovation can be traced to policy aspirations aiming at stimulating science and technology-based development at the urban level. For instance, in March 2014 the Chinese Government issued the first outline of their urbanization plan *National New-Type Urbanization Plan (2014−2020)* that sets out a blueprint for China's future urbanization and economic development. The new plan aims to promote efficient, people-oriented, just, and ecologically livable development (Fang, Ma, & Wang, 2015). China's leadership has recognized that achieving such goals requires a new growth model that among others is based on productivity increases and innovations, and that this itself is predicated upon the role of urban areas. If well managed, cities can support continued productivity increases through agglomeration effects and enable innovation and new ideas to emerge (The World Bank and Development Research Center of the PRC State Council, 2014). It is then no surprise that the call of the State Council (China's cabinet) issued in 2015 for ministries and local governments at all levels was to support innovation and startups as a way of leveraging nationwide economic growth and job creation (SCMP, 2015).

Such political aspirations take the form of central governmental policies aiming to facilitate the development of local innovation ecosystems. For example, in 2012 the Ministry of Housing and Urban Rural Development issued the "Notice of Carrying out the National Smart City Pilot" and approved over 90 pilot smart city projects. By 2013 the number of approved smart city pilot projects increased to 193. Such trends reflect the importance assigned by the central government to smart cities as a strategy for accelerating China's industrialization and informatization. In addition, smart city development is viewed by central authorities as an effective means toward utilizing ICT science and technology areas such as Internet of Things, cloud computing, big data, and spatial geographic information, for improving urban planning and management (Li, Lin, & Geertman, 2015). At the same time, China's innovation ecosystem is characterized by a strong position of the local government (World Economic Forum, 2016).

A manifestation of China's influential central-local policy frameworks for local innovation ecosystems can be observed in a recent national pilot scheme of science and technology innovation zones, the so-called Future Sci-Tech Cities, applicable in the cities of Hangzhou, Beijing, Nanjing, and Wuhan. Accordingly the FSTC was launched in 2010 over a master-planned area of 123 km^2 at the Yuhang district of Hangzhou in the northwest part of the city (Management Committee of Hangzhou Chengxi Scientific Zone, 2015). The FSTC project is driven by the triptych[1] of "talented individuals−innovative industries−resource development." In this

---

[1] The triptych is case specific and neither constitute an official term in the Chinese context nor relate to the mainstream triple helix model, widely used to explain local innovation systems including as regards to smart cities (Komninos, 2008; Leydesdorff & Deakin, 2011).

context a core FSTC objective is the resettlement of high-quality overseas talents and professionals in strategic economic areas such as the information economy, biomedicine, new energy, and financial services (ZOTP, 2016). The "triptych" is considered by provincial and municipal authorities as instrumental in improving the innovation ability of the Zhejiang Province and the city of Hangzhou as a whole. This aspiration involves special attention to the potential role of agglomeration of suburban spaces toward enacting a billion-dollar order smart urban economy. At the same time, innovation and the Internet sector fit well with political aspirations toward making Hangzhou a city of global importance. In the words of the Chinese Communist Party chief of Hangzhou (Zhao Yide) (Hangzhou Municipal Government, 2017):

> *We have to speed up the creation of a center for innovation and entrepreneurship, which is based on 'Internet Plus' strategy and has global influence, so that Hangzhou can develop into a beautiful international city.*

Indeed the central level policy demand for the FSTC project converged with local policy rationales for innovation-based economic restructuring that took a firmer position in the late 2000s. Specifically, in 2008 the municipal government of Hangzhou directed the Yuhang district government to set up a special committee with remit to improve spatial planning and development at the district level. Over time the committee spotted the key role of talents and creativity as drivers for catalyzing area-based economic development and diversification. The activities of the Yuhang Committee in the period 2008–10 then offered a basis for the formulation of the FSTC Management Committee.

Other than multilevel policy rationales, broader factors also created a conducive environment for the development of the Dream Town Internet village. Most notable ones were the rapid development of the Zhejiang information economy over the last decade, the presence of an active venture capital (VC) industry in the wider Hangzhou–Shanghai territory as well as the location of the Alibaba Group Internet Corporation within the FSTC. The Dream Town innovation site, as part of the FSTC, also relates to broader policy goals revolving around promoting polycentric spatial and economic restructuring in Hangzhou. For instance, the FSTC holds the administrative status of a "city subcenter." In addition a key objective of Dream Town master plan is that the site ultimately develops into a model urban space that balances social, economic, and ecological considerations.

9.2.2 Theoretical context and organization schemas

Research theoretical frameworks and empirical studies centered on the interplay of growth and actor coalitions have been put forward to explain underlying factors and processes behind urbanization and development. Such a mainstream theoretical perspective originally developed for western contexts and, in particular, US cities is the Urban Regime Theory (URT) (Molotch, 1976). A baseline URT point is that municipal governance is characterized by an arrangement between public and private actors in the pursuit of economic growth (Douay, 2010). In doing so, powerful actors tend to organize around a partnership approach to urban space use and exploitation (Jianga, Waley, & Gonzalez, 2016). Chinese urbanization dynamics have been well examined through URT-informed empirical studies looking at the role of dominant politico-economic actors organized around a pro-growth agenda, which is driven by the specificities of land development (e.g., Jianga et al., 2016; Qian, 2007, 2011; Wu & Waley, 2018; Zhang, 2002, 2014). The relevance of URT perspectives for the Chinese context touches ground with two urban-related aspects of the country's transition to a new governance system. The first is the opening to a market-driven economy, which is accompanied by the reforming of state-owned enterprises (SOEs) and a strong input by non-SOE sectors (e.g., township enterprises and private businesses) in urban affairs (Wang, 2014; Wei, 2012). The second is the "decentralization" of economic and administrative responsibilities, which has constituted subnational state authorities, particularly at the municipal and district level, key actors in urban planning and development. Economic decentralization in particular serves as an instrument for growth and empowers local authorities to act as resource mobilizers (Wu, 2007).

As described in Section 9.1 the Dream Town innovation site in the context of the FSTC is a growth-oriented project driven by multilevel governmental priorities. It also involves strong input by diverse innovation-related nonstate actors (e.g., startups and incubators; VC industry; Alibaba Group). The Dream Town thus represents an exemplary project of China's contemporary efforts for promoting the smart economy on the basis of an entrepreneurial mode of urban governance operationalized by public—private collaborative frameworks. As such, it is examined through a URT-informed analytical framework, at the intersection of urbanization and smart innovation, that incorporates a substantial dimension (content and project) and a procedural dimension (actors and process) (Dror, 1973) in order to unfold underlying project-related policy and actor organizational frameworks, as depicted in Fig. 9.1:

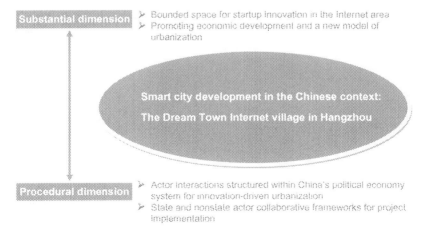

Figure 9.1 Analytical framework for the Dream Town smart project in Hangzhou, China.

9.3 Research methodology: case study

Hangzhou, the capital of Zhejiang Province, is located at the southern part of the Yangtze River Delta about 180 km southwest of Shanghai. Hangzhou's history extends over 5000 years making it one of China's Seven Ancient Capitals. Called as "the Paradise on the Earth" by scholars and writers, and well-known for its picturesque natural landscape and environment, Hangzhou is the origin city of Grand Canal—the world's longest artificial canal. Hangzhou's city properly consists of nine urban administrative districts that form the core of the Hangzhou metropolitan area (Qian, 2015). Fig. 9.2 presents Hangzhou's location in China:

In addition, Table 9.1 presents key economic and socio-spatial data for Hangzhou:

Hangzhou represents a Chinese coastal metropolis that has experienced major urban challenges and governance reforms over the regime's restructuring period. Importantly, devolved political and economic responsibilities to municipal authorities and a public—private collaborative approach marked by strong input by nonstate actors (e.g., property and VC industry; town and village enterprises; domestic private industries) largely determine the city's affairs (Qian, 2015). Hangzhou's economy has evolved too over time, placing emphasis since the mid-2000s on various technology and knowledge-intensive sectors such as financial services, e-commerce, IT, biomedicine, and tourism. In fact, since the mid-1990s, a new

Figure 9.2 The location of Hangzhou in China (Wikipedia, 2018).

Table 9.1 Key data for Hangzhou.

Index	Figures as of 2013 (unless otherwise noted)
Urban population	7.08 million
Territory	4876 km^2
Economic output	$160 billion (2016)
GDP/capita	$19,000
Economic production share	Primary: 3.2%; secondary: 43.9%; tertiary: 52.9%
Added value of information economy	$39 billion (2016), contributing to over 50% of city GDP growth

Source: Based on Qian, Z. (2015). Hangzhou: City profile. *Cities*, 48, 42−54; Hangzhou Municipal Government. *Innovative Hangzhou ranks top developed city in China (news provided by Hangzhou Municipal Government)*. (2017). Available from https://www.prnewswire.com/news-releases/innovative-hangzhou-ranks-top-developed-city-in-china-300436538.html.

political leadership in Hangzhou has put forward bold reforms to strengthen the city's economy in a globalization and information age. Part of this revolves around creating an economic basis that merges IT technologies with smart applications under the reputable motto of developing the "Silicon Valley in Paradise" (Wei, 2012).

The city's affairs have become an increasingly political-bound sphere largely defined by the interests of local political elites and administrative leaders (e.g., mayors; general secretaries of the Municipal Communist Party Committee) as well as the formation of pro-growth coalitions with nonstate actors toward a market-oriented urban development approach. In this context, reflecting on the specificities of the Chinese regime, Hangzhou authorities embark into collaborative relations with private actors from the position of an "owner and manager of production means" (e.g., land; financial institutions). In this regard the authorities act in essence as prime market agents that reap multiple benefits from the urban space developmental process (Wu, 2015). Such state−nonstate actor relations take place within the Chinese hierarchical urban planning system whereby city master plans ought to be approved by higher tiers of authority (e.g., upward from People's City Congress to the Provincial Government and the Chinese State Council). However, in practice fast urban development often outpaces formal planning frameworks. Lastly, some elements of empowered civic society in urban affairs can be observed in Hangzhou (Qian, 2015). The analysis of the project management context of the Dream Town smart case in the remaining of Section 9.3 draws from 32 semistructured problem-centered interviews conducted with local actors over the period March−June 2016 (Appendix A).

9.3.1 Scope

A grounding study of the smart cities literature suggests the evaluation of smart projects versus six areas—economy, governance, people, mobility, environment, and living (Giffinger et al., 2007). A bounding factor of the Dream Town, in terms of project scope, is that employed startups should relate to Internet. The official

Dream Town policy document (FSTC, 2015) defines that eligible smart applications should fall in the areas of e-business, software design, information services, integrated circuit, big data, cloud computing, network security, and animation design. At the time of the primary data collection, most of the Dream Town startup projects were related to two smart areas: "economy" and "quality of life."

Specifically, many of the projects were revolving around digital economy applications, with Alibaba's online platforms offering a mainstream promotion channel. The Dream Town also depicts a more subtle "smart economy" aspect: the aspiration by governmental authorities that the innovation site will lead to a new Alibaba corporation. This in turn is expected to bring various benefits to the state revolving around increased revenues through employment and corporate taxes, the stimulation of consumption-based urbanization (e.g., Alibaba's workforce in the order of thousand employees is itself a large consumption urban group) or increase in land values that would be factored in prospective large-scale urban development.

Regarding the "quality of life" dimension, it can be mostly discerned at a personal rather than community level. For example, many startup projects were about applications (APPs) for issues such as job seeking advice, management of everyday activities (e.g., time-wise), improvement of indoor living environment, and personal entertainment. To a much lesser extent a couple of projects were targeting broader issues such as facilitation of online communication for potential common issues of interest (e.g., self-organized forms of community employment with emphasis on marginalized people) or online discussion forums aiming at fostering greater interest for "serious" (as put by the startup CEO) socioeconomic issues. In addition a key goal of the Dream Town master plan is to showcase a model space that fosters social openness while merging economic and environmental considerations. Fig. 9.3 shows the main entrance area of the Dream Town Internet village.

Figure 9.3 The main entrance area of the Dream Town Internet village, with the administrative building on the left.

9.3.2 Integration

The Dream Town innovation site has been developed in response to policy goals at various governmental levels. So, it is an implementation platform of the central level pilot FSTC innovation zone in Hangzhou. It is also closely related to the prospects, and entrepreneurial dynamics, of the Zhejiang provincial and Hangzhou city economy. It is then no surprise that the Zhejiang Governor aspires Dream Town to form a new motor of the provincial information economy and to become the new norm for urban to regional economic restructuring nationwide.

The overarching logic behind the Dream Town project is that innovation and talent creativity drive growth and place-based competitiveness. Accordingly, governmental authorities, involved in the visioning and planning of Dream Town, placed emphasis on offering the best possible means of support to innovation subjects (startup companies) but with expectations for yielding outstanding outcomes. The FSTC Deputy Director stated, when referring to prospective startups, "I am responsible for the sun and rain, you are responsible to thrive" (*China Daily Asia*, 2015). To this end, Dream Town incorporates various soft "means of governance" aiming at creating a stimulating and flexible environment for innovation activities on the basis of multiple support (organizational, financial, technical). Granting of admission to startups follows a typical procedure whereby project proposals are submitted to a selection committee comprising external experts from the industrial, business, and academic sector. Companies may also enter Dream Town through informal interaction with incubators (nearly twenty in total)—the companies located onsite that host startups and serve as their innovation mentor.

In either case a memorandum of agreement is signed between the Dream Town administration office (which is a branch of FSTC organizational structure) and startups defining formal aspects such as onsite settling, the type of support available as well as broad expectations for innovation outcomes. However, there is no formal authority residing with the Dream Town administration office or incubators to command a startup company to withdraw from the site (e.g., due to low performance). However, incubators themselves can make a decision whether or not to continue supporting. Also, startups are not obliged to belong to an incubator—they can still enter Dream Town and follow their own plans. However, such cases are sparse as the bulk of startups consider incubation critical for their prospects. In addition, formal FSTC administrative documents define the broad scope of activities for the Dream Town site. This is the case regarding the role of onsite entities (e.g., incubators; the Dream Town company, a private company located onsite that is responsible for the day-to-day management of the site) as well as external stakeholders potentially interacting with startups (e.g., institutional or VC investors).

9.3.3 Organization

The Dream Town is a key delivery platform of FSTC, a state project established in 2010 as part of China's National Strategy on Talents. It is also a formal project of the Zhejiang provincial and Hangzhou municipal master plans. Its operational expenses are covered by the city and provincial governments. In principle, Dream Town startups are mandated to involve college graduates from universities of the Zhejiang Province who ought to serve as the enterprise legal persons of the company (contributing at minimum 30% of the total registered business capital) and comprise at least 70% of the company's staff. The programmatic goals for Dream Town over the period 2015–18 involve 2000 startup projects, set up by 10,000 graduates, which would attract more than 300 VC funds and over $45 billion of investment (FSTC, 2015).

The site's day-to-day operation is outsourced to the private sector, the so-called Dream Town company, located onsite and comprising offices that specialize in various areas such as financial management, business planning, law, marketing, and advertising. Startups are granted every year $3000 in electronic form (the "creative digital tickets"), which can be used to buy out services from the Dream Town company.

The first point of contact for startups is their hosting incubator, a private company settled onsite, which acts as an "umbrella entity" offering various supports. A typical incubator can host many startups (e.g., up to 30) that are typically located in the same building with the incubator. Incubators are staffed with a few individuals (normally up to 10) and assist startups in three main ways: routine issues (e.g., office facilities and management); networking with internal (e.g., peers) and external entities (e.g., investors); and technical and business support for the innovation process (e.g., know-how; financial planning; advice on market issues). In certain cases, incubators may themselves invest in projects by offering capital in exchange of shares which would then be cashed out if the startup decides to withdraw from incubation. Incubators can invest directly (e.g., own funds) or through their wider organizational structure (e.g., parent companies that may or may not belong to the VC industry).

In addition, in order to maximize opportunities for investing, a designated space for VC companies, the Angel Village, has been positioned across the Internet village (formally consisting an integral part of Dream Town) to facilitate interactions between startups and VCs that, in principle, specialize in science and technology financing. However, based on a field site visit and interviews with two Angel Village VC companies, it appears that such interactions are limited.

A core stakeholder for the Dream Town project is also Alibaba Group, the Internet retailing global corporation, which is headquartered in FSTC, within just a mile distance from Dream Town, over a 400,000 m^2 work facility—the Taobao Town. Founded in 1999 by Jack Ma, a former college student of Hangzhou Normal University, Alibaba grew by the late 2000s not only to be one of the largest online worldwide retailers but also to be a multinational company diversified to business areas such as Wi-Fi applications, mobile operating systems, Internet-based TV as well as the media sector through the purchase of the South China Morning Post (Hong Kong) in 2015. Due to its importance for the broader innovation and economic prospects of the city and province (e.g., in terms of turning FSTC into a global spotlight that brings in resources and companies which would boost development), Alibaba enjoys a privileged position in urban affairs. For example, it is one of the few private companies that communicate directly with municipal authorities on spatial and economic development issues. To give an example, Alibaba was given the option to select the specific land plot upon which to develop the Taobao site. In fact the land allocation did not follow the standard procedures of the formal auction system of land-use certificate provision but was agreed informally.

The company's influence for Dream Town is multifaceted. First, Alibaba as a global (Chinese) corporation in the Internet area originating from Hangzhou serves as a role model for startups. In addition, it offers onsite technical resources (e.g., cloud computing) available for free while its online platform serves as a promotion channel for the startup innovation products. However, by far the most important influence of Alibaba is in the area of capacity building. Specifically the company is considered an outstanding environment for the development of competent employees in various segments of the Internet sector (e.g., technical, operational, financial, sales, marketing). Indeed, many founding members or employees of startups and incubators were once working for Alibaba at various levels (seniors, office staff, interns) acquiring thus valuable knowledge and expertise. Startups also interact informally with Alibaba employees in order to share experiences or seek advice. In addition, Alibaba is considered as a potential attractor of VC funding in FSTC, an aspect which in principle could increase financing prospects for the startups.

Besides the above-described core stakeholders, there is virtually no involvement of universities in the Dream Town project. Relevant interactions are merely confined to informal exchange of views between startup staff and university researchers or to product testing and promotion activities (e.g., college students as end-users of innovation products). Such interactions are limited and do not seem to play any major role for startups. In fact, startups reported that a factor that constraints interactions with outside stakeholders like universities or FSTC entities is their (startup) focus on internal tasks. This is particularly the case over the first months of the incubation period, which are considered critical for their overall success. Lastly, there are almost no local community-related interactions around Dream Town projects. As mentioned, few startup projects incorporate broader community aspects and while doing so, the focus is on promoting online communication forums. When startups, active in such projects, were asked whether they plan to get involved with community issues beyond the online sphere, they reported that traditional community activities (e.g., actual events or face-to-face meetings) are outside the scope of their innovation plans. Figs. 9.4 and 9.5 present key actors and functions for the development (Fig. 9.4) and implementation (Fig. 9.5) parts of the Dream Town smart project.

9.3.4 Time

Four main time-periods can be identified for the Dream Town smart project from conceptualization to implementation. The first, which extends from 2008 to 2010, relates to the convergence of political priorities on innovation policy-making at multiple governmental levels that created the ground for the establishment of the FSTC innovation zone in Hangzhou, of which Dream Town is a key delivery

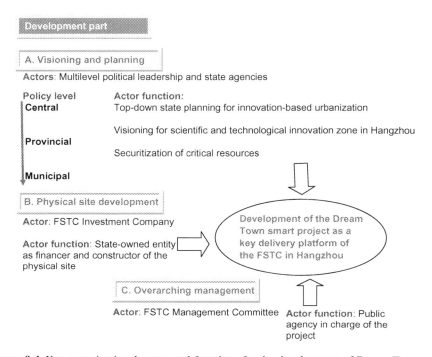

Figure 9.4 Key organizational actors and functions for the development of Dream Town.

platform. Specifically the national pilot scheme of the four urban zones, including Hangzhou's FSTC, was promoted as part of national policy-making on innovation-driven development. In addition, subnational political leadership at the provincial level and shortly thereafter at the municipal government level (e.g., Secretary of the Hangzhou Municipal P.R. China Communist Party who was later on appointed at the central governmental party) favored the development of a science and technology innovation zone in the city. In roughly the same period the Chinese National Development Reform Commission put forward a projection of expected GDP growth increase in Hangzhou's Yuhang district based on the area's innovation-related economic potential and offered an overall economic plan for the district. Such spatio-economic planning aspects framed a general context for city and provincial authorities within which to justify and plan the FSTC project in the context of the national pilot scheme. As a result the FSTC project was officially included in Hangzhou's municipal government planning by 2010 and was officially launched in 2010.

In what forms the second period, 2010−14, the Dream Town project was put forward by the FSTC Management Committee and preceded to materialization promptly. Relevant debates became well structured by 2014 and in December of that year the construction began and lasted 3 months so that the innovation site was ready to start off in Spring 2015. The third period, March−September 2015,

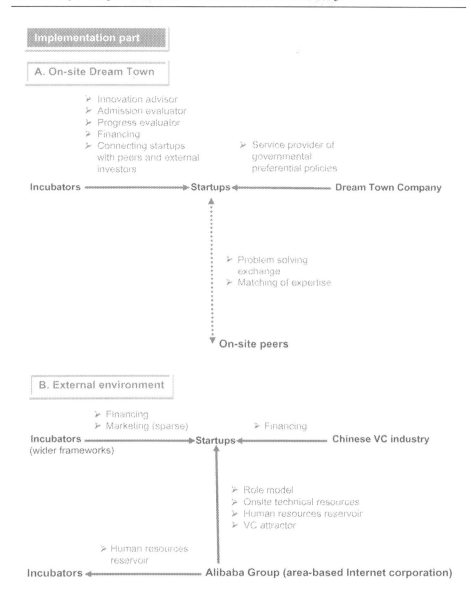

Figure 9.5 Key organizational actors and functions for the implementation of Dream Town.

involves the first wave of incubators that were asked by the FSTC Management Committee to locate onsite promptly in exchange of a straightforward settling process and supportive resources. This was because incubators were considered by the committee as key for bringing in a critical mass of initial startups. Subsequently a fourth period can be observed from September 2015 onward where startup

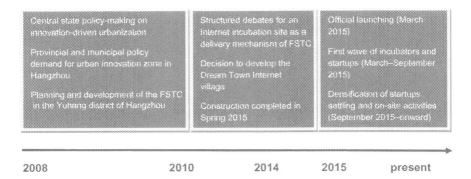

Figure 9.6 Timeline of the Dream Town project.

recruitment and onsite activities are regularized. Fig. 9.6 presents a timeline of the above-described main periods:

9.3.5 Cost

The first main cost-block for Dream Town is the site construction that was undertaken by the FSTC Investment Company, a state-owned asset management and construction company, through a combination of public (municipal and provincial government) and private finance.[2] The second main cost-block is the operational expenses that are addressed through funding provided mostly by the municipal government at an annual level of around $15 million (Maslak, 2018) and to a lesser extent by the provincial government. These funds cover among others various subsidies (e.g., creative tickets—$3000 per year; market research studies; onsite housing rent for startup employees) as well as seasonal competition prizes (up to $30,000 per proposal). Startups are also eligible for low-cost lending (e.g., discounted loans) of over $150,000 through the Venture Loan Risk Pool mechanism set up by the FSTC (2015).

9.3.6 Quality

Smart specifications for the startup projects are secured in two ways. The first relates to the formal admission process where an independent committee decides on whether proposals should be supported or not. Besides that, startup proposals are also evaluated by interested incubators informally. Once a startup enters the site, its performance and potential are assessed by the hosting incubators. Typically a

---

[2] There are no publicly available data for the costing of the site construction or the relative contribution of public/private funds, while no such data could be retrieved from the interviews.

6-month period is adequate for incubators to conclude whether a project goes into a promising direction. If this is the case, incubators would normally decide whether to connect startups with potential investors (typically VCs) or invest themselves in their projects. In addition, external investors who finance a startup act in essence as an evaluator. In such a context, neither the Dream Town administration office nor incubators hold authority to command the withdrawal of a startup from the site.

9.3.7 Risks

There are five main aspects through which risks are attempted to be managed in the Dream Town smart project. The first is the Angel Village site that was established across Dream Town to promote VC infusion, although such an outcome appears weak to date. Second, Dream Town was strategically placed adjacent to Alibaba Taobao Town for several reasons. Alibaba is considered by authorities as a potential VC attractor, an expectation that is exemplified by the recent general investment environment throughout China. As reported by an incubator,

> *VC investments all over China have difficulties in sustaining similar levels of profits like in the near past. So, many VC companies tend to pay attention to Alibaba as a potential human resource pool for startup projects because it is considered that its employees have good working experience.*

Third the startup incubation aims at lowering risks related to the innovation process. In this regard, incubators are a constant source of support for startups in terms of know-how and connectivity with peers and external entities. Fourth, Dream Town was planned and implemented within the specificities of China's hierarchical political system, in effect reflecting the priorities of powerful governmental agencies and leadership at various levels. However, its operational framework, within such a dominant state regime, incorporates flexibility regarding stakeholder interactions and innovation-related arrangements. For example, there is no restriction on financial streams for the startup projects; they can include startup personnel funds as well as VC and institutional capital from all over China. In addition, incubators can invest own funds or bring in finance through their wider organizational frameworks. For instance a cofounder of an incubator (who is also coowner of a Chinese VC company with investments in over 40 startups in China some of which have a stock value in the order of a billion dollar) has invested in hosted projects. In another case the Seventh Universe incubator mediates to facilitate finance infusion from its parent Hangzhou Daily Media Company, a traditional media firm located in Hangzhou. As of June 2016 the incubator was in the process of setting up an investment foundation, to be called "Dream Come True," within its parent company in order to accelerate the process of finance channeling. In few cases, incubators try to facilitate startups to access the market. For instance, one incubator reported that its sister company that is active in the media sector, and located within FSTC, is used to promote startup innovation products when they are ready to try the market.

Lastly, economic assistance in various forms, with the most notable ones such as the various subsidies and financial incentives (see Section 3.2), helps startups to manage financial risks. Such supports, in particular, the granting of free office space for up to 3 years, are considered by startups important for reducing investment risks by lowering considerably the operational costs. In addition a risk pool mechanism has been set up that offers low-cost loans to startups. This is the "Venture Loan Risk Pool," which is funded by three parties—the FSTC Management Committee, the Hangzhou Yuhang Sci-tech Guarantee Ltd. and a pool of eligible Chinese corporate banks in a 4:4:2 ratio. It is a nonprofit loan mechanism where the FSTC Committee and the Sci-Tech Guarantee Ltd. offer around $1.5 million each while banks provide $750k raising the total underwriting fund to nearly $3.75 million. A single application by a startup can get a maximum loan of up to $150,000. The total loan amount that can put forward through the banks is around $30 million.

9.3.8 Procurement

Assigned procurement tasks can be identified only in the outsourcing of the site's day-to-day operation to the Dream Town company, in which case responsibilities are defined by a MOA between the company and the FSTC. Other relations involving internal stakeholders (startups, incubators, the Dream Town administration) are subject to MOAs too. Incubators also respect their wider organizational frameworks (e.g., finance channeling through a parent VC or other types of parent companies). MOA agreements also exist between startups and external investors. The MOA between incubators and the Dream Town administration is defined in broad terms. Accordingly, incubators do not have to adhere to very specific tasks as startup hosts while they are simply obliged to report basic data; for example, how many projects do they support or the level of profit.

9.3.9 Discussion—the fringes

The Dream Town project incorporates specific programmatic goals as well as broader objectives. Progress to date on programmatic goals is presented in Table 9.2, which includes the most recent data that could be retrieved from (online) official sources:

The data suggest that Dream Town is well on track regarding attracted entrepreneurs while the VC capital funds target has been already exceeded. However, the target of 2000 startup projects by 2018 seems challenging. In addition, no public data for the total investment value of undertaken projects is available in order to compare with the $47 billion target. Hence, overall there is a mixed performance on official goals.

Besides programmatic startup project-related goals, the Dream Town is related to two broad policy goals. The first is the enactment of innovation-driven urban

Table 9.2 Dream Town programmatic goals and performance (2015−18).

Programmatic goal	Target (2015−18 time-frame)	Performance (Spring 2017)
Number of startup entrepreneurs	10,000	7000
Number of startup projects	2000	700
Number of attracted VC capital funds	300	500
Project financing value[a]	–	$232 million
Total investment value	$47 billion	N/A

VC, Venture capital.
[a]Not an official goal but provided as supplementary data.
Source: Based on Hangzhou Municipal Government. *Innovative Hangzhou ranks top developed city in China (news provided by Hangzhou Municipal Government)*. (2017). Available from https://www.prnewswire.com/news-releases/innovative-hangzhou-ranks-top-developed-city-in-china-300436538.html.

development. The second involves turning the Dream Town site into an exemplary urban space that balances social, economic, and environmental considerations. For the first goal, it can be argued that Dream Town does promote regular interactions between startups and economic actors (mainly the VC industry) while around 90 projects (as of Spring 2017) have surpassed the $150,000 investment threshold (1 million Chinese RMB) (*Top News*, 2017). In addition, diversified financial streams are infused into startups—for example, through incubators and their wider organizational frameworks as well as from institutional investors. If one also considers the site's engaging entrepreneurial atmosphere, as widely reported by startups, and the interest showed by external investors, which according to the local press tend to stop by on a daily basis (*China Daily Asia*, 2015), it becomes evident that Dream Town's financial-related arrangements and stakeholder relationships have adopted a structured character. However, a market-related issue appears to hamper the project's broader impact on the urban economy. That is, startups and the produced innovation are disconnected from prospective end-users. This can be related to both a physical and a processual dimension. For example, startups raised the point that the Dream Town site is remotely located from the city core area, an aspect that adds difficulties for market promotion. At the same time, concerns were raised about whether the project is well designed to support the full cycle of the innovation process from initial steps to market diffusion. For instance, as reported by a startup CEO:

> We currently build-up our operational team which will try to promote our brand and make it accessible to end-users. We have to step-out of Dream Town and get close to customers so over the next months you might not be able to see me a lot in Dream Town. I think that Dream Town offers good infrastructures for the company's period 0−1 but for the period 1−10 maybe this is not the ideal choice for you. So, in the period 1−10 maybe the main task for me as a CEO is to step-out and require resources. Also I believe that when you are in the 1−10 period you have to be very close to prospective customers. But they are not around Dream Town.

Furthermore, despite aspirations for turning Dream Town into the "Silicon Valley" of Hangzhou, it appears questionable the extent to which innovation outcomes truly reflect high-tech standards. For instance, based on the fieldwork, it appears that many of the surveyed smart projects reflect new ideas in the Internet of Things sector for the Chinese environment. To offer an example, some smart Apps are aimed at creating online communication forums between stakeholders, for instance, for social issues or a specific business sector such as housing industry. This was described as a novelty for Hangzhou's environment (e.g., in relation to the ways that housing stakeholder interactions are typically organized). However, it does not necessarily signify advanced technological artifacts in the broader sense. As put by a surveyed startup:

> *I think that Dream Town is not really about high technology like in the U.S. style but it's more conservative although people tend to talk about it in a similar way like for U.S. innovation sites.*

An indicative point that potentially aligns to the above argument is that the Dream Town smart project to date does not seem to exert substantial influence at the international level. For example, a recent Internet search (March 09, 2018) did not bring up concrete information regarding international debates or implications out of the project—for instance, as regards to constituting a best practice in material/discursive terms or in terms of setting new innovation standards. Hence, it remains to be seen whether and what kind of broader influence would the smart project may exert in the future. Also, with respect to potential exposure to international factors such as competition pressure, the Dream Town project seems fairly insulated. This is largely because it was envisioned and implemented in response to domestic policy rationales of powerful state agencies and political leadership. As such the various preferential policies together with place-based factors such as the embeddedness in the FSTC or the physical, material, and discursive relevance to the dominant Alibaba Corporation constitute the innovation site a favorable destination for Chinese startups.

Lastly the Dream Town has not lived up to the expectation of transforming into a comprehensive socio-ecological urban space. Specifically, there is no major social activity taking place onsite other than informal visits by individuals and social groups (e.g., schools; university students), nor a strong environmental dimension in pursued innovation products or within the 3 km^2 master-planned site territory. In fact, such broader social and environmental issues were not raised by any of the interviewees. The lack of a socio-environmental perspective in the project can be also observed by looking at the core built environment attributes of the site: Dream Town is wholly occupied by the incubator buildings that host the startups as well as by few buildings devoted for housing accommodation, administration (e.g., Dream Town company) and recreation purposes. Figs. 9.7–9.10 offer an inside view of the site.

The smart city of Hangzhou, China: the case of Dream Town Internet village 213

Figure 9.7 A wider view inside Dream Town: incubator buildings along a water canal.

Figure 9.8 The Seventh Universe incubator—one of the nearly 25 such buildings in Dream Town.

Figure 9.9 Once a new startup company joins Dream Town, its logo is displaced publicly.

Figure 9.10 Visitors in Dream Town.

9.4 Conclusions

Examining smart cities in diverse contexts contributes to gaining a richer understanding of the underlying policy factors, and project frameworks are put forward for promoting more livable urban places but also of the on-the-ground challenges and realities underpinning the pursuit of smart urban futures. This chapter discussed a smart project in the Chinese urban context by looking at the case of the Dream Town site for the promotion of Internet-related startups. Reflecting on the case study's specificities can offer insight on broader issues that could be of relevance to wider efforts of smart city development. First the Dream Town case in Hangzhou, a prefecture-level city in the Chinese urbanization system, revealed a key role for the state in the envisioning and implementation of the smart project in question: political leadership and policy rationales at the central, provincial, and city level were central for the planning of the project, and the allocation of critical resources for its operationalization through a collaborative approach with private actors. In this regard the examined case suggests that governmental priorities and agencies may be a core factor, if not the most critical one, in efforts to enact smart city development. In particular the Dream Town case pointed that institutions and political contexts spanning from the national to the local level do matter regarding the conceptualization of smart projects and the mobilization of resources and actor relations for project implementation. The presented case thus suggests that the governing of the smart city may extend well beyond, but not instead of, the "government." In this regard the Dream Town project confirms an underlying factor of the URT perspective in the Chinese context—the central role of public–private collaborative frameworks for the planning and implementation of growth-oriented urban projects. Accordingly the case study showed that political economy plans for innovation-based urban futures can lead to a facilitative environment for private agency involvement under a potentially "win–win" situation: pursuing multilevel policy goals for innovation-driven urbanization while creating a structured space for startups to innovate and potentially enter the market.

In such a context the operational part of the Dream Town smart project revealed the key role of certain private actors. Specifically the Alibaba Group and onsite incubators were found to influence the startup innovation process along various dimensions, including routine tasks, human resource pooling, business planning, financing, networking, and so on. Whereas Alibaba can be considered as a representative aspect of the Hangzhou context, its multifaceted role for the Dream Town case may highlight a more generalized processual characteristic for the contemporary smart city: the centrality of the spatiality, expertise, and reputable status of leading smart-related private actors for the broader environment within which smart projects are pursued. In addition the Dream Town case highlighted two other broader implications. The first is the extent to which planned smart projects take into account market diffusion issues. The second is whether pursued projects truly reflect innovation or business-as-usual, an issue for which data availability and quality are integral toward a well-rounded evaluation. In the Dream Town case, such data were either not in the public domain or could not be retrieved from the discussions with stakeholders. Having then in place accredited information clearinghouses can assist with a fuller and more transparent evaluation of smart projects as they evolve over time.

Closing-off the Dream Town case revealed that in spite of aspirations to embed an integrated socio-ecological dimension in the innovation site, this issue received less attention in the process and stayed at the level of policy rhetoric despite constituting a main objective of the master plan. This highlights the likely difficulties for balancing economic, environmental, and social considerations when planning and implementing smart city projects, and the need for paying close attention to potential repercussions of smart activities as regards to the generation and distribution of relevant costs and benefits throughout socioeconomic groups.

Acknowledgments

This research work was conducted in the context of the MEDIUM project (New pathways for sustainable development in Chinese MEDIUM size-cities). The author would like to acknowledge the support of the French National Center for Scientific Research (CNRS) and the UMR 8504 Géographie-cités and to thank MEDIUM partners, in particular Hangzhou Normal University. The author would also like to thank all interview participants for their valuable insight on this research, as well as Ms. Li Yang from Hangzhou Normal University for her assistance on the interviews. The MEDIUM project has received funding from the European Union under the External actions of the EU—Grant Contract ICI + /2014/348-005.

About the author

Iraklis Argyriou
UMR 8504 Géographie-cités, Centre National de la Recherche Scientifique (CNRS), Paris, France
Iraklis Argyriou holds a PhD in energy and environmental policy from the University of Delaware, United States. He then undertook a postdoctoral fellowship position, based in China, with the UMR 8504 Géographie-cités research unit of the French National Center for Scientific Research. His research involves theoretical and empirical questions revolving around the political and social dynamics of sustainable urban development, in particular as regards to the multilevel and multiactor governance of sustainability in diversified urban contexts. Iraklis has been involved in research projects for various urban sustainability topics (sustainable energy, climate change mitigation, urban planning for innovation) at the international level (United States, United Kingdom, and China).

References

China Daily Asia. *Entrepreneurs of tomorrow inspired by Dream Town*. (2015). Available from http://www.chinadailyasia.com/business/2015-09/07/content_15313058.html.
Douay, N. (2010). The emergence of a collaborative approach challenges Hong Kong's urban planning model. *China Perspectives*, *1*, 97−109.
Douay, N., & Henriot, C. (2016). La Chine à l'heure des villes intelligentes. *L'information géographique*, *80*, 89−104.
Dror, Y. (1973). The planning process: A facet design. In A. Faludi (Ed.), *A reader in planning theory* (pp. 323−345). Oxford: Pergamon Press.
Fang, C., Ma, H., & Wang, J. (2015). A regional categorization for "New-Type Urbanization" in China. *PLoS One*, *10*, e0134253. Available from https://doi.org/10.1371/journal.pone.0134253.

Fang, C., Ma, H., Wang, Z., & Li, G. (2014). The sustainable development of innovative cities in China: Comprehensive assessment and future configuration. *Journal of Geographical Sciences*, 24, 1095−1114.
FSTC. (2015). *The Dream Town policy assembly*. Hangzhou: Hangzhou Future Sci-Tech City.
Giffinger, R., et al. (2007). Smart Cities—Ranking of European medium sized cities. In *Technical report*. Centre of Regional Science at Vienna UT.
Hangzhou Municipal Government. *Innovative Hangzhou ranks top developed city in China* (news provided by Hangzhou Municipal Government). (2017). Available from https://www.prnewswire.com/news-releases/innovative-hangzhou-ranks-top-developed-city-in-china-300436538.html.
Jianga, Y., Waley, P., & Gonzalez, S. (2016). Shifting land-based coalitions in Shanghai's second hub. *Cities*, 52, 30−38.
Komninos, N. (2008). *Intelligent cities and globalisation of innovation networks*. London: Taylor & Francis.
Leydesdorff, L., & Deakin, M. (2011). The triple-helix model of smart cities: A neo-evolutionary perspective. *Journal of Urban Technology*, 18, 53−63.
Li, Y., Lin, Y., & Geertman, S. (2015). The development of smart cities in China. Proceedings of the 14th international conference on computers in urban planning and urban management CUPUM 2015, paper 291. Cambridge, MA: Massachusetts Institute of Technology.
Management Committee of Hangzhou Chengxi Scientific Zone. (2015). *Hangzhou Chengxi scientific innovation industry cluster zone talent service guidance*. Hangzhou: Management Committee of Hangzhou Chengxi Scientific Zone.
Maslak, M. A. (2018). *Education and female entrepreneurship in Asia: Public policies and private practices*. New York: Palgrave Mcmillan.
Molotch, H. L. (1976). The city as a growth machine: Toward a political economy of place. *American Journal of Sociology*, 82, 309−332.
PRC Central Committee of Communist Party. (2016). *The 13th five-year plan for economic and social development of the People's Republic of China (2016-2020)*. Beijing: Central Compilation & Translation Press.
PRC State Council. *China approves technological innovation plan to refuel growth*. (2016). <http://english.gov.cn/premier/news/2016/07/21/content_281475398570246.htm> Accessed 03.09.17.
Qian, Z. (2007). Institutions and local growth coalitions in China's urban land reform: The case of Hangzhou High-Technology Zone. *Asia Pacific Viewpoint*, 48, 219−233.
Qian, Z. (2011). Building Hangzhou's new city center: Mega project development and entrepreneurial urban governance in China. *Asian Geographer*, 28, 3−19.
Qian, Z. (2015). Hangzhou: City profile. *Cities*, 48, 42−54.
SCMP. *State Council calls for angel investors to help grow startups and jobs in China*. (2015). Available from https://www.scmp.com/news/china/article/1735905/state-council-calls-angel-investors-help-grow-startups-and-jobs-china.
The World Bank and Development Research Center of the PRC State Council. (2014). *Urban China: Toward efficient, inclusive, and sustainable urbanization*. Washington, DC: The World Bank.
Top News. *Hangzhou dream town welcome two birthday: Abandoned granary transformation business paradise*. (2017). Available from http://www.top-news.top/news-12803685.html.
Wang, L. (2014). Forging growth by governing the market in reform-era urban China. *Cities*, 41, 187−193.
Wei, Y.-D. (2012). Restructuring for growth in urban China: Transitional institutions, urban development, and spatial transformation. *Habitat International*, 36, 396−405.

Wikipedia. *Location of Hangzhou in China*. (2018). Available from https://en.wikipedia.org/wiki/Hangzhou#/media/File:China_edcp_location_map.svg.
World Economic Forum. (2016). *White Paper: China's innovation ecosystem*. Geneva: World Economic Forum. Available from http://www3.weforum.org/docs/WEF_GAC_On_China_Innovation_WhitePaper_2016.pdf.
Wu, F. (2007). Re-orientation of the city plan: Strategic planning and design competition in China. *Geoforum, 38*, 379–392.
Wu, F. (2015). *Planning for growth: Urban and regional planning in China*. New York: Routledge.
Wu, Q., & Waley, P. (2018). Configuring growth coalitions among the projects of urban aggrandizement in Kunming, Southwest China. *Urban Geography, 39*, 282–298.
Zhang, S. (2014). Land-centered urban politics in transitional China – Can they be explained by Growth Machine Theory? *Cities, 41*, 179–186.
Zhang, T. (2002). Urban development and a socialist pro-growth coalition in Shanghai. *Urban Affairs Review, 37*, 475–499.
ZOTP. (2016). *Talents service manual of Hangzhou Future Sci-Tech City*. Hangzhou: Hangzhou Future Sci-Tech City.

Appendix A Actors interviewed for the Dream Town smart city case

Respondents	Actors
1–19	Startup companies
20–24	Incubators
25	FSTC Management Committee
26	FSTC Planning Committee
27	FSTC Investment Company
28	Hangzhou Municipal Planning Bureau
29	Local journal on real estate issues
30	Provincial-level policy journal of China's Communist Party
31–32	VC companies of the Dream Town Angel Village

FSTC, Zhejiang Hangzhou Future Sci-Tech City; *VC*, venture capital.

The smart city of Changsha, China 10

Qiaomei Yang
Department of Public Administration and Sociology, Erasmus School of Social and Behavioral Sciences, Erasmus University Rotterdam, Rotterdam, The Netherlands

Chapter Outline

10.1 Introduction 219
10.2 Background 222
    10.2.1 National strategy: informationization development in China and electronic government 222
    10.2.2 The organizational scheme of smart city construction 223
    10.2.3 The outline for construction of new smart city and optimization of public service modes 225
    10.2.4 The impacts of urbanization step onto the era 3.0 and Changsha is practicing to construct smart city 228
    10.2.5 Huawei internet of things (IOT) platform development tendency in the arena of smart city 228
10.3 Research methodology: case study 229
    10.3.1 Scope 229
    10.3.2 Time series for the diffusion of smart city evolution 231
    10.3.3 Discussion—the fringes 235
10.4 Conclusions 237
Acknowledgment 239
About the author 239
References 239
Further reading 240

10.1 Introduction

Ever since the concept of smart city was introduced by IBM Corporation in 2009 as the "Smart Planet winning in China" proposal in response to the concept of "Smart Planet," a number of new concepts, including "smart planet" and "smart city," have triggered the wide attention across the nation. From central government to local level governments, many cities have viewed it as the key development and proactively explore and pilot. "Smart city" is defined by IBM as the use of information and communication technology to sense, analyze, and integrate the key information of core systems in running cities. At the same time, smart city can make intelligent response to different kinds of needs, including daily livelihood, environmental protection, public safety and city services, and industrial and commercial activities.

Komninos (2002) sees intelligent (smart) cities as territories with high capacity for learning and innovation, which is built in the creativity of their population, their institutions of knowledge creation, and their digital infrastructure for communication and knowledge management.

A smart city was viewed with four disciplinary perspectives that were documented to form the corresponding smart city fundamental theories: ICT, urban planning and growth, living labs as large-scale testing beds, eco or green city and corresponding ecological aspects, and creative industry in a city (Anthopoulos, 2014, 2015). It might be argued that beneath the emphases on human capital, social learning, and the creation of smart communities, lay a more limited political agenda of "high-tech urban entrepreneurialism" (Hollands, 2008). In the proposal of IBM in 2009, there are three features of smart city, that is, instrument [via monitoring camera, sensor, radio frequency identification (RFID), mobile and handed facilities, etc.] to form into more thorough sense; interconnection (by broadband, wireless, and mobile information communication web) to connect into "more thorough Internet connection"; and intelligent (by high-speed analysis instruments and collective IT platform) to realize deeper intelligentsia.

Some perceived benefits that in current days IBM's statement reinforces are the perceived benefits of smart city initiatives for solving urban problems through technological solutions that have wide-ranging applications between cities around the world. The description of smart city consultation held a vision of sharing policy strategies that used responsive and adaptive information technologies to improve on urban issues for "current and prospective residents and businesses." Explicit in the presentation of the smart city was that technology could improve nearly every aspect of urban life: health, safety, education, and general prosperity (Chatterton, 2000). Smart city initiatives acted as a localization of globally circulating policy concepts (Chatteron & Hollands, 2002; Wiig, 2016), where the smart city's technological potential signaled inventive ideas for urban changes but rarely targeted marginalized neighborhoods outright (Shelton, 2015).

In China, in order to facilitate and regulate the healthy development of smart city, the Ministry of Housing and Construction, the Ministry of Science, the Ministry of Industry and Information, the Committee of Development and Reform, etc. subsequently embarked on the pilot work in relation to the smart city, among the national smart cities (district and town) led by the Ministry of Housing and Construction that played the main role. On December 5 the Ministry of Housing and Construction launched "the interim management method of the national smart city pilots" and "the pilot index system (temporary) for the national smart city (district, town)." According to these two files, there are altogether three piles of approvals amount to approximately 300 cities (districts and town) to launch the national smart city pilots. In March 2014 the Central Committee of Communist Party of China (CPC) and the National State Council jointly launched the "national new urbanization regulation (the year 2014−2020)" which pointed out that the new urbanization should focus on the inherent meaning and the quality. This was the first time that smart city construction was introduced into national strategy planning, in which it proposed that by the year 2020 a couple of specific featured smart cities will be built. Later in August of that year, regarding the problems exposed in the constructive process during the smart pilots, the eight sectors and committees collaboratively printed "the opinion guidance regarding the facilitation of healthy development for smart city" in which it stresses "the strengthening of top-level designation, and in different areas the people's government should research and make up the smart city constructive proposal from the strategic blueprint of city development."

In Changsha, the capital of Hunan and a central southern geographically located municipality, the authority also takes measures in marginalizing the impacts of advanced Internet technology, the penetration of artificial intelligence. In general, it has passed several stages from the early stage that the civil society started to apply the information technology to communicate with the public agencies and seek public resources in virtual world. Subsequently, the municipal authority stepped further to confront the prosperity of social media, for example, Weixin, Alipayment, Didi traveling, and Mobike, to shape the emergence of artificial intelligence. There are several reasons for the municipality to adopt the latest technology in bringing the whole community in mutual interactions. The existing smart infrastructure contains the bases of shared economy, big data, and artificial intelligence and maintains the latest smart services such as "one door entry service" and "remote courses." One of the side products in this informative wave is that new organizations are like the bamboos after the rain, and they created enormous power in pursuing the maximization of social benefits. Meanwhile, the emergence of new organizations in public management arenas that also reversely motivated the other walks of life in this region burst into creativity for the continuity in energy consumption, and frequent social mobility; therefore there are much space for the investment and social entrepreneurs to involve the social transformations so as to create better lifestyle for the residents.

However, alongside the opportunities for the renovations within the public mechanism, such as the prosperity of the employee market and the redistribution of wealth among the differed social stratification, there are in the meantime occurrences of technical, social, and ethical challenges. In order to address the wicked problems or uncertainties, efforts in the renovation in the aspects of organizations and other walks of life have been indispensable for the entire community to jointly adopt and diffuse the new technological transformation.

This chapter aims at exploring the tensions between the smart city policy script of improving on urban problems and the underlying benefits of these policies, which was oriented to the globalized information economy. It provides an empirical case study of how one city did so, and the divide between stated desires for workforce education and civic engagement and outcomes much more focused on global economic promotion through innovative policy-making. Hence, the author formulated the following research questions: what is the architectural smart city construction in the municipality of Changsha, how did the attributes come into being during the visible evolution, and what could be the potential mechanism for authorities to take into account for further advancement?

10.2 Background

10.2.1 National strategy: informationization development in China and electronic government

On May 8, 2006 the Central Office of CPC, State Council has launched the "National Informationization Development Strategy 2006−2020" and requested all regions and departments to combine the reality to fully implement and carry out. In this strategy, it is stated that the informationization is the big tendency of the world development and the significant power in facilitating the economic−societal transformation. To powerfully facilitate the informationization, there are the strategic measures to cover the modernized overall goal of our nation, to implement the scientific development values, to comprehensibly build the good society, and to construct the socialist harmonious society and build the innovative national urgent desire and necessary option. The informationization is to fully make use of the information technology, to use the information resources, to facilitate information exchange and knowledge sharing, to improve economic increase in quality, and to facilitate economic−societal development transformation of historical process. Since the 1990s, the information technology has gradually innovated and continuously developed, and the information network popularity has become prevalent. The informationization is the significant feature of the global economic−societal development and gradually evolves into all-in social transformation while entering into the 21st century. The informationization has exerted deeper influence on the economic−societal development. The wide application of highly penetrating information technology is cultivating new huge breakthroughs, and the information resources are becoming significant provocative elements, for the inadvisable assets, and social wealth. The information network has become more prevalent and increasingly integrated.

The 13th five-year plan outline for the national economic and societal development of the People's Republic of China has proposed that "focus on the infrastructure transformation, public service convienientalised [conventionalized], social governance refinement, and sufficiently utilize modern information technology and big data to construct a new pile of model smart cities." The general secretary Jinping Xi has stressed on the workshop of cybersecurity and information.[1] The notions of the new urbanization (1) Centering on citizens enhance the technology provision capacity, pillared at new infrastructure, rooted with new services, focused on new governance; explore the new patterns of constructive executive; build long-term development mechanism; insist on the clarified new development path, further to continuously enhance the level of city modernization, and gradually satisfy the needs of citizens' happy life. (2) Intensive integration: The "three integrations and five crosses" has become the new type of smart city main tune. (3) Green low carbon is the titled meaning of the construction of smart cities. (4) The interactions between the virtuality and reality bring the harmonious unity of the physical world

---

[1] Data source: Chinese information and communication research institution monitoring.

and cyberspace. From the perspective of technology notions, new type of smart cities are the comprehensive collective application platform and are showcased by wide application of new generation of information technology to realize the mutual reflections and collaborative interactions of the city's physical world, cyber virtual space, further to construct a twin digital city systems based on data-driven, software definition, platform support, and the interaction of virtuality and reality (city information modeling). (5) Open multiple: smart city systems are a complicated huge system that is not only surrounding the city energy infrastructure, Internet facilities, the business service, medical education, industries and fields, etc. but also face up to the citizen's groups for providing high-level personalized intelligent services. A new type of smart cities provides mutual reciprocal services to multiple groups and cross-digital gaps, which soothes the city running systems, and the citizens mutually construct and participate, innovate political commercial think tanks, scientific research agencies, and investors cooperative mechanism, to construct the inclusive ecological system.[2]

"Digital Architecture White Paper," which was formally realized on January 11, 2018, states that the digital transformation facilitated the development of China. The world economic forum launched "the advocate for digital transformation," which indicated that during the decade of 2016−25 the digital transformation is expected to bring industrial value and societal value of over 1000 billion. "Digital Architecture White Paper" proposed a "one recognition," that is, mental world (human), physical world, and digital world (cyber), the three-dimensional world of mutual developments. Digital world has become the new engine of the world. Digital architecture is conceptualized to lead the transformation of and update on the industry by using Building Information Modelling (BIM) and cloud computation, big data, logistical net, mobile Internet, and artificial intelligence. It combines the advanced refined construction of theoretical methods, clustering human flow, data, technology, and business system, to realize all processes, elements, participant's digitization, online, and intelligence, so as to construct the projects, enterprises, and industrial platforms of ecological new system (Fig. 10.1).

10.2.2 The organizational scheme of smart city construction

Smart city is a new mode via comprehensive utilization of modern scientific technology to integrate information resources, manage business application systems, strengthen city planning, construction, and management, and it is a new ecological system for city management. Being different from digital city, smart city is featured as to comprehensively utilize logistics network, cloud computation, and public information platform as a representative of modern scientific technology and approaches to comprehensively sense the city information resources, to integrate, dig, analyze, share, and collaborate, to enhance the city management and service level (the housing and construction ministry). The overall framework for smart city contains the network layer (web layer is the foundation for smart city, which

[2] *Digital Architecture White Paper* was formally promulgated on January 11, 2018.

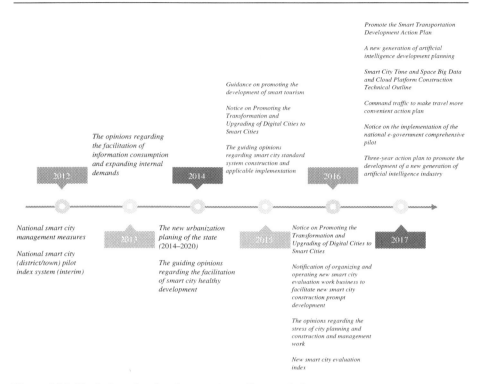

Figure 10.1 Evolution of national smart city policy regulations.

includes electronic information network, Internet, and broadcast and TV network, as well as the three-network integration, logistic network, etc.). The sensory layer is one of the significant features for the smart city, which differs from that for the digital city, and the primary source for the smart city to run data. From the perspective of technology, several main sensory technologies are the watching the land testing sensory technology, RFID technology, wireless sensor network (WSN) technology, Zigbee sensory technology, etc. from the sensory data sources; the main sensory methods are the satellites in the sky, the airplane in the sky, and various sensory equipment on and underground. Planet observation sensing technology, RFID technology, WSN technology, and Zigbee sensing technology use public facilities, including computing resources, Internet resources, storage resources and security facilities, sensory layer, infrastructure public data-set, public information platform, smart application, and user layers.

The structure of smart city includes perception, network, and application layers, which can make the future world increasingly appreciable and measurable, interconnected and interoperable, and intelligent (Liu & Hou, 2010). During the construction of smart city, according to the actual situations and combining the latest technologies, public facilities could adopt the cloud computation or traditional mode, and under the cloud technology mode, make use of virtual technology to virtually process public facilities resources and form a virtual resource pool to make use of cloud service technology, provide the independently running service resources as services and complete public facilities services for the construction of smart city.

The public service database consists of all kinds of application database. The public service data is the service-type data-set formalized via public fundamental data and public business data to cleanly conduct, dig, analyze, provide the themed application resource services for the application units. Wisdom application uses public database and application unit business data as data sources to integrate public data and application unit business data via public information platform, to provide information services to the smart application after the integration, and to improve the application service level and collaborative capability.

The public information platform aims to realize the different departments' systems in the city for resource sharing and business collaboration to effectively avoid the multiple head investment in the city, the repeated construction, the waste of resources, problems, etc. to effectively support the city to normally and healthily run the management. It is the infrastructure of smart city. Public information platform is the entrance and existence of city public data to realize the exchange of city public data as well as the clean integration and processing. It helps one to achieve the sharing service of public data in the city to reshape the city government—specific network and public network with data services and time and space carrier services on the basis of the city public database, and the decision knowledge services based on data mining.

10.2.3 The outline for construction of new smart city and optimization of public service modes

The Communist Party's 18th National People's Congress and the Fourth and Fifth Plenary Session of the 18th CPC Central Committee as guidelines proposed the outline for construction of new smart city and optimization of public service modes to insist on the innovation, coordination, green, open, sharing development notions; to catch up the state to implement the Internet strengthening strategy, Chinese manufacture 2025 strategy, big data strategy, and Internet plus action plan opportunity, surrounding the two-type society and Changsha six on the frontline demands, with four internationalized emerging city, information benefits citizens as goal; to construct the broadband-wide information infrastructure facilities, smart integration informationized application, high-end green modernized industrial system, sustainable innovative development environment, and reliable information security system; to highly enhance Changsha informationized level, and gradually satisfy the government, enterprise, and citizens' demands for informationization; to effectively enhance the city's comprehensive carrier capability and residents happiness index; to create the social environment of "benefitting citizens, prosperous businesses, and good governance; and to build Changsha into the modern regional smart city with international influence, eventually to lead the fulfillment of good life dream, two types of dream, and happiness dream.

The main approaches: Smart Changsha implements the 669 plan, that is, to complete six tasks (to improve information fundamental infrastructure, to construct citizens digital life, develop smart industries, innovate the city comprehensive management, to facilitate the four modernization integration development, and to facilitate the two types of harmonious society) and constructs six stress projects (broadband Changsha project, wireless Changsha project, three-network integration project, Changsha big data center project, network and information security project, new generation information technology industry fostering, and expanding project) to construct nine clouds (citizens' livelihood cloud, governance cloud, benefit the peasants cloud, industrial cloud, business cloud, innovative start-up cloud, police cloud, traffic cloud, and city construction management cloud).[3]

By the year 2020 the informationization of Changsha will step into the leading team of the country, and the digitization application covers each dimension of the economic society; the smart economy becomes the main shape of the economy; smart lifestyle was prevalent; and the city comprehensively realized the smart implementation, where the information overall index reached over 90, to build informationization to facilitate two types of industry development initiative cities, three-network coverage of the urban and city Internet cities, the electronic commerce and digital culture prosperous vibrant cities, smart management and efficient governance—served cities, digitized credit and information security reliable cities, and to make efforts to build Changsha into the smart capital, via two types, that is, innovative capital and green capital in the western and central region, to support Changsha in building into the national intelligent manufacture center, national innovation creativeness center, and the national transportation logistics center.

10.2.3.1 Changsha public security big data application

The Changsha emergency connected the guide system, the sky-net project, the smart transport, smart firework, application systems data by using the cloud computation organically connected via big data processing technology to build the police cloud big data platform; to realize the overload data analysis process, deep mining, comprehensive applications; to overall enhance all kinds of businesses to resolve the cases, seek and allocate, coordinately battle, etc. capability; and gradually to operate the prediction police exploration represented by the security tendency analysis, transport prediction, the sources of the cars analysis, on the basis of the cloud search application; and to provide with all kinds of benefit service information to citizens to innovate the Changsha public security police service pattern.

10.2.3.2 Transport cloud

By integrating the Changsha information resources in the transport field, and based on the Changsha big data center to build a transport cloud, there occurs the facilitating of the Internet plus transport service. To operate the land, water, air, metro, and city commute railways, etc., transport information to improve the coordinate

---

[3] "One cloud, two webs, six data-sets, and nine clouds" (in Chinese: *yiyun liangwang liuku jiuduoyun*).

management and public service capability is required. To explore the transport industry, public security, weather security, earthquake test, etc., cross-departments, cross-region data integration and construction of the transport industry database are required. To actively attract the socially fine resources, and to utilize the transportation big data to deliver the travel information, the transportation disguise add-value services and construction of the convenient transportation service system based on the Internet platform.

10.2.3.3 Smart environmental protection

To combine the logistics technology influence on water body, water sources, air, noise, and polluted sources, abandons to conduct the sensory, the processor, and management formalize the resources environmental shouldering capability dynamics monitoring network covering the main ecological elements. To build a new generation of network smart environmental protection system clustering the smart censoring capability, smart sensory process capability and comprehensive management capability is required as a whole, realizes the data mutual connection and open sharing for the ecological environmental data, and fulfills the overall goal of "precise test, swift delivery, clear calculation, good management," which is aiming at the facilitating of anti-pollution and reduce the elimination process, to strengthen the environmental protection and realize the harmonious development of the environment and humans (Table 10.1).

Table 10.1 The industrial allocation for the smart city applications in Changsha.

Industries	The instructions for the industries' situation
Government services conventionalize citizens	City service has covered social insurance, regional tax, traffic police, etc. Key businesses regarding convenient citizens and the city service visit quantity have stably increased
Traveling	The airport, stations, connecting Weixin payment, the smart purchase, service check, etc. Convenient services were fully online, and the high-speed railway, high press, and underground railway industries embarked on collaboration
Shopping	There were pilots for the smart Tianxin, over 30,000 among all shopping centers, supermarkets, stores, and chain-stores were connected with Weixin payment
Food and entertainment	Over 10,000 shops among all food canteens, KTV, and entertainment industries were connected with Weixin payment
Medical care	Six hospitals and medical institutions realized the reservation of payment, electronic report, etc. Smart medical service capability
Tourism	All touristic venues, hotels, etc. prevalently open the Weixin reservation and selling of tickets businesses

In Changsha, the industries are involved in convenient citizens, traveling, shopping, canteen and entertainment, medical care, and tourism. The city service has covered social insurance, regional tax traffic police, etc. Due to the key services for the citizen conveniences , the city service visit number has stably increased. For traveling, the airport and stations have been connected with Weixin payment, smart purchase of tickets, service inquiry, etc. For the sake of citizens, conveniences were fully made online, and the high-speed railway and high-press underground railway industries have embarked on collaboration.

10.2.4 The impacts of urbanization step onto the era 3.0 and Changsha is practicing to construct smart city

Smart city is to utilize a smart technology approach, such as big data, cloud computation, logistics network, etc. to integrate into the business arenas of the city and provide services to the government, enterprise, and residents. Changsha, as one of the central cities, has taken trials and practices in smart city areas, for instance, in the west side of Changsha Xiang River, one of the core blocks of Meixi Lake district, there has been an organized Meixi smart city limited company, which has built the contents, including the city pass, smart campus, smart tourism, smart community, smart environmental protection (water), smart buildings, to increasingly enhance the living environment and quality.

The public service mode transform is the issue of public service informationization. In the process of smart city developments, there is a need to carry out and gradually upgrade the public service informationization that has become the current public service development, which is a necessary tendency. The national state council that is concerned with the aspect of facilitating information consumption extension and broadening of internal demand opinions (national 2013 No. 32) points out that it is essential to facilitate the public information resources sharing and development and utilization, to enhance the civil arenas information service level, to accelerate three aspects to improve public service informationization level for smart city construction. In the process of smart city construction, by building the smart governance, smart medical care, smart transportation, smart social insurance, smart tourism, etc., public service platforms are required to enable each of the function in the city to coordinate, to operate, to facilitate the government public administration and public service systemically and efficiently, to provide enterprises with qualified service and unlimited innovative space, and to provide all kinds of governance, livelihood, business, etc. with all dimensional information.

10.2.5 Huawei internet of things (IOT) platform development tendency in the arena of smart city

Along with the human society's urbanization, the city's transportation, medical care, housing, and higher environmental pressures further increased. How to realize the smart city management and facilitate the sustainable development of the cities has become one of the themes in contemporary society. The construction of smart city is the reversible trend for contemporary world development.

In the first year of 13th Five-Year Plan, the city plans all over the nation have gradually been carried out, and revealed the new times feature. Some smart city pilots have preferred the comprehensive solution plans at the beginning of construction. From the designation at the top structure, data sharing, and service platform, to consultancy schedule, operation services steps that are to be uniformly built by the professional agencies, as well as their deployment and maintenance. Currently, the smart cities manifested two main tendencies: first the technological tendency aspect platform technology and low power wide area (LPWA) technology swiftly emerge, and protected the powerfully secure aspect for the construction of smart cities; and the ecological tendencies aspect for the industrial ecology from the monotonous to the complicated.

The construction of smart city cannot stand without the innovative development of information technology. It is with the development of cloud computation, mobile Internet, logistics network, and big data continuous development that the time for smart city construction becomes increasingly mature, and more cities hope to apply new technology and new plans to enhance the city management capability to realize the sustainable development.

10.3   Research methodology: case study

10.3.1   Scope

In the rhetoric of the smart city, wireless, ubiquitous computing offered the potential to connect residents to digitized information that could take the place of these civic services formerly found in physical locations, such as what Digital On-Ramps proposed, to move educational services from schools and community centers to a digital application.

Echoing Kitchin (2014a, 2014b) claimed that scholars engaging the smart city research need to move beyond critiquing IBM and the rest of the "urban intelligence industrial complex" (Hill, 2013) to consider why, how, and where cities have enrolled in smart city policy-making.

Methodologically, the research consisted of fieldwork, discourse analysis and narrative analysis of policy documents, press releases from the corresponding municipal office, as well as speeches from relevant parties, and interviews with the midlevel planners involved in implementing Digital On-Ramps. This study focused on Changsha as the research case. Interviews, based on the smart city initiatives framework, were used to qualitatively understand concepts and factors that characterize smart city initiatives. Semistructured interviews were conducted with individuals who are responsible for projects and initiatives that are underway (Fig. 10.2).

Changsha has attracted a substantial level of foreign investment. In 2005, for example, nearly US$1 billion worth of foreign direct investment (FDI) poured into

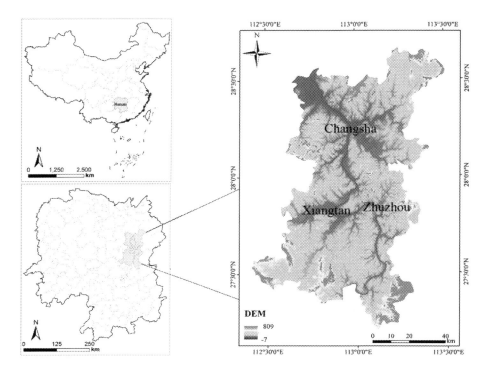

Figure 10.2 Location of the Changsha−Zhuzhou−Xiangtan area.
Zhang, M., Lin, H., Wang, G., Sun, H., Cai, Y. (2019). Estimation of vegetation productivity using a landsat 8 time series in a heavily urbanized area, central China. *Remote Sensing 11*, 133.

the city, mainly in hi-tech, manufacturing, food production, and services. This figure is up 40% in 2001; 59% of the total FDI has come from Hong Kong, South Korea, Singapore, and Japan; 28% has come from the Unite States and 9% from Europe. By the end of 2008, more than 500 foreign companies had made over US $10 million worth of investments in Changsha. Changsha had total retail sales of 74 RMB billion in 2006. But rapid economic growth has made environmental pollution a serious problem in Changsha, caused by rapidly increasing numbers of private cars, widespread construction sites, and numerous industrial facilities on the outskirts of the city.

The politics of Changsha in Hunan province in the People's Republic of China is structured as a dual-party-government system like all other governing institutions in mainland China. Changsha Municipal Government today is deeply influenced by its long past. The Mayor of Changsha is the highest ranking official in the People's Government of Changsha or Changsha Municipal Government. Changsha is governed by a democratically elected People's Congress, which corresponds to the parliament of democratic country. The Head of the Changsha Municipal Government is the Mayor. The Mayor's agreement is required for an Act of Changsha People's

Congress to become law. The People's Congress has a number of different functions. First and foremost, it scrutinizes the execution of constitution, laws, regulations in the city. Another important function is to debate the major issues of the city. Its other roles are provided by the means of carrying on the work of government by voting for leaders, including chairman and vice chairman of the People's Congress, and mayor, deputy mayor, president of the municipal court and president of the municipal procuratorate.[4] Smart construction is a smartened platform, which is targeted at "smart city construction," which comprehensively applies to mobile Internet, cloud computation, big data, and logistic web, etc. and modern information technology and proactively facilitates the transformation of the business management of housing and urban constructive system's information sharing, mutually communicate and connect eventually to realize the goal of "urban construction more orderly, urban management more refined, government services more convenient, the industrial management more effective."[5]

10.3.2 Time series for the diffusion of smart city evolution

Till 2014, the urbanization rate in China was 54.77%, which is much lower than the developed countries. It is predicted that in 2030 the urbanization rate will reach 70%, which is a significant factor and the pillar of Chinese real estate development, interpreted from the Chinese new urbanization development model and the development of Hunan's urbanization. There are several facilitators for the success of urbanization: sufficient funding preparation, reasonable overall plan, orderly industrial development, refined transport sets and effective development ordinance, etc. In the future, a multitude of population continuously entering the cities will also make the urbanization toward development more soundly. The urbanization in era 3.0 is featured as the geographical edge advantage, facilitating the inclusive development of the first, second, and third industries.

On November 7, 2014, in order to facilitate the healthy development of smart cities, the central Internet and information office, national development reform committee, etc.; 26 related departments, formulating into the smart city healthy development departmental coordination working group held the "China smart city innovation conference" in Guangzhou, interpreting to the localities and stakeholders of the "guiding opinions with regard to the facilitation of the healthy development of smart cities," which introduced the next step of promoting smart city construction working key points to related departments.

To build smart cities is a systematic and innovative work, which catches up the new generation of web technology, new generation intelligence manufacture industry, new generation service industry, and the opportunity of urbanization, to decode the city development puzzles, to win the significant strategic decision making,

---
[4] http://www.hnup.com/webapp/solutionzhzj.html.
[5] Red.net 2016-08-10. *The impacts of urbanization step onto the era 3.0 and Changsha is practicing to construct smart city.*

which also relates to the economic transformation and upgrade, social management innovation, and people's life quality enhancement.

Changsha City People's Government Office Printed "Smart Changsha Development Overall Plan (2016–2020)," which indicated the development goal, overall infrastructure, the main tasks, focused projects, and implemented procedures for Changsha City in the future 5 years to comprehensively deploy several basic principles including (1) centering on citizens, and benefitting the entire population; (2) resource integration and mutual connection as well as common sharing; (3) the deeply integration and innovative development; (4) the government guiding and market driven; (5) the application leading and solidating the industries; (6) refining the foundation and controlling the security in this plan.

Meanwhile, there is the development goal that by year 2020 the information level of Changsha will enter the leading rank of the nation, and the digitized application will cover every single dimension of the economic society, and the smart economy will become the main status, the lifestyle of the smart life will be prevalent, the city will comprehensively realize digitized operation, and information index will reach 90, to construct the informationization and promote the "two-type industry" development innovative city, vibrant city of the Internet city, the e-commerce and digital culture prosperity, the service city of digitized management, and effective governance service city, the reliable city of digital trust and information security, to strive to make the Changsha City the capital of smartness, for two types, viz., innovation and green.

Therefore there are six highlighted projects, including: (1) broadbelt Changsha project. In accordance with the national "broadband China" strategy as opportunity, actively promoting major operators to speed up the construction of "urban optical network" process, to build the city light network clustering IP, broad belt, and the integration as a whole, and to realize the network service capability of realizing the entire city network smoothly, and built an information highway for "Smart Changsha," to broaden the business arenas and facilitate the consumption of information; (2) the wireless Changsha project is executed by the network basic infrastructure, mobile data center and platform as well as the application construction, to promote the project. Till 2020 to realize the wireless broadband network profound coverage and promote the social management, public security, public service etc., mobile applications will extend the electronic governance and electronic commerce to gradually extend to the mobile Internet and reduce the government and enterprise running costs, and simultaneously fulfill the goal of prevalent service in citizens' livelihood fields. (3) Three-network integration projects: These projects are responsible to continuously promote the three-network integration modeling project, and realize the network's mutual connection and communication, and resources sharing. (4) Changsha Big data center project: The foundation of Smart Changsha, the Changsha big data center is built upon the national supercomputer Changsha center and cloud base to construct the Changsha big data center, and the information sharing, exchange, open data hub to gradually formalize the clustering, analysis, and decision making smart core; (5) network and information security guarantee project: it comprehensibly constructs the network and information security hierarchically systematic security covering the sense level, network level, the platform level, and the application level of standardized unity to build and refine the network and information security proof system, security responsibility system, the emergency, and save system and service system to effectively protect the information collection, salvage, delivery, process steps information security, and stress the information security management capability construction, and build the entire unified, refined smart city network and information security guarantee system. (6) New generation information technology industry foster and grow project: To strive to develop the cloud computation, big data, logistics network, mobile Internet, etc., new generation of information technology industries facilitates all technological industries' deep integration and constructs the smart city industrial ecological system.

In order to facilitate the city management "Internet plus" series integrative work, and compressible implementation for the decision allocation of the communist party central, the state council concerning the city management work, further to level up the social governance specialization, legalization, smartness, and professional, are to construct the "one platform, big data, and big service." In other venues the smart city trials have embraced with the large achievements with regard to the urbanization and social mobility.

At the start of the 13th Five-Year Plan, the smart city plans across the nation has subsequently been carried out and presents the new era characteristics. Some of the smart city pilots stress the comprehensive solution plan, from the designation of the top structure, the data sharing, and service platform construction, to the consultancy plan, the operation service, etc. Every knot was delivered to the professional institution to unite formally build, allocate, and maintain. So far, the smart city construction has revealed two main tendencies: first, the technology tendency has secured powerfully the construction of the smart city, along with the technology tendencies of platform technology and LPWA technology.

There is the principle of "insisting on six consistence, three separation, and two divides." The six consistencies include one unified standard, unified resources, unified mutual exchange, and unified common applicable development. Three separations refer to the concrete business applicable departments, layers, steps promotion; two do not refer to the finance and no longer arrange the construction of lap room alone, and the budgeted funding to procurators of various basic resources, and not plan to transfer to the smart government cloud platform and no more arrangement of the maintenance funding. The construction of smart city project must adopt the open structure and extendable infrastructure to ensure the comprehensiveness and security and to consider the locality and advances.

Smart city policies were folded into existing, entrepreneurial governance strategies that prioritized economic promotion even as they presented a script of widespread social benefit (Harvey, 2000; Hollands, 2008). In the analysis of policy discourse and outcomes the logic of digital efficiency and technological improvement stayed outside of critique, an example of the positivist belief that the Internet, digital connectivity, and social media hold the capacity to transform cities and social–spatial exchange (Rabari & Storper, 2015) (Fig. 10.3).

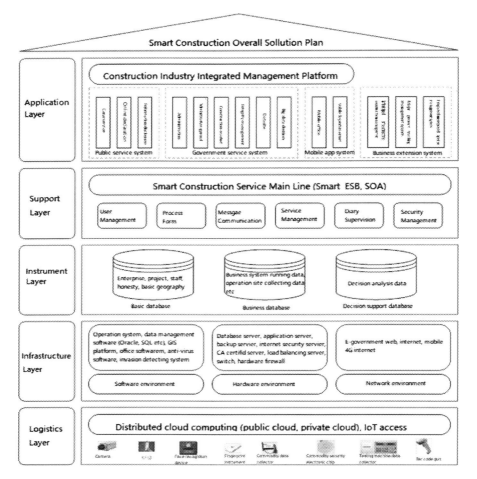

Figure 10.3 The architecture of smart construction project in Changsha.
Source: Changsha Planning Information Service Center, used by permission.

Smart governance cloud platform works as the data interactive core of Changsha city's new smart city construction to realize the contentedness and communication between the departments, construct the information sharing, exchange, open data hub, and gradually formulate the cluster, analysis, decision-making smart core to provide public information service. In accordance with the principle of "up on cloud as the common status, not on layer as exception," all department's extant cloud service or information system should gradually transfer to the smart governance cloud platform. In the case of special reasons, it cannot be proposed to the smart governance cloud platform; it is a must to consult the expert argumentation of the experts' council and report to the new smart city construction management application leading team office (i.e., short for the smart office) to approve.

The six fundamental databases act as the public data core of smart city construction and are dependent on the smart governance, cloud platform to break the departmental data barriers, to realize the unitary construction of public infrastructure database that unify the sources of the data and to avoid the repeated construction.

The nine-cloud application as the presentation of the application effectiveness for the Changsha city's new smart city construction need to highlight the city management's ability enhancement, the citizens' livelihood services respiratory, industrial economics development, etc. aspects construction, and stresses the applicable effective evaluation, and enhance the sense of fulfillment for the masses. The construction of smart city was phased into three stages as digital city, smart city, intelligent city, and currently, we have stepped into the second stage which is referred as smart city, and it has transmitted into the creature from mechanics, to form into the symbiotic, cogoverning, and win–win ecosystem. The highlight of smart city is the application of big data.

10.3.3 Discussion—the fringes

The overall solution proposal can be summarized as one standard system, and one data center, surrounding two business lines, and eventually form into an integrative solution proposal and realize the aim of constructive industry "data one pool, manage one line, and monitor one web." The core of smart city construction data service, and the unified information service standards, includes the building of basic data pool (enterprise, staff, project, honesty, the basic geographical data, the policy regulations, etc.), the business data-set, and the decision-making support pool, the catalog system of information resources, the realization of basic data resources mutual construction and sharing, the data-support for constructing the project administrative approval, the biding, the quality monitoring management, security monitoring management, the enterprise honesty, and decision-making support.

Information sharing to construct a large platform: the construction of integrative information platform, gathering constructive project application, management approval, monitoring, statistics, analyzing as a whole, by business process measurement, information sharing, dynamics update, and big data mining, etc. Information technology instruments, to comprehensively enhance the capability of constructive department's macro adaptation, the market monitoring and the public service capacity, to build the precision decision-making platform and smartened monitoring platform for the responsible departments' information.[6]

One card pass: the future gatekeeper obtains the universe. In the future of Changsha, it will fulfill the "one machine all pass" plan, the Hunan green travel information system limited firm researched smartened life "one pass" and "all know" cellphone app for smart and happy life. The project has been simulated as an IC card via smart phone NFC close payment system, to simulate the cellphone as an IC card, by related standards of the People's Bank, to prepare safe and convenient payment for the users. In the future, Changsha citizens only need to carry one

[6] http://www.changsha.gov.cn/xxgk/szfxxgkml/gzdt/zwdt/201509/t20150923_811067.html.

cellphone to realize the public transport, smartened parking, supermarket convenient store, the living water, electricity, gas charge, the drug store payment, etc.

Meanwhile, in order to resolve the parking problems in the urban area, the Pass Transport Facilities Limited Firm leading to promote the "urban smart parking system" in Changsha, and currently, they are planning to construct two intelligent parking lot and realize the smartened testing parking lot, the smartened inducing parking, the intelligent timing for charge, the comprehensive parking management.

In 2003 the whole nation started to promote the "city one pass"; in 2009 Changsha has embarked on this work, and now the city IC card has deeply integrated in people's daily life. It is claimed that under setting of Internet plus, the urban one pass will bring extreme improvement for the service of smart city. So far the city one pass project has reached a coverage of over 0.65 billion citizen population, and 180 cities. In the development of Internet plus city, the city one pass owns the specialty of small, sticky, and activity, extending to all walks of life in the dressing, eating, living, traveling, and happy, etc. aspect, which can be applied to the communities, the campus, etc. Settings for the application areas contain comprehensive transport, the municipal charge, the small-scale consumption, etc. 40 fields, and forming into thousands of enterprises for the entire industrial chain of upstream and downstream[7].

The smart community is the innovative mode for the facilitation of public service, the conventionalize citizens service digitization of community management and service. The Yuhua District of Changsha city as the innovative experiment field of national community governance and service innovation leads to comprehensively organize, and inject the societal resources and power. In October this year, Hunan Province has started to pilot the socialized running of "happy smart community" project to construct the government information release and public affairs functions. This project has achieved preliminary effects in the pilot of Jinhuan community at Gaoqiao Street of Yuhua District. Nearly 60% of the residents have experienced the more conventionalized real life aspect from the expectations of science, through the easy participation of interactive community and governance; the sufficient verification of the convenience, efficiency of smart communities, further to improve the public management and service capacity. This project will use 1 year to run at 105 communities, to discover the community management service work pinpoints, tough points, and blind points, which also opened the hotlines of 400-80890-590 hotlines and the platform complaint and advice channels. A few days ago, Jingdong city and Changsha People's Government organized the signing ceremony for the smart city project, and both sides will make full use of the technological advantage of Jingdong's big data and AI, depending on the smartened applicable constructive fruits, and build Changsha into the future city model with international competitiveness.

It is acknowledged that the cooperation of both sides will combine the analyzing models of the censoring system of Changsha city and Jingdong city headquarter, relying on the smart government cloud of Changsha city and the constructive fruits of smartened application fruits, combining the multiple timing and space big data

---

[7] http://hn.people.com.cn/n/2014/1203/c337651-23093290.html.

analysis models, and borrow the big data accumulations of Jingdong Group on the aspects of e-commerce, finance, logistics, etc.; on the big data platform: the mayors driving cab project, the credit city, intelligent transport, etc. Nine arenas to deeply cooperate on the project will be operated by phases, and the first phase is mainly for building credit evaluation system, which could be applied to different settings in the credit city, based on the mayors driving cab project on basis of smart government cloud in Changsha city.[8]

10.4 Conclusions

Ever since 2012, Changsha has become the national smart city pilot, via several years' construction. There have been achievements in information basic infrastructure as a pilot city of the state two integration pilot cities, three networks emergent pilot cities, the state next generation Internet pilot city, information convenience city, broadband pilot city. These pilot cities' implementation have laid the foundation, and these basic infrastructures were placed at the first half level, by the five-star Changsha construction in recent years; the infrastructure have basically been refined.

All the European cases have been initiated by local governments, while central initiatives try to develop network of smart cities. The transformation with-respect to ICT in cities in China has taken place since the beginning of this century. Anthopoulos (2014, 2015) classified the existing competition between cities to a "smart" competition, where innovation and ICT are utilized to attract residents, visitors, and investments. One significant finding is that although smart cities mostly begin as public projects, recently they do not compete only in the domains of innovation and of state-of-art technology that transforms them into extensive test-beds and attracts international attention to living labs, but smart cities suggest an extensive niche market.

The progressive smart city needs to create a real shift in the balance of power between the use of information technology by business, government, communities, and ordinary people who live in cities, as well as seek to balance economic growth with sustainability.

Social sustainability implies social cohesion and sense of belonging, while environmental sustainability refers to the ecological and "green" implications of urban growth and development (Gleeson & Low, 2000) in unproblematically adopting some of the assumptions from the IT model of urban development. While smart cities may fly the banner of creativity, diversity, tolerance and culture, the balance appears to be tipped toward appealing to knowledge and creative workers, rather than using IT and arts to promote social inclusion (Graham, 2002; Solnit & Schwartzenberg, 2000). Such shifts would involve the progressive smart city

---

[8] *Jingdong Smart City signs Changsha to jointly build a model of the future city* http://mini.eastday.com/a/180907105309737.html.

addressing issues of power and inequality in the city (Harvey, 2000) as well as begin to seriously respect diversity and build a democratic urban pluralism (Sandercock, 1998). One thing that is patently clear, however, is the degree to which cities have become more unequal through IT (Graham, 2002), the processes of globalization (Harvey, 2000), changes in urban labor markets and increased gentrification (Smith, 1996a, 1996b).

The regulations and institutions have provided evidences and securities for the effective operation and continuous promotion of the smart city construction. Currently, the domestic smart city construction mainly relate to the areas of governance, finance, transport, medical care, education, tourism, logistics, and community governance. With differed focuses in the construction of smart city, there are three types of development modes. Type one concentrates on the intellectualized "links" of the infrastructure and builds an Internet infrastructure everywhere. Type two is directed by the industries and paid more attention to the development of information, including the science development trend; and the third type is stressed by the resolution of urgent demands of city development and the improvement of citizen's living standard, where it focuses on the digitized application of the enterprises citizens, and governments further to facilitate the industrial development by applications.

Changsha city is constructing the smart city and building the comforting railway new city (people's net) not only for the smart cities, but also for the high press new district when first plan and construct has added the "sponge city," "comprehensive launch," etc. to new city design notions, by using information and communication technologies to test, analyze, and integrate the city operation core system. Each item of the key information gives smart reaction to all the demands including citizens' livelihood, environmental protection, public security, city service, business commercial activities, which will be the future city management notions for the high railway new city.

The sources of smart city construction form a refined market economy that runs mechanism, while the decisive role of deploying resource is to create a healthy and fine market environment. To rationalize the relationship between the government and market, it is the precondition to make use of their decisive roles in smart city construction resources allocation. At this moment, all levels of governments have played the role of leaders, constructors, supervisors, assessors, etc. When the obligations and authority restraints in aspects of providing city management and public services are difficult to differ and precisely defined, it is in need of the government to scientifically recognize their own roles in city plan construction. To steer rather than row, and to clarify the concrete contents of their power and obligation lists, it is required to respect and follow the development discipline of market economy and to manifest the significant role of market in the smart city construction. Therefore it is the urgent desire to combine the actual situations, the policy demands, and the actual problems to make the personalized smart city development strategy and encourage the participation of multiple interest—related bodies to truthfully realize the sustainable and harmonious development of the city.

Acknowledgment

The author would like to thank Dr. Leonidas Anthopoulos for the invitation in drafting the chapter story in southern central China, his appropriate review comments and the anonymous reviewer remarks in adjusting it into one region instead of multiple cities. Thanks go to the related contributors for the figures used in this chapter.

About the author

Qiaomei Yang is a PhD candidate at Department of Public Administration and Sociology at Erasmus School of Social and Behavioral Sciences, Rotterdam. Prior to coming to Europe, Qiaomei studied public administration in China and got her research master degree in July 2014. Her PhD project is *The Diffusion and Adoption of Government Use of Official Microblogging Services in relation to G2C Interactions in Chinese Local Governments*. In 2015 she presented her research in 2015 EGPA Annual Conference PhD Symposium Meeting and 2015 Conference of the Transatlantic Policy Consortium (TPC). In 2016 she presented her paper *Government-to-Citizen Interaction on Government Microblogging Services* at The 20th Annual Conference of International Research Society of Public Management (IRSPM). In 2017 she presented her paper *Intention Survey of Citizens' Use of Government Microblogging Service* in 2017 Fall International Research Conference of Association for Public Policy Analysis & Management Conference (APPAM). In 2018 she presented her paper *The Value Orientation of Cross-Sectorial Collaboration on Chinese Government Microblogging Platform* in The Social Innovation and Change Initiative (SICI) research conference Rethinking Cross-Sector Social Innovation, and her paper *Promises and Pressures in China's Digital Democracy* in Scandinavian Workshop on E-Government (SWEG). At the same year, her article *Microblogging and Authoritarian Governance Regimes: Results from a Survey on the Use of Sina Weibo by Chinese Citizens* got published on *The Electronic Journal of e-Government*, 2018, 16(2). Her main research interest includes social media, e-government in China, and decision-making.

References

Anthopoulos. (2014). Smart cities and their roles in city competition: A classification. *International Journal of Electronic Government Research, 10*(1), 63−77.
Anthopoulos. (2015). Understanding the smart city domain: A literature review. In M. P. Rodríguez-Bolívar (Ed.), *Transforming city governments for successful smart cities* (Vol. 8, pp. 9−18). Public Administration and Information Technology. Available from https://doi.org/10.1007/978-3-319-03167-5_2.
Chatterton, P. (2000). Will the real creative city please stand up. *City, 4*(3), 390−397.
Chatteron, P., & Hollands, R. (2002). Theorising urban playscapes: Producing, regulating and consuming youthful nightlife city spaces. *Urban Studies, 39*(1), 95−116.

Gleeson, B., & Low, N. (2000). Unfinished business': Neoliberal planning reform in Australia. *Urban Policy & Research, 18*(1), 7−28.

Graham, S. (2002). *Bridging urban digital divides: Urban polarisation and information and communication.*

Harvey, D. (2000). *Spaces of hope.* Edinburgh University Press.

Hill, D. (2013). Essay: On the smart city; Or, a "manifesto" for smart citizens instead. *City of sound.* Retrieved from <http://www.cityofsound.com/blog/2013/02/on-the-smart-city-a-call-forsmart-citizens-instead.html>.

Hollands, R. G. (2008). Will the real smart city please stand up? *City, 12*(3), 303−320. Available from https://doi.org/10.1080/13604810802479126.

Kitchin, R. (2014a). Big data, new epistemologies and paradigm shifts. *Big Data & Society, 1*(1), 1−12.

Kitchin, R. (2014b). Making sense of smart cities: Addressing present shortcomings. *Cambridge Journal of Regions, Economy and Society.* Available from https://doi.org/10.1093/cjres/rsu027.

Komninos, N. (2002). *Intelligent cities: Innovation, knowledge systems and digital spaces.* London: Taylor and Francis.

Liu, Y., & Hou, R. (2010). About the sensing layer in Internet of Things. *Computer Study*(5), 55, 62.

Rabari and Storper. (2015). The digital skin of cities: Urban theory and research in the age of the sensored and metered city, ubiquitous computing and big data. *Cambridge Journal of Regions Economy & Society.* Available from https://doi.org/10.1007/978-94-011-5450-5_34.

Sandercock, L. (1998). *Towards cosmopolis: Planning for multicultural cities* (p. 258) Chichester: John Wiley.

Shelton. (2015). The 'actually existing smart city'. *Cambridge Journal of Regions, Economy and Society, 8*(1), 13−25.

Smith. (1996a). *Environmental hazards: Assessing risk and reducing disaster* (6th ed.). Routledge. (4 Jan. 2013).

Smith, N. (1996b). *The new urban frontier: Gentrification and the revanchist city.* London: Routledge.

Solnit, R., & Schwartzenberg, S. (2000). *Hollow city: Gentrification and the eviction of urban culture.* London, UK: Verso Books.

Wiig, A. (2016). The empty rhetoric of the smart city: From digital inclusion to economic promotion in Philadelphia. *Urban Geography, 37*(4), 535−553. Available from https://doi.org/10.1080/02723638.2015.1065686.

Further reading

Anthopoulos, L. (2017). *Understanding smart cities − A tool for smart government or an industrial trick? Public administration and information technology* (Vol. 22). New York: Springer Science + Business Media.

Balakrishna. Enabling technologies for smart city services and applications. In *2012 Sixth international conference on next generation mobile applications, services and technologies.*

Boyle, T., Giurco, D., Mukheibir, P., Liu, A., Moy, C., White, S., & Stewart, R. (2013). Intelligent metering for urban water: A review. *Water, 5*(3), 1052−1081.

Campbell, H. S. (1999). Professional sports and urban development: A brief review of issues and studies. *Review of Regional Studies, 29*(3), 272−292.

Changsha People's Government Office printed. *Smart Changsha Development Overall plan (2016−2020)*. <http://www.cs-icloud.gov.cn/news/detail/1691> 15.03.17.

Cocchia, A. (2014). Smart and digital city: A systematic literature review. In R. P. Dameri, & C. Rosenthal-Sabroux (Eds.), *Smart city: How to create public and economic value with high technology in urban space* (pp. 13−43). Springer, Cham. Available from https://doi.org/10.1007/978-3-319-06160-3_2.

Cosgrave, E., Arbuthnot, K., & Tryfonas, T. (2013). Living labs, innovation districts and information marketplaces: A systems approach for smart cities. *Procedia Computer Science, 16*, 668−677.

Kaufmann, D., Leautier, F., & Mustruzzi, M. (2005). *Governance and the city: An empirical exploration into global determinants of urban performance. World Bank Policy Research Working Paper No. 3712*. Available at SSRN: <https://ssrn.com/abstract = 545723> or <https://doi.org/10.2139/ssrn.545723>.

Hollands, R., & Chatteron, P. (2004). The London of the north?: Youth cultures, urban change and nightlife in Leeds. In R. Unsworth, & J. Stillwell (Eds.), *Twenty first century Leeds: Geographies of a regional city*. Leeds University Press.

Mechant, P., Stevens, I., Evens, T., & Verdegem, P. (2012). E-deliberation 2.0 for smart cities: A critical assessment of two "idea generation" cases. *International Journal of Electronic Governance, 5*, 82−98.

National Development and Reform *Committee and Internet and Information Office of Central Government*. <http://www.hnup.com/webapp/solutionZHZJ.html>.

National Economy and Societal Development Statistics Report. <http://www.gov.cn/shuju/2017-02/28/content_5171643.htm>.

Paskaleva, K. (2011). The smart city: A nexus for open innovation? *Intelligent Buildings International, 3*, 153−171.

Peck, J., Siemiatycki, E., & Wyly, E. (2014). Vancouver's suburban involution. *City, 18*(4−5), 386−415.

Red.net. *The interpretation of the urbanization wisdom in era 3.0*. <http://www.csgy.gov.cn/ztpd/ydhlw/201703/t20170307_1934636.htm> Accessed 12.08.16.

Sandercock, L. (2003). *Cosmopolis II: Mongrel cities of the 21st century* (2nd ed.). London: Continuum.

Schuurman, D., Baccarne, B., Mechant, P., & De Marez, L. (2012). Smart ideas for smart cities: Investigating crowdsourcing for generating and selecting ideas for ICT innovation in a city context. *Journal of Theoretical and Applied Electronic Commerce Research, 7*, 11−12.

The notice of Changsha city government in printing. *Changsha city new smart city construction management applicable method*. <http://www.changsha.gov.cn/xxgk/gfxwj/srmzf/201709/t20170922_2050071.html>.

Young, R. F., & Wolf, S. A. (2006). Goal attainment in urban ecology research: A bibliometric review 1975−2004. *Urban Ecosystems, 9*(3), 179−193.

Smart city evolution in India: the cases of Dehradun, Nagpur, and Allahabad

Vinay Kandpal
University of Petroleum & Energy Studies, Dehradun, India

Chapter Outline

11.1 Introduction 243
11.2 Background 244
11.3 Research methodology 246
    11.3.1 Dehradun 246
    11.3.2 Nagpur city 249
    11.3.3 Allahabad 252
11.4 Conclusions 256
Acknowledgment 257
About the author 257
References 257
Further reading 258

11.1 Introduction

The speedy increase of Indian economy has put a stress on physical infrastructure. As the worldwide population continues to rise at a steady pace, more and more people are moving from rural or hilly areas to semiurban or urban cities on an everyday basis. The percentage of India's urban population has grown steadily during the past few decades, jumping from 6.2% in 1951 to 31.2% in 2011, and it is expected to reach 40% by 2031. As per 2011 Census, cities accommodate nearly 31% of India's current population and contribute 63% of Gross Domestic Product (GDP). Urban regions are expected to put up 40% of India's population and contribute 75% of India's GDP by 2030. This necessitates a comprehensive development of physical, institutional, social, and economic infrastructure. Smart future cities could be a crucial step toward the simplicity of life of people. There is a need for aspiring smart future cities in emerging economies to address the deep-seated structural issues of municipal governments and engage in the process of governance transformation rather than adopting temporary solutions. The flagship smart city mission of the Prime Minister of India Mr. Narendra Modi was inspired by Gujarat International Finance Tec-city in the state of Gujarat, which is a smart city still under construction influenced by the Chinese city, Shanghai. The Government of

India (GoI) has approved the Smart Cities Mission under which 100 smart cities would be made. Smart city is a great prospect for infrastructure companies. In India, given its demographics and diversity, unique challenges and opportunities exist for developing "smarter" cities, which attract increased investment, employ innovative technology, create environmentally sustainable solutions, grow operational efficiencies, and improve the lives of urban citizens.

Most of the countries are trying to provide excellent facilities to its citizens, and India is gearing up to make its smart city project a success. Both private sector and government departments along with citizens are attempting to ferment together to accomplish this goal (Chatterjee & Kar, 2018). A study by Mckinsey Report (2018) suggests that in the next 15 years, about 200 million people will transport from rural to urban areas in India. Smartness in the city means smart design, smart utilities, smart housing, smart mobility, and smart technology. There is a need for the cities to get smarter to manage complexity, increase efficiency, reduce expenses, and improve quality of life. Smart cities focus on their most pressing demands and on the greatest opportunities to better lives. They tap a range of approaches—digital and information technologies, urban planning best practices, public–private partnerships (PPPs), and policy change—to make a difference. They always put people first. In the approach to the Smart Cities Mission of GoI the objective is to promote cities that provide core infrastructure and give a decent quality of life to its citizens, a clean and sustainable environment and application of "smart" solutions. The focus is on sustainable and inclusive development, and the idea is to look at compact areas, create a replicable model, which will act like a lighthouse to other aspiring cities. The concept of smart city, which has become really popular these days (Albino, Berardi, & Dangelico, 2015), is based on the adoption of ICT (Information and Communication Technologies) as ways to revitalize economic opportunities and to increase global competitiveness. In this sense the GoI is devoted to raise the quality of life for citizens through its urban development agenda (Bloomberg Philanthropies, 2017; Nair, 2017). Cities generate new varieties of physical problems such as scarcity of resources, air pollution, difficulty in waste management, traffic congestions, and inadequate, deteriorating, and aging infrastructures, etc. (Chourabi et al., 2012). Another set of challenges arise from the massive levels of digitization and generation of data (Chauhan, Agarwal, & Kar, 2016).

11.2 Background

Smart cities have been realized as intelligent digital ecosystems installed in the urban space (Chourabi et al., 2012; Desouza & Flanery, 2013; Giffinger, Fertner, Kramar, Meijer, & Pichler-Milanovic, 2007; Lee, Phaal, & Lee, 2013; Neirotti, De Marco, Cagliano, Mangano, & Scorrano, 2014; Piro, Cianci, Grieco, Boggia, & Camarda, 2014; Wey & Hsu, 2014). Angelidou (2014) approached smart city using a civil engineering and urban architecture lens and classified smart cities as new versus existing cities, and corresponding smart city projects to "soft" versus "hard" implementations. More than 150 smart city cases can be observed around the world, which can be classified into (1) from scratch city cases; (2) hard ICT infrastructure focused cases; and (3) soft ICT infrastructures in the urban space (Anthopoulos, Janssen, & Weerakkody, 2016). Since there is no clear smart city approach yet, there have been several attempts by international organizations to standardize smart city solutions, such as for smart water, energy, transportation, buildings, etc. Smartness in city means smart design, smart utilities, smart housing, smart mobility, and smart technology. There is a need for the cities to get smarter to manage complexity, increase efficiency, reduce expenses, and improve quality of life.

Smart cities focus on their most pressing demands and on the greatest opportunities to better lives. They tap a range of approaches—digital and information technologies, urban planning best practices, PPPs, and policy changes—to make a difference. They always put people first.

The UK Department of Business, Innovation and Skills considers smart cities a process rather than as a static outcome, in which increased citizen engagement, hard infrastructure, social capital, and digital technologies make cities more livable, resilient, and better able to respond to challenges.

The British Standards Institute defines smart city as "the efficient integration of physical, digital and human systems in the built environment to deliver sustainable, comfortable and inclusive future of its citizens."

India's economy is spreading out quickly. By 2030, it is expected to have risen by five times, buoyed largely by the country's urban centers. During the same period the country's labor force is expected to grow by 270 million workers, with urban jobs accounting for 70% of that growth. Today, India is less than 30% urban, and the quality of life in its cities is chronically low. However, with the two-thirds of GDP already generated in India's cities and rural urban migration patterns accelerating, the country faces a critical challenge: managing this rapid urbanization in a way that enhances the livability of India's urban spaces.

The GoI has proposed USD 333 million under "safe city" project, to make seven big cities (Delhi, Mumbai, Kolkata, Chennai, Ahmedabad, Bangalore, and Hyderabad) to center on technological progress rather than workforce. The Ministry of Urban Development plans to invest more than USD 20 billion in the metro rail projects in coming years. The GoI has planned to have an electric vehicle charging station in all urban areas and along all state and national highways by 2027. India has invested $1.2 billion so far and hopes to attract more funding from private investors and from abroad. Developing a new or greenfield smart city with target population of 5–10 lakh is likely to require financial investment ranging between INR 75,000 and 150,000 crore and may require 8–10 years for implementation.

The societal and economic features of the urban population also help to understand the notion of Indian cities. Indian cities do not represent examples of planned, equitable, safe, and sustainable or inclusive growth. Indian cities are in desperate need of better urban planning and administration, and fresh ideas are urgently required. Instead of the entire city, one part will be selected for carrying out the improvement work.

Accordingly, during the 5-year duration of the mission, only one part of the city will undergo a transformation, whereas during the same period, the remaining parts of the city will be developed and governed in the usual manner, which is currently marked by numerous inefficiencies. Poor and vulnerable groups may be found living within the specific areas selected from the city for the purpose of transformation. The smart city plan has to look into the living and livelihood condition of slum dwellers, beggars, and poor people.

Slum areas are a focal point for redevelopment plans, and Greenfield projects feature inclusionary zoning, with a requirement for 15% of housing to be affordable. However, urban poverty is complex. Many of the urban poor have migrated from rural areas and lack skills, often finding their way into menial jobs. The smart cities will be adjudicated for their ability to train and impart skills to the urban poor, as well as to provide affordable housing.

11.3 Research methodology

The study mainly focuses on an effective analysis of SWOT (strengths, weaknesses, opportunities, and threats) based on the smart city, to promote urban development of Nagpur, Allahabad, and Dehradun. An attempt is made to present the manuscript in the form of analysis of the case. It shows the scenario of the cities, which includes its history, demographics, data of its economy, the stakeholders involved, and SWOT analysis.

11.3.1 Dehradun

Dehradun is the capital of the Indian state of Uttarakhand, near the Himalayan foothills (Fig. 11.1). At its core is the six-sided Ghanta Ghar clock tower. To the southwest is Paltan Bazaar, a busy shopping area. Just east is the Sikh temple Gurdwara Nanaksar, topped with ornate white and golden domes. In Clement town to the city's southwest, Mindrolling Monastery is a Tibetan Buddhist center with shrine rooms in its Great Stupa. Dehradun Municipal Corporation is locally known as Nagar Nigam Dehradun. Other urban entities involved in civic services and city governance and management include Mussoorie Dehradun Development Authority, Special Area Development Authority, Jal Sansthan, and Jal Nigam among others. Dehradun is also known for its basmati rice and bakery products.

11.3.1.1 Strengths

1. *Strategic location:* Dehradun is strategically located and has good connectivity to New Delhi by air, rail, and road. It serves as gateway for the key tourist destinations of the state. The floating population recorded for Dehradun is 20,000 people per day. It is well connected and in proximity to popular Himalayan tourist destinations and Hindu holy cities of Haridwar and Rishikesh. Industrial and educational hub of Roorkee is also nearby.

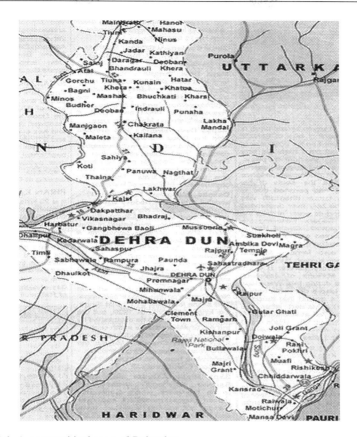

Figure 11.1 A geographical map of Dehradun.

2. *City of schools:* Dehradun is an important educational hub of India embraced with large number of leading public schools and colleges in both government and private sectors with over 1.70 lakh students enrolled. Dehradun is considered the citadel of prestigious public schools such as The Doon School, Welham Girls and Boys School, Convent of Jesus & Mary, St Thomas School, and Rashtriya Indian Military College.
3. *Literacy rate:* The average literacy rate is over 84%, quite high when compared to the national average of 74%. This augments the quality of human resource available in the city.
4. *Dehradun is anchor to organizations of national importance*, namely, Geological Survey of India, Wadia Institute of Himalayan Geology, Indian Institute of Remote Sensing, Forest Research Institute (FRI), and Indian Military Academy and Headquarters of Oil and Natural Corporation.
5. *Colonial age heritage structures*, namely, Astley hall, Clock Tower (hexagonal form), Jesus Mary Church, FRI, Indian Military Academy, Khalanga War memorial, Ashoka's Rock Edict (under Archeological Survey of India), and Ashwamedh Sthal of Raja Sheel Barman (Under Archeological Survey of India).

11.3.1.2 Weaknesses

1. *Less than expected level of urban utilities:* While the Dehradun Municipal Corporation has been taking initiatives toward Solid Waste Management and sanitation issues, the identified municipal services are below the expected level to cater to ever-increasing migration.
2. *High population density:* The population density of Dehradun is 1900 km^2 persons per km^2. In 2001−11, Dehradun had a growth rate of around 32.48%, higher than the national average of 7.64%, resulting in congestion in the city core.
3. *Inefficient transport and parking:* Total 48.1% of roads in Dehradun are used for on-street parking on both the sides. Weak public transportation system has led to plying of vikrams without permits adding to the level of pollution in the city. There is significant amount of mismanagement in terms of the route planning for the vikrams and city buses.
4. *Lack of employment opportunities:* As per low workforce participation, in 2011, the workforce participation ratio was about 34:66. The share of main workers is 30% in the total workforce, 4% is shared by the marginal workers, and share of nonworkers is 66%. There is absence of enough employment opportunities in the service sector in line with the employable population of the city.

11.3.1.3 Opportunities

1. *Gateway to tourist destinations:* Investment toward promotion and development of facilities catering to floating population could serve as making the city a "Hub" for key tourist cities under Hub & Spoke model wherein the routes to the identified cities could be strengthened, promoting *Regional Rapid Transit System* (RRTS), implementing the Mussoorie−Dehradun ropeway. Significant volume of tourist footfall could be retained for an extra day in the city by restoration and conservation of the heritage structures in the city and creating places of tourists' interests and information within the city.
2. *Infotainment hub (hospitality, vocational, higher education, information, and entertainment centers for kids and tourist):* Given the high number of schools and educational institutions, policy incentives toward attracting institutions of repute would help to start a Dehradun center. At present, the city has only one Institute of Hotel Management (IHM), and given the hospitality sector growth opportunities in the city, such institutes could be set up. Given the high number of educational institutes, the convergence with GoI schemes, namely, skill India, could be undertaken through tie-ups with the existing institutes. The city presents the opportunity to set up facilities with informational, educational, and entertainment values for the large mass of students and tourists.
3. *Qualified employable workforce:* About 75% of the population in Dehradun is below the age of 45 years. Because of high literacy rate and good institutions, the city has good quality of employable population. This provides an opportunity for strengthening employment opportunities in line with the strength of the city, that is, in hospitality and tourism-related sectors within the city to provide more employment opportunities to captive human resources.
4. *Potential to develop as counter magnet city to National Capital Region (NCR):* Situated at around 250 km from Delhi and with over saturation of NCR due to immigration and good infrastructure of rail, road, and air connectivity with NCR, National Capital Region Planning Board (NCRPB) has already included Dehradun in the list of counter magnet cities to NCR.

11.3.1.4 Threats

1. *Depleting environment resources:* There is a decline in the urban green spaces in Dehradun city from 22.98% of total area in 2004 to 15.13% in 2009. In addition, growing environmental pollution personalized vehicles has adversely affected the livability in the city.
2. *Possibility of unplanned growth along the Haridwar road:* The city has found natural expansion along the Haridwar road, and with the ongoing strengthening of the highway; there is high chance of further unplanned growth along the corridor.
3. *Crime rate:* The large section of nonworking population can give rise to an increased crime rate in the city if not channelized productively.
4. *Migration:* There is likelihood of large-scale migration to the city from the nearby peri-urban areas and other parts of the state putting strain on its infrastructure and creating further housing shortages.

11.3.2 Nagpur city

Nagpur is the third largest city of the Indian state of Maharashtra after Mumbai and Pune (Fig.11.2). Nagpur is the 13th largest Indian city in terms of population. It has been proposed as one of the smart cities in Maharashtra. Nagpur is the seat of the

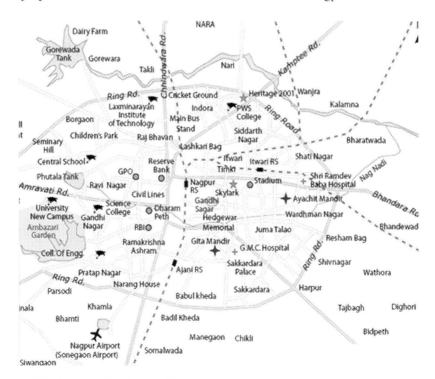

Figure 11.2 A geographical map of Nagpur.

annual winter session of the Maharashtra state assembly. It is a major commercial and political center of the Vidarbha region of Maharashtra. According to a survey by a news channel, Nagpur was identified as the best city in India in livability, greenery, public transport, and health-care indices.

The SWOT analysis for Nagpur is discussed in the following sections:

11.3.2.1 Strengths

1. *Strategic location:* Nagpur is the geographical center of the country and enjoys an efficient transportation infrastructure with road, rail, and air connectivity to major urban or metropolitan cities. Nagpur has the potential to become a key hub of central India.
2. *Rich in natural resources:* The presence of perennial rivers such as Pench, Kanhan, and Vena endow the Nagpur region with abundant water resources; Vena dam has a capacity of 23.5 million cubic meters, and the total line storage capacity is 380 million cubic meters. Nagpur is also one of the greenest cities in the country. For every 10 persons, there are nine trees in Nagpur. In addition, industrial land available in Butibori (Asia's largest industrial estate) and other industrial areas can propel industrial growth with industrial land prices being only 10% and 14% of the industrial land prices in Thane and Pune, respectively. A variety of minerals such as coal (23% of state's reserves), manganese (45% of state's reserves), and limestone and iron ore (76% state's reserves) are found in the Nagpur Metropolitan Region.
3. *Competence to implement PPP projects successfully:* Nagpur is perhaps the only city in the country with a broad-based PPP implementation competence. Nagpur's marquee PPP success is the 24 × 7 water supply project, a pilot project. With the immense success of the pilot the project is now being scaled up to the entire city and will be completed by 2019. In addition, Nagpur has also implemented projects such as recycling and reuse of 130 million liters per day wastewater, installation of LED street lights in place of conventional street lights, city bus operations and collection, and treatment of solid waste management. The city has cleverly leveraged private sector efficiencies for efficient service delivery.
4. *Established medical and education hub of central India:* With nearly 625 hospitals the city has a total bed capacity of 12,000. With three beds per 1000 population, Nagpur is a medical hub for the central India region. With 35 engineering colleges, three medical colleges, and a host of research and professional education institutions, Nagpur has emerged as the education hub of central India. Reputed institutions such as Visvesvaraya National Institute of Technology, National Environmental Engineering Research Institute Indian Institute of Management Nagpur, Animal Husbandry and Fisheries University, and Nagpur University are present in the city. With the upcoming Indian Institute of Information Technology, Nagpur, All India Institute of Medical Sciences, Nagpur will be able to expand on its reputation as an education hub and facilitate setting up of startups and other entrepreneurial ventures.
5. *Vicinity of tiger tourism hot spots*: There are an estimated 243 tigers and 3 Project Tiger within the Vidarbha region. The region also has four national parks that attract tourists in large number (520,000 in 2009). Nagpur is the key access point for reaching these tourist locations that add to the city's economic potential.
6. *Experience in setup and management of special purpose vehicles:* The Nagpur Municipal Corporation (NMC) has already set up an Special Purpose Vehicle (SPV) in the form of the Nagpur Environment Services Ltd. for implementing the 24 × 7 water supply project

in Nagpur. In addition, the Nagpur Improvement Trust is also akin to an SPV that has been executing urban development projects in the city's periphery. Thus Nagpur has substantial experience in setting up and management of special purpose vehicles.

11.3.2.2 Weaknesses

1. *Multiple planning institutions:* Nagpur has multiple planning agencies that shape urban growth but in an uncoordinated manner. This has resulted in dichotomous urban growth with a significant portion of the city's population living in unplanned, haphazard, and vulnerable areas with the paucity of services and a subpar quality of life.
2. *Unplanned and haphazard development:* The eastern periphery of Nagpur is made up of a number of unplanned layouts inconsistent with the development plan land use provisions. It is estimated that there are over 2450 layouts where existing land use is inconsistent with proposed land use of the development plan of Nagpur. This includes mauzas such as Nara, Nari, Wanjara, Wanjri, Bharatwada, Pardi, Watoda, Tajbagh, Dighori, Manewada, and Somalwada.
3. *Inequitable distribution of civic services:* The 2450 unplanned layouts are estimated to house 30% of the city's population. Being unplanned, these layouts are unable to access civic services and continue to subsist in squalor. Services such as adequate water supply, sanitation and sewerage, public transport, and street lighting are hardly available to this section of the city. This has severely affected livability parameters and offers compromised quality of life to the residents of such layouts.
4. *Weak local public transportation systems:* Bus services are the only means of public transport available in the city, which has led to an increasing number of private vehicles plying on the city roads. At present, public bus transport caters to only 12% of the commuting population. Despite efforts such as route rationalization and procurement of additional buses, the city has had limited success in shifting its commuting population to the public transport system.
5. *Administrative and operational inefficiencies affecting quality of public service delivery:* While NMC has developed more than 60 e-governance modules, reach of these services is limited. Further, limited convergence and compartmental approach of departments has also affected overall service delivery. The use of IT/smart technology for operations is extremely limited at present, and hence, it is critical to scale up the use of technology to achieve incremental benefits of improved operations.
6. *Lack of employment opportunities:* Nagpur's economic growth has not picked up pace over the years, which has resulted in the young and educated people not finding adequate employment opportunities. An estimated 11,000 engineers, 800 management graduates, and 250 doctors graduate from Nagpur each year.

11.3.2.3 Opportunities

1. *Potential to become a multimodal logistics hub with Multimodal International Cargo Hub Airport Nagpur (MIHAN) playing a key role:* While Goods and Service Tax (GST) will make Nagpur a cost-effective distribution center, its connectivity via rail, road, and air will make it an attractive location for multimodal logistics activity. The growth of MIHAN will also ensure creation of a diverse economic base propelling all round development in Nagpur.
2. *Potential for Transit-Oriented Development (TOD) due to metro rail project:* Two metro routes of 38 km have been planned across the city. Works for 6 km are already underway.

High density mixed development, through *Forest Survey of India* (FSI) of 4 or more, along the metro alignment will encourage TOD in areas like Sitabuldi and Jail ward. Shifting the Central Jail will unlock prime real estate, which can be utilized for developing high-density retail/medical/entertainment zones.

3. *Availability of government land:* A large number of government, industrial, and NMC land are available for development. Leveraging the government institutions' land bank can generate resources to fund infrastructure expansion.
4. *A host of infrastructure projects will add to the city's economic agenda for implementation of in-pipeline projects*: Orange city street project, 142 acre International Standard Sport Complex and sports university complex at Wathoda, 100 acre skill development center at Watoda, Gorewada International Zoo, and Nagpur–Mumbai super communication expressway will exert much needed push to the local economy.
5. *Rejuvenation of water sources due to Nag riverfront development:* The Nag riverfront development project focuses on pollution abatement as well as place making by developing promenades and open spaces for recreation. The pollution abatement Detailed Project Report (DPR) has received in-principle funding approval from the Ministry of Environment, Forest and Climate Change (MoEF). The Nag river will be rejuvenated through these interventions.
6. *Potential to boost tourism:* Deekshabhoomi, a much-vaunted Buddhist memorial, can be aggressively marketed as a tourist destination. The Gorewada International Zoo can add to the tourism potential of the city.

11.3.2.4 Threats

1. *Brain drain phenomenon:* The young and educated are increasingly moving out of Nagpur in search of employment. The lack of employment opportunities compels the youth to migrate out of Nagpur to other centers. This out-migration is evidenced by the Census 2011 figures; the decadal growth rate declined from 27% to 19%.
2. *Underdevelopment in MIHAN:* The industrial growth in Nagpur has not been dynamic enough to create a vibrant economy. In addition, MIHAN was expected to fuel the economic growth of Nagpur with an estimated 125,000 direct jobs. However, the slow growth of MIHAN has further accentuated the lack of employment avenues in Nagpur. With the political capital that Nagpur currently has, growth of MIHAN can be accelerated. However, if the growth in MIHAN continues to be slow, Nagpur will continue to witness out-migration, which can impact the city's all-round growth prospects.

11.3.3 Allahabad

Allahabad is one of the largest cities of Uttar Pradesh (Fig. 11.3). The city is known worldwide for its magical confluence of history, culture, and religion (City Development Plan of Allahabad, 2006). The city may be divided into three physical parts: (1) Trans-Ganga or the Gangapar plain, (2) the Ganga–Yamuna doab (confluence), and (3) Trans-Yamuna or the Yamunapar tract, all three of which are formed by Ganga and its tributary Yamuna, the latter joining the former at Allahabad, the confluence being known as sangam. General topography of the city is plain with moderate undulations. As per Census of India, 2011, total area of the city is approximately 70 km^2 and population is 1168,385.

Figure 11.3 A geographical map of Allahabad.

11.3.3.1 Strengths

1. *Strong historical and cultural identity:* Well established pilgrimage center, one of the four sites in India hosting the Kumbh fair every 12 years
   a. Annually 4 crore tourists visit Allahabad; around 0.3% comprise foreign tourists; over the last 5 years, there is a 27% increase in tourist inflow. The Maha Kumbh Mela (fair) in 2013 itself hosted close to 7.5 crore visitors (with 3.5 lakh foreigners).
   b. Fairly large inventory of built heritage comprising nearly 30 temples of various styles; Ananda Bhawan and other colonial era spaces such as Khusro Bagh; Chandrasekhar Azad Park and Minto Park.
   c. River shoreline of around 40 km comprising both Yamuna and Ganga.
2. *Known zonal center for higher education:* A number of renowned and premier educational institutions of higher learning are present in the city.
   a. Allahabad University (central), Motilal Nehru National Institution of Technology, Motilal Nehru Medical College; Indian Institute of Information Technology, Govind Ballabh Pant Social Sciences Institute, Agricultural University, and the Allahabad State University
   b. Coaching classes for competitive examinations comprise a major industry in the city

3. *Natural resource base of agricultural produce and silica:*
   a. has a history of glass manufacturing works and
   b. high yield of guava, amla, and bananas
4. *Well-connected transport and water:*
   a. Rail connectivity: Located along the rail route of New Delhi−Howrah
   b. Starting point on the proposed National Waterway no. 1 (Allahabad and Haldia)
5. *Urban services well developed*:
   a. Water supply exceeds national standard of 135 L per capita per day.
   b. High capacity of wastewater treatment and disposal inventory created under Ganga Action Plan and National Ganga River Basin Authority schemes, present capacity is over 280 million liters per day.
   c. Integrated solid waste management programs operational for almost a decade

11.3.3.2 Weaknesses

1. *Lack of integrated strategy to support and sustain tourism:*
   a. Most of the state support is "reactive," that is, responds to specific events and not targeted at maintaining tourism-based infrastructure.
   b. Lack of formal approach to guide visitors on the pilgrimage and other sites in the city.
2. *Higher education centers do not foster the local economy:* Most students move on to other cities and towns after completing education; institutions have limited engagement with industry.
3. *Stagnant manufacturing and industry:*
   a. Most large industrial units have closed down or are exiting the state.
   b. Micro, Small and Medium Enterprises (MSME) sector is not supported well in terms of new, emerging areas, namely, skill-based support services.
   c. Limited focus on knowledge-based industries.
4. *Limited air connectivity to the city:*
   Only one airline with a single flight is servicing between Allahabad and Delhi which is impacting tourism.
5. *Urban form does not encourage compact development:*
   a. Most areas show considerably lesser density than what is supported except organic and unplanned built-up areas, very few flatted systems in the city.
   b. No provision for mixed use development in master plan.
   c. New residential schemes are heavy on "plots" of land and are increasing urban sprawl more than compacting; viability of many line services suspects on account of high sprawl and low density. This is because the development authority is not encouraging redevelopment of high-density areas.
   d. "Own vehicle"−centered development—modal share of buses is 8% only; even as motorized trips have an average length of just under 7 km.
   e. Only 1% of the road network has footpaths; high instances of on-street parking.
   f. Limited focus on street and intersection design; increase in road accidents over last 3 years (844−1019); and limited signages.
   g. New rolling stock for buses has not been acquired since 2009; most buses have reached condemnation stage.

11.3.3.3 Opportunities

1. *Organizing and formalizing the Triveni and Sangam experience:*
    a. Provision of infrastructure and other amenities in all over the riverfront, positioning the same as a group of "managed" sites, which improves visitor experience, including developing areas for new activities, namely, boating.
    b. Development of a comprehensive and easily accessible information base of cultural elements, potential itinerary for visiting and support services that would essentially (1) market Allahabad's cultural and historical identity, (2) facilitate smooth visits, and passage of tourists and pilgrims alike.
2. *Positioning the other new Allahabad:*
    a. Areas of the city, which generate economic activities, may also be used to attract tourists and visitors, namely, civil lines, Katra as elements of "contemporary and living culture."
    b. Certain old and run-down areas offer potential to be resuscitated and redeveloped (urban renewal) as centers of mixed use supporting local economic development; government lands, which are vastly underutilized.
    c. Option for retrofitting/adaptive reuse of old premises with a Victorian character, namely, Nagar Nigam premises for mixed use and commercial capitalization.
3. *Rich deposits of silica:* Even though the glass industry has all but closed, potential lies in ceramic and other such materials which now have advanced applications in power, aerospace, and defense.
4. *High yields of agroproduce, particularly guavas and amla:* Potential for development of cooperative or privately owned manufacturing units for fruit-based products.
5. *Making education work for the city:*
    a. Establishing centers for excellence, innovation hubs, and R&D centers within Allahabad University and other similar setups.
    b. Fostering start-ups, industry–academia linkages for laboratory testing and application development.
    c. Improving market access and outreach of major university setups to improve employability.
6. *Connectivity:*
    a. Airport Authority of India fund (Rs.300 Cr.) sanctioned for the modernization of airport to increase tourists' footfalls.
    b. Land available for Infrastructure Development and *Instrument Landing System* (ILS) system being implemented for night landing.
7. *Urban amenities:*
    a. City-wide implementation and upscaling of Hari-Bhari PPP initiative for door-to-door waste collection planned. The initiative has potential to support waste to energy initiative.
    b. Availability of funds under Urban Transport Fund, Employment Generation and Self-income development scheme by District Urban Development Authority (DUDA) and development of Intelligent Traffic Management System (ITMS) plan.
    c. Redevelopment of unutilized and encroached "Nala's" (open drains), and creation of recharge ponds within the city.
    d. A metro rail is proposed (feasibility study ongoing) to be taken up within the city.

11.3.3.4 Threats

1. Flooding in Ganga; encroachments within flood plain.
2. Continuing practice of development of housing schemes resulting in uncontrolled urban sprawl and an imbalanced property market; ad-hoc changes in land use with limited land consolidation.

3. Minimal focus on affordable housing; last 2 years have seen only about 850 units produced.
4. Overdependence on the existing tube wells for water supply will lead to the depletion of water levels.

11.4 Conclusions

Nagpur has developed as the topmost city in India. In only 5 months, Nagpur competed and overcame other areas that were previously chosen for becoming smart future cities. An ongoing stock-taking activity directed by urban development ministry has uncovered that although Nagpur started becoming a smart city in September 2016, substantially later compared to the 33 rest urban areas' smart transformation initiation; it has accomplished the best investment−conversion ratio. India's smart future city program would like to alter city life and enhance personal satisfaction for India's urban population.

On the other hand, without a clear zone arrangement, numerous parts of Dehradun have seen erratic advancement throughout the years, which harmed the vision of a smart city. Smart city would require smart economy, splendid individuals, smart organization, smart correspondence, effective information services, hassle-free travel, clear environment, and ease of living. Largely, with mass movement prompting essential issues, similar to water deficiencies and congestion, the rate at which these urban areas will be developed is crucial. Uttarakhand's first "smart city" will be constructed in Dehradun, which will be equipped to provide its residents with information-based services, all monitored through a 24 × 7 online integrated command and control system. The low-floor bus equipped with camera, global positioning system, panic button, and air suspension has started between Dehradun and Mussoorie, which is quite crucial as in smart city issues like governance, security, and ease of travel has to be taken into consideration. The real test before the government is to create self-sustaining cities for everyone, paying little mind to whether they are rich or poor. Making a smart city is not just about installing the physical infrastructure, like streets and water, energy, and transportation networks. Open private organizations (PPP) are required to convey, yet the component seems to require a ton of culling with the end goal for it to work, a reality perceived in the ongoing budget. The enormous test will be to make self-maintaining urban communities, which make employments, utilize assets admirably, and furthermore prepare individuals. The idea ought to be to influence urban areas to work for the majority. India needs to now take an imperative choice with regard to making brilliant urban communities. It needs to decide whether it wants to select making new urban areas or update existing ones. Government officers in India should react in a legitimate and capable way if the vision is to be accomplished. Focus, State, and municipal administration must cooperate to discover approaches to manage the complicated political condition that at present hampers urban advancement in a big way. With smart cities' mission in mind, the GoI officials are working hard to develop Allahabad as smart city. By January

2019, Allahabad would be able to enjoy facilities, such as intelligent traffic management system, a smart parking system, environmental sensors, an efficient solid waste management system, pan−tilt−zoom camera, and crowd management analytic. Allahabad police have launched a smart mobile app for its personnel. With the preparations for the Kumbh Mela, a Hindu religious event, the work of smart city in Sangam Nagar is also running very fast in Allahabad.

Acknowledgment

A part of this paper has been presented in AW4City 2018 workshop, Lyon, France—April 23−27, 2018.

About the author

Dr Vinay Kandpal holds Ph.D. in Management from Department of Management Studies, Kumaun University, Nainital. He is honors graduate in Commerce from University of Calcutta and did his MBA with dual specialization in Finance & Marketing. He is assistant professor in Department of Accounting & Finance, College of Management & Economic Studies, University of Petroleum & Energy Studies, Dehradun. He has over 12 years of experience in Academics. He has published 25 research papers in the areas of topics, such as Banking, Smart Cities, CSR, Corporate Governance and Infrastructure Finance in leading refereed and indexed Journals. He has presented papers in National and International Seminars and Conferences on various topics in Institutes, such as IIM Ahmedabad, IIM Kozhikode, IIM Bangalore, IIM Indore, IIM Raipur, and IIT Delhi to name a few. He has participated in the UGC Refresher Course organized by Academic Staff College Kumaun University, Nainital and FDPs in IIT Kharagpur and Banaras Hindu University. His fields of Teaching and Research Interest are Financial Accounting, Management Accounting & Cost Accounting, Working Capital Management, Capital Market, Mutual Fund, Financial Management, Banking, Financial Inclusion, and Financial Institutions. He is a member of All India Management Association Indian Accounting Association and Indian Commerce Association. He has published four books in the area of Accounting and Finance.

References

Albino, V., Berardi, U., & Dangelico, R. M. (2015). Smart cities: Definitions, dimensions, performance, and initiatives. *Journal of Urban Technology*, *22*(1), 3−21. Available from https://doi.org/10.1080/10630732.2014.942092.

Angelidou, M. (2014). Smart city policies: A spatial approach. *Cities*, *41*(S1), S3−S11.

Anthopoulos, L., Janssen, M., & Weerakkody, V. (2016). A Unified Smart City Model (USCM) for smart city conceptualization and benchmarking. *International Journal of e-Government Research*, *12*(2), 76−92.

Bloomberg Philanthropies. *India Smart Cities Mission*. (2017). Available from <https://www.bloomberg.org/program/government-innovation/india-smart-cities-mission> Accessed 02.08.18.

Chatterjee, S., & Kar, A. K. (2018). Alignment of IT authority and citizens of proposed smart cities in India: System security and privacy perspective. *Global Journal of Flexible Systems Management*, *19*(1), 95−107.

Chauhan, S., Agarwal, N., & Kar, A. K. (2016). Addressing big data challenges in smart cities: A systematic literature review. *info*, *18*(4), 73−90.

Chourabi, H., Nam, T., Walker, S., Gil-Garcia, J. R., Mellouli, S., Nahon, K., et al. (2012). Understanding smart cities: An integrative framework. In *45th Hawaii International Conference on System Science* (pp. 2289−2297).

Desouza, K. C., & Flanery, T. H. (2013). Designing, planning, and managing resilient cities: A conceptual framework. *Cities*, *35*, 88−89.

Giffinger, R., Fertner, C., Kramar, H., Meijer, E., & Pichler-Milanovic, N. (2007). *Smart cities: Ranking of European medium-sized cities* [Online]. <http://www.smart-cities.eu/download/smart_cities_final_report.pdf> Retrieved June 2018.

Lee, J.-H., Phaal, R., & Lee, S.-H. (2013). An integrated service-device-technology roadmap for smart city development. *Technological Forecasting & Social Change*, *80*, 286−306.

Mckinsey Report. *Combating the challenges of urbanization in emerging markets: Lessons from India*. (2018). <https://www.mckinsey.com/industries/capital-projects-and-infrastructure/our-insights/combating-the-challenges-of-urbanization-in-emerging-markets-lessons-from-india> Accessed 22.04.18.

Nair, S. (2017). *The too smart city*. Indian Express. Available from <http://indianexpress.com/article/opinion/columns/smart-city-mission-urban-development-4721785/> Accessed 28.12.17.

Neirotti, P., De Marco, A., Cagliano, A. C., Mangano, G., & Scorrano. (2014). Current trends in smart city initiatives: Some stylised facts. *Cities*, *38*, 25−36.

Piro, G., Cianci, I., Grieco., Boggia, G., & Camarda, P. (2014). Information centric services in smart cities. *The Journal of Systems and Software*, *88*, 169−188.

Wey, W.-M., & Hsu, J. (2014). New Urbanism and Smart Growth: Toward achieving a smart National Taipei University District. *Habitat International*, *42*, 164−174, City development plan, 2015.

Further reading

Albino, V., Berardi, U., & Dangelico, R. (2014). Smart cities: Definitions, dimensions, performance and initiatives. *Journal of Urban Technology*, *50*(6).

Allahabad as a smart city: SWOT analysis. Available from <https://www.researchgate.net/publication/316666894_ALLAHABAD_AS_A_SMART_CITY_SWOT_ANALYSIS> Accessed 21.01.18.

Anthopoulos, L. (2017). *Understanding smart cities—A tool for smart government or an industrial trick? Public Administration and Information Technology* (Vol. 22). New York: Springer Science + Business Media, ISBN: 978-3-319-57014-3 (Print) 978-3-319-57015-0 (Online).

Anthopoulos, L. G., & Vakali, A. (2011). *Urban planning and smart cities: Interrelations and reciprocities* (pp. 1−12). Berlin Heidelberg: Springer-Verlag.

Government of India. Concept note on smart cities dated 3rd Dec. 2014 from Ministry of Urban development Government of India (pp. 3−4). Retrieved from https://india.smartcitiescouncil.com/system/tdf/india/public_resources/Concept-Note-on-Smart-City-Scheme_0.pdf?file = 1&type = node&id = 2229. Accessed 15.01.16.

Gopal, K. (2014, May). Smart India will be ushered in sooner than we believe is possible. *Construction Opportunities*, pp. 30−31.

Khan, Y. Z. (2015). Smart city "A Dream to be true". *International Journal of Linguistics and Computational Applications (IJLCA)*, 2(1), 1−5.

Koo, C., Ricci, F., Cobanoglu, C., & Okumus, F. (2017). Special issue on smart, connected hospitality and tourism. *Information Systems Frontiers*, 19(4), 699−703.

Laartz, J., & Lulf, S. (2011). Partnering to build smart cities. McKinsey & Company, Available from https://www.mckinsey.com/~/media/McKinsey/dotcom/client_service/Public%20Sector/GDNT/GDNT_SmartCities_v5.ashx. Accessed 14.03.15

Mookerji, N., & Taneja, M. (2014, September 18). Flexible PPP pact to woo industry for smart city. *Business Standard*. <http://www.business-standard.com/article/economy-policy/flexible-ppp-pact-to-woo-industry-for-smart-city-114091701235_1.html> Retrieved 20.04.15.

Mori, K., & Christodoulou, A. (2012). Review of sustainability indices and indicators: Towards a new City Sustainability Index (CSI). *Environmental Impact Assessment Review*, 32, 94−106.

Pandey, M. (2014, September 13). Narendra Modi's imprint on smart city project. *India Today*. <http://indiatoday.intoday.in/story/narendra-modi-imprint-on-smart-city-project/1/382571.html> Retrieved 10.03.15.

Rana, N. P., Luthra, S., Mangla, S. K., Islam, R., Roderick, S., & Dwivedi, Y. K. (2018). *Information Systems Frontiers*. <https://doi.org/10.1007/s10796-018-9873-4>.

Ryser, J. (2014). Planning smart cities ... sustainable, healthy, liveable, creative cities ... or just planning cities? In *Proceedings REAL CORP 2014 Tagungsband* (pp. 447−456). May 21−23, 2014, Vienna, Austria: REAL CORP.

Regional Centre for Urban and Environmental Studies (2016). Slum Free City Plan of Action − Allahabad, OU, Hyderabad. Retrieved from http://mohua.gov.in/upload/uploadfiles/files/19UP_Allahabad_sfcp-min.pdf. Accessed 25.01.18

The Smart City Perspective, PwC India (2014). Retrieved from https://www.pwc.in/assets/pdfs/industries/.../pwc-india-the-smart-city-perspective.pdf. Accessed 17.05.18.

The smart city of Pune

Zeenat Rehena[1] and Marijn Janssen[2]
[1]Aliah University, Kolkata, India, [2]Delft University of Technology, Delft, The Netherlands

Chapter Outline

12.1 Introduction   261
12.2 Background   263
12.3 Major challenges   265
12.4 Smart city of Pune   267
    12.4.1 Scope   269
    12.4.2 Integration   269
    12.4.3 Organization   272
    12.4.4 Cost   273
    12.4.5 Quality   275
    12.4.6 Risks   276
    12.4.7 Procurement   277
    12.4.8 Discussion—the fringes   279
12.5 Conclusion   280
About the authors   280
References   281
Further reading   282

12.1 Introduction

The term "smart city" was introduced near the end of the 20th century (Anthopoulos, Janssen, & Weerakkody, 2016). Smart cities are rooted in the implementation of the citizen-centric use of information and communication technologies (ICT) developed for urban spaces. Its meaning has since then been expanded to refer to the future of cities and their development.

In recent years, Internet of Things (IoT), social media combined with data analytics, has become a hub for the agglomeration of collective intelligence, collaboration that is supported by the internet and different forms of participation opportunities (Komninos, 2009). Due to the huge growth and the domination by technology, traditional approaches to city management and maintaining urban lifestyle can be improved. Many governments at different levels—regional, national, international—have initiated programs on digital and smart cities (Anthopoulos, 2017). The conceptualization and interpretation of what constitutes a smart city varies from city to city and country to country, depending on the level of development, willingness of the government to change and reform the city, typical societal challenges, available resources, and goal of the citizen (Chourabi et al., 2012). The effects of globalization, emerging technology, virtuality, and intelligence of the web have a direct effect on the India's economy, education, and social system greatly (Janssen, Matheus, & Zuiderwijk, 2015).

India is the second largest populated country in the world after China. Currently, 32% of India's population lives in cities. These numbers are rapidly increasing due to the growth inurbanization, and it is predicted that almost half of the population will be going to live in cities by 2030 (Kumar & Prakash, 2016).

The intention to develop smart cities in India was declared in 2014 of now ruling Government of India (GoI). The initial idea was to build 100 new smart cities with state-of-the-art technology. Instead the government selected three existing cities from each state for development under the *National Sustainable Habitat and Smart City Mission*. Thus the original thought changed from building *100 new smart cities* to making *existing cities smart*.

Initially, 20 cities were designated as building smart cities in 2015. After that, in two phases 40 more cities were designated in 2016 and 2017, respectively. The stages are categorized as follows:

- Stage-1: Past track record under Jawaharlal Nehru National Urban Renewal Mission, service levels, and financial strength.
- Stage-2: Economic impact of smart city plan, inclusivity, e-governance, and citizen participation to decide financing of smart cities.

Fig. 12.1 shows the 100 smart cities under "Smart Cities Mission." In city Pune, the Pune Smart City Development Corporation Limited (PSCDCL) has decided to implement different pilot projects in this mission. Initially, 15 pilot projects are started to process focusing on the redesigning of streets, footpath retrofitting, making space on roads for social activities, junction redesigning, rainwater harvesting, low-income skill development and health care, LED lighting, solar roof top, e-governance center to provide single-point place to enable citizens to avail various civic facilities (https://indianexpress.com/article/cities/pune/pune-smart-city-company-gives-nod-to-15-projects-2759638/).

Although "Smart City Mission" has started to take its shape, there is still not a clear understanding of the concept among practitioners, academia, and citizens (Chourabi et al., 2012). The main objectives of this chapter are identify the key areas influencing for the development of smart city and the challenges faced during this phases to become a smart city. By studying and exploring background literature from various government's reports, web portal, blogs, research papers, urban studies, public administration web portals, we identify the potential challenges during the development process.

The remainder of this chapter is organized as follows. The historical and socioeconomical background of city Pune is elaborately discussed in Section 12.2. Major challenges are discussed in Section 12.3. The challenges faced mainly during the development phases, that is, from a city to become a smart city are explained in this section. In Section 12.4, different development stages of the city Pune are analyzed and discussed briefly. Concluding remarks are given in Section 12.5.

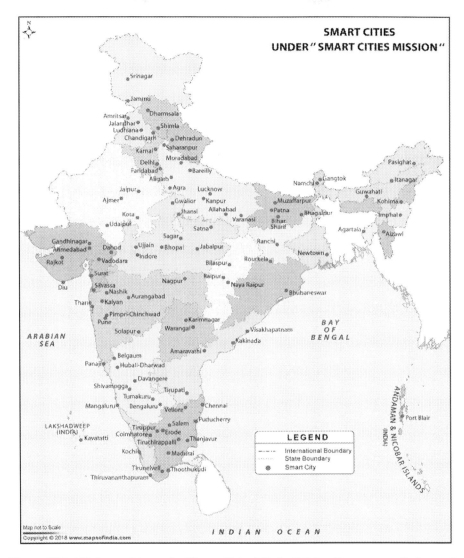

Figure 12.1 100 Smart cities under "Smart Cities Mission" (https://www.mapsofindia.com/government-of-india/smart-cities-project.html).

12.2 Background

With 29 states and 7 union territories, India is the second largest populated country in the world after China. Currently, 32% of India's population lives in cities. These numbers are rapidly increasing due to the growth in urbanization, and it is predicted that almost half of the population will be going to live in cities by 2030 (Kumar & Prakash, 2016). As people are moving, this in turn results in heavy demand on energy, transportation, water, building, public facilities, etc. Urbanization in India is in alarming sign. The rapid growth in cities involves huge challenges but also has big opportunities for smart cities. Fig. 12.2 shows the growth rate of urban population in India. As a result, it disrupts the balance of the urban life of the citizen. Although the rate of urbanization is increasing, the statistics says that the country still has about 69% of its population living in rural areas (http://hlrn.org.in/documents/Smart_Cities_Report_2018.pdf). On the other hand, six urban dwellers live in an inadequate settlement without basic services. Also, nearly two-thirds of urban households do not have access to water within the house, and about 85 million urban Indians lack adequate sanitation facilities. It is also seen that about 1% of the population in cities is estimated to be homeless.

The concept of a "smart city" is a relatively new phenomenon in India. In order to provide the better services, such as clean drinking water, affordable housing, good and low-cost education, proper waste management to the citizen, the GoI has initiated the "100 Smart Cities Mission" to promote Wealthier, Healthier, and Happier cities for better urban life for citizens in 2014. The main aim of the smart city is to build a city that is solely for its citizens. The mission has triggered discussions across the country on the concept of smart cities. The main focus of the mission is to fulfill the need and proper direction toward the urbanization in the context of India's present scenario.

The proposed Reference Framework by CSTEP (Centre for Study of Science, Technology and Policy) for the Smart Cities Mission in India has various aspects

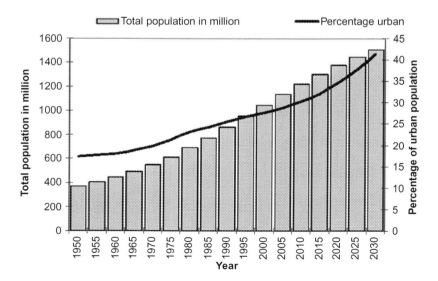

Figure 12.2 Growing trend of urban population in India (http://www.governoruk.gov.in/files/Smart_City_Dehardun.pdf).
Source: UN population statistics.

related to smart cities. The study report of CSTEP is expected to guide policy makers and urban practitioners in making critical decisions in a positive direction to make Indian cities smart (CSTEP report, 2015).

The Smart City Reference Framework shows directions to both practitioners and scientists as well. The Framework is driven by guiding principles from the United Nations' (UN's) draft Sustainable Development Goals. The guiding principles are well-being, equity, efficiency, and foresight.

12.3 Major challenges

ICT was identified as a key enabled for smart city governance (CSTEP report, 2015). It represents a collection of technologies, people, policies, resources, social norms, practices, and information that interact to support governing activities (Chourabi et al., 2012). The objective of the smart city governance is to investigate the way a smart city runs and proposes tools for monitoring and policy making (https://smartcitygovernance.eu/). Only through the proper management of different segments, such as transportation, health care, education, and security, the administrations and the governments can design and implement policies that are effective for society as a whole. Thus smart governance is also a big challenge to implement a smart city.

Smart city projects and initiatives have a big impact on the quality of life of citizens (Berntzen & Johannessen, 2016). Citizens are the heart of a city and the main actors in a multitude of city challenges faced through ongoing urbanization and demographic growth, consumption habits, and increasing expectations (Recupero et al., 2016). With the existing city infrastructure, it is not possible to manage and provide better city life to mass of the citizen. Perhaps the most feasible solution is to implement smart city projects. But while implanting it in India's sociopolitical context, it suffers from several potential challenges.

The following are the major challenges raised in various platforms, such as local people, local government, central government, industrialists, investors, academia, during the development phase of the Smart Cities Mission, in India.

- *The right framework for smart cities*

    According to the India's social and political status, it is very important to identify the right model for smart cities. There has been no consensus on defining the indicators for an Indian smart city till date. This may result in fragmented concepts of smart cities being implemented in different cities.

- *Social acceptability*

    In the 21st century our urban life is mostly controlled by the new innovations of technology. We have new devices that are able to communicate with each other allowing more and more activities to be optimized and automated. Therefore we can do more and more with less number of resources. There is a lack of clarity in understanding the smart city and the ICT. The image of smart cities is projected as heavily instrumented and automated. Also, in India where maximum people are struggling with their basic needs (food,

education, employment, shelter, and drinking water), understanding the smart city project and ICT are the major challenges for the social acceptability.
- *Livability*

    Livability has been considered an important dimension for measuring any urban city. It is a guiding principle that shapes the social, economic, physical, and biological urban environment. It has also been associated with dimensions, such as safety, climate, infrastructure, public policies, and business environment (Kashef, 2015), making the concept multidimensional in nature. Thus it is a big concern to provide a livable, healthy, safe environment to the citizens for the huge demand of the resources.
- *Sustainability*

    Sustainable urban development aiming at environmental awareness in the use of natural resources in smart cities (Komninos, 2016). Sustainable development includes little waste, lower consumption, moving toward green, using environmentally sustainable energy resources, such as solar or wind energy. Therefore it is a big challenge on the environmental sustainability of these cities.
- *Multiple or conflicting goals*

    There are other urban sector programs, such as New Urban Rejuvenation Mission, that are running. Recent developments suggest that there are some convergences between the Smart City Mission and the New Urban Rejuvenation Mission. However, a clear milestone is required.
- *Roadmap of the smart cities*

    If the Smart Cities Mission is an attempt to upgrade existing cities and prepare them for the future, then there is a need for a universal approach/framework to be developed under the Mission. The design and development of a sustainable, economically viable framework will help in achieving a city's growth altogether.
- *Funding strategy*

    It is anticipated that developing smart cities will entail substantial investments, which will be locked-in for a long term, and in turn shape India's urban future. According to the High Powered Empowered Committee on Urban Infrastructure, INR 7 lakh crore is required for the next 20 years to bridge the existing gaps in India's urban infrastructure. This amounts to INR 35,000 crore per year. The need for private sector investment in urban development, including smart cities, is thus important.
- *Lack of coordination*

    There is a lack of center–state government coordination. Effective implementation of the project can be done when there is a coordination between various government bodies of different states.
- *Smart governance*

    There is a need of proper monitoring of the project. It is important to take the experiences from the previous schemes or programs and should address by the Mission. There is a need to control over program implementation and sanctioning of funds by the GoI, otherwise it may lead to delays.
- *Digital literacy*

    There is a knowledge gap between technology and citizens who are benefited by using these technologies in their everyday life. Thus it is a challenge to train with digital literacy to underprivileged youth.

Table 12.1 describes the overview of the different challenges mentioned earlier.

Table 12.1 Overview of challenges.

Challenges	Descriptions
Right design for smart city	There are no proper indicators for smart city. Therefore it is very important to find out right design for it
Social acceptability	The social acceptance of technology is a challenge
Livability	It is an important dimension to measure the urban city lifestyle. Thus it is a big challenge how to provide a good, safe, healthy, and easy life to the citizen to fulfill their demand
Sustainability	Development of the smart city needs the existing resources. It is a challenge to develop environmental sustainability of these smart cities for future
Multiple or conflicting goals	Lack of clear milestones between several programs
Proper roadmap of smart city	There is a lack of universal approach or framework for upgrading the existing cities for future generation
Funding strategy	Funding is needed to ensure that the projects continue
Lack of coordination	There is no proper coordination between center—state governments
Smart governance	Lack of proper monitoring, control, and policy making over the program and funds
Digital literacy	To train with digital literacy is a challenge

12.4 Smart city of Pune

The mission of the 100 smart cities in India is to provide a healthy, wealthy, and happier country to the citizens. Pune is one of the popular cities to contribute to these objectives. According to the geographical location and industrial growth of it, it has a lot of advantages mainly strong human capital, strong business environment, huge number of universities and colleges, top IT companies, Delhi—Mumbai-industrial corridor, sufficient water supply, comfortable climate with temperature varying from 12°C to 38°C to become a smart city. In this section a case study of city Pune is thoroughly studied and explained. The primary goal is to explore the key areas for the development of smart city.

Pune is the ninth-most populated city in India and the second largest city in the state of Maharashtra after the state capital city of Mumbai. The estimated population is of 3.13 million (Census of India, 2011) and is also the 101st largest city in the world, by population. Pune is considered the cultural capital of Maharashtra. The "Mercer 2015 Quality of Living rankings" evaluated local living conditions in more than 440 cities around the world where Pune ranked at 145, second in India after Hyderabad (138).

Pune has been able to create one of the strongest human capital and economic growth engines among Indian cities (Top Ten Wealthiest Towns of India, 2012; Haritas, 2018). It has the eighth largest metropolitan economy and sixth highest per capita income in the country (https://pwc.blogs.com/files/global-city-gdp-rankings-

2008-2025.pdf). Furthermore, with 811 colleges, it is often called the "Oxford of the East," and it has resulted in more than 30% graduate personnel, which has triggered the IT revolution in the city. On the other hand, almost all of the top IT companies in the country located here, making it the second biggest software hub in the country. Thus Pune is among the top five foreign direct investment locations in India. Pune's educated citizens have also been instrumental in driving participative governance, which is again one of the best across Indian cities.

Pune has a diverse economic structure and a well-connected infrastructure. It is part of a larger urban development corridor stretching from Ahmadabad via Mumbai to Pune (Shaw, 2005). This urban corridor (namely with the districts of Mumbai, Thane, and Pune) shows the highest values of the Human Development Index (YASHADA (Yashwantrao Chavan Academy of Development Administration), 2014). The future plans envisage an integration into the Delhi−Mumbai Industrial Corridor (DMIC) with an infrastructural upgrade and the creation of a large industrial zone (planned as "node 19": Pune−Khed-industrial area, about 100 km^2) (GoI, 2007). Currently, Pune aims at transforming into a "smart" city, the "most livable city in India" (Pune Smart City).

The population growth and the increasing socioeconomic polarization are linked to the economic development of the city (Benninger, 1998). The first industrial production unit in Pune, an ammunition factory, was built in 1869. In 1885 the Deccan Paper Mill, in 1888, a copper and brassware factory, and in 1893, a textile mill were founded (Benninger, 1998).

The orientation toward knowledge-based sectors (IT) in combination with manufacturing and production of food and pharmaceuticals offers future proof jobs for different skills, and the city's economy does not depend on one branch. However, as in many cities of the Global South, the informal economy is for large parts of the population which is the most relevant source of income. According to Kumar, the workforce participation rate in the Pune urban agglomeration stood at 38.8% (Batty et al., 2012). This relatively low figure indicates that there are a large number of persons working in the informal sector. Informal occupations come along with a large number of disadvantages, such as lack of revenue and security. However, the informal sector also creates income for a majority of the population, it is shaped by highly dynamic, often creative- and solution-oriented processes, and informal institutions contribute to the efficiency of the city's economy (Batty et al., 2012).

Pune Municipal Corporation (PMC) (2012), the civic body of Pune city, stood second in the smart cities challenge launched by Ministry of Urban Development (MoUD), GoI in 2015. PMC is committed for making governance citizen friendly and cost effective by delivering services electronically to ensure accountability and transparency. In 2016 Pune city won three awards for smart city project in a competition organized by Business World.

In 2017 Pune city was identified and ranked 13th among 134 major cities worldwide from United States, Europe, Asia Pacific, Middle East, and Africa by JLL City Momentum Index 2017 where Pune ranked 7th in Asia pacific and 3rd in India.

12.4.1 Scope

A Smart City System comprises six key building blocks: (1) smart people, (2) smart city economy, (3) smart mobility, (4) smart environment, (5) smart living, and (6) smart governance (Anthopoulos & Reddick, 2016). These six building blocks are closely interlinked and contribute to the Smart City System and will be used to describe the smart city of Pune. These six pillars have their own contributions toward the development of the smart city. These are briefly demonstrated in this section.

These have equal weightage on building smart city, however, following Vinod Kumar (2015), "smart people" was given more prominence because without their active participation and involvement a Smart City System would not function in the first place.

1. Smart People are the fundamental building block of a Smart City System. It includes many crucial attributes. People in a smart city are highly flexible and resilient to the changing circumstances.
2. On the other hand, Smart Economy is the second building block of smart city. It understands its economic DNA.
3. While smart mobility is the third building block of a Smart City System, which focuses on the mobility of people, and not only that of vehicles. It should effectively manage vehicular and pedestrian traffic and traffic congestions.
4. The fourth building block of smart city is smart environment that values and capitalizes on scenic resources without harming the ecological system, natural resources, and biodiversity.
5. Living is the fifth building block of a Smart City System, which provides the necessary safety and security to women, children, and senior citizens.
6. The final and most important building block of Smart City System is Smart Governance without whose support it is impossible to manage the Smart City System.

Table 12.2 represents these six pillars to build a smart city having the different attributes.

12.4.2 Integration

Rapid urbanization in India has been noticed significantly. As estimated by the McKinsey Global Institute, around 590 million people will live in cities by 2030, up from 340 million in 2008. Compared to this exponential growth, it took 40 years for India's urban population to rise by 230 million between 1971 and 2008. In the next two to three decades, urbanization will be the most important growth engine, with cities driving more than 70% of new job creation and 70% of Indian GDP by 2030. While urban development will be the most important growth engine for India, but it will also put dominating pressure on resources and environment. With most cities planned many decades ago, unanticipated population explosion and rapid migration have seriously disrupted the urban lifestyle, which in turn lower the livability index. Most cities suffer from unending traffic congestions, water shortages, and challenges around waste disposal. The performance of Indian cities

Table 12.2 Smart city components with attributes.

Components	Attributes
Smart people	1. Smart people excel in what they do professionally 2. Smart people have a high Human Development Index 3. A smart city integrates its universities and colleges into all aspects of city life 4. It attracts high human capital, for example, knowledge workers 5. A smart city maintains high graduate enrollment ratio and has people with high level of qualifications and expertise 6. People in a smart city are highly flexible and resilient to the changing circumstances 7. Smart city inhabitants excel in creativity and find unique solutions to challenging issues
Smart economy	1. A smart city is driven by innovation and supported by universities that focus on cutting-edge research. Also it is supported by cultural heritage, architecture, planning, and development of the city 2. A smart city highly values creativity and welcomes new ideas 3. A smart city has enlightened entrepreneurial leadership 4. A smart city offers its citizens diverse economic opportunities 5. A smart city knows that all economics works at the local level 6. A smart city is prepared for the challenges posed by and opportunities of economic globalization
Smart mobility	1. A smart city focuses on the mobility of people, and not only that of vehicles 2. A smart city will advocate walk ability and cycling 3. A smart city has vibrant streets (at no additional cost) 4. A smart city effectively manages vehicular and pedestrian traffic, and traffic congestion 5. A smart city will have mass rapid transit system, such as metro rail, light metro, monorail, or sky-train for high-speed mobility 6. A smart city will have integrated high-mobility system linking residential areas, work places, recreational areas, and transport notes (e.g., bus/railway station/s and airport) 7. A smart city has seamless mobility for differently-abled people
Smart environment	1. A smart city lives with and protects the nature 2. A smart city is attractive and is rooted in its natural setting 3. A smart city values its natural heritage, unique natural resources, biodiversity, and environment 4. A smart city conserves and preserves the ecological system in the city region 5. A smart city embraces and sustains biodiversity in the city region 6. A smart city is a green city and clean city 7. A smart city has an integrated system to manage its water resources, water supply system, wastewater, natural drainage, floods and inundation, especially in the watersheds where it is located, especially in view of the (impending) climate change

(Continued)

Table 12.2 (Continued)

Components	Attributes
	8. A smart city focuses on water conservation and minimizes the unnecessary consumption of water for residential, institutional, commercial, and industrial use, especially in the arid and semi-arid areas
	9. A smart city has an efficient management system for the treatment and disposal of wastewater, and reuse of treated wastewater, particularly in the arid and semi-arid areas
	10. A smart city has an efficient management system for the collection, treatment, and disposal of industrial wastewater
	11. A smart city has an integrated and efficient management system for the collection, transfer, transportation, treatment, recycling, reuse, and disposal of municipal, hospital, industrial, and hazardous solid waste
	12. A smart city has an efficient system to control air pollution and maintain clear air, especially in the air sheds where it is located
	13. A smart city has an efficient and effective system for disaster risk reduction, response, recovery, and management
Smart living	1. A smart city records and celebrates local history, culture, and nature
	2. A smart city has a vibrant downtown, 24 h and 7 days a week
	3. A smart city builds natural and cultural assets to build a good quality of life
	4. A smart city not only understands the big picture of urban livability, but also pays attention to small details
	5. A smart city has high-quality open and accessible public spaces
	6. A smart city is an ideal place of living, especially for women, children, and senior citizens
	7. A smart city organizes festivals that celebrate people, life, and nature in city
	8. A smart city has a ritual event (or more) that symbolizes the values and aspirations of the community
	9. A smart city celebrates and promotes art, cultural, and natural heritage in the city
Smart governance	1. A smart city practices accountability, responsiveness, and transparency (ART) in its governance
	2. A smart city uses big data, spatial decision support systems and related geospatial technologies in urban and city regional governance
	3. A smart city constantly innovates e-governance for the benefit of all its residents
	4. A smart city constantly improves its ability to deliver public services efficiently and effectively
	5. A smart city practices participatory policy-making, planning, budgeting, implementation, and monitoring

(*Continued*)

Table 12.2 (Continued)

Components	Attributes
	6. A smart city has a clear sustainable urban development strategy and perspectives known to all
7. A smart city utilizes creative urban and regional planning with focus on the integration of economic, social, and environmental dimensions of urban development
8. A smart city practices E-Democracy to achieve better development outcomes for all
9. A smart city embraces a triple helix model in which government, Academia, and Business/Industry practice changing roles in governance

needs significant improvement across multiple parameters related to the "quality of life" (*Source:* McKinsey Global Institute).

Conceived as an innovative way to drive infrastructural, economic, environmental, and social growth, the Smart Cities Mission aims to do so by enabling local development and harnessing technology to improve the quality of life of citizens. The proposal for smart city, Pune, will be developed and implemented with citizens' participation, using the processes described in this section.

Any citizen engagement of this scale requires significant preparation and planning. The Smart City Pune team, which consisted of multistakeholders, such as government officials, corporate, NGOs and social foundations, consulting firms, students from schools and colleges, and local media, drove a four-pronged effort before launching the citizen engagement initiative, which consisted of the following criteria:

- Defining the stages of citizen engagement and objectives for each stage
- Defining different modes of citizen engagement
- Creating a partner ecosystem to drive an effort of this scale
- Creating a "war room" to monitor and track the entire effort

In correspondence to the Smart Cities Mission in India guidelines, the smart city team of city Pune has structured the entire citizen engagement effort into nine phases as shown in Fig. 12.3. The first five phases of the structure were for the entire city while the last four were run for the area identified for the local area development initiative. The output for each phase has been shared with the citizens with the help of local media for the betterment of the system.

12.4.3 Organization

The Smart City Mission has been launched by the Indian government in June, 2015 with the aim of providing better quality life in the 100 cities in India.

Phase-I	Phase-II	Phase-III	Phase-IV	Phase-V
17–28th Sep • Ask citizen on inputs on creating a vision for the city • Ask citizen the major areas of concern in the 12 sectors. • Playback results at the end of the phase	28th Sep–12th Oct • Ask citizen about development opportunities ans issues in each core sector and help identify the most vital issues that need to be waived	13th–23rd Oct • Ask a citizen for detailed solutions to key pan city	Over a period of 3 days • Conduct delivery labs for extensive problem-solving with key experts and citizens to refine solutions • Open citizen discussion forums	15th Nov–23th Dec • Share the final set of solutions with citizens and open for suggestions and discussions

Phase-VI	Phase-VII	Phase-VIII	Phase-IX
• Selection od development type • Define assessment criteria for selection • Short-listing of areas • Evaluation by citizens • Evaluation by sector experts • Evaluation by elected representatives	• Participation of 50+ teams from arch. colleges in pune • Extensive a profiling done through walk through and workshops	• Citizen asked issues they face in basic sciences • Visions for the area and the smart features it should have were understand	• >60% of the households to pleadge support for this initiative planned

Figure 12.3 Different phases of structure of the Smart City Pune.

Central governments as well as local state governments, private sector companies, local community, universities are cooperating to each other for making the Pune Smart City. The PSCDCL is developed with PMC. The PMC and PSCDCL have signed memorandum of understanding between private sector companies, NGO's, local communities to success of the Pune Smart City Vision and Mission.

PMC has interacted with other administrative areas, such as Pimpri Chinchwad Municipal Corporation, Khadki Cantonment Board, and Pune Cantonment Board, and works along with other stakeholder entities. Table 12.3 shows the type of service and the associated authority and their allied bodies for other related functions within the jurisdiction boundary of PMC. On the other hand the quadruple helix of different organizations is shown in Fig. 12.4. It consists of private sectors, local community, universities, and local government.

12.4.4 Cost

In this section the cost for implementing Pune Smart City projects is described. Two different type of cost are used, implementation cost and operating cost. Implementation cost is referred as capital expenses, and operating cost is named operating expenses cost. Table 12.4 describes the different projects and their cost in rupees (crore).

Table 12.3 The power–interest levels of various stakeholders for city Pune.

Sector/power–interest level	Stakeholders
Sewerage	PMC
Roads, bridges, flyovers/RoB/multilevel parking	PWD, MSRDC, NHAI, PMC
Traffic control and management system	Police Dept (Traffic)
Public transport system	PMPML
Street lighting	PMC
Storm water drainage	PMC
Solid waste management	PMC
Parks/Playgrounds	PMC
Slum development	SRA, PMC
Housing	MHADA, PMC
Air, water, and noise pollution control	PMC, MPCB
Tourism	MTDC
River protection	PMC, MPCB
Public health	PMC
Education	MSBSHSE, PMC, DEO

PMC, Pune Municipal Corporation; *PWD*, Public Works Development; *MSRDC*, Maharashtra State Road Development Corporation; *PMPML*, Pune Maharashtra Parivahan Mahamandal Ltd.; *SRA*, Slum Rehabilitation Authority; *MHADA*, Maharashtra Housing and Area Development Authority; *MPCB*, Maharashtra Pollution Control Board; *MTDC*, Maharashtra Tourism Development Corporation; *MSBSHSE*, Maharashtra State Board of Secondary and Higher Secondary Education; *DEO*, District Education Officer; *RoB*, Road over Bridge.

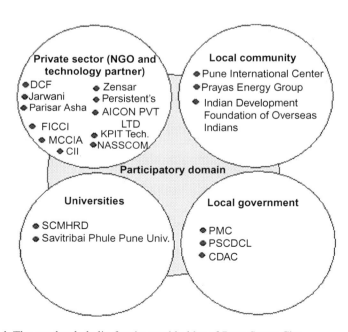

Figure 12.4 The quadruple helix for the stockholder of Pune Smart City.

Table 12.4 Different cost distribution for individual smart city projects.

Sl. no.	Project name	Total cost (Cr.)	capEx (Cr.)	opEx (Cr.)
1	Riverfront Development	105	100	5
2	24 × 7 electricity supply smart, grid and solar panels	420	364	56
3	*Water and sewage*			
	(i) Reservoir	100	87	13
	(ii) Smart metering	24	22	2
	(iii) Society level slums	10.4	6.4	4
	(iv) Storm water drains	44	43	1
	(v) STP augmentation	105	100	5
4	*Waste and sanitation*			
	(i) SWM	37	16	21
	(ii) Public toilets	2	1.5	0.5
5	*Public transport*			
	(i) BRT	216	210	6
	(ii) E-Buses	240	125	115
	(iii) E-Rickshaw	1.1	1.1	
	(iv) ICT-enabled bus	31	27	4
6	*Citizen services and security*			
	(i) CCTV	35	27	8
	(ii) IT connectivity	151	146	5
	(iii) Digital literacy	2		
	(iv) Smart parking	50	50	
7	Adaptive traffic management	123	123	0
8	Bus system ITMS	105	70	34
9	Smart parking initiative	62	15	47
10	Intelligent road management	5	3	2
11	Smart bulk meter	86	83	3
12	Smart commercial meter	68	60	8

capEx, Capital expenses; *ICT*, information and communication technologies; *opEx*, operating expenses; *SWM*, solid waste management; *STP*, sewage treatment plant; *BRT*, bus rapid transmit; *ITMS*, intelligent traffic management system.

12.4.5 Quality

Public transport and facilities, water supply, sanitation, energy, food, and security are some of the pressure points that will be affected by rising urbanization. There are lot of standards that provide cities with an overall framework for defining what "being smart" means for them and how they can get there.

There are three most important resources that may consider a standardization framework for smart cities (CSTEP report, 2015). These are as follows:

1. *International Organization for Standards (ISO)*

    ISO's smart cities–related work falls under the Technical Committee 268 (TC 268)- Sustainable Development in Communities, which was constituted in March 2012.

The primary objective of TC 268 is to build consensus among international communities on sustainable development standards. There are many standards that are discussed as follows:

a. ISO 37120: It is for sustainable development and resilience of communities. It provides metrics for Smart Community Infrastructure based on *global city indicators for city services and quality of life*, which in turn help harmonize performance indicators in these fields.

b. ISO/TR 37150 and ISO 37151: It represents technical report on Smart Urban Infrastructures around the world. It will serve as a base for the development of the future ISO 37151 standards metrics for benchmarking smartness of infrastructures.

c. ISO 3710: It provides an output that is built on ISO 26000:2010. It describes Guidance on Social Responsibility.

Apart from these well-known standards mentioned here, there are other standards in ISO, which can be linked to a city's environment. These are ISO 15686 (Buildings and construction assets), ISO 13153 (Framework and design process for energy saving single family residential and small commercial buildings), ISO 14001(Environmental management system), ISO 50001 (Energy management system), ISO 27001 (Information security management), and ISO 20121 (Sustainable events).

2. *International Electrotechnical Commission (IEC)*

IEC was developed to coordinate the activities of smart city development in conjunction with the ISO in September 2013. It publishes consensus-based International Standards and manages conformity assessment systems for electric and electronic products, systems, and services with the aim to serve as a reference for national and international standardization.

3. *International Telecommunication Union (ITU)*

ITU is the UN's specialized agency for ICT. ITU releases recommendations on standards relating to telecommunication networks. ITU-T Study Group 5 established a Focus Group on Sustainable Smart Cities (FG-SSC) in February 2013. FG-SSC has four main Working Groups (WGs): WG1 (ICT and roadmap for smart sustainable cities), WG2 (ICT infrastructure), WG3 (standardization gaps, Key Performance Indicators (KPIs), and metrics), and WG4 (policy and positioning).

Although there are standardizations for various components of a city system, such as ICT and various physical and social infrastructure facilities, still there is no single standard till date, which is accepted globally as the standard method to certify a city as "smart." Thus there are always to be worry in viewing cities as a sum of products or services in comparison with a single dynamic entity within which the products and services are is in a constant mode of interaction to deliver on the ever-changing expectations.

12.4.6 Risks

Every innovation has own high uncertainties and risks. There are lots of opportunities to help Pune becomes a smart city. First, the municipal area of Pune comes under the PMR area that has a number of economic opportunities. Second, Pune comes under the DMIC influence zone that can be the catalyst in the city's economic growth. It also further increases the growing demand of services. Third, the proximity of Pune city to DMIC Project will have a potential of integration with other urban nodes in the region. The other important opportunities are as follows:

1. DMIC will increase ample human resource availability and hence requirement for creation of job opportunities.
2. Due to its strategic location and favorable climate, the city can be developed as the center point for all business transit and has potential for heritage tourism as well.
3. As compared with other peer cities, Pune has the lowest density in the last decade, which indicates land availability, except in the core old city.
4. There is strong inflow of talent as Pune is an IT hub and pioneer educational hub of India.
5. Due to high economic growth in the city and region, there is a lot of potential for investment in Pune's real estate. About 40% of the total land, which is reserved for residential use in DP (Delhi–Pune road), has a potential that can absorb the transfer development rights (TDR) generated.
6. This TDR can be utilized into the suburbs of the city, the land available into the areas where large land parcel having bigger plot sizes are available.

On the other hand the risks for Pune Smart City are as follows:

1. Pune city has shown a lot of focus on urbanization and economic development. Definitely, this in turn will increase the pressure on the current physical and transport infrastructure. It also hugely impacts on the local environment, which can act as a danger to the image of Pune as one of the most livable cities.
2. The migrant population involved in the IT, industrial, and real estate sectors is likely to increase the demand for housing, particularly for Economically Weaker Sections (EWS)/low-income groups (LIG) and need for basic amenities. If housing for these groups is not planned, slums are likely to increase.
3. The percentage of recreational areas has reduced from 9.2% in 1987 DP to 7.4% in 2001 DP.
4. Awareness of the e-governance to the underprivileged citizens to use the ICT-enabled platform.

Table 12.5 explains the different types of risks and their potential managing activities.

The risks includes tremendous pressure on existing physical and transport infrastructure due to economic growth, availability of the dwelling for mainly LIG people, reduction of open green spaces, and lack of skill and awareness of the ICT.

12.4.7 Procurement

The Pune Smart City proposal was selected for priority financing under Smart City Mission by MoUD, GoI. Thereafter, the PMC has incorporated a special purpose vehicle company called PSCDCL, under the Companies Act 2013, solely for the purpose of implementing the smart city proposal.

PSCDCL will receive funding from GoI and PMC or from the State Government for implementing the smart city projects. Given the wide range of technical-and sector-specific expertise required to implement the smart city projects, PSCDCL shall be supported by a team of consultants for strategic, technical, and project management support.

Table 12.5 Different types of risks and managing activities.

Risk	Managing activity
Nonpayment of user charges for car parking especially multilevel car parking	Parking should be PPP structuring for proper and effective objective and maintains
Awareness and consciousness of the lower level of citizens across the city to use ICT platforms for smart mobility and e-governance	Create more awareness on usage of e-governance platform especially targeting the BPL class
Timely availability of funds from other schemes of the state or central government converged with Smart City Project Scheme	Organizations shall have sufficient reserve funds to deal with such delays and state govt./city corporation shall have the financial implementation plan well in advance to tackle such situations
With the rapid growth of urbanization and economic development this in turn will increase the pressure on the current physical and transport infrastructure	If counter magnets are not developed simultaneously, then Pune city may have to face overcrowding. Further, industrial development along the growth corridors for example, Pune–Ahmednagar highway will lead to over population

ICT, information and communication technologies; *PPP*, public private partnership.

There are some steps or process from where the Pune Smart City projects been assigned through contractors or bidder.

1. *Scope of proposal*:

    PSCDCL intends to select the General Consultants (GC) to provide Strategic Advisory and Project Management Support to PSCDCL, through an open competitive bidding process. Therefore in this regard, PSCDCL invites proposals from interested and eligible firms to provide the consultancy services.

2. *Eligibility for consultants*:

    The bidder shall be a private company, firm incorporated in India under the (Indian) Companies Act 1956/2013, or a company incorporated under equivalent law abroad. Further, the bidder must have a valid service tax registration. They must have at least one office in India, which has been operational for the last 3 years or more.

    The other two eligibility criteria are technical capability and financial capability.

    The bidder shall enclose with its proposal, certificate(s) from its statutory auditors stating its total revenues from professional fees during each of the 3 (three) financial years.

3. *Conflict of interest*:

    Bidders shall not have a conflict of interest that may affect the selection process or the consultancy. Any bidder found to have a conflict of interest shall be disqualified. The bidder and any entity affiliated with the bidder, including subconsultants and their affiliates shall be disqualified from providing goods, works, or services, resulting from or directly related to the GC's services as defined in the scope of this assignment.

4. *Number of proposals*:

    A bidder applying individually or as an associate shall not be entitled to submit another application either individually or as a member of any other consortium.

5. *Right to reject any proposal:*
PSCDCL reserves the right to accept or reject any proposal at any time without any liability or any obligation for such acceptance, rejection, or annulment, and without assigning any reasons therefore.
6. *Evaluation of proposals:*
There are a lot of conditions imposed for contracts of the case such as security deposit, compensation for delay, action when whole of security deposit is forfeited, action when the progress of any particular portion of the work is unsatisfactory, and extension of time limit.

12.4.8 Discussion—the fringes

The background story of city Pune to become "smart city" is described elaborately in this chapter. After launching the first phase of "Smart City Mission" the PSCDCL has identified the current challenges of Pune and framed a plan to address the challenges. They have decided to implement different pilot projects for this mission. Initially, 15 pilot projects are started to process focusing on the redesigning of streets, footpath retrofitting, making space on roads for social activities, junction redesigning, rainwater harvesting, low-income skill development and health care, LED lighting, energy saving, digital technology to residents, empowering underprivileged youth, e-governance center to enable citizens to avail various civic facilities (https://indianexpress.com/article/cities/pune/pune-smart-city-company-gives-nod-to-15-projects-2759638/). In most of the projects the ideas basically came from the citizen. The PSCDCL authorities have engaged over 60% of the population in the first phase to determine which challenges need to be prioritized. They continued citizen engagement meetings twice a month to get the feedback for a better understanding of the flaws (http://www.urban-hub.com/cities/pune-uses-smart-city-concepts-for-residents/). Among the 15 pilot projects, Smart LED, E-Bikes, Placemaking are successfully completed and run. Smart LED is a smart and sustainable street lighting solution. It is controlled from a command center and gives safer neighborhoods. On the other hand, E-Bikes is the world's first dock-less bike-sharing platform, which is operated by mobile app, whereas Placemaking is a project to develop vacant spaces mainly for social activities. Many other large infrastructural projects are under development stage, for example, the construction of e-connectivity, transit hub, and river rejuvenation project. Smart technology companies such as Google and thyssenkrupp are working together with this smart city project. Google will provide 150 Google hotspot station to Pune for providing internet connectivity in the public spaces and thyssenkrupp elevator will open an elevator manufacturing site to deliver the mobile products. In spite of the several challenges discussed previously, Pune owns the "One Planet City Challenge" by World Wildlife Fund in 2017/18. Pune was also named as "a best governed city" by the Annual Survey of India's City Systems in 2017 (http://www.urban-hub.com/cities/pune-uses-smart-city-concepts-for-residents/).

12.5 Conclusion

Making cities smart will take time and enormous effort. It is critical to create an enabling policy and regulatory environment. Smart cities need to be sustainable and also ensure the successful returns on investment to make them as well. The objective of this chapter is to investigate the key areas influencing the development of smart city and the challenges faced during the development process in the country like India where the smart cities often confronted with multiple problems, such as unplanned development, inevitable population growth, lack of infrastructure, inadequate transport facilities, traffic congestion, and poor power supply. To identify the potential challenges, we took a case study of Pune. From the thorough study of the city Pune, it was seen that prospering cities also face severe challenges in long-term development. The challenges arise from several factors, for example, planning rules and regulations, resources, coordination between central—state governments, financing and population pressure. Another important demand is to establish a powerful planning authorities who developed integrated plans for urban and its surroundings development and also have the power to enforce their establishment.

Furthermore, in our study it was seen that several approaches toward the development can be found in city Pune. Although a comprehensive strategy for a transition toward smart city does not exist. A true vision for the agglomeration has to be developed for the growth of Pune in future.

About the authors

Dr. Zeenat Rehena is an Assistant Professor in the Dept. of Computer Science and Engineering at Aliah University, India since 2012. She received her B.Tech. and M.E. degree in Computer Science and Engineering in 2005 and 2009, respectively. From the year 2009 to 2012, she worked in the School of Mobile Computing and Communication, Jadavpur University, Kolkata, India, as a research fellow. She received her Ph.D. in Engineering from the Jadavpur University in 2016. She also completed her Postdoctoral research work from Delft University of Technology, the Netherlands in 2017—18.

Her research interests are Wireless Sensor Network, Ad-Hoc Network, Smart City, IoT, Big Data, etc. She has published many papers in reputed conferences and journals. She is a member of IEEE since 2012.

Prof. Dr. Marijn Janssen is a full professor in ICT & Governance and chair of the Information and Communication Technology (ICT) research group of the Technology, Policy and Management Faculty of Delft University of Technology. He was ranked as one of the leading e-government researchers in surveys in 2009, 2014, and 2016 and has published over 450 refereed publications. He was nominated in 2018 by Apolitical as one of the 100 Most Influential People in the Digital Government https://apolitical.co/lists/digital-government-world100. More information: www.tbm.tudelft.nl/marijnj.

References

Anthopoulos, L. (2017). Smart utopia VS smart reality: Learning by experience from 10 smart city cases. *Cities*, *63*(Suppl. C), 128−148. Available from https://doi.org/10.1016/j.cities.2016.10.005.

Anthopoulos, L., Janssen, M., & Weerakkody, V. (2016). A Unified Smart City Model (USCM) for smart city conceptualization and benchmarking. *International Journal of Electronic Government Research (IJEGR)*, *12*(2), 77−93.

Anthopoulos, L. G., & Reddick, C. G. (2016). Smart city and smart government: Synonymous or complementary?. In *Proceedings of the 25th international conference companion on World Wide Web* (pp. 351−355). International World Wide Web Conferences Steering Committee, April 2016.

Batty, M., Axhausen, K. W., Giannotti, F., Pozdnoukhov, A., Bazzani, A., Wachowicz, M., . . . Portugali, Y. (2012). Smart cities of the future. *The European Physical Journal Special Topics*, *214*, 481−518.

Benninger, C. C. (1998). Poona the emergence of a metropolis. In R. P. Misra, & K. Misra (Eds.), *Million cities of India growth dynamics, internal structure, quality of life and planning perspective* (Vol, I, pp. 384−417). New Delhi, India: Sustainable Development Foundation.

Berntzen, L., & Johannessen M. R. (2016). The role of citizens in "Smart Cities". In *Conference: Management—International conference*. Slovakia.

Census of India. *Pune city census*. (2011). Available online <http://www.census2011.co.in/census/city/375- pune.html> Accessed 02.09.17.

Chourabi, H., Nam, T., Walker, S., Gil-Garcia, J. R., Mellouli, S., Nahon, K., . . . Scholl, H. J. (2012). *Understanding smart cities: An integrative framework*. 2012 45th Hawaii international conference on system science (HICSS) (pp. 2289−2297). IEEE.

CSTEP. (2015). *CSTEP report*. <http://niti.gov.in/content/cstep-report-smart-cities-framework>.

GoI (Government of India); Ministry of Commerce and Industry. (2007). *Concept paper Delhi—Mumbai Industrial Corridor*. New Delhi: GoI.

Haritas, B. (2018). Richest cities of India. *BW Businessworld*. Retrieved 26.06.18.

Janssen, M., Matheus, R., & Zuiderwijk, A. (2015). *Big and open linked data (BOLD) to create smart cities and citizens: Insights from smart energy and mobility cases*. International conference on electronic government (pp. 79−90). Cham: Springer.

Kashef, M. (2015). *Urban livability across disciplinary and professional boundaries*. Frontiers of Architectural Research.

Komninos, N. (2009). Intelligent cities: Towards interactive and global innovation environments. *International Journal of Innovation and Regional Development*, *1*(4), 337−355.

Komninos, N. (2016). Smart environments and smart growth: Connecting innovation strategies and digital growth strategies. *International Journal of Knowledge-Based Development*, *7*(3), 240−263.

Kumar, S., & Prakash, A. (2016). Role of big data and analytics in smart cities. *The International Journal of Science and Research*, *5*(2), 12−23.

PMC (Pune Municipal Corporation). (2012). *Revising/Updating the City Development Plan (CPD) of Pune City—2041 under JNNURM*.

Pune Smart City. *Pune Smart City Vision*. Available online <http://www.punesmartcity.in/?wicket:bookmarkablePage = :Com.SmartCity.Page.Internal.Cityvision> Accessed 02.09.17.

Recupero, D. R., et al. (2016). An innovative, open, interoperable citizen engagement cloud platform for smart government and users' interaction. *Journal of the Knowledge Economy, 7*, 388−412. Available from https://doi.org/10.1007/s13132-016-0361-0.

Shaw, A. (2005). Peri-urban interface of Indian cities: Growth, governance and local initiatives. *Economic and Political Weekly, 40*, 129−136.

Top ten wealthiest towns of India. (2012). Maps of India. Retrieved 01.03.12.

Vinod Kumar, T. M. (2015). E-Governance for smart cities. In T. M. Vinod Kumar (Ed.), *E-Governance for smart cities*. Singapore: Springer.

YASHADA (Yashwantrao Chavan Academy of Development Administration. (2014). *Maharashtra Human Development report 2012*. New Delhi, India: YASHADA.

Further reading

Pune City Census Department. *Official website of PMC.*

Bapat, M. (1981). Shanty town and city: The case of Poona. *Progress in Planning, 15*, 151−269.

<http://smartcities.gov.in/content/>.

<https://smartnet.niua.org>.

<https://smartnet.niua.org/sites/default/files/resources/Smart%20Pune-Citizen%20Engagement%20Case%20Study.pdf>.

<https://www.geospatialworld.net/blogs/role-of-citizens-in-building-smart-city/>.

UN-HABITAT. (2013). *Planning and design for sustainable urban mobility: Global report on human settlements 2013*. Abingdon, Oxon: Routledge.

The smart city of Nara, Japan

Narutoshi Sakano
Public Sector Consulting Division, Fujitsu Research Institute (FRI), Tokyo, Japan

Chapter Outline

13.1 **Introduction** 283
13.2 **Background** 285
13.3 **Research methodology: case study** 286
  13.3.1 Utilizing renewable energies in the three major projects 286
  13.3.2 Evaluation 287
13.4 **Conclusion** 290
About the author 291
Reference 293
Further reading 293

13.1 Introduction

The Paris agreement, which is an international framework to reduce greenhouse gas (GHG) emissions from 2020 following the Kyoto Protocol and the Cancun Agreement, came into effect in November 2016. The Paris agreement aims to reduce GHG emissions virtually to zero by the late this century in order to curb the temperature rise below 2°C. Participating countries, including Japan, need to reduce GHG emissions dramatically. So far many governments and companies have been trying to reduce GHG emissions by individually reducing fuel energy, but they are required to cooperate with each other by creating renewable energy to achieve the dramatic target. Japan, with a CO_2 emission reduction target, is promoting the smart city concept in many areas through providing subsidies to regional governments as stated by the Ministry of Economy, Trade and Industry and the Ministry of Environment. Nara Medical University and its hospital try to introduce the smart city concept utilizing the subsidy.

Nara is located in the Kansai region of Japan and is famous for its history and culture (Fig. 13.1). Nara was a capital in the 8th century, and there are famous temples, shrines, and ruins as "Historic Monuments of Ancient Nara," a UNESCO World Heritage Site.

The Nara Medical University and its hospital in Nara plan to move to a vacant area (approximately 10 ha) in 2021 where the Nara Research and Development Center in Agriculture used to exist (Fig. 13.2). Private companies, regional governments (Nara-shi and Kashihara-shi), and Nara Medical

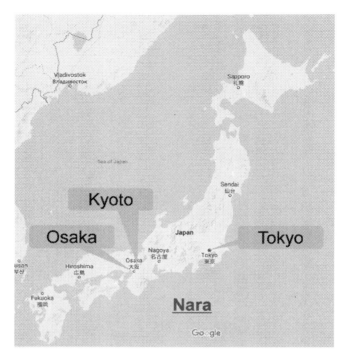

Figure 13.1 Location of Nara.
Source: Google Map.

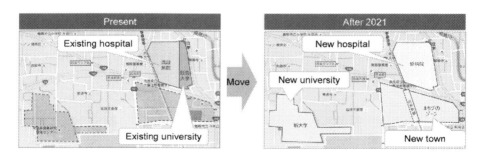

Figure 13.2 Moving plan of Nara Medical University and its hospital.

University have been deliberating the development of a town, which mainly consists of a new university, a new hospital, and a new town, aiming to revitalize the local economy based on medical services with the smart city concept. This activity was selected as a model case of revitalizing the local economy by the Cabinet Office in 2014, and its local revitalizing plan was endorsed in 2015.

Utilizing a subsidy from the New Energy Promotion Council, Fujitsu Research Institute (FRI) and Kansai Electric Power conducted a feasibility study on building regional energy management system as community-based renewable energy of local production and local consumption in FY 2014. This feasibility study estimates CO_2 emission reductions and evaluates the profitability of projects under the regional energy management system.

13.2 Background

The feasibility study outlines the projects of utilizing renewable energy in a new university (New University), a new hospital (New Hospital), and a new town (New Town) under the regional energy management system. In New Town, solar thermal systems on 60% of the building roofs and a sewage thermal system will be introduced for hot water and for providing excess heat for New Hospital through a heat pipe (Fig. 13.3). At New University a solar power system is to be introduced on the roof of 50% of buildings for electricity and providing excess electricity to New Hospital utilizing batteries. The New Hospital, a large consumer of energy, will introduce a well water thermal system for air conditioning while receiving heat and electricity from New Town and New University. Therefore the following three projects are chosen as major projects under the regional energy management system:

1. Regional thermal management between New Town and New Hospital;
2. Regional electricity management between New University and New Hospital;
3. Utilizing well water thermal in New Hospital.

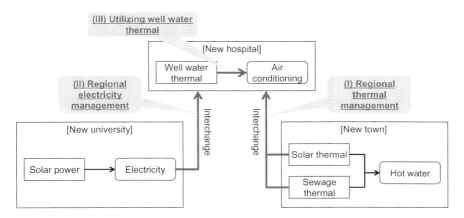

Figure 13.3 Three major projects in the regional energy management system.

13.3 Research methodology: case study

13.3.1 Utilizing renewable energies in the three major projects

13.3.1.1 Regional thermal management between New Town and New Hospital

The project introduces a solar thermal system and sewage thermal system for hot water in New Town. The heat collection of the solar thermal system exceeds the demand for hot water in New Town, but if the demand for hot water in New Hospital and the loss in heat pipes are added to the demand for New Town, the demand exceeds the heat collection of the solar thermal system in New Town (Fig. 13.4). The shortage is greatest (253 MW h) in January when people need a great deal of hot water in the cold winter.

As shown in Fig. 13.4 the thermal system can only cover the demand for hot water in New Town but cannot cover the demand for New Town and New Hospital plus the loss in heat pipes. Therefore the project introduces a sewage thermal system to fill the shortage. If eight 47.4 kW sewage heat pumps are introduced, the sewage thermal system can supply 282 MW h and cover the shortage for all year (Fig. 13.5). The potentiality of sewage thermal is estimated as 767 kW, and such sewage thermal system can be introduced.

13.3.1.2 Regional electricity management between New University and New Hospital

The project introduces solar power system in New University for the peak cut of New University as well as New Hospital through providing excess electricity from

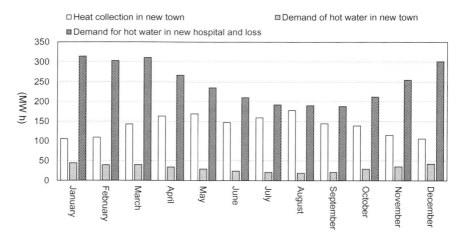

Figure 13.4 Supply and demand of solar thermal.
Source: "Community based Renewable Energy of Local Production and Local Consumption" [Fujitsu Research Institute and Kansai Electric Power. (2016). *Feasibility study of Nara Medical University and its hospital*. New Energy Promotion Council].

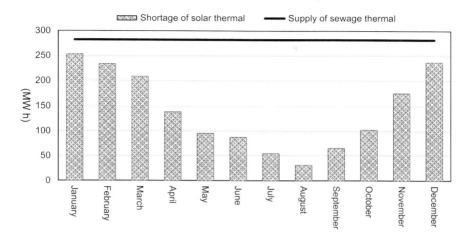

Figure 13.5 Supply of sewage thermal and shortage solar thermal.
Source: "Community based Renewable Energy of Local Production and Local Consumption" [Fujitsu Research Institute and Kansai Electric Power. (2016). *Feasibility Study of Nara Medical University and its hospital*. New Energy Promotion Council].

New University. The demands for electricity of New University and New Hospital are estimated to be largest in July when people need much cooling air in the hot weather. Therefore the volumes of the peak cut of New University and New Hospital are assumed to be the differences between the electricity consumptions with in-house electricity generators in a sunny day and the electricity consumptions without in-house electricity generators in a rainy day. Based on this assumption, the peak cut volume of New University is calculated as 442 kW and that of New Hospital is 597 kW (Fig. 13.6).

The solar power system is to be introduced on the roofs of 50% of the buildings in New University but cannot cover the afternoon demand (1500 to 1800) (Fig. 13.7). Therefore the solar power system will charge the battery during the morning and noontime, and the battery will supply electricity in the afternoon to New University and New Hospital for peak cut.

13.3.1.3 Utilizing well water thermal in New Hospital

The potential of well water thermal in New Hospital is estimated as 170 kW year around. The volume is 1.9% of cooling air (9105 kW) and 2.8% of heating air (6125 kW).

13.3.2 Evaluation

The investment for the regional electricity management between New University and New Hospital is estimated at 797.6 million yen (about $7.25 million), the regional thermal management between New Town and New Hospital at 593.768

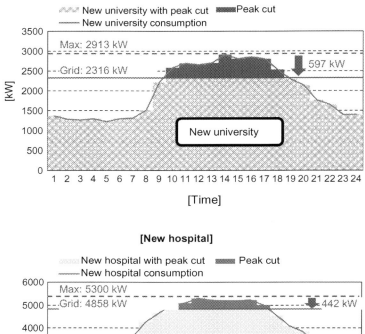
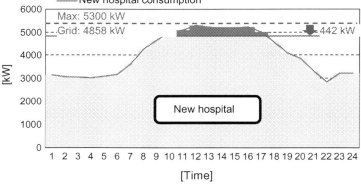

Figure 13.6 Volumes of peak cut (July).
Source: "Community based Renewable Energy of Local Production and Local Consumption" [Fujitsu Research Institute and Kansai Electric Power. (2016). *Feasibility Study of Nara Medical University and its hospital*. New Energy Promotion Council].

million yen (about $5.4 million), and utilizing well water thermal in New Hospital at 40.912 million yen (about $372,000) (Table 13.1). The three major projects will create renewable energy such as solar thermal and solar power and reduce CO_2 over consuming grid power. Regional electricity management between New University and New Hospital, regional thermal management between New Town and New Hospital, and utilizing well water thermal in New Hospital are expected to reduce 1080 t-CO_2, 284 t-CO_2, and 63 t-CO_2, respectively. Among the three major projects, regional electricity management between New University and New Hospital is expected to create the greatest amount of renewable energy (19,947 GJ) and achieve the largest CO_2 reduction with the largest investment amount.

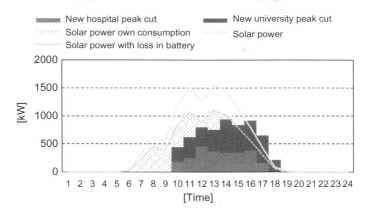

Figure 13.7 Supply of solar power and volumes of peak cut (July).
Source: "Community based Renewable Energy of Local Production and Local Consumption" [Fujitsu Research Institute and Kansai Electric Power. (2016). *Feasibility Study of Nara Medical University and its hospital*. New Energy Promotion Council].

Table 13.1 Estimates of investment amounts and effects of the three major projects.

Major projects	Investment amount		Renewable energy	CO_2 reduction
	Yen in thousands	$ in thousands		
(I) Regional thermal management between New Town and New Hospital	593,768	5398	5308 GJ	284 t-CO_2
(II) Regional electricity management between New University and New Hospital	797,600	7251	1,967,893 kW h (19,947 GJ)	1080 t-CO_2
(III) Utilizing well water thermal in New Hospital	40,912	372	1177 GJ	63 t-CO_2

Source: "Community based Renewable Energy of Local Production and Local Consumption" [Fujitsu Research Institute and Kansai Electric Power. (2016). *Feasibility Study of Nara Medical University and its hospital*. New Energy Promotion Council].

When looking at the profitability of the three major projects, profits are generated from the total reduction of the cost of purchasing grid power. The energy cost reductions are estimated at 32.462 million yen (about $295,000) for regional electricity management between New University and New Hospital, 24.170 million yen

Table 13.2 Profitability of the three major projects.

Major projects	Energy cost reduction		Investment recovery period	
	Yen in thousands	$ in thousands	Without subsidy (years)	With subsidy of half investment (years)
(I) Regional thermal management between New Town and New Hospital	24,170	220	24.6	12.3
(II) Regional electricity management between New University and New Hospital	32,462	295	24.6	12.3
(III) Utilizing well water thermal in New Hospital	1952	18	21.0	10.5

Source: "Community based Renewable Energy of Local Production and Local Consumption" [Fujitsu Research Institute and Kansai Electric Power. (2016). *Feasibility Study of Nara Medical University and its hospital*. New Energy Promotion Council].

(about $220,000) for regional thermal management between New Town and New Hospital, and 1.952 million yen (about $18,000) for utilizing well water thermal in New Hospital (Table 13.2). Note that feed-in tariff has been introduced since 2012 in Japan, and solar power is purchased by power companies for 18 yen (about $0.20) per kW h in FY 2016. Regional electricity management between New University and New Hospital is expected to generate solar power but the volume is not enough to sell to power companies.

The investment recovery periods are estimated at 24.6 years for regional thermal management between New Town and New Hospital and regional electricity management between New University and New Hospital, and 21.0 years for utilizing well water thermal in New Hospital. With subsidies covering half of the investment amounts the investment recovery periods are estimated at 12.3 years for regional thermal management between New Town and New Hospital and regional electricity management between New University and New Hospital, and 10.5 years for utilizing well water thermal in New Hospital. Considering that the usual investment recovery period in Japan is less than 10 years, the investment recovery periods of the three major projects are long. It is necessary to reduce the investment cost for facilities and equipment of the three major projects.

13.4 Conclusion

As discussed above, the three major projects under the regional energy management in Nara Medical University and its hospital with the smart city concept can reduce

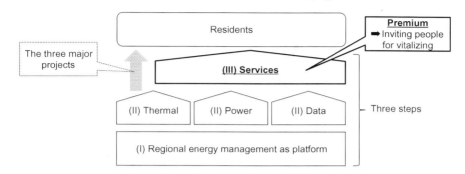

Figure 13.8 Steps of improving services in the smart city concept.

CO_2 emissions through utilizing renewable energies, but it will take a long time to recover the investments even with subsidies. As the population has been decreasing in Japan, the smart city concept can provide a premium value to attract people, thus revitalizing the local economy while reducing the cost of providing services.

The following three steps are to be implemented for improving services under the smart city concept (Fig. 13.8):

1. Regional energy management as platform;
2. Developing thermal, power, and data resources;
3. Services utilizing thermal, power, and data.

The outcome will be to expand the smart city concept with attractive services while the cost of related facilities and equipment is reduced due to economies of scale.

The possible services of the smart city concept in Nara Medical University and its hospital are shown in Table 13.3. As Japan's population ages, there will be increasing demand for social welfare and medical services. With the recent developments in vehicle technologies, services related to electric vehicles and autonomous vehicles are worth giving consideration.

About the author

Narutoshi Sakano (as of February 5, 2019)

1. Business affiliation

Managing Consultant, Public Sector Management Consulting Group, Fujitsu Research Institute

2. Summary

April 2001–present:

Engaged in research projects commissioned by central government on smart cities, expanding overseas transport/information and communication technology (ICT) business mainly in ASEAN countries and road safety as well as providing consulting services for regional governments on administration reform.

Table 13.3 Possible services of the smart city concept.

Facilities	Services	Aspects		
		Thermal	**Power**	**Data**
Social welfare and medical services				
Houses for elderly people	• Watching services • Temperature and humidity management • Product development (providing data for producers) • Building energy management	—	• Air conditioning • Saving power	• Monitoring facilities and residents
Day service centers	• Temperature and humidity management • Building energy management	—	• Air conditioning • Saving power	• Monitoring facilities and residents
Health centers	• Expert consultation on diet and exercise based on medical data • Management of taking medicines	—	—	• Medical, dietary, and biological data • Monitoring stocks of medicines
Gyms	• Temperature and humidity management • Heated indoor pool	• Thermal for pool	• Air conditioning	• Monitoring facilities and users
Rehabilitation centers	• Temperature and humidity management • Product development (providing data for producers)	—	• Air conditioning	• Monitoring facilities and users

(*Continued*)

Table 13.3 (Continued)

Facilities	Services	Aspects		
		Thermal	**Power**	**Data**
Transport and shipping services				
Stations	• Temperature and humidity management • Providing thermal	• Thermal for energy	• Air conditioning	• Monitoring facilities and passengers
Shopping malls	• Temperature and humidity management • Building energy management • Product development (providing data for producers)	—	• Air conditioning • Saving power	• Monitoring purchasing behavior
Vehicle sharing				
Rental car facilities	• Rental car services of electric vehicles • Providing information for autonomous vehicles	—	• Battery charging	• Eco-point for shopping • Monitoring vehicle travel

Source: "Community based Renewable Energy of Local Production and Local Consumption" [Fujitsu Research Institute and Kansai Electric Power. (2016). *Feasibility Study of Nara Medical University and its hospital*. New Energy Promotion Council].

Reference

Fujitsu Research Institute and Kansai Electric Power. (2016). *Feasibility study of Nara Medical University and its hospital*. New Energy Promotion Council.

Further reading

Case Studies of Smart Communities. (2017). *Ministry of Economy, Trade and Industry*. From <http://www.meti.go.jp/press/2017/06/20170623002/20170623002-1.pdf> Retrieved Oct. 2018.

Ministry of Environment. (2018). *Accelerating and maximising renewable energy program.* From <https://www.env.go.jp/earth/ondanka/lca/2018/mat06.pdf> Retrieved Oct. 2018.

Public Foundation of Kansai Research Institute, Keihanna Science City. From <https://www.kri.or.jp/know/> Retrieved Oct. 2018.

A smart city case study of Singapore—*Is Singapore truly smart?*

Marianna Cavada, Miles R. Tight and Christopher D.F. Rogers
University of Birmingham, Birmingham, United Kingdom

Chapter Outline

14.1 Background 295
14.2 Singapore's vision—a smart nation 296
14.3 Research methodology: the Smart Model Assessment Resilient Tool 296
    14.3.1 Introduction to assessment of Smart Model Assessment Resilient Tool 296
    14.3.2 Integration 298
    14.3.3 Organization 298
    14.3.4 Timescale 299
    14.3.5 Singapore's smart initiatives 300
    14.3.6 Reach—star ratings of Singapore's initiatives 303
    14.3.7 Risks 304
    14.3.8 Procurement 304
    14.3.9 Benefits of Singapore's initiatives on liveability actions 304
    14.3.10 Direct impact on lenses 306
    14.3.11 Indirect impact on lenses 307
14.4 Conclusions and recommendations 308
Acknowledgments 310
About the authors 310
References 311
Further reading 314

14.1 Background

Singapore's location in Asia was its primary asset in the 19th century trading era, but cheap manufacturing in the 1960s and the production of digital products in the mid-1980s led to a flourishing information technology (IT) infrastructure and significant economic development (Mahizhnan, 1999). Since then, Singapore has grown from a country of relatively limited opportunities into a contemporary nation that has become globally renowned and increasingly smart (Cohen, 2012b; Warwick, 1998). Efforts by Juniper Research Limited (a consulting firm focusing on digital products and telecommunications) suggest that it was the first smart city, and Singapore is often included in the worldwide smart city rankings (IESE, 2016; Juniper Research, 2018; Smith, 2016). For example, it was ranked first in the world's top five smart cities (Buntz, 2016) and was a big winner (along with New Zealand) in the IDC Smart City Development Index (IDC, 2016). Consequently, Singapore is often considered the smartest city (Watson, 2017). This chapter seeks to test the claim to greatest smartness.

14.2 Singapore's vision—a smart nation

A smart city is often a blurred concept, viewed differently by stakeholders (Cavada, Hunt, & Rogers, 2014). Smartness has been associated with recent innovative technologies and positive outcomes in the urban context (Anthopoulos, 2017). Singapore is the first nation that is considered smart, a notion that extends further than the city scale, Singapore, as a city, is unique in a worldwide context considering itself a Smart Nation. Unlike a city (when smart operations are in a city scale and governed locally, a Smart Nation is directly linked to the national government operation, both enabled and potentially constrained, by national policies. In particular, Singapore has ministries and government agencies (Digital Communication Agencies, Infocomm Media Development Authority, 2018) that work in partnership with Smart Nation Singapore (SNS) (2018a) and have a strong presence in the smart agenda. The SNS (2018b) gives priority to the digital aspect of smart, innovative digital technologies and economy. In the context of this case study, it is essential to perceive smart also as a complete entity (i.e., take a holistic view that one could claim is aligned with Singapore's vision of national smartness). Ideally, smartness perceives all liveable aspects to be just as important as functional digital aspects, and this needs to be better understood in order for liveability to function, and be maintained, in smart cities (Adair, 1985; Cavada, Hunt, & Rogers, 2017; Melvin, 2012). A liveable vision usually involves a sequence of choices (or initiatives adopted in the smart agenda) over time, which lead to an optimal set of policies, decisions, and actions for truly smart cities (Cavada, Hunt, & Rogers, 2016; Roebuck, 2011). This process is explored in the Smart Model Assessment Resilient Tool (SMART), a methodology for the assessment of smart city initiatives that is explained in Section 14.3, which adopts a similar approach to that used in a Hong Kong planning regeneration scheme, where three core aspects—economic, societal, and the physical mode of development—were analyzed (Cavada et al., 2016; Shen, Wang, & Tang, 2014).

14.3 Research methodology: the Smart Model Assessment Resilient Tool

14.3.1 Introduction to assessment of Smart Model Assessment Resilient Tool

This section describes the implementation of SMART, which was developed to support the stakeholder groups taking part in decision-making processes aiming to achieve liveability in smart cities, and, we would suggest without exception, a city's vision will claim to enhance the well-being and quality of life of its citizens, as well as (usually) the natural environment in which the city is embedded. SMART does this by providing a transparent and repeatable analysis of proposed initiatives [or interventions in city systems, as described by Rogers (2018)] in the context in which they need to work. This involves examining the impacts on a city's performance criteria and their connections (i.e., dependencies and interdependencies) until they reach a consensus on how to achieve liveability in smart cities (Communities GovUK, 2009; Kurka & Blackwood, 2013; Montibeller and Franco, 2010). SMART is described here in assessing the Singaporean case using its Strand One (S1) analysis, as outlined in Fig. 14.1, it achieves this by analyzing the initiatives adopted by the city in relation to its smart agenda.

There are 52 initiatives that have been introduced by Singapore in its goal to become "smart," together with a simple three-star rating assessment used to describe the impact on Singapore's population (three stars represents a potential for impact on the whole of Singapore's population, while one star represents an impact on a small subset of its population, of whatever nature). We analyzed the benefits deriving from the initiatives to evaluate how the direct and indirect impacts of the initiatives are distributed in supporting the "actions toward liveability," identified by Leach et al. (2017). In total it shows that there were direct (i.e., specifically targeted benefits described as intended outcomes of the initiative) and indirect (benefits that are judged indirectly to support the actions—advantageous by-products) beneficial impacts on the Liveability Actions across 125 cells. The tool has been further developed (via the addition of Strand Two—S2 analysis) to include discussions and local expert opinions to evaluate the initiatives adopted in the smart agenda of a city, and thereby enrich the S1 analysis. S2 also enables the application of a fuller analysis using multicriteria analysis and the analytical hierarchy process to establish priorities among the criteria and initiatives, and thereby determine the appropriate sequencing that would help to inform decision-making founded on the evidence base created by SMART, which would in turn result in enhanced

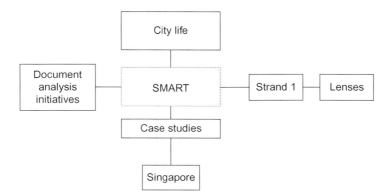

Figure 14.1 SMART (S1) used to assess Smart (Nation) Singapore. *S1*, Strand One; *SMART*, Smart Model Assessment Resilient Tool.

liveability in smart cities (Cavada et al., 2016; Communities GovUk, 2009; Halepoto, Sahito, Uqaili, & Chowdhry, 2015; Lazaroiu & Roscia, 2012; Lombardi, Leach, & Rogers, 2012). However it was not possible to employ S2 for the Singapore case study reported here.

14.3.2 Integration

Singapore's vision to become a leader in terms of the quality of life was initially conceived during the 1980s in the form of the government's information technology plan to improve services, which led to increasing socioeconomic opportunities in governance advances, technology, and industry collaborations (Foo & Pan, 2016). Singapore has scaled up its ambitions from being a smart city to being the first Smart Nation, focused on citizens and businesses, with input that will enable innovative actions and government regulation (SNS, 2018a). Singapore's vision is founded on two factors: the Singaporean Prime Ministerial leadership, aiming to strengthen the economy and liveability, and the implementation of national policies (Strategic National Projects, Open Data, Living Laboratory, Industry and Start-Up Ecosystem, Cybersecurity and Data Privacy, and Computational Capabilities and Digital Inclusion; SNS, 2018c). The relationship between liveability and the economy is clearly perceived in terms of the citizens' ability to connect to the government's digital service system, which specifically aims to support the Singaporean community, provide access to information for efficiency and the prospective creation of businesses through open data (GovTech Singapore, 2018). It becomes evident that digitalization is the main factor in enhancing liveability—connecting the community to government services and digital technology—and this can equally provide economic benefits. Lastly, in Singapore, all initiatives are led by SNS (2018d), developed by the main government through the Prime Minister's office. Smart Nation Singapore (SNS) also supports other agencies, such as GovTech Singapore (2016) and National Youth Council Singapore (NYCS) (2016).

14.3.3 Organization

Delivery of the digital transformation was enabled by the Infocomm Media Development Authority, a government regulator for digital innovation, and was supported by GovTech Singapore (GovTechSingapore, 2016; IMDA, 2018). The IMDA (2018) published the "Intelligent Nation" report, a collection of endeavours for the 2025 governance plan vision, based on *innovation, integration, internationalisation*, to enhance liveability through information technology learning, initiated by the supply of laptops and internet access for everyone; and digital health care and governance, aiming to spread the benefits of technology to the wider society (IDA, 2008, pp. 7−9).

The Government of Singapore's efforts to create a liveable and economically successful nation are organized by the originators of the SNS (SNS, 2018a). The financial aims of the Research, Innovation and Enterprise 2020 RIE2020 (2018) scheme prioritized government funding for early founded businesses, and collaborations to enhance knowledge, investment, and confidence in industrial involvement (National Research Foundation (NRF), 2017). Reforms and the effects on the economy of collaborations involving private organizations, such as Cisco, working with Singapore's Smart Nation showed that, in 2014, the fiscal advantages of digitalization would exceed $4.6 trillion within a decade. These are expected to arise from 40 smart cases that promote innovative systems in engineering, health, and trade and bridge further collaborations of the IDA and the Ministry of Communications and Information (Bradley, Reberger, Dixit, & Gupta, 2014). The NRF (2017) has also focused on fiscal efforts; supported by the government in the "Innovation & Enterprise Cluster Fund" manufacturing scheme, with $54.4 million of funding for industry led projects.

SNS is a long-term plan and continues to address challenges at a governmental decision-making level to emphasize digital infrastructure interventions, to improve citizens' lives (Hoe, 2016). Therefore Singapore's step-wise view of a Smart Nation recognizes four pillars of initiatives (health, living, mobility, and services) to address ways of improving the quality of life issues through the implementation of digital technologies (SNS, 2018a,b,c,d). According to the SNS (2018a,b,c,d), mobility and service initiatives have adopted technological advancements to improve transportation with driverless automobiles and real-time data analytics, whereas health care and housing can be considered the main focal points of standards of living/quality of life. Further initiatives, promoting a car-free agenda, contribute to the smart and liveable agenda through local initiatives and car ownership being *from 0.25% to 0%*, according to the Land Transport Authority Singapore (Land Transport Authority of Singapore, 2018; Urban Redevelopment Authority, 2018). Part of the smart liveable agenda support human capacity and commerce extends to the support of younger generations (enabled by National Youth Council Singapore—NYCS) in collaboration with Spring Singapore, supported by the Ministry of Trade and Industry for collaborations, development programs and finances (NYCS, 2016; Spring Singapore, 2015). It is evident that government collaborations have developed through the RIE2020 Plan, arranged in four areas—scientific collaboration and scientific funding from the government; funding for prospective economic development, collaboration with the commercial sector for fiscal gains; and empowerment of the human workforce. One of the main scientific collaborations is the Singapore-MIT Alliance for Research and Technology Innovation Centre SMART making Singapore a smart and outward looking nation (NRF, 2016, 2018; SMART, 2016).

14.3.4 Timescale

This section examines current initiatives in the Smart Nation agenda—most of the initiatives, in their descriptions, indicate a timescale during which they are active, although benefits will usually extend beyond the life of the initiative itself. There is a strong indication that the Smart Nation agenda was founded on the long digitalization that Singapore has been through since the 1960s (1966 when the Ministry of Defence introduced computing) through the 1980s (when the National

Table 14.1 Timescale of initiatives for Singapore.

Timescale	Singapore initiatives
Total	*52*
A = active	41
C = completed	6
U = unknown	5

Computerisation Programme was introduced) and in the 1990s (National Science and Technology Board and Infocommunications Development Authority of Signapore was founded), and these led to the recent (2017) converge of the national digital systems and the smart agenda of Singapore (Tan & Yimin, 2018, pp. 106−115).

Table 14.1 shows the distribution of initiatives that are currently active or have been completed (or participation has concluded), or in five cases where the descriptions do not specify a timescale.

Active initiatives include those initiated by the SNS and GovTech, mostly relating to government digital systems and access to them (i.e., health-care solutions—digital, ageing, and homecare; electric and self-driving vehicles; and access to grants; along with cashless society). Those for which there is no indication of timescale are Singapore's Youth Council, Government IT Security Incident Response, National Authentication Framework, Technology Associate Programme, and Agile Development. This shows that the smart agenda is very much active in Singapore.

14.3.5 Singapore's smart initiatives

Smartness in Singapore is not thought of as a city-level consideration, as happens in smart cities elsewhere, it is rather considered one of the main strategies, if not the main strategy, for the national government, a unique concept in the smart realm because of Singapore's situation as a city state. SNS (2018a) is the mechanism for Singapore's national smartness, which explains how the technology is used for the city's services and how it improves citizens' quality of life. SNS is the umbrella agency connecting to further government agencies and has a brief to carry out smart and other programs, as exemplified by initiatives from GovTech Singapore and NYCS. Singapore has adopted 52 initiatives so far. Since Singapore has 5.184 million people (MoFA, 2011), this equates to about 10 initiatives per 1 million people. The main agency, SNS, has adopted 14 initiatives categorized in four areas, also shown in Fig. 14.2.

> Health: Four initiatives aim to assist with patient care by developing health-related analytics, supporting elderly mobility using robotics, an app linked with citizens' wearables to encourage exercise, and monitoring health for those patients at home.

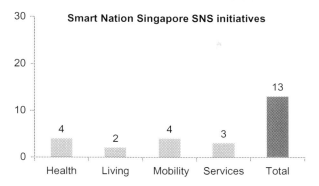

Figure 14.2 Number of SNS initiatives. *SNS*, Smart Nation Singapore.

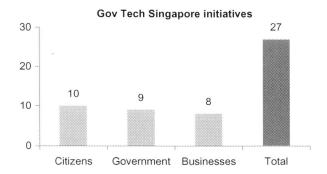

Figure 14.3 Number of Gov Tech initiatives.

Living: Two initiatives, both apps, one aiming to improve interaction between the municipality and citizens on environmental issues, and the second—aimed both at citizens and professionals—to better understand the living conditions of a home, apartment tower, or at neighborhood level and achieve more efficient living.

Mobility: The four initiatives here are focused on a crowd-based mobility technology, for example, technologies to aid citizen access to public transportation and mobility analytics—mostly on public mobility, but also parking. Singapore particularly supports autonomous mobility testing and research on requirements for public mobility.

Services: Three initiatives here aim to support the citizen−government interaction through a citizen database platform (MyInfo), providing access to 100 public services; a financial database to support the economy and create business opportunities; and an initiative for digital transaction for citizens and businesses.

GovTech Singapore (2018) is the main digital technology agency of Singapore, which delivers the Singaporean Smart Nation; here, there are 27 initiatives (shown in Fig. 14.3) clustered into three categories that are mostly concerned with developing digital interventions for citizens.

- Citizens: There are 10 initiatives aimed at connecting citizens with digital government services, open datasets (also containing personal information on banking and health),

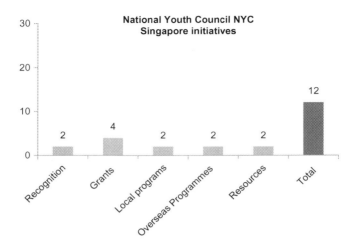

Figure 14.4 Number of NYC initiatives. *NYC*, National Youth Council.

digital training programs and fellowships, further agencies to assist with citizens' questions, and a crowd platform for sharing new ideas.
- Government: While some of the government initiatives are also part of the citizens' initiatives, the government-focused initiatives are mainly on research grants, national collaborations and logistical platforms, public services developments, and digital tools for innovative development.
- Businesses: These initiatives are typically shared with the other two categories; for example, grants coming from the government or having access to online sharing platforms, and also IT safety, and access to academic collaboration.

The NYC is part of the Ministry of Culture, which aims to empower the younger generations and currently has 12 initiatives in five categories, shown in Fig. 14.4.

- Recognition: Two initiatives accepting applications for awards on leadership and youth.
- Grants: There are four grants to support research and development actions that benefit the wider community, to provide support for projects led by the youth, and to facilitate participation in international projects as a way to enhance resilience in the younger generations. Like the initiatives described so far, there is some overlap here across the categories.
- Local programs: Initiatives include volunteering schemes and surveys recording the youths' opinion, along with recreational activities, festivals, and celebrations.
- Overseas programs: These are mostly exchange programs in countries abroad (notably Southeast Asian countries) and include recreational activities that enhance resilience.
- Resources: Statistics for teenagers and young citizens up to mid-thirties and electronic news on youth matters.

However, the ultimate purpose of this chapter is to explore whether Singapore is truly smart. This is achieved using SMART to assess the intended (direct) benefits of the initiatives and their beneficial wider positive impacts (indirect benefits). The conceptualization of true smartness concerns the enhancement of liveability in smart cities (see Liveable Cities, 2013), and it is the assessment method for the liveability performance of cities that underpins the SMART analysis (Leach, Lee, Hunt, & Rogers, 2017a,b). The analysis is described in Sections 14.3.9–14.3.11.

As described later, the analysis explores how an initiative supports a series of what are termed actions toward liveability—and any one initiative might support several actions either as a direct result of its design or as a helpful by-product of beneficially changing something else. For convenience the actions are clustered under four lenses—Society, Environment, Economy & Finance, and Governance & Policy—and each lens focuses on a set of high-level goals, which are in turn supported by the actions (see Leach et al., 2016). However, there are three other perspectives to introduce so that this analysis can be viewed in context.

14.3.6 Reach—star ratings of Singapore's initiatives

A simple three-star rating has been applied to the 52 initiatives adopted in Singapore to reflect the "reach" of the initiatives. Three-star initiatives are those that benefit the whole population of Singapore, and two-star initiatives benefit a substantial proportion of the population, but they are more narrowly focussed—those of working age provides a good example; while a one-starred initiative would benefit only a small, highly targeted subset of the population, school leavers, perhaps, or those in need of retraining from a shrinking industry. Singapore's 52 initiatives support the Liveability Actions (directly or indirectly) in 125 identified ways (i.e., there are 125 impacts in total). Applying engineering judgment to the descriptions of each initiative, and thus allocating a star rating, to estimate the reach of the initiatives and summing the star ratings yields a total of 266. The average reach of the initiatives (266 divided by 125 impacts) is 2.12, which shows that the initiatives were more generally beneficial, whether directly or indirectly, for the majority of the population rather than narrow subgroups or sectors.

More specifically, 19 three-star initiatives were judged to benefit the whole population of Singapore (e.g., Assistive Technology, Telehealth, Contactless Payment, Digital Government, Citizen Connect, Smart Nation, Social Service), 17 two-star initiatives showed a somewhat narrower focus of beneficiaries (e.g., Leveraging Technology, Business Grants Portal, Design Challenge, Call for Proposals, Smart Nation Fellowship, National Trade Platform, TRANS Grant, SME Portal), while there were judged to be 16 one-star initiatives (e.g., Self-Driving Vehicles and Standards, GovTech Cloudstore, Young Change Makers, Leadership and Service Award, Singapore Youth Award, Singapore-ASEAN Youth Fund) that affect a small proportion of the population, such as young people or those interested in autonomous vehicles or other more narrowly focused technology.

Singapore takes a strong top-down view on smartness that depends highly on the government's implemented policies, with a much stronger focus on the Society Lens than the Environmental Lens. Here, the citizens benefit from improved connection to government systems, while at the same time data collection (by the government) can lead to new polices and help the economy—a symbiotic relationship. However, that does not lend itself to delivery of the broader spectrum of enhanced liveability for the wide Singaporean population.

14.3.7 Risks

Risk in the SNS is a real threat, as demonstrated by the (July 2018) data breach of a medical clinic. This was a major event that compromised the privacy and security of citizens by releasing details of 1.5 million patients—it not only shows that potential attack is a real threat to the technological system that supports smartness, but that it can have drastic effects on the population in general (SingHealth, 2018). Singapore's immediate action on the matter was to conduct an investigation with the Cyber Security Agency, one of Singapore's government agencies. The Ministry of Communications and Information communicated the incident to patients and has been responsible since then to improve safety in digital services, and especially in health care (Cyber Security Agency, 2018; SingHealth, 2018). However, attacks like these might occur again in digital systems, where the risk is continually upgraded because of new technologies and where national agencies need both to provide assurance of safety for users and secure smartness not only for the systems themselves but also for people. Furthermore, since "smart" refers to a nation, rather than a particular city, in Singapore's case, safety emerges as a national issue in collaborations and procurement.

14.3.8 Procurement

SNS follows the national procedures when it comes to procurement for smart cities projects: the tender process notices are posted openly on the GeBIZ website listing bidding opportunities, while selected interested parties can be shortlisted or bidding tenders can be sought by invitation only (MoF, 2017). Similar to other national operations, funding for smart projects is distributed through the government agencies, where also alternative collaborations can be established through public–private partnerships and other arrangements, such as joint ventures or partnerships (MoF, 2017). It might be that the process being governed by the central administration enables a faster processing of smart initiatives and projects across Singapore that would be the case if it were attempted by a local administration working within national guidelines and dealing with other competing local demands. The Ministry of Finance claims that such a tender procurement process provides transparency and supports competition between the bidding agencies, while the Singaporean Government is able to establish international collaborations at a government level with international partners, such as the delivery of blockchain in Chongqing in China (MoF, 2017).

14.3.9 Benefits of Singapore's initiatives on liveability actions

Overall Singapore as a smart city—or a Smart Nation in a city context—is renowned for smartness and has achieved the highest positions in international rankings (Buntz, 2016; Cohen, 2012a; IDC, 2016; IESE, 2016; Juniper Research, 2018; Smith, 2016; Warwick, 1998; Watson, 2017). Singapore's

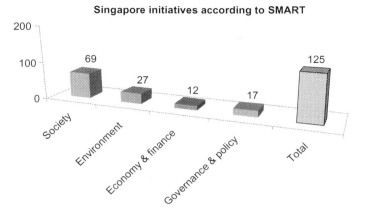

Figure 14.5 Initiatives benefits according to Liveability Goals.

society is highly digitalized, where locals are often computer literate, and as a nation Singapore is open to international collaborations and exchange. A more in-depth view of the initiatives can be found in the descriptions and assessment of Singapore's initiatives. Here, the results of the overview are analyzed, showing the direct and indirect beneficial impacts on Liveability Actions of the 52 adopted initiatives (Fig. 14.5). In total there are judged to be 125 areas of beneficial impact across the four liveability lenses (64 are marked as direct impacts and 61 as indirect impacts). These will be analyzed separately in Sections 14.3.10 and 14.3.11.

Most of the impacted Liveability Actions are found in the Society Lens. This is because the initiatives largely use digital interventions to deliver efficient communications between citizens and government services, and this has a wider societal benefit. There is less benefit in the Environment Lens; evidently the smart agenda in Singapore does not focus as strongly on environmental benefits, in contrast to certain other highly acclaimed smart cities, such as Copenhagen (Cavada et al., 2016). There is even less benefit in Economy & Finance and Governance & Policy Lenses, potentially due to the strong top-down administration that might consider smart solutions need not to address these issues. The analysis further shows the distribution of the initiatives' direct and indirect impacts (Fig. 14.6). It is clear that there is a more even distribution of direct impact on the Liveability Actions across the four lenses, yet interestingly the initiatives have been shaped with societal benefits in mind since there is markedly more indirect impact on the Society Lens; as previously stated, the societal benefit is shown in the indirect impact of the digital interventions for governmental services to citizens.

In the next two sections the direct and indirect impacts on the Liveability Actions, as reflect the overview.

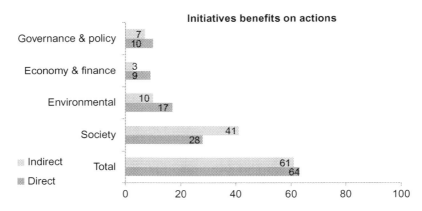

Figure 14.6 Benefits (direct/indirect impact) on Liveability Actions.

14.3.10 Direct impact on lenses

In total, there are 64 direct impacts (Fig. 14.6), with the greatest impact on the Society Lens (28 cells). This section uses each Lens to understand in more detail the initiatives' impact on the Liveability Actions and hence support in achieving Liveability Goals. For example, the "increase the match between city dweller aspirations and well-being" action is impacted directly by 12 initiatives (12 cells are marked), while "maximize cultural benefit" is also well supported (with 7 cells marked), both Liveability Actions supporting in turn the "enhance community and individual well-being" goal. The "Ensure equity (fairness)" goal is impacted less, although the "ensure an enabling social environment to maximize individual capabilities in the context of carbon reduction and resource security" action is impacted directly by five initiatives so this is clearly a government priority in Singapore. Otherwise the "ensure an enabling physical environment to maximize individual capabilities in the context of carbon reduction and resource security" action is directly targeted by one initiative, while the other two Liveability Actions supporting this goal are not targeted, and likewise there is no direct impact on the action supporting the "enhance biodiversity and ecosystem services" goal.

Interestingly, the Environmental Lens has been far less directly targeted by Singapore's smart initiatives (17 cells are marked), and indeed this is true for both direct and indirect impacts thus making it clear where Singapore's priorities lie: people before planet. Moreover, where the environmental goals have been supported it is in terms of the most "socially beneficial" Liveability Actions in the Environmental Lens (i.e., supporting health and well-being and making provision for local people in the workforce as opposed to addressing resources). In support of the "ensure resource efficiency" goal, there is direct impact on the "maximize cultural services (health benefits, recreation, opportunities for outdoor learning)" action (seven cells are marked) and the "increase the match between well-being and minimizing high-carbon mobilities, while maximizing low-carbon mobilities and immobilities of people and objects" action (three cells marked). In support of the "ensure resource security" goal, "maximize sustainable use of local people first (e.g., utilizing the local workforce and leveraging local skills) and then maximize the security of supply of nonlocal people" is directly impacted by six initiatives, while the "increase the match between city dwellers' aspirations and resource secure living" action is impacted only once, and the remainder show no impact at all.

In the Economy & Finance Lens (targeted directly by nine initiatives), the "maximize investment to support liveability objectives (maximizing well-being, resource security and efficiency, and minimizing CO_2 emissions)" action is clearly the highest priority (eight cells marked)—again it is the action with a stronger people focus—while only one initiative directly supports the "uncouple economic vitality from the CO_2 emissions associated with economic growth" action—which has a stronger environmental focus. In the Governance & Policy Lens (targeted directly by 10 initiatives), there is direct impact on the "uncouple governance structures and timescales from political cycles and 'color' of governing bodies" action (six cells marked) and the "uncouple policy making and policy timescales from political cycles and 'color' of governing bodies" action (four cells marked).

14.3.11 Indirect impact on lenses

The number of indirect impacts on Liveability Actions is close to the number of direct impacts, this shows a healthy outcome from the design of the initiatives—it is far more effective if smart initiatives are able to deliver multiple benefits rather than being targeted on a single benefit (Rogers, 2018). Interestingly, and in support of the earlier analysis, the 61 indirect impacts are strongly weighted toward the Social Lens (41 cells), with 10 indirect impacts in the Environmental Lens, 3 in the Economy & Finance Lens, and 7 in the Governance & Policy Lens. This reinforces the idea that Singapore is putting its people first when it comes to the digital interventions.

In support of the "enhance community and individual well-being" goal, there is much indirect impact in support of the "increase the match between city dweller aspirations and well-being" and "maximize cultural benefit" Liveability Actions (15 cells marked each), while the "promote healthy living and healthy long lives" and "minimize ill-being" Liveability Actions are each supported by four initiatives. The "ensure equity (fairness)" goal is evidently far less important (only two indirect impacts), and there is zero indirect impact on the "enhance biodiversity and ecosystem services" goal.

There is even less indirect (compared to direct) impact on Liveability Actions in the Environmental Lens (41 cells marked), with only the "maximize cultural services (health benefits, recreation, opportunities for outdoor learning)" action (3 cells) and the "maximize sustainable use of local people first (e.g., utilizing the local workforce and leveraging local skills) and then maximize the security of supply of nonlocal people" action (7 cells) being supported. All other Liveability Actions have zero indirect impact that shows little indirect consideration for the Environment Lens.

The Economy & Finance Lens shows little indirect impact: "maximize investment to support liveability objectives (maximizing well-being, resource security and efficiency, and minimizing CO_2 emissions)" is indirectly supported by two initiatives and "uncouple economic vitality from the CO_2 emissions associated with economic growth" by one.

In the Governance & Policy Lens, there are seven indirect impacts from Singapore's smart initiatives: the "uncouple governance structures and timescales from political cycles and 'color' of governing bodies" action is indirectly impacted by four initiatives and the "uncouple policy making and policy timescales from political cycles and 'color' of governing bodies" action by three.

14.4 Conclusions and recommendations

The broad spectrum of smart cities research has shown a considerable diversity of perspectives making it hard to distil a universal meaning of smartness, and this creates further complexities not only in the assessment of smartness but also in characterization of smart cities using rating systems. Smart for many is related to digital technology, this research goes beyond this single concept to develop an assessment as to whether cities are truly smart—that they are enhancing liveability by promoting societal and individual well-being. For this reason, this research has explored the delivery of liveability via a city's smart initiatives, where the assessment has been focusing on what makes smart cities truly smart. Smartness has been evaluated in terms of support by the initiatives in advancing Liveability Goals (and more specifically Liveability Actions), along with their reach in terms of time frame and population impact (using a simple three-star rating). The means of assessment—the SMART—is an approach that can be used to support decision-making when developing city initiatives to deliver truly smart cities.

Various limitations in smart conceptualizations make it difficult to assess all smart cities equally, and this defines the biggest limitation facing this research (Cavada et al., 2014). Furthermore, smart city agendas adopt smart initiatives according to context and time constraints and are funding specific, often following an agenda of appropriate city aspirations (Rogers, 2018) that are open to interpretation. Of course, Singapore is a distinct case due to the fact that the leadership agendas are influenced by current national considerations—international collaboration and competition—and therefore, even more than in other smart cities, national political agendas and fiscal priorities determine priorities for Singapore's smart agendas and initiatives.

SMART has been used to capture the city aspirations of contemporary and prospective smart cities, as revealed by Future Urban Living (Rogers et al., 2012) and the Foresight Future of Cities (Hunt & Rogers, 2015) activities and adopted in the Urban Futures Methodology (Lombardi et al., 2012; Rogers et al., 2012) and in turn incorporated in the Liveable Cities Methodology (Leach et al., 2017a,b). These aspirations inevitably involve the aspects of sustainability, resilience, and liveability. Notably, the assessment of resilience (the R in SMART stands for resilient) could provide information on the risks inherent in smart city development and provide further clarification of the smart city vision — an assessment of resilience is often used by corporations to make decisions on technological aspects (Twiss & Jones, 1978).

Singapore's uniqueness as a smart city−state is an interesting factor. The national government has set the smart agenda, and initiatives were supported by government organizations, to enhance citizen services using digital systems (GovTech Singapore, 2018; SNS, 2018a,b,c,d). Although it has adopted a high number of initiatives (52) to achieve its smart aspirations, it however achieved the lowest score of 125 impacts on Liveability Actions in comparison with similar case studies reported by Cavada (2019)—London (46 initiatives, 193 impacts), Copenhagen (59 initiatives, 235 impacts), and Birmingham, the United Kingdom (39 initiatives, 194 impacts)—implying that Singapore's initiatives were narrowly focussed and not designed with multiple benefits in mind (Rogers, 2018).

However, the expectations of SNS can be argued to have fallen short, as the analysis shows that digitalization does not necessarily support truly smart, liveable cities. The implementation of the smart agenda in Singapore, however, is a faster process due to the links enabled by the governmental collaboration. It is therefore recommended that in the future, liveability could (and should) be considered in the decision-making process of the city, and this might be achieved by emphasizing liveability in its overall smart vision. This, in turn should be reflected in the design of new smart city initiatives—governed by the idea that it is desirable that a truly smart agenda supports the highest number of Liveability Actions and delivers the widest impact on the population—and in this endeavor the Lens framework (Leach et al, 2017a,b) and SMART (Cavada, 2019) provide helpful tools. Moreover, there is particular encouragement in Singapore that change can occur relatively fast, and therefore if this were considered a priority, then government-assisted implementation of these new initiatives could see liveability—true smartness—enhance the performance of the city and enrich the lives of its citizens.

A further consideration in this respect is that support for Liveability Actions in Singapore is not distributed uniformly across all Lenses, and a balance of impacts is needed to contribute most effectively to the city's liveability. Having identified the need using the various approaches developed by the members of the Liveable Cities team, techniques such as cost−benefit analysis and/or cost effective analysis could be used to explore initiative priorities according to Government and local funding.

In conclusion, therefore, this research has set the liveability paradigm as an addition to the existing state-of-the-art in smartness, hoping that further leverage will be based on what this research considers truly smart. If these arguments are accepted, SNS is ideally placed to develop its own agenda, noting that it already provides a lead in developing the smart concept internationally, based on Singapore's context, vision, and liveability assessment for the future. If it did, it would provide a clearer understanding of how to perceive, assess, and implement smartness.

Acknowledgments

The authors gratefully acknowledge the financial support of the UK Engineering and Physical Sciences Research Council (EPSRC) under grant numbers EP/J017698 (Liveable Cities), EP/K012398 (iBUILD), EP/N010523 (Self-Repairing Cities), and EP/R017727 (the UKCRIC Coordination Node), and the contributions to thinking on smart cities provided by their colleagues from these programs.

About the authors

Marianna Cavada is a research fellow working on "Monitoring Birmingham's metabolism as it 'goes for gold' in 2022" IAA EPSRC funded, previously a researcher (Liveable Cities) and received her PhD from the Department of Civil Engineering, University of Birmingham, United Kingdom, on the subject of smart cities. Her research focuses are on smart cities from a liveability angle, and her work has been published in academic journals and conferences. She has a background in (international) architecture and has practiced internationally, in the Middle East (Al Falah, Abu Dhabi) and in China (Shanghai; Twin Cities—Kunming) and has also worked in large organizations (ATKINS).

Christopher D.F. Rogers is a professor of geotechnical engineering in the School of Engineering at the University of Birmingham. He researches urban sustainability, resilience, and liveability and has a particular interest in far-distant city futures. Alongside his cities research portfolio, he also researches infrastructure systems, with a particular focus on buried infrastructure, utility services, use of underground space, and infrastructure systems' interdependencies, following a history of research in pipelines, roads, and trenchless technologies. He leads EPSRC's £10 million Mapping and Assessing the Underworld programme, alongside a £10 million program on future cities, notably the Urban Futures and Liveable Cities consortium grants exploring how future cities might deliver urban resilience and liveability, respectively. He is currently a member of a research consortium that is exploring the use of robots for street works.

He chairs the Research, Development & Innovation towards Engineering Excellence Panel and the Futures Group at the Institution of Civil Engineers and was a member of the UK Government Foresight Future of Cities Lead Expert Group, and now he is a central figure in UKCRIC—the UK Collaboratorium for Research on Infrastructure and Cities. He leads the development of the new £27.6 million UKCRIC National Buried Infrastructure Facility at Birmingham and PLEXUS—a pump-priming grant that combines all 11 of UKCRIC's new laboratories—and he serves as the Director of Research Integration of UKCRIC's Coordination Node.

Miles R. Tight is a professor of transport of energy and environment at the School of Engineering, University of Birmingham. He has been actively researching sustainable transport for more than 30 years and most recently has been very interested in the role of walking and cycling in urban transport and how long-term change in transport occurs. He has led a number of high-profile research projects in these areas, most recently the EPSRC-funded projects STEPCHANGE (Sustainable Transport Evidence and modelling Paradigms: Cohort Household Analysis to support New Goals in Engineering design) and "Visions of the role of walking and cycling in 2030." He has received international funding through the "IMPACT" project (Implementation Paths for Action towards Sustainable Mobility) funded through the Swedish MISTRA programme, and the EU-funded "TRANSLINK" project (Transportation Research Links for Sustainable Development) and "MIME" (Market-based Impact Mitigation for the Environment) projects. He has recently been involved in the SMArt CitIES Network for Sustainable Urban Futures (SMARTIES Net) funded by ESRC, which is looking specifically at future urban development in Indian cities and is currently working as part of the EU-funded 3SRecipe project looking at shrinking cities.

References

Adair, J. (1985). *Effective decision making: A guide to thinking for managment success.* London: Pan Books Ltd.

Anthopoulos, L. (2017). *Understanding smart cities—A tool for smart government or an industrial trick? Public administration and information technology* (Vol. 22). New York: Springer Science + Business Media. ISBN: 978-3-319-57014-3 (Print) 978-3-319-57015-0 (Online). <https://link.springer.com/book/10.1007%2F978-3-319-57015-0>.

Bradley, J., Reberger, C., Dixit, A., & Gupta, V. (2014). Singapore employs IoE connections as foundation for "smart nation" vision. In E. Summary (Ed.), *White paper.* Chicago, IL: Cisco.

Buntz, B. (2016). *The World's 5 smartest cities* [Online]. The Internet of Things Institute. Available from <http://www.ioti.com/smart-cities/world-s-5-smartest-cities>.

Cavada, M., Hunt, D., & Rogers, C.D.F. (2014) Smart cities: Contradicting definitions and unclear measures. *Forum*, 1–30 November 2014; Sciforum Electronic Conference Series, Vol. 4, 2015, f004; doi:10.3390/wsf-4-f004.

Cavada, M., Hunt, D., & Rogers, C.D.F. (2016) *Do Smart Cities realise their potential for lower Co2 emissions?* In *Proceedings of the institution of civil engineers institute of civil engineers engineering sustainability*, Themed issue 2016.

Cavada, M., Hunt, D., & Rogers, C.D.F. (2017) *The little book of smart cities* (Liveable cities publication) presented at the House of Commons, UK.

Cavada, M. (2019). *Smart model assessment resilent tool (S.M.A.R.T.): A tool for assessing truly smart cities* (PhD thesis). UK: University of Birmingham.

Cohen, B. (2012a) *Singapore is on its way to becoming an iconic Smart City* [Online]. FastCoExist. Available from https://www.fastcodesign.com/1679819/singapore-is-on-its-way-to-becoming-an-iconic-smart-city. Accessed 10.02.2018.

Cohen, B. (2012b) *The top 10 smart cities on the planet* [Online]. FastCoDesign. Available from https://www.fastcodesign.com/1679127/the-top-10-smart-cities-on-the-planet. Accessed 03.05.2018.

Communities Gov, U. K. (2009). In C. A. L. Goverment (Ed.), *Multi-criteria analysis: A manual.* Wetherby: Crown.

Cyber Security Agency. (2018). *About us*. Government of Singapore. Available from <https://www.csa.gov.sg/> Accessed 05.09.18.
Foo, S. L., & Pan, G. (2016). Singapore's vision of a smart nation. *Asian Management Insights, 3*(1), 76−82, Research Collection School Of Accountancy. Available from http://ink.library.smu.edu.sg/soa_research/1531.
GovTech Singapore. (2016). *eGov Masterplan* [Online]. Singapore. Available from <https://www.tech.gov.sg/About-Us/Corporate-Publications/eGov-Masterplan> Accessed 04.02.17.
GovTech Singapore. (2018). *Programmes & Partnerships*. Available from <https://www.tech.gov.sg/Programmes-Partnerships> Accessed 01.07.18.
Halepoto, I., Sahito, A., Uqaili, M. & Chowdhry, B. (2015) Multi-criteria assessment of smart city transformation based on SWOT analysis. In *Information technology: Towards new smart world*, 5th National Symposium, Saudi Arabia.
Hoe, S. L. (2016). Defining a smart nation: The case of Singapore. *Journal of Information, Communication and Ethics in Society, 14*, 323−333.
Hunt, D. V. L., & Rogers, C. D. F. (2015). *Aspirational city futures: Three models for city living. Foresight future of cities project*, 16 pp. UK: Government Office for Science. <www.gov.uk/government/publications/future-of-cities-aspirational-scenarios>.
IDA. (2008). *Innovation. Integration. Internationalisation. Report by the iN2015 Steering Committee iN Imagine your world*. Singapore: Info-communications Development Authority of Singapore, An Intelligent Nation, a Global City, powered by Infocomm.
IDC. (2016). *IDC announces 2016 Top Smart City Projects in Asia/Pacific—Singapore and New Zealand as Big Winners*. International Data Corporation. Found at <https://www.idc.com/getdoc.jsp?containerId = prAP41679316> Accessed 09.10.16.
IESE. (2016). *Ranking the World's 'Smartest' cities* [Online]. Available from <https://www.forbes.com/sites/iese/2016/07/06/the-worlds-smartest-cities/#2aef8cb84ab9> Accessed 16.09.16.
IMDA. (2018). *InfoComm Media Development Authority*. Singapore: Singapore Government. Available from <https://www.imda.gov.sg/about/what-we-do> Accessed 04.02.18.
Infocomm Media Development Authority. (2018). *Road to Chongqing: Delivering a blockchain solution to China*. Available from <https://www.imda.gov.sg/infocomm-and-media-news/sg-spotlight/2018/8/road-to-chongqing-delivering-blockchain-platform-to-china> Accessed 01.09.18.
Juniper Research. (2018). *Your advantage through intelligence*. Found at <https://www.juniperresearch.com/home> Accessed 20.12.18.
Kurka, T., & Blackwood, D. J. (2013). Selection of MCA methods to support decision making for renewable energy developments. *Renewable and Sustainable Energy Reviews, 27*, 225−233. Available from https://doi.org/10.1016/j.rser.2013.07.001.
Lazaroiu, C. G., & Roscia, M. (2012). Definition methodology for the smart cities model. *Energy, 47*, 326−332.
Leach, J. M., Braithwaite, P. A., Lee, S. E., Bouch, C. J., Hunt, D. V. L., & Rogers, C. D. F. (2016). Measuring urban sustainability and liveability performance: The City Analysis Methodology (CAM). *International Journal of Complexity in Applied Science and Technology (IJCAST), 1*(1), 86−106.
Leach, J. M., Lee, S. E., Hunt, D. V. L., & Rogers, C. D. F. (2017a). Improving city-scale measures of livable sustainability: A study of urban measurement and assessment through application to the city of Birmingham, UK. *Cities, 71*, 80−87.
Leach, J. M., Lee, S. E., Boyko, C. T., Coulton, C. J., Cooper, R., Smith, N., et al. (2017b). Dataset of the livability performance of the city of Birmingham, UK, as measured by its citizen wellbeing, resource security, resource efficiency and carbon emissions. *Data in Brief, 15*, 691−695.

Liveable Cities. (2013). *The Liveable cities project.* Birmingham. Found at <http://liveablecities.org.uk/> Accessed 10.05.15.

Lombardi, D. R., Leach, J. M., & Rogers, C. D. F. (2012). *Designing resilient cities: A guide to good practice* (p. 164) Bracknell, UK: IHS BRE Press.

LTAS Land Transport Authority of Singapore. (2018). *Certificate of entitlement quota for November 2017 to January 2018 and vehicle growth rate from February 2018.* Found at <https://www.lta.gov.sg/apps/news/page.aspx?c = 2&id = b010406e-6edf-4224-9cd1-928706cd6fe7> Accessed 02.10.18.

Mahizhnan, A. (1999). Smart cities: The Singapore case. *Cities, 16*(1), 13−18.

Melvin, A. (2012). *Decision-making using the analytic hierarchy process* (AHP) and SAS/IML. In Group, S. S. U. (Ed.), *20th Annual SouthEast SAS Users Group.* Durham, NC.

MoF. (2017). *Procurement process.* Ministry of Finance. Available from <https://www.mof.gov.sg/Policies/Government-Procurement/Procurement-Process> Accessed 05.09.18.

MoFA Ministry of Foreign Affairs (2011). *Population in brief national population and talent division*, Prime Minister's Office Singapore Department of Statistics Ministry of Home Affairs Immigration & Checkpoints Authority.

Montibeller, G., & Franco, A. (2010). Multi-criteria decision analysis for strategic decision making. In C. Zopounidis, & P. M. Pardalos (Eds.), Handbook of multicriteria analysis, applied optimization (Vol. 103, pp. 25−48).

National Research Foundation (NRF). (2016). *Research Innovation Enterprise 2020 Plan.* Singapore: RIE.

National Research Foundation (NRF). (2017). *Growing a vibrant national innovation system.* (2017). Found at <https://www.nrf.gov.sg/rie2020/growing> Accessed 02.10.18.

National Research Foundation (NRF). (2018). *Research, innovation, enterprise 2020 plan: Winning the future through science and technology.* Found at https://www.nrf.gov.sg/docs/default-source/default-document-library/rie2020-publication-(final-web).pdf >. Accessed 10.07.2018.

National Youth Council Singapore (NYCS). (2016). *National Youth Council Initiatives* [Online]. Singapore: Singapore Government. Available from <https://www.nyc.gov.sg/initiatives> Accessed 18.01.17.

Research, Innovation and Enterprise 2020 RIE2020 (2018). *Plan winning the future through science and technology.* Singapore: National Research Foundation, Prime Minister's Office. Available from <www.research.gov.sg/RIE2020> Accessed 01.07.18.

Roebuck, K. (2011). *Decision theory: High-impact strategies - what you need to know: Definitions, adoptions, impact, benefits, maturity, vendors.* Australia: Tebbo.

Rogers, C. D. F., Lombardi, D. R., Leach, J. M., & Cooper, R. F. D. (2012). The urban futures methodology applied to urban regeneration. *Proceedings of the Institution of Civil Engineers, Engineering Sustainability, 165*(1), 5−20.

Rogers, C. D. F. (2018). Engineering future liveable, resilient, sustainable cities using foresight. *Civil Engineering, Proceedings of the Institution of Civil Engineers, 171*(6). Available from https://doi.org/10.1680/jcien.17.00031.

Shen, Q., Wang, H., & Tang, B. S. (2014). A decision-making framework for sustainable land use in Hong Kong's urban renewal projects. *Smart and Sustainable Built Environment, 3*, 35−53.

SingHealth. (2018). *Joint press release by MCI and MOH—SingHealth's IT system target of cyberattack. Safeguard measures taken, no further exfiltration detected.* Available from <https://www.singhealth.com.sg/AboutSingHealth/CorporateOverview/Newsroom/NewsReleases/2018/Pages/cyberattack.aspx> Accessed 05.09.2018.

SMART. (2016). *Singapore MIT Alliance for Research and Technology* [Online]. Singapore. Available from <http://smart.mit.edu/> Accessed 12.04.18.

Smart Nation Singapore (SNS). (2018a). *Many Smart ideas, one SmartNation* [Online]. Singapore. Available from <https://www.smartnation.sg/> Accessed 01.20.17.
Smart Nation Singapore (SNS). (2018b). *Digital government blueprint.* Available from <https://www.smartnation.sg/DGB> Accessed 01.09.18.
Smart Nation Singapore (SNS). (2018c). *Why Smart Nation.* Available from <https://www.smartnation.sg/about/Smart-Nation> Accessed 20.08.18.
Smart Nation Singapore (SNS). (2018d). Available from <https://www.smartnation.sg/about/sndgg> Accessed 20.08.18.
Smith, S. (2016). *Singapore named 'Global Smart City 2016'.* Hampshire, UK: Juniper Research. Found at <https://www.juniperresearch.com/press/press-releases/singapore-named-global-smart-city-2016>.
Spring Singapore. (2015). *Spring Singapore Enabling Enterprise.* Found at <https://www.spring.gov.sg/About-Us/Pages/spring-singapore.aspx> Accessed 10.11.16.
Tan, B., & Yimin, Z. (2018). *Urban Systems Studies. Technology and the city: Foundation for a Smart Nation* (1st ed.). Singapore: Centre for Liveable Cities.
Twiss, B., & Jones, H. (1978). *Forecasting technology for planning decisions.* London & Basingstoke: The Macmillan Press Ltd.
Urban Redevelopment Authority. (2018). *To make Singapore a great city to live, work, and play: Car Free Zones.* Found at <https://www.ura.gov.sg/ms/CarFreeZones> Accessed 09.02.18.
Warwick, N. (1998). Managing the smart city-state: Singapore approaches the 21st Century. *The New Zealand Journal of History, 32.*
Watson, J. (2017). *Where are the 10 smartest cities in the world?* [Online]. Hot Topics. Found at <https://www.hottopics.ht/stories/tech-hubs/where-are-the-10-smartest-cities-in-the-world/> Accessed 10.03.17.

Further reading

EBSCOhost. (2018). *'Country reports—Singapore' 2018* (pp. 1–33). Business Source Premier, EBSCOhost. Viewed September 12, 2018.
iDA Singapore. (2015). *Media factsheet Smart Nation Platform. Annex A.* Available from <https://www.imda.gov.sg/~/media/imda/files/inner/about%20us/newsroom/media%20releases/2015/0422_snv/annexa.pdf> Accessed 20.08.18.
Ministry of Communications and Information (MCI). (2018) *Infocom Media Manpower Development.* Available from <https://www.mci.gov.sg/portfolios/infocomm-media/initiatives/factsheets/cross-carriage-measure> Accessed 20.08.18.

The smart city of Newark, NJ: data analytics platform for economic development and policy assessment

Soon Ae Chun[1], Kevin Lyons[2] and Nabil R. Adam[2]
[1]City University of New York, New York, NY, United States, [2]Rutgers University, Newark, NJ, United States

Chapter Outline

15.1 Introduction 315
15.2 *Smart city* data analytics platform 317
    15.2.1 Smart city platform architecture 317
15.3 Case studies: analytics for information needs and decision support 318
    15.3.1 Analysis for Newark industrial manufacturing 318
    15.3.2 Anchor institution analysis 319
    15.3.3 Smart city governance analytics 320
    15.3.4 Anchor institution—Beth-Israel Medical Center 321
    15.3.5 City government—economic impact analysis 321
15.4 Discussions 324
    15.4.1 Scope 324
    15.4.2 Integration 326
    15.4.3 Organization 327
    15.4.4 Time 327
    15.4.5 Cost 328
    15.4.6 Quality 328
    15.4.7 Risks 328
    15.4.8 Procurement 329
15.5 Conclusion 329
Acknowledgments 329
About the authors 330
References 331
Further reading 331

15.1 Introduction

Urban cities, such as Newark, face a tremendous challenge in terms of economic development for the community and for the local workforce (Kitchin, 2015). Brookings study (Mistry, Vey, & Shearer, 2013) reports a great promise of the

Newark manufacturing sector that consists of around 400 small companies, which can shift a local and regional economy to a more resilient new economy driven by the creation of quality jobs and broad-based inclusion in innovative, low-carbon, export-intensive industries (New Jersey Manufacturing Extension Program, 2011). This promise has basis on the great assets that the City of Newark has such as the Newark's prime location and density of human resources as well as business concentrations in New York City nearby; Newark is a transportation hub with rails, ports, and airports where goods and exports can be easily moved to nationally and globally. Newark has diverse and scalable market concentration around it.

However, even with these opportunities, Newark manufacturers showed limited investment in new product and process development, lacking in-house innovation capabilities. A lack of coordination and capabilities also create dark data, not utilizing the data efficiently for optimal supply chain management or sustainability efforts with green businesses. Small Newark manufacturers are isolated from resources and tools to maximize access to new clients in regional and global markets. There is a skills gap in workforce to enter with readiness for the manufacturing industry.

With the analyses of the opportunities and challenges, the report recommends some of the strategic plans to make small manufacturing industry more competitive and sustainable. The recommended strategic plans include the following:

- Accelerated innovation via open innovations by sharing ideas and technologies with other manufacturers and from outside partners, for example, educational institutions. Sharing and colocation of the value ideation, design and production, and technologies can promote more productivity and facilitate the city-wide ecosystem.
- Create a network of Newark manufacturers to easily access existing business-to-business (B2B) networks and promote local and regional supply chain competitiveness (e.g., procurements and contracts) through local and domestic sourcing. This networked resource can support Newark manufacturers to view the supplier opportunities and production and employment planning, which can contribute to Newark's "sustainable economy" goals.
- Predict and promote manufacturing career opportunities for the small manufacturing sector and develop Newark talents to have readiness with the knowledge and skill sets. The educational opportunities with local educational institutions can provide manufacturing talent pipelines for the credentialing, internships and apprenticeships to develop manufacturing workforce locally and regionally.

In response to the suggested strategic goals, the Newark City Mayor's Office, Rutgers University Research Centers, including Rutgers Public–Private Community Partnership (PPCP) Program, Rutgers Institute of Data Science Learning and Applications (I-DSLA), have been collaborating on developing a smart city project to boost the economic development by fostering the collaborations among local manufacturing industries and businesses to share information to increase local procurement (sourcing) by anchor institutions that will increase the production levels of manufacturers. The production increase may entail boosting employment and skilled workforce education, which may also contribute to reducing crimes.

The smart city project is to develop the *smart city data analytics platform* that provides the data and analytics service infrastructure, enabling the three major stakeholders (government, manufacturing companies, and anchor institutions) to share the procurement data between anchor institutions and manufacturing companies and between government and manufacturing companies, and to provide data analytics services to allow these stakeholders to be informed and aware of their business productivities within the city. In addition to the B2B business data and B2G government procurement data, the platform made open government data sets and citizen generated data sets of the Newark city to provide the comprehensive understanding of the economic entities, activities and their relationships, in the context of other factors, such as crimes, vacant lots, workforce, and employment data.

The major challenges the project faced was the data collection, because the business data in transaction level is difficult to obtain and businesses that are often in competition with other businesses were not willing to share their data, not only the business revenues, but also employment data. Unlike other smart city solutions where the sensors could be used for data generation and collection, the economic activities data that are within the perimeters of proprietary businesses are difficult to obtain or monitor. The willing partners have to agree to share the data sets.

15.2 *Smart city* data analytics platform

In order to make manufacturing decisions, such as how much products should be produced, the manufacturer needs the understanding of the historical and projected market demands. In order to fulfill the business tasks, anchor institutions should have understood how much goods they could purchase from existing and potential suppliers. In addition, the local government needs qualified suppliers to fulfill their service requirements. These major economic parties have their own isolated systems and do not share the data in order to make decisions to promote local sourcing and manufacturing. To enable the collaborative economic development in the city of Newark, and to promote Newark's industrial manufacturers' competitiveness, we have developed the *Newark Smart City Infrastructure for Real-Time Data Analytics* to support the decision-making. This infrastructure will provide a network to industrial manufacturers to access the government and business procurement opportunities, and to share manufacturing data to facilitate supply-chain visibility and business development planning.

This is a private—public—academic partnership among the Newark City Mayor's Office, Rutgers University Research Centers, including Rutgers PPCP Program, Rutgers I-DSLA, industrial manufacturing companies in Newark, and major anchor institutions.

15.2.1 *Smart city platform architecture*

The smart city platform we developed has the architecture as shown in Fig. 15.1.
Our system has the capacity to integrate the procurement and corporate data from the 42 anchor institutions with the 400 manufacturing and business data. This

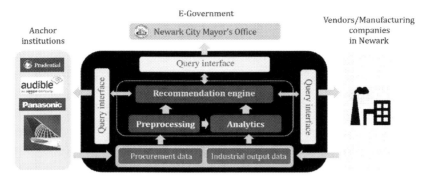

Figure 15.1 Architecture of smart city platform for real-time industrial data analytics.

integration is then used to identify procurement and contracting opportunities for the anchors and manufacturers. In addition, it integrates open government data sets, such as crime data, property data, vacant lots, and demographic data.

The system supports multiple decision-making opportunities by three major stakeholders, namely, Newark manufacturing companies, Newark anchor institutions, and the Newark city government, based on all the integrated financial, social, production and environmental data. The machine learning models and visualization analytics modules provide stakeholders to view not only the data sets but also the business trends, predictions on production levels or employment demands. In addition, the evaluation tool for economic policy impacts and alternative policy analyses tools for alternative policy impacts are currently developed. It serves as an integrated resource sharing and analysis hub, which could provide visibilities and notifications to the industries indicating potential contracting and bidding opportunities, potential production levels, and policy directions.

15.3 Case studies: analytics for information needs and decision support

15.3.1 Analysis for Newark industrial manufacturing

The industrial manufacturing companies could enter their own production level data, employment data, employee benefits, and contracting data into the platform. The voluntary data sharing as well as regular reminder for data entry and updates are notified. These manufacturing companies' data are used for visual analytics to inform

- the number of companies in different cities by manufacturing types,
- annual trend of new industries founded in different parts in New Jersey,
- the number of employees by primary industry types,
- Newark's production capacity compared to other cities within New Jersey,
- the trend analysis of manufacturing employment,

The smart city of Newark, NJ

City rank Industry wise

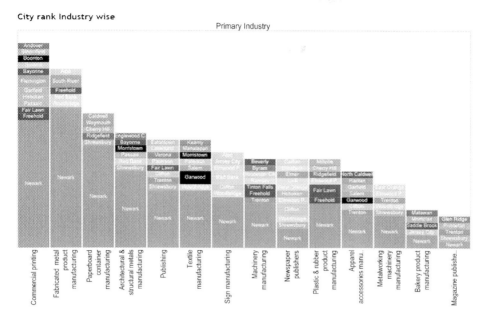

Figure 15.2 Number of companies in different cities by manufacturing types (the number of companies in Newark in each category is shown in the bottom portion).

- prediction model of manufacturing based on the volume of procurements, and historical hiring data, and
- cooperative clustering for bid responses and workforce sustainability.

Fig. 15.2 shows the number of companies in different cities by manufacturing types.

In addition to these information provisions, the platform provides tools to analyze the hiring trends over the years, and to predict the hiring potentials based on the historical hiring data, production plans according to the procurement amount. The prediction is modeled with applying a machine learning approach trained with historical data sets on hiring, production and procurement demand volumes.

15.3.2 Anchor institution analysis

Anchor institutions in Newark make large purchases, but in order to promote the local economic growth, it is crucial to know how the anchor fulfills its orders and procurement demands. It is important to know whether an anchor institution is primarily sourcing outsiders, or tapping into the local manufacturers. Thus the platform provides tools to analyze the anchor institution data for their decision support. The data analytics platform provides functionalities to answer the following questions:

- What is the number of employees?
- What are the revenue breakdowns?
- What is the total procurement value by industry type?

Fig. 15.3 shows the procurement values by Newark manufacturing type.

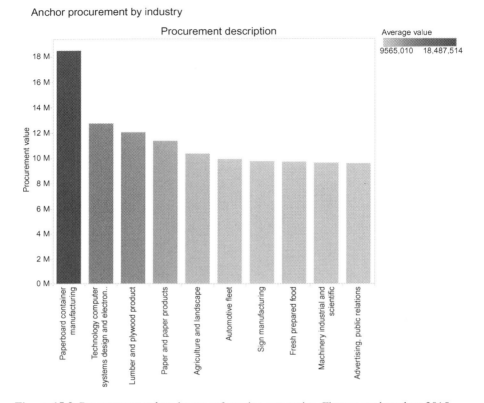

Figure 15.3 Procurement values by manufacturing categories. Figures are based on 2015.

15.3.3 Smart city governance analytics

Newark city government invests funds for the economic development and sustainability. Below are sample resource allocations decision supported by the infrastructure.

- assess employment trends and plan job training programs,
- analyze the city government procurement statistics to ensure inclusive policy,
- assess fairness in vendor selection, and
- design the city planning with integrated view of the economic activities and trends.

The employment monitoring by manufacturing sector and anchor institutions allows the city to promote job training programs. For instance the hiring predictions can prompt the city government or academic institutions to assess the gap in the workforce with specific manufacturing skills and plan educational programs to meet the demands.

The city's contract award decisions also depend on the geographic inclusion of manufacturer vendors, or on the minority- and women-owned businesses. The economic development decisions, such as a location selection to develop new businesses, or equitable vendor selections for government procurement, need the data and information support. The smart city platform provides the visualization tools, such as mapping and dashboard tools, to support the city policy decisions. In addition, the city needs to design policies fit to the needs of community and industry. In order to design the responsive and adaptive policies, the city needs integrated view of the industry's trends, and the interaction of connected data sets. The data analytics platform is to provide these policy analytics support.

15.3.4 Anchor Institution—Beth-Israel Medical Center

Newark Beth-Israel Medical Center/RWJBarnabas Health is a 665-bed quaternary care, teaching hospital located in Newark. It provides comprehensive health care for the region with more than 800 physicians, 3200 employees, and 150 volunteers. It is part of RWJBarnabas Health, the largest health-care delivery system in the state. It houses an advanced robotic surgery center and a variety of medical speciality areas. It is one of the anchor institution. It procures $150k worth of textile products from two local manufacturers, while at the same time it procures $5 million worth of textile products from outside of Newark area.

Our smart city data analytics can allow this anchor institution to locate the local manufacturing companies of textile products via mapping visualization. Fig. 15.4 shows the anchor institutions marked with house icons. One of them in lower left side shows Beth-Israel Medical Center with its textile procurement information, and its two local textile manufacturers shown as small triangle icons in the circle in the lower left corner.

The analytics of the system also allows users to discover that there is a large potential companies in Newark, which are in the textile manufacturing (shown in bar graph on the right corner). When drilled down, it shows nine more potential textile manufacturers, with total 170 employees, and the total product capacity worth $15 million. Thus the analytics platform can provide the information needed to promote more local procurement, which will contribute to the economic development of Newark. The fact that Newark has additional capacity to fulfill Beth Israel's textile needs is not readily available without the smart city data analytics platform.

15.3.5 City government—economic impact analysis

The city government of Newark is planning to utilize the vacant lots in the city for different neighborhoods. In order to do that the visualization of vacant lots for each district and the crime map can be overlayed to see the heat map of troubled neighbors. In order to invest on these areas the economic development's impact on the neighborhood is important for the city government for future planning.

Fig. 15.5 shows the vacant lots on the map, and the analytics also shows the visual distribution of vacant lots by different neighborhood. When one neighborhood is chosen on the graph, the yellow area on the map is highlighted. The city officials could analyze the impact on crimes and employment if vacant property could be used by manufacturers.

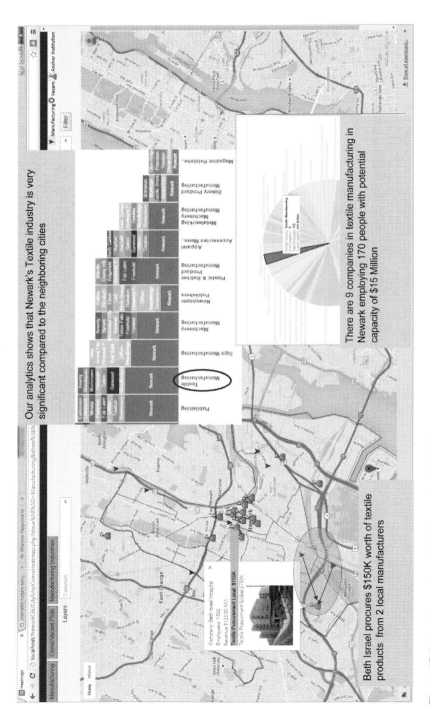

Figure 15.4 *Local sourcing analysis for anchor institution.*

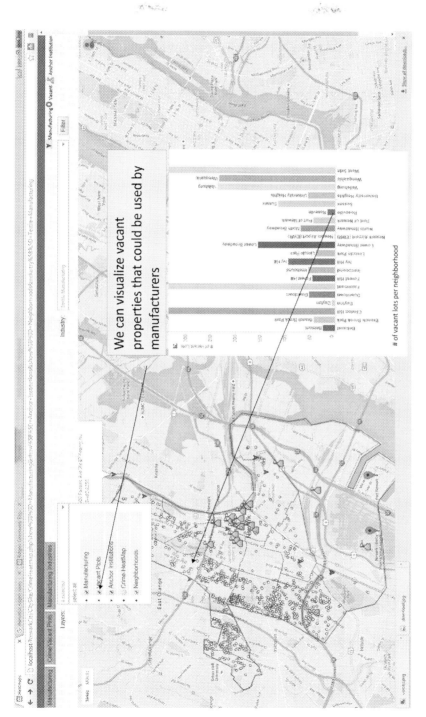

Figure 15.5 Vacant lots mapping and analysis.

Given the potential capacity expansion (e.g., textile manufacturing as seen in Section 15.3.4), the city officials could see the projected employment growth that is generated by the employment prediction model (such as a regression model on the number of employment on manufacturing capacity). Similarly, the crime reduction model in relationship with multiple predictors, such as the number of vacant lots and employment number, can generate the projected number of crime incidents.

Fig. 15.6 shows the heat map of crimes in different neighborhoods in Newark, and it shows the impact-related analytics results, where the particular neighborhood can have the employment growth due to the capacity expansion from Beth-Israel Medical Center (shown in upper graph on the right top). Given the employment generated by the capacity expansion, the system also projects the drop in number of crimes (shown on the lower bottom graph on the right.).

As illustrated, this analytics tool can support the city officials to identify and select the impactful policies for economic development in the neighborhood.

15.4 Discussions

Newark Industrial Data Analytics Platform (NIDAP) also serves as a permanent "one-stop" clearinghouse database for the partners to deliver leading-edge, customized research and advisory support to 400 small and mid-sized manufacturers and provide near real-time information and predictive analytics of local supply chain capabilities for the city government to assess their economic policies and planning. This data and predictive power help understand the greater Newark supply chain competitiveness and sustainability, market readiness, exports, and logistics and offer relevant support and expertise to regional economic/community development and workforce retention and growth.

From the case studies in Section 15.3 the data analytics infrastructure can promote the development of collaborative procurement opportunities for our Newark anchor institutions. The Initiative for a Competitive Inner City (ICIC) November 2014 report (Zeuli, Ferguson, & Nijhuis, 2014) identified and provided data that showed that on an annual basis, our 42 Newark-based anchor institutions procure only 3% of the goods and services they need from our Newark manufacturers and businesses. The 3% represents approximately $30 million of procurement activity. Our research has identified another 15%−20% of additional procurement activity that could be targeted at the Newark manufacturing and business community if the 42 anchor institutions targeted their purchasing power toward the Newark business that could competitively provide the goods and services they need.

15.4.1 Scope

The data analytics infrastructure project is innovation that was greatly needed in economic development decision-making and informing. The ability to project the economic trends and employments and crimes was possible independently and

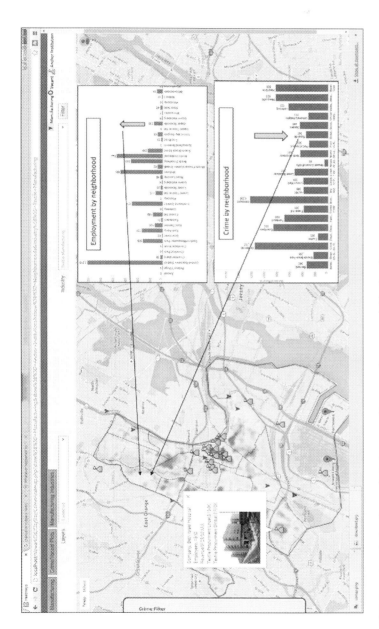

Figure 15.6 Impact analysis of manufacturing capacity expansion on a neighborhood.

separately within each anchor institution, but the global visibility of collective economic potentials within the city equips not only the manufacturers to discover their supply chain possibilities but also the anchor institutions to plan their procurement sourcing decisions to contribute to the local economy. In addition, the city government has the ability to see the possible policy impact analyses based on the data to address the hard problems to make sustainable development. The city has known that an expansion of manufacturing capability can influence the employment, job training programs, and crimes, but they can now quantify these potential impacts and make a data-driven policy with the analytics. This helps the urban planning in general by allocating the resources in the right places.

The chain of impacts is not limited in the illustrated cases, but they can impact the viability of tourism potentials due to the economic development, enhancing the cultural activities and the quality of life. So the economic development can create a long chain of transformations in the city.

- Enhancing Outreach and Support Services
- Participation in Business Networks and Working Groups
- involved in strategic planning and resource alignment/coordination related to the upcoming expansion of Port Newark
- Scaling to sustainable economic development
- Interactive map showing urban heat islands in Newark measured by the Urban Heat Island Index
- Overlay the manufacturing industries, anchor institutions, and abandoned properties on crime heat map to visualize the collective impact

15.4.2 Integration

The data and analytics infrastructure for big data management interlinks Newark anchor institutions and manufacturing industry businesses to display in a holistic and visual mapping platform the connections between the entire Newark business infrastructure complemented by several other important and relevant Newark city data (e.g., financial, commodity, permits, employment, crime, and vacant lot data). It also interconnects with the Newark city government.

The aims to develop, strengthen, and increase Newark anchor institution-to-local business transactions and local spending. Further its goal includes developing and deploying the Newark anchor-to-local business B2B system. By directly linking and integrating local procurement contracts to local hiring requirements established by the Newark 2020 Buy, LiveHire program (https://www.hirebuylive.com/), this data analytics infrastructure intends to help achieve the goal of reducing Newark's unemployment rate by 50% by 2020. Businesses can also benefit from this initiative since the increase in local procurement and B2B transactions can lead to 65% new business growth opportunities, as identified in a report by the ICIC (Zeuli et al., 2014).

The infrastructure will serve as a permanent "one-stop" clearinghouse of business data and associated analytics. Thus this will make the comprehensive procurement transaction data between businesses. With proper easy-to-use analytics tools the academic and business experts could leverage the infrastructure to deliver leading-edge, customized research and advisory support to the entire Newark business community. The support will span several areas, including business (supply and services) with supply chain/procurement contracts (demands), competitiveness, sustainability, market readiness, exports, and logistics. In addition, it can support data-driven government policy planning for the regional economic, community development and a sustaining policy for promoting urban industrial workforce retention and growth.

15.4.3 Organization

Our research and development project is designed to enhance and sustain the resource-based and collaborative capacity of the Newark Industrial Solutions Center (NISC) that was launched in December 2014. NISC's mission is to develop, strengthen, and promote Newark's industrial competitiveness and economic development utilizing Rutgers PPCP applied and embedded supply-chain and business development tools and hands-on capabilities. This mission is informed by a demonstrated vision for civic engagement, capacity building, and problem-solving with local and regional collaborators, including the following:

- City of Newark,
- Newark Regional Business Partnership,
- Rutgers Cornwall Center,
- Newark Workforce Investment Board,
- Rutgers Academic Research Community (Rutgers Energy Institute, Rutgers EcoComplex),
- Newark anchor institutions,
- New Jersey Manufacturing Extension Program,
- Rutgers Business School PPCP Program, and
- Rutgers I-DSLA.

15.4.4 Time

The project started in 2016, following strategic goals proposed by the Brookings report (2013), and by 2017 the first prototype of the infrastructure has been shared by participating consortium and evaluated the timeline for the remaining tasks:

- Q1: 2016 Formation of partnership of industry organizations (manufacturing sector and anchor institutions), city government and university centers. sharing vision for the smart city data analytics platform development and its possibilities
- Q2–Q3 2016: Gathering data and requirements gathering and a use case analysis
- Q4 2016: A rapid prototype components of visualization analytics of data sets, and sharing to get further functional and nonfunctional requirements
- Q1–Q2 2017: Development of prototype specifications and developing database. Develop data capturing components, and visual interface (e.g., mapping and graphs) to display different layers of data sets
- Q3–Q4 2017–Q1–Q2 2018: System prototype components development

- Creating manufacturing and procurement data and information access component and visualization
    - Creating employment projection models
    - Creating crime projection models
    - Creating impact analysis components for the city
    - Creating hiring projection models for decision makers
- Q1−Q2 2018: Demonstration to other city and vendor companies (e.g., city of Baltimore), and gathering of further requirements specifications
- Q3−Q4 2018: Implement the policy impact analyses and procurement recommender models
- Q1−Q4 2019: Expansion of functionalities (e.g., inclusive policy analysis)
- Q3−Q4 2019: User feedback collection and prepare evaluation criteria for development of a full system and adoption. Estimate the probability of success and the cost estimates
- Q1−Q4 2020: In parallel identify a technology start-up to develop a full-scale working system and launching

15.4.5 Cost

The project development cost was partially funded by the NSF (National Science Foundation) IUCRC (Industry−University Cooperative for Research Centers) that was awarded to the Rutgers I-DSLA. The IUCRC Program was initiated in 1973 to develop long-term partnerships among industry, academe, and government. The NSF invests in these partnerships to promote research programs of mutual interest, contribute to the nation's research infrastructure base, enhance the intellectual capacity of the engineering or science workforce through the integration of research and education, and facilitate technology transfer (NSF IUCRC).

15.4.6 Quality

The standards specification in ISO 37120:2018 (2018) addresses the indicators of city services for sustainable development in communities. It focuses on economy, employment, urban planning, water quality, transportation, etc. that are relevant to measure the smart city−related efforts. We have consulted the ISO 37122 subcommittee standards for the smart cities indicators that included the following economy indicators (ISO/CD 37122, 2017):

- Percentage of local businesses contracted to provide city services, which have data communication openly available
- Annual number of new start-ups
- Percentage of labor force employed in the information and communications technology sector
- Percentage of the labor force employed in the education and research and development sectors

15.4.7 Risks

The project was initiated with the assumption that the coalition of manufacturing industry, anchor institutions, and the city government are fully participating to construct the digital artifact that all could benefits. The challenge is that the coalition is not binding but voluntary, thus, the data shared by each party may not be complete, thus, posing some partiality or incomplete portrayal of the economic potentials and prediction models.

Another risk is the adoption and management issues. The industrial manufacturers are small businesses, mostly without electronic information systems capabilities. The information infrastructure for the manufacturers may be more challenging to adopt, while the anchor institutions may resort to their own system and not sharing the critical data.

15.4.8 Procurement

So far, the project has developed the proof of concept prototype funded by the grants. To uptake the efforts the community leaders (the Newark city government or the consortia of anchor institutions) need to plan the implementation across industry within the region. One option is to procure a start-up company by the leadership organization and speed up the process of robust implementation with data acquisitions.

15.5 Conclusion

The case described the project of developing a data and analytics infrastructure for economic development as part of the smart city initiative in Newark, NJ. The focused area is the interconnection smart city model to enhance the sharing and interactions among the city economic entities, that is, small manufacturing industry, Anchor institutions, and the city government. The intent is to provide not only the information but analytics framework where the economic entities could utilize the tools for planning, auditing, and exploring alternative solutions.

The prototype developed by the university research team was partially funded by the grant to promote a long-term relationship between industry and university to address real-life problems. The economic agents are volunteer based, thus, it needs a strong leadership to guide the initial momentum to move to the next phase of development, that is, developing more robust and more comprehensive system building on the prototype system project.

The remaining challenges include the data sharing and completeness of data sets for more accurate prediction models, and governance and ownership issues of the project. The end user adoptions issues are also a challenge to the project's success.

Acknowledgments

This project is funded by NSF CNS 1624503 and CNS 1747728, partially supported by the National Research Foundation of Korea Grant from the Korean Government (NRF-2017S1A3A2066084) and by the Fulbright Scholarship Program. We acknowledge I-DSLA research team, who has developed the system, including P. Varsayni, E. Kurien, S. Yuan, and graduate associate members, and the Newark City Office of Information Technology team who has provided data sets and discussion sessions. All data sets were shared between 2015-2016, and the tool's capabilities are described with the simulated anchor procurement dataset.

About the authors

Soon Ae Chun is a professor of information systems and informatics program, and a graduate center professor of computer science doctoral program. She is the director of the Information Security Research and Education Lab (iSecure Lab). She is the recipient of the Fulbright Senior Scholarship and the CSI Dolphin Award for Outstanding Scholarly Achievement. She served as the President for the Digital Government Society. Her research area includes security and privacy, semantic data integration, social data analytics and workflow, focusing on digital government, security and privacy, and public health. She is an IEEE senior member, a member of ACM Computing Society, the Digital Government Society, and the Beta Gamma Sigma Honor Society.

Kevin Lyons is an associate professor in Rutgers School of Business and serves as director of the Rutgers Business School Public Private Community Partnership Program. Dr. Lyons conducts research on developing and integrating global environmental, social, economic, ethical criteria and data into supply chain/procurement systems and processes. His research work includes the environmental and economic impacts on raw material extraction, logistics, manufacturing, consumption, consumer of multiple products and services research, designing and implementing local, national, and international environmental economic development systems, waste-to-energy systems, and environmental and sustainable social policy and financial impact forecasting (e.g., Sarbanes Oxley Corporate Social and Environmental Impact Reporting). He has also created the supply chain archeology and supply chain waste archeology research disciplines and has researched and written extensively on conducting environmental health checks on global supply chains and the resulting benefits of reduced risk management impacts and costs. He is the recipient of many awards, including Sierra Club Annual Professional of the Year Award, New Jersey State Governor's Award for Environmental Leadership and Excellence, NSF-IGERT grants (2).

Nabil R. Adam is a distinguished professor of Computers and Information Systems at Rutgers University; the founding director of the Rutgers of the Institute for Data Science, Learning, and Applications (I-DSLA); and the founding director of the Rutgers CIMIC Research Center. He is a cofounder and past director of the Meadowlands Environmental Research Institute. He was on loan as a fellow to the US Department of Homeland Security-Science & Technology Directorate where he served as a Senior Program Manager, a Branch Chief and managed the Complex Event Modeling, Simulation, and Analysis program, served as the technical lead for the Unified Incident Command and Decision Support System program, and initiated the Cyber−physical Systems Security initiative and the Social Media Alert and Response to Threats to Citizens initiative.

References

ISO/CD 37122. (2017). *Sustainable development in communities—Indicators for smart cities.*

New Jersey Manufacturing Extension Program. (2011). *Next Generation Manufacturing Study: New Jersey Executive Summary.*

ISO 37120:2018. (2018). *Sustainable cities and communities—Indicators for city services and quality of life.*

Kitchin, R. (2015). Making sense of smart cities: addressing present shortcomings. *Cambridge Journal of Regions, Economy and Society*, 8(1), 131–136.

Mistry, N., Vey, J. S., & Shearer, R. (2013). Newark's Manufacturing Competitiveness: Findings and Strategies. In: The *Brookings Metropolitan Policy Program report*. Brookings Institution. <https://www.brookings.edu/wp-content/uploads/2016/06/NewarkManufacturingMay28.pdf>.

NSF IUCRC. *About the IUCRC Program.* <https://www.nsf.gov/eng/iip/iucrc/about.jsp> Accessed November 2018.

Zeuli, K., Ferguson, L., & Nijhuis, A. (2014). *Creating an Anchored Local Economy in Newark recommendations for implementing a comprehensive local procurement strategy.* <http://icic.org/wp-content/uploads/2016/04/ICIC_NEWARK_rprt_REV.pdf>.

Further reading

Gibson, D. V., Kozmetsky, G., & Smilor, R. W. (Eds.), (1992). *The technopolis phenomenon: Smart cities, fast systems, global networks.* Rowman & Littlefield Co.

The case of Quayside, Toronto, Canada

Pamela Robinson[1] and Steven Coutts[2]
[1]School of Urban and Regional Planning, Ryerson University, Toronto, ON, Canada,
[2]Civic Sandbox: Research and Practice Group, Toronto, ON, Canada

Chapter Outline

16.1 Introduction 333
16.2 Background 335
    16.2.1 History 335
    16.2.2 Theoretical context 337
16.3 Research methodology: case study 338
    16.3.1 Scope 338
    16.3.2 Integration 339
    16.3.3 Organization 340
    16.3.4 Time 341
    16.3.5 Cost 342
    16.3.6 Quality 342
    16.3.7 Risks 342
    16.3.8 Procurement 343
    16.3.9 Discussion—the fringes 344
16.4 Conclusions 345
Acknowledgment 346
About the authors 346
References 347

16.1 Introduction

In October 2017, news outlets and social media were abuzz with the announcement that Toronto's waterfront was soon to be home to "the first neighborhood built from the Internet up" (Badger, 2017). Sidewalk Labs, the urban technology subsidiary of Alphabet (Google's parent company) had won a bid to plan a smart city development on a 4.9-ha (12 acres) waterfront site known as Quayside (Waterfront Toronto, 2017c) (Fig. 16.1). Overnight, a forgotten corner of Toronto's industrial landscape became a "very big sandbox in which to conduct [...] high-tech experiments" (Hawkins, 2017).

Toronto, Canada is the political capital of the Province of Ontario and the economic engine of the country. It is situated on the north shore of Lake Ontario, on the traditional lands of several indigenous nations—the Mississaugas of the Credit, the Anishnabeg, the Chippewa, the Haudenosaunee, and the Wendat

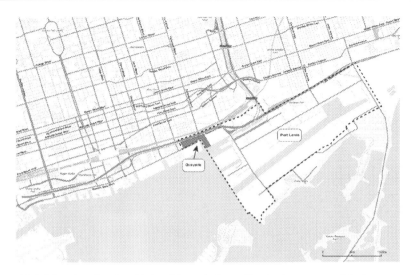

Figure 16.1 Map showing the 4.9-ha (12-acre) Quayside site in context with the approximately 325-ha (803-acre) Port Lands.

peoples. The word "Toronto" itself, originates from the Kanienke'haka word "Tkaronto" which translates to, "the place in the water where the trees are standing" (Tabobondung, 2016). While these peoples have always had a relationship with the land and water, much of Toronto's contemporary waterfront is the result of the European settler's activity; infilling has seen the water's edge gradually migrate southward since the 19th century. The iconic postcard skyline views of the city, dominated by the presence of the western hemisphere's tallest free-standing structure, the CN Tower, have their foundations in sediment dredged from the lakebed.

Experimentation and resistance have both made their mark on Toronto's urban history. The St. Lawrence neighborhood was one of the earliest successful mixed-use, mixed-income developments. The opposition mobilized against the proposed Spadina Expressway in the late 1960s, which was considered to be a watershed moment in the city's history. Activists (including famed writer and urban activist, Jane Jacobs) forced a halt to a project, which would have bisected vibrant neighborhoods, destroyed thousands of homes, and opened the way for a network of expressways crisscrossing the city and its suburbs (White, 2016). It is therefore fitting that these two parallel themes should play a role in Canada's first "smart city" project.

This case study examines the Sidewalk Toronto—Quayside project, approximately 16 months after it was first announced. This case is important for two reasons. First, as a joint venture with Sidewalk Labs, sister company to Google—one of the most ubiquitous and valuable companies in the world—the reception of this project is bound to set a precedent for similar projects worldwide. Second, this case likely differs from others presented in this volume in that this project has not yet been built or even approved. At the time this chapter was written the project's overall master plan had not yet been submitted.

16.2 Background

16.2.1 History

Toronto's waterfront—the place in which the Quayside project will be built—has seen its share of ambitious master plans over the years. Efforts to reshape the waterfront stretch back over five decades as Toronto, like many port cities worldwide, has seen its manufacturing and resource-based industries retreat from the water's edge, revealing opportunities for a broader range of economic activities and increased public access on the underutilized land (Fig. 16.2). Eidelman (2013) has identified three distinct eras of planning ambitions for the waterfront:

- 1960–72: City planners put forward a high-density, modernist vision for a new "Harbor City."
- 1972–88: Civic leaders eschew master planning in favor of small-scale improvements to the public realm, parklands, and stimulation of job growth in the eastern harbor.
- 1988–2000: Shift in focus towards brownfield remediation, restoration of ecosystems, and encouragement of mixed-use development.

However, none of these plans came to fruition for various reasons including legal challenges, leadership changes, convoluted governance structures, and especially land ownership conflicts between different government actors (Eidelman, 2013).

Figure 16.2 The Quayside site (top left) has historically been home to low-density industrial uses.
Source: City of Toronto Archives, Fonds 1257, Series 1057, Item 5657.

16.2.1.1 Waterfront Toronto

In 2002 the Toronto Waterfront Revitalization Corporation (rebranded as Waterfront Toronto in 2007) was created through provincial legislation, with a CAD 1.5 billion funding commitment from the municipal, provincial, and federal governments. It was given legal jurisdiction to direct strategic planning and remediation initiatives and seek development partners for 2840 acres (1149 ha) of waterfront lands [Office of the Auditor General of Ontario (OAG), 2018]. Since 2004, the development policies and strategies of Waterfront Toronto have been guided by a concept of sustainability encompassing the three pillars of economic development, social growth, and environmental protection (Bunce, 2009; Robinson, 2012). Their most recent sustainability framework that guides the redevelopment efforts includes the additional goals of resilience and innovation (Waterfront Toronto, 2017d).

While Waterfront Toronto had an ambitious planning mandate, the Corporation was only given ownership and control over 1% of the lands that it was tasked with revitalizing (OAG, 2018); the authority to conduct large-scale planning and zoning of lands remained with the City of Toronto. Furthermore, close to half (CAD 700 million) of promised government funding never materialized (OAG, 2018). Despite these limitations, Waterfront Toronto successfully led the redevelopment of mixed land use communities and public spaces and between 2007 and 2009, Waterfront Toronto was able to negotiate the purchase of 4.9 ha adjacent to the Port Lands—to be known as "Quayside."

With the Quayside lands unencumbered by private or government ownership, Waterfront Toronto had the opportunity to advance its planning agenda. In March 2017, Waterfront Toronto issued a request-for-proposals (RFP) in which it sought an innovation and funding partner for Quayside (Waterfront Toronto, 2017c). Observers have noted that financial realities may have driven the decision to seek an external partner taken at a time when, in 2017, Waterfront Toronto had largely depleted its initial funding and "need[ed] a new partner with deep pockets to continue its mission" (Sauter, 2018). The RFP also expressed a desire for the Quayside site to be used as a "test bed" for new and emerging technologies. On October 17, 2017 a news release announced that Sidewalk Labs—the winning bidder—and Waterfront Toronto had entered into a framework agreement the previous day to build a district that would "tackle the challenges of urban growth" (Waterfront Toronto, 2017b).

16.2.1.2 Sidewalk Labs

Sidewalk Labs—the New York-based urban innovation firm owned by Google's parent company, Alphabet—was founded in June 2015 by Daniel L. Doctoroff. As former deputy mayor of New York City for economic development during the Bloomberg administration and former chief executive of Bloomberg L.P, Doctoroff shared Sidewalk Labs' ambitions to build a city "from the Internet up" as early as April 2016:

> *I'm sure many of you are thinking this is a crazy idea: building a city new — the most innovative, urban district in the world, something at scale that can actually have the catalytic impact among cities around the world [...] We don't think it's*

crazy at all. People thought it was crazy when Google decided to connect all the world's information, people thought it was crazy to think about the concept of a self-driving car. (Roberts, 2017)

After Sidewalk Labs was named the winning bidder, Sidewalk Toronto, Limited Partnership, was formed as an "entity through which Waterfront Toronto and Sidewalk will collaborate to create the MIDP for Quayside and the Eastern Waterfront" (Waterfront Toronto, 2017a, p. 2). While it appeared that Sidewalk Labs had its sights set on a U.S. city for its first significant project (Williams, 2017), Waterfront Toronto's RFP for an "innovation and funding partner" proved to be an attractive opportunity for Sidewalk Labs to test its ideas on the ground on a highly visible urban stage.

16.2.2 Theoretical context

Smart city planning and development in the North American context is still in its early days. At first glance the Sidewalk Toronto's proposal appears to share certain characteristics of the "test bed urbanism" model documented in Songdo in South Korea (Halpern, LeCavalier, Calvillo, & Pietsch, 2013) and Masdar in Abu Dhabi. Indeed, Waterfront Toronto's press material openly states that the Quayside development "will provide [a] test bed for solutions to pressing urban challenges" (Waterfront Toronto, 2017d). However, the idealized theories of smart city planning that have emerged from those contexts may have limited utility in helping us make sense of what is happening on the ground in "actually existing smart city" (Shelton, Zook, & Wiig, 2015, p. 14).

As a conceptual tool, the "assemblage" helps us approach the complexity of urban problems by emphasizing the relations between social and spatial relationships at different scales (Allen, 2012; Legg, 2009). Kitchin and Lauriault (2018, p. 8) propose that "data assemblages" can map the relationships between "apparatuses and elements that are thoroughly entwined, and develop and mutate over time and space." These apparatuses include: systems of thought, forms of knowledge, finance, political economy, governmentalities and legalities, materialities and infrastructures, practices, organizations and institutions, subjectivities and communities, places, and the data marketplace (Kitchin, 2014, p. 25).

"Platform urbanism" can be seen as an assemblage at work in the Quayside project. Platforms can be broadly understood as the "reconfiguration of production, consumption, distribution and monetization of cultural goods and services" enabled by the Internet-as-infrastructure (Van der Graaf, 2018, p. 153). Platform urbanism is a "complex platform-based urban ecosystem encompassing private and public organizations and citizens"(Van der Graaf, 2018, p. 155); an ostensibly neutral digital infrastructure that facilitates connections between different groups, mediates their interactions, sets governance conditions and—crucially—profits from the extraction and analysis of their data (Srnicek, 2016). The politics of platform urbanism can be seen at work in the case of the popular short-term rental platform, Airbnb, as municipal governments struggle to manage its negative externalities: decreased housing affordability and availability as well as wholesale gentrification of neighborhoods (Nieuwland & van Melik, 2018).

Besides the enormous competitive advantage to be gained by being the first to integrate and "lock-in" their products into urban systems, it is difficult to understate the political power accruing to firms that are able to position themselves as gatekeepers of vast flows of data about the city and its inhabitants. Asymmetries in access arising from the ownership and terms of usage of data extracted through the smart city platform create challenges for government, civil society, and individual actors who face seeking access to information used in planning decisions or seeking open data for a broad range of purposes. In the first 16 months of this project, similar questions about data ownership, access, and uses have arisen as Quayside is imagined.

16.3 Research methodology: case study

16.3.1 Scope

In the 16 months since its announcement the Quayside project has undergone substantial changes in scope. While the original extent of the project was the 4.9-ha Quayside parcel, a project update released in early 2019 proposed an expanded planning footprint (Sidewalk Toronto, 2019) (Table 16.1).

During the first public consultation event the Chief Policy Officer for Sidewalk Labs presented the eight high-level principles (pillars) that would guide the development on the 4.9-ha Quayside parcel: sustainability, mobility, public realm, buildings, community and city services, digital platform, housing affordability, and privacy and data governance (Sidewalk Toronto, 2018). These mostly align with smart city advocates' who claims that by better connecting the analysis of data with urban governance and planning, cities can encourage economic innovation, competitiveness, and efficiency; advance sustainability through energy efficiency, reduced congestion, and improved public transit; and help make local government more accessible to citizens with expanded opportunities for citizen

Table 16.1 Proposed project phases.

	Phase 1 (Quayside):	**Phase 1 + 2 (complete project):**
Site area (acres)	12	190
Gross floor area (million sq. ft.)	3	35
Residents	~5000 (3000 units of housing)	~50,000 (33,000 units of housing)
Jobs (jobs "on-site")	~3900	~45,000

Source: Adapted from Sidewalk Toronto. *Project update: February 14th, 2019* (p. 18). (2019). Retrieved from <https://sidewalktoronto.ca/wp-content/uploads/2019/02/FEB14-SWTO-Business-Case-Overview.pdf>.

participation and engagement (Hollands, 2008; Kitchin, 2015; Luque-Ayala & Marvin, 2015; Puron-Cid, Gil-Garcia, & Zhang, 2015).

An early vision document gives some clues as to what residents could expect from the Quayside project (Sidewalk Labs, 2017). From an urban design perspective the project is visually inviting—seamlessly integrating technology with high quality design in the public realm. Its 4.9 ha are envisioned to incorporate modular, tall-timber buildings, self-driving shuttles, robot delivery. To further convey their thinking about what this community might look like, Sidewalk Labs has renovated an old fish-processing plant at 307 Lakeshore Boulevard East as a space for showcasing new technologies. One proposed solution is dynamic, reconfigurable pavement, allowing the street to accommodate different mixes of users and activities throughout the day. Building envelope technologies (raincoats) are envisioned to increase pedestrian comfort by shielding them from extreme temperature and inclement weather.

16.3.2 Integration

Given that this chapter was written before the Master Innovation and Development Plan (MIDP—the site master planning document), efforts to formally assess the integration of different project components would be premature. By reference to the project's governing agreements, we can gain an understanding of the roles set out for each of the actors involved.

Established as a result of Waterfront Toronto's RFP, the Framework Agreement entered into by Waterfront Toronto and Sidewalk Labs set the terms of the working relationship between the two entities with the ultimate expected result being the development of the MIDP for the Quayside site. The initial agreement provided for the establishment of a Project Management Committee—consisting of equal representation from senior representatives from Waterfront Toronto and Sidewalk Labs—but the detailed governance structure was to be developed through subsequent discussions (Waterfront Toronto, 2017a).

A revised agreement—the Plan Development Agreement—was released on July 31, 2018, superseding the original Framework Agreement (Waterfront Toronto & Sidewalk Labs, 2018). It departed from the original agreement in that it: clarified that no public lands would be transferred to Sidewalk Labs, no land outside the Quayside parcel (i.e., the Port Lands/Eastern Waterfront) would be involved in the development, and Sidewalk Labs' role would no longer be "comaster developer" but the "innovation and funding partner" while Waterfront Toronto would be the "revitalization lead" (Rider, 2018a).

But over the last 16 months, this list of roles Sidewalk Labs envisions for itself has grown to include: planning partner; real estate research and development; real estate economic development catalyst; infrastructure financing; horizontal development partner; advanced infrastructure facilitator; technology deployment; investments in economic development, and; value sharing (Sidewalk Toronto, 2019).

The planning, governance, and framing of this project have been dynamic from the beginning. It is not surprising that these changes have emerged given the complexity of the project, but the dynamic nature of the project also makes it hard for the public to follow and poses a challenge for all interested parties to foresee what might happen next.

16.3.3 Organization

In October 2017 when the project was announced the Sidewalk Toronto partnership between Waterfront Toronto and Sidewalk Labs appeared to be the leading entity. A draft organizational chart (Waterfront Toronto, 2018b) (Fig. 16.3) circulated at the meeting of Waterfront Toronto's Quayside committee showed the Quayside project's multilayered governance structure.

Information flows up from various work streams through committees eventually accountable to Waterfront Toronto's governing bodies: the Intergovernmental Steering Committee (composed of a voting and a staff member from each level of government, who provide governance and oversight) and the Board of Directors

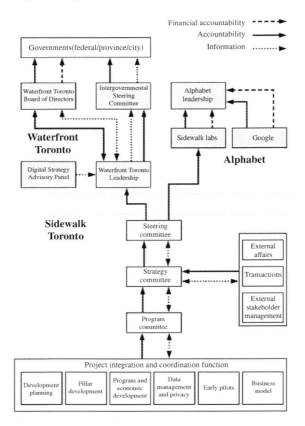

Figure 16.3 Diagram outlining proposed governance relationships in Quayside project (Waterfront Toronto, 2018b).

(composed of members appointed by each level of government, who approve projects and capital expenditures). The joint venture, Sidewalk Toronto, Limited Partnership, has three major committees:

- Steering committee (aka project committee as per original framework agreement): To discuss and address the highest level strategic and political considerations. A forum for issues resolution.
- Strategy committee: To address strategic and external facing components of the project. This committee is also responsible for decision-making and guidance related to the development of the MIDP, as determined by the program committee.
- Program committee: To integrate all content produced by work streams.

The complexity of this organization chart demonstrates the complexity of the governance framework needed for a precedent-setting project.

16.3.4 Time

When the project was first announced, the initial timeline anticipated that the entire planning process would be completed in 2018 (Sidewalk Toronto, 2018). However, as the project has progressed, the timelines have been extended (Waterfront Toronto, 2018a). This is perhaps not surprising given the complexity of the project and its

Table 16.2 Timeline of key events.

Date	Event
March 17, 2017	Waterfront Toronto issues the Quayside request for proposal on various international tender services to develop and fund a plan for a community in the 4.9 ha (12-acre) Quayside site
October 17, 2017	Project agreement is announced by Prime Minister of Canada, the Premier of Ontario, the Mayor of Toronto, Waterfront Toronto and the Executive Chairman of Alphabet Inc
March 20, 2018	Public open house 1
May 1, 2018	Sidewalk Labs releases a document called "Responsible Data Use Policy Framework," which contains high-level visions of how data use and privacy would be addressed
May 3, 2018	Public open house 2
July 31, 2018	Signing of a second agreement, the Plan Development Agreement, with Sidewalk Labs, which supersedes the October 2017 Framework Agreement. This agreement further defines the role and responsibilities for each party in developing a plan for the Quayside community
August 14–15, 2018	Public open house 3
December 8, 2018	Public open house 4
Mid-2019	Draft MIDP released for consultation and preliminary review
September 30, 2019	MIDP for Quayside to be finalized
Late 2019	MIDP consideration by Waterfront Toronto Board of Directors

Source: Office of the Auditor General of Ontario (OAG). *2018 Annual report* (p. 706). (2018). Retrieved from <http://www.auditor.on.ca/en/content/annualreports/arreports/en18/2018AR_v1_en_web.pdf>.

politics. It is also important to remember that the current timeline (Table 16.2) presented only encompass the delivery of the actual smart city precinct plan; planning approvals, land development, and occupancy are still many years away.

16.3.5 Cost

As the plan is still in development and given the amount of novel technology proposed for Quayside, it is still too early to properly predict the full cost or value of the development. However, Sidewalk Labs' initial investment of USD 50 million to fund pilot projects and plan development throughout 2018—combined with a land value estimated at CAD 675 million (Roth, 2018b)—are indicators of the economic potential of this project.

16.3.6 Quality

The Quayside case presents a challenge for the traditional planning process and shows that when new technology is added to a land use planning process, this addition requires new governance and oversight (Barth, 2019). When the MIDP is delivered by Sidewalk Labs to Waterfront Toronto a comprehensive review process will take place with significant input from Waterfront Toronto itself, the Federal, Provincial, and local governments and public consultation.

The Framework Agreement gives Waterfront Toronto or Sidewalk Labs the power to terminate the agreement if project milestones are not met or if the final MIDP does not meet with board's approval (Waterfront Toronto & Sidewalk Labs, 2018). As the City of Toronto's Waterfront Secretariat website states,

> *To implement the MIDP, Waterfront Toronto and Sidewalk Labs will have to initiate various municipal application and evaluation processes, given the City's role as a regulator, landowner, and provider of municipal infrastructure and services. The precise list of required regulatory processes will be determined when the MIDP is submitted. Going forward, many of these processes will require Council approvals and public processes, such as planning, building and environmental approvals, right-of-way permits, road closings, real estate transactions, and affordable housing agreements.*
>
> *City of Toronto (2019b).*

Indeed, this plan will present many approvals challenges, not just in terms of built form, but also in terms of data privacy and governance rules across all three levels of governments.

16.3.7 Risks

Early on, public debate centered on data ownership and privacy concerns, with Sidewalk Labs receiving criticism for its reluctance to release specific details on if or how collected data would be used commercially (Scassa, 2017; Wylie, 2017). In response, Sidewalk Lab's introduced its Responsible Data Use Framework as a tool to speak to public concerns with how data will be used and what role data plays in the business model, including the following components: responsible data use guidelines; a civic data trust; responsible data impact assessments, and; use of open standards (Sidewalk Labs, 2018). However, Sidewalk Labs' relationship to Google and other ongoing data-related cases emerging across the broader technology sector [e.g., the Facebook–Cambridge Analytica data harvesting scandal (Cadwalladr & Graham-Harrison, 2018)] continue to be issues of concern in public dialogue around this project.

Perhaps the biggest challenge this project has faced thus far is the mixed reactions by the public toward the project and its vision as it has unfolded. Public critics of this project have raised several issues: how the year-long stakeholder consultation process has taken place, how and when key project details have been shared, the evolving and relationship between Waterfront Toronto and Sidewalk Labs, and data privacy and ownership concerns among many (Crawford, 2018; Rattan, 2018; Roth, 2018a; Wylie, 2018a, 2019). Upon Sidewalk Labs' announcement of its plans for expansion into the Port Land, critics have called for the entire process to be scrapped, mobilizing via the #BlockSidewalk campaign (#BlockSidewalk, 2019; Balsillie, 2018; Wylie, 2019).

There has also been internal turbulence at Waterfront Toronto, as evidenced by the "stepping down" of CEO Will Fleissig in July 2018 (Roy, 2018) followed by the resignation of a board member over concerns about how the Plan Development Agreement process had unfolded (Rider, 2018b). In October 2018, Saadia Muzaffar, founder of TechGirls Canada, resigned from Waterfront Toronto's Digital Strategy Advisory Panel citing "Waterfront Toronto's apathy and utter lack of leadership regarding shaky public trust and social license" (OAG, 2018, p. 708). Shortly after the 2018 provincial election—with a progressive conservative government now in power—the Province's three appointed members on Waterfront Toronto's Board of Directors were removed with their replacements taking their seats in the spring of 2019 (Rider, 2018c).

While the MIDP has yet to be delivered, once public, it is certain to ignite intense responses. As it turns out, building a "city from the Internet up" may be more difficult to achieve than anyone expected.

16.3.8 Procurement

The prevailing climate of fiscal restraint (if not austerity) in which many North American governments find themselves often translates into reluctance to commit to major infrastructure investments. The Quayside RFP summed up this state of affairs as follows:

> Government funding is constrained and there exists a large list of competing infrastructure projects. In collaboration with the private, public and not-for-profit sectors, Waterfront Toronto must seek out new and innovative partnerships,

funding and investment models that enable our projects, address our goals and recognize and mitigate diminishing government funds.
Waterfront Toronto (2017c, p. 8).

The privatization and competitive management of public infrastructure is not a new phenomenon (Grossi & Pianezzi, 2017; Harvey, 1989); smart cities merely provide a new context in which this process can be enacted (de Cordova, 2018).

Given the innovative nature of this project and its scale, it is not surprising that procurement issues are challenging. Despite Sidewalk Labs' insistence that their platform will be vendor-neutral, the Plan Development Agreement states that third-party procurement (e.g., issuance of RFPs for developers) will be undertaken jointly by Waterfront Toronto and Sidewalk Labs—with a provision that Sidewalk Labs may provide "Purposeful Solutions" in circumstances where there is no suitable alternative on the market (Waterfront Toronto, 2017c). Sidewalk Labs' position, not only as a consultant but as a potential vendor and developer of considerable volumes of intellectual property, has raised questions about whether their involvement at this stage of the project gives them a competitive advantage down the road (Wylie, 2018b). These procurement issues, like many other elements of this project, demonstrate how new approaches to urban technology developments challenge conventional public–private relationships.

As noted by others, much of the current driving force behind adoption of smart city infrastructure and products has originated from "vendor push (as opposed to) city government push". Therefore it is reasonable to ask: do smart "solutions" address actually-existing problems, or if smart technology is a "hammer", are complex urban issues simply the "nails?" In the post-New Public Management era, cities have ample experience with public–private partnerships (P3s), wherein after a certain period of time, the asset or infrastructure designed and built (and/or operated, managed, etc.) through the P3 reverts back to public ownership. While this model can work for traditional bricks-and-mortar infrastructure, it may present challenges when applied to smart city platforms. In the case of new, rapidly changing (and potentially untested) technologies, municipalities may be challenged to fully evaluate these products before procuring them. As Kitchin, Coletta, Evans, Heaphy, and Mac Donncha note (2017, p. 15), "cities have a long history of purchasing technologies that are costly and do not always deliver on their promises." Thus far, this project signals that in order for municipalities to effectively procure urban technology systems, new capacity and expertise will need to be developed in-house.

16.3.9 Discussion—the fringes

Sidewalk Labs is not the only technology company to announce bold smart city plans. A subsidiary of Bill Gates' investment firm has taken the "greenfield" approach, investing USD 80 million to build a smart city in the desert outside Phoenix, Arizona (Garfield, 2017); Amazon garnered bids from North American cities (including Toronto) to compete against one another by offering the most generous subsidies to play host to its second corporate headquarters (Day, 2017), eventually selecting two sites in Queens, New York City, and northern Virginia. However, subsequent backlash from legislators and civil society against the USD 3 billion in incentives that had been offered to Amazon resulted in the cancellation of the Queens' corporate campus (Goodman, 2019).

These proposals exemplify a new environment in which we no longer see cities procuring technology solutions from vendors; but smart technology vendors now procure an urban area on which to deploy themselves. While tax giveaways and business location incentives offered by local governments are nothing new, technology companies taking on city building roles challenge established local government norms and processes in ways that we are only just beginning to understand.

Interestingly, concurrent to the Quayside project, a different approach to smart city building is unfolding in Canada. In 2017, Infrastructure Canada launched the Smart Cities Challenge, a cross-Canada competition, which sought to encourage communities of all sizes, including municipalities, regional governments, and indigenous communities (First Nations, Métis, and Inuit) to identify a pressing issue in their community and adopt a smart cities approach to create a solution through innovation, data, and connected technology (Infrastructure Canada, 2017). With three prize categories (CAD 5 million, 10 million, and 50 million), the challenge garnered 130 eligible submissions from over 200 communities (communities were encouraged to partner with one another). The winners of this first round will be announced in May 2019.

For cash-strapped local governments the prospect of a large economic development windfall is enticing. However, this raises important questions: do these projects—whether driven by the private or public sector—actually help local governments make progress on priority issues, or are they big ticket distractions that divert staff time, creativity, and focus away from other important works?

There is currently no precedent in Canadian municipal planning processes for receiving and evaluating a proposal such as Quayside. This gap was highlighted by a motion brought forward by Toronto City councilor Joe Cressy, which noted that "to date, those essential frameworks have yet to be defined for Toronto's civic data, and we must ask ourselves what we want from a smart city and from digital infrastructure" (City of Toronto, 2019a). Internationally Barcelona, Amsterdam and New York are taking leadership through their "Cities Coalition for Digital Rights" initiative. Efforts like this one will help build city-to-city learning and also create a common platform of expectations that should positively impact government−private sector-community interactions around new smart city projects.

16.4 Conclusions

Constellations of sensors embedded in sidewalks and buildings may have the ability to collect and analyze vast amounts of data, leading to great potential for these technologies to optimize service delivery and produce operational efficiencies over the long run. However, as Hollands (2008, p. 13) put it, "the real smart city has to begin to think with its collective social and political brain, rather than through its 'technological tools.'"

The Quayside case provides an illustrative counterexample to the Silicon Valley ideology that says smart city solutions will usher in a rational, postpolitical planning climate. Planning will remain a contested, political process in the era of the smart city, and this will require that the planning profession adapt to this new paradigm.

Sidewalk Labs' efforts to plan a new neighborhood in an existing urban area "from the Internet up" has met with citizen and civil society concerns alike, galvanizing critics, and mobilizing new capacity within the community. If Scott (1998, p. 5) was correct when he noted, "an incapacitated civil society provides the leveled social terrain on which to build," then the robust citizen opposition to the Quayside project may have proven the inverse.

The delivery of the MIDP (in late spring 2019) and the subsequent government and public responses will determine whether the vision for Quayside becomes a reality. However, the concerns raised thus far about proposed uses of technology signal that this project will continue to meet with resistance. If any lessons can be drawn from this project, it is that municipal governments everywhere should take stock of their preparedness on data and technology governance issues—including ownership, control, access, privacy, and procurement—and anticipate pushback from civil society and the public before smart city technology companies come knocking at their door.

Acknowledgment

The authors would like to thank the Social Sciences and Humanities Research Council of Canada for its support through the Geothink partnership project.

About the authors

Pamela Robinson (PhD, MCIP, RPP) is an associate professor in the School of Urban and Regional Planning at Ryerson University in Toronto, Canada. She is also a registered professional planner. As part of the Geothink research team, Robinson's research and practice focus on urban sustainability issues with a particular focus on cities and climate change and the use of open data and civic technology to support open government transformations. She is a member of Waterfront Toronto's Digital Strategy Advisory Committee and served as an academic advisor to the Sidewalk Toronto Fellows Program. Robinson is an editor of *Urban Sustainability: Reconnecting Space and Place* (University of Toronto Press, 2013), *Teaching as Scholarship: Preparing Students for Professional Practice in Community Services* (WLU Press, 2016) and is a columnist for *Spacing* magazine.

Steven Coutts [M.Pl, BA (Hons)] is a researcher and planning associate with Civic Sandbox: Research and Practice Group based in Toronto, Canada. He also worked as a facilitator at several Sidewalk Toronto public engagement events.

References

#BlockSidewalk. *Press release.* (2019). Retrieved from <https://www.blocksidewalk.ca/media>.

Allen, J. (2012). A more than relational geography? *Dialogues in Human Geography, 2*(2), 190−193.

Badger, E. (2017, October 18). Google's founders wanted to shape a city. Toronto is their chance. *The New York Times.* Retrieved from <https://www.nytimes.com/2017/10/18/upshot/taxibots-sensors-and-self-driving-shuttles-a-glimpse-at-an-internet-city-in-toronto.html>.

Balsillie, J. (2018, October 5). Sidewalk Toronto has only one beneficiary, and it is not Toronto. *The Globe and Mail.* Retrieved from <https://www.theglobeandmail.com/opinion/article-sidewalk-toronto-is-not-a-smart-city/>.

Barth, B. (2019, March). Smart cities or surveillance cities? *Planning.* Retrieved from <https://www.planning.org/planning/2019/mar/smartcities/>.

Bunce, S. (2009). Developing sustainability: Sustainability policy and gentrification on Toronto's waterfront. *Local Environment, 14*(7), 651−667.

Cadwalladr, C., & Graham-Harrison, E. (2018, March 17). Revealed: 50 Million Facebook profiles harvested for Cambridge Analytica in major data breach. *The Guardian.* Retrieved from <https://www.theguardian.com/news/2018/mar/17/cambridge-analytica-facebook-influence-us-election>.

City of Toronto. (2019a). *Data governance and smart cities − By Councillor Joe Cressy, seconded by Councillor Paul Ainslie.* Adopted by City Council on February 26. Retrieved from <http://app.toronto.ca/tmmis/viewAgendaItemHistory.do?item = 2019.MM3.2>.

City of Toronto. (2019b).*Quayside: Project status and review.* Retrieved from <https://www.toronto.ca/city-government/planning-development/waterfront/initiatives/current-projects/quayside/>.

Crawford, S. (2018, February 1). Beware of Google's intentions. *Wired.* Retrieved from <https://www.wired.com/story/sidewalk-labs-toronto-google-risks/>.

Day, M. (2017, October 23). Amazon receives 238 bids for its second headquarters. *The Seattle Times.* Retrieved from <https://www.seattletimes.com/business/amazon/amazon-receives-238-bids-for-its-second-headquarters/>.

de Cordova, S. F. (2018, January 5). Smart cities are changing: The rise of the city as a public-private partnership service model. *Medium.* Retrieved from <https://medium.com/@sfdecordova/smart-cities-are-changing-93251a46884a>.

Eidelman, G. (2013). *Landlocked: Politics, property, and the Toronto waterfront, 1960-2000.* University of Toronto. Retrieved from <http://hdl.handle.net/1807/35812>.

Garfield, L. (2017, November 22). Bill Gates' investment group spent $80 million to build a "smart city" in the desert—And urban planners are divided. *Business Insider.* Retrieved from <http://uk.businessinsider.com/bill-gates-smart-city-pros-cons-arizona-urban-planners-2017-11>.

Goodman, J. D. (2019, February 14). Amazon pulls out of planned New York city headquarters. *The New York Times.* Retrieved from <https://www.nytimes.com/2019/02/14/nyregion/amazon-hq2-queens.html>.

Grossi, G., & Pianezzi, D. (2017). Smart cities: Utopia or neoliberal ideology? *Cities, 69,* 79−85. Available from https://doi.org/10.1016/j.cities.2017.07.012.

Halpern, O., LeCavalier, J., Calvillo, N., & Pietsch, W. (2013). Test-bed urbanism. *Public Culture, 25*(270), 272−306. Available from https://doi.org/10.1215/08992363-2020602.

Harvey, D. (1989). From managerialism to entrepreneurialism: The transformation in urban governance in late capitalism. *Geografiska Annaler. Series B, Human Geography*, *71*(1), 3. Available from https://doi.org/10.2307/490503.

Hawkins, A. J. (2017, October 17). Alphabet's Sidewalk Labs strikes deal to turn 800 acres of Toronto into an 'internet city.' *The Verge*. Retrieved from <https://www.theverge.com/2017/10/17/16488942/alphabet-sidewalk-labs-toronto-quayside>.

Hollands, R. G. (2008). Will the real smart city please stand up? *City*, *12*(3), 303−320. Available from https://doi.org/10.1080/13604810802479126.

Infrastructure Canada. (2017). *Smart cities challenge*. Canada. Retrieved from <https://www.infrastructure.gc.ca/cities-villes/index-eng.html>.

Kitchin, R. (2014). *The data revolution: Big data, open data, data infrastructures and their consequences*. London, UK: SAGE.

Kitchin, R. (2015). Making sense of smart cities: Addressing present shortcomings. *Cambridge Journal of Regions, Economy and Society*, *8*(1), 131−136. Available from https://doi.org/10.1093/cjres/rsu027.

Kitchin, R., Coletta, C., Evans, L., Heaphy, L., & Mac Donncha, D. (2017). Smart cities, urban technocrats, epistemic communities and advocacy coalitions. In *The programmable city working paper no. 26*. Retrieved from <https://osf.io/preprints/socarxiv/rxk4r/>.

Kitchin, R., & Lauriault, T. P. (2018). Toward critical data studies: Charting and unpacking data assemblages and their work. In J. Thatcher, A. Shears, & J. Eckert (Eds.), *Thinking big data in geography: New regimes, new research* (pp. 3−20). Lincoln, NE: University of Nebraska Press.

Legg, S. (2009). Of scales, networks and assemblages: The League of Nations apparatus and the scalar sovereignty of the Government of India. *Transactions of the Institute of British Geographers*, *34*(2), 234−253. Available from https://doi.org/10.1111/j.1475-5661.2009.00338.x.

Luque-Ayala, A., & Marvin, S. (2015). Developing a critical understanding of smart urbanism? *Urban Studies*, *52*(12), 2105−2116. Available from https://doi.org/10.1177/0042098015577319.

Nieuwland, S., & van Melik, R. (2018). Regulating Airbnb: How cities deal with perceived negative externalities of short-term rentals. *Current Issues in Tourism*, 1−15. Available from https://doi.org/10.1080/13683500.2018.1504899.

Office of the Auditor General of Ontario (OAG). *2018 Annual report*. (2018). Retrieved from <http://www.auditor.on.ca/en/content/annualreports/arreports/en18/2018AR_v1_en_web.pdf>

Puron-Cid, G., Gil-Garcia, J. R., & Zhang, J. (2015). Smart cities, smart governments and smart citizens: A brief introduction. *International Journal of E-Planning Research*, *4*(2), iv−vii.

Rattan, C. (2018, May 23). Torontonians should take control of their data. *NOW Toronto*. Retrieved from <https://nowtoronto.com/news/owns-data-toronto-smart-city/>.

Rider, D. (2018a, July 31). Toronto's high-tech Quayside district takes 'next step' as new deal reached with Google sister company. *Toronto Star*. Retrieved from <https://www.thestar.com/news/city_hall/2018/07/31/sidewalk-labs-deal-unlocks-40-million-us-for-quayside-high-tech-district.html>.

Rider, D. (2018b, August 2). Waterfront Toronto deal with Google sister company is 'short-changing' city, says board member who quit. *Toronto Star*. Retrieved from <https://www.thestar.com/news/city_hall/2018/08/02/waterfront-toronto-deal-with-google-sister-company-is-shortchanging-city-says-board-member-who-quit.html>.

Rider, D. (2018c, December 7). Ontario government fires three Waterfront Toronto board members after Quayside deal. *Toronto Star*. Retrieved from <https://www.thestar.com/news/gta/2018/12/07/province-fires-three-waterfront-toronto-board-members-after-google-deal.html>.

Roberts, J. J. (2017, May 9). Google is planning a 12-acre high-tech city in Canada. *Fortune*. Retrieved from <http://fortune.com/2017/05/09/google-alphabet-toronto-canada/>.

Robinson, P. J. (2012). Planning for sustainability: Moving from plan to action. In A. Dale, W. T. Dushenko, & P. J. Robinson (Eds.), *Urban sustainability: Reconnecting space and place* (pp. 83−105). Toronto: University of Toronto Press.

Roth, A. (2018a, June 18). Three affiliated companies registered to lobby the City of Toronto after Sidewalk Labs won Quayside bid. *The Logic*. Retrieved from <https://thelogic.co/news/exclusive/three-affiliated-companies-registered-to-lobby-the-city-of-toronto-after-sidewalk-labs-won-quayside-bid/>.

Roth, A. (2018b, September 17). Estimates show Waterfront Toronto's portion of land, sought by Google's sister company, worth over half a billion dollars. *The Logic*. Retrieved from <https://thelogic.co/news/exclusive/estimates-show-waterfront-torontos-portion-of-land-sought-by-googles-sister-company-is-worth-over-half-a-billion-dollars/>.

Roy, I. (2018, July 4). Waterfront Toronto CEO Will Fleissig to step down. *Toronto Star*. Retrieved from <https://www.thestar.com/news/gta/2018/07/04/waterfront-toronto-ceo-will-fleissig-to-step-down.html>.

Sauter, M. (2018, February 13). Google's guinea pig city. *The Atlantic*. Retrieved from <https://www.theatlantic.com/technology/archive/2018/02/googles-guinea-pig-city/552932/>.

Scassa, T. (2017, November 23). Who owns all the data collected by 'smart cities'? *Toronto Star*. Retrieved from <https://www.thestar.com/opinion/contributors/2017/11/23/who-owns-all-the-data-collected-by-smart-cities.html>.

Scott, J. C. (1998). *Seeing like a state: How certain schemes to improve the human condition have failed.*. New Haven, CT: Yale University Press.

Shelton, T., Zook, M., & Wiig, A. (2015). The 'actually existing smart city'. *Cambridge Journal of Regions, Economy and Society*, 8(1), 13−25. Available from https://doi.org/10.1093/cjres/rsu026.

Sidewalk Labs. *Project vision*. (2017). Retrieved from <https://sidewalktoronto.ca/wp-content/uploads/2017/10/Sidewalk-Labs-Vision-Sections-of-RFP-Submission.pdf>.

Sidewalk Labs. *Digital governance proposals for DSAP consultation*. (2018). Retrieved from <https://www.waterfrontoronto.ca/nbe/wcm/connect/waterfront/41979265-8044-442a-9351-e28ef6c76d70/18.10.16_SWT_Draft + Proposals + Regarding + Data + Use + and + Governance_Tuesday_730pm.pdf?MOD = AJPERES&CONVERT_TO = url&CACHEID = 41979265-8044-442a-9351-e28ef6c76d70>.

Sidewalk Toronto. *Roundtable 1 − Presentation*. (2018). Retrieved from <https://sidewalk-toronto.ca/wp-content/uploads/2018/04/18.03.20_Sidewalk_Toronto_Roundtable.pdf>.

Sidewalk Toronto. *Project update: February 14th, 2019*. (2019). Retrieved from <https://sidewalktoronto.ca/wp-content/uploads/2019/02/FEB14-SWTO-Business-Case-Overview.pdf>.

Srnicek, N. (2016). *Platform capitalism*. Cambridge, UK: Polity Press.

Tabobondung, R. (2016). Wasauksing−Vancouver−Toronto: My path home. In J. Pitter, & J. Lorinc (Eds.), *Subdivided: City-building in an age of hyper-diversity* (pp. 46−54). Toronto: Coach House Books.

Van der Graaf, S. (2018). In waze we trust: Algorithmic governance of the public sphere. *Media and Communication*, 6(4), 153. Available from https://doi.org/10.17645/mac.v6i4.1710.

Waterfront Toronto. *Innovation and funding partner framework agreement: Summary of key terms for public disclosure.* (2017a). Retrieved from <https://sidewalktoronto.ca/wp-content/uploads/2018/05/Waterfront-Toronto-Agreement-Summary.pdf>.

Waterfront Toronto. *New district in Toronto will tackle the challenges of urban growth.* (2017b). Retrieved from <https://www.waterfrontoronto.ca/nbe/portal/waterfront/Home/waterfronthome/newsroom/newsarchive/news/2017/october/newdistrict in toronto will tackle the challenges of urban growth>.

Waterfront Toronto. *Request for proposals: Innovation and funding partner for the quayside development opportunity.* (2017c). Retrieved from <https://sidewalktoronto.ca/wp-content/uploads/2017/10/Waterfront-Toronto-RFP-No.-2017-13.pdf>.

Waterfront Toronto. *Resilience and innovation framework for sustainability.* (2017d). Retrieved from <https://waterfrontoronto.ca/nbe/wcm/connect/waterfront/4a8f0eea-ad2c-44f6-85f8-0024c70dada2/WTRI- + Framework.20171013 + FINAL.pdf?MOD = AJPERES>.

Waterfront Toronto. (2018a). *Digital strategy advisory panel—Meeting #6 (December 13, 2018).* Retrieved from <https://www.waterfrontoronto.ca/nbe/wcm/connect/waterfront/246c0b92-a561-45bb-8b6c-2ede39e3b492/meeting + book + - + digital + strategy + advisory + panel + - + meeting + _ + 6 + December + 13 + 2018 + revised + 12-12.pdf? MOD = AJPERES>.

Waterfront Toronto. (2018b). *Quayside committee meeting: Item 6a—Project management structure (January 17, 2018).* Retrieved from <https://waterfrontoronto.ca/nbe/wcm/connect/waterfront/3f177ee0-3bf2-4a4f-8144-ef421ed04a5e/Item + 6a + - + Project + Management + Structure + - + January + 17%2C + 2018 + consolidated.pdf?MOD = AJPERES>.

Waterfront Toronto, & Sidewalk Labs. *Plan development agreement between Toronto Waterfront Revitalization Corporation and Sidewalk Labs LLC, dated the 31st of July, 2018.* (2018). Retrieved from <https://sidewalktoronto.ca/wp-content/uploads/2018/07/Plan-Development-Agreement_July312018_Fully-Executed.pdf>.

White, R. (2016). *Planning Toronto: The planners, the plans, their legacies, 1940-80.* Vancouver: UBC Press.

Williams, J. (2017, May 4). Google wants to build a city. *StateScoop.* Retrieved from <https://statescoop.com/google-wants-to-build-a-city/>.

Wylie, B. (2017, November 8). Think hard before handing tech firms the rights to our cities' data. *The Huffington Post.* Retrieved from <http://www.huffingtonpost.ca/bianca-wylie/think-hard-before-handing-tech-firms-the-rights-to-our-cities-data_a_23270793/>.

Wylie, B. (2018a, June 2). Sidewalk Toronto, social license, and the limits of a borrowed reputation. *Medium.* Retrieved from <https://medium.com/@biancawylie/sidewalk-toronto-social-license-and-the-limits-of-a-borrowed-reputation-6a9bfaa4db3c>.

Wylie, B. (2018b, September 1). Sidewalk Toronto—Intellectual property, innovation, and the politics of choice. *Medium.* Retrieved from <https://medium.com/@biancawylie/sidewalk-toronto-intellectual-property-innovation-and-the-politics-of-choice-8e795e67aaef>.

Wylie, B. (2019, February 26). Is sidewalk labs going too far in the port lands? Yes. *Toronto Star.* Retrieved from <https://www.thestar.com/opinion/contributors/thebigdebate/2019/02/26/is-sidewalk-labs-going-too-far-in-the-port-lands-yes.html>.

The Brazilian smart cities: a national literature review and cases examples

Luiz Pinheiro Junior[1,2]
[1]Positivo University, Curitiba, Brazil, [2]Getulio Vargas Foundation - FGV-EAESP, São Paulo, Brazil

Chapter Outline

17.1 Introduction 351
17.2 Smart cities—background theoretical 353
17.3 Research methodology: literature review and cases cited 356
    17.3.1 Brazilian literature and cases about smart cities 356
    17.3.2 Smart cities discussion in the Brazilian context 358
17.4 Conclusions 360
Acknowledgments 361
About the author 361
References 362
Further reading 365

17.1 Introduction

Information technology has been disseminated through its use in companies, government, institutions, and universities and is also present in the population, through smartphones, tablets, and notebooks and recently has used as a strategic artifact for the development of cities.

In terms of Brazilian cities, there is a large percentage of concentration in the urban population, since according to IBGE (2010), 82% of the population is in urban areas with 160,925,792 inhabitants in the cities and 29,830,007 inhabitants in rural areas. This large number of people in cities has become a challenge for public managers in providing services in various sectors, such as infrastructure, governance, education, mobility, and health, and has propelled a search for solutions that can help in the quality and agility of these services.

In the 1990s scientific research started a discussion that cities could become digital, with the use of information technology in their management. Singapore is an Asian city-state that was cited by Mahizhnan (1999) in a study on the use of information technology in education, infrastructure, and economics with the aim of playing a superior quality of life through the use of technological artifacts.

The European Union (EU, 2017) has also come together and discussed agendas in this direction through the use of technologies in cities making them smarter. In this context, it is possible to cite the case of the city of Barcelona in Spain that has been cited as a model of application of solutions and innovations for the management of urban resources and services.

Initiatives by companies that provide solutions such as IBM, CISCO, Telefonica, Qualcomm, and Oracle have recently appeared on the market as platforms that can be implemented in cities for the modernization of their services, but academic studies have also been interested in this topic, which can be perceived through a large number of publications on smart cities.

In mapping literature about smart cities at academic databases, according to the graph of Fig. 17.1, collected in the Scopus database that presents approximately 400 papers in international journals relating the words smart city and smart cities in the areas of administration, public administration, and management with an expansive line as of 2010.

The growth of publications on this topic has been reviewed by international researchers for the contributions, discussions, and development of theoretical models and empirical research on the smart cities (Anthopoulos, 2015; Meijer & Bolívar, 2015).

In the Brazilian academy, research on smart cities has appeared lightly in conferences, rarely in national journal because it is an emerging issue, but in practical contexts, public managers and suppliers (FGV — Fundação Getulio Vargas — Smart Cities Forum Brasil, 2017) have discussed it. In Brazil, government

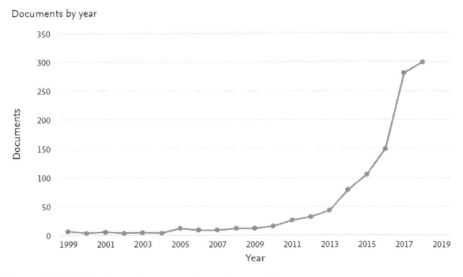

Figure 17.1 Publications about smart city and smart cities.
Source: Scopus-Academic Database - Search Papers about Smart Cities (2018). Available from <http://bit.ly/2FtfKq1> Accessed 10.04.18.

initiatives, such as the National Front of Mayors, My Intelligent City Program of the Ministry of Science, Technology, Innovation, and Communications, contributed as public policies for the implementation of the smart cities concept in interested cities (Przeybilovicz, Cunha, & Meirelles, 2018).

To contribute to this field in a theoretical and applied way the aim of this chapter is to propose a discussion about smart cities in Brazil from a literature review on the topic. The international literature has already been reviewed by some authors (Anthopoulos, 2015; Meijer & Bolívar, 2015); however, in the Brazilian context a paper in this format was not found until the moment, which highlights the relevance of the paper to be used as a guide to the new researchers who will delve into this theme by disseminating research on current and future Brazilian smart cities.

For this, in this chapter a contextualization on smart cities is carried out as well as an analysis of the national publications comparing them with global contexts discussing them and later a research agenda for the Brazilian literature is defined.

The chapter is structured first in the background theoretical with international references. In Chapter 3, we explain the methodology used and sequence, Section 3.1 explains the national literature and cases from Brazil. In Section 3.2, this realized a discussion about smart cities in Brazilian context, and sequence has been made in this conclusions.

17.2 Smart cities—background theoretical

Smart cities concept appeared in the literature in the middle of the century when Mahizhnan (1999) presents the case of Singapore in the use of information technology in education, infrastructure, and economy with the aim of improving the quality of life of those people. After this period a great number of publications are available, with the aim of discussing how information technology can assist cities and managers in managing, innovating, and providing services to citizens, making them smart cities (Anthopoulos, 2015).

However, because these are publications related to cities from different contexts, there is an interdisciplinary set of areas that discuss the same subject, but with different perspectives such as public administration and business, architecture and urbanism, geography, information technology, computing, information systems, sociology, information management, economics, engineering, among other areas, and it is verified in this conglomerate that there are different definitions of what is smart city, as can be observed some of them in Table 17.1.

The diversity of definitions about smart cities can be understood in Table 17.1, since the researches are related to the areas of study and performance of researchers, providing interdisciplinary research and with the intention of investigating and understanding a phenomenon in common in different contexts (Anastasia, 2012; Anthopoulos, 2015; Chourabi et al., 2012; Komninos, 2006; Meijer & Bolívar, 2015; Nam & Pardo, 2011).

Table 17.1 Concepts about smart cities.

Authors	Area	Definition of smart cities
Komninos (2006)	Urban development	Smart growth, cybercities, smart communities, smart innovation environments
Nam and Pardo (2011)	Public administration	Set of technologies, people, and institutions
Anastasia (2012)	Geography and regional planning	Development of communications, networks, interconnecting diverse actors, such as individuals, companies, institutions, and governments, with the aim of gaining and competitiveness
Chourabi et al. (2012)	Information technology	Set of technology, management and organization, governance, politics, people, communities, economy, infrastructure, and environment
Meijer and Bolívar (2015)	Public administration and governance	Technologies, people, and governance
Anthopoulos (2015)	Business administration	Innovation based on ICT helping urban life in terms of people, economy, environment, mobility, and quality of life
International Standards Organization (2014)	Governance	Environmental context, history and societal characteristics, governance, and subsystems
International Telecommunications Union (2014)	Governance	Sustainability, quality of life, urban aspects, smartness, society, economy, environment, and governance
IEEE — Smart Cities (2017)	Engineering	Technologies, government, and society

ICT, Information and communication technologies.

It is possible to identify that the research carried out around the smart cities concept comes from research centers or specific universities distributed in a global way in which they develop great projects related to public management, specifically in the modernization of cities, such as the Center for Technology in Government (CTG) from the University of Albany in the United States (Chourabi et al., 2012; Gil-Garcia, Helbig, & Ojo, 2014; Nam & Pardo, 2011), researchers in Greece (Anastasia, 2012; Anthopoulos, 2015; Komninos, 2006), Europe (Kuk & Janssen, 2011; Meijer & Bolívar, 2015), and South Korea (Lee, Hancock, & Hu, 2013; Li, Nucciarelli, Roden, & Graham, 2016), which are countries with significant publications in this area. There are also other regions, but at an embryonic stage or with isolated publications not mentioned in this text.

Komninos (2006) points out that the environment in which smart cities are inserted promotes a favorable context for innovation, and how this environment can aid in the dissemination of technology transfers, collaborative innovation, collective strategic intelligence, promoting innovative clusters and systems in a city context. Nam and Pardo (2011) cite the integration of human, technological, and institutional factors, because for the authors, an ever-changing city has health, transport, environment, education, and energy services all of which are smart, and the set of these services disseminates new suppliers, as well as a system conducive to innovation in services and research and development (Komninos, 2006; Nam & Pardo, 2011).

The new services provided by smart cities can be the enhancement of existing services, or new services developed through technologies, and propel new business models. Kuk and Janssen (2011) investigated whether innovation of business models in services already existing in smart cities was a faster alternative than the development of new projects and verified that in terms of value added, new services are slower but have a higher sustainability than the improvement of existing services (Kuk & Janssen, 2011).

Technological changes involve various areas of a city, such as infrastructure, economy, environment, management, politics, and governance, and in which Chourabi et al. (2012) propose an integrated framework of how a smart city can interfere in these specific areas or sectors.

However, by specifying the areas of activity in a smart city according to IEEE – Smart Cities (2017), it can provide new characteristics within cities such as smart economy, smart mobility, smart environment, smart people, smart life, smart governance, and according to this, these are the new challenges for cities by 2050 (IEEE – Smart Cities, 2017).

However, in government contexts, eGovernment (eGov) initiatives are advancing at a local level, where smart cities provide their own digital services with superior efficiency, which was supported by the initiatives of level the digitization of their services through eGov. There is a tendency in the literature to separate smart government from smart cities through smartness in government, (Gil-Garcia, Zhang, & Puron-Cid, 2016) which can spread the concept of smart services to a national level.

There are constant revisions of the literature to understand the concept of smart cities, a fact that was observed in a bibliometric review in 27 international journals with relevant and interdisciplinary impact factors, in the period 1997–2005 authors Anthopoulos and Reddick (2016) or related concepts that appear in the smart cities literature, such as digital city, virtual city, information city, knowledge-based city, broadband city, ubiquitous city, and eco-city. These concepts aim to explain how cities have evolved with the use and adoption of technologies in their management.

In this article, the author uses the concept of smart city, the one that uses information technology artifacts in the improvement of its services, making them more effective and smart in all areas (Anastasia, 2012; Anthopoulos, 2015; Chourabi et al., 2012; IEEE – Smart Cities, 2017; Komninos, 2006; Meijer & Bolívar, 2015; Nam & Pardo, 2011).

17.3 Research methodology: literature review and cases cited

This research uses a methodological strategy to review the national literature on a given topic. As justification, it is intended to explore the published works on smart cities in the Brazilian context to propose a research agenda in this field.

The keywords "smart city," "smart city," "smart cities," "digital city," "digital city," and "digital cities" were used because they coincide with words used in literature reviews by international researchers (Meijer & Bolívar, 2015). Because it is a recent topic, it was searched in several national databases such as Spell, Journal Capes, Brazilian Digital Library of Theses and Dissertations, and in Google Scholar filtering Brazilian researches related to the keywords and related to the topic of cities from the year 0 to the present.

As researches on the topic returned through keywords, their references were also analyzed, leading to new findings. There were 20 national works, being theses, dissertations, papers in journals and conferences being a small but significant amount for an emerging theme that is in international growth according to introduction in Fig. 17.1.

After tabulation the texts were analyzed in full by researchers involved with the topic, discussed their content, and reported briefly in the topic in sequence.

17.3.1 Brazilian literature and cases about smart cities

In Brazil the publications about smart cities began in 2006 with digital city initiatives, in a case cited by Rezende (2006), investigate the digital city of Mossoro. In this case the technology has helped the digital city and promotes a local environment of innovation. Subsequently, Câmara, Carvalho, de, Pinto, and Júnior (2012) discuss the proposal of a framework for smart and innovative cities in the Brazilian Northeast to assist public and private managers in the elaboration and discussion of public policies aimed at the development of this region.

Gama, Alvaro, and Peixoto (2012) present a technological maturity model for the smart cities, and Farias, Alencar, Ísis, and Alencar (2011) describe an architecture for this configuration of cities, in the infrastructure part of digital communication whether via optical fiber or Wi-Fi.

The city of Buzios was studied by Freitas (2014) and Vilaca et al. (2014) in which the first author developed his research in order to understand the interpretation that the citizens had of the smart city concept. Vilaca et al. (2014) analyzed the implementation of the Brazilian smart cities in the area of energy, in which the project was described by the authors addressing three central elements, such as city sustainability, electricity rationality, and efficiency. The Project was emphasized in partnership with an energy company.

Falcão (2015) has also researched the relationship of energy and smart cities, with the development of smart grid through smart meters and photovoltaic systems, and it is emphasized that studying these artifacts is in line with international publications (Kramers, Höjer, Lövehagen, & Wangel, 2014).

In the area of information technology, Silva (2014) presents a model of privacy provision in smart cities in which people can act as sensors in these cases, and Tomas (2014) develops at the same time a software architecture for smart cities in which the development of solutions for these cities is based on artifacts Internet of Things.

Paletta, Vasconselos, and Gonçalves (2015) and Afonso, Lima, da Costa, Garcia, and Álvaro (2014) work in isolated areas of smart cities in the Brazilian context, the first authors discuss how public and university libraries can assist as strategic resources in the development of smart cities. Afonso et al. (2014) justify a gap in the area of smart health through a literature review in the area of the use of information technologies in health as the approaches of smart health in smart cities.

Weiss (2013) develops his research in the city of Porto Alegre in order to explore how the smart cities have become a new practice in the management of services and urban infrastructure. The author expands his research citing the internet as a channel in which the citizen can use as channels of relationship with the public power, arguing as a criticism by the Brazilian cities to be in the initial phase of adoption and use of these digital resources (Weiss, 2014).

Madeira (2015) presents a prescriptive and applied model of electronic governance of cities, explained by four elements: municipal intelligence, strategic leadership, technology management, and characteristics of the change process and how this model can aid in the development of a smart city.

Lins, Ramos, Viana, and Frey (2015) discuss the incorporation of smart cities in the Latin American countries, where they mention four themes that can help the smart cities achieve innovations and their technological development which are smart mobility, mobile localization, monitoring smart natural resources and buildings or smart spaces, and the authors discuss techniques and topics related to these solutions.

In the sequence, Cunha, Przeybilovicz, Macaya, and Burgos (2016) present a comparative research Brazil−Spain, about the visions of the citizen and managers between the two countries in relation to smart cities. The authors suggest steps that can help in the development of these implementations in cities, especially in Brazil, through factors such as the development of a city vision with broad participation, managerial leadership, legislative updates, service integration, data availability, planning, participatory and governance mechanisms, independent open platforms, and interoperability.

There are also cases of research carried out in national territory, but they were published in international conferences but were developed by Brazilian researchers who act and foment the field of smart cities in the Brazilian academic research (Macadar & Lheureux-de-Freitas, 2013; Pereira, Macadar, & Testa, 2016; Porto & Macadar, 2016).

The Connected Smart Cities ranking that lists the most intelligent cities in Brazil elected in 2018 announced the city of Curitiba as the most intelligent and

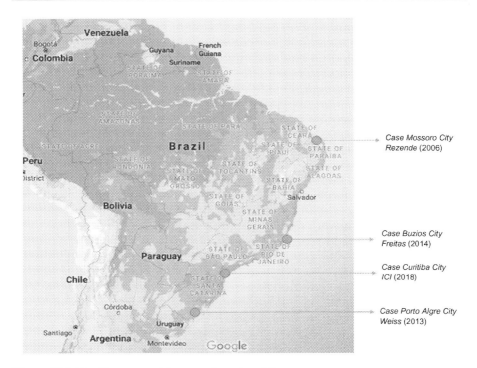

Figure 17.2 Brazilian smart cities cases in national literature.

connected. For that the indicators of mobility, urbanism, environment, energy, technology, innovation, economy, education, health, safety, entrepreneurship, and innovation were analyzed. As the Institute of Intelligent Cities of Curitiba (ICI — Instituto Cidades Inteligentes de Curitiba, 2018) uses technology in management, it makes the transformation of data into strategic information, and this can contribute to management and citizens.

Finally, the most evidenced cases in the national literature were cities: Mossoro, Buzios, Curitiba, and Porto Alegre, which can be visualized in Fig. 17.2, according to their geographical location in South America. Other cases such as Sao Paulo, Rio de Janeiro, and Brasilia were mentioned in the literature but not necessarily investigated in depth.

17.3.2 Smart cities discussion in the Brazilian context

It is possible to observe from the previous topic that the publications related to smart cities in Brazil are still in an initial phase, with isolated publications in 2006 and with an increase in quantity after 2010. Multidisciplinary as well as international publications (Table 17.1) occur in the Brazilian academy related to the theme (Table 17.2). This fact shows a trend in which each area explores the phenomenon

Table 17.2 Comparison of Brazilian publications about smart cities and international frameworks used.

National publications	Brazilian city	Area	International framework
Weiss (2013, 2014), Weiss, Bernardes, and Consoni (2015)	Porto Alegre	Business administration	Allwinkle and Cruickshank (2011), Nam and Pardo (2011), Chourabi et al. (2012)
Freitas (2014)	Buzios	History	Chourabi et al. (2012)
Paletta et al. (2015)	Not identified	Information management	Chourabi et al. (2012)
Silva (2014)	Not identified	Information technology	Nam and Pardo (2011)
Tomas (2014)	Not identified	Information technology	Nam and Pardo (2011)
Madeira (2015)	27 Cities from Rio Grande do Sul, Parana, Sao Paulo, Rio de Janeiro, and Ceara state	Engineering	Nam and Pardo (2011)
Porto and Macadar (2016)	Not identified	Business administration	Chourabi et al. (2012)

of cities in depth, contributing to the field in general, and to the advancement of knowledge in this area.

In national surveys, an alignment with the international academy, through the theoretical basis, the use of frameworks and international bibliographical references is evident, a fact that demonstrates proximity and alignment with the international scope of smart cities. In Table 17.2, it is possible to verify that four papers use a theoretical model proposed by Chourabi et al. (2012) in smart analysis and definition of cities. This model of authors has been replicated internationally, and Brazil follows this trend up to the present moment.

It is possible to verify that the national publications are decentralized in terms of areas and citations, fact as it is a contemporary phenomenon and its multidisciplinary, or because the researchers are in different schools, such as administration, engineering, IT, and social sciences. It is worth exploring that integration among researchers, or the development of joint research, with different theoretical lenses, approaches, and methods may contribute to a Brazilian advance in the development of Brazilian cities.

To illustrate the development of collaborative publications, researchers in Greece are already developing studies with the United States (Anthopoulos & Reddick, 2016) or even Brazilian researchers are seeking space for international publications, in order to collaborate with the field, or to develop new research partnerships in the smart cities area, breaking the frontiers of knowledge (Macadar & Lheureux-de-Freitas, 2013; Miranda, Cunha, & Pugas Filho, 2016; Pereira et al. 2016).

Nam and Pardo Smart Cities models (2011, 2014) are also referenced and used in Brazilian research, which can be seen in Table 17.2, being cited four times in relevant researches such as dissertations or national theses. According to Chourabi et al. (2012), it is possible to observe a predominance of American School models in national surveys, especially references developed by the CTG of the University of Albany.

It is proposed to advance this national research to use and compare other models of other schools, such as Greece and Italy (Anthopoulos, 2015; Neirotti, De Marco, Cagliano, Mangano, & Scorrano, 2014) and the Netherlands and Spain (Meijer & Bolívar, 2015) of a Latin American or Brazilian model, in a developing economy.

Management and other areas such as the Getulio Vargas Foundation (FGV) Business School develop academic–applied projects to mobilize and advance the discussion of smart cities in Brazil, such as the Smart Cities Forum Brazil (FGV – Fundação Getulio Vargas – Smart Cities Forum Brasil, 2017) public managers presenting Brazilian cases and how to proceed in this direction.

The Pontifical Catholic University of Rio Grande do Sul state has an innovation center for smart cities (PUC-RS, 2016) that allows to develop academic research and applied to the development of solutions that aim at the innovation of cities as a whole.

In Brazil, there is also a Master's program in smart and sustainable cities with the objective of training teachers with technical and scientific skills in urban development (Uninove, 2017).

The Brazilian participation in research on smart cities is still embryonic but arouses interests in some areas such as public administration and business, computing, engineering, and social sciences with the emergence of recent publications, mobilizations of researchers' academic–applied guidelines to new challenges for this field.

17.4 Conclusions

Information technology has encompassed organizational processes and has even been mass used by federal, state, and municipal governments. In the search for modernization of public services, in an applied context, the use of technology in cities brought the concept of smart cities (Smart Cities) through the implementation of technological platforms. In a theoretical counterpoint the concept of smart city has appeared in the literature in periodicals of public administration or business, engineering, computing, humanities, and social sciences (Anthopoulos, 2015) proposing emerging formats of city management, use of technologies, and citizen participation.

This chapter aims to propose a discussion of studies and cases on smart cities in Brazil based on a review of the literature on the subject, with a brief discussion on this field. It is observed in the literature, both international and national, about the subject that the researches are multidisciplinary and permeate several areas, since they are related to a broad phenomenon that permeates several actors or research areas. Also in this review, it was possible to observe the development of conceptual models that aim to propose and manage environments of smart cities.

Comparing the international literature framework with a small number of Brazilian articles, theses, dissertations, and books, it can be verified that the Brazilian research on smart cities is at an embryonic stage in academic or applied studies, permeating interdisciplinary areas, and such studies have an alignment with international research in terms of models, using frameworks by the authors Chourabi et al. (2012) and Nam and Pardo (2011). International studies and Brazilian research permeate interdisciplinary areas, yet all investigate the context of cities and seek to explore how technologies can help in this direction, making them smarter.

As a theoretical contribution, the present study has the characteristic of advancing in the scientific field of smart cities in a Brazilian context, presenting then characteristics, concepts, and a brief discussion with the publications on the subject, besides proposing gaps or studies that will collaborate and with the aim to advance on the frontier of knowledge.

The study has limitations because it is a theoretical chapter, but it is suggested that future empirical research in this field be carried out at the national level, since Brazil can become a model for the use of technological resources in cities located in a country, which can be used by other countries with similar characteristics.

As a suggestion of future studies, it is investigated whether other cases of Brazilian cities are being researched, mainly in the western and northern regions, since there is a predominance of capitals of the Brazilian east. In addition, issues such as the future of smart cities and alignment with international models are possible insights for researchers of the theme.

Acknowledgments

Many thanks the organizer of the book for his patience and honored invitation to participate in an important publication for the Latin American context.

About the author

Luiz Pinheiro Junior is a professor in Business School at Positivo University—Brazil and has expertise with research in information systems (IS), electronic government (eGov), smart cities, electronic invoicing, and cloud computing. He is a professor in MBA, conferencist in information technology (IT) and information systems, and reviser in conferences and journals in Brazil, Europe, and Latin America. His personal website is http://www.luizpinheirojunior.com.

References

Afonso, R. A., Lima, L. C., da Costa, L. C., Garcia, V. C., & Álvaro, A. (2014). Mapeamento Sistemático de Informática Médica para Cidades Inteligentes. In *XIV Congresso Brasileiro em Informática em Saúde — CBIS* (1–7).

Allwinkle, S., & Cruickshank, P. (2011). Creating smarter cities: An overview. *Journal of Urban Technology, 18*(2), 1–16.

Anastasia, S. (2012). The concept of "smart cities". Towards community development? *Networks and Communication Studies, NETCOM, 26*, 375–388. Retrieved from http://netcom.revues.org/1105.

Anthopoulos, L. (2015). Defining smart city architecture for sustainability. In *Electronic government and electronic participation: Joint proceedings of ongoing research and projects of IFIP WG 8.5 EGOV and ePart 2015*, (AUGUST) (pp. 140–147). <https://doi.org/10.3233/978-1-61499-570-8-140>.

Anthopoulos, L. G. (2015). Understanding the smart city domain: A literature review. *Transforming City Governments for Successful Smart Cities*, 1–185. Available from https://doi.org/10.1007/978-3-319-03167-5.

Anthopoulos, L. G., & Reddick, C. G. (2016). Understanding electronic government research and smart city: A framework and empirical evidence. *Information Polity, 21*(1), 99–117. Available from https://doi.org/10.3233/IP-150371.

Câmara, S. F., Carvalho, H. J. B. de, Pinto, F. R., & Júnior, N. A. (2012). É possível o Nordeste brasileiro ter cidades Inteligentes e Inovadoras? A proposta de um Framework. In *ENAPAG — Encontro de Administração Pública E Governo* (1–16).

Chourabi, H., Nam, T., Walker, S., Gil-Garcia, J. R., Mellouli, S., Nahon, K., ... Scholl, H. J. (2012). Understanding smart cities: An integrative framework. In *Proceedings of the annual Hawaii international conference on system sciences* (pp. 2289–2297). <https://doi.org/10.1109/HICSS.2012.615>.

Cunha, M. A. C., Przeybilovicz, E., Macaya, J. F. M. & Burgos, F. (2016). *Smart Cities: Transformação digital de cidades*. São Paulo: PGPC.

EU—European Union-Digital Economy & Society—Smart Cities. (2017). Available from https://ec.europa.eu/digital-single-market/en/smart-cities, Accessed 23.06.17.

Falcão, M. C. (2015). *Análise do impacto de sistemas fotovoltaicos conectados à rede de distribuição na qualidade da energia de uma Smart City* (Dissertação de Mestrado). Universidade Estadual Paulista — Unesp, Ilha Solteira.

Farias, J. E. P. De, Alencar, M. S., Ísis, A., & Alencar, R. T. (2011). Cidades Inteligentes e Comunicações. *Revista de Tecnologia Da Informação e Comunicação, 1*(i), 28–32. Available from https://doi.org/10.12721/2237-5112.v01n01a06.

FGV — Fundação Getulio Vargas — Smart Cities Forum Brasil. (2017). In <http://fgvprojetos.fgv.br/eventos/smart-cities-forum-brasil> Accessed 10.03.18.

Freitas, J. A. (2014). *Cidade inteligente Búzios: entre paradigmas e percepções* (Master Dissertation). Fundação Getulio Vargas — FGV, Rio de Janeiro.

Gama, K., Alvaro, A., & Peixoto, E. (2012). Em Direção a um Modelo de Maturidade Tecnológica para Cidades Inteligentes. In *VIII Simpósio Brasileiro de Sistemas de Informação*, (Sbsi) (pp. 150–155).

Gil-Garcia, J. R., Helbig, N., & Ojo, A. (2014). Being smart: Emerging technologies and innovation in the public sector. *Government Information Quarterly, 31*(S1), I1–I8. Available from http://doi.org/10.1016/j.giq.2014.09.001.

Gil-Garcia, J. R., Zhang, J., & Puron-Cid, G. (2016). Conceptualizing smartness in government: An integrative and multi-dimensional view. *Government Information Quarterly*. Available from https://doi.org/10.1016/j.giq.2016.03.002.

IBGE — *Instituto Brasileiro de Geografia e Estatística — Sinopse do Censo Demográfico*. (2010). In <http://www.censo2010.ibge.gov.br/sinopse/index.php?dados = 8> Accessed 05.05.18.

ICI — Instituto Cidades Inteligentes de Curitiba. (2018). In <https://www.ici.curitiba.org.br/noticias/curitiba-lidera-ranking-de-cidades-inteligentes-no-brasil/2137> Accessed 10.07.18.

IEEE — Smart Cities. (2017). In <http://smartcities.ieee.org> Accessed 01.06.18.

International Standards Organization (ISO). (2014). Smart cities Preliminary Report 2014. Retrieved from http://www.iso.org/iso/smart_cities_report-jtc1.pdf, April 2019.

International Telecommunications Union (ITU). (2014). Smart sustainable cities: An analysis of definitions. Retrieved from www.itu.int/en/ITU-T/focusgroups/ssc/Documents/Approved_Deliverables/TR-Definitions.docx, March 2019.

Komninos, N. (2006). The architecture of intelligent cities. In *Second international conference on intelligent environments* (Vol. 1, pp. 13—20). Retrieved from <http://www.urenio.org/komninos/wp-content/uploads/2014/01/2006-The-Architecture-of-Intel-Cities-IE06.pdf>.

Kramers, A., Höjer, M., Lövehagen, N., & Wangel, J. (2014). Smart sustainable cities — Exploring ICT solutions for reduced energy use in cities. *Environmental Modelling and Software*, *56*, 52—62. Available from https://doi.org/10.1016/j.envsoft.2013.12.019.

Kuk, G., & Janssen, M. (2011). The business models and information architectures of smart cities. *Journal of Urban Technology*, *18*(2), 39—52. Available from https://doi.org/10.1080/10630732.2011.601109.

Lee, J. H., Hancock, M. G., & Hu, M.-C. (2013). Towards an effective framework for building smart cities: Lessons from Seoul and San Francisco. *Technological Forecasting and Social Change*, *89*, 80—99. Available from https://doi.org/10.1016/j.techfore.2013.08.033.

Li, F., Nucciarelli, A., Roden, S., & Graham, G. (2016). How smart cities transform operations models: A new research agenda for operations management in the digital economy. *Production Planning & Control*, *27*(6), 514—528. Available from https://doi.org/10.1080/09537287.2016.1147096.

Lins, A., Ramos, H. S., Viana, L. P. & Frey, A. C. (2015). Cidades Inteligentes, um Novo Paradigma da Sociedade do Conhecimento. In C. A. Z. Vasconcellos (Org.). *Cuba e Brasil no Século XXI* (pp. 165—178). Blucher.

Macadar, M. A. & Lheureux-de-Freitas, J. (2013). Porto Alegre : A Brazilian city searching to be smarter. In *Proceedings of the 14th annual international conference on digital government research* (pp. 56—64).

Madeira, G. S. (2015). *Construindo Governança Eletrônica de Cidades: Um modelo de implementação de soluções para inovação e otimização da gestão pública* (Ph.D. thesis). Universidade Estadual de Campinas — UNICAMP, Campinas.

Mahizhnan, A. (1999). Smart cities: The Singapore case. *Cities*, *16*(1), 13—18. Available from https://doi.org/10.1016/S0264-2751(98)00050-X.

Meijer, A., & Bolívar, M. P. R. (2015). Governing the smart city: A review of the literature on smart urban governance. *International Review of Administrative Sciences*, *0*(0), 1—17. Available from https://doi.org/10.1177/0020852314564308.

Miranda, P. R. M., Cunha, M. A. V. C., & Pugas Filho, J. M. (2016). eParticipation in smart cities of developing countries: Research-based practical recommendations. In J. R. Gil-Garcia, T. A. Pardo, & T. Nam (Eds.), *Smarter as the new urban agenda: A comprehensive view of the 21st century city* (pp. 315—332). Springer International Publishing.

Nam, T., & Pardo, T. A. (2011). *Conceptualizing smart city with dimensions of technology, people, and institutions,* 282−291. Available from https://doi.org/10.1145/2037556.2037602.

Neirotti, P., De Marco, A., Cagliano, A. C., Mangano, G., & Scorrano, F. (2014). Current trends in smart city initiatives: Some stylised facts. *Cities, 38,* 25−36. Available from https://doi.org/10.1016/j.cities.2013.12.010.

Paletta, F. C., Vasconselos, P. O., & Gonçalves, Y. S. (2015). A Biblioteca no Contexto das Cidades Inteligentes. *Pesquisa Brasileira Em Ciência Da Informação E Biblioteconomia, 10*(1), 001−018.

Pereira, G. V., Macadar, M. A. & Testa, M. G. A. (2016) Framework for understanding smart city governance as a sociotechnical system. In *Ninth international conference on theory and practice of electronic governance − ICEGOV* (pp. 11−12).

Porto, J. B. & Macadar, M. A. (2016). *Smart city: a rigorous literature review of the concept from 2000 to 2015* (Relatório de Doutorado em Administração). Programa de Pós-Graduação em Administração, Pontifícia Universidade Católica do Rio Grande do Sul (PUCRS), Porto Alegre.

Przeybilovicz, E., Cunha, M. A., & Meirelles, F. de S. (2018). O uso da tecnologia da informação e comunicação para caracterizar os municípios: quem são e o que precisam para desenvolver ações de governo eletrônico e smart city. *Revista de Administração Pública, 52*(4), 630−649. Available from https://doi.org/10.1590/0034-7612170582.

PUC-RS − *Pontifícia Universidade Católica do Rio Grande do Sul − RS − ganha centro de inovação para Cidades Inteligentes.* (2016). In <http://www.pucrs.br/facin/rio-grande-do-sul-ganha-centro-de-inovacao-para-cidades-inteligentes> Accessed 19.03.18.

Rezende, J. F. D. de. (2006). Mossoró Cidade Digital e o Sistema Local de Inovação em TI e Inclusão Digital de Mossoró. In *XXIV Simpósio de Gestão da Inovação Tecnológica* (1−15).

Silva, W. M. (2014). *Go!SIP: um framework de privacidade para cidades inteligentes baseado em pessoas como sensores* (Dissertação de Mestrado). Universidade Federal do Pernambuco − UFPE, Recife.

Tomas, G. H. R. P. (2014). *Uma arquitetura para cidades inteligentes baseada na internet das coisas* (Dissertação de Mestrado). Universidade Federal do Pernambuco, UFPE, Recife.

Uninove. *Universidade Nove de Julho − Programa de Mestrado em Cidades Inteligentes e Sustentáveis* (2017). In <http://www.uninove.br/mestrado-e-doutorado/programa-de-pos-graduacao-em-cidades-inteligentes-e-sustentaveis-ppg-cis> Accessed 10.01.18.

Vilaca, N. M. C. A. A., Figueiredo, V. N., Oliveira, L. B., de, Ferreira, V. H., Fortes, M. Z., Correia, W. F., & Pacheco, O. L. C. (2014). Smart City − Caso da Implantação em Búzios. *Revista SODEBRAS, 9*(98), 16−22.

Weiss, M. C. (2013). *Cidades inteligentes como nova prática para o gerenciamento dos serviços e infraestruturas urbanos: estudo de caso da cidade de Porto Alegre* (Master dissertation). Centro Universitário da FEI, São Paulo.

Weiss, M. C. (2014). A internet como canal de comunicação entre o poder público e os cidadãos em tempos de cidades inteligentes. In *IV Congresso de Administração, Sociedade e Inovação − CASI* (1−14).

Weiss, M. C., Bernardes, R. C., & Consoni, F. L. (2015). Cidades inteligentes como nova prática para o gerenciamento dos serviços e infraestruturas urbanos: a experiência da cidade de Porto Alegre. *URBE − Revista Brasileira de Gestão Urbana, 7*(3), 310−324. Available from https://doi.org/10.1590/2175-3369.007.003.AO01.

Further reading

Telles, M. J., Barbosa, J. L. V., & Righi, R. R. (2017). Um Modelo Computacional para Cidades Inteligentes Assistivas. *iSys | Revista Brasileira de Sistemas de Informação, 10* (1), 52−79.

UE − União Européia − *Digital Economy & Society − Smart Cities*. (2017). In <https://ec.europa.eu/digital-single-market/en/smart-cities> Accessed 23.05.18.

Porto Alegre, Brazil: the smart health case of Gerint

Paulo R. Miranda[1], Clarice S. Porciuncula[2] and Maria A. Cunha[3]
[1]Procempa, ICT Services Company of the Municipality of Porto Alegre, Porto Alegre, Brazil, [2]Procempa, Gerint Project, Porto Alegre, Brazil, [3]Getulio Vargas Foundation (FGV), Center for Studies in Public Administration and Government, São Paulo, Brazil

Chapter Outline

18.1 Introduction   367
18.2 Background   369
    18.2.1 The Brazilian health service   370
    18.2.2 The regulation of access to health services   371
    18.2.3 Dimensions of the regulation of health services   371
18.3 Research methodology: case study   372
    18.3.1 Porto Alegre Smart City   372
    18.3.2 Scope   375
    18.3.3 Integration   381
    18.3.4 Organization   382
    18.3.5 Time   383
    18.3.6 Cost   383
    18.3.7 Quality   384
    18.3.8 Risks   384
    18.3.9 Procurement   385
    18.3.10 Discussion—the fringes   385
18.4 Conclusions   386
Acknowledgments   387
About the author   387
References   388
Further reading   390

18.1 Introduction

Brazilian cities, such as São Paulo, Rio de Janeiro, Porto Alegre, and Curitiba, have appeared in international smart city rankings, although it could be difficult to argue that these actually are smart cities in the country. However, numerous initiatives may be described as smart. Anthopoulos (2015) highlights that the expression smart city does not describe a city with specific attributes but rather is used to characterize different cases of "smartness" in urban spaces. In 2017 18% of local governments in Brazil claimed to have some form of smart city plan or project. This number rises to 77% when considering only state capitals and 70% in municipalities with over half a million inhabitants (Comitê Gestor da Internet no Brasil, 2018). While some are relatively simple implementations, others require a complex effort of articulation between the public sector, private sector, and citizens: requalification of urban areas, intelligent lighting and traffic lights, incentives for the development of a creative economy, coworking spaces, and incentives for start-ups. Other requirements include electronic participation, open data, administrative modernization, operational control centers, environmental monitoring, use of big data, and analytics in public policies, public bicycles, structure for electric cars, and many others (Cunha, Przeybilovicz, Macaya, & Santos, 2016).

This chapter describes the Gerint Hospital Admissions Management system that regulates admissions through the Brazilian health system in the city of Porto Alegre (Fig. 18.1). A Brazilian study has shown that, among the areas of smart initiatives, health services are one of the greatest priorities (Cunha et al., 2016). Porto Alegre is the southernmost Brazilian state capital. Rio Grande do Sul state is on the border with Uruguay and Argentina. With approximately 1.5 million residents the municipality treats 364,000 patients per month. Of these, over 18,000 are admitted to hospitals. A major challenge facing the city is to guarantee universal and equal access to health services for the entire population while dealing with limited resources, high-complexity procedures, and a complex network that provide public and private services.

The Gerint system was developed through a partnership between public and private institutions. Following this experience in Porto Alegre, it is being implemented in a large number of cities in Rio Grande do Sul state. Its main functions are registration, blocking, occupying, and freeing up hospital beds in every hospital, managing requests for admission with information and monitoring of the patients' health, management tools for regulators, management tools for applicants, map of hospital beds (occupied, free, or blocked by hospital and type of bed), sharing of information, and communication between service centers, management of referrals[1] by municipality or region, patients' records, and integration of services with external systems (web services).

The remaining of this chapter is organized as follows: the following background Section 18.2 presents the Brazilian public health service and describes the regulatory procedures to manage the access to health services. Then, Section 18.3 introduces the case of Porto Alegre, reporting some initiatives in the context of smart cities. Then, the scope of the Gerint project is analyzed, with details of the solution and the analysis of some aspects of the case, such as interoperability, integration, organization, time, costs, quality, risks, and procurement. Section 18.4 of this chapter presents some conclusions and points out some improvements, and next steps already have been planned for the future of this case.

---

[1] Referrals: When a service or specialist is not available in a city or region, patients that need them are forwarded to hospitals or agencies previously established in the system. These cases are known as "referrals."

Figure 18.1 Porto Alegre in Brazil.

18.2 Background

Brazil is the largest country in Latin America. Its 8.5 million km² account for 47% of South America. With a population of 208.4 million [Brazilian Institute of Geography and Statistics (IBGE), 2018], it is the 5th most populated country in the world, with the 9th highest gross domestic product (GDP) [International Monetary Fund (IMF), 2018] and the 50th highest per capita GDP. The country is a federative republic made up of 26 states and the federal district, in which the capital, Brasilia, is located, and 5570 municipalities. The country suffers from great regional and social inequality, and offering quality healthcare services to most of the population is a huge challenge (Castro & Machado, 2010).

18.2.1 The Brazilian health service

The Brazilian public health service is made up of a combination of public and private organizations constituted throughout the 20th century, forming a complex network of socioeconomic and historical relationships (Elias, 2004). In 1988 as part of the country's redemocratization process, the new constitution defined health as "a citizen's right and a duty of the State" (Brasil, 1988; Article 196). It attributed to the state the duty of drafting social and economic policies to ensure universal and equal access to procedures and services to promote, protect, and recover health, promoting the "decommodification" of healthcare (Elias, 2004). The Constitution, from Articles 198 to 200, delegated to the Brazilian health service [Sistema Único de Saúde (SUS)] the coordination and execution of policies to protect and promote health in Brazil (Moura, 2013). The SUS is therefore the main public healthcare policy. To a certain extent, it mirrors the developments that began in the United Kingdom in the early 20th century, spreading across Europe and consolidated in the form of the welfare state after the Second World War (Elias, 2004).

Changes in the demographic and epidemiological profile of the population, such as aging, and a falling birth rate, people opting for the public health system as they can no longer afford private health insurance (due to the economic downturn and unemployment), the urbanization process (Matos, 2012), and the search for diagnosis and treatment, have resulted in pressure to adopt new techniques. This is one of the dilemmas facing the public healthcare system. Nevertheless, there are risks associated with adopting technologies and procedures whose results have not been fully tried and tested, and their costs may be high, compromising the ability to meet the healthcare needs of the population at large (CONASS, 2011). Healthcare expenditure is growing and consumes a large part of the budget of citizens and governments. Thus there is a need to establish regulation processes to mediate the pressures between supply and demand for healthcare services.

It is important to highlight that the Constitution of 1988 promoted the decentralization of healthcare services. Some should be provided by the states, but most of the services constitutionally fall to the municipalities. Decentralization was a tool to strengthen the regionalization, hierarchy, and integration process of healthcare actions and services in every region of the country, respecting the competencies of the three spheres of management (federal, state, and municipal governments) (Paim, Travassos, Almeida, Bahia, & Macinko, 2012). In Brazil, a country of large territorial dimensions and social and economic inequalities, this decentralization of the healthcare system is highly complex (Assis & Jesus, 2012). Making it feasible required complementary legislation, new rules, and an administrative reform at all levels of government (Farias, Gurgel, Costa, Brito, & Buarque, 2011). The Ministry of Health established measures to strengthen primary care and access to specialized services through regulation (Paim et al., 2012). From the early 1990s, it published norms intended to redefine responsibilities, establishing mechanisms for the transfer of funds, for instance, the amount per capita transferred to municipalities to fund primary care, and new representative councils and management committees at all levels of government. These norms were replaced in 2006 by the Healthcare Pact, defining mutual commitments between levels of government regarding the goals and responsibilities involved in healthcare, expanding the decision-making mechanisms in the system, with social participation and alliances between interested parties. New modalities are sought to manage the public/private relationship to guarantee the social characteristics of the healthcare system (Elias, 2004). There have been innovations in the governance of health in Brazil, such as national healthcare participatory conferences and the institutionalization of the structure that established health councils and intermanagerial committees at the state (bipartite) and federal (tripartite) levels, in which decisions are made by consensus. These structures helped to provide clearer definitions of the areas of institutional responsibility and allowed the participation of more diverse actors in the decision-making process, committing each level of government through the implementation of the national health policy (Paim et al., 2012).

18.2.2 The regulation of access to health services

In 2008 the Brazilian Ministry of Health, through an edict (Brasil, 2008), defined the so-called regulatory complex that manages the occupation of hospital beds and the agendas of healthcare units (Brasil, 2006), allowing it to become fully involved in the authorization of service billing, controlling the physical and financial limits established in contracts with private healthcare services, setting and executing the criteria for the classification of risk, and other aspects (CONASS, 2011).

Municipal Health Secretaries, public health managers in municipalities, along with the State Health Secretary, the manager of public health in a state, are responsible for providing the population with the resources they need for their universal healthcare. Municipalities and states should seek to correct shortages and inequalities, which frequently occur due to distortions in the funding of the sector and the widespread participation of the private sector in the healthcare system, to ensure that the population has access to healthcare according to their needs (Rodrigues, 2016).

18.2.3 Dimensions of the regulation of health services

In the complex Brazilian health system, it is necessary to implement adequate controls on costs and, at the same time, ensure the principles of universality and equality in access to services. The coordination of primary care (basic treatment), secondary care (provision of specialist services), and tertiary and hospital care (the latter two predominantly provided by private services and including high-cost procedures) has required a permanent effort in terms of creating and improving regulation mechanisms (Menicucci, 2009).

The National Regulation Policy organizes regulatory procedures into three dimensions: regulation of health systems, regulation of healthcare, and regulation of access to healthcare. The first two dimensions, respectively, involve (1) directives for monitoring, controlling, evaluating, auditing, and inspecting national, state, and municipal health systems; and (2) monitoring the provision of services by public and private providers, conducted by the health secretariats of the states and municipalities, in order to ensure the adequate provision of health services to the population. The third dimension is especially important in our case. Access to healthcare is regulated by making more adequate alternative care available to meet citizens' needs through attending urgent cases, consultations, beds, and other services. Guaranteed access is based on protocols, risk classification, and other priority criteria. This set of norms is intended to organize, control, manage, and prioritize access to and the flow of healthcare services in the Brazilian Health System. It encompasses the medical regulation of prehospital and hospital care for emergencies, the control of available beds, and schedules for appointments and specialized procedures. It also includes the standardization of procedures through healthcare protocols, the establishment of referrals between units with different levels of complexity and local, intermunicipal and interstate capacity for complexity in accordance with the agreed flows and protocols. Each municipality is responsible for operationalizing the regulations in its territory.

18.3 Research methodology: case study

Porto Alegre is the capital city of Rio Grande do Sul, in the south of Brazil. The city has become well known internationally for its participative budget model, which has been in use since 1989 and has inspired cities all around the world. With a population of 1.479 million (IBGE, 2018) and GDP of approximately U$21 million and per capita GDP of approximately U$14,000, the city is important regionally and nationally. It is also known for its active participation and for having hosted the World Social Forum (WSF) in 2001, 2002 and 2003, 2005, 2012, and 2014. The WSF is an event organized by social movements from several continents with the goal of preparing alternatives for a global social transformation. Its slogan is "Another World is Possible."[2]

18.3.1 Porto Alegre Smart City

Porto Alegre has often been referred to for its initiatives that place it in the context of smart cities (Macadar & Lheureux-De-Freitas, 2013). The IBM Smarter Cities Challenge Program Summit chose Porto Alegre as one of the 31 winning cities from around the world in 2012. The project that integrates surveillance cameras, speed cameras on the streets, and smartphones for identification and alarms for undocumented vehicles in real time was awarded the Excellence in Electronic Government prize by the Brazilian Association of Public ICT Agencies [Associação Brasileira de Entidades Estaduais de Tecnologia da Informação e Comunicação (ABEP)] in 2017.

[2] http://forumsocialportoalegre.org.br/.

The diverse range of smart initiatives developed in the city can be described using the Smart City Integrative Framework proposed by Chourabi et al. (2012), although there is no smart city master plan. To characterize the initiatives of the city, actions of technology, governance, political context, and others are described. Cunha and Miranda (2013) proposed that to describe the use of technology by governments, besides the development of applications focusing on improving the management processes of administration, in the provision of better public services and with easy access, and in the promotion of electronic democracy, it is also necessary to address issues related to the governance of IT, technological infrastructure and digital inclusion, economic development, and the generation of jobs and income.

In technology, Porto Alegre operates its own fiber optics network, with over 800 km, interconnecting 100% of the administration agencies and urban equipment (schools, clinics, traffic and security units, convention centers, cameras, and traffic lights, etc.). The city has its integrated command center [Centro Integrado de Comando (CEIC)], with resources for video monitoring, communication, and specialist teams that enable the management of large events in the city, cultural or sports events, storms, floods and accidents, etc. (Fig. 18.2). Porto Alegre also has a system of geographical information that makes a set of over 100 georeferenced data sets available.

The city has registered governance initiatives that were highlighted before in the text. The municipal administration promoted an administrative reform to improve the integration and transversal management of strategic programs. The strategic management board of directors is directly linked to the Mayor's office. The

Figure 18.2 Integrated command center (CEIC) (by Helena Rocha—Porto Alegre City Hall).

articulation between the government, universities, and businesses is coordinated by an Innovation Board, which works to stimulate and support interaction between them, develop projects, promote innovation and technological decisions to promote businesses and articulate public policies on technology. Another important initiative is the Alliance for the Innovation of Porto Alegre, a pact formed by the three largest universities in the city [Federal University of Rio Grande do Sul (UFRGS), Pontifical Catholic University of Rio Grande do Sul (PUCRS), and the University of Vale do Rio dos Sinos]. This alliance led to the Innovation Pact, which involves, besides the universities, the business sector, organizations from the third sector, and the government. The governance of the pact is exercised by a board, at which the principal leaders of all the segments committed to the goals of this initiatives have a seat. The pact focuses on transforming the city into a model in the area of innovation and entrepreneurship in the country, creating a potential for local, national, and international connections to boost social and economic development.

In the political context, two initiatives stand out, the participative budget and the World Social Forum. It is also important to highlight that the International Free Software Forum is held in Porto Alegre, the most important free software meeting in Latin America and one of the major free software events in the world.

Other initiatives include

- Network of 35 telecenters (with training programs and access to technological resources), distributed among the poorest populated areas of the city, aiding literacy and digital inclusion and facilitating inclusion in the labor market;
- "Bike PoA"—offering bicycle-sharing services;
- "Porto Alegre Free"—offering free Wi-Fi access in parks, squares, and public buildings, expanding to reach over 200 hot spots in 2019;
- Biomonitoring—based on an agreement established in 2008 with the UFRGS, using the methodology of biomonitoring of air at 12 distinct points (6 municipal schools). At each site where a native tree, the strawberry guava (the object of biomonitoring), was planted, information is gathered and used in priority areas for studies of major pollutants;
- Reference Center for Renewable Energies and Energy Efficiency, involving several interested parties to develop public policies, projects, and actions to promote and encourage the use of renewable energies;
- Porto Alegre Master Planting Plan to preserve, manage, and increase the number of trees in the city. Based on an inventory of trees in the city, it publishes directives for the planning, production, conservation, and management of public trees.

The three largest universities located in Porto Alegre have science parks that attract high technology companies such as HP, Microsoft, and Dell, and incubators and accelerators that encourage the creation of new businesses. Tecnopuc, belonging to the PUCRS, has a Smart City Innovation Center, which conducts research and develops solutions related to smart cities and the Internet of Things. This is the result of a partnership between PUCRS and Huawei, a global leader in global Information and Communications Technologies (ICT). The research center can be used by the community of the Science and Technology Park and the university to develop projects in the fields of public management, health, and education. It can also be used for the development of an operational system for smart cities and their applications.

These and a number of other initiatives jointly help to make up the framework of a city that seeks innovation, collaboration, and good practices to face the challenges of the global urbanization process and the typical lack of resources in developing countries. Smart cities should provide environments of collaboration, supported by ICT (Miranda, Cunha, & Pugas Filho, 2016).

In the field of public health, smart initiatives in Porto Alegre serve as a model in Brazil. All the units of the basic treatment networks, specialist and tertiary networks (hospitals) have been interconnected with the management systems of the Municipal Health Secretariat using the fiber optic information highway. Its telemedicine system, operational since 2008, improves the quality of primary diagnoses and reduces waiting times for specialist treatment. In 2018 public health programs in the city were awarded the InovaCidade prize at the Smart City America Congress & Expo, and the Excellence in Electronic Government prize from the Brazilian Association of Public ICT Agencies (ABEP) for the Hospital Admissions and Scheduling Management System (Gerint/Gercon).

18.3.2 Scope

Although smart city concepts continue to produce highly different views from one to the other and lead to a certain amount of confusion among specialists (Anthopoulos & Fitsilis, 2013), the Gerint initiative is classified as a Smart City initiative. Considering the model that analyzes smart cities in six areas (economy, mobility, environment, living, people, and governance), adopted by many specialists (Anthopoulos & Fitsilis, 2013), the project fits the dimensions of Smart Governance and Smart Living. It is placed in the context of using ICT to make public services smarter and more focused on improving citizens' quality of life, in this case, municipal health services.

The Gerint system was developed for the municipality of Porto Alegre. After Porto Alegre, it has been available to the municipalities of Rio Grande do Sul since January 2018. It is being implemented gradually, except in Porto Alegre, which already uses the system in all its services.

Rio Grande do Sul is made up of 497 municipalities and has 307 hospitals and 111 emergency care services.[3] Of these, 29 hospitals and 4 emergency care services[4] are located in Porto Alegre. The state has a total of 30,151 hospital beds.[5] Of these, 20,641 are available to the public health system (SUS). The Gerint currently monitors the occupation of the 4575[6] beds in the city of Porto Alegre.

---

[3] Information available on the website of the CNES system: http://cnes2.datasus.gov.br/Mod_Ind_Unidade.asp?VEstado = 43&VMun = &VComp = 00&VUni = .

[4] Information available on the website of the CNES system: http://cnes2.datasus.gov.br/Mod_Ind_Unidade.asp?VEstado = 43&VMun = 431490.

[5] Information available on the website of the CNES system: http://cnes2.datasus.gov.br/Mod_Ind_Tipo_Leito.asp?VEstado = 43.

[6] Map of hospital beds in the Gerint system at https://gerint.procempa.com.br.

It is estimated that 71% of the Brazilian population uses the SUS.[7] The National Health Research Project,[8] conducted by the Brazilian Institute of Geography and Statistics in 2013, concluded that 65.7% of the population that required hospital admissions for 24 hours or more used the SUS services. Therefore it is calculated that approximately 7025,911 citizens of Rio Grande do Sul state could be treated through the Gerint system.

The system allows real-time monitoring of the occupation situation of each bed in the municipal hospital network and the beds hired from private hospitals by the municipal administration, enabling the optimized occupation of these beds. At the same time the sharing of information regarding patient's clinical condition with recommendations for admission between the Regulation Centers (of the city, state government, and other cities in the state), and of these with hospitals, allows decisions to be made based on shared information, improving the governance of the regulation. This approach is innovative in Brazil, where the major challenge is to adjust the demand for specialist services in the primary care network, or that is generated by it, with the availability of beds and services offered by the components of the network, whether public, community, or private (Barbosa, Barbosa, & Najberg, 2016; Paim et al., 2012).

Sharing a patient's information between Regulation Centers makes it possible to seek the best treatment for this patient in more than one place at the same time. The centers also share information simultaneously with more than one hospital. Every hospital has a team of doctors capable of evaluating these requests forwarded by the center and gauge the hospital's capacity to meet this demand. The patient's case is discussed by specialists, and the most suitable hospital is authorized to receive and admit that patient. The center that first identifies a bed that meets the requirements authorizes the admission, and the system informs the service that requested the treatment to enable the immediate transfer of the patient. The process is operated within the system and is transparent and traceable.

Porto Alegre's Municipal Health Secretariat and the hospitals in the city have found that there has been a substantial improvement in the quality of care provided to patients since the implementation of the system.

18.3.2.1 Description of the solution

The system was developed to meet this set of requirements and functions:

- High availability.
- Easy use and navigation of the system.
- Friendly interface.
- Aspects of security, creation of access profiles with permission to view and alter information in the system.

---

[7] News published by the Brazilian government at http://www.brasil.gov.br/noticias/saude/2015/06/71-dos-brasileiros-tem-os-servicos-publicos-de-saude-como-referencia.
[8] Results available at ftp://ftp.ibge.gov.br/PNS/2013/pns2013.pdf.

- Register of operations executed in the system by creating a log, enabling the traceability and auditing of this information.
- Availability of managerial information, with the use of business intelligence tools.
- Updated map of beds per hospital.
- Patient identification through a national identification register of SUS users (national health card).
- Configuration of more than one regulation center, with the registration of connected applicant and executing establishments. The regulation centers may be emergency units (ambulance services, admissions, and consultations and examinations).
- Implementation of the transfer or sharing of requests for admissions between centers.
- Integration services for receiving and sending information to the systems of the applicant or executing units.
- Integration with the specialist appointment management system.
- Integration with the system that supports the authorization of accounts and billing.
- Integration with the national register of healthcare establishments of the Ministry of Health.
- Forwarding to hospitals and exchanging messages between the regulation centers and the internal regulation of hospitals for the assessment of patients (traceable).
- Detailed information of the vital signs and principal signs and symptoms of patients.
- Specific questions regarding type of bed to streamline admission requests.
- Classification of gravity using the MEWS protocol[9].
- Regulation's classification of priority.
- Regulation criteria that determine whether a request from a hospital (hospital's own admission) will be regulated or not: in this case, the application of these criteria could determine that the hospital cannot admit a patient without authorization from the respective center.

18.3.2.2 Diagram of the system: architecture and technology

The system is divided into two parts, the frontend and backend (Fig. 18.3). The frontend is developed using HTML[10] 5, JavaScript, and CSS[11] 3. The screen control and access to services of the backend are developed using AngularJS,[12] version 1.3. The backend is developed in Java 7, on the Java Enterprise platform, Edition 7[13] (JEE7), and executed on the WildFly application server[14] 10. This backend is accessed through web services available in the REST layer,[15] which access the business layer developed in Enterprise JavaBeans[16] 3, which accesses the database using Hibernate[17] 4. The database used is Oracle 10g.

---

[9] Scale of alert for the early identification of risk: Modified Early Warning Scoring https://en.wikipedia.org/wiki/Early_warning_score.
[10] Hypertext Markup Language.
[11] Cascading Style Sheets.
[12] https://angularjs.org/.
[13] https://docs.oracle.com/javaee/7/index.html.
[14] http://wildfly.org/.
[15] https://en.wikipedia.org/wiki/Representational_state_transfer.
[16] https://www.oracle.com/technetwork/testcontent/ejb-3-085455.html.
[17] Information available at http://hibernate.org/.

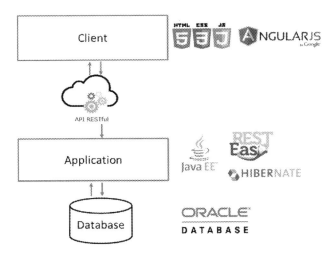

Figure 18.3 Architecture of the Gerint system.

Users are authenticated using Keycloak.[18] Authorization is given through the system itself, as Keycloak does not meet the particular needs of the system.

- *Interoperability*

The Gerint system uses integration services with the national identification systems of SUS users and registers of healthcare establishments and professionals, through SOAP web services.[19] Furthermore, to ensure that the information regarding requests for admissions is available as quickly as possible to seek a bed for the patient, the system provides hospitals with a set of integration services (Fig. 18.4). All services are accessed with unique access keys, which identify the hospital and ensure that the information remains secure. Access to these services is managed by the APIMAN[20] tool.

- *Innovation*

The major challenge of this project in terms of technology was implementing integration services that allowed hospitals and emergency rooms to integrate their information systems with the Gerint fully and securely, sending and receiving data on requests for admissions and the occupation and freeing up of beds, as one of the main goals of the system is to provide a map of hospital beds in the city in real time.

A set of 22 integration services was developed, working 24 hours a day, 7 days a week, and available to the network of specialist service providers, guaranteeing the parity and simultaneousness of information between systems, avoiding communication breakdowns between those involved in seeking the best treatment for patients.

---

[18] Information available at https://www.keycloak.org/.
[19] Simple Object Access Protocol https://www.w3.org/TR/soap/.
[20] Information available at http://www.apiman.io/latest/.

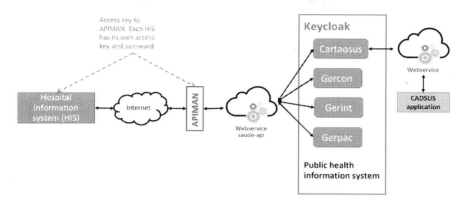

Figure 18.4 Diagram of interoperability.

Another innovation implemented in the Gerint was the structure of a number of Regulation Centers, allowing a request for admission to be shared between more than one center. Every center can work on the regulation of this request, seeking the most suitable hospital. The center that locates the best service forward the patient, meeting his needs more effectively.

The system also implements a process that allows messages to be exchanged between applicants, hospitals, and regulation centers. This exchange of messages through the system dispenses with the need for telephone calls, messages through WhatsApp[21] or Short Message Service[22] text messages. Every message sent generates a flag in the admission request, warning professionals that a communication needs to be evaluated. When read, the message is flagged, and the alert is removed. Messages marked as important generate specific alerts to professionals. As every message is recorded in the system, it is possible to conduct audits to evaluate the effectiveness of the service for a request for admission.

. Monitoring panels were created in the system in order to present the admission requests according to operator's access profile. The goal is to assist request monitoring process. Services that only register requests, such as emergency rooms, can view and access only their own requests and can monitor the development of the regulator's work through an exchange of the situation of their requests. Hospitals visualize and access their own requests and those that the regulation centers forward to them to evaluate the possibility of admitting the patient, in addition to those that are already authorized for admission in this service.

The regulatory professionals have their own panel (Fig. 18.5). All requests for admissions that are registered in the system and need the intervention of a regulator are presented on a panel in accordance with their situation, showing the doctors at

---

[21] https://www.whatsapp.com/.
[22] https://en.wikipedia.org/wiki/SMS.

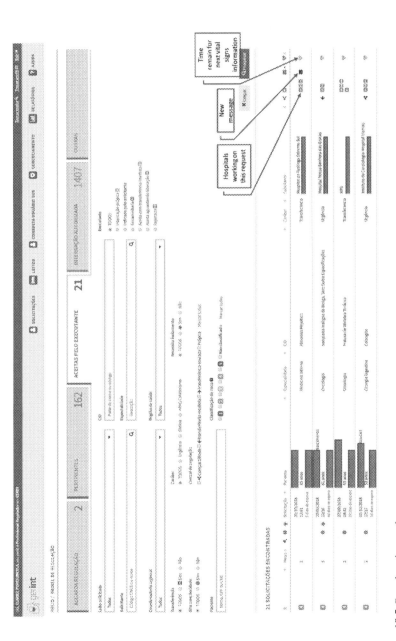

Figure 18.5 Regulator's panel.

the regulation center the specific alerts, such as unread messages, the hospitals to which the request has been sent, and the time remaining for the next development of the patient.

18.3.3 Integration

The responsibilities of the Municipal Health Secretariat as the manager of health services in the city entail integration with other services in the region (Fig. 18.6). It is in this context that the regulatory complex operates, with the following requirements:

- To regulate, monitor, and operationalize the control (quantitative and financial) of beds available.
- To standardize admission requests through treatment and regulatory protocols.
- To establish mechanisms for forwarding patients from one health service to another, in accordance with standardized flows and protocols.
- To establish, provide training for, orient, and monitor prioritization of access and the use of services with more adequate levels of complexity.
- To promote the use and improvement of information from national identification registers of users of the Brazilian public health service, healthcare establishments and professionals.
- To aid planning, control, evaluation, and auditing in healthcare.
- To aid the organization of flows of references between healthcare regions, in keeping with the agreement made for the state (regionalization).
- To regulate medical processes through the regulation and authorization centers.

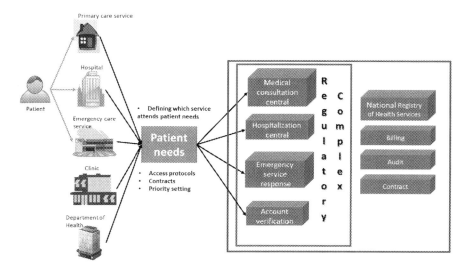

Figure 18.6 Illustration of the regulatory complex of Porto Alegre.

A look at the duties and competencies of the regulatory complex shows that integration is a basic requirement of the information system, from the viewpoint of access by different teams of the Municipal Health Secretariat, service providers, other secretariats, and the Health Secretariat of the State of Rio Grande do Sul. This is also true from the viewpoint of using basic information made available by the systems of the Ministry of Health, such as the National Health Card, a document that identifies users of the SUS, and the National Registry of Healthcare Establishments and Professionals, a registration system for all health services and professionals that treat SUS patients nationwide.

18.3.4 Organization

The Gerint is the result of cooperation between the ICT Service Company of the Municipality of Porto Alegre (Procempa), the Municipal Health Secretariat of Porto Alegre, and the Health Secretariat of the State of Rio Grande do Sul. Its purpose is to organize the access to the health system and support the flow of treatment based on epidemiological, sanitary, and social demands, guaranteeing treatment at different levels of complexity and in geographical territories (Assis & Jesus, 2012). The project involved the teams of the health secretariats of the state and city, with management professionals, field technicians, including two large hospitals in the city, and the Procempa systems development team. To analysis and design the system, in 2016, a work group of healthcare professionals and systems analysts was formed. The work group held meetings to define the scope of the project, redesign the flows of the regulatory complex, and defining system requirements and functions. These meetings were held three times a week for 4 months. The result of this work was registered in a document called the Product Vision Document, presented to all the coordinators of the Health Secretariat and submitted for the approval of the municipal and state health secretaries. For the development, Procempa used agile methods,[23] which advocate better communication between client and development team, more frequent deliveries of software and a faster response to possible changes in the project. The Procempa development team established iterations of 2 weeks, where the functionalities prioritized by the client and that would add value to the project more quickly were developed. At each iteration a version of the system was delivered to the client for evaluation and ratification.

After the first version that was considered functional the system was validated by the teams from two major hospitals in Porto Alegre, Nossa Senhora da Conceição (federal government) and Santa Casa de Misericórdia Hospital of Porto Alegre (private). With the collaboration of the teams from these two hospitals, in addition to validating the implemented processes, it was possible to make improvements in the functionalities of the system. A pilot project was implemented at Nossa Senhora da Conceição Hospital, where the system was tested for a month. Following this test, the other hospitals in Porto Alegre were added. In the phase of expanding the system to the whole city the teams form the other hospitals, mostly private, were responsible for redefining and enhancing the integration services of the systems.

[23] Further information at http://agilemanifesto.org/.

18.3.5 Time

Porto Alegre was one of the first cities in Brazil to implement Emergency Regulation Centers [Serviço de Atendimento Móvel de Urgência (SAMU)] for Admission and Regulation of Consultations and Examinations in the late 1990s, soon after assuming full management of health in the municipalization process and a few years after the promulgation of Federal Law no. 8.080, which regulated the Brazilian Public Health System.

In the early 2000s, there was a gradual increase in the volume of regulations in the city. It was only in 2008 that the Ministry of Health instituted a national policy for the regulation of the Brazilian Public Health System (SUS). With the growing volume of regulations and the need to have better controls on demand, Porto Alegre acquired on the market its first computerized system for regulating appointments and admissions and implemented it from 2010 to 2011. This system was also used by Rio Grande do Sul state. However, in the beginning of 2013, the system started showing signs of operational instability, and the supplier had difficulty in making adjustments and developing new functionalities.

To meet the need to conduct the regulatory process in keeping with legislation and facing the impossibility of maintaining the current system, in December 2014, the Municipal Health Secretariat decided to develop a new information system in partnership with the ICT Service Company of the Municipality of Porto Alegre (Procempa).

On the June 22, 2015, the work group was made official. The project was developed in integrated modules for scheduling management (Gercon) (Fig. 18.7) and admissions management (Gerint) (Fig. 18.8). The first module to be specified and developed was the one for the management of specialist appointments.

18.3.6 Cost

So far, the project has occupied around 16,000 hours of the Procempa technicians' time to specify, develop, and monitor its implementation. Following

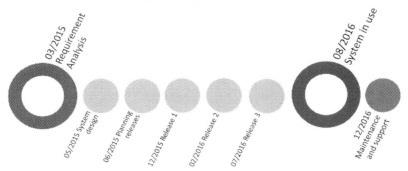

Figure 18.7 Schedule of the Gercon project.

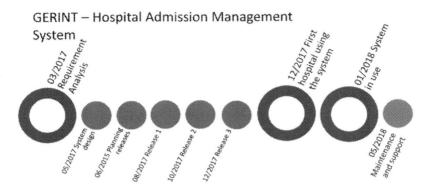

Figure 18.8 Schedule of the Gerint project.

implementation in January 2018, other implementations and versions of the system were agreed on with the Secretariat. The total sum of resources applied to the project by September 2018 was U$812,000.

To operate the two regulation centers of Porto Alegre the Health Secretariat has an annual total expenditure of U$6.2 million.

18.3.7 Quality

The project management group monitors the results of the system through indicators extracted from data warehouse[24] using a business intelligence[25] tool. This group has been defining a set of new indicators to continuously improve the process, such as number of hospitalizations by type of bed and average time of regulation by type of bed and priority. These are now being implemented and will permit the establishment of new metrics.

In order to monitor the performance of the regulation center the management group uses an effectiveness indicator. It's possible to observe an increase of about 26% on the effectiveness of the regulation process (see Fig. 18.9) if compared with last year results.

18.3.8 Risks

The main risk of the project was the possibility that hospitals would not participate in the integration process. As it is a system for forwarding patients that need to be admitted to hospital, the greatest demand is for information to be available to healthcare professionals as quickly and as accurately as possible. Without adequate integration services, hospitals and emergency rooms, which have their own information systems, would have to operate their systems and the Gerint, duplicating data, causing delays in the process and losses of information. This risk was

---

[24] https://en.wikipedia.org/wiki/Data_warehouse.
[25] https://en.wikipedia.org/wiki/Business_intelligence.

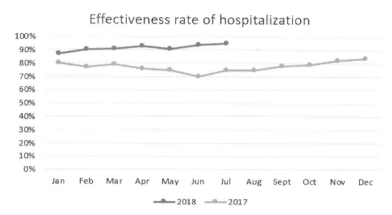

Figure 18.9 Effectiveness rate of hospitalization represents the rate of hospitalizations successfully resolved over the total number of requests made by emergency services.

mitigated through negotiations for contracts and partnerships held by the Municipal Health Secretariat of Porto Alegre.

The main hospitals of Porto Alegre are already 100% integrated into the Gerint. Consequently, the occupation and freeing up of over 60% of the beds in the city are updated in real time. All the specialized hospitals and services of the SUS in the city are integrated into the Gerint.

18.3.9 Procurement

Procempa is the ICT service company of the municipality of Porto Alegre. Its contract specifies that it should meet the requirements of diverse administration agencies, including those involved in healthcare. Every project is specified, budgeted and, following approval, managed in accordance with project management requirements.

18.3.10 Discussion—the fringes

The system was tested in a pilot implementation project in December 2017 with a single federal hospital, Nossa Senhora da Conceição. In January 2018 the other hospitals in the city were incorporated into the system, along with all the emergency services. The hospitals and emergency services in the rest of the state, which need to forward patients to the capital, have gradually been trained to use the Gerint system.

The interoperability between Gerint and hospital systems was developed originally with reference to two large hospitals in Porto Alegre. Further integration with other hospitals was challenging, and the development of these integration services was surely the most complex part of the project and required a great deal of reworking. The flaws in defining the scope of a project are the cause of flaws in many government technology projects (Anthopoulos, Reddick, Giannakidou, & Mavridis, 2016). In this case the project team redesigned these services in collaboration with the hospital staff involved. Each hospital has its own peculiarities in terms of processes and systems.

Although the system has only been completely implemented in Porto Alegre for 4 months, the results can already be evaluated.

- The map of hospital beds in Porto Alegre is already available to the Health Secretariat in real time.
- Around 60% of the SUS beds in the city are monitored through integration services between the Gerint and the systems of the largest hospitals.
- The other hospitals, which do not yet use the integration system, update information directly in the system.
- Obtaining information and the possibility of sharing requests between the municipal and state centers means a more effective search for a bed to guarantee that patients are forwarded to the service that best suits their needs.
- The exchange of messages between regulators and doctors in hospitals improves the understanding of a patient's case and the evaluation of his medical conditions.
- All requests for admission to hospitals in Porto Alegre are registered in the Gerint.

18.4 Conclusions

One of the major motivations of this project was the failure of the previous system, which had numerous problems, such as the lack of integration with hospitals and other specialist services, nor did it meet the requirements for regulation with other municipalities in the state. Regulation centers worked on each case by telephone, contacting other centers, and hospitals.

The new Gerint system can be integrated with the systems of service providers. The demands of the health secretariats included sharing information among diverse actors. The municipal and state secretariats and their regulation centers operate today in the same virtual space. They share patient's information while seeking to satisfy their needs. The one that solves the problem first is the one that forward the patient. When addressing a request, the system obeys the criteria of regionalization and targets referral institutions.

The connectivity infrastructure in Porto Alegre is good, which facilitates the interconnection of the network. However, the system meets the needs of regulation of other cities in the state, leading to the emergence of communication infrastructure problems that continue to be an obstacle to the expansion of the network to the outlying regions of the state.

Cooperation with the State Health Secretariat (SES) was fundamental when it came to achieving results. The SES team was integrated with the work group, and the system was designed to serve the entire state. By recognizing that healthcare is not limited to the borders of the city, both the state and the municipality can have an overview of how the patient moves within the health system and can provide a better service. This is a major differential compared with the other systems in the country, which conduct their regional regulation using telephone and messaging systems.

New modules are being developed that will complement the project. The integrated billing model for hospitals and the Health Secretariat will implement the billing rules defined by the Ministry of Health for SUS admissions to streamline payments to hospitals for the services they provide.

Dashboards for monitoring hospital services in the city are also under construction, based on a set of evaluation indicators for the regulation process and the effectiveness of hospitals in responding to requests. These indicators are defined in collaboration with the Municipal Health Secretariat of Porto Alegre.

The next challenge in improving public health services in Porto Alegre is the Electronic Patient Record project. The project, in the planning phase, scheduled to roll out on the beginning of 2020, will aggregate information from the various systems that support public health services. This medical record will aggregate information from systems, such as Gerint, with hospitalization information, Gercon, with specialist consultations, the dispensing system for medicines in municipal pharmacies [Sistema de Dispensação de Medicamentos (DIS)], as well as city's emergency services.

The challenge of this project is to seek and integrate citizen's entire health history, including care taken in the basic network, in specialized services, hospitals, clinics, and exams. In addition, this information must be presented succinctly and clearly to health professionals, ensuring safety, privacy, reliability, and traceability. Once again, the integration process between the various systems that serve the city's health services is essential for the success of this initiative.

Acknowledgments

This work was made possible by the municipal administration of Porto Alegre and the management of Procempa that freed the access to project information.

About the author

Paulo Roberto Miranda—CEO of the ICT Services Company of the Municipality of Porto Alegre (Procempa). He is a civil engineer with a Master's Degree in Management from the Federal University of Rio Grande do Sul. He has worked as the Municipal Secretary of Information and Technology for the Municipal Government of Curitiba, CEO of CELEPAR ICT Company of Paraná state, Technical Director of PROCERGS (ICT Company of Rio Grande do Sul state), and Superintendent of Federal ICT Services (SERPRO) in the states of Rio Grande do Sul and São Paulo. He has held the position of Executive Secretary for the Information Technology Council of Rio Grande do Sul state and Executive Director of the Computing Council of Paraná state. He has also worked as the Director of

Consultancy for BRISA (Partnership for the Development of Information Technology). He has over 30 years of experience in the fields of Information and Communications Technology, Strategic Planning and Technology Management in the public and private sector.

Clarice Stella Porciuncula is a systems analyst with a degree for the Pontifical Catholic University of Rio Grande do Sul (PUCRS), a specialist in Information Systems and Telematics through the Federal University of Rio Grande do Sul (UFRGS). She has worked at Procempa since 1985, in charge of serving the Municipal Health Secretariat of Porto Alegre. She has participated in a number of projects at the company, such as the Cooperative Health Project, which she coordinated. This project involved three other Brazilian capital cities in addition to Porto Alegre. She was responsible for the development and implementation of the Management Portal, a system for registering and monitoring the municipal government's strategic projects. Since 2014, she has coordinated the development of the Regulator Complex project, which includes the Gercon (Scheduling Management), Gerint (Hospital Admission Management), and GERPAC (High-Complexity Procedure Management) systems.

Maria Alexandra Cunha has 30 years of experience as a professor, IT professional, and consultant. She holds a Doctor's Degree in Business Administration from Universidade de São Paulo (USP), and she is a professor at Escola de Administração de Empresas de São Paulo (Sao Paulo Business School) of Fundação Getulio Vargas (FGV), in Master's Degree Program and Doctorate Program, where her line of research is Information Technology Management. She has been leading academic research and professional projects in IT governance, e-government, e-governance, and e-democracy, and on models for administering computerization in governments. More recently, her research interests are IT for development and smart cities. Professor Cunha is the author of several articles, technical reports, researches, chapters, and books, and she is the member of the editorial board of Brazilian academic journals in Business Administration. She coordinated for two mandates the "Information Management" area at ANPAD (Brazilian Academy of Management).

References

Anthopoulos, L., & Fitsilis, P. (2013). Using classification and roadmapping techniques for smart city viability's realization. *Electronic Journal of e-Government, 11*(2), 326–336.

Anthopoulos, L., Reddick, C. G., Giannakidou, I., & Mavridis, N. (2016). Why e-government projects fail? An analysis of the Healthcare.gov website. *Government Information Quarterly, 33*(1), 161–173.

Anthopoulos, L. G. (2015). *Understanding the smart city domain: A literature review. Transforming city governments for successful smart cities* (pp. 9–21). Cham: Springer.

Assis, M. M. A., & Jesus, W. L. A. D. (2012). Acesso aos serviços de saúde: abordagens, conceitos, políticas e modelo de análise. *Ciência & Saúde Coletiva, 17*, 2865–2875.

Barbosa, D. V. S., Barbosa, N. B., & Najberg, E. (2016). Regulação em Saúde: desafios à governança do SUS. *Cadernos Saúde Coletiva, 24*(1).

Brasil. (1988). *Constituição federal de 1988.*
Brasil. (2006). *Ministério da Saúde. Diretrizes para a implantação de Complexos Reguladores/ Ministério da Saúde, Secretaria de Atenção à Saúde, Departamento de Regulação, Avaliação e Controle de Sistemas.* Brasília: Ministério da Saúde. Available at <http://bvsms.saude.gov.br/bvs/publicacoes/DiretrizesImplantComplexosReg2811.pdf>.
Brasil. (2008). *Portaria No. 1.559/2008 do Ministério da Saúde do Brasil que institui a Política Nacional de Regulação do Sistema Único de Saúde—SUS.* Available at <http://bvsms.saude.gov.br/bvs/saudelegis/gm/2008/prt1559_01_08_2008.html>.
Brazilian Institute of Geography and Statistics (IBGE). (2018). *Projeção de População.* revisão 2018.
Castro, A. L. B. D., & Machado, C. V. (2010). A política de atenção primária à saúde no Brasil: notas sobre a regulação e o financiamento federal. *Cadernos de saúde pública, 26,* 693–705.
Chourabi, H., Nam, T., Walker, S., Gil-Garcia, J. R., Mellouli, S., Nahon, K., ... Scholl, H.J. (2012). Understanding smart cities: An integrative framework. In *45th Hawaii International Conference on System Science (HICSS), January 2012* (pp. 2289–2297). IEEE.
Comitê Gestor da Internet no Brasil. (2018). *Pesquisa TIC—Governo Eletrônico 2017.* São Paulo: Comitê Gestor da Internet no Brasil. <https://cetic.br/media/docs/publicacoes/2/TIC_eGOV_2017_livro_eletronico.pdf>.
CONASS. (2011). *Brasil. Conselho Nacional de Secretários de Saúde. Regulação em Saúde/ Conselho Nacional de Secretários de Saúde* (pp. 126). Brasília: CONASS. (Coleção Para Entender a Gestão do SUS2011, 10) ISBN: 978-85-89545-70-9.
Cunha, M. A., & Miranda, P. R. D. M. (2013). *O uso de TIC pelos governos:* uma proposta de agenda de pesquisa a partir da produção acadêmica e da prática nacional. *Organizações & sociedade, 20*(66), 543–566.
Cunha, M. A., Przeybiloviez, E., Macaya, J. F. M., & Santos, F. B. P. D. (2016). *Smart cities: Transformação digital de cidades.* São Paulo: Fundação Getulio Vargas.
Elias, P. E. (2004). Estado e saúde: os desafios do Brasil contemporâneo. *São Paulo em perspectiva, 18*(3), 41–46.
Farias, S. F., Gurgel, G. D., Jr., Costa, A. M., Brito, R. D. L., & Buarque, R. R. (2011). A regulação no setor público de saúde no Brasil: os (des) caminhos da assistência médico-hospitalar. *Ciência & saúde coletiva, 16,* 1043–1053.
IMF. (2018). *Country report—Brazil.* Available at <https://www.imf.org/en/Countries/BRA>.
Macadar, M. A., & Lheureux-De-Freitas, J. (2013). Porto Alegre: a Brazilian city searching to be smarter. In *Proceedings of the 14th annual international conference on digital government research* (pp. 56–64). ACM; June 2013.
Matos, R. (2012). Migração e urbanização no Brasil. *Revista Geografias, 8*(1), 7–23.
Menicucci, T. M. G. (2009). O Sistema Único de Saúde, 20 anos: balanço e perspectivas. *Cadernos de saúde pública, 25,* 1620–1625.
Miranda, P. R. M., Cunha, M. A. V. C., & Pugas Filho, J. M. (2016). *eParticipation in smart cities of developing countries: Research-based practical recommendations. Smarter as the New Urban Agenda* (pp. 315–332). Cham: Springer.
Moura, E. S. D. (2013). O direito à saúde na Constituição Federal de 1988. *Âmbito Jurídico,* Rio Grande, XVI, (114).
Paim, J., Travassos, C., Almeida, C., Bahia, L., & Macinko, J. (2012). Saúde no Brasil 1—O sistema de saúde brasileiro: história, avanços e desafios. *Veja, 6736*(11), 60054–60058.
Rodrigues, P. H. D. A. (2016). Os 'donos' do SUS. RECIIS. *Revista Eletrônica de Comunicação, Informação e Inovação em Saúde, 10*(4).

Further reading

Porto Alegre City Hall. *OP—25 anos em Porto Alegre (2014)*. <http://www2.portoalegre.rs.gov.br/smgl/default.php?p_secao = 86>.

Sinaleira 2020 Porto Alegre. *Agenda 2020*. (2018). <http://agenda2020.com.br/sinaleira/porto-alegre/> Acesso em 30.10.18.

Smart city of Algiers: defining its context

Kamila Ghidouche Ait-Yahia[1], Faouzi Ghidouche[1] and Gilles N'Goala[2]
[1]Ecole des Hautes Etudes Commerciales — EHEC, Kolea, Algeria,
[2]Montpellier Management Institute — MOMA Institute, Montpellier, France

Chapter Outline

19.1 Introduction 391
19.2 Background 392
    19.2.1 Concept evolution 392
    19.2.2 Definitions and dimensions 393
    19.2.3 Smart city limits 393
19.3 Project definition methodology 394
    19.3.1 Study area 394
    19.3.2 Integration and organization 395
    19.3.3 Schedule 396
    19.3.4 Funding 396
19.4 Research methodology: the case of Algiers 397
    19.4.1 Methodological approach 397
    19.4.2 Emerging results and discussion 398
19.5 Conclusion 403
About the authors 403
References 404
Further reading 405

19.1 Introduction

Around the world, several countries have initiated smart city projects to develop cities into "smarter" and more "residential" ones. Thus technology is deployed to solve problems and dysfunctions common to all major cities or metropolitan areas, such as high population growth, security problems, road traffic density, pollution, etc. The aim is to offer citizens a better quality of life.

Mahizhnan (1999) was the first to mention the concept of "smart city" by addressing Singapore case in a research paper. Since then, several authors have proposed to conceptualize and define the smart city that has become "popular" for both researchers and governments (Albino, Berardi, & Dangelico, 2015). While most authors agree that this concept is the provision of innovative solutions to improve citizens' daily lives, some still consider it to be ambiguous (Nam & Pardo, 2011) given the "cacophony" of existing definitions (Chourabi et al., 2012).

Referring to the work of Kitchin (2015) or Angelidou (2014), the success of smart city development strategies depends on the ability of political leaders to adapt to the local context and the needs of citizens. There is therefore no universal approach to start a smart city project; each city will have to find suitable solutions to the specific problems previously identified.

There are many cases in the academic literature of smart cities, which have been addressed, particularly in North America, Europe, and Asia. However, there is little research on African cities. Nonetheless, some, such as Zenâta in Morocco, Kigali in Rwanda, or Cotonou in Benin, have experienced considerable growth and are pioneers in innovation.

With regard to our research, we decided to address the case of Algeria (the largest country in Africa) and the city of Algiers in particular since it is one of the 10 most populated cities in Africa with almost 8 million inhabitants. As the project is still in its early stages, it seemed interesting to us to understand how and from what angle the smart city will be approached. In order to meet this objective, we opted for a qualitative approach by interviewing a group of information and communication technologies (ICT) experts as well as potential and/or involved stakeholders in the Algiers smart city project. The objective is to find out how the latter represent a smart city, how they plan to design it, and which dimensions should be integrated.

This chapter is planned as follows: after the introduction, we will present in Section 19.2 a general background on smart cities projects, while in Section 19.3, we will explain Algiers smart city project definition methodology and the scope of the study. Finally, in Section 19.4, we will discuss the main results of the exploratory study and draw conclusions.

19.2 Background

19.2.1 Concept evolution

At first, researchers used the terms "virtual city" (Graham & Aurigi, 1997) then "digital city" or "information city" to designate cities that took the opportunities offered by the web and ICT to promote the socialization of citizens, support local democracy (in the absence of public space), and develop urban marketing (Anthopoulos, 2017). In his literature review, Komninos (2018) explains that the concept of smart cities dates back to the late 1980s and can be found in the work of Hall (1988), Raynal (1988), and Lipman et al. (1986).

The concept of digital city was also mentioned in 1998 by Besselaar and Beckers who explained it as a broad infrastructure for virtual communities and as a space for exchange and sharing of common interests. However, Anthopoulos (2017, p. 15) highlighted the fact that the term "digital" goes beyond a single urban space and that the services provided could also benefit people who were not part of the "physical" community. At that time the most eloquent examples of digital cities were Amsterdam (as a result of an activist's efforts to open dialog between politicians and the community) and also the case of Kyoto where citizens' interactions were recorded using sensors and then reproduced in animation to analyze their behavior.

All these concepts have subsequently evolved toward "ubiquitous city" (omnipresent city); in this type of city the "data" (data) are omnipresent and integrated into the various urban infrastructure (Anthopoulos & Fitsilis, 2014). In fact, it is the South Korean government that has initiated this terminology with reference to cities that provide content and services to their users via fixed and mobile networks.

Over time, these concepts have evolved into more "sophisticated" ecosystems offering more intelligent services and allowing technological integration. This technological implementation can vary from simple information transmission (low level) to more intelligent systems taking into account quality of life and sustainable development (Anttiroiko, Valkama, & Bailey, 2014). Some researchers also show the concept of "intelligent city," which is much more focused on inventiveness, creativity, collective intelligence, and artificial intelligence (Lee, Hancock, & Hu, 2014). According to Anthopoulos (2017), the term "smart" should not be limited to the use of ICT; smartness can also refer to creative design or a new organization, so intelligence of a city is its ability to effectively mobilize all its resources.

19.2.2 Definitions and dimensions

Based on previous research, there are a variety of definitions for smart cities: Anthopoulos and Reddick (2016) describe them as cities that offer innovative solutions based mainly (but not exclusively) on ICT in order to improve citizens' daily lives and promote local sustainable development. Meijer and Bolívar (2016) define the concept of the smart city as the ability of a territory to attract and mobilize human capital in collaboration with stakeholders (individuals and organizations) using ICT.

Other authors, such as Van Kemenade (2017), prefer the definition of Giffinger et al. (2007) because it stresses on the importance of the citizen and describes the main dimensions of an intelligent city. In his work, "Understanding Smart Cities," published in 2017, Anthopoulos (2017) summarizes all these definitions by exposing the eight dimensions of a smart city: smart infrastructure, smart mobility (or transport), smart environment, smart services, smart governance, smart citizens, smart living environment, and smart economy.

19.2.3 Smart city limits

However, many authors have pointed out certain limitations of smart cities: first, they do not result directly from an assessment of user needs (Kitchin, 2015), but rather from the supply of large companies aimed at profit making (Douay and Henriot, 2016, p. 89). This often results in a mismatch between user needs and the available supply. Second is the risk of widening the digital divide and social and territorial inequalities. Thus if we take the example of certain cities, such as Rio or Singapore, only certain districts are concerned by these intelligent services and infrastructures, while others are simply disadvantaged. Finally, Hollands (2008) had published an article criticizing these cities "designated" or "labeled" "smart city" for promotional purposes only.

19.3 Project definition methodology

As previously mentioned, there are few studies on smart cities and their specificities in African countries, therefore in this section, we will discuss the case of a major North African city: Algiers (Fig. 19.1).

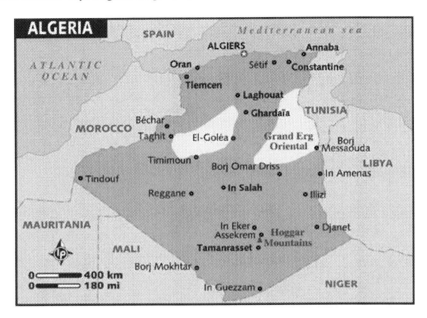

Figure 19.1 Algeria map.
Source: From www.lonelyplanet.com. Reproduced with permission from LonelyPlanet © 2019, Lonely Planet.

The first experiment had already been initiated in Algeria involving the new city of Sidi Abdellah (located to the west side of Algiers and inaugurated in 2011). This city introduced as "smart and integrative" promoted "high-tech" infrastructures as well as parks and extensive green spaces, but to date, this project is still unfinished. The additional projects for new cities as well as smart cities have been initiated but remained elusive.

19.3.1 Study area

The "Algiers smart city" project whose strategic plan was defined by the *Plan Directeur d'Aménagement et d'Urbanisme* (PDAU) up to 2035 aims to solve the major problems concerning Algiers in order to transform it into a cleaner, safer, more modern, more accessible, and more attractive city.

The strategic approach for the success of this project is based on the following principles (The Report, 2018):

- Initiate encouragement measures to motivate local start-ups and innovative companies to get involved in the project.

- Monitor, compare, and analyze previous experiences of smart cities in order to understand the reasons of their failure or their success. Moreover, the organization of the *Smart Cities Global technology and investment summit* on June 27 and 28, 2018 aimed to promote exchanges and partnerships between different stakeholders around the world.
- Introduce more flexible and favorable measures to attract technology giants and encourage them to invest in these projects.
- Investing in local talents, whether in Algeria or abroad, also to limit the flight of talents, a series of competitions for young talents are organized rewarding the best projects with considerable funding.

According to Algiers smart city implementation team, water, transport, and energy are the priority sectors to be considered.

Moreover, the city of Guenzet (located only 250 km far from Algiers) succeeded in saving 55% of energy in 1 year by setting up a center to manage in real time the public services connected to the city's system. Thanks to this center, it will be possible to detect technical problems and accelerate the intervention of municipal agents.

19.3.2 Integration and organization

The ICT sector in Algeria is considerably underdeveloped, and the current legislation is a major obstacle to its expansion. An experimental laboratory (Fig. 19.2) and a technological innovation hub were launched in April 2018. This laboratory will make it possible to test different solutions before their large-scale launch and will serve to set up a regulatory framework favorable to innovation. This common space should bring together companies, academic institutions, research laboratories, and

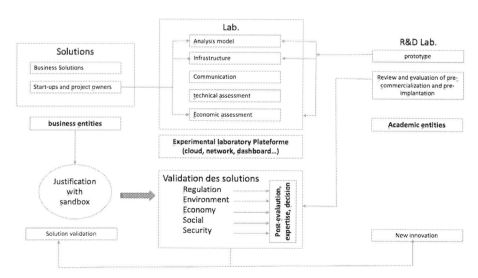

Figure 19.2 Large-scale experimental laboratory—fundamentals.
Source: From http://www.wilaya-alger.dz/fr/lancement-du-laboratoire-experimental-dinnovation-technologique/

politicians in order to generate synergies that will enable Algiers smart city project to develop more quickly and efficiently.

The innovation hub (Fig. 19.3) will be responsible for bringing local technological actors closer to the international community in order to provide them with adequate support and guarantee the success of their projects.

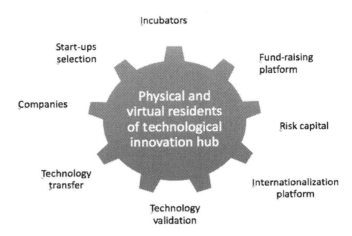

Figure 19.3 Hub of innovation—toolkit.
Source: From http://www.wilaya-alger.dz/fr/lancement-du-laboratoire-experimental-dinnovation-technologique/

19.3.3 Schedule

A first call for collaboration was launched in early June 2017 for different interested parties (start-ups, investors, research and development laboratories, universities, large companies, etc.) in order to gather different proposals. These proposals were used to develop a preliminary project plan in discussions between the city and potential solution providers. In April 2018 the experimental laboratory and innovation hub were launched, and a second call for proposals was made. In June 2018 the Smart Cities Global technology and Investment Summit was held in Algiers, and a progress report was presented.

19.3.4 Funding

In an interview conducted by The Report (2018), Riad Hartani (architect and designer of Algiers smart city project), who worked on other smart cities around the world, explained that the budget devoted to information systems was relatively low and that the biggest challenge would be to generate sustainable revenues through technology transfer.

To date the type of financing has taken the form of venture capital and prospective investments (The Report, 2018), but it is mainly the government that will initially have to provide funding for the project in the form of grants and subsidies.

19.4 Research methodology: the case of Algiers

19.4.1 Methodological approach

Given the rather broad and multidisciplinary nature of the field of research on smart cities and to understand the cultural context of our study, we opted for an exploratory study. We have therefore developed a semidirective interview guide based on three main themes: first, the representation of smart cities and the view of Algiers smart city project; second, the issues and expected impacts on all parties involved; and finally, the obstacles and limits relating to smart cities.

Once the guidelines were prepared, we conducted individual interviews with eight[1] persons: ICT experts, urban planners, and potential partners in the Algiers smart city project. For 2 months (between August 2017 and September 2017), we interviewed these persons either face to face, by telephone, or by Skype. The recorded interviews were transcribed and returned to the interviewees for final validation. Table 19.1 describes the profile of the interviewees, the manner in which the interview was conducted, and the duration.

Table 19.1 Profile and description of interviewees.

Names and companies	Time duration (h:min)	Function	Area of activity/years of experience
Iheb Tekkour Digitalex	1:15	Business manager/founder of Hawess	ICT and digital Experience: 15 years
Lilia Saïbi Systra	0:30	Project manager/training architect	Transport/mobility Experience: 11 years
Ali Abassen CDTA	0:25	Researcher	Technology Experience: 12 years
Youcef Boucherim ZTE Corporation	0:25	Director O&M and network services	Telecom and network solutions Experience: 22 years
Abdel Moula Karim On market	0:53	Associate director—cofounder	Marketing-oriented technologies Experience: 20 years
Riad Hartani Wilaya (gouvernorat)	1:00	Consultant and advisor on behalf of the Wilaya of Algiers for the Algiers smart city project	A.I. technological engineering Experience: 15 years
Mourad Hadj Saïd Algérie smart city Dz Ad displays	1:00	Managing director/founder	Communication and urban advertising Experience: 20 years
Raouf Ourzeddine Ad displays	1:00	Marketing and communication manager	Communication and urban advertising Experience: 3 years

ICT, Information and communication technologies.

---

[1] The number of people interviewed was determined according to the saturation criterion defined by Mucchielli, that is, from the eighth interview onward, we considered that the information collected was no longer current.

Regarding the processing and analysis of responses, we opted for a lexical analysis by context and a content analysis. In view of this type of analysis, the Sphinx IQ2 software seemed to be the most appropriate.

19.4.2 Emerging results and discussion

19.4.2.1 Methods

In this part of the research work, two sections were organized: the first presents the results of the lexical analysis by context and the orientation of responses and feelings. This technique seemed particularly appropriate since it intended to best illustrate the representation of smart cities by our interviewees (Mathieu, 2004). The second section will focus on content analysis, in particular to identify the dimensions to be given priority in the smart city project, the issues and expected impacts as well as the perceived obstacles and limitations.

19.4.2.2 Smart city representation (lexical and semantic analysis)

The word clusters presented in Fig. 19.4 were developed using the words that were most frequently cited and the dominant themes in the interviewees' speech (global word cluster and cluster per interviewee). This allowed us to deduce the respondents' representation of an intelligent city.

Figure 19.4 Representation of smart cities.
Source: Word cloud adapted from Sphinx IQ2.

The first observation that can be made from this is the predominance of themes and words related to "technology" (cited 138 times), which suggests that interviewees easily associate smart cities with technology. The "citizen" comes second with 100 quotes; in their discourses, interviewees insist that there can be no smart city without citizen involvement and participation. Finally, the major concern highlighted in the interviewees' comments concerns "transport and mobility" (cited 68 times). Everyone believes that mobility is a key dimension to be integrated into the Algiers smart city project.

However, if we examine the discourses more carefully, we can see that two trends emerging: one group (mainly that of the actors involved and/or potential actors) whose discourse is essentially focused on the technological aspects of the smart city, and the other group (mainly experts) highlights the citizen and the problems concerning Algiers. It also appears that issues related to the environment and sustainable development are rarely mentioned, except for waste treatment mentioned by two interviewees.

Although many difficulties were raised in the speeches (transport, mobility, population growth, etc.), the tendency of the responses reflects a positive orientation (46.8%), the rest being classified by the program as neutral or negative responses.

19.4.2.3 Content analysis

To carry out this content analysis, we focused on the three main categories identified through the interviews: first, we will outline the priority dimensions to be integrated into the Algiers smart city project, then we will discuss the challenges and expected impacts on the various stakeholders, and finally we will end with the project's obstacles and limits (Table 19.2).

Table 19.2 Themes distribution.

Mobility	14.5%
Transport	11.8%
Accessibility	3.9%
Roads	3.3%
Governance	**14.5%**
Online services	5.3%
Informative	3.9%
Organized	3.3%
Modern	2.6%
Digital inclusive	2%
Citizens	**11.8%**
Involved/concerned	6.6%
Participate	4.6%
Collaborate/cocreate	2%

19.4.2.4 A key aspect of the Algiers smart city project

If we refer to the preliminary results, two aspects seem to be a priority according to our interviewees: mobility and governance. One of the major problems in Algiers is the traffic density, traffic jams, and the relatively poor road conditions. For this reason, actors and experts believe that this aspect should be given priority, as should the governance aspect, which should be more modern and encourage digital inclusion. In addition, the interviewees agree that the citizen is a key dimension of the project. Besides being involved, informed, and aware, it must be the departure point and the purpose of any smart city project. Finally, contrary to the trends and concerns of developed countries, it is also noted that the environmental and sustainable development dimension is very little present in the discourse of the interviewees, only waste management was mentioned (Table 19.3).

Table 19.3 Identified topics and example of verbatim.

Identified topics	Verbatim
Mobility	• "An efficient city where it is easy to find your way around and access various public and private services (transport, shops, etc.)" (Lilia Saïbi) • "One of the main problems of Algiers is the road network, which is not up to date" (Iheb Tekkour) "The second aspect, very important that one, is transport (mobility), the time spent in transport is enormous" (Mourad Hadj Said)
Governance	• There is also a particular culture to instill in citizens and a major communication and awareness-raising effort to be carried out with them • Before speaking about smart city, you need an intelligent citizen who is the central core of the smart city, so he must be involved in the heart of the project by offering simple services (Y. Boucherim)
Citizen	• The citizen has a user role, so he must be sensitized in this sense (Ali Abassen) • The human being must be at the core of the discussion and so it is necessary to consider citizens' lives, solving their problems and optimizing the way these problems are managed (Abdel Moula Karim)

19.4.2.5 Challenges and impact for participants

According to the responses of the interviewees, the challenges are mainly technological, economic, and security. In terms of impact and fallouts, this should be a "win−win" situation for everyone: first of all, an intelligent city would allow the development of a high-performance ecosystem in which companies, start-ups, research centers, and political decision-makers could work together in the interest of all.

The citizen, for his part, would gain in quality of life. He would be more productive and less stressed, since he is at the center of the project priorities. Therefore the solutions provided in the smart city project must be concrete and quickly noticeable. Finally, the fallouts will also be economic, and in terms of attractiveness and influence, Algiers has a strategic geographical location constituting one of the gateways to other African countries; moreover, many infrastructures are planned: for example, the Trans-Saharan road Algiers-Lagos (Nigeria) (end of 2018) (Table 19.4).

Table 19.4 Expected challenges and impacts of the smart city project.

Topics	Verbatim "challenges and impacts"
Development of a high-performance ecosystem	• The strategic challenge is to know how to integrate information technology into city management, and enhance the intelligent city aspect, so that it can be a catalyzer for the development of technological ecosystems (as Singapore) (an interview with Riad Hartani) • "The participation of large companies, especially those which provide services on a large scale such as energy, water, cleaning services, etc.), must be involved by providing access to their data (open data) (...). Start-ups will then be the main motor of innovation and will deploy services and applications" (Ali Abassen) • "Everyone contributes to the structure. With his level of competence and requirement, citizens are supposed to express their problems, start-ups must provide technological solutions and this constitutes a global ecosystem, politicians are supposed to initiate a willingness and a development strategy in regard to all this" (interview with Abdel Moula Karim)
Life quality	• "In theory, the interest of the citizen comes first, since his quality of life will be improved, he will be more productive, and spend less time in transport (traffic jams), he will live in a cleaner city and be less stressed, he will be able to lead a decent life and his vision of the future will be better" (Mourad Hadj Said) • The motivation is the quality of life, but it is an abstract concept, we must find a way to show concrete results that have a direct impact on citizen daily life (Riad Hartani)
Economic impact/ territorial attractiveness	• "Encourage the digital economy and provide work for innovative companies. The main issue is twofold: the citizen's quality of life and the economic situation in Algeria, which could lead to export in the digital field (software)" (Ali Abassen) • "Algiers' strategic location requires it to be part of a smart city approach. The capital is compelled to rise to the challenge, particularly with the 4600 km Trans-Saharan road network that will link Algeria to Lagos (Nigeria). Algiers therefore does not have the right to be an ordinary capital but a reference point. Unfortunately, considering the way things are done, we are not close to achieve it. Just observe the difficulty we have in managing garbage collection, and you will understand everything" (Iheb Tekkour) • "Several issues, including economic ones. Just by solving traffic jam problems, most parties would benefit" (Raouf Ourzeddine)
Security measures	• "Algerian websites are hosted abroad. Most people's data are stored on hard disks that can be lost at any time. This implies the priority of creating data centers and setting up an optical fiber network" (Youcef Boucherim) • "Obviously, we must not forget the aspect of data protection, infrastructure security and the fight against cybercrime" (Youcef Boucherim)

19.4.2.6 Obstacles and constraints

According to our interviewees, since a smart city project requires a very long time (between 20 and 40 years), several obstacles can arise: first, aspects relating to the slowness of the authorities' decisions and consequently the budgets allocated will necessarily create a time lag because of technology quick evolution. The second important point is the lack of visibility and concrete solutions for the citizen.

Interviewees believe that if politicians communicate on smart city with a futuristic vision focused on technology, there will be a demobilization and distrust from citizens.

In conclusion the smart cities constraints are related to digital divide and social cohesion. However, respondents minimized this risk, arguing that they have confidence in the Algerian government, which has always "promoted digital inclusion." Others believe that a smart city project is not "supposed to be a war against inequalities" (Table 19.5).

Table 19.5 Obstacles and constraints.

Topics	Verbatim (obstacles and constraints)
Budget/ organization long procedure	• "The most challenging aspect is the complexity of choosing the sector and the solution to these problems. They are also long-term projects that require a large budget and as previously reported, it takes perseverance" (Riad Hartani) • "You know, the biggest constraint in smart city is that technology advances fast while governmental decision process is slow, so there is a gap between technology and execution and that is the problem that must be solved first" (Riad Hartani)
Overly futuristic vision of the project	• We must not go into "futuristic raves." A smart city requires smart citizens, technical skills, and appropriate structure (which is not yet the case in Algeria) (Iheb Tekkour) • "An intelligent city (…), not just about the futuristic aspects of the city, 'space,' flying cars, robots (at least it's not just that)" (Karim Abdel Moula)
Concern/distrust/ fear	• "We must not use the term 'smart city,' this imported term that may frighten citizens, it is better to talk about a new organization, about simplification" (Iheb Tekkour) • "If they play too much on the futuristic aspect, they will only accentuate the complex and the Algerian resistance against ICTs" (Iheb Tekkour) • Fear of new technologies, either for difficulties in understanding these tools, or losing confidentiality about personal data (Lilia Saïbi) • "Of course, there must be a high speed network, which allows data transfer, especially in the era of big data. We also need a powerful security system" (Youcef Boucherim)
Digital divide and social cohesion	• "Unequal conditions are part of our world, it would be utopian to say to ourselves that we are all the same, (…). There are all social classes in a city, it is not war against inequality. Politically the government is supposed to reduce the gap between categories, but its mission is to ensure the minimum social level to offer the new generations the same chances of success" (Abdel Moula Karim) • "Algeria has always adopted a policy of digital inclusion (universal service), since the project will have public funding" (Ali Abassen)

ICT, Information and communication technologies.

19.5 Conclusion

The global interest of public authorities in smart cities is now an established fact. If the importance of this type of project is well known, the most difficult is to identify the issues related to strategic sectors of each city and to know where to start. Previous research illustrated specific priorities and challenges in the developed countries: environment and sustainable development. This is not the case for emerging countries where literature scarcity in African countries is evident. The objective of this research is to illustrate the specificities of a North African city (Algiers) in order to understand how a smart city project can be implemented there.

Given the innovation of the project, we opted for an exploratory approach by conducting interviews with Algerian ICT experts and potential actors. A lexical and semantic method allowed us to get their representation of a smart city: technology and mobility.

Therefore in order to determine the key dimensions, issues, and barriers, we choose to conduct a content analysis: it appears that mobility and governance were priority dimensions, and that the issues and impacts would affect the city's economy, quality of life, and attractiveness. As for the obstacles and limits, the experts expressed that a too "futuristic" vision could frighten the citizen and create a gap between their perceptions and reality.

Finally, the limits relating to digital divide and social cohesion were highlighted but underestimated, particularly because the government has always adopted a "digital inclusion" policy, or because it was "utopian" to design an "ideal city."

This contribution enriches the literature by shedding light on the specificities of a North African smart city. Concerning the managerial implications, it is essential for citizens to be more involved and for politicians to pay more attention to their needs and problems.

One of the limits of our work is that we did not take into account urban planners and sociologists point of views, who may have approached the subject from a different perspective. In our future research, we also plan to consider citizens' point of views and compare them with the results of this study. An intercultural approach (developed vs emerging countries) would also be valuable in identifying possible similarities and discrepancies.

About the authors

Kamila Ghidouche Aït-Yahia is a senior lecturer at Ecole des Hautes Etudes Commerciales (EHEC) Business School (Kolea University Center—Algeria). She currently teaches marketing principles, consumer behavior, and communication. Her major research interests are related to different marketing applications, more specifically, place branding, smart cities, city image assessment and improvement, events' effect on cities, territorial attractiveness, and citizen participation. She is the member of scientific committee in various international conferences on marketing and tourism in North Africa.

Faouzi Ghidouche is a senior lecturer at HEC Algiers (business school—Kolea University Center—Algeria). He teaches supply chain management, inventory management, and merchandizing. He completed his PhD in business sciences and received an accreditation to direct researches from HEC Algiers. His major research interests are large-scale trade, supply chain management, and place branding. He contributed in many conferences related with trade and services in the emergent countries.

Gilles N'Goala is a professor in Montpellier Management Institute. He is also the president of French Marketing Association (AFM). He is the head of marketing innovation and territories master. His research interests are related to customer relationship, smart cities, and digital.

References

Albino, V., Berardi, U., & Dangelico, R. M. (2015). Smart cities: Definitions, dimensions, performance, and initiatives. *Journal of Urban Technology*, 22(1), 3−21.

Angelidou, M. (2014). Smart city policies: A spatial approach. *Cities*, 41, S3−S11.

Anthopoulos, L. G. (2017). *Smart government: A new adjective to government transformation or a trick? Understanding smart cities: A tool for smart government or an industrial trick?* Springer International Publishing.

Anthopoulos, L. G., & Fitsilis, P. (2014). Smart cities and their roles in city competition: A classification. *International Journal of Electronic Government Research (IJEGR)*, 10(1), 63−77.

Anthopoulos, L. G. & Reddick, C. G. (2016). Smart city and smart government: Synonymous or complementary? In *Proceedings of the 25th international conference companion on world wide web* (pp. 351−355). International World Wide Web Conferences Steering Committee.

Anttiroiko, A. V., Valkama, P., & Bailey, S. J. (2014). Smart cities in the new service economy: Building platforms for smart services. *AI & Society*, 29(3), 323−334.

Chourabi, H., Nam, T., Walker, S., Gil-Garcia, J. R., Mellouli, S., Nahon, K., & Scholl, H. J. (2012). Understanding smart cities: An integrative framework. In *2012 45th Hawaii international conference on system science (HICSS)* (pp. 2289−2297). IEEE.

Douay, N., & Henriot, C. (2016). La Chine à l'heure des villes intelligentes. *L'Information géographique*, 80(3), 89−102.

Giffinger, R., Fertner, C., Kramar, H., Kalasek, R., Pichler-Milanovic, N., & Meijers, E. (2007). *Smart cities. Ranking of European medium-sized cities, final report*. Vienna, UT: Centre of Regional Science.

Graham, S., & Aurigi, A. (1997). Virtual cities, social polarization, and the crisis in urban public space. *Journal of Urban Technology*, 4(1), 19−52.

Hall, P. (1988). *Cities of tomorrow: An intellectual history of urban planning and design*. Oxford: Blackwell Publishing.

Hollands, R. G. (2008). Will the real smart city please stand up? Intelligent, progressive or entrepreneurial? *City*, 12(3), 303−320.

Kitchin, R. (2015). The promise and peril of smart cities. *Computers and Law: The Journal of the Society for Computers and Law*, 26(2). Available from https://www.scl.org/articles/3385-the-promise-and-perils-of-smart-cities, Accessed 13 January 2018.

Komninos, N. (2018). Smart cities. In B. Warf (Ed.), *The SAGE encyclopedia of the Internet* (pp. 783−789). Sage Publications.

Lee, J. H., Hancock, M. G., & Hu, M.-C. (2014). Towards an effective framework for building smart cities: Lessons from Seoul and San Francisco. *Technological Forecasting and Social Change, 89*, 80−99.

Lipman, A. D., et al. (1986). *Teleports and the intelligent city*. Homewood, IL: Dow Jones-Irwin.

Mahizhnan, A. (1999). Smart cities: The Singapore case. *Cities, 16*(1), 13−18.

Mathieu, J. P. (2004). L'analyse lexicale par contexte: Une méthode pertinente pour la recherche exploratoire en marketing. *Décisions Marketing, 34*, 67−77.

Meijer, A., & Bolívar, M. P. R. (2016). Governing the smart city: A review of the literature on smart urban governance. *International Review of Administrative Sciences, 82*(2), 392−408.

Nam, T. & Pardo, T. A. (2011). Conceptualizing smart city with dimensions of technology, people, and institutions. In *Proceedings of the 12th annual international digital government research conference: Digital government innovation in challenging times* (pp. 282−291). ACM.

Raynal, M. (1988). *Distributed algorithms and protocols*. New York City: John Wiley & Sons.

The Report. (2018). *Alger smart city: Practical and pragmatic*. Oxford Business Group.

Van Kemenade, E. (2017). Smart universities walk the talk of commitment. In *International conference on quality in education and training 2017, innovative universities for smart cities, Kenitra, 12−13 May*.

Further reading

Marsal-Llacuna, M. L., Colomer-Llinàs, J., & Meléndez-Frigola, J. (2015). Lessons in urban monitoring taken from sustainable and livable cities to better address the smart cities initiative. *Technological Forecasting and Social Change, 90*, 611−622.

Van den Besselaar, P., & Beckers, D. (1998). Demographics and sociographics of the Digital City. In T. Ishida (Ed.), *Community computing and support systems. Social interaction in networked communities* (pp. 108−124). Springer.

Zubizarreta, I., Seravalli, A., & Arrizabalaga, S. (2015). Smart city concept: What it is and what it should be. *Journal of Urban Planning and Development, 142*(1), 04015005.

The smart city of Johannesburg, South Africa

Kelvin Joseph Bwalya
University of Johannesburg, Johannesburg, South Africa

Chapter Outline

20.1 Introduction 407
20.2 Background 409
20.3 Research methodology: case study 411
    20.3.1 Scope and timeline 412
    20.3.2 Integration 413
    20.3.3 Organization 413
    20.3.4 Time 414
    20.3.5 Cost 414
    20.3.6 Discussion—the fringes 415
Conclusions 416
Acknowledgments 417
About the authors 417
References 418

20.1 Introduction

The Johannesburg Smart City project was conceived under the leadership of President Thabo Mbeki, further conceptualized under the leadership of President Jacob Zuma, and currently being realized for operationalization by the Johannesburg city (Dlodlo, Mbecke, Mofolo, & Mhlanga, 2013). The orientation toward smart city is espoused upon the desire to position Johannesburg as one of the world class cities. The inclination toward a smart city will help the city of Johannesburg to position itself as an agile city, which has the capacity to rigorously overcome its problems and future challenges. Unlike other cities in Africa, Johannesburg faces unique problems that need to be overcome using strategic and sustainable means. Some of these include ever-increasing noise levels, growing urbanization, energy problems, unmanageable traffic woes, congestion, pollution, crime, information overload, unemployment, etc. This chapter explores that Johannesburg positioning itself as a smart city by presenting the different strategic initiatives being implemented.

According to Lea (2017), smart cities are conceptualized upon many different concepts that form a complex ecosystem geared to improving different aspects of individual citizens, city authorities (toward intelligent public administration and policy-making), local companies and organizations, and community groupings (Asimakopoulou & Bessis, 2011; Dlodlo et al., 2013). A smart city is a multidimensional and multifaceted conceptualization that can manifest in many aspects of the socioeconomic establishment. According to the ISO standards, smart cities are geared toward cities that can easily adapt to changing environmental settings, where information can pervasively be accessed, and decisions made intelligently in a sustainable manner. (Anthopoulos, 2017). The conceptualization of smart cities is conceptualized upon *"ISO/TC 268, sustainable cities and communities," "ISO 37100, sustainable cities and communities—Vocabulary,"* and *"ISO 37120, sustainable development in communities—Indicators for city services and quality of life."* Some of the specific standards include *"ISO 26000, guidance on social responsibility," "ISO 17742, energy efficiency and savings calculation for countries, regions and cities," "ISO 39001, road traffic safety (RTS) management systems," "ISO 24510, activities relating to drinking water and wastewater services—Guidelines for the assessment and for the improvement of the service to users," "ISO/IEC 30182, smart city concept model—Guidance for establishing a model for data interoperability,"* etc. There are also three standards in development such as *"ISO/IEC 21972, information technology—An upper level ontology for smart city indicators," "ISO/IEC 27550, information technology—Security techniques—Privacy engineering," "ISO/IEC 27551, information technology—Security techniques—Requirements for attribute-based unlinkable entity authentication"*. A full list of standards can be seen at (https://www.iso.org/files/live/sites/isoorg/files/store/en/PUB100423.pdf).

Despite the occupancy of technology as the central prerequisite for a city's transition toward a smart city, it is not the only requirement. Smart city entails improvement of different socioeconomic infrastructures such as having in place smart university and education, which is inspired by context and desired future orientation hinged on global principles (Gil-Garcia, Pardo, & Nam, 2016). Because of the relative newness of the concept, there are no globally accepted principles or single-route strategies that can be followed toward design and realization of smart cities. However, the consensus is building around the interplay and balance of smart public administration, smart governance, smart resources, city planning and design, and Information and Communications Technology (ICT) integration into the urban and regional spaces for a connected and integrated city socioeconomic infrastructure (Nfuka & Rusu, 2010).

The realization of a smart city requires a lot of city's design attributes to dovetail together (Paroutis, Bennett, & Heracleous, 2012). The different requirement for achieving spatial intelligence where different information resources can be accessed pervasively anywhere, anytime, and using any device (Marcelino-Sádaba, González-Jaen, & Pérez-Ezcurdia, 2015). There are equally important requirements such as community engagement into the governance infrastructure of the city (citizen inclusiveness), overall city administration styles, information integration transcending toward ubiquitous information management that can service the different information needs in the citizens living cycles, data quality, privacy and security, city design taking into consideration sustainability requirements. These requirements are integrated into the overall design of the smart city concept (Hall, 2000; Harrison et al., 2014).

Despite the advancements toward smart city development in Johannesburg, there are still so many challenges that need to be addressed. These key challenges need to be solved if the city of Johannesburg were to be able to accommodate a variety of individuals and businesses coming from diverse backgrounds. Many of these challenges have been accumulating from the time of apartheid to now where the socioeconomic dimensions have kept changing in order to be abreast with the globalization trends. Some of the entrenched problems were brought about by the apartheid policies, such as the Group Areas Act that ensured that whites and blacks settled in designated areas and had to obtain permission to go to another area. Because of the Areas Act, many social infrastructures in the city of Johannesburg metropolitan are not developed to the desired levels.

With the ever-increasing population of people in Johannesburg and a lot of people migrating to the cities in the realm of economic migration and increased urbanization, there is more pressure on merger resources (NIUA & PEARL, 2014). Increased urbanization will ultimately culminate into increased pressure on the merger resources, such as water, electricity/gas, sanitation/waste management, Internet connectivity, and transportation or traffic management. For example, at the moment, a distance of 23 km may end up taking 3 hours during peak hours, which is a notorious loss of productivity on the city. Intelligent traffic management in the realm of smart city is more than needed in such a contextual setting. How do you design cities to reduce pollution? Despite the aforementioned contextual challenges, Johannesburg is ranked first in Africa in terms of urban development and ICT maturity (BusinessTech., 2017). However, in order to keep this competitiveness, there is need to keep pushing the peddle of strategic innovation as a lacunae for a sustained smart city orientation. Currently, there are two fronts of creating a smart city that are underway—the main Johannesburg polity and Modderfontein. This chapter explores the different initiatives that are currently being explored in Johannesburg. The different interventions being explored in the context of smart city Johannesburg dovetail into the contemporary and anticipated urban planning.

This chapter is arranged as follows: the next section presents the background that articulates the formulaic and principle concepts attributed to the conceptualization of smart cities. Then, the methodological nuances of this research are discussed together with the scope defining this research. Further, the concepts of integration, time, cost, and organization with regards to the Johannesburg Smart City project are discussed. The discussion section presents both the technical and managerial aspects of the Johannesburg Smart City project enshrined onto the Modderfontein project. The chapter concludes by giving a recap of the different issues that have been discussed in this chapter.

20.2 Background

The smart city conceptualization in Johannesburg is as a result of the international campaign going around the globe to have competitive cities delve toward smart cities. There is a unison understanding that cities built upon the concepts of smart cities will be competitive and will go a long way in being sustainable (Kramers, Hojer, Lovehagen, & Wangel, 2014). The other motivation is that many of the government departments are standalone and do not easily and readily share information as most of the government business processes are not integrated. The result of such an infrastructure is that it is difficult to achieve the desired service levels in the public services. Smart city advocate for a socioeconomic infrastructure hinged on ICTs where government and private organizations can easily share information and business processes.

The design and establishment of smart city Johannesburg is done in two phases and spread over a period of 40 years. In the first phase the key organizational schema pursued in the design of a smart city Johannesburg is initially a public spending initiative led by the Mayoral office. The key spending in the first phase is toward the erection of public Wi-Fi hotspots to increase Internet accessibility. In the second phase the key organizational schema will be a public—private coalition where the key developer of the Modderfontein city will source funding from China to build a brand-new city from starch. As a key stakeholder, the city of Johannesburg will be involved in the different phases of the development.

This case specifically looks at the establishment of smart health and intelligent transportation that can be achieved in the realm of smart cities. Although this is the case, it is clear that the case of Johannesburg is still in its nascent stages and has a lot to do with regards to establish a requisite and sustainable and connected socioeconomic infrastructure.

Sustainable development is benchmarked against the UN Sustainable Development Goals (SDGs) that include entities, such as climate action, financial and social inclusion, poverty reduction, better health, and sanitation (Bate & Robert, 2007). Smart cities will have their socioeconomic infrastructure geared toward being a key player in the attainment of the SDGs. Sustainability in the contemporary ICT era entails the integration of ICTs in various socioeconomic value chains such as in transport (toward intelligent transport systems) and energy sector (toward renewable and green energy systems), communications sphere, public service delivery platforms; so sustainability is rightly achieved by continued innovation in all sectors of the economy. Johannesburg presents itself as a ripe ground to bleed innovation given its relatively easiness to access to capital and markets, good policy resumes, etc. Generally, there have been different efforts propagated by the city of Johannesburg government in a view to nurture innovation. Most of these efforts are embedded into the different official and nonofficial interventions and projects (Dlodlo et al., 2013). As a result, there has been an increased emphasis on the need for increased innovation at different levels of the socioeconomic hierarchy.

Johannesburg has been ranked as the city at the forefront of urban development propagated by higher maturity and massive penetration of ICTs. The level of development of smart cities is measured by the Ericsson Networked Society City Index that measures the level of sustainable urban socioeconomic development and ICT maturity. Using the 2016 version of this index, Johannesburg ranked 35th out of 41 cities around the world ahead of cities, such as Dhaka, Mumbai, Cairo, Delhi. The city of Johannesburg has entered into smart partnerships, such as triple/quadruple helix, public—private partnerships, citizen participation in order to overcome the challenges that act as roadblocks in the realization of smart cities.

20.3 Research methodology: case study

The chapter is a case study focusing on Johannesburg hinged on the extensive review of policy documents, journal articles, and anecdotal evidence on the status of development of Johannesburg toward smart city. Johannesburg is situated in Gauteng province houses 13.39 million of the 56 million people in South Africa. Johannesburg itself has a population of 4.94 million people as of 2016. It is estimated that Johannesburg receives about 3027 migrants each month demonstrating its ever-increasing pressure on its socioeconomic infrastructure and opportunities. The city has a current average gross domestic product per capita of around US$ 9000 pushing Johannesburg into the middle-income economy bracket.

Johannesburg has higher levels of unemployment (28%) and has one of the highest levels of inequality in the world (Gini = 0.66). There are generally disparities in the annual earnings according to race: white are the highest, followed by the Indians, colored and then Africans. Almost half (42%) of the poor population are food insecure—live below the recommended minimum dietary energy consumption.

Johannesburg faces entrenched challenges, such as slow economic growth cemented by a weaker currency, ever-increasing interest rates thereby culminating into massive youth unemployment; massive environmental decay brought about by consistent climate change makes the city to be ranked 13th in the world of greenhouse gas emission—making Johannesburg susceptible to wave-related death, floods, etc.; breakdown in the service delivery due to decaying socioeconomic infrastructure, such as broken traffic lights, potholes; entrenched poverty and inequality exacerbated by income inequality (Gini of 0.66 way above the UN distress level of 0.4), lack of food security and resilience, and the negative effect of the Apartheid Department Trajectory has made the poor to be densely populated in the same territories; ever-increasing social disconnect brought about by increased xenophobic attacks and crime putting a direct demand on the authorities to come up with strategies on building an inclusive and cohesive community.

The overarching agenda for the establishment of smart city is hinged on the Johannesburg 2040 Growth and Development Strategy. The 2040 Strategy is a set of initiatives designed by the Johannesburg city government and other stakeholders to achieve the different national and international developmental strategies. The 2040 Strategy is hinged upon the adopted SDGs, the New Urban Agenda (roadmap for driving the implementation of the SDGs), the Africa Agenda toward 2063 (advancing the pan-African vision of a prosperous, integrated, and peaceful Africa driven by its citizens), and the different national development plans.

20.3.1 Scope and timeline

The city of Johannesburg (also referred to as Jozi, Joburg, or Egoli) is South Africa's biggest city located in the Witwatersrand range of hills. The city has an area of 1645 km^2. The city was discovered around the early 19th century as a gold-mining settlement. Historical and contemporary information about Johannesburg can be found on www.joburg.co.za.

The city of Johannesburg has many suburbs separated by different levels of economics. Basically, the city is surrounded by inner suburbs, such as Eastern (Bedfordview, Edenvale), South-Eastern (Soweto, Roodepoort), Northern (Sandton, Midrand, Saxonwold, Rosebank), North-Western (Randburg). In order to peddle the smart city agenda, the city government has municipal companies that help in achieving transition toward a smart city. In order to manage waste a municipal company Pikitup was formed to manage refuse collection and Joburg City Power to manage the collection of electricity tariffs.

The quality of life in Johannesburg, especially in the northern suburbs, is comparable to most advanced cities in the world. There are different apps available that are used to enhance the quality of life for citizens and visitors. Some of the apps include Namola—a free app that enables crime response keeping oneself and others safe; Cell 411—a safety application that can be used to capture videos of crime or alert others about the incidence bypassing the police and calling groups of friends and relatives to respond to crime; Kitestring—a web-based service that checks works through inaction to determine the safety of an individual; 911 Response App— it is specially meant to protect tourists in case of an emergency; Uber for police—it is used when stationary and can be used to call the police when in panic; Iceplus—this gives access to country-wide armed response, etc. These different apps are used in a bid to overcome the hurdles for defeating crime in Johannesburg.

Through the intelligent transport system partners in South Africa, there have been workshops on "transport data" and "sustainability," which are cornerstones of smart cities today. Today, the Gautrain is a flagship green transport mode, which is smart in the true sense of the word. This intelligent transport mode has significantly reduced congestion on the roads in Gauteng province. The Gautrain uses electrical power so there are no significant carbon emissions into the environment and a timed transport service culminating into smart and intelligent service.

There are so many applications attributed to smart cities especially in the context of Johannesburg. For example, health-care system can be designed in such a way that it is interconnected allowing the exchange of patient records and medical history allowing informed treatment of ailments by any medical facility. Because of standardized records and integrated systems, a patient will be able to visit any hospital of choice and still expect to get the same quality health service that could have been received anywhere. The intelligent transport system that comes with full development of smart cities will unlock opportunities where citizens will be able to know which transport roadways will be congested at a given time so as to avoid them. Further, citizens will be able to know the exact location and status of the transport they are waiting for at any time. Intelligent transport systems entail that there will be few road traffic accidents. Since there will be pervasive access to information given the installation of public Wi-Fi hotspots throughout the city of Johannesburg, citizens will be able to make informed instantaneous decisions thereby avoiding being the subjects of crime and understanding where contemporary opportunities may be. Because of the advanced information infrastructure, many of the citizens will be able to work from the comfort of their homes.

The conceptualization of the US$8 billion Johannesburg Smart City project anchored by the Modderfontein project started almost a decade ago. Construction on the project began in early 2015. Although the project was originally designed to be done and fully operational by 2040, there is now talk of a delay that could extend the project life span to 2060. One thing is good though—there is commitment from different stakeholders that this project will go on despite all the odds.

20.3.2 Integration

The different initiatives toward positioning Johannesburg as a smart city are espoused upon the Johannesburg 2040 Growth and Development Strategy and motivated by the international movement toward smart cities. As shown in Fig. 20.1, the central stakeholders are the Johannesburg city government that has already progressively put in place several projects geared toward positioning Johannesburg as a smart city, Shanghai's Zendai development company that is the lead stakeholder in the conceptualization and development of Modderfontein smart city within the confines of Johannesburg, and private constructors and community that will be interested in the development of the smart cities.

Zendai has committed to spend around US$8 billion in putting in place the necessarily socioeconomic infrastructure to support the different aspects of contemporary and future smart city requirements.

20.3.3 Organization

In the context of Johannesburg the smart city is primarily owned by the city government, which is the smart city champion. The different projects of smart city are managed by government departments with specific project teams and individuals

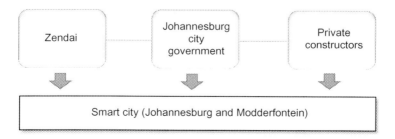

Figure 20.1 Stakeholders for the development of smart city Johannesburg.

appointed to lead the different aspects of the interventions. Private entities, such as Sebata and Deloitte, are directly involved in the conceptualization, design, and implementation of smart city projects in Johannesburg. Other business entities are also invited to join the bandwagon in innopreneurship toward smart cities.

The quadruple helix arrangements brings the local government (Johannesburg city government), the private sector (such as Sebata and Deloitte), universities (such as the smart city project at the University of Johannesburg and other projects in different universities), and the local community.

20.3.4 Time

As articulated earlier, the design and implementation of smart city Johannesburg is in twofold. The first phase is the current one that starts around 2014 and go through until 2030/40. In this phase the different aspects of the socioeconomic infrastructure is gradually revised or revamped to accommodate the different principles espoused in smart city characteristics set. The prominent effort in this phase is to improve individuals' accessibility of Internet access through the erection of planned 1000 Wi-Fi hotspots.

The second phase is the erection of a brand-new Modderfontein smart city within Johannesburg bordering the city of Midrand. This city is to be developed with the help of the Chinese development firm Shanghai Zendai that has acquired 1600 hectares in Modderfontein.

20.3.5 Cost

Other than the US$8 billion budgeted for the establishment of the Modderfontein project from the scratch, there are other interventions within the wider city of Johannesburg to transform the city into a truly smart city. In this regard, other stakeholders have jumped onto the bandwagon of ensuring that the other parts of Johannesburg are not completely left out of the smart city drive. For example, the Mayoral office has been actively leading initiatives toward transforming the greater Johannesburg into a smart city. In this regard, in the first phase, it is difficult to put a single cost to the transformation of Johannesburg into a smart city. The Mayoral office keeps locating funds to the development of the city on an annual basis to fund different initiatives, such as the erection of Wi-Fi hotspots. A sum of at least US$3 billion will have been spent by 2019. Since the ultimate project cycle runs until 2030/40 the actual cost will depend on the initiatives funded. At least there is commitment from the city government to fund initiatives that are going to position Johannesburg a smart city. It is expected that along the way there will be private stakeholders coming on bold during the project cycle.

In the second phase an explicit cost of around US$8 billion will be invested by Shanghai's Zendai to erect the city from scratch. The design of Modderfontein will incorporate a lot of fluidity to accommodate the changing tastes and smart city expectations over time so as to achieve a truly sustainable smart city. This entails that a huge junk of the budget will go into design initiatives.

20.3.6 Discussion—the fringes

Because of acute challenges in different aspects of personal life in Johannesburg, the idea of smart cities is a welcome one for a majority of individuals and businesses in Johannesburg. It can therefore be anticipated that a majority of the people will support the implementation of smart city concept given the anticipated benefits. Apart from the anticipated nonwavering support the development of the smart cities has been encouraged by developments in the Internet of Things and cloud or fog computing (Zanella & Vangelista, 2014). Because of envisaged development toward a smart city, it is expected that Johannesburg will continue turning into a contiguous conurbation, which will be more accommodative to different types of people and businesses.

Since the realization of smart cities depend on reliable Internet access provided with Wi-Fi hotspots, mobile service providers, cable, etc., Johannesburg may stand to miss out on the different opportunities that come with smart city implementation. This is because Johannesburg does not provide universal access to its citizens and businesses. Currently, a majority of Internet access is achieved through subscriptions to mobile telephone providers with 100 MB of data costing around US$1.5. This is relatively expensive. In recognizing the gravity of this problem the city of Johannesburg is responding to the problem by erecting reliable Wi-Fi hotspots across different public spaces, such as clinics, swimming pools, *Rea Vaya* Rapid Transit Bus System bus stations, so far, over 400 hotspots have been erected across the city. There are also plans to have the installation of over 1000 hotspots across the city, which will connect over 4 million people in the city. These initiatives are ongoing and may not be enough at the moment.

The smart city agenda for Johannesburg is led by the Mayor's office and focuses on traditional smart city including green technology and transport. On the transport domain, key transport initiatives aimed at decongesting the road networks, such as Rea Vaya, Gautrain (semiunderground speed train), Metrobus, need to be connected to the overall intelligent networks. The sustainable transport model entails all different users of the different pathways (spatial environment) are appropriately accommodated, and the discomfort is reduced as much as possible. Thus public transport pathways and motorways accommodate commuters, pedestrians, and motorists in such a way that they enjoy these media as public social spaces. In order to facilitate intelligent transport systems, the Gauteng Department of Roads and Transport has built an interactive app "Gauteng on the move" by using XP to inform transport users of available transport to take them from points A to B.

Hinged on artificial intelligence and cognitive computing, the city of Johannesburg is just on the brink of deploying smart computers in repetitive, routine, and mundane tasks such as in the call centers. If this is successful, it is anticipated that interactive voice response machines will be deployed in many service platforms where callers will be able to type or speak to a machine, which will further route them to the most appropriate and free customer care agent.

Self-service options driven by technology but delivered by people, such as self-service machines and interactive displays at the airport terminals, are mainly

Figure 20.2 City of Johannesburg (online noncopyrighted photos).

preferred by Generation 21. Smart airports such as the OR Tambo International Airport in Johannesburg has socio-technical infrastructure designed to allow pervasive and seamless access to dynamic information allowing an improved airport experience of individuals. This includes electronically managed car parking systems that show available parking slots allowing easy navigation through a massive car park.

Fig. 20.2 shows two uncopyrighted images obtained from the Internet. The one on the left shows a major transport hub showing a motor vehicle bridge over a busy rail system, which is considered a reliable transport system connecting the inner Johannesburg to outskirt suburbs. The image on the right shows the city center of Johannesburg littered with a lot of buildings.

The infrastructural outlay shows that there could be a lot of challenges that city dwellers and tourists may face if the different aspects of the city are not integrated and connected. Therefore the implementation of smart cities will go a long way in transforming Johannesburg into an intelligent city.

Conclusions

The current smart city initiatives under the Johannesburg 2040 Strategy will contribute to the future orientation of Johannesburg's positioning toward smart city such as the Johannesburg's 2060 city—the Modderfontein smart city. This city will be built from scratch on 1600 hectare land, which will have state-of-the-art socio-economic infrastructure.

In cahoots with the many higher level initiatives implemented in Johannesburg, educational institutions, such as the University of Johannesburg, have jumped on the bandwagon by pursuing institutional-level projects expounding the different research and practical dimensions of smart cities. Further still, there is a general increase in research interest of smart cities at individual levels. The understanding is that the different initiatives will dovetail to the higher level initiatives geared toward positioning Johannesburg as a smart city.

Some of the challenges include low Internet penetration, seemingly unrealistic and low budgetary location toward the achievement of smart city, and unclear scope as one of the key roadblocks to smart city development. Other challenges include underdevelopment, lack of skills, lack of well-trained and tech-savvy individuals who might advance the innovation agenda needed in smart city environments. In this context, implementing education programs on the citizens is a strategic initiative that will further catapult Johannesburg into a smart city. Education is a critical skill for citizens in the smart city arrangement (PwC, 2013).

With regards to sustainability, smart cities will aim to reduce gas emissions and the city's carbon footprint, protect the impact of humans and industry on the natural environment and pursuing green energy solutions such as renewable energy for a better future (Batty et al., 2012). Sustainable economic development is geared toward designing the socioeconomic and cultural infrastructure in such a way that the different infrastructural elements are networked and integrated thereby making it easy to do business.

Regarding the realization of Johannesburg smart city project, it is worth asking "what is coming next?". It is clear that this project will come to fruition given a multisectoral commitment that has been shown by different stakeholders. The end result will be that many of the South African cities will aim to jump onto the bandwagon of implementing smart cities.

Acknowledgments

Special thanks to the School of Consumer Intelligence and Information Systems, College of Business and Economics for the enabling research environment.

About the authors

Kelvin Joseph Bwalya is an associate professor at the School of Consumer Intelligence and Information Systems, Department for Information and Knowledge Management, University of Johannesburg. He has a PhD in Information Management (University of Johannesburg), Masters of Computer Science (Korea Advanced Institute of Science and Technology—KAIST), and Bachelors in Electronics and Electrical Power Engineering (Moscow Power Engineering Technical University). He is also a member of the Board of Directors—Mosi-o-Tunya University of Science and Technology (MUST). He is also a PhD supervisor and member of the board of exams at various universities around the world. He has supervised five PhDs to completion, several masters and undergraduate projects. He has examined 24 PhD dissertations from nine universities in Africa and abroad, and several masters theses. By the end of 2017, he had already published seven academic and research books and over 100 pieces of peer-reviewed articles and has also managed numerous research funds. He is also a member of various professional bodies and editorial teams. He is busy researching on disruptive technologies, cloud and fog computing, big data and predictive analytics, data genomics, spatial−temporal data modeling, competitive intelligence, database design, m-Government, open governance data, etc. He is actively pushing for establishing himself as a quality assurance expert on higher education in the SADC region. Currently, he is a member of team of experts at the Higher Education Authority (Zambia).

References

Anthopoulos, L. (2017). Understanding smart cities—A tool for smart government or an Industrial Trick? In *Public administration and information technology* (Vol. 22). New York: Springer Science + Business Media. ISBN: 978-3-319-57014-3 (Print) 978-3-319-57015-0. Available at: <https://link.springer.com/book/10.1007%2F978-3-319-57015-0> Accessed 14.08.18.

Asimakopoulou, E., & Bessis, N. (2011). Buildings and crowds: Forming smart cities for more effective disaster management. In *Fifth international conference on innovative mobile and internet services in the ubiquitous computing*. 30 June−2 July 2011, Seoul, South Korea, ISBN: 9780769543727.

Bate, P., & Robert, G. (2007). *Bringing user experience to healthcare improvement: The concepts, methods and practices of experience based design*. Oxford: Radcliffe.

Batty, M., Axhausen, K. W., Giannotti, F., Pozdnoukhov, A., Bazzani, A., Wachowicz, M., ... Portugali, Y. (2012). Smart cities of the future. *The European Physical Journal Special Topics, 214*(1), 481−518.

BusinessTech. (2017). Joburg ranks as the top financial market in Africa in 2017. *BusinessTech*, 9th September 2017. Available at <https://businesstech.co.za/news/business/196888/joburg-ranks-as-the-top-financial-market-in-africa-in-2017/> Accessed 05.12.17.

Dlodlo, N., Mbecke, P., Mofolo, M., & Mhlanga, M. (2013). The Internet of Things in community safety and crime prevention in South Africa. In *International joint conference computers, information and systems sciences and engineering CISSE 2013*. University of Bridgeport.

Exploring the nature of the smart cities research landscape. In J. R. Gil-Garcia, T. A. Pardo, & T. Nam (Eds.), *Smarter as the New Urban Agenda: A comprehensive view of the 21st century city*. Switzerland: Springer International Publishing.

Hall, R. E. (2000). The vision of a smart city. In *Proceedings of the second international life extension technology workshop*. Paris, France.

Harrison, C., Eckman, B., Hamilton, R., Hatswick, P., Kalagnanam, J., Paraszczak, J., & Williams, P. (2014). Foundations of smarter cities. *IBM Journal of Research and Development, 54*(4), 1−16.

Kramers, A., Hojer, M., Lovehagen, N., & Wangel, J. (2014). Smart sustainable cities-exploring ICT solutions for reduced energy use in cities. *Environmental Modelling and Software, 56*, 52−62.

Lea, R. *Smart cities: An overview of technology trends driving smart cities*. (2017). Available at <https://www.ieee.org/publications_standards/publications/periodicals/ieee-smart-cities-trend-paper-2017.pdf> Accessed 21.09.17.

Marcelino-Sádaba, S., González-Jaen, L. F., & Pérez-Ezcurdia, A. (2015). Using project management as a way to sustainability. From a comprehensive review to a framework definition. *Journal of Cleaner Production, 99*, 1−16.

Nfuka, E. N., & Rusu, L. (2010). Critical success factors for effective IT governance in the public sector organization in a developing: The case of Tanzania. In *Proceeding of the 18th European conference on information systems (ECIS)*. Pretoria, South Africa, June 7−9, 2010.

NIUA & PEARL. *Exploratory research on smart cities: Theory, policy and practice.* (2014). Available at <https://smartnet.niua.org/content/e6bb6d10-74bc-441d-8094-741a04a96034> Accessed 20.03.19.

Paroutis, S., Bennett, M., & Heracleous, L. (2012). A strategic view on smart city technology: The case of IBM Smarter Cities during a recession. *Technological Forecasting and Social Change, 89*, 262−272.

PwC. *Cities of opportunity: Building the future.* (2013). Available at <https://www.pwc.com/gx/en/capital-projects-infrastructure/publications/assets/pwc-cities-of-opportunity-building-the-future.pdf> Accessed 04.12.17.

Zanella, A., & Vangelista, L. (2014). Internet of Things for smart cities. *IEEE Internet of Things Journal, 1*(1), 1−10.

The smart city of Tunisia

Aroua Taamallah[1], Maha Khemaja[2] and Sami Faiz[3]
[1]ISITCom, University of Soussa, Sousse, Tunisia, [2]ISSATS, University of Soussa, Sousse, Tunisia, [3]ISAMM, University of Tunisia, Sousse, Tunisia

Chapter Outline

21.1 Introduction 421
21.2 Background 422
21.3 Research methodology: case study 423
    21.3.1 Scope 423
    21.3.2 Integration 426
    21.3.3 Organization 428
    21.3.4 Time 429
    21.3.5 Cost 429
    21.3.6 Quality 430
    21.3.7 Risks 430
    21.3.8 Procurement 430
    21.3.9 Discussion 430
21.4 Conclusions 431
Acknowledgments 431
About the authors 432
References 432

21.1 Introduction

Tunisians protested to solve their social problems, including poverty and joblessness. The revolution therefore has occurred in January 2011 to change not only the social state but also the political state inside and outside Tunisia (Ayeb, 2011). Tunisia still has suffered from problems in security, economy, and social areas. Maintaining security was one of the challenges that the country faced, especially after the Libyan war and the three successive attacks: the first was in Bardo Museum in Tunis on March 18, 2015; the second was in a hotel in Sousse on June 26, 2015; and the third attack was in the Presidential Guard on November 27, 2015. The problems of security also affect the tourism that is an important economy contributor (7% of gross domestic product (GDP)) and has created 400,000 jobs before the revolution. Tourism deterioration also implies lower foreign exchange earnings. Economy suffers from difficulties that are basically linked to the financial crisis of the Eurozone, the decrease in the Tourism sector, and the decrease in the production of the phosphate and hydrocarbon in 2015. The average of the growth rate was 3.6% over the period 2008−10 and slowed down to 1.4% over the period of 2011−16. Social challenges that Tunisia suffers from are basically poverty and unemployment. The poverty rate was 15.5% in 2013. Poverty is most prevalent in rural areas (4.6% of rural areas were in an extreme poverty in 2010). The unemployment rate reached 15% in 2013, especially for young (23% of young graduates were unemployed).

Despite the problems that Tunisia faces, it offers strengths and opportunities like its strategic situation on the intersection of Europe, the Middle East, and North Africa (MENA) and sub-Saharan Africa. Its strategic situation is an opportunity for partnerships with those regions. Tunisia is also characterized by a network of high-quality public infrastructure and services in different domains, such as water, transportation, and energy. It also gets benefited from its highly developed industries in domains, such as textile, pharmaceutical products, mechanical and electrical components, agri-food, and aeronautic. Tunisia has also made innovations in the domains of electronics and machinery. It is also the first in North Africa in terms of innovation, information and communication technology (ICT) development, talent competitiveness, and entrepreneurship ecosystem. Tunisia is the first world exporter of dates and olive oil for the 2015−16. Tunisia is also classified as the second exporter of organic produce and of car components in Africa. Tunisia is considered the first democratic country in the Arab world. The Quartet of the Tunisian National Dialogue was awarded the Nobel Prize in 2015 for its decisive contribution to building pluralist democracy in Tunisia. Stakeholders do many efforts in terms of strategies [Strategic Development Plan (2016−20); Tunisia Solar Plan (2014−30), green economy (2014−20), and Digital Tunisia 2020 National Strategic Plan] and projects to transform the city into a smart one, to increase the quality of life and transform it to an economic hub.

In this chapter, we focus Digital Tunisia 2020 National Strategic Plan, how it has been conceived and was implemented, what is the difference between the theory and the practice in implementing this strategy. The aim is therefore to identify if Tunisia is really a smart city or it claims to be smart. The reminder of the chapter is as follows: Section 21.2 contains a background of the ICT domain, Section 21.3 contains the case study how the strategy was conceived, implemented, and what are the impacts on Tunisia. Section 21.4 concludes and presents perspectives.

21.2 Background

In the literature, there exist various smart city definitions. Anthopoulos (2017) defines a smart city as the use of ICT and innovation to mitigate city's challenges in economic, social, and environmental domains.

Stakeholders are also making efforts to transform Tunisia into a smart city. The Tunisian government has adopted many ICT strategies before and after 2011. Since the 1990, Tunisia has adopted a national cybersecurity strategy to increase the security of information systems (ISs) in the country and to improve the use of e-services and e-commerce. Another ICT strategy named e-Tunisia was adopted by the Tunisian government in 2005 and was modified in 2011. The e-Tunisia aims to offer public services in a digital form and to provide transactional services (Ouerghi, 2014). Various programs have been adopted to integrate ICT in all sectors (tourism, finance, education, etc.) and for the training of experts in different domains. To modernize the public administration and facilitate communications between governmental organizations (G2G), between government and citizens (G2C), and between government and businesses (G2B), Digital Tunisia 2020 National Strategic Plan is adopted. It also allows to render Tunisia an economic hub of the region.

The legal framework of ICT in Tunisia has existed since the late 1990s. A telecommunication code aims to organize the ICT sector. Other measures are included such as the National Telecommunication Authority, the National Frequency Agency. In 1999 a law was conceived to define cybercrime and to specify sanctions against IT hackers. The National Agency for Computer Security was the first operational center in Africa. It aims to assist government and businesses during the security of their ISs.

21.3 Research methodology: case study

Tunisia is a small country of 11 million inhabitants with a surface of 16,360 km^2. It has a strategic situation between Europe, the MENA region, and sub-Saharan Africa as shown in Fig. 21.1. Tunisia has a diversified nature: seas, mountains, Sahara, forests, and is characterized by its beautiful places in all regions of the country (Table 21.1).

Tunisia is marked by the mixing of cultures and civilizations of Berber, Carthaginian, Arabe, Turkish, and French. It used to be a French colony during 75 years. In 1956 Tunisia obtained its autonomy. Since 1957, women got rights to vote and to be a candidate during elections where Habib Bourguiba was named the president of Tunisia. Habib Bourguiba supported the vision to create a well-educated and open-minded society. Bourguiba's vision succeeded. Zine El Abidine Ben Ali has become the president of the country over the 1987–2011 period. The revolution took place from December 2010 to January 2011, and Ben Ali's government fell. Tunisia enters in a transition period from 2011 to 2014 where presidential elections occur. From 2014 until now, El Beji Kayed ElSebsi is the president of Tunisia.

21.3.1 Scope

The smart city of Tunisia covers many sectors including ICT that is one of the most dynamic sectors in the Tunisian economy before, during, and after the revolution. The added value in economic development is 4.5 billion dinars in 2014, and digital exports are 0.95 billion dinars in 2014. Tunisia is characterized by the most

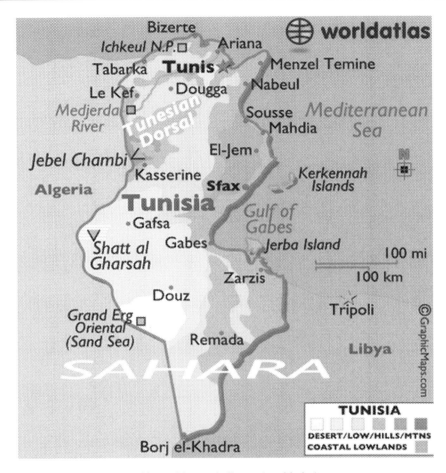

Figure 21.1 Tunisia geographic position and climate (worldatlas).

developed telecommunication infrastructure in the region, which is strengthened to render the country an international digital destination by 2020.

In this section, we focus on innovations in ICT domain in Tunisia in terms of enterprises, uses of ICT, and infrastructure. The main goal behind the investment in this sector is to render Tunisia one of the continent's leading digital destination (world: 87, Africa 4, and Arab countries 8) in terms of jobs creation (7500 jobs every year) and ICT use in all sectors. Studies show that ICT is more and more servicing other activity sectors in Tunisia (Table 21.2).

To reinforce science-industry links and develop a knowledge-based economy a technological infrastructure has been developed. It is composed of El Ghazala technological park. After that a network of 15 technology parks has been created all over the country (Gafsa, Kef, Kasserine, Monastir, Siliana, Kairouan, Sousse,

Table 21.1 Beautiful landscapes from all over the country.

Table 21.2 National survey about professional activities (National Institute of Statistics, 2018).

Activity sector	2015	
	Existence on the web	**Internet usage**
Extractive industries	72.8	30.6
Manufacturing industries	59.7	20.4
Production and distribution of electricity, gas, steam, and air	59.4	32.8
Building	55.4	31.1
Commerce; automobile, and motorcycle repair	61.9	51.9
Transportation and warehousing	59.4	35.4
Accommodation and catering	40.0	15.5
Information and communication	91.2	92.3
Real estate activities	70.0	92.3
Specific scientific and technological activities	78.8	77.1
Administrative and support services activities	74.3	56.2
Public administration	100.0	85.4
Education	81.5	57.3
Health and social actions	58.3	38.7
Art, shows, and recreational activities	70.3	33.3
Other services activities	54.8	34.9

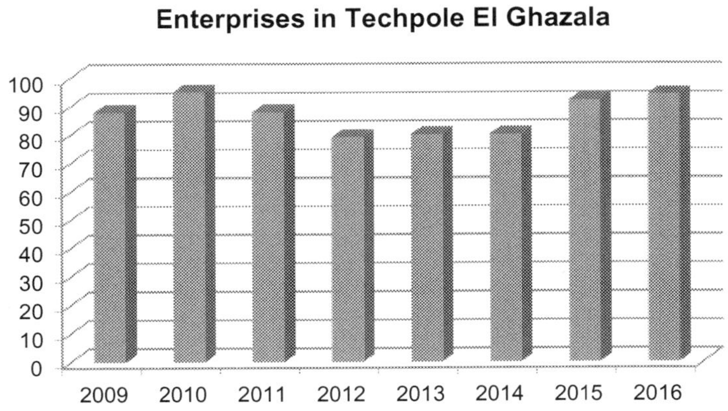

Enterprises in Techpole El Ghazala

Figure 21.2 Enterprises in Technopark El Ghazala.

Tozeur, Medenine, Tataouine, Zaghouan, Beja, Jendouba, and Sidi Bouzid). They help to develop technology-based partnerships and to create start-ups and enterprises (entrepreneurship). Statistics from 2009 to 2016 show a small decrease of enterprises number in El Ghazala in the period 2011−12, and growth has started to pick after 2013 (Fig. 21.2).

Statistics from 2009 to 2016 show a sustained growth of enterprises number in cyberparks in the period 2009−12, a small decrease in the period 2013−14, and growth has started to pick after 2014 (Fig. 21.3).

There are also initiatives that increase citizen, enterprises participation in Tunisia development. E-collectivity is a pilot project that is developed to achieve this objective by offering services, such as e-citizen and e-service. E-citizen is a service that allows the citizen participation in decision-making using tools like survey and e-participation tools. E-service allows the citizen to create and track tax payments.

21.3.2 Integration

The sector of new technologies in Tunisia is a sector that creates value and jobs. In 2014 it accounted for 7% of the country's GDP. If Tunisia wants to change its economic model, it must quickly adhere to the digital, which is a locomotive boosting to all the economic sectors of the country, going from the private to the public.

The sector of the digital economy is now made up of about 600 companies, of which only 60 are operational. It can solve the problem of unemployment and fight against parallel trade.

The Assid's government priority in 2015 was to develop the Digital Tunisia 2020 National Development Plan (NDP) that solves the country issues over the 2016−20 period. The NDP encourages the public−private partnership (PPP) and was officially presented at the Tunisia 2020 International Conference that occurred

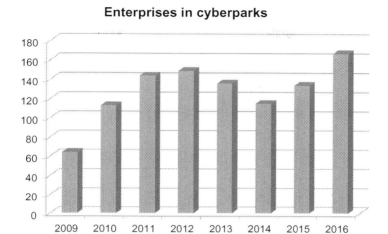

Figure 21.3 Enterprises in cyberparks.

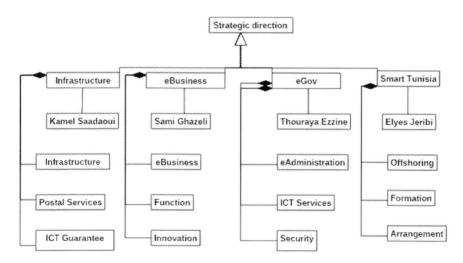

Figure 21.4 Digital Tunisia strategic orientations.

in November 28–29, 2016. The conference leads to many partnerships with a funding of Euro 14 billion.

Digital Tunisia 2020 is mainly composed of four strategic directions that are infrastructure, e-Gov, e-Business, and Smart Tunisia (Fig. 21.4).

The infrastructure axe aims to develop an infrastructure that offers an ultrahigh-speed Internet. The digital infrastructure ensures social inclusion and an easy access to information. The e-Gov will offer transparent and open administrative services to citizens using digital technologies. It aims to transform to administration with zero waste. E-business axe aims to enhance the use of digital technologies and innovation in businesses and industries. This increases the competitiveness of enterprises and the use of digital economy. Smart Tunisia (2017) aims to place Tunisia on top of Africa-Middle east region in offshoring and IT offshoring. It is proposed within the framework of the PPP. It is a program designed to make Tunisia an attractive digital hub to facilitate the polarization of foreign investors.

In this chapter, we focus on the e-Gov strategic direction, especially the Smart Gov 2020 program.

Smart Gov 2020 has four pillars that are (1) to offer an integrated administration by providing sharable state infrastructure and systems and allowing exchangeable e-data; (2) to offer an opened administration through transparency, data reuse, and citizen participation; (3) to provide a user-centric governance by offering simple and citizen-oriented services; and (4) digitalizing the administration and encouraging citizens to use digital administrative services.

The project has basically three components that are smart gov, institutional support and capacity building, and project management.

Smart gov component aims to modernize administrative ISs to move toward open and paperless administration. This will allow the citizen who will have a unique identifier and an electronic card to have access to administrative services. There are also plans to implement a platform that ensures data exchange and interoperability of state ISs. An e-gov infrastructure is also implemented including a national cloud and government intranet. To promote transparent and reuse of public data an open data framework is established. The project includes an extension of the Integrated National Network of the Administration to interconnect 550 administrative sites, 650 government sites, and over 400 sites of justice ministry.

Institutional support and capacity building component supports legal, human, and statistical aspects during the implementation of Digital Tunisia 2020.

Project management component supports the delivery unit and technical expertise.

21.3.3 Organization

The governance of the Digital Tunisia 2020 project is ensured by the government (Youssef el Chahed's government), the private sector, and the society. The government is the sponsor of the project. African Development Bank (AfDB) helps Tunisia during the transitional phase and finances the Digital Tunisia 2020. Tunisia has also other partners, such as World Bank, European Investment Bank. The government, especially the Ministry of Information Technologies and the Digital Economy (MTCEN), is the first responsible of the execution of the planned strategies. The strategic orientations are supported by three structures of piloting (governance, communication, and financing and budget) and three support structures (legal and regulatory, expertise building, and digital trust) (Fig. 21.5).

The smart city of Tunisia

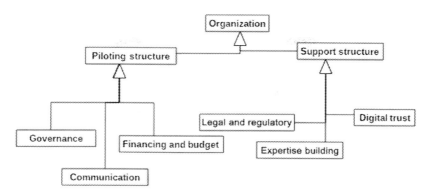

Figure 21.5 Organization structure of Digital Tunisia 2020.

Table 21.3 The timeline of the Smart Gov 2020 execution (Digital Tunisia 2020, 2017).

Task name	Semester 1		Semester 2		Semester 3		Semester 4		Semester 5	
	Tri 1	Tri 3	Tri 1	Tri 3	Tri 1	Tri 3	Tri 1	Tri 3	Tri 1	Tri 3
General activities										
Smart Gov										
Institutional support and capacity building										
Financial and accounting audits										
Project implementation management and monitoring										

21.3.4 Time

The Smart Gov 2020 implementation schedule is illustrated by Table 21.3.

It contains mainly five tasks of Smart Gov 2020, which are general activities, smart gov, institutional support and capacity building, financial and accounting audits and project implementation, and management and monitory. The duration of the first task lasts one semester and a half, whereas the other tasks occur simultaneously and last four semesters.

21.3.5 Cost

The budget of Smart Gov 2020 is EUR 134.96 million: EUR 71.56 million coming from AfDB, and EUR 63.4 million coming from the Tunisian government. Table 21.4 illustrates a description of the estimated costs with reference to the project's components.

Table 21.4 The estimated costs of the project (Digital Tunisia, 2020, 2017).

Components	EUR million
Smart Gov	109.9
Institutional support and capacity building	11.96
Project management	0.60
Baseline cost	122.46
Physical contingencies (7%)	8.57
Financial contingencies (3%)	3.93
Total	134.96

21.3.6 Quality

During the initial steps of the project implementation the problems unexpectedly encountered are the lack of human resources and slow procurements. The AfDB deals with the procurement of the project by offering a technical assistance and by providing a consultancy firm during the implementation of the project.

21.3.7 Risks

The risks that the MTCEN faces during the implementation of the project are (1) the lack of high-speed internet infrastructure, (2) failure of ministries to provide interoperable platform, and (3) limited use of online services.

Collaboration between ministries to provide an interoperable platform. The Digital Economy Strategic Council gives to the ministries their tasks to do during the fulfillment of the project. The use of additional financial resources to improve ICT infrastructure.

21.3.8 Procurement

During the Digital Tunisia 2020 projects, many contracts have been signed with the AfDB for the procurement policy related to the consultancy services, the procurements for the Smart Tunisia initiative, and the procurement of IT equipment and networks.

21.3.9 Discussion

The Digital Tunisia 2020 is under implementation, and MTCEN will create annual reports about the results of the project since the end of 2018. The delivery unit of the project is being established and will monitor the execution of the project. The MTCEN needs to collaborate with other ministries to fulfill the financial needs for the accomplishment of the project. Since the project is not yet finished the real impact cannot be visualized.

As initial results of the project, various initiatives appear offering services to citizens and ensuring open data exchange among governmental organizations. The project is intended to reduce citizens' travels and to reduce greenhouse gas emissions and paper consumption. Various e-services have been implemented and are available for citizens' needs: governmental information (Open Data Portal, 2017), sites for citizen's participation in decision-making (E-participation Portal, 2016), portals to address economic operator's needs (E-Commerce Portal, 2017), e-payment services (e.g., dinar Web Site, 2017). Ministries sites and other governmental services are available (Finance Ministry Portal, 2017; General Direction of Customs, 2017 etc.) and are up to date for users' needs.

During the design phase, there are interventions from private sector in the conceptualization of Digital Tunisia 2020. We recommend then to increase citizens' engagement in strategies definition to fulfill a unified vision that considers social, economic, and environmental issues of Tunisia.

There is a focus on the impact of the project on citizens using indicators, such as the percentage of households with access to online government services, the number of digital technologies jobs created per year, the use of e-participation platforms by citizens.

The smart city of Tunisia is in its infancy and needs more efforts to ameliorate it. It follows the development process of any smart city, which is composed of four phases: predesign phase, design phase, implementation phase, and evaluation phase (Taamallah et al., 2017). However, as we know, stakeholders do not use tools that facilitate this transformational process to a smart city of Tunisia.

For this aim, we propose to the stakeholders to use automatic learning from existing smart cities to acquire expertise from them (Taamallah, Khemaja, & Faiz, 2017). We also suggest them to use the strategy design platform that offers a set of tools and services for the design of smart city strategies (Taamallah et al., 2018a,b). We also propose to use a smart city simulator to test and evaluate strategies before their implementation in the city (Taamallah et al., 2018c). This will solve the problem of the lack of financial funds during the real implementation of the strategies in Tunisia.

21.4 Conclusions

Tunisia is moving toward becoming a smart and sustainable city. Investments are taking place in many domains including green economy and sustainable development, smart governance, ICT, smart transportation, smart energy, and smart education. Collaboration between government, industries, universities, and citizens is necessary to develop an integrative and a coherent smart city approach that considers economic, social, and environmental factors. In this chapter, we analyze the ICT sector and focus on the Digital Tunisia 2020 strategy implementation. The initial results mention that Tunisia is evolving the ICT domain. The strategy is under implementation, and the results will show the real impact of the strategy on the improvement of the ICT domain. The chapter also offers solutions and recommendations to solve the weaknesses of this domain.

Acknowledgments

I want to thank Walid Helali, a well-known Tunisian photographer and painter, and Safwen Ladhari, a Tunisian computer science engineer, for the photos.

About the authors

Aroua Taamallah received her research master degree in Networking and Telecommunications in 2014. Now, she is a PhD student in Informatics Sciences at ISITCom. She published papers in specialized conferences and journals.

Maha Khemaja has a PhD in Computer Science from Paul Sabatier University (Toulouse 3) and is a member of PRINCE laboratory. She is an assistant professor at the University of Sousse, Tunisia. She published numerous papers in specialized conferences and journals, and she is the member of many national and international projects.

Sami Faiz has a PhD in Computer Science from the Orsay University (Paris 11) and is a member of the Remote Sensing and Information Systems Research Unit (TSIRS). He is a full professor. He published numerous papers in specialized conferences and journals, and he is the founder of many national and international projects.

References

Anthopoulos, L. G. (2017). *Understanding smart cities: A tool for smart government or an industrial trick?* (Vol. 22). Basel: Springer.

Ayeb, H. (2011). Social and political geography of the Tunisian revolution: The alfa grass revolution. *Review of African Political Economy*, *38*(129), 467–479. Available from https://doi.org/10.1080/03056244.2011.604250.

Digital Tunisie 2020. (2017). <https://www.afdb.org/fileadmin/uploads/afdb/Documents/Project-and-Operations/Tunisia_Support_Project_for_the_Implementation_of_the_%E2%80%9CDigital_Tunisia_2020%E2%80%9D_National_Strategic_Plan.pdf> Accessed October 2018.

E-Commerce Portal. (2017). <http://www.marchespublics.gov.tn> Last Accessed on November 2018.

E-dinar Web Site. (2017). <www.e-dinar.poste.tn> Last Accessed on November 2018.

E-participation Portal. (2016). <http://www.e-participation.tn/> Last Accessed on November 2018.

Finance Ministry Portal. (2017). <http://www.finances.gov.tn/index.php?lang = fr> Last Accessed on November 2018.

General Direction of Customs. (2017). <https://www.douane.gov.tn/> Last Accessed on November 2018.

National Institute of Statistics. (2018). <http://www.ins.tn/fr/publication/indicateurs-fondamentaux-sur-l%E2%80%99utilisation-des-technologies-de-l%E2%80%99information-et-de-la-1> Last Accessed on November 2018.

Open Data Portal. (2017). <http://www.data.gov.tn/> Last Accessed on November 2018.

Ouerghi, M. S. (2014). ICT strategy in Tunisia: The case of e-Tunisia and Tunisan2. Open Movement. In: *Computer applications and information systems (WCCAIS), 2014 World Congress on* (pp. 1–8). IEEE.

Smart Tunisia. (2017). <http://www.smarttunisia.tn/> Last Accessed on November 2018.

Taamallah, A., Khemaja, M., & Faiz, S. (2017). Strategy ontology construction and learning: Insights from smart city strategies. *International Journal of Knowledge-Based Development, 8*(3), 206−228.

Taamallah, A., Khemaja, M., & Faiz, S. (2018a). *Toward a framework for smart city strategies design. Proceedings of the 3rd international conference on smart city applications* (p. 56) ACM.

Taamallah, A., Khemaja, M., & Faiz, S. (2018b). *Towards a framework for participatory strategy design in smart cities. The proceedings of the third international conference on smart city applications* (pp. 179−192). Cham: Springer.

Taamallah, A., Khemaja, M., & Faiz, S. (2018c). A web-based platform for strategy design in smart cities. *International Jouranl of Web Based Communities.* Available from https://doi.org/10.1504/IJWBC.2019.10019198.

Conclusions: putting "sustainable" in smart cities

Maria Cristina Bueti and Chris Ip
International Telecommunications Union, Geneva, Switzerland

The process of technological innovation—from invention, commercialization, to widespread adaption—is intrinsically connected to the well-being of citizens.[1] This mutually transformative relationship shapes the outcomes of smart city development and applications, which promise new knowledge and positive disruption that would improve the quality of life of all city dwellers. This is indeed the case as demonstrated in the many cases illustrated in this book.

Yet, this unguided expedition often carries economic, environmental, and societal risks that are commonly overlooked and required further attention. For example, cybersecurity plays an important role in safeguarding the data and information that the economic well-being of a smart city relies heavily upon. The energy consumption and information and communication technology (ICT) infrastructures required to transfer and manage the massive volume of data generated by smart sensors and other emerging technologies are leaving behind significant environmental footprint. The rapid adoption of advanced technologies is also threatening to further marginalize vulnerable population groups that lack access to or operational knowledge of these new technologies (e.g., the poor, women, and people with disabilities).

Therefore at the heart of smart city development should be—the human being. This is to go beyond the current market-driven model of smart city development, which often emphasizes on creating an ICT-led market to devise a positive city and business environment through short-term resource optimization.[2] Fostering long-term urban sustainability and inclusive innovation requires smart governance and active citizen participation.[3] The inputs and feedback from civil society and the private sector are the source for monitoring and revaluating city policies to ensure they serve the needs of all population groups, contributing to the sustainability of the entire smart city ecosystem.

---

[1] "Shaping the future of the fourth industrial revolution"—Klaus Schwab, 2018.
[2] "Sustainable smart cities: Applying complexity science to achieve urban sustainability"—United Nations University, 2017.
[3] "Enhancing innovation and participation in smart sustainable cities"—United for Smart Sustainable Cities, 2016.

That is why the term "smart sustainable cities (SSCs)" is preferred when discussing smart city development at the international level. By putting "sustainable" in smart city, greater emphasis would be placed on creating high-quality and sustainable economic, social, and cultural growth. This creates a new mindset for urban stakeholders, incentivizing them to take sustainability and global development agenda, such as the Sustainable Development Goals (SDGs), into consideration when implementing smart city strategies.

In October 2015 the International Telecommunications Union (ITU) and the United Nations Economic Commission of Europe (UNECE) developed the following definition of a smart sustainable city:

> *A smart sustainable city is an innovative city that uses information and communication technologies (ICTs) and other means to improve quality of life, efficiency of urban operation and services, and competitiveness, while ensuring that it meets the needs of present and future generations with respect to economic, social, environmental as well as cultural aspects.*
>
> UNECE and ITU, October 2015

This definition highlights the multifaceted nature of an SSC. It gives attention to the social, environmental, and cultural aspects of city development that are often overlooked while emphasizing the need of creating an enabling environment for meeting the needs of both present and future generations. This definition would serve as a good starting point for urban stakeholders to take collaborative actions on incorporating sustainability and human centric aspects of development in a smart city.

A.1 An agile and multilateral approach to smart sustainable cities

To unlock the full potential of smart city technologies, urban stakeholders must align their smart city strategies with the SDGs. Empirical research has pointed to the fact that smart city technologies and applications have an untapped potential of helping cities to meet 70% of the SDGs. Data-driven applications, which serve as the foundation of many smart city solutions, can improve the key indicators of cities by 10%−30%, from reducing fatalities by 8%−10%, accelerating emergency response times by 20%−35%, to reducing the average commute time by 15%−20%, lowering greenhouse gas emission by 10%−15%, and reducing water consumption by 20%−30%.[4]

Realizing this untapped potential in this complex space requires city stakeholders to adopt an agile and multilateral approach to SSCs development which would see the involvement of all stakeholders in the process. This approach entails that policymakers should aim to create mechanisms for knowledge sharing and collaborative actions at the city, regional, and international levels, while adopting a flexible and

---

[4] "Smart cities: Digital solutions for a more livable future"—McKinsey Global Institute, June 2018.

agile governance strategy that could cope with the pace of technological development; the academia is encouraged to conduct research on the sociological and environmental perspectives of implementing smart city applications;[5] and other urban stakeholders should also look for ways to match new digital and data technologies with international standards, such as ITU-T Recommendations, in order to disseminate the vital technical knowledge at the global level, to ensure interoperability of data platforms between government entities and technology providers as well as cross-border interoperability, and ultimately to distribute the benefits of technological innovation equally across all sectors.

Indeed, international organizations and platforms could play a decisive role in catalyzing this multilateral approach to SSCs. For example, ITU—the United Nations specialized agency in ICTs—has been actively engaged with policymakers and major ICTs providers in setting the interoperability and environmental requirements of emerging technologies such as Internet of Things, artificial intelligence, blockchain, and 5G. The United for Smart Sustainable Cities initiative—a global platform coordinated by ITU, UN-Habitat, and UNECE and supported by other 13 UN bodies to advocate for the use of ICTs in facilitating the transition to SSC—has developed a set of key performance indicators for smart sustainable cities, which have already assisted over 50 cities worldwide in evaluating their smart strategies and progress in meeting the SDGs.[6] The results have not only helped refining their smart projects but also served as an important reference point for other aspiring SSCs.

A.2 Conclusion

This book has delivered exceptional insights on how cities worldwide have implemented their smart strategies. They have demonstrated that smart city project management requires a different strategic approach than the traditional city management strategy. In order to overcome challenges, such as the adverse environmental effects of smart city infrastructures and growing social inequality, it is imperative that all urban stakeholders are involved in the discourse of smart development. Different population groups shape how technologies are being deployed. Their involvement embeds the desirable values and characteristics in these technologies that would otherwise be forgotten.

The emergence of smart city is merely the beginning of a revolution. New technologies will inevitably appear, and more challenges as well as more opportunities will be arisen. It is up to us to ensure that emerging technologies will be developed, deployed, and consumed responsibly and with the perspectives of multiple stakeholders in mind. It is only through common dialogs and collaboration that we can realize the full benefits of smart technologies and to collectively move forward as a society.

---

[5] "Shaping the future of the fourth industrial revolution"—Klaus Schwab, 2018.
[6] "Collection methodology for key performance indicators for smart sustainable cities"—U4SSC, 2016.

Author index

A
Adlbrecht, G., 13−14
Afonso, R. A., 357
Afzalan, N., 343
Agarwal, N., 244
Ahmed, K. P., 162
Ahmed, N., 339
Alawadhi, S., 101−102
Albino, V., 391
Alencar, M.S., 356
Alencar, R.T., 356
Alexandrou, E., 132
Allen, J., 336
Allwinkle, S., 359*t*
Almeida, C., 370−371
Almonacid, G., 35
Alvaro, A., 356
Álvaro, A., 356−357
Amralla, S.M., 15
Anastasia, S., 353−355, 354*t*
Andersen, P., 16
Angelidou, M., 105, 392
Anthopoulos, L. G., 105−106, 130, 149−150, 151*f*, 158*f*, 161, 166−167, 220, 237, 244−245, 261−262, 269, 296, 352−355, 354*t*, 360, 367−368, 375, 385−386, 392−393, 407−408, 422
Anttiroiko, A.V., 393
Asimakopoulou, E., 407−408
Assis, M.M.A., 370−371, 382
Attri, A., 101−102
Aurigi, A., 392
Aversano, P., 105−106
Ayeb, H., 421−422

B
Baccarini, D., 12−15
Baccarne, B., 96−97
Bahia, L., 370−371
Bailey, S.J., 393
Bakhshi, J., 13−14
Ballon, P., 84, 93
Balsillie, J., 337, 343
Bannister, F., 95−96
Barbosa, D.V.S., 376
Barbosa, N.B., 376
Baron, G., 130, 136
Bate, P., 410
Batini, C., 95
Batty, M., 268, 417
Ben Letaifa, S., 84, 99−100
Bennett, M., 408
Benninger, C.C., 268
Berardi, U., 391
Beretta, I., 51−52
Bernardes, R.C., 359*t*
Bernow, S., 35
Berntzen, L., 265
Bessis, N., 407−408
Bilo, N., 28−29
Blackwood, D. J., 296−297
Bocquet, J., 13−14
Bódi, Z., 105−106
Boggia, G., 244−245
Bolívar, M.P.R., 352−356, 354*t*, 360, 393
Boogert, G., 142−143
Borchiellini, R., 52, 65−66
Bosch-Rekveldt, M., 13−15
Bower, D., 13
Bradley, J., 298−299
Brandoni, C., 29−30
Brans, J., 35
Braun, E., 132−133, 133*f*
Bria, F., 105
Brito, R.D.L., 370−371
Bruni, E., 67−68
Buarque, R.R., 370−371
Bunce, S., 334

Buntz, B., 125, 295–296, 304–305
Burgos, F., 357

C
Cagliano, A.C., 244–245, 360
Calvillo, N., 336
Câmara, S. F., 356
Camarda, P., 244–245
Capra, C.F., 130–131
Carvalho, H. J. B., 356
Carvalho, J., 23
Carver, S., 13–14
Castelnovo, W., 95–97
Castro, A.L.B.D., 369
Cattolica, U., 51–52
Chapman, C., 14–15
Chapman, R., 12–14
Charalabidis, Y., 95–96
Charette, R.N., 12
Chatterjee, S., 244
Chatteron, P., 220
Chatterton, P., 220
Chauhan, S., 244
Chourabi, H., 244–245, 261–262, 265, 353–355, 354*t*, 359–361, 359*t*, 373, 391
Cianci, I., 244–245
Cocchia, A., 129
Coletta, C., 97, 341
Connolly, D., 23
Connolly, R., 95–96
Consoni, F.L., 359*t*
Conti, S., 98
Cooper, R. F. D., 296–297
Corgnati, S. P., 55–56
Costa, A.M., 370–371
Costa, G., 71*t*
Costa, L. C., 357
Crawford, S., 343
Creazzo, L., 105–106
Crompvoets, J., 87–88
Cruickshank, P., 359*t*
Cunha, M. A., 352–353, 368, 373
Cunha, M. A. C., 357
Cunha, M.A.V.C., 360, 375
Curry, E., 129

D
da, Garcia, V. C., 357
Dalal-Clayton, B., 28
Dall'O, G., 67–68
Damasiotis, V., 13–16
Dameri, R.P., 130
Dang, C.N., 13–14
Dangelico, R.M., 391
David, R. F., 162
Day, M., 344–345
de, Pinto, F. R., 356
De Marco, A., 244–245, 360
Deakin, M., 83–84, 197–198
Deleuze, G., 336
Delmastro, C., 55–56
Demaria, M., 71*t*
Desouza, K.C., 244–245
Dias, L., 26*f*, 28–30, 29*f*, 32, 35–36
Diaz-Diaz, R., 134–135
Dickson, A., 13–14
Dixit, A., 298–299
Dlodlo, N., 407–408, 410
Dodman, D., 28
Dombkins, D., 13–14
Dombkins, P., 13–14
Dong, H., 101–102
Douay, N., 195–196, 198–199
Drechsler, W., 105
Dror, Y., 199
Dulac, J., 56
Dzhusupova, Z., 129

E
Eidelman, G., 333–334
El Saddik, A., 101–102
Elias, P.E., 370–371
Erenda, I., 105–106
Evans, L., 97, 341

F
Faiz, S., 431
Falcão, M. C., 356–357
Fang, C., 195–197
Farias, J.E.P.De, 356
Farias, S.F., 370–371
Farrington, B., 162
Fathy, R. A., 149–150
Fazli, S., 14
Ferguson, L., 324
Fertner, C., 244–245
Fioretti, G., 13
Fitsilis, P., 13–16, 375, 393

Flanery, T.H., 244−245
Foo, S. L., 298
Fraefel, M., 93
Freitas, J. A., 356, 359t
Frey, A. C., 357

G

Galang, J., 339−340
Gama, K., 356
Garfield, L., 344−345
Gargiulo, M., 27−28, 55−56
Gasiorowski-Denis, E., 5
Geertman, S., 197
Gemma, P., 149−150
Geraldi, J., 12−15
Ghazarian, A., 15
Giannakidis, G., 25−26, 26f
Giannakidou, I., 385−386
Giffinger, R., 201−202, 244−245, 393
Gil-Garcia, J.R., 337, 354−355
Gleeson, B., 237−238
Gonçalves, Y.S., 357
Gonzalez, S., 198−199
González-Jaen, L.F., 408
Gorod, A., 13−14
Gouveia, J. P., 25−26, 26f, 28−32, 29f, 31f, 35−36
Graham, G., 354
Graham, S., 237−238, 392
Gray, J., 136
Greening, L., 35
Grieco, 244−245
Griffon, A., 105−106
Grossi, G., 344
Gschwend, A., 93
Guattari, F., 336
Guelpa, E., 56
Gupta, V., 298−299
Gurgel Jr., G.D., 370−371

H

Hagan, G., 13
Hall, P., 392
Hall, R. E., 408
Haller, S., 93
Halpern, O., 336
Han, H., 105−106
Hancock, M. G., 84, 354
Haritas, B., 267−268

Harrison, C., 408
Harvey, D., 233, 237−238, 344
Hass, K., 13−14
Havelaar, R., 131−132, 135
Hawken, S., 105−106
Heaphy, L., 97, 341
Heijlen, R., 87−88
Helbig, N., 354
Henriot, C., 195−196
Heracleous, L., 408
Hill, D., 229
Hoe, S. L., 299
Höjer, M., 356−357, 409−410
Hollands, R., 220
Hollands, R. G., 95−98, 220, 233, 337, 343, 393
Holtzman, J., 6−7
Hornstein, H., 1−2
Hou, R., 224−225
Hsu, J., 244−245
Hu, M., 84
Hu, M.-C., 354
Hunt, D. V. L., 302, 308−309
Huynink, S., 2

I

Ipsilantis, P., 166−167
Ireland, V., 13−14
Ísis, A., 356
Ivy, J., 162

J

Jakhar, A.K., 13
Janssen, M., 95−96, 101−102, 149−150, 244−245, 261−262, 354−355
Jesus, W.L.A.D., 370−371, 382
Jianga, Y., 198−199
Jing, Y., 35
Johannessen M. R., 265
Johnson, P.A., 342
Júnior, N. A., 356

K

Kanter, M. R., 98
Kaplan, S. R., 162
Kar, A.K., 244
Kashef, M., 266
Kazantzi, V., 166−167
Kerzner, H., 1−2

Keshavarz, G., 15
Khan, A.A., 15
Khayatian, F., 67−68
Khemaja, M., 431
Kiridena, S., 12
Kirytopoulos, K., 13−14
Kitchin, R., 84, 95, 97, 229, 315−316, 336−337, 341, 392−393
Klauser, F., 105
Komninos, N., 197−198, 219−220, 261−262, 266, 392
Kostakis, V., 105
Kramar, H., 244−245
Kramers, A., 356−357, 409−410
Kuk, G., 354−355
Kumar, S., 262−264
Kurka, T., 296−297
Kushwaha, D., 15
Kushwaha, D.S., 15

L
Lauriault, T.P., 336
Lea, R., 407−408
Leach, J. M., 296−298, 302−303, 308−309
Lecavalier, J., 336
Lee, G., 14−15
Lee, H. J., 84
Lee, J. Y., 184f
Lee, J.-H., 244−245
Lee, J.H., 354
Lee, J.Y., 185f
Lee, S. E., 302
Lee, S.-H., 244−245
Legg, S., 336
Leydesdorff, L., 83−84, 197−198
Lheureux-de-Freitas, J., 357, 360, 372
Li, F., 354
Li, G., 195−196
Li, Y., 197
Lima, L. C., 357
Lin, Y., 197
Lins, A., 357
Lipman, A.D., 392
Litow, S. S., 98
Liu, Y., 224−225
Lombardi, D. R., 296−298, 308−309
Long, G., 31−32
Long, L., 13−14

Lopes, E., 11−12
Lourenc,o P., 30
Lövehagen, N., 356−357, 409−410
Low, N., 237−238
Lu, Y., 13−15
Lund, H., 23
Luque, A., 336−337
Luque-Ayala, A., 341−342
Lysons, K., 162

M
Ma, H., 195−197
Mac Donncha, D., 97, 341
Macadar, M. A., 357, 359t, 360, 372
Macaya, J. F. M., 357
Machado, C.V., 369
Macinko, J., 370−371
Madeira, G. S., 359t
Mahizhnan, A., 351, 353, 391
Mahmood, A., 15
Mangano, G., 244−245, 360
Mantel, B., 142−143
Marcelino-Sádaba, S., 408
Markatou, M., 132
Marle, F., 13−14
Martinsson, F., 56
Marvin, S., 336−337, 341−342
Maslak, M.A., 208
Matheus, R., 261−262
Mathiesen, B. V., 23
Mathieu, J.P., 398
Matos, R., 370
Matos, S., 11−12
Mavridis, N., 385−386
Maylor, H., 12−14
Mbecke, P., 407
McGranahan, G., 28
McNeill, D., 105
Mechant, P., 96−97
Meijer, A., 84, 352−356, 354t, 360, 393
Meijer, E., 244−245
Meirelles, F. de S., 352−353
Menicucci, T.M.G., 371
Mertens, B., 95
Meško, M., 105−106
Mestre, A., 31−32
Mhlanga, M., 407
Miranda, P.R.D.M., 373

Miranda, P.R.M., 360, 375
Mirza, T.H., 15
Misra, A.K., 15
Mistry, N., 315−316
Misurac, G., 95
Mitchell, S., 26−27
Modiri, N., 15
Mofolo, M., 407
Molina, F., 12
Mollay, U., 142−143
Molotch, H.L., 198−199
Morozov, E., 105
Moura, E. S. D., 370
Mozaffari, M.M., 14
Muñoz, L., 134−135
Mutani, G., 55−56, 57f

N
Nair, S., 244
Najberg, E., 376
Nam, T., 353, 391
Neirotti, P., 244−245, 360
Newman, J., 136
Nfuka, E. N., 407−408
Nguyen, A.T., 13−15
Nguyen, L.D., 13−14
Niaros, V., 105
Nijhuis, A., 324
Norton, P. D., 162
Nucciarelli, A., 354
Nunes, V., 31−32

O
Oehmen, J., 14
Ojo, A., 129, 354
Oskam, I., 130, 139f, 140f
Ostergaard, P. A., 23
Osterwalder, A., 134−135
Otgaar, A., 132−133, 133f
Otto, B., 95
Ouerghi, M. S., 422−423

P
Paasche, T., 105
Paim, J., 370−371, 376
Paletta, F.C., 357
Pan, G., 298
Panza, A., 67−68

Pardo, T. A., 353, 391
Paroutis, S., 408
Pedram, M., 15
Peixoto, E., 356
Pereira, G. V., 357, 360
Pérez-Ezcurdia, A., 408
Pérez-González, D., 134−135
Perez-Higueras, P., 35
Phaal, R., 244−245
Pianezzi, D., 344
Pichler-Milanovic, N., 244−245
Pietsch, W., 336
Pigneur, Y., 134−135
Piro, G., 244−245
Polonara, F., 29−30
Porter, M., 162
Porto, J. B., 357, 359t
Prabhakar, G.P., 12
Prakash, A., 262−264
Przeybilovicz, E., 352−353, 357
Pugas Filho, J.M., 360, 375
Puron-Cid, G., 337, 355
Putra, Z.D.W., 136

Q
Qazi, A., 13−14
Qian, Z., 198−201, 201t
Quigley, J., 13−14

R
Rabari, 233
Rafiq, M., 162
Rajnish, K., 13
Ramos, H. S., 357
Rattan, C., 339−340, 343
Raynal, M., 392
Reberger, C., 298−299
Recupero, D.R., 265
Reddick, C. G., 269, 355, 360, 385−386, 393
Rehacek, P., 6
Remington, K., 13−15
Rezende, J. F. D. de, 356
Ribbers, M. A., 15
Rider, D., 338−339
Robert, G., 410
Robinson, D., 26f
Robinson, P.J., 342

Roblek, V., 105−106
Roden, S., 354
Rodrigues, A. M., 31−32
Rodrigues, P.H.D.A., 371
Rodriguez Bolivar, M. P., 84
Rogers, C. D. F., 00014#p0115, 00014#p0120, 00014#p0235., 307−309
Rosati, U., 98
Roth, A., 339−340
Ruiz, P., 14
Rusu, L., 407−408

S
Saarikoski, H., 35
Sandercock, L., 237−238
Sang, Z., 149−150
Santonen, T., 105−106
Sanz, L., 28
Sarto, L., 67−68
Sauter, M., 334, 343
Savoldelli, A., 95
Scholl, C., 133−134
Scholl, H. J., 101−102
Schoo, K. C., 15
Schrama, W., 130, 139f, 140f
Schremmer, C., 142−143
Schuurman, D., 96−97
Schwartzenberg, S., 237−238
Schweitzer, L.A., 343
Scorrano, 244−245
Scorrano, F., 360
Scott, J.C., 343
Sedaghat-Seresht, A., 14
Seixas, J., 25−26, 26f, 28−32, 29f, 31f, 35−36
Sense, A., 12
Sharma, A., 15
Shaw, A., 268
Shearer, R., 315−316
Shelton, 220
Shin, D., 180f, 181f
Silva, W. M., 357, 359t
Simão, T., 31−32
Simoes, S., 32, 35−37, 35f, 36t, 37t, 38t, 45−46
Simões, S., 26f
Singh, G., 101−102
Smith, 237−238
Smith, N., 13, 237−238

Smith, S., 295−296, 304−305
Söderström, O., 105
Solnit, R., 237−238
Srnicek, N., 336, 341−342
Štáhlavský, R., 130−131, 135
Steen, K., 133−134, 134f
Stellingwerf, R., 6
Storper, 233
Stroscia, M., 71t
Sudhakar, G.P., 12
Svejvig, P., 16

T
Taamallah, A., 431
Tan, B., 299−300
Terrados, J., 35
Testa, M. G. A., 357
Thuesen, C., 14
Tibau, F., 85
Todeschi, V., 56
Tomas, G. H. R. P., 357
Toval, A., 12
Townsend, A., 84, 100
Travassos, C., 370−371
Trieste, V., 51−52
Tsoukalas, I. A., 161
Turner, R., 13

V
Valentim, A., 28−29
Valkama, P., 393
van Bueren, E., 133−134, 134f
Van Cauter, L., 101−102
van den Buuse, D., 130, 139f, 140f
van Dijck, E., 130, 139f, 140f
Van Kemenade, E., 393
van Winden, W., 130, 132−133, 133f, 136−142, 139f, 140f
Vangelista, L., 415
Vasconselos, P.O., 357
Verda, V., 56
Vey, J. S., 315−316
Viana, L. P., 357
Vidal, L., 13−14
Vidal, L.A., 13−15
Vidgen, R., 13−14
Vilaca, N.M.C.A.A., 356
Villa, N., 26−27
Vinod Kumar, T.M., 269

Violi, P., 105
Visser, B., 13
Vukomanović, M., 2–3, 11

W

Waley, P., 198–199
Walravens, N., 95–96
Wang, J., 35–36, 196–197
Wang, L., 198–199
Wang, Z., 195–196
Wangel, J., 356–357, 409–410
Ward, S., 14–15
Watson, J., 295–296, 304–305
Weerakkody, V., 149–150, 244–245, 261
Wei, Y.-D., 198–201
Weiss, M. C., 357, 359t
Weiss, M.C., 359t
Wey, W.-M., 244–245
Whitty, S.J., 12–13
Wiig, A., 220
Williams, J., 335
Williams, T., 12–14
Williams, T.M., 14–15
Winch, G., 158
Witte, J.-J., 132–133, 133f

Wu, F., 198–199, 201
Wu, Q., 198–199
Wylie, B., 337, 342–343

X

Xia, W., 14–15

Y

Yigitcanlar, T., 105
Yimin, Z., 299–300
Young, M., 2

Z

Zandhuis, A., 6
Zanella, A., 415
Zebgarini, N., 71t
Zeuli, K., 324, 326
Zhang, C., 35
Zhang, J., 337, 355
Zhang, S., 198–199
Zhang, T., 198–199
Zhao, J., 35
Zollin, R., 13
Zuiderwijk, A., 95–96, 261–262
Zuse, H., 15

Subject index

Note: Page numbers followed by "*f*" and "*t*" refer to figures and tables, respectively.

A

Access to health services, regulation of, 371
ADRAL (Regional Development Agency of Alentejo), 37
AEB. *See* Amsterdam Economic Board (AEB)
African Development Bank (AfDB), 428, 430
Agile, 436–437
 PMBOK and, 7–9
Agile Alliance, 7–9
Agile Practice Guide, 7–9
AIM. *See* Amsterdam Innovation Motor (AIM)
Alentejo Regional Development Agency, 26–27
Algiers smart city
 background of, 392–393
 map of, 394*f*
 project definition methodology, 394–396
  funding, 396
  integration and organization, 395–396
  schedule, 396
  study area, 394–395, 395*f*, 396*f*
 research methodology, 397–402
  challenges and impact for participants, 400–401, 401*t*
  content analysis, 399, 399*t*
  key aspect, 399–400, 400*t*
  methodological approach, 397–398, 397*t*
  methods, 398
  obstacles and constraints, 402, 402*t*
  representation (lexical and semantic analysis), 398–399, 398*f*
Alibaba Group Internet Corporation, 198–199, 202, 204–205, 212, 215
Alipayment, 221
Allahabad, 252–256
 geographical map of, 253*f*
 opportunities, 255
 strengths, 253–254
 threats, 255–256
 weaknesses, 254
Alliander, 131
Amazon HQ2 process, 342
Amsterdam Arena, 131
Amsterdam Economic Board (AEB), 131, 136
Amsterdam Innovation Motor (AIM), 130–131
Amsterdam Municipality, 131
 departments in Amsterdam Smart City, involvement of, 137*f*
Amsterdam Smart City (ASC), 130
 Amsterdam Municipality departments, involvement of, 137*f*
 background of, 130–136
 organization of, 135–136, 135*f*
 research methodology, 136–144
  cost, 140–141, 141*t*
  integration, 137–138
  organization, 138–140, 139*f*
  procurement, 142
  quality, 141
  risks, 141–142
  scope, 136–137, 138*f*
  timescale, 140, 140*f*
 theoretical approach for, 132–135
  business model, 134–135
  urban innovation system, 132–133, 133*f*
  urban living lab, 133–134, 134*f*
 timeline of, 131*f*

Anchor institution analysis, 319, 320f
ANCI (National Association of Italian Municipalities), 52
ANSI, 6–7
App4Torino, 64–65
Appropriation, 101
Arcadis, 131
ASC. *See* Amsterdam Smart City (ASC)
Aspern Smart City Research, 107
Association for Project Management, 13
Austrian Association of Cities and Towns, 106
Austrian Federal Ministry of Transport, Innovation and Technology (BMVIT), 106
AXELOS Ltd., 3
AxTO Program, 75–76

B

Belgium
  facts and figures of, 88t
  Leuven. *See* Smart City Leuven
  map of, 91f
Ben Ali, Zine El Abidine, 423
Beth-Israel Medical Center, 321, 324
Biotope City, 108t
BMVIT. *See* Austrian Federal Ministry of Transport, Innovation and Technology (BMVIT)
BoostInno, 64
Bourguiba, Habib, 423
Brazil
  Ministry of Health, 371
  National Regulation Policy, 371–372
Brazilian Association of Public ICT Agencies, 372
Brazilian intelligent cities
  publications, 352f
  research methodology, 356–360
    discussion, 358–360, 359t
    literature and cases, 356–358, 358f
    theoretical background, 353–355
British Standards Institute, 245
BTL method, 189
BTO method, 189
BuildyourCity2gether Wien Aspern, 108t
Busan Eco Delta City, 176, 192

C

CapaCity program, 107
CEIC, 373
CEIIA, 26–27
Cell 411, 412
Center for Environmental and Sustainability Research (CENSE), NOVA University of Lisbon, 28
Central Alentejo Intermunicipal Community (CIMAC), 26–27
Central Committee of CPC, 220–221
Central Office of CPC, 222
Centre for Study of Science, Technology and Policy (CSTEP), 264–265
Changsha smart city
  background of, 222–229
    informationization development and electronic government, 222–223, 224f
    IoT platform development tendency, 228–229
    organizational scheme of smart city construction, 223–225
    public security big data application, 226
    public service modes, optimization of, 225–228
    smart environmental protection, 227–228, 227t
    transport cloud, 226–227
    urbanization, impacts of, 228
  research methodology, 229–237
    fringes, 235–237
    scope, 229–231, 230f
    time series, 231–235, 234f
CHAOS report, 12
Chief Technology Officer (CTO), 131, 136
China
  Ministry of Housing and Construction, China, 220–221
  Ministry of Housing and Urban Rural Development, China, 197
  Ministry of Industry and Information, China, 220–221
Chinese National Development Reform Commission, 205–206
Chinese State Council, 197, 201, 222
CIMAC (Intermunicipal Community of Central Alentejo), 37

Subject index 449

CIP—EIP. *See* Competitive and Innovation Program—Entrepreneurship and Innovation Program (CIP—EIP)
CIP—ICT Policy Support Programme, 66
CISCO, 26—27, 105, 159, 298—299, 352
  Connected Digital Platform, 156—157
Citizen engagement, 272, 279
City Council of Leuven, 83—84
City Hall of Leuven, 95—96
CityMobil2, 161
Climate and Energy Fund, 106—107, 108*t*
CN Tower, 333—334
Co-City, 64, 75
Cocreation, 100—101
Committee of Development and Reform, 220—221
Commscope, 83—84, 91, 97—98
Competence Baseline, 1—2
Competitive and Innovation Program—Entrepreneurship and Innovation Program (CIP—EIP), 66
Connected Smart Cities, 357—358
Consultants ETA, 107
Control Group, 336
Covenant of Mayor Initiative, 51—52
Cronos, 83—84, 91, 97—98
CROSS project, 66
CSTEP. *See* Centre for Study of Science, Technology and Policy (CSTEP)
CTO. *See* Chief Technology Officer (CTO)
Cyberpark enterprises, 426, 427*f*
Cyber-physical approach, 158—161
Cyber Security Agency, 304
Cycloid, 37

D

Decentralization, 198—199
DecidiTorino, 75—76
DECO (Portuguese Association for the Defense of the Consumer, Évora University), 37
Decsis, 26—27
Dehradun, 246—249
  geographical map of, 247*f*
  opportunities, 248
  strengths, 246—247
  threats, 249
  weaknesses, 248

Dell, 374
DEYAT, 154
Didi traveling, 221
"Digital Architecture White Paper", 223
Digital city, 392—393
Digital City Wien, 118—119, 125
Digital Economy Strategic Council, 430
Digital On-Ramps, 229
Digital Strategy Advisory Panel, 339
Digital Tunisia 2020 National Strategic Plan, 422—423, 426—427, 430—431
Distribution system operator (DSO), 23—24, 31—32
Doctoroff, Daniel L., 335, 339—340
Dream Town Internet village, Hangzhou
  background of, 196—199
  innovation-based urbanization, designated space for promoting, 196—198
  theoretical context and organization schemas, 198—199, 199*f*
  programmatic goals and performance, 211*t*
  research methodology, 200—213
  cost, 208
  fringes, 210—213, 213*f*, 214*f*
  integration, 202*f*, 203
  organization, 203—205, 206*f*, 207*f*
  procurement, 210
  quality, 208—209
  risks, 209—210
  scope, 201—202
  time, 205—208, 208*f*
DSO. *See* Distribution system operator (DSO)
"Dynamic Street, The", 340—341

E

E-Bikes, 279
e-car sharing, 126
EcoBusiness Plan, 124—125
E-collectivity, 426
Economic impact analysis, 321—324, 322*f*, 323*f*, 325*f*
EDIA S.A., 37
EDP Distribuição S.A., 23—24, 26—27, 37
eGovernment (eGov), 355
EIP-SCC, 106

El Chahed, Youssef, 428
Electronic government, 222−223
ELENA mechanism, 43
ElSebsi, El Beji Kayed, 423
e-mobility, 126
Empowerment, 279
Energy Atlas project, 136−138, 142−145
   cost of, 140−141, 141*t*
   development of, 142*f*
   organization of, 138
   procurement of, 142
   stakeholder analysis, 139*f*
   stakeholders, 139*f*
   timeline of development, 140*f*
   visualization, 138*f*
Energy Fund, 140−141
Energy system, 24
Engie, 131
Ericsson Networked Society City Index, 410−411
e-Trikala, 150
Europe 2020 Strategy, 129
European Commission, 56−57, 66, 136, 138, 140−141
European Community, 52
European Horizon 2020 program, 57−58
European Innovation Partnership "Smart City & Communities", 52
European Investment, 428
European Investment Bank, 43
European Regional Development Funds, 43
European Union, 51−52, 93−94, 129−131, 351−352
European Union LIFE Programme, 43
Évora InovCity, 23−25, 46
Évora Municipality, 23−25, 27−28, 30, 37
Évora smart city, 21, 45*f*
   background of, 23−27
   Évora InovCity, 23−25
   integrated city planning toward Évora Action Plan for sustainable energy, 25−26
   research methodology, 27−46
      cost, 39−43, 41*t*
      fringes, 42*t*, 44−46
      integration, 29−34, 31*f*, 32*f*, 33*t*, 35*f*
      organization, 34−39, 36*t*, 37*t*, 38*t*
      risks, 43−44
      scope, 28−29, 29*f*
      time, 39, 40*t*
   "Smart Cities" Memorandum of Understanding, 26−27
Exclusion mechanisms, 98−99

F

"FaciliTo Giovani e Innovazione Sociale", 63−64
FDI. *See* Foreign direct investment (FDI)
Feasibility study, 285−286
Federal University of Rio Grande do Sul (UFRGS), 373−374
FGV. *See* Getulio Vargas Foundation (FGV) Business School
FIWARE European project, 64
Flemish Agency for Innovation and Entrepreneurship, 93
Foreign direct investment (FDI), 229−230
Foresight Future of Cities, 308−309
Fourth industrial revolution, 174, 184−185, 191
FRI. *See* Fujitsu Research Institute (FRI)
FSTC. *See* Zhejiang Hangzhou Future Sci-Tech City (FSTC)
Fujitsu Research Institute (FRI), 285
Future Sci-Tech Cities, 197−198
Future Urban Living, 308−309

G

GARE (Association for the Promotion of a Culture of Road Security), 37
Geographic information systems (GIS), 30, 44
GERCON, 383, 387
Gerint Hospital Admissions Management system, 368, 375, 378*f*, 382−385, 384*f*
"GerOs—Networking in Osteoporosi", 65
GESAMB (Environment and Waste Management), 37
Getulio Vargas Foundation (FGV) Business School, 360
GHG. *See* Greenhouse gas (GHG) emissions
GIS. *See* Geographic information systems (GIS)
GoBike, 61
GOI. *See* Government of India (GoI)
Google, 279
Governance analytics, 320−321

Subject index

Government of India (GoI)
  Ministry of Urban Development (MoUD), 268
  smart city evolution in
    Allahabad, 252–256, 253f
    background, 244–246
    Dehradun, 246–249, 247f
    Nagpur city, 249–252, 249f
    Pune, 261
  urban population, growing trend of, 264f
GovTech Singapore
  "Intelligent Nation" report, 298
  smart initiatives, 300–302, 301f
Green economy (2014–20), 422
Greenhouse gas (GHG) emissions, 21–22, 25–26
Group Areas Act, 409
GRÜNEzukunftSCHULEN (green future schools), 108t
"Guardando la Città Metro per Metro", 64–65
GUGLE Wien Penzing und Alsergrund, 108t
Gujarat International Finance Tec-city, 243–244

H

Hangzhou
  Dream Town Internet village. *See* Dream Town Internet village, Hangzhou
  key data for, 201t
  location of, 200f
Hangzhou Daily Media Company, 209
Hangzhou Yuhang Sci-tech Guarantee Ltd., 210
Hartani, Riad, 396
HEAT_re_USE.vienna Probing, 108t
Hendrick de Keyser Exchange Centre, 130, 136
High-tech infrastructure, 175, 177–178, 184–186, 188
Horizon 2020, 93–94
HP, 374
Human Development Index, 268

I

IBM, 105, 219–220, 229, 352
  Intelligent Operations Center, 341–342
ICB. *See* Individual Competence Baseline (ICB)
ICBv4, 2–3, 11
  competence elements, 2, 3t
  guideline, 2
ICIC. *See* Initiative for a Competitive Inner City (ICIC)
ICity rate, 69
ICT. *See* Information and communications technologies (ICT)
IDC Smart City Development Index, 295–296
I-DSLA. *See* Rutgers Institute of Data Science Learning and Applications (I-DSLA)
Imec, 83–84, 91
(Indian) Companies Act 1956/2013, 278–279
Individual Competence Baseline (ICB), 1–3, 11
Industrial manufacturing analysis, 318–319, 319f
Industry–University Cooperative for Research Centers (IUCRC), 328
Infocommunications Development Authority of Signapore, 299–300
Information and Communications Technologies (ICT), 21, 95, 118–120, 129, 149–150, 154–157, 167, 174, 178–181, 184–185, 191–192, 237, 244–245, 261, 265, 276, 374–375, 435–436
  Integration for Buildings and Electrical Grid Wien-Aspern, 108t
  standardization, 157
Information city, 392
Informationization development, 222–223
Infrastructure Canada, 342
Infrastructure financing, 252
Initiative for a Competitive Inner City (ICIC), 324, 326
Innovation, 378
Innovation & Enterprise Cluster Fund, 298–299
Innovation-based urbanization, designated space for promoting, 196–198
Innovation Center of the City of Turin, 76
InSMART. *See* Integrative Smart City Planning (InSMART) project

Integrated City Energy Planning Tool, 30
Integrated energy planning, 29—34, 31f, 32f, 33t, 35f
Integrated National Network of the Administration, 428
Integrated Operation Control Center (IOCC), 178—182
Integrative Smart City Planning (InSMART) project, 25, 27—29, 34, 39, 45—46
   FP7 project, 157
   Integrated City Energy Planning Framework, 25—26, 26f
Intelligent city, 393
Intelligent decisions, 407—408
International Electrotechnical Commission (IEC), 276
International Free Software Forum, Porto Alegre, 374
International Project Management Association (IPMA), 1—2
   Individual Competence Baseline guide, 1—3, 3t, 11
International Telecommunications Union (ITU), 149—150, 276, 436—437
Internet plus service, 233
Internet startups, 195—197, 199, 201—212, 214—215
Interoperability, 378, 379f
IOCC. *See* Integrated Operation Control Center (IOCC)
IoTorino, 75—76
IoT platform development tendency, 228—229
IPMA. *See* International Project Management Association (IPMA)
ISO10006:2003, 5
ISO10007:2003, 5
ISO 13153, 276
ISO 14001, 276
ISO 15686, 276
ISO 17742, 407—408
ISO 20121, 276
ISO 21500, 1—2, 5—7, 11
   structure, 6t
ISO 21500:2012, 3—5
ISO 24510, 407—408
ISO 26000, 407—408
ISO 27001, 276
ISO 31000:2009, 5
ISO 37100, 407—408
ISO 37101, 149—150
ISO 37120, 52—53, 70, 276
   core indicators, 71t
ISO 37122, 328
ISO 37151, 276
ISO 39001, 407—408
ISO 50001 (Energy management system), 276
ISO/IEC 21972, 407—408
ISO/IEC 27550, 407—408
ISO/IEC 27551, 407—408
ISO/IEC 30182, 407—408
ISO/TC 268, 407—408
ISO/TR 37150, 276
Italian National Institute of Statistics, 53—54
ITU. *See* International Telecommunications Union (ITU)
ITU-T Recommendations, 436—437
IUCRC. *See* Industry—University Cooperative for Research Centers (IUCRC)

J
Jacobs, Jane, 333—334
Jae-in, Moon, 184
Japan
   Ministry of Economy, Trade and Industry, 283
   Ministry of Environment, 283
JESSICA Holding Fund Portugal, 43
Johannesburg 2040 Growth and Development Strategy, 411
Johannesburg Smart City
   background, 409—411
   cost, 414
   fringes, 415—416, 416f
   integration, 413, 413f
   organization, 413—414
   research methodology, 411—416
   scope and timeline, 412—413
   time, 414
Juniper Research Limited, 295—296

K
Kansai Electric Power, 285
Key performance indicators (KPIs), 53
Kitestring, 412

Subject index

Korean smart city policy, evolution of
  background, 175–176
  fringes, 189–191
  research methodology, 176–191
    cost, 186–187
    integration, 179–181, 181f
    organization, 181–184, 183t
    procurement, 188–189
    quality, 187–188
    risks, 188
    scope, 177–179, 177t, 178f, 180f
    time, 184–186, 184f, 185f
  types and goals, 190t
KPIs. *See* Key performance indicators (KPIs)
KPN, 131
Kumbh Mela, 256–257

L

Land & Housing Corporation (LH), 188–189
Land Transport Authority Singapore, 299
LEDs. *See* Light-emitting diodes (LEDs)
Legislative sandbox, 176
Leuven MindGate, 83–88, 91, 93, 98, 100
Leuven smart city. *See* Smart City Leuven
LH. *See* Land & Housing Corporation (LH)
Liander, 143–144
Life-cycle management, 164–166, 165t, 166t
Light-emitting diodes (LEDs), 23–25, 39
Light regulators, 23–24
LinkNYC, 336
Liveability, 304–305, 305f, 306f
Liveable Cities Methodology, 308–309
LONgevity—OPLON project, 64
LPWA technology, 229, 233

M

Ma, Jack, 204–205
"Make your city smart" project, 108t
Manufacturing industry, 318–319, 319f
Market-driven economy, 198–199
Master Innovation and Development Plan (MIDP), 337, 339–340, 342
MCDA. *See* Multicriteria decision analysis (MCDA)
McKinsey Global Institute, 269–272
Meta-architecture, 151f

Microsoft, 374
MIDP. *See* Master Innovation and Development Plan (MIDP)
MIHAN. *See* Multimodal International Cargo Hub Airport Nagpur (MIHAN)
Ministry for Research, University, and Instruction (MIUR), 67
Ministry of Land, Infrastructure, and Transport (MLIT), 182
Ministry of Science, China, 220–221
"Mischung: Nordbahnhof", 108t
"Mischung: Possible!,", 108t
MIUR. *See* Ministry for Research, University, and Instruction (MIUR)
MLIT. *See* Ministry of Land, Infrastructure, and Transport (MLIT)
Mobike, 221
Modderfontein, 409–410, 413–414, 416
Modi, Narendra, 243–244
Most Ancient European Towns Network, 23, 27
MSW. *See* Municipal solid waste (MSW)
Mt. Lemmon Holdings, 336
Multicriteria decision analysis (MCDA), 35–40, 45
Multidisciplinarity, 100–101
Multilateral approach to smart sustainable cities, 436–437
Multimodal International Cargo Hub Airport Nagpur (MIHAN), 251–252
Municipal Communist Party Committee, 201
Municipal Department for Environmental Protection, 124
Municipality of Torino, 51–52, 59–60
Municipality of Trikala, 150, 153, 163–164
Municipal solid waste (MSW), 28–29
"My Generation@Work", 64
My Intelligent City Program of the Ministry of Science, Technology, Innovation, and Communications, Brazil, 352–353

N

Nagpur city, 249–252
  geographical map of, 249f
  opportunities, 251–252
  strengths, 250–251
  threats, 252
  weaknesses, 251

Namola, 412
Nara Medical University, 283−284, 284f, 290−291
Nara Research and Development Center in Agriculture, 283−284
Nara smart city, Japan
  background of, 285
  location of, 284f
  research methodology, 286−290
    evaluation, 287−290, 289t, 290t, 292t
    renewable energies, utilization of, 286−287
  service improvement, 291f
National Agency for Computer Security, 423
National Computerisation Programme, 299−300
National Emergency Management Agency, 182
National Energy Efficiency Fund, 43
National Frequency Agency, 423
National Front of Mayors, 352−353
National Health Card, 382
National Health Research Project, 376
National Informationization Development Strategy 2006−2020, 222
National Land Planning and Using Act, 179
National New-Type Urbanization Plan (2014−2020), 196−197
National Registry of Healthcare Establishments and Professionals, 382
National Science and Technology Board, 299−300
National Science Foundation (NSF), 328
National State Council, 220−221
National Strategy on Talents, China, 195−196, 203−204
National Sustainable Habitat and Smart City Mission, 262
National Telecommunication Authority, 423
National Youth Council Singapore (NYCS), 299
  initiatives, 300−302, 302f
Newark 2020 Buy, LiveHire program, 326
Newark City Mayor's Office, 316−317

Newark Industrial Data Analytics Platform (NIDAP), 317−318
  anchor institution analysis, 319, 320f
  architecture, 317−318, 318f
  Beth-Israel Medical Center, 321
  economic impact analysis, 321−324, 322f, 323f, 325f
  governance analytics, 320−321
  industrial manufacturing analysis, 318−319, 319f
Newark Industrial Solutions Center (NISC), 327
Newark smart city, NJ
  cost of, 328
  data analytics platform. *See* Newark Industrial Data Analytics Platform (NIDAP)
  integration of, 326−327
  organization of, 327
  procurement of, 329
  quality of, 328
  risks of, 328−329
  scope of, 324−326
  timeline of, 327−328
Newark Smart City Infrastructure for Real-Time Data Analytics, 317
New Energy Promotion Council, 285
NIDAP. *See* Newark Industrial Data Analytics Platform (NIDAP)
911 Response App, 412
NISC. *See* Newark Industrial Solutions Center (NISC)
Non-University Research, 107
Nossa Senhora da Conceição, 382
"Notice of Carrying out the National Smart City Pilot", 197
NSF. *See* National Science Foundation (NSF)
NYCS. *See* National Youth Council Singapore (NYCS)

O

Office of Government Commerce, 3
One door entry service, 221
Open Data platform, 94−96, 101−102
Open Incet, 76
OPTICITIES project, 67, 67f
Oracle, 352
Organizational scheme of smart city construction, 223−225

P

Pakhuis De Zwijger, 131
Paris agreement, 283
People competencies
  project management standards, 2, 3t
Perspective competencies
  project management standards, 2, 3t
Pervasive access, 407−408, 412−413, 415−416
Phillips, 26−27
Placemaking, 279
Plan Development Agreement, 338−339
Plan Directeur d'Aménagement et d'Urbanisme (PDAU), 394
Plan—Do—Check—Act, 6
Planet Smart Square, 63, 63f
"Platform capitalism" business model, 336
PLISION, 155
PM. *See* Project management (PM)
PMBOK. *See* Project management body of knowledge (PMBOK)
PMI. *See* Project Management Institute (PMI)
Pocket Mannerhatten, 108t
PON (National operative program for Research and Competitiveness) funds, 75
Pontifical Catholic University of Rio Grande do Sul (PUCRS), 360, 373−374
Porto Alegre Smart City, Brazil
  background of, 369−372
    access to health services, regulation of, 371
    Brazilian health service, 370−371
    regulation of health services, dimensions of, 371−372
  research methodology, 372−386
    architecture and technology, 377−381
    cost, 383−384
    fringes, 385−386
    integration, 381−382
    organization, 382
    procurement, 385
    quality, 384, 385f
    requirements and functions, 376−377
    risks, 384−385
    scope, 375−381
    time, 383
PostNL, 131
PPCP. *See* Rutgers Public−Private Community Partnership (PPCP) Program
PPP. *See* Public−private partnerships (PPP)
Practice competencies
  project management standards, 2, 3t
Presidential Committee on the Fourth Industrial Revolution, 173−174
PRINCE2. *See* Projects IN a Controlled Environment (PRINCE2)
PROCEMPA, 383
ProGiReg, 75
Project coalition management, 166−167
Project communications management, 8t
Project complexity, 12−16
  approaches to, 13−15
  software, 15−16
  types of, 13
Project cost management, 8t
Project integration management, 8t
Project management (PM), 1−2
Project management body of knowledge (PMBOK), 1−2, 5−12, 15−16
  and agile, 7−9
  areas, 7, 8t
  process groups, 6−7
  project manager, role of, 10−11
Project Management Body of Knowledge (PMBOK), 150−152, 158, 161, 165−167, 169
Project Management Institute (PMI), 1−2, 7−10, 14−16
  talent triangle, 10−11
Project management standards, 2−12
  comparison, 11−12
  IPMA's ICB guide, 2−3, 3t
  ISO 21500:2012, 3−5
  PMBOK, 6−11
    and agile, 7−9
    areas, 7, 8t
    project manager, role of, 10−11
  PRINCE2, 2−3
Project manager, role of, 10−11
Project procurement management, 8t
Project quality management, 8t
Project resource management, 8t
Project risk management, 8t

Project schedule management, 8t
Project scope management, 8t
Projects IN a Controlled Environment (PRINCE2), 1–3, 11–12
  Agile guide, 5
  principles, 4–5
  process groups, 4
  themes, 4
Project stakeholder management, 8t
Pro-LITE (Procurement of Lighting Innovation and Technology in Europe) project, 66
PROMETHEE method, 35–36
PSCDCL. See Pune Smart City Development Corporation Limited (PSCDCL)
PT, 26–27
Public health, 370–371
Public–private partnerships (PPPs), 74, 163, 166–167, 199–201, 214–215, 244–245, 250, 255–257, 426–427
Public security big data application, 226
Public service modes, optimization of, 225–228
PUMAS (Planning Sustainable Regional/Urban Mobility in the Alpine Space) project, 61
Pune Municipal Corporation (PMC), 272–273
Pune Smart City
  background of, 263–265
  challenges, 265–266, 267t
  cost, 273–274, 275t
  fringes, 279
  integration, 269–272
  organization, 272–273, 274f, 274t
  phases of structure, 273f
  procurement, 277–279
  quality, 275–276
  risks, 276–277, 278t
  scope, 269, 270t
Pune Smart City Development Corporation Limited (PSCDCL), 262, 272–273, 277–279

Q

Quadruple Helix model, 92, 97, 100
Qualcomm, 352
Quality of life, 202

Quayside smart city, Toronto, Canada
  background, 335–338
  history, 335–337
  innovations, 335f
  map of, 334f
  pillars of, 340f
  research methodology, 338–345
    cost, 342
    fringes, 344–345
    integration, 339–340
    organization, 340–341
    procurement, 343–344
    quality, 342
    risks, 342–343
    scope, 338–339
    time, 341–342

R

"Radiologia domiciliare—R@dhome", 65
Regional Bank of Thessaly, 153
Regional energy management system, 285f
Remote courses, 221
Renewable energies, utilization of, 286–287
  regional electricity management, 286–287, 288f, 289f
  regional thermal management, 286, 286f, 287f
  well water thermal, 287
Responsible Data Use Policy Framework, 339–340
Rutgers Institute of Data Science Learning and Applications (I-DSLA), 316–317, 328
Rutgers Public–Private Community Partnership (PPCP) Program, 316–317, 327
Rutgers University Research Centers, 316–317
RWJBarnabas Health, 321

S

S + CC. See Smart & Connected Communities (S + CC)
Santa Casa de Misericórdia Hospital, 382
SC. See Smart city (SC)
SCWA. See Smart City Wien Agency (SCWA)
SDGs. See Sustainable Development Goals (SDGs)

Subject index 457

SDP. *See* Software development process (SDP)
SEAPs. *See* Sustainable energy action plans (SEAPs)
Sejong 5-1 District, 192
Sejong New Administrative City, 176–178
Sensing Safety at Work (SEeS@W), 64
SET Plan Industry Initiative Smart Cities and Communities, 106
Sewage thermal system, 286
  supply of, 287*f*
Sidewalk Labs, 333–334, 336–337, 339–340, 342
SiEBEN, 159
Siemens, 105
Singapore
  Ministry of Communications and Information, 304
  Ministry of Culture, 302
  Ministry of Defence, 299–300
  smart city. *See* Smart Nation Singapore (SNS)
Singapore-MIT Alliance for Research and Technology Innovation Centre, 299
Slums, 246
Smart & Connected Communities (S + CC), 26–27
Smart Block Step II Wien, 108*t*
Smart Changsha Development Overall Plan (2016–2020), 232–233
Smart cities. *See also individual entries*
  concepts, 354*t*
  definitions of, 192, 245, 393
  dimensions of, 393
  evolution of concepts, 392–393
  limits of, 393
Smart Cities and Regions Platform, 106
Smart Cities Demo Aspern, 108*t*
"Smart Cities" Memorandum of Understanding (MoU), 26–27
Smart Cities Mission, India, 262, 263*f*, 264–266, 272–273, 279
Smart City Act, 176, 185–187
Smart City Challenge, 342
Smart City Days, 64–65
Smart City Expert Advisory Board, 107
Smart City im Gemeindebau, 108*t*
Smart city index, 70
Smart City Innovation Center, 374

Smart City Integrative Framework, 373
Smart City Leuven
  appropriation, 101
  background of, 85–86
  context, 85–86
  focus areas, 86
  case analysis, 87–99
    actions and projects, 89*t*
    costs and funding channels, 92–94
    integration and organization, 90–92
    privacy matters and data sensitivities, 95–96
    quality and procurement criteria, 94
    risks and anticipation, 94–99
    scope, 89–90
    time, 92, 92*f*, 96*f*
  low involvement from stakeholders, 96–98
    citizens, 96–97
    civil servants, 97
    companies, 97–98
    exclusion mechanisms, 98–99
    reluctance to intercity collaboration, 99
  map of, 87*f*
  multidisciplinarity (and cocreation), 100–101
  road map, 101
  strategy, 100
  technology, 101–102
Smart City National Observatory, 52
Smart City Reference Framework, 264–265
Smart City Vienna
  background of, 106–117
  implementation of, 108*t*
  research methodology, 118–126
    digital city, 118–119
    educational projects, 118
    energy, 119–120
    fringes, 125–126
    health and social affairs, 120
    integration, 120–122, 121*f*
    organization, 123, 124*f*
    scope, 118–120
    time, 123–125
  strategy objectives, 122*t*
Smart City Vienna Laxenburger Straße, 108*t*
Smart City Vienna—Liesing Mitte, 108*t*
Smart City Wien, 108*t*
Smart City Wien Agency (SCWA), 123

Smart City Wien Framework Strategy, 118, 121, 123
Smart economy, 202
Smart energy systems, 23
Smart environmental protection, 227–228, 227t
Smart Évora, 32–33, 33t
Smart Flanders program, 93
Smart Gov 2020 program, 428–429
Smart LED, 279
Smart Living, 375
SMART model, 99–100
Smart Model Assessment Resilient Tool (SMART). See Smart Nation Singapore (SNS), Smart Model Assessment Resilient Tool
Smart Nation Singapore (SNS), 297f, 298–299
　recommendations for, 308–309
　Smart Model Assessment Resilient Tool, 296–308
　　assessment, 296–298, 297f
　　direct impact on lenses, 304–305
　　indirect impact on lenses, 306–307
　　initiatives on Liveability Actions, benefits of, 304–305, 305f, 306f
　　initiatives, 300–303, 301f, 302f
　　integration, 298
　　organization, 298–299
　　procurement, 304
　　risks, 304
　　star ratings of initiatives, 303
　　timescale, 299–300, 300t
　vision of, 296
Smart Planet, 219–220
Smart sustainable cities (SSCs), 435–437
Smart Tunisia, 427–428
"SMILE (Smart Mobility, Inclusion, Life & Health, Energy), 53, 57–60, 59f, 61f, 65–66
SNS. See Smart Nation Singapore (SNS)
Social insurance, 228
SOEs. See State-owned enterprises (SOEs)
Software development process (SDP), 15–16
Software project complexity, 15–16
Solar thermal system, 286
　demand of, 287f
　supply and demand of, 286f

South China Morning Post, 204–205
SSCs. See Smart sustainable cities (SSCs)
State-owned enterprises (SOEs), 198–199
Steering Group of Smart City Leuven, 100
STORY project, 93
Strategic Development Plan (2016–20), 422
Sustainability, 67–68, 69f, 266, 410, 412
Sustainable Action Plan, 25
Sustainable Development Goals (SDGs), 435–437
Sustainable Development Goals (SDGs), 410–411
Sustainable energy action plans (SEAPs), 25, 46
Sustainable Energy Measures Plan (SEAP), 51–53, 58
SWOT (strengths, weaknesses, opportunities, and threats) analysis, 246
　Allahabad, 253–256
　Dehradun, 246–249
　Nagpur city, 250–252

T
Taobao Town, 204–205, 209
TAPE. See Turin Action Plan for Energy (TAPE)
Technical University Vienna, 107
Technological-economic model (TIMES model), 30, 32–36, 32f, 33t, 39–40
Technological innovation, 435
Technology, 261–262, 265–266, 272, 279
Technopark El Ghazala enterprises, 424–426, 426f
Telefonica, 352
13th Five-Year Plan, 222–223, 229, 233
13th National Five-Year Plan for Economic and Social Development 2016–20, 196–197
TIMES model. See Technological-economic model (TIMES model)
TINA Vienna Urban Technologies + Strategies, 107, 123
Titan, 336
TNO. See Toegepast Natuurwetenschappelijk Onderzoek (TNO)
TOD. See Transit-Oriented Development (TOD)

Toegepast Natuurwetenschappelijk
    Onderzoek (TNO), 130
"Torino as a Platform" project, 75–76
Torino smart city
  background of, 53
  indicators of, 54t
  energy consumption and CO_2 emissions,
    55t
  research methodology, 53–76, 57f
    cost, 65–67, 66t, 67f, 68t
    fringes, 75–76
    integration, 57–58
    organization, 59–60, 59f, 60f, 61f
    procurement, 74
    quality, 67–70, 69f
    risks, 70–74
    scope, 56–57
    time, 60–65, 62f
  smart mobility, 61, 62f
  smart environment, 61–63, 63f
  smart economy, 63–64
  smart living, 64
  smart people, 64–65
  smart governance, 65
  Turin Action Plan for Energy, 65
Torino Smart City Foundation, 53, 57–60
Torino Social Impact, 76
Torino Social Innovation, 64
Torino Wireless, 53, 57–60
Toronto Waterfront Revitalization
    Corporation. *See* Waterfront
    Toronto
"TRANSFORM plus" project, 107, 108t
TRANSFORM project, 107, 138, 140
  cost of, 140–141
  procurement of, 142
  timescale of, 140
Transit-Oriented Development (TOD),
    251–252
Transport cloud, 226–227
TRIBUTE project, 66–67
Trikala smart city
  background of, 152–157
  evolution timeline of, 152f
  figures of, 156t
  fringes, 167–168
  geographic map, 153f
  initial project portfolio, 152t
  meta-architecture, 151f
  project mission definition, 158f
  research methodology, 158–168
    life-cycle management, 164–166, 165t,
      166t
    organization of, 164f
    power, 162t
    project coalition management,
      166–167
    project mission definition, 158–163,
      159f, 160f, 161f
    resource-based motivation, 163–164
  view of, 154f
Triple Helix model, 83–86, 90–91, 96,
    99–100
Tsitsanis, Vassilis, 152–153
Tunisia
  geographic position and climate, 424f
  landscapes, 425t
  Ministry of Information Technologies and
    the Digital Economy (MTCEN), 428,
    430
  national survey of professional activities,
    425t
Tunisia smart city
  background of, 422–423
  research methodology, 423–431
    cost, 429, 430t
    integration, 426–428
    organization, 428, 429f
    procurement, 430
    quality, 430
    risks, 430
    scope, 423–426
    time, 429, 429t
  strategic orientations, 427f
Tunisia Solar Plan (2014–30), 422
Turin Action Plan for Energy (TAPE),
    51–52, 58, 60, 65–66

U

Uber for police, 412
Ubiquitous city (U-City), 174, 178f, 181f,
    393
  construction, legal framework for, 180f
U-City Act, 175, 178–181, 185–187
UC Leuven-Limburg, 83–84, 91, 93
UK Department of Business, Innovation and
    Skills, 245
Uncertainty, 14–15

UNECE. *See* United Nations Economic Commission of Europe (UNECE)
UN-Habitat, 437
United for Smart Sustainable Cities initiative, 437
United Nations Economic Commission of Europe (UNECE), 436–437
University of Albany
  Center for Technology in Government (CTG), 354, 360
University of KU Leuven, 83–86, 88, 91, 95, 101
University of Vale do Rio dos Sinos, 373–374
UN Paris Agreement on Climate Change, 21
UN Refugee Agency, 155
Urban assemblage, 336
Urban Cool Down, 108*t*
Urban Futures Methodology, 308–309
Urban innovation system, 132–133
  components of, 133*f*
Urbanization, 262–265, 269–272, 275, 277
Urban living lab, 133–134, 134*f*
Urban Regime Theory (URT), 198–199, 214–215
Urban technocrats, 341–342
URT. *See* Urban Regime Theory (URT)
Uttarakhand, 256–257

V
Venture Loan Risk Pool mechanism, 208, 210
Vienna Business Agency, 107
Vienna Research Festival, 107
Vienna smart city. *See* Smart City Vienna
Vienna University of Economics and Business, 107
Virtual city, 392

W
Waag Society, 131
Waterfront Toronto
  committees, 337
  Quayside. *See* Quayside smart city, Toronto, Canada
WeGovNow project, 76
Weixin, 221
Well water thermal system, 287
Wien Energie, 107
Wiener Linien, 107
Wiener Netze, 107
Wiener Wohnen, 107
World Bank, 428
World Council of City Data (WCCD), 52, 70, 77, 149–150
World Wildlife Fund, 279

X
Xi, Jinping, 222–223

Y
Yide, Zhao, 197–198
Yuhang Committee, 198

Z
Zhejiang Hangzhou Future Sci-Tech City (FSTC), 195–199, 203–206, 209–210, 212
  Investment Company, 208
  Management Committee, 198, 206–208, 210

Printed in the United States
By Bookmasters